Ancient Literary Criticism

Ancient Literary Criticism

The Principal Texts in New Translations

EDITED BY

D. A. RUSSELL

Fellow of St. John's College, Oxford

AND

M. WINTERBOTTOM

Fellow of Worcester College, Oxford

CLARENDON PRESS · OXFORD

Oxford University Press, Walton Street, Oxford OX2 6DP

OXFORD LONDON GLASGOW
NEW YORK TORONTO MELBOURNE WELLINGTON
KUALA LUMPUR SINGAPORE JAKARTA HONG KONG TOKYO
DELHI BOMBAY CALCUTTA MADRAS KARACHI
IBADAN NAIROBI DAR ES SALAAM CAPE TOWN

© OXFORD UNIVERSITY PRESS 1972

I.S.B.N. 0 19 814360 5

First Published 1972
Reprinted   *1978*

Printed in Great Britain
by J. W. Arrowsmith Ltd, Bristol

PREFACE

WE are extremely grateful to Miss M. E. Hubbard for allowing us to include her translations of Aristotle, to Miss D. C. Innes for her Demetrius, and to Mr. T. F. Higham for his *Frogs*. Of the rest, Mr. D. A. Russell is responsible for the Greek texts, and for the *Ars Poetica*, and Dr. M. Winterbottom for the remainder of the Latin texts.

We have not attempted to ensure complete uniformity in presentation or in the style or scale of annotation throughout the book. The Indexes are meant to supplement the notes, especially in explaining proper names. They have been made possible by the help of Mrs. S. Argyle, to whom we should like to express here our gratitude and appreciation.

Other texts might, and perhaps should, have been included; but we hope we have made a sufficient selection to give the reader who wishes to study this subject in English a fair and intelligible view of ancient criticism within the compass of a single volume.

D. A. R.

M. W.

CONTENTS

INTRODUCTION

THERE are a number of recent surveys, both long and short, of the Greek and Roman contribution to literary criticism.[1] The purpose of this book is to provide, in English and with brief explanatory comments, the most important texts on which any judgement must be based. We have tried to keep in mind the intrinsic interest of what our authors say, its importance as a commentary on ancient literature, and its influence on later criticism. Some of the texts are well known and have often been translated; others, especially the later Greek ones, are less familiar.

In date, these texts are concentrated—by the accident of survival—in two main periods: the century which ended with Aristotle, and the two centuries beginning with Cicero. Of the first beginnings of Greek critical thought in the casual but illuminating remarks of poets, we have only scraps: enough however to show that the basic ideas of inspiration, social or didactic commitment, and levels of style and genre, were present and natural in the Greek approach to literature long before speculation became articulate. Yet most of the first part of this book (chaps. 2–3) is devoted to the two great philosophers, Plato and Aristotle. Plato's view of literature is indeed a curiously negative one; concerned always with his moral counter-revolution, his attempt to defend inherited values in a hostile world, he seems to give most of his attention to the task of counteracting the bad effects of poetry and rhetoric. It is obvious that Aristotle in the *Poetics* is activated by the need to answer Plato's austerity; the contrast between master and pupil is perhaps more interesting in this marginally philosophical field than in the issues of logic and metaphysics. We see how Aristotle's detachment from civic emotion and the limitations of his own literary talent lead him to a saner and more illuminating view of what poets do and ought to do for their fellow men.

It is, as we said, the accident of survival that determines the chronological pattern of our texts. The Hellenistic age is a blank. One candidate presented himself, but could not be included: Philodemus the Epicurean, a contemporary indeed of Cicero, but an active debater in the controversies of the Hellenistic schools. The fragments of his work (papyri from Herculaneum) are obscure and thorny; it is often difficult to distinguish his own views from those he is arguing against. But the reader who wishes

---

[1] G. M. A. Grube, *The Greek and Roman Critics*, Toronto, 1965, is now a standard book; miniature surveys by D. A. Russell in *Oxford Classical Dictionary*, 2nd edn., s.v. Literary Criticism, and in *A Social History of Western Literature*, ed. D. Daiches, vol. i.

to take a fair view of the whole development can hardly avoid taking him into account. Like Horace, he was a poet as well as a critic; and it is clear that he protested both against the current didactic view of the poet's function and against the ordinary rhetorical assumption that content and form can be treated separately.[1]

All the rest of this book (chaps. 4–15) dates from a long but fairly homogeneous period: that of the imitative, bilingual literature of the Roman empire, an age of standardized rhetorical teaching and very great concern with form, especially stylistic form. Only Demetrius (chap. 4) and Strabo (chap. 7, A) open the window a little on the preceding darkness: Demetrius by his obvious connections with stylistic problems as seen in the late fourth century B.C., Strabo by his 'didactic' reaction to the Hellenistic opinion that the essence of poetry lies in its entertainment value. The rest of our authors should be seen against the background of the changing fashions of oratory and prose style generally in the first two centuries of the Empire. There are of course great differences between the Greeks and the Romans; there are also strikingly close connections— the 'survey of literature' which Quintilian gives as a guide to the orator's reading (chap. 9, D) is largely derived, in its Greek part, from Dionysius' book 'On Imitation', written perhaps a century earlier.

The Greek picture is both simpler and more baffling. Dionysius (chap. 7) is the prophet of a reformation: he has a vision of a new literature arising out of the intelligent imitation of the classics, discarding the extravagance, banality, and illiteracy which he sees in Hellenistic prose. But of course this reformation did not produce a clean sheet. 'Longinus' (chap. 11) shares Dionysius' historical view—but neither is his own writing classicizing nor is the quality of 'sublimity' with which he is concerned one that is particularly prominent in Attic prose. He does battle with a friend of Dionysius—Caecilius of Caleacte—over the crucial subject of the evaluation of Plato: his admiration for the rich metaphorical abundance of the *Timaeus* ('Longinus' 32) is symptomatic of a 'baroque' taste which is very far from jejune Atticism.

But it is difficult to follow the fluctuations of Greek taste—the texts we have (apart from Dionysius) are of doubtful date, the successive waves of 'reform' are hard to distinguish from one another. We are on much firmer historical ground with the Romans.

Here the dominance of rhetoric in our texts is particularly obvious. We have not only Cicero (chap. 5) and Quintilian (chap. 9), but a selection (chap. 8) of practical examples of 'declamation' and comments on the practice. It is clear that the habit of debating general themes and imaginary

---

[1] See Grube, 193 ff., for a useful and intelligent summary of what is known of Philodemus.

cases in rhetorical schools had pervasive effects on all kinds of Latin writing under the Empire. It is important to see why this happened. It is an adaptation to new circumstances of something very fundamental in all classical literature. Right from the time of Gorgias (chap. I, G), the practical 'art of speaking' was thought to give a guide to the evaluation even of poetry. This was natural, because the Greeks (and the Romans after them) always seem to have been primarily concerned with the element of persuasiveness or convincingness in literature—its reference not to the writer's needs nor to the subject's, but to the impact on the audience. This persuasiveness involved reasoning, giving pleasure, and —most important—inducing emotional responses. It seems doubtful whether self-release and self-expression were ever thought of as impulses to write—even though the irrationality of the poet's drive was recognized and treated as divine or daemonic. Normally, two motives were understood: the need to make people do what you wanted, and the desire for reputation as a master of men's minds. Now, in the age of Cicero (as in classical Athens) much energy was naturally occupied in the political and forensic activities of civic life; these produced real 'urgency' (agōn, contentio) and hence real oratorical literature. With the fall of the Republic, which meant both the establishment of a monarchy and the transfer of power from assemblies to armies and their commanders, this 'real' oratory began to fade. The practice of declamation did something to replace it. Addressed to a leisured and expert audience, the imaginary speeches encouraged ingenuity, sophistication, a rapid development of tricks and devices. The first-century literary scene, with the theories and comments that rose out of it, is impregnated with all this.

Much of the most interesting material in these later texts is concerned with the classical authors of the past. The Romans, it is true, maintained a tradition of commenting on contemporary developments: Horace (often under a veil of talk about Greek literature) deals with Augustan problems; we have Seneca on his predecessors (chap. 8, J) and Quintilian on Seneca (chap. 9, D); Pliny discusses his own works (chap. 9, H); Tacitus (chap. 10) gives one of the speakers in his Dialogue an apologia for the modern manner. But the Greeks hardly ever do this. Plutarch (chap. 12) is concerned, following in Plato's footsteps, to save the young from the perils of poetry: he means Homer and classical tragedy and comedy. His criticism of Aristophanes and Herodotus is in the same vein. It is only Lucian (chap. 13, B) who strikes a more contemporary note—his targets are archaizing historians of the second-century Parthian wars. Yet there can be no doubt that the attention to the classics which the educational system of these centuries demanded led to very considerable critical virtues: clear standards of 'true' and 'false' sublime; minute and appreciative observation of style, tone, and genre; balance and common sense.

But the authors must speak for themselves. To generalize about them is inevitably to point out limitations. Rhetoric, ethics, education—what has all this to do with literature? The answer lies in the spirit and intelligence with which they undertook such enterprises of criticism as they understood; on this score, Aristotle and 'Longinus', Cicero, Tacitus, and Quintilian, need have no fears.

D. A. R.

1

BEGINNINGS

In this chapter we collect passages from early Greek poets and other writers to illustrate the beginnings of aesthetic reflection and criticism. Many of the original texts are printed (with Italian commentary and translation) in G. Lanata, *Poetica pre-platonica*, Firenze, 1963. See also R. Harriott, *Poetry and Criticism before Plato*, London, 1969.

A. HOMER

The epics, and especially the *Odyssey*, contain a number of passages which express views on the function and nature of poetry (the poet's dependence on the Muse, his divine skill, and so on) and the power of speech. See Grube, pp. 1-4; H. Maehler, *Die Auffassung des Dichterberufs im frühen Griechentum*, Göttingen, 1963, pp. 9-34.

1. Tell me now, Muses who dwell on Olympus—for you are goddesses, you are there, you know everything, while we hear only repute and know nothing—tell me who were the leaders and princes of the Danaoi. Their number I could not tell or name, no, not if I had ten tongues and ten mouths, a voice that would not tire, a heart of bronze, if the Olympian Muses, daughters of aegis-bearing Zeus, did not tell me how many there were who went to Troy. (*Iliad* 2. 484–92)

2. And the famous bard (*aoidos*) sang to them, and they sat quietly listening. He sang of the dreadful return of the Achaeans that Pallas Athene sent them on their way home from Troy . . . And Penelope wept and said to the divine bard: 'Phemius, you know many ways to charm men with deeds of men and gods, that bards commemorate. Sit by me and sing one of those; let them drink their wine in silence; but stop *this* song, this dreadful song, that always pains my heart in my breast, for intolerable grief touches me deeply. For I always remember and yearn for the head of a man whose fame is great in Hellas and Argos.'

Wise Telemachus answered: 'Mother, why grudge the trusted bard giving such pleasure as his mind commands him? Bards are not to blame; it is Zeus who is to blame, because he gives what lot he pleases to every man on earth. No blame to Phemius, either, for singing the bad fortune of the Danaoi: men give most praise always to the newest song they hear.' (*Odyssey* 1. 325–8, 336–52)

B

3. 'Herald, come here, take this meat for Demodocus to eat; let me embrace him, for all my sorrows. Bards earn honour and respect among all men on earth, because the Muse has taught them the ways of song (*oimai*), and loves the race of bards . . .

'Demodocus, I praise you above all men. Either the Muse taught you, the daughter of Zeus, or else Apollo. Very beautifully you sing the fate of the Achaeans, their deeds and sufferings and toils, as if you were there yourself or had heard from someone else. But change your tune now, and sing of the making of the Wooden Horse . . . If you will sing me that tale properly, I shall tell all mankind that god in kindness gave you the divine power of song.'   (*Odyssey* 8. 477 ff.)

4. [Phemius] . . . seized Odysseus by the knees and spoke to him, begging:

'I beg you, Odysseus, respect me and pity me. You will suffer hereafter if you kill a bard who sings to gods and men. I taught myself; god put all kinds of ways of song into my mind; I am fit to sing at your side as at a god's; do not desire to cut my throat.'   (*Odyssey* 22. 342 ff.)

B. HESIOD: THE POET AND THE MUSES

Hesiod's *Theogony* (*c.* 700 B.C.) opens with a hymn to the Muses, in which the poet describes his encounter with them while he was keeping his sheep on Helicon. They gave him a staff of bay, inspired him to sing, and prescribed his subject.

There may well be elements in this narrative which were already convention. Shepherd-poets are found in other literatures: Amos and Cædmon come to mind. There are also of course many imitations, especially in Hellenistic and Roman poetry. But the familiarity of the symbolism in later literature should not cause us to deny to Hesiod a sincere conviction of the divine origin of his calling.

Text and commentary: M. L. West, Oxford, 1966.

With the Muses of Helicon let us begin our song.
They dwell on the high and holy mountain of Helicon
and dance on their dainty feet
round the dark spring and the altar of mighty Kronion.[1]
In Permessos or Hippokrēnē
or Olmeios divine
they wash their delicate skin.
They form their lovely dances on Helicon's highest summit,
nimble and strong of foot;
and thence they arise and go in the night, in darkness enveloped,
uttering marvellous music, singing the praises of Zeus,

[1] 'Son of Kronos', i.e. Zeus.

of Zeus who carries the aigis, and Hera queen of Argos...
and the holy race of the other immortals.

It was they who taught Hesiod once their beautiful song,
as he kept his sheep under holy Helicon.
Yes, me, whom you hear, the goddesses spoke to unbidden,
the Muses of Olympus, the daughters of aigis-bearing Zeus:
'Shepherds dwelling in the fields,' they said,
'living scandals, greedy guts,
we know how to tell many lies that resemble the truth,
but we know also how to tell the truth when we wish.'
With these words
the eloquent daughters of Zeus plucked and gave me as a staff
a splendid branch of growing bay.
And they breathed divine song into me
that I might tell of the past and of the future,
and they commanded me to sing of the race of the immortal, blessed Gods,
and always to sing of themselves, both first and last.

(*Theogony* 1–11, 21–34)

C. THEOGNIS: IMMORTALITY IN POETRY

This passage—sixth- or fifth-century B.C.—is an early, perhaps the earliest,
statement of the poet's claim to confer immortality. It is a love poem.

I give you wings to fly over the boundless sea, soaring easily over every
land. You shall be at every feast and banquet, in many men's mouths.
Lovely young men will sing clear and beautiful songs about you to the
clear notes of the flute. And when you go down to Hades' house of mourning in the hollow places of the murky earth, even in death you will not
lose your fame; you will always be thought of among men, with a name
that will last for ever, Cyrnus, as you rove round Greece and among the
islands, passing over the unharvested, fish-teeming sea—not riding on
a horse's back, but escorted by the splendid gifts of the violet-crowned
Muses. You will be a song for all men who care, even in time to come, so
long as earth and sun endure.

But scant is the regard I get from you: you cheat me as though I were
a little child.   (237 ff.)

D. PINDAR

The greatest lyric poet of the fifth century speaks now and then, in his own
person, about the making and purpose of poetry. See especially C. M. Bowra.
Pindar, Oxford, 1964, chap. 1.

1. Under my arm are many sharp arrows in the quiver, that speak to those that understand. For the world at large, they need interpreters. Wise is he who knows many things by nature. But those who have merely learned gabble incessantly, like crows insatiate of chatter, against the holy bird of Zeus... (*Olympian* 2. 83 ff.)

2. A man successful in his deeds gives a pleasant cause for the Muses' streams to flow. Great valour dwells in deep darkness for need of song. In one way only we know a mirror for noble deeds—if thanks to bright-clad Memory reward is found for labour in the famous songs of poetry ... I fancy Odysseus' story has become greater than his sufferings because of the sweet poetry of Homer. There is something grand about his lies and winged devices. Wisdom deceives, misleading with fables. But the mass of men have a blind heart... (*Nemean* 7. 11 ff.)

3. Prophesy (*manteueo*), Muse, and I will be your interpreter (*propha-teusō*). (fr. 137 Bowra)

E. FRAGMENTS OF PHILOSOPHERS

Xenophanes (*c*. 565–470 B.C.) was both poet and philosopher. To him is assigned the first criticism of early poetry on moral grounds; he seems to anticipate the view that Plato develops in the *Republic* (below, chap. 2, B).

Homer and Hesiod attributed to the gods all the reproaches and disgraces of men—theft, adultery, deceit. (fr. B 11 Diels–Kranz)

Democritus (*c*. 460–360 B.C.), the greatest of the atomists, is often quoted as an authority for the doctrine that poets need divine inspiration (cf. Horace, *The Art of Poetry*, 295 ff.: below, p. 287).

Whatsoever a poet writes under possession (*enthousiasmos*) and the divine spirit (*hieron pneuma*) is very beautiful. (fr. B 18)

Homer, being endowed with a nature subject to divine influences (*phusis theazousa*), constructed a fair work of poetry of every kind. (fr. B 21)

F. ANECDOTES OF THE POETS

In classical Greece, poets were famous men and there were many stories about them. We give first a contemporary anecdote of Sophocles by another tragic poet, Ion of Chios.

The boy blushed even deeper, and Sophocles said to his neighbour at dinner:

'How right Phrynichus was:

"On red cheeks shines the light of love!"'[1]

[1] Fr. 13 Nauck.

The Eretrian, who was a schoolmaster, took this up. 'Of course, Sophocles, you are an expert in poetry. But Phrynichus was surely wrong in calling the boy's jaws "red". If a painter were to colour this boy's jaws red, he wouldn't be beautiful any more. It's not right to liken the beautiful to what isn't beautiful.' Sophocles laughed. 'Then I take it, sir,' he said, 'that you don't approve either of Simonides' much-admired line:

"the maid from red lips speaking"—[1]

or of Homer's "gold-haired Apollo".[2] For if the painter had made the god's hair gold and not black, the painting would have been worse. And what about "rosy-fingered"?[3] If you dipped your fingers in rose colour, the result would be a dye-worker's hands, not a beautiful woman's.'

(Ion of Chios, fr. 8 von Blumenthal)

Next, Sophocles on his own development—perhaps a paraphrase in Plutarch's Greek rather than the original words. See C. M. Bowra, *Problems in Greek Poetry*, Oxford, 1953, pp. 108–125; the translation dissents from his interpretation because we take *lexis* as '(ordinary) speech'.

Sophocles used to say that, having played through the magniloquence of Aeschylus, and then the sharp artificiality of his own manner, he turned finally to the style of (ordinary) speech, the best and most expressive of character. (Plutarch, *Moralia* 79 b)

It is again to Plutarch that we owe the following stories and sayings, embedded in the sophisticated and involved argument of a declamation on 'whether the glory of Athens is due more to war or to wisdom'.

But Simonides calls painting 'silent poetry' and poetry 'talking painting'. For literature relates and sets down as having happened the same events that painters represent as happening. And the colours and shapes of the painters and the words and expressions of the writers make manifest the same things; they differ in material and manner of imitation, but they both have the same goal. The best historian then is he who brings his narrative to life like a picture with emotions and personalities. Thucydides always strives after this vividness (*enargeia*), in his desire to make the hearer a spectator and to rouse in the reader's mind all the emotions of dismay and disturbance which the eyewitness felt . . .

Poetry owed its charm and honour to its power to express things in a lifelike way: as Homer says, she

'spoke many lies, resembling truth'.[4]

One of Menander's friends is supposed to have said to him, 'Menandeh the festival's coming up, and you haven't done your comedy yet.' 'Or,

---

[1] Fr. 80 Page.   [2] Not in Homer, but (e.g.) in Tyrtaeus.
[3] Frequent Homeric epithet of dawn.   [4] *Odyssey* 19. 203.

yes, I have,' he replied, 'the plot is arranged, there's only the verses to add'—because, no doubt, poets themselves believe the action to be much more essential and important than the words. When Pindar was a young man and flaunted his learning, Corinna took him to task for tastelessness, because instead of composing myths, the proper function of poetry, he heightened the flavour of his subject with rare words, catachreses, metaphors, song, and rhythm. Pindar listened to what she had to say, and then produced the following and showed it to her:

> Ismenos or Melias of golden spindle,
> Cadmus or the holy race of the Spartoi,
> Heracles' mighty strength
> or Dionysus' glorious honour.[1]

Corinna laughed: 'Sow with the hand,' she said, 'not with the sack.' For in fact Pindar had mixed a complete hotchpotch of myths into the poem. But that poetry is concerned with myths is testified also by Plato.[2] And a myth is a false statement resembling a true one; hence it is far removed from reality, since a statement is an image or ghost of an action, and a myth of a statement . . .

Athens possessed no notable practitioner of epic or lyric poetry. Cinesias seems to have been a poor dithyrambist—himself a (? sterile) dim creature, he has had a bad reputation because of the jokes and jeers of the comic poets. As for the drama, comedy was thought such a low, vulgar activity that no Areopagite was allowed, by law, to compose a comedy. Tragedy did flourish, and was famous: a wonderful experience for the eyes and ears of that generation. It lent to myth and emotion a deceit wherein, as Gorgias[3] says, the deceiver is more just than the non-deceiver, and the deceived is wiser than the undeceived. The deceiver is more just because he has fulfilled his promise; the deceived is wiser, because it takes a measure of sensibility to be accessible to the pleasures of literature . . . (*Moralia* 346 f–348 d)

G. GORGIAS: THE POWER OF LOGOS

The passage just quoted contains a characteristically ingenious remark of Gorgias of Leontini (*c*. 483–*c*. 376). He was among the earliest teachers of rhetoric. At Athens (*c*. 427) his fantastic style, with its elaborate antitheses and figures, was a dazzling success. We translate—without attempting to reproduce the often bizarre verbal effects of the original—a passage from *A Defence of Helen* in which Gorgias discusses the irresistible power of speech: one possible excuse for

---

[1] Fr. 9 Bowra.
[2] *Phaedo* 61 b.
[3] See the next section. Cf. also Plutarch, *On the Study of Poetry* 1 (below, p. 509).

Helen is that she was beguiled by *logos*. The text is not well preserved; we have indicated places where there is serious doubt.

Text: L. Radermacher, *Artium Scriptores*, Vienna, 1951, 52 ff.; commentary by O. Immisch, Berlin, 1927. Discussion: Grube, 17 ff.

If it was speech that persuaded her and deceived her soul, it is not 8 difficult to make her defence and get the charge dismissed.
Thus:
Speech is a great prince. With tiny body and (? strength) unseen, he performs marvellous works. He can make fear cease, take away pain, instil joy, increase pity. I will explain how; the audience[1] must feel convinced of this. I hold all poetry to be speech with metre, and that is 9 how I use the word. Those who hear poetry feel the shudders of fear, the tears of pity, the longings of grief. Through the words, the soul experiences its own reaction to successes and misfortunes in the affairs and persons of others.

Let me shift my ground. Inspired charms which use speech are sum- 10 moners of pleasure and banishers of pain. The force of the charm meets the conviction of the mind and bewitches, persuades, and changes it by sorcery. Of sorcery and magic, two arts have been discovered, to mislead the mind and deceive the judgement.

Think how many people, by inventing false words, have deceived, and 11 do every day deceive, many minds on many matters! If everyone had memory of all the past, knowledge of the present, and foresight of the future, speech would not be (? like this). But as it is, we have no facility in remembering the past or viewing the present or divining the future; so that on most subjects most people summon opinion to be the mind's adviser. But opinion is treacherous and unstable, and involves her employers in treacherous and unstable successes . . . [*corrupt sentence omitted*].

For speech the persuader forces the persuaded mind to agree with what 12 is said and approve what is done. The persuader therefore does wrong because he compels, and the persuaded, because she is compelled by speech, deserves no abuse.

The alliance of speech and persuasion shapes the mind as it wishes. 13 We can see this in various ways. First, in the talk of the scientists, who rob us of one opinion to give us another, and make the incredible and unseen apparent to the eyes of opinion. Secondly, in the debates which events force upon men, wherein a single speech pleases and persuades a multitude, by the skill of its writing, not the sincerity of its utterance. Thirdly, in the contentions of philosophers, where is displayed a rapidity

[1] i.e. the imaginary jury which has to be persuaded of the validity of the defence.

of intellect that makes it easy to change the conviction with which an
opinion is held.

14   The effect of speech bears the same relation to the constitution of the
mind as the prescribing of drugs does to the nature of the body. For just
as various drugs expel various humours from the body, some ending
disease and some ending life, so some speeches give pain, some pleasure,
some fear, some confidence, while others again poison and bewitch the
mind with a malevolent persuasiveness.   (*Helena* 8–14)

H. ARISTOPHANES, *FROGS* 830–1481

INTRODUCTION

1. *The play in its time*

1. Aristophanes produced the first of his comedies in 427 B.C. at the age of
about 23, and the last of the eleven which survive in 388, shortly before his death.
The *Frogs* was first shown in late January or early February 405. It was awarded
the first prize and also received the rare honour of a second performance,
perhaps later in the same year. Theatrical performances at Athens formed part
of the festivals of Dionysus, god at this time not only of wine but of all the
creative or recreative fluids in nature.

The god himself is a central figure in the *Frogs*; and in the first half of it
mainly but not entirely a figure of fun. This role would surprise no anthropo-
logist and no student of medieval Christian festivities. On set occasions ribald
fun at the god's expense was thought to give him both honour and delight, as
certainly as it gave his worshippers the pleasures of release. Dionysus (whose
High Priest presided at the theatre) and his half-brother Herakles were constant
butts of comedy. Very few of the other gods, not even Zeus, were spared.

2. To write any comedy in the early months of 405 must have been a desper-
ately baffling task. The preceding year, marking half a century since the death of
Aeschylus, had been marked also by the deaths of his great successors in Tragedy.
First Euripides, aged about 75, had been mourned; then Sophocles, older by
12 years or more, whose death, if much later, may well have caused some revision
in the draft of the play. Over and above all this, the time was one of military
exhaustion, acute political unrest, and subversive free thought. By prayers and
plans Athens was seeking deliverance in a war destined to bring her downfall
in 404. It had begun in 431 and had continued with only one brief intermission.
In 413 the disaster suffered by Athenian arms in Sicily had been followed by
Sparta's occupation of part of Attica. Since then the city had been crowded
with refugees; and economic resources, for this and other reasons, were severely
strained. They depended not only on local supplies but on command of the seas
—an uncertain factor even after the naval victory of Arginusae (off Mytilene) in
406. Meanwhile party faction had increased the sum of trouble. It had driven
Alkibiades, the most brilliant, if egoistic, of Athenian war-leaders, into voluntary

exile and had made of him a political adventurer. He had even gone over to the Spartans for a time and given advice most damaging to his native land (cf. 1427-9). In 411 continuing unrest had come to the surface in 'The Revolution of the 400', an oligarchical movement. This was followed in 410 by a restoration of the democracy; which meant that some of the revolutionaries lost their lives, and others their civil rights, in whole or in part.

It is for these disfranchised citizens that Aristophanes pleads in the 'Parabasis' of the *Frogs* (686-705), a part of the play traditional in comedy, where the Chorus 'comes forward' and the playwright, speaking through the mouth of its leader, freely expresses his own views on public affairs and personalities. Aristophanes' pleading was widely approved and contributed much to the play's success. It was no time for vindictive party feeling. Athens needed the whole-hearted service of all good men.

One question which divided the country was whether to conclude an early peace on honourable terms or to fight on for higher stakes. Aristophanes almost certainly shared the feelings of the landowners and other refugees from occupied Attica. These desired an end to the war and welcomed an offer of peace made by Sparta soon after Arginusae. But the offer had been refused, mainly under the influence of Kleophon, a demagogue openly attacked in *Frogs* 679-85, 1532 f.

Seventy Spartan ships had been lost at Arginusae, together with the admiral in command. In gratitude for victory the Athenians set free all slaves who had served on board. But the price of victory had been high—twenty-five triremes, with casualties which saddened the whole city; and finally all joy was soured by the impeachment of the victorious commanders for having failed to recover the crews of disabled ships and the floating dead.

3. Theramenes, a leading politician twice satirized in the *Frogs* (534-41, 967-70), was closely concerned in these events. Some account of him is necessary because Euripides, so prominent in the play, is made (in line 967) to boast of him and of Kleitophon as typical products of his own teaching. Both were 'moderns', conversant with the New Learning, Kleitophon being a member of the Socratic circle; both, like Euripides himself, were right-wing democrats, favouring a restricted franchise, but not a narrow oligarchy; and in 411 Theramenes, backed by Kleitophon, had been a prime agent in establishing a dominant 'Four Hundred'. Later he had advocated their deposition and the execution of two of his former friends. Behaviour of this kind earned him the name of a turncoat— in Greek 'a buskin' that would fit either foot. At Arginusae he himself, together with other subordinates, had been charged with the work of recovery. In self-defence they laid the blame on dilatory action by their superiors, eight of whom were eventually condemned to death, Erasinides, mentioned in *Frogs* 1196, among them. This result was largely due to the cleverness and eloquence of Theramenes.

In ancient times his character was violently attacked by writers of extreme views, but as warmly defended by others, including Aristotle, who thought of him as willing to serve Athens under any government that was constitutional. Today, as A. W. Gomme writes, 'we have no means of judging Theramenes' sincerity'.[1] That discussion is closed. But writers still take sides in discussing the kindred question: what did Aristophanes really think of Theramenes? And their answer to this must also determine, to some extent, their opinion of his views on Euripides.

According to A. W. Gomme, Aristophanes 'makes fun of Theramenes' cleverness, but genially'. Gilbert Murray, on the other hand, finds that in *Frogs* 534–41 the tone of Aristophanes 'is peculiarly soft and venomous, unlike his ordinary loud railing', because Theramenes 'was unpleasantly stained with the blood of his companions'.[2] I share this view and would add that the venom is made all the more deadly by the context of the lines, viz. Dionysus' cowardly exchanges of dress with Xanthias. Anything to save his own skin!—which, as we are reminded in 968–70 is the principle so ably acted upon by Theramenes.

Gomme's opinion is in keeping with the tenet of most modern scholars that Aristophanes wrote his plays not as political pamphlets, but with the main, if not the sole, object of raising the laughter and applause by which the judges were mainly guided in awarding the prizes. On that assumption one may read the lines on Theramenes as ambivalent. His supporters might take them as a 'genial' flick at his cleverness; his opponents as a 'venomed' shot at his duplicity. The laughs and applause could come from both sides.

4. Aristophanes paid Euripides the high compliment of parody. There is no doubt that he knew his plays through and through and admired his creative genius and technical skill. But he was also in touch with the Socratic circle and could see the plays as documents of the religious, social, and literary changes which the New Learning was bringing about. These changes included the gradual erosion of the old religion (cf. 890 ff.) and of time-honoured conventions in the drama that had sprung from it. In tragedy elevation of style had been demanded by tradition, which also governed music, metre, and dress; in comedy tradition had protected extreme freedom of speech and the ritual use of broad humour. Aristophanes may well have viewed the modern trends with some real dislike and misgiving. In the final scene of the *Frogs* the Chorus sing: 'It's bad form, then, to sit chatting with Socrates; to discard the rules of composition; and to neglect the chief canons of tragedy. Anyone who idles his time away in pretentious discussion and in scratching up trivialities as food for thought is out of his mind' (1491–9). Aeschylus, soon after, is more outright. He says to Pluto: 'Hand over the Chair of Poetry to Sophocles against my return. On no account let Euripides sit there, even by accident. He sticks at nothing, he's a liar, and scurrilous too' (1515 ff.).

It is difficult to read that last scene without feeling that Aristophanes combined a great professional admiration for Euripides with some personal dislike both of the man and of the intellectual movement he represented. In the *Frogs*, so ably constructed to get laughs and to stir memories of happier days when the countryside was open to the Mystae and to all country-lovers, a challenging, old-fashioned glance sometimes flashes out from the mask of fun.

---

[1] *Oxford Classical Dictionary*, s.v. 'Theramenes'.
[2] *The Frogs Translated into English Verse*, London, 1908, p. 117.

5. It is noticeable that Dionysus in judging between the two poets makes up his mind only after putting to them two questions of a non-literary kind. This was fair enough, because both had agreed (1008–12) that admonition and advice were a function of poetry. The two questions (1422 f., 1435 f.) are both political 'feelers'. Asked simply for their views on Alkibiades—which meant their views on the question of his recall from exile at this critical moment—Euripides gives no advice, but generalizes, expressing his hatred for Alkibiades by implication. Aeschylus, by contrast, urges the need for tolerance: 'If you rear a lion-cub, you must humour him.' This comes near to suggesting a policy and matches the frame of mind pleaded for by Aristophanes in the Parabasis. Finally the merits of the two replies are summed up by Dionysus with diplomatic ambiguity, which must have released political tension and earned a laugh.

Unfortunately the replies to the second question—how to save the country—cannot be determined with certainty, because the Greek text from 1435 to 1466 is very much confused. But of course (or so I think!) Dionysus' verdict had to go to Aeschylus. The veteran of Marathon and Salamis was clearly the man for the moment. He represented the fighting spirit and high-mindedness and single-hearted patriotism that were required.

2. *Scenes previous to the literary contest*

The first 172 lines of the *Frogs* suggest to the audience what they may expect as its main theme: the rescue of Euripides from Pluto's realm of Hades, the Underworld of the dead. But this expectation is disappointed.

Dionysus, accompanied by the slave Xanthias, his porter on donkey-back, sets out intent on the rescue. A club and lion-skin disguise him, not very convincingly, as Herakles, his more masculine and less literate half-brother, who had once stolen the dog Cerberus from Hades. The impersonation, he hoped, might prove protective.

A first stop is made at Herakles' house. Dionysus explains to him the lack of truly skilful and creative poets in Athens and the crying need for restoring Euripides to life. The prior claims of Sophocles (whose comic value to Aristophanes would be less) are neatly brushed aside: 'He must not come back', says Dionysus, 'until I've learned how well his son, the poet Iophon, can write without his father's help.' Herakles, with his pioneer's knowledge of the Underworld, is then consulted on the best routes to take and on the provision made there for human needs. He describes 'the great big lake' and its ferryman, Charon; the region of snakes and fearful monsters; and the huge slough and rivers of ordure where the worst of wrong-doers lie. Then follow sights and sounds which move even Herakles to eloquence: 'The musical breath of flutes will float around you and you'll look on the finest daylight, such as our own up here, and myrtle groves and happy throngs of men and women and a great clapping of hands. For there go the Mystae . . . They live just at Pluto's gate and will direct you.'

Aristophanes chose, at a time of public mourning and acute anxiety, to give his play a Chorus of Mystae, the Initiates of a mystical religion. In the longest of their choral interludes (316–459) they re-enact the processional rites, part solemn and part festive, of one or other of the two chief Mysteries at Athens;[1] or, in my guess, combine elements of both, to please as many spectators as possible. We know very little about these Mysteries, except that they promised happiness in a life after death on certain conditions. That was a theme suitable to a time of great recent losses in war. But the festival required, and everyone also needed, the release of a really good laugh and of pleasant memories. The first choral song (209–68), which gave the play its name, very skilfully provided both. It was sung off-stage, beginning when Dionysus, a comical oarsman, is about to row across 'the great big lake' and has been told by Charon that 'frogs as musical as swans' will help him to keep a rhythmical stroke. The frogs' refrain 'Brekekekex koax koax' (a sound still to be heard in Romney marshes, with Kentish variations) must have brought to mind scenes dear to country-bred refugees from occupied Attica; and Dionysus' efforts to match the frogs in their changes of rhythm and finally to outpace them have remained 'good theatre' and cheerful reading to this day.

High comedy continues in the adventures which follow and lead up to the long interludes by the Mystae and to Aristophanes' political pleading in the Parabasis. Then come further adventures at the gate of Pluto's domain. Of these it is enough to say that Dionysus' impersonation of Herakles brings more danger than protection. Herakles is 'wanted' by Pluto's janitor and legal luminary Aeacus for dog-stealing; and by the mistress of an Underworld lodging-house for robbery with violence. Dionysus, true to his character from Homeric days (*Iliad* 6. 135 f.) onwards, plays the coward throughout, forcing or wheedling Xanthias to exchange clothes with him whenever trouble is likely to come and to change back again if some pleasant invitation comes first. In the third of these exchanges—much as Theramenes after the battle of Arginusae rounded on his superiors—Dionysus, now dressed as the slave, actively encourages the arrest by Aeacus of Xanthias, now dressed as the master. Xanthias protests his complete innocence of dog-stealing and offers Dionysus, his supposed slave, for interrogation by torture. He, in this crisis, declares his divinity. Aeacus, however, is not convinced; and assuming that if one of the two is really a god he will show no signs of pain, flogs them both—but without clear result. The matter is then referred to Pluto and his wife Persephone; the true Dionysus is recognized; and a final exchange of clothes takes place.

Tony Hancock, a leading comedian in his time, 'always maintained that the best of comedy was written by the Greeks'[2]—and he, if anyone, must have known. I suspect that he had in mind these closely-packed, quick-moving scenes of the *Frogs*.

In front of Pluto's gateway the switch to the second half of the play is made,

---

[1] These two were the Mysteries of Demeter and Persephone, centred in the precinct of Demeter at Eleusis, 12 miles from Athens, and the Dionysian Mysteries, traced back to Orpheus and connected with the 'Lenaean' festival of Dionysus, the name of which may be derived from 'Lenai', female followers of the god. It was at this festival the *Frogs* was first shown. Its setting was the southern slopes of the Acropolis.

[2] Cf. 'Death of a Comedian' by Michael Wade, in *The Times Saturday Review*, 1 Feb. 1969, p. 19.

with amusing inconsequence. A servant from Pluto's household exchanges confidences with Xanthias on domestic service. Their dialogue is of great interest because it forms a link between the 'Old Comedy' of Aristophanes and the Comedy of Manners that was to develop in the next century and pass on through the Romans to us. Suddenly the talk is interrupted by noises off—confused shouts and abusive language. These are explained to Xanthias as a brawl between Aeschylus and Euripides arising from an old local custom. Maintenance in Pluto's dining hall and Chairs aligned with his were granted to Great Masters in all the major arts. Only Masters greater still could displace the holders. Euripides, encouraged by a mob of crooks who were crazy about his verbal dexterities, was now laying claim to the Chair of Poetry, held for the last 50 years by Aeschylus. There was popular clamour for an official trial of skill. Sophocles was not competing. On arrival he had kissed Aeschylus and clasped his hand and withdrawn. He would stand for the Chair only if Euripides became the new holder. Xanthias' master Dionysus had been appointed by Pluto to judge the contest; and all the necessary apparatus had been provided.

The slaves' dialogue is followed by a choral ode characterizing the two contestants in elaborately metaphorical style. It is after this ode that the English translation begins.

In this part of the play the Chorus has a less important role than before. It comments briefly on the action that has preceded, or invites interest in what is to come. On the whole it is impartial, but seems in one or two places to be a mentor and partisan of Aeschylus. In itself it nowhere serves to hold the play together; but it does at one point (384 ff.) give a clue to the structural plan. For it prays for grace from Demeter 'to say much in jest and much in earnest' and thereby to win the first prize. This prayer favours a view that such unity as the play can be said to possess derives entirely from its central figure, Dionysus himself.[1] His character has two sides. The comic side reflects the fruitful, positive aspects of social life and the laughing acceptance by mankind of their own limitations; or their equally gay self-assertion, in drunken release, as subject to no will but their own.[2] The other side, thoughtful and serious, is revealed in Dionysus as god also of the tragic stage, where individual men and women play out their part in agonizing struggles for and against society. This serious side appears in the opening scenes of the play, where Dionysus avows his intention of giving Athenian tragedy—and Euripides—a new lease of life. In the Parabasis it makes a brief reappearance, if the Chorus may be regarded as spokesmen of their god. Finally, in the Literary Contest, Dionysus strives throughout to maintain the gravity befitting a judge. If gaiety breaks in, it is snubbed (1150) or kept in check (1399 f.) until judgement is pronounced (1467–78).

---

[1] See C. P. Segal, 'The Character of Dionysus and the Unity of the *Frogs*', *Harvard Studies in Classical Philology*, 65, 1961, as revised for *Twentieth Century Interpretations of the 'Frogs'*, ed. D. J. Littlefield, New Jersey, 1968, pp. 55 f. and reff.

[2] Cf. Arthur Platt, *Nine Essays*, Cambridge, 1927, pp. 55 f.

NOTE ON THE TRANSLATION

The nature of a translation must always depend very largely on its purpose. The translation I have made for this book is to illustrate a chapter of history —the history of ancient literary criticism. I have therefore thought it right to keep closely to the text of Aristophanes, translating line for line, and, except in the rendering of expletives, making only a sparing use of modernizations, though these might well be used in versions written for the stage of today. The text I have followed, with only a few deviations, is that of Professor W. B. Stanford's second edition of the play. I am much indebted to him also for his commentary.

To represent the ordinary dialogue metre of Greek comedy—an iambic six-foot line ('trimeter') much more freely constructed than that of tragedy— I have used a five-beat verse with an indeterminate number of 'slack' syllables. This makes it possible to render line for line without padding or other embarrassment; and when the speaker quotes from tragedy, or plays at being tragic, the line can be contracted to the more formal measure of our own tragic blank-verse.

Fidelity to the spirit of the Greek really involves fidelity to its metrical forms; for metres have a way of asserting their own personality. I have therefore tried, outside the ordinary dialogue, to reproduce these forms. Metre in ancient Greek depended upon measurements of time. Syllables were regarded as either 'long' (–) or 'short' (◡) in duration, usually called 'quantity'; and Greek syllabation differed from our own, except when we sing, e.g. they said *pe-ri-phe-ry*, not *per-iph-er-y*. In English, by contrast, the incidence of stress ('), meaning loudness or emphasis however slight, is the guiding metrical principle. This being so, the only practical method, in my opinion, of conveying some notion of Greek metrical patterns is to represent the longs and shorts by stressed and unstressed syllables respectively. But preferably, the stressed syllables should also be 'true-timed', i.e. actually long in duration as judged by the ear; and the short should have naturally short vowels, uncluttered by consonants. What will then be written—and what I have tried myself to write—is best called 'true-timed accentual verse'. The 'quantitative' translation of classical metres, which attempts to observe most of the ancient rules of prosody, is quite different. On it see *The Oxford Book of Greek Verse in Translation* (1938), pp. lvi–ix and Robert Bridges' quantitative hexameters on pp. 55–60 of the same book.

In writing true-timed verse by ear one soon finds that the quantity of one and the same syllable varies with its context. Contrast, for example, an angry 'Húrry úp!' with '*Shé* won't hurry up for anyone!' where the '*Shé*' is followed by a flurry of shorts. Or take the word 'and'. In some places it bears sufficient stress to count as a long; but with stressed syllables next to it on either side, as in 'bréad and bútter' it is little more than ''n'. There are other discoveries to be made—but here's a caution. Readers of my translation should not, in the act of reading, try to work out the metrical patterns. My hope is that if they go ahead, as naturally as they would in reading the morning paper, most of the metrical patterns will assert themselves.

Some of the patterns are not foreign to English poetry; and among that number is one which is well worth reproducing both because of its recurrence in the *Frogs* and because Euripides, at one point, is criticized for a fault in his use of it. It is known as the 'Glyconic' metre and was adapted by Tennyson on an accentual basis (mostly true-timed) for a poem 'On the Jubilee of Queen Victoria'. For example:

> You then joyfully, all of you,
> Set the mountain aflame to-night,
> Shoot your stars to the firmament . . .

In Greek the basic form with its common variations is $\cup \circ \mid -\cup\cup- \mid \cup -$. Metrists mark it off, as shown, into 3 constituents or 'feet', of which the most distinctive is the central 'nucleus' $-\cup\cup-$, a 'choriambus'. Variations shown in the 1st foot are an iambus ($\cup -$), a spondee ($--$), or a trochee ($-\cup$); and in the last $\cup -$, or $--$. In certain places and on certain conditions further variation could be made by 'resolving' a long into two shorts. Such 'resolutions' both in dialogue and in lyrics are commoner in Euripides than in Aeschylus or Sophocles and may perhaps be classed among his dietary methods (cf. 939–43) of slimming the Tragic Muse. Associated with glyconics is a metre, the 'Pherecratean', exactly the same except in the last foot, which consists of a single long syllable. See 1253, 1256, 1258–60.

Nine glyconics are quoted from or attributed to Euripides by Aeschylus in the course of lines 1310–28. Five of these keep to the basic form, viz. 1311, 1318, 1320, 1324, 1326. Two show 'resolutions' in the 1st foot, viz. 1317, 1327. There is nothing uncommon in these. But the remaining two are unique. In 1322 Aeschylus quotes from Euripides:

> put an arm | round mother, child | of mine,

where the 1st foot is an 'anapaest' ($\cup\cup-$). In theory this could be explained as a spondee ($--$) with the first long 'resolved'; but in normal practice that licence was ruled out. So Aeschylus, himself beginning a glyconic of basic form, asks Dionysus 'This foot's | curious, see | it?' To which Dionysus replies not with a monosyllabic 'yes', which would have completed the line regularly, but with 'I do', making a licentious anapaest ('it? I do') in the 3rd foot and showing that he had taken Aeschylus' point.

Aristophanes had great metrical versatility. This translation may perhaps give some conception of it to readers with no knowledge of Greek.

EURIPIDES   DIONYSUS   AESCHYLUS   CHORUS   PLUTO

EURIPIDES (*To Dionysus*) I claim the Chair and won't give up. Don't
lecture me.
In the art of poetry I say I'm the better man.
DIONYSUS. You see his point, Aeschylus. Then why so mum?
EUR. First he'll assume a proud reserve, that trick
of mystification common to his tragic heroes.
DIO. My dear good fellow, take a moderate tone.
EUR. I know the man, long ago I saw clean through him,

    the creator of boorish characters, tongue-tied when he will,
    or mouthing with no curb, no continence, no closure,
    a narrow-ranging big-mouthed-bundle-of-bombast.
AESCHYLUS. Is that so, you son of a market-garden goddess?[1]   840
    Do you speak so of me, you picker-up of tittle-tattle,
    you stager of beggar-men, you rag-and-tatters-patcher?
    O but you'll soon be sorry for it!
DIO.   Aeschylus, stop!
    'And let no passionate rancour fire your soul.'
AES. I shall not stop until I have clearly shown
    what this stager of cripples is worth, for all his bluff.
DIO. (*Playfully suggesting a sacrifice to appease the Storm god*)
    A lamb, boys, a black lamb, go, fetch it out;
    there's a hurricane here, working up for a sortie.
AES. (*To Euripides*) You picker-up of Cretan monodies, you importer
    of sacrilegious unions into the art of Tragedy.   850
DIO. Hi, you! Hold hard, most honourable Aeschylus;
    and you, my poor Euripides, if you're wise,
    go off, well away from the hailstones falling,
    or else he'll strike in his rage, coming down on your head
    with some capital phrase that will knock your *Telephus* out of it.
    You, Aeschylus, don't be wild, but give and take
    criticism gently. Poets should not exchange
    volleys of abuse like bake-house wives; but you
    flare up all at once with the roar of an oak on fire.
EUR. *I* am ready for battle, *I* am not shirking;   860
    ready, if *he*'s game, to give or get first bite,
    probing dialogue, lyrics, and sinews of structure;
    and I'll submit, 'fore god, my *Peleus*, my *Aeolus*,
    my *Meleager* too, and even the *Telephus* as well.
DIO. (*To Aeschylus*) What plan do *you* suggest? Speak, Aeschylus.
AES. I have never wished to hold a contest here;
    we are not meeting, you see, on equal terms. DIO. How's that?
AES. *My* works have not died with me, as his with him;
    his will be handy here, when he wishes to quote.
    However, since you approve, I too must comply.   870
DIO. (*Preparing to invoke the Muses*) Come, then, bring me frankincense,
        someone, and fire;
    then I, before the battle of wits begins,
    can pray for grace to judge with professional skill.

---

  [1] Cf. 947. Whatever the real social status of Euripides' mother, Aristophanes likes
to refer to her as a market-gardener or greengrocer.

(*Turning to the Chorus*) You'll accompany my prayer with a hymn to the Muses.

CHO.   Virginal Nine, the begotten of Zeus,
Muses, who gaze from above on our masters of speech subtly-woven,
coiners of wise aphorisms, that are stamped with their learning and insight,
—sharp witted, too, in the turns and the twists of a wrestle at word-
                                                                    play—
          Muses, descend! For the ablest of men,
          marvels at shaping a phrase, with a wealth of   880
          lexical carpentry, square up to fight—
see, the stupendous professional bout now waits the word to open!

DIO. (*To Aesch. and Eur.*) Now you two pray, before you speak your
     lines.   885
AES. Demeter, who informed and fed my mind,
     may I prove worthy of thy Mysteries.
DIO. (*To Eur.*) It's your turn now. Put some incense on. EUR. No, thank
     you.
     The gods I pray to are other ones than these.
DIO. Personal gods, new coinages? EUR. For sure.   890
DIO. Pray, then, to your private, nonconformist gods.
EUR. Upper Air, my nutriment! Pivoted, wagging Tongue!
     Intellectual Power! Nostrils that scent out faults!
     Right well may I expose the flaws I pounce upon.

CHO.   All ears are we! Let us hear, speak out!
          what is the strife estranging you, most clever of men?
               Where is the warpath like to lead?
               Tongues of both are stirred to fury,
               stout of heart are both and daring,
               both have minds soon roused to act;
                 so to one we look for something   900
                 smart, of piquant urban flavour,
                 some refined, smooth style of wit;
               while a Titan's strength uproots him
               arguments and all, confounding
          countless twists and turns of speechcraft's wrestling holds.

(*Dionysus gives a lead with the long iambic measure commonly used in
attack and bids Euripides open the debate.*)

DIO. Now speak and hurry; making sure that all you say is witty;
　jocose comparisons are out and commonplace expressions.

EUR. My observations on myself as poet I'll put second;
　at first I'll deal with Aeschylus and shortly I'll expose him
　as nothing else than charlatan and cheat. I'll show the dodges
　by which he fooled the simple souls of Phrýnichus'[1] upbringing.　910
　He'd stage at first some lonely form, seated and veiled, and faceless,
　Achilles, say, or Níobë—a piece of window dressing,
　for there they'd sit without a word, never so much as grunting.

DIO. Quite true, not even a grunt.

EUR.   Meanwhile the choir would force upon us
　string after string of lyric verse—and still that form was silent.

DIO. I revelled in the silence and I found it no less pleasant
　than listening to our talkers of to-day.

EUR.   But you were simple,
　depend upon it.

DIO.   I agree. But *why* did the feller do it?

EUR. A charlatan's device to hold his audience: they'd be waiting
　for Níobë to say something. On went the play and on.　920

DIO. The utter scoundrel! How I was imposed upon!
　　　　　　　　　(*Turning to Aeschylus*) Hi, you there!
　What makes you fume and fidget so?

EUR.   He knows when he is beaten.
　Then after all this choral stuff, when half the play was over
　came twelve big words from the ox-hide age, browbeaters, helmed and
　　　crested,
　unheard-of horrors, bogywords.

AES.   Oh my, oh my!

DIO.   Be silent.

EUR. Not one intelligible thing he'd say.

DIO. (*To Aeschylus*)   Don't gnash your teeth, man.

EUR. His talk was all Scamanders, trenches, shields with griffin-eagles
　embossed in beaten bronze, and heaps of towering, craggy phrases
　of meaning hard to gather.

DIO.   Yes, my word, I've lain before now　930
　'sleepless the long night-watches through' and inwardly debating
　whatever kind of bird the phrase 'a brown horse-cock' denoted.

AES. An emblem, that was, painted on the ships, you ignoramus.

DIO. And all the time I thought it meant Philóxenos' boy, Eryxis!

EUR. But should one write in tragic verse of even a barn-door rooster?

AES. And you, you god-forsaken rogue, of what, I ask, did you write?

　　　　[1] The greatest of Aeschylus' predecessors: cf. 1300.

EUR. Of horse-cocks never! Good god, no! Nor antlered goats, as you did—
the things one sees depicted on those tapestries from Persia.
Oh no! When I took over tragic art, and found our mistress
blown out with your bombastic stuff and phrases stomach-loading, 940
a slimming course was first my care. To take off weight, I gave her
versicles, constitutionals, some white beetroot for purges,
and verbal flux, strained off from books, presented in decoction.
Next, monodies to plump her—DIO. With Kephisophon[1] for dressing.
EUR. Again, no prating prologues mine; no slapdash, clueless forewords!
My prologist at once explained the drama's antecedents.
DIO. And more respectable than yours, god knows, he must have shown them!
EUR. And further, from the play's first lines I'd have no unemployment;
the women I'd keep talking, and the servants just as freely, 949
the master of the house, young girl and aged crone—AES. Then surely
you should have died the death for such effrontery. EUR. Good lord, no!
I acted in a democratic spirit. DIO. Let that be, friend;
for you it's not a subject that would warrant an excursus.[2]
EUR. (*With a gesture to the audience*) What's more, I taught our people here
the way to talk. AES. I'll say so!
And better if your guts had split before you started teaching!
EUR. I taught them to apply a subtler *Metrik*; trim their verses
by set-square; ponder, pry, perceive; love twisting and sharp practice;
think evil and be always hypercritical. AES. I'll say so!
I showed our common life, familiar things, the things around us,
which could themselves have proved me wrong, because my audience
knew them 960
and could have faulted me. I never used pretentious language
to make the listeners lose their heads, staging to stupefy them
a Kyknos or a Memnon with-bell-harness-and-cheek-pieces.
Our pupils mark the difference between us: two of his are
Phormīsius the hearth-rug and Megaínetus the cock-shy,[3]
the-trumpet-lance-and-whiskers-breed whose-arched-pine-stems-
disrupt-you.
Kleitophon's mine, and mine Therámenes, the Smartie.
DIO. Therámenes? Ah, there's an artist! Up to every challenge!

[1] An Athenian, living in Euripides' house; supposed to help him with his plays and
to have an affair with his wife. Cf. 1408; also 1046, 1440–4.
[2] An insinuation that Euripides had oligarchic leanings, like his 'pupils' Theramenes
and Kleitophon, and that spending his last years at the Macedonian court was far from
democratic.
[3] Phormisius was shaggy in appearance; a part of his name suggests the Greek for a
rug. Megainetus may have resembled the bronze figure which formed part of the target
for heel-taps thrown from a wine-cup in the game of 'Kottabos'.

Wherever trouble faces him and brinkmanship is needed,
he's trouble-free the trimmer's way—if Chians lose, he's Keian.   970

> (*The short iambic lines which follow form the traditional 'breathless piece'*
> (pnīgos), *so called because delivered at high speed. These mark the end
> of the attacking speech of the first debater.*)

EUR. Such sound advice on how to think
I gave our friends the audience
by blending my tragedian's art
with Reasoning and Searching Thought,
that no one now could name a thing
beyond their grasp: they know what's what,
including new, progressive ways
of keeping house: 'Is all well here?'
they ask, 'Where's this?' and 'Who's got that?'

DIO. Lord, yes! The menfolk, everyone,   980
in Athens now, no sooner home,
bawl out to their domestic staff
'Where *is* the crock? This sprat's head, where?
Who wolfed it? Can the bowl I used
last year have died on me? We had
some garlic yesterday: what's left?
This olive's partly gnawed: by whom?'
The times are gone when they'd sit round
as feeble-minded as you please,
with jaws agape, mere suckers all   990
and simple sugar-babies.

CHO. (*To Aeschylus*) 'You behold these things, lustrous Achilles?'[1]
What on earth will you say? How refute them? Look to it, or
passion may be sweeping you
off the race-course, past the olives.[2]
Grave your rival's accusations!
O beware, my noble friend!
Do not state your case in anger;
reef to just one edge of canvas,
inch by inch then ease her on.   1000
Keep a wary eye the meanwhile,
wait the moment ripe for sail and
open out to catch a constant, gentle breeze.

> (*The leader of the Chorus urges Aeschylus to the counter-attack, giving
> him a lead in the anapaestic measure he will adopt.*)

[1] From the lost *Myrmidons* of Aeschylus.   [2] Flanking the course.

Prime builder in all our Hellene race of majestic, towering phrases, endowing tragedians' stuff with a style, take heart, throw open the sluices.

AES. I'm bridling with rage at this turn of events and my innards revolt at the notion

of a counter attack on the likes of my foe. But in case he should say I am cornered—

(*To Euripides*) first answer me this: for a gift of what kind is it right to admire any poet?

EUR. For his expertise and his sound advice and because we improve by our teaching

mankind's civic sense and their natures too. AES. Very well, if you've failed to improve them　　　　　1010

and have made finished rascals of those who were sound and of noble demeanour aforetime,

what is due, will you say, for amends? DIO. It is death. Spare *him* such a personal question.

AES. Now please to reflect what the breed of my day proved like, when I handed them over;

they were noble, upstanding, of four cubits' height, not malingering skrimshankerburghers,

not your idlers or tricksters, the type of today, nor the rogues whose kind stick at nothing;

for the spear and the lance were the breath of their lives and the whiteness of plumes coruscating

and the casque and the greave and a heart fear-proofed sevenfold, as a buckler of oxhide!

EUR. It's his curse, getting worse—DIO. And will bore me to death, if he *will* knock away at his helmets.

EUR. (*To Aeschylus*) What in fact did you do to instruct and produce so noble a breed of our manhood?

DIO. Speak, Aeschylus, speak, no longer persist in your obstinate pride and displeasure.　　　　　1020

AES. There's a drama I wrote, full of war. DIO. How so? AES. 'Seven leagued against Thebes' was the title.

Not a soul could have seen it without the desire himself to give proof of his mettle.

DIO. How wrong of you, that! It's the army of Thebes that your warlike play has emboldened

—and to side with our foes! For that service at least the reward you receive is—a hiding!

AES. You Athenians, too, could have trained for the field, but you turned
  to your own avocations.

To resume: in my *Persians* again, let me add, I extolled a superlative
  action;

and the lesson I taught was to crave always for supremacy over
  opponents.

DIO. I rejoiced in that scene where the King's crown prince wailed loud
  for his father departed

and the chorus at once clapped their hands—like so!—with a hullabaloo
  of 'i-au-oi'.

AES. (*Disregarding interruption*) It's the duty of poets to practise their art
  in the ways I have told; reckon only   1030

how helpful the nobler among them have been, to this day from the
  earliest ages.

First Orpheus showed us his mystical rites and barred foods taken by
  slaughter;

Musaeus, again, taught cures of disease and oracular lore; and from
  Hesiod

field-work we have learned, when to reap, when to plough. Or reflect
  on the genius of Homer—

whence came all his glory and fame? Was it not from his teaching us
  practical lessons?

Battle-order he showed and the deeds that excel and the way to bear
  arms— DIO. That is something

Pantoklés never learned; for our greatest of fools, t'other day, on parade
  as an escort,

strapped a helmet on first, then was mounting a plume—as if plumes
  could be fixed from the outside!

AES. Yet he taught many more, fine soldiers and brave, such as Lámachus,[1]
  known as 'the Hero'.

I too, being shaped to the mould of his mind, bodied forth many
  patterns of greatness—   1040

a Patróklos, or Teucer, the old lion-hearts; and I hoped that my fellow
  Athenians

might take on the stamp of heroical types at the sound of the trumpeter
  calling.

Never once, god knows, did my hand portray loose Phaedras or loose
  Sthenoboias,[2]

---

[1] One of the three generals commanding in Sicily in 415 B.C. He was killed there.

[2] Phaedra, wife of Theseus, who loved her stepson Hippolytus: the reference is to
Euripides' *Hippolytus*—the earlier version shocked more than the one extant. For
Sthenoboia (or Anteia) and Bellerophon see *Iliad* 6.

not in one of my plays could you find anywhere any lovelorn woman presented.

EUR. God knows, Aphrodítë can hardly have made any mark upon *you*!

AES. Never may she!

What a burden she was, what a cumbersome weight, when she lighted on you and your household!

And she tumbled your own very self to the ground. DIO. That's a fact, god's truth, very much so!

Those plays, written round other folk and their wives, struck painfully back at their author!

EUR. (*To Aeschylus*) What's the harm, you bigot, you're thinking I do to our country by my Sthenoboias?

AES. If the noblest of wives from our noblest of homes drained poison to end their abasement,   1050

it was all *your* fault, with the lure of your plays and the shame your Bellérophons brought them.

EUR. Do you think there was no foundation of fact in the play I composed about Phaedra?

AES. Lord knows, it was true; but a poet should veil and conceal what is base and immoral,

not stage and propound it. Our infants are taught by whoever is near to instruct them;

but the poets alone are the teachers of youth—so, for sure, what we say in our poems

should adhere to what's morally sound. EUR. I suppose if your vocables dwarf Lycabettus,

Parnassus-big mouthfuls of speech, that's the way to impart sound moral instruction?

No, rather be human and speak man to man. AES. Poor fool, by a law of their nature

sublime ideas and greatness of thought are begetters of lofty expression,[1]

and, again, demigods as of right should excel mere mortals in grandeur of phrasing,   1060

since greater magnificence, too, than our own is the outward mark of their clothing.

I preached sound doctrine in all these points. *You* ruined the show.

EUR. By what action?

AES. By your treatment of Royalty. Time and again, to arouse compassion, you staged them

not in royal array but in bundles of rags. EUR. And whatever was harmful in that?

---

[1] Cf. 'Longinus' (below, p. 468).

AES. A result is that now there is no one of means who will stand running-costs of a trireme.

Ostensibly clothed in a costume of rags he'll weep and declare he's a pauper.

DIO. By our Lady, that's true! And beneath, all the time, he is swathed in the warmest of woollens

and when once well away with his fraudulent tale—up he bobs buying delicatessen!

AES. And another effect of the views you professed is the talkative, tongue-wagging fashion;

for it emptied the gyms, it was hard on the rumps of the young, sitting long in discussion,   1070

and encouraged indiscipline. Admirals' crews give an officer back-chat. In *my* day

they knew little else than to shout for their loaves and to bawl 'pull away' at a send-off.

DIO. Lord, yes! And to blow from abaft in the face of a rower behind in the galley,

or to crown a messmate with a load of their dirt and to filch civvy clothes on a shore-leave.

Nowadays whole crews give you cheek and won't row, spreading sail on their slightest occasions.

(*To match* 971–91 *a 'breathless piece' follows in shorter lines of the preceding metre.*)

AES. Is there *any* disgrace for which *he*'s not to blame?
It was *he*, was it not, who put bawds[1] in the cast;
He wrote of *accouchements* in shrines of the gods
and of sisters incestuous, mating with brothers,   1080
and of women who swear that in life we are dead.
Now, thanks to such ploys, *who* are crowding our streets?
Here, legions of clerks, petty servants of State;
there, sly jackanapes with a hold on the mob—

---

[1] *Bawds*: e.g. the old nurses of Phaedra and Sthenoboia (1043), who in pity for their mistresses became go-betweens. *Accouchements in shrines*: the reference may be to Augë in Euripides' play of that name. *Sisters incestuous*: e.g. Cánacë, in a play bearing the name of her father Aeolus, god of the winds, who is said in Homer, *Odyssey* 10. 6 f., to have married his six daughters to his six sons. Cf. the Ptolemies in ancient Egypt. *In life we are dead*: the sentiment occurs in fragments of two lost plays of Euripides, e.g. in the *Polyidus*, as translated by Sir Maurice Bowra: 'Who knows if living after all is death, / While death is counted life by those below?' (*The Oxford Book of Greek Verse in Translation*, 1938, p. 460). The quotation is used by Dionysus with devastating effect in 1477.

expertly bamboozling it, time after time.
There's nobody left who can race with a torch,
  not a soul with a notion of training.
DIO. Not a soul, that's a fact! I was hoarse with guffaws
at the All-Athens Show when I saw one who raced
pale, paunchy, bent over. With how much ado   1090
he was pounding on, left ever further behind!
Then the crowd at the Potteries, hard by the gates,
had a whack at him, paunch, rib and flank and backside;
and this oaf, at the feel of the flats of their hands
    with a feeble back-fire
flew, blowing the flame to revive it.

CHO. Big is the crisis, bitter the quarrel, massive hostilities now impend.
  Is there a judge could make decision   1100
  when, of the two, one throws his weight in,
yet his opponent, ably wheeling, scores a fine, sharp counter-blow?
  Now for both it's 'úp and át him!'
Openings there are in dozens, ways for new inroads of wit.
  If any quarrel is to be settled,
  tell of it, go ahead, bring you up, both of you,
  incriminations, new or ancient.
Take a chance with subtle wisecracks phrased with knowledgeable skill.
Should you feel alarm, mistrusting these your listeners' competence,
  thinking they will fail to see the   1110
  finer points in what you're saying,
feel no fear, the whole position is today completely changed.
  All by now are old campaigners,
  one and all possess a textbook and perceive the smarter hits.[1]

---

[1] The references in these lines to the intelligence of the audience, who are 'old campaigners, each one with a book', are best taken as (i) advance notice of the literary fare Aristophanes is about to provide; (ii) a jest, appearing to deprecate the spread of learning and bookishness—his *Clouds* in 423 B.C. had been above the heads of most of the audience. The very word 'book' had become a good gag, as its use in Aristophanes elsewhere shows, from at least 414 B.C.; cf. line 943 above. Books, in the form of a papyrus roll (or papyrus folded horizontally for short memoranda), had become available from the second half of the fifth century or earlier. Aristophanes makes only one certain reference to the text of a written play, viz. in *Frogs* 52, where Dionysus 'had been reading Euripides' *Andromeda* on board ship'. It seems that books were sometimes distributed to friends by their authors after a public reading and eventually traded in the market-place from sold-up estates. There is no trace at this time of professional publishers, speculating on public demand. See E. G. Turner, *Athenian Books in the 5th and 4th centuries B.C.*, London, 1952.

Now their minds, by grace of nature
sharp before, are sharper still.
Forge ahead, then, do not worry,
you've no need to doubt your audience, they're a highly cultured lot!

EUR. (*To Dionysus*) Mark, then, his prologues[1] in themselves. I'll turn
at first to them, testing the part that's first   1120
in this accomplished author's tragic dramas;
for some preliminary facts he'd not make clear.

DIO. And which of his prologues will you test? EUR. A good number.
(*To Aeschylus*) Recite me first the one from the myth of Orestes.

AES. 'Thou Nether Hermes, watchman of realms paternal,
be thou my saviour and ally, I pray thee,
for I am come to this country and return.'[2]

DIO. (*To Euripides*) Have you any faults to find there? EUR. Twelve or more.

DIO. But the lines recited are only three in all.   1130

EUR. With a score of faults in every single line.

DIO. Aeschylus, take my advice and quote no more,
or amends will clearly be owing for more than three.

AES. Am *I* to shut up to please *him*?

DIO.   If you take my advice.

EUR. At the very start a blunder, huge as high Olympus![3]

AES. (*To Dionysus*) Do you see what rot your advice is?

DIO.   I couldn't care less.

AES. (*To Euripides*) How do you say I went wrong?

EUR.   Repeat, from the start.

AES. 'Thou Nether Hermes, watchman of realms paternal . . .'

EUR. Orestes is speaking, isn't he, close to the tomb
of his father, who is dead?

AES.   That's nothing but what I say.   1140

EUR. Then was it the death which Orestes' *own* father died,
'By stealthy cunning slain at a woman's hand'
— was it *that* of which Hermes, he said, was the watchman?

AES. No, no! he invoked not Hermes the God of Stealth
but Nether Hermes, the Helpful, making this clear

---

[1] Formal prologues are found in all but four of the extant Greek tragedies. They are
spoken by one of the characters or by a divine being closely in touch with the events
concerned. The prologist by explaining the situation out of which the plot develops
gave useful help to the audience, for the myths on which plays were based had more
than one version.

[2] The beginning of the *Choephori*—known only through Aristophanes.

[3] I borrow the translation from Shakespeare, *Julius Caesar*, iv. 3. 90 ff.: *Cassius*. A
friendly eye could never see such faults. *Brutus*. A flatterer's would not, though they do
appear | As huge as high Olympus.

by calling that role a paternal, inherited power.

EUR. There's a bigger fault, then, than the one I was meaning;
for if he holds his nether-world power by inheritance—

DIO. (*Interrupting*) That would make him a grave-robber on his father's
side.

AES. Dionysus, that is not a vintage joke![1]   1150

DIO. (*To Aeschylus*) Give him another verse. (*To Euripides*) You, watch
the costs.

AES. 'Be thou my saviour and ally, I pray thee,
for I am come to this country and return.'

EUR. The accomplished Aeschylus has told us the same thing twice.

AES. How so?

EUR.   Consider the phrasing—but I'll inform you.
'I am come to this country', he says, and 'I return' says he;
but to 'come to the country' and to 'return' are one and the same.

DIO. Lord, yes! it's just as if one begged from a neighbour like this:
'Please lend me a bowl, or a crock, if you will, to mix in.'

AES. It's not 'one and the same', you talked-silly creature!   1160
Far from it. The verse is excellently phrased.

EUR. In what respect? Tell me your reason for saying so.

AES. A man with civic rights can be said to 'come home',
for without more ado he arrives home and is there;
but an exile does more than to 'come': he 'returns' or 'is restored'.

DIO. By Apollo, well said! Your answer, Euripides?

EUR. I deny that Orestes was ever 'restored' to his home.
He came home secretly, without official leave.

DIO. By Hermes, well said—but, search me, *what* does he mean?

EUR. (*To Aeschylus*) Go ahead now with another verse.

DIO.   Go on, Aeschylus, do,   1170
and *jump* to it! (*To Euripides*) You, keep a close look out for faults.

AES. 'On this heaped tomb I call upon my father
to hear and hearken . . .'

EUR.   Two words for one again!
'To hear and hearken', says he. A clear tautology!

DIO. It's the dead he was addressing, you insufferable fool,
to whom we cry out thrice, yet never get through.

AES. (*To Euripides*) And how did *you* compose your prologues?

EUR.   I'll explain.
And if ever I say the same thing twice, or if

[1] I have some recollection that an unnamed pupil offered the translation I print of
this line to his tutor the late J. D. Denniston of Hertford College, Oxford, who passed
it on to me. I wish I could make fuller acknowledgement.

you detect any padding or irrelevance—spit on me!
DIO. Come, then, recite. Clearly it's up to me   1180
to hear how correctly written your prologues are.
EUR. 'Oedipus was at first a happy man . . .'[1]
AES. Good god, no! In misery he was born and bred.
Why, Apollo foretold even before his birth
that he would kill his father, aye, spoke it of one unborn.
How *could* he have been 'at first a happy man'?
EUR. (*Continuing*) 'to prove in turn of all men wretchedest'.
AES. Good god, no! He never 'proved' that way 'in turn',
his wretchedness never ceased. From his earliest hour
they exposed him, in winter, abandoned in a crock,   1190
to prevent his growing up and killing his father;
then ill-chance linked him with Polybus, his feet all swollen;
next, he was married young to an old beldame,
and his own mother she was, to make it worse;
lastly, he gouged his eyes out.
DIO.   Happy still, even if
he had shared Erasínidës' command—and execution.[2]
EUR. (*To Aeschylus*) You drivel, sir. My prologues are elegantly
    written.
AES. I won't now carp at your phrasing word by word,
'fore heaven no! but demolish, so help me god,
your prologues with the aid of a litt'l old flask.[3]   1200
EUR. *My* prologues? With a litt'l old flask?
AES.   A single one,
for your style is such that the meanest things are in place—
a litt'l old fleece, or flask, or shopping bag;
they suit your iambic verse, as I'll prove on the spot.
EUR. You'll prove it, will you? AES. Yes. DIO. (*To Euripides*) Recite away.
EUR. (*Quoting from a prologue of his*)
'Aegyptus, in the tale most widely told,
with fifty sons took ship; and driven by oar
to port in Argos . . .'

---

[1] Euripides' *Antigone*.
[2] See above, p. 9.
[3] The word (*lēkuthion*) for flask in 1200 and the two words coupled with it are all diminutives, i.e. expressive of affection or, more often, contempt, and mostly of collo-quial use. A small, globular flask, often containing oil such as sunbathers use, was carried about by Athenians or their slaves. In translating I found that a plain English diminutive ('little flask', 'flasklet', etc.) did not convey the undertones and the flat colloquial bathos of the diminutive in Greek. Hence 'litt'l old flask'.

AES.   lost his litt'l old flask.[1]

DIO. What ever's the point of this litt'l old flask? Doggone it!
Recite him another prologue, let's see once more.   1210

EUR. 'Dionysus, who with wands and fawn-skins dight
among the pine-flares on Parnassus' wold
leaps with the dancers . . .'

AES.   lost his litt'l old flask.

DIO. Oh my! The flask has struck again and caught us!

EUR. It won't matter at all, he won't be able
to attach a flask to the prologue I've got here:
'There lives no man in all things fortunate;
of noble nature is one, but wants his bread;
another, ignoble . . .'

AES.   lost his litt'l old flask.

DIO. Euripides—EUR. Well? DIO. We'd better reef in a bit,   1220
this litt'l old flask will blow a nasty gale.

EUR. Bah! By our Lady I wouldn't give it a thought,
it'll now be knocked from his hand, once and for all.

DIO. Come, then, try another—and keep well clear of the flask.

EUR. 'Faring from Sidon, Cadmus long ago
son of Agenor . . .'

AES.   lost his litt'l old flask.

DIO. (*To Euripides*) My dear, good fellow, buy back that litt'l old flask
and stop him from tearing our prologues to shreds. EUR. What's that?
Buy it? *I*? To please *him*? DIO. If you'll take my advice.

EUR. No, no! There's many a prologue I'll manage to quote   1230
that will baffle him yet in attaching a litt'l old flask.

---

[1] The Greeks sometimes amused themselves by completing the structure of a broken quotation with a fixed phrase or 'tag' such as 'and the partridge leg'. So, in modern versions of the same pastime, tags used are 'pork and greens' or 'grandmother's big red toe'. Sometimes, as in this scene, when the game was for two players, an object of some kind could be staked, and won or forfeited according to success or failure in attaching the tag, cf. 1227, 1235 f.

All the simpler souls among the audience of the *Frogs* could enjoy the familiar fooling. Perhaps the scene has nothing more to it. But it can be argued that beneath the fooling Euripides is criticized partly for incongruity of style, cf. 1202 f.; that he deserves it because of his boasts in 959, 971-9; and that the point is emphasized by choosing from his prologues lines of perfectly suitable diction for tragedy and then rounding them off with a tag of ridiculously humble and prosaic associations.

Further, the lines chosen have a wearisome sameness of syntactical structure, all of them, except 1217 ff., opening with a proper name and an attached participial clause. Lines 1232 f. are the only examples of this structure found in his extant plays, but others may have shown it becoming a habit.

(*Quoting again*) 'Pelops of Tantalus' line to Pisa driven
by mares of mettle . . .'

AES.   lost his litt'l old flask.

DIO. You see? He's attached the litt'l old flask again.
Pay up, my good fellow, by hook or crook, even now;
you'll get it for an obol, a sound and shapely flask.

EUR. Not yet, good Lord no! I've many a prologue still!
(*Quoting again*) 'Oeneus, one harvest . . .'

AES.   lost his litt'l old flask.

EUR. Allow me first to recite the verse complete:
'Oeneus, one harvest, from his fields' rich crop   1240
offering first-fruits . . .'

AES.   lost his litt'l old flask.

DIO. In the act of offering? What sneakthief pinched it from him?

EUR. Let it pass, friend. I defy him to chip in to this one:
'Zeus, as the very voice of Truth has told . . .'

DIO. (*Interrupting to close the scene*) You'll bore me stiff! 'Lost his litt'l
old flask', he'll say.
The flasket sprouts on your prologues like styes on the eye.
For god's sake turn instead to his choral songs.

EUR. Of course, for I've got the means of showing him up
as a bad song-writer who makes all his songs the same.   1250

CHO. What is afoot? What is starting now?
So I ponder, and ask myself
what are his incriminations?
How fault one who in wealth of song
prized for beauty has far surpassed
all his kind to this moment?
I *do* wonder what line he'll take—
how on earth will he fault him,
King by Bacchus appointed?
Fears have I for his fortune.   1260

EUR. Wonderful songs indeed!—as will soon appear.
I'll cut them all down to a single unit of metre.

DIO. All right. With some of these pebbles I'll keep the score.

(*Interlude follows on the flute, which then accompanies the lyrics.*)

EUR.[1] 'Phthiôt Achilles,
at the sound of men's hacking and hewing . . .'

[1] Euripides recites (with offensive intonation?) isolated lines from Aeschylus' plays,
making no continuous sense. To each he adds, as a kind of refrain, a shorter line, the

        O pain
upon pain! Come you not to the rescue?
   'Hermes, Sire of our race,
we adore thee, a breed of the lake-lands . . .'
        O pain
upon pain! Come you not to the rescue?
DIO. That is two against Aeschylus, two pains.
EUR. 'My lesson learn, great king of kings,   1270
in Achaia supreme, son of Atreus . . .'
        O pain
upon pain! Come you not to the rescue?
DIO. That's a third against Aeschylus, three pains.
EUR. 'Silence! Artemis' honey-bee maids
are approaching to open her temple . . .'
        O pain
upon pain! Come you not to the rescue?
   '*I* am well able to speak
of their march and their Chiefs, sped by Heaven . . .'
        O pain
upon pain! Come you not to the rescue?
DIO. Zeus, King of Heaven! What a bellyful of 'pains'!
I'm for the bathroom, a douche is the thing for me,
pains upon pains have set my kidneys aching.   1280
EUR. Don't go, first hear another set of his songs,
worked up from modes accompanied on the lyre.[1]

same every time, which picks up the dactylic rhythm into which the quotations invariably fall. Very possibly the rhythm was commoner in lost plays than in those we possess.

Dionysus meanwhile keeps the score with pebbles for counters. His two interjections match the rhythm of the refrain, which the line-arrangement of the translation helps to mark.

1264. *Phthiôt*: of Phthia or Phthiotis, just N. of the Euboic gulf.

This quotation (from the *Myrmidons*) and the next three are all from plays known to us by little more than their titles. The last is from the *Agamemnon*.

[1] Tragic choruses were normally accompanied by the flute, not the lyre as here. Loss of the music obscures the point made by Euripides in this second set of quotations from Aeschylus. As before, the prevailing rhythm is dactylic, the dactyls being preceded in the 1st and 4th quotations by an iambic metron ($\cup - \cup -$); and, as before, the line-arrangement in the translation aims at marking the recurrent dactylic run. By contrast, the metre of the refrain 'tophlattothrat' is iambic and suggests that Euripides made play of thrumming on a lyre as he sang. It seems that he is charging Aeschylus with musical as well as metrical monotony.

The 1st and 3rd quotations are from the *Agamemnon*, the 4th is of unknown origin, and the 2nd and 5th are from plays known to us only by their titles. Stitched together they make a crazy kind of continuous sense. The 5th matches the refrain in metre, except in the last foot ($- \cup$ for $\cup -$). It is incomplete, gives no clear sense, and may be an interpolation.

DIO. Proceed, proceed—and don't go tacking on 'pains'.

EUR. 'How kings, twin-throned,
                           of Achaia and spearmen of Hellas'
  to-phlat-to-thrat to-phlat-to-thrat
    'dire as the Sphinx,
                           a dispenser of evil, a hell-hound',
  to-phlat-to-thrat to-phlat-to-thrat
    'marched to avenge,
                           bidden on by a heartening omen',
  to-phlat-to-thrat to-phlat-to-thrat   1290
    'a find for vultures,
                           for the tear-away hounds heaven-ranging',
  to-phlat-to-thrat to-phlat-to-thrat
    'and how converged against Ajax . . .'
  to-phlat-to-thrat to-phlat-to-thrat . . .

DIO. What's this to-phlat-to-thrat? Was it from Marathon, or where,
that you got together these chanties of the rope-walk?

AES. I brought them, at any rate, from an honoured source and put them
to honourable purpose, that none should see me culling
flowers where Phrýnichus had culled, a holy close, Muse-haunted; 1300
but *he* (*pointing to Euripides*) gets his honey from every whoreson
    frippet,
from Melétus' drinking-catches, from Carian flute-songs,
from dirges and dance-music. I'll soon prove my point.
Bring me the lyre, someone—but hold, what need
of a lyre for *his* stuff? Where's she that clacks the bones?
Come, woman, only you are Euripides' true Muse,
his songs are fit for no other lead than yours.

  (*Here enters an unlovely female figure, possibly with large ill-matched
  feet (line 1323), who marks with the castanets, as she dances, the
  metrical patterns attributed by Aeschylus to Euripides. The song is
  mainly a patchwork of quotations, without consecutive sense.*)

DIO. She's never practised Lesbian arts,[1] not she!

AES.[2] Halcyons, who float along in a buzz of small-talk

  [1] Lesbos was famous for lyric poetry, as well as for sexual perversion.
  [2] The first few lines of this song have a faint semblance of continuity, but soon pass
into a series of disjointed quotations from Euripides. The point of some, such as 1319,
is lost to us, but most are clearly chosen to illustrate technical faults, including confused
imagery, as in lines 1313–16, or questionable diction, music, and metre—a trio that are
sometimes not merely technical but exemplify ways in which Aeschylus thought a
stately choral tradition had been debased. This debasement is his main concern. He also

o'er the sea-waves tireless flood,   1310
bathed meanwhile in a dewy spray
of liquid atomies thrown from your wings;
you, too, spiders, who crouched in the rafter-nooks,
twi-i-i-i-i-ine with your toes the yarn, that tightly
drawn to fit a loom-hung webbing
moves the busy reed-sley to a song—
many a flute-loving dolphin there
leapt, enchanting the dark ships' prows!
Race-courses and oracles!
Sapful sheen of the vine in bud!   1320
Agony-banishing cluster of grapes!
Put an arm round mother, child of mine!

(*The grotesque feet of Euripides' 'Muse' are now displayed, while Aeschylus savours with distaste the initial anapaestic foot 'put an arm' and provokes from Dionysus, in response, an equally licentious final anapaest 'it? I do', making a pair of them.*)

This foot's curious—see it? DIO. I do.

AES. What's that? See you its pair? DIO. I do.

AES. (*To Euripides*)
Sure, Kȳrēnē taught you her style!
How dare *you* to disparage *mine*?
Fit model she! For the songs you write
ape twelve tricks of the whore's trade!

(*Relapsing into dialogue*) So much for your choric songs. I also wish thoroughly to expound the style of your lyric solos.[1]   1330

finds Euripides too fond of trivialities, e.g. the 'small-talk' (a colloquialism in the Greek) and spray-baths of halcyons, or the activities of spiders in the attic. On the musical side he evidently objects to roulades (1314), but we do not know enough of the facts to say more, except that music and morals were intimately connected according to Plato and other Greek thinkers.

[1] The burlesque solo which Aeschylus sings is a mixture of quotation and parody much as before, but with greater originality in their setting. They are integral parts of a central story which serves to ridicule Euripides' proud boast of having democratized tragedy (948–52). The narrator is a working woman. She begins with the tale of her ill-boding dream, the taint of which demands a ritual purification. Then, invoking the Sea-god, she relates her dream's horrible fulfilment: her rooster has been stolen! And the thief is a female slave called *Glykē*, a name roughly equivalent to 'Dulcie'.

This disaster prompts invocations of her housemates, or maybe townsfolk; of the mountain nymphs; and of a menial whose name *Māniā* is the same as that of a Phrygian prostitute.

Next she tells how she was working far into the night at her spinning—perhaps implying that she fell asleep at the task. Meanwhile the theft occurred and the cock, as pictured in her imagination, soared up and away in temporary escape from Glykē—or did she dream of it as flying away from herself for ever?   (*footnote continued overleaf*)

AES.   O Night, darkly luminous Night,
whose ghost, in my dream, do you rouse from the murk,
whose nightmare shape dead-alive, living-death,
from his Hell steals forth
night-spawned, very creature of darkness?
Deep-black grave-cloths shroud those bones—
O most dire
most horrible is the sight of him!
A blood lust, a blood lust peers from his eyes
and his nails are talons—enormous!

O to be clean! Hurry, maids, with a light for me!
Go, dip your pails in the dewy fresh streams and prepare me a bathful;
I'd be cleansed of my demonic phantasy.   1340

O help, Sea-god, O help me!
This is *it*! O help me, housemates!
Witness a sight to astound you!
He is gone, the cock I loved! Glykē has pinched him—
and she's decamped!
Nymphs of the hills, rally round!
You, Mánĭā, lend a hand!

Ah me, *how* intently
did I strive to finish a skein's length,
hands working the packed spindle of flax thread,
whir-ir-ir-irring it round,
so early I planned to rise
and darkling go on my way   1350
to find me a market!
Then he flew, up he flew to the height of heav'n,
bird never soared on a lighter wing!

Invocations follow of *Cretan bowmen*; of the huntress *Artemis*, here called '*Dictynna*'
and 'beauty queen'; and of *Hekate*, all in the hope of making a posse to catch Glykē at
home bearing evidence of her guilt.

Subordinate to the main theme, but important, is burlesque of Euripides' metrical
and musical extravagances; of his inconsequent narrative style; of his love for uniting
opposites in a single, striking expression, e.g. 'darkly luminous' (cf. D. H. Lawrence on
'Bavarian Gentians' in *Last Poems*: 'Bavarian gentians, big and dark, only dark / darken-
ing the daytime torch-like with smoking blueness of Pluto's gloom'); of his addiction to
invocations and to words for light and darkness and flight; and of his many repetitions
of emotive words, 'a blood lust, a blood lust', etc. Lapses into colloquialism, such as
'This is it!', add to the picture of democratized Tragedy.

In 1331–7 ('O Night . . . enormous') the line-division, but not the substance or the
metre, varies from that of Stanford's Greek text.

To me bitter, bitter is his legacy,
drop upon drop ever my eyes let fall,
showering, showering, oh, poor me!

Cretans![1]
Ida's breed, hasten hither,
aid me with the archers, your artillerymen,   1357
haste along, lithely stepping, round the household form a ring!
Hither O Dictynna, named 'beauty queen',
bring your own bitchlet pack, cast around, thoroughly search all
the house!   1360

Come child of Zeus, Hekatē, to my aid,
your torch, double-branched, penetrating, hold!
Let it blaze, lift it high and show me in
to catch Glykē the raider, bird and all!

DIO. Now both of you stop the songs. AES. I've had enough too,
I want to take him up to the weighing machine.
Only the scales can put our poetry to the test;
the weight of our phrases will try us and find us out.
DIO. Then both come here, if I really must weigh up
slabs of poetic art like any cheesemonger.

CHO.   Clever men *do* take endless pains!   1370
Another oddity's soon to come,
novel, and fully as strange could be.
Who could have figured it out? None other!
Dammit, if I for onc had heard it,
said by a sound authority even,—
man in the street, say,[2]—I'd have thought him
talking arrant nonsense!

DIO. Come on, stand each to his scale-pan. AES. and EUR. So!
And each take hold of it and say his say in turn,
not letting go until I call 'kokku'.[3]   1380
AES. and EUR. We're holding. DIO. Speak, then, down into the scales.
EUR. 'Would the ship Argos never had winged through . . .'[4]
AES. 'Spercheios' river and grazing grounds of kine.'

---

[1] After the initial cry 'Cretans!' the metrical system is based on the 'cretic' foot
–∪– with substitutions, typical of Euripides, of two shorts for a long syllable. In 1358
two cretics are followed by a trochaic run cut short in the last foot (–∪–|––|–∪–|–).
Hekate is invoked in a system combining iambs and anapaests.
[2] A hit at the way rumour spreads, especially in war-time.
[3] The cock's crow—or the cuckoo's cry.   [4] *Medea* 1.

DIO. Kokku! AES. and EUR. It's freed. DIO. And actually far the lower (*pointing to Aeschylus*) is this one's scale-pan.

EUR. However can that be so?

DIO. 'How?' ask you? Why, he placed a river in, moistening
his utterance, just as a woolman damps his wool;
but yours was a featherweight, it had wings to it.

EUR. Let him speak another and counterbalance mine.

DIO. Take hold again, then. AES. and EUR. See, it's done. DIO. Speak on.

EUR. 'Persuasion has no other shrine than speech.' 1391

AES. 'Death is the only god who loves not gifts.'

DIO. Let go! AES. and EUR. It's freed. DIO. Yes, again it's *his* scale sinking,
he placed Death in, the heaviest bane of all.

EUR. And I, Persuasion. My saying's a masterpiece.

DIO. Persuasion's an airy, irrational kind of thing.
Go, search for something else, one of your heavyweights,
something to draw your scale down, brawny and big.

EUR. Let's see . . . Where, oh where, have I such a line? DIO. I'll tell you:
'Achilles has thrown two singles and a four.'[1] 1400
Speak on, please, both of you. This is your last round.

EUR. 'Heavy with iron the club his right hand grasped.'

AES. 'Chariot on chariot piled, corpse upon corpse.'

DIO. He's thoroughly tricked you once again. EUR. How so?

DIO. He placed two 'chariots' in and 'corpses' two,
a weight not a hundred Egyptians could lift up.

AES. For me, then, no more tests by single sayings!
Into the scale himself let him step, and sit,
with children, wife, Kēphísophon and all,
taking his library with him. I, for my part,
shall speak but twice, two sayings, and outweigh them. 1410

DIO. (*To Pluto*) They're both my friends. I won't decide between them,
I'll not become embroiled myself with either;
One I consider clever—and one delights me.[2]

PLU. What? Will you leave undone all that you came for?

DIO. Suppose I *do* judge? PLU. Off you'll go with one of them,
the one you pick, and won't have come here to no purpose.

DIO. Thanks, and god bless you. (*To Aeschylus and Euripides*) Look,
now, I'd have you know
I came down here in search of a poet. EUR. And why?

DIO. That Athens, saved by him, might keep her choirs.

[1] A trifling line, said to come from Euripides' much-ridiculed *Telephus* (cf. 855, 864).

[2] In view of 1468 I agree with those who think that the one who 'delights' Dionysus is Aeschylus; but lines can be adduced to support the opposite opinion.

And so, whichever one gives her the sounder advice   1420
on policy, he is the man I am minded to take.
(*He turns to Aeschylus and Euripides*)
First, then, about Alkibíades. What views
have you? The country's in travail, painfully, for an answer.
EUR. What are her own views, pray? DIO. 'Her own', you ask.
'She yearns and hates and fain would have him back.'
But tell me, you two, what *you* think about it.
EUR. I hate a citizen should he prove slow
to help his country and swift to do much harm,
meeting his own needs well, shiftless in hers.
DIO. Lord bless me, that's well said. (*Turning to Aeschylus*) And what's
your view?   1430
AES. ''Twere best to rear no lion in the State;
if one be reared, best humour his caprice.'
DIO. Lord help me, I'm in a torment of indecision!
One's given a clever, one a lucid answer.
But state your views once more, you two, and tell us
what means of saving the country you envisage.
EUR. Suppose Kleókritos were given the featherweight
Kinésias for wings and blown to sea—
DIO. That sight would be a laugh, but what's the idea?
EUR. Suppose a sea-fight and the pair with flasks   1440
of vinegar, showering it into our enemies' eyes!   1441
DIO. Well done, my Palamédes, a born genius you!   1451[1]
Your own thought was it? Or Kēphísophon's?
EUR. My own, barring the vinegar flasks. That's his.
DIO. (*To Aeschylus*) And what say you? AES. First tell me about the country,
   —is she served by serviceable men? DIO. Of course not,
she hates their guts. AES. And likes the ne'er-do-wells?
DIO. Not she, oh no! Bad lots are forced upon her.
AES. What means, then, are there of saving such a country,
'unsuited both by smooth wear and the rough'?
DIO. Find means, good heavens, if you're to rise from the dead.   1460
AES. Above ground I'll speak: here I would rather not.
DIO. Please, please, not that! Send up and save from here.   1462
AES. I know a way to do it and will show. DIO. Speak on.   1442
AES. When we think trusty what we now mistrust
and what we trust untrusty. DIO. How? I'm lost.
Less learning, please, and more lucidity.

           [1] 1442–62 rearranged as shown.

AES. If we mistrusted citizens whom now
we trust, and used the services of those
we do not use, we should, perhaps, be saved;
and if in present courses we fare badly,
would not the opposite ways be our salvation? 1450
    (*Here it is assumed that two lines, in which Aeschylus was asked to
    elaborate his advice, are missing.*)
AES. When they regard their enemy's land as theirs, 1463
their own as free to him; and find sea-power
means full State-banks: tax-levies, bankruptcy.
DIO. Good! But *all* gains are swiped by soak-the-rich courts.
PLU. (*To Dionysus*) Your judgement, please. DIO. I'll judge this way
between you:
'choosing the one my soul is pleased to choose'.
EUR. Mindful of gods you named in sworn assurance
that you would take me home again, choose your friends. 1470
DIO. 'My tongue has sworn, but'—I'll choose Aeschylus.
EUR. What have you done, you bloody man? DIO. Meaning me?
Aeschylus I judged the winner. And why not?
EUR. 'Can you meet my eyes, fresh from your deed of shame?'[1]
DIO. 'What's shameful, if the audience think not so?'[2]
EUR. Have you no heart? Will you really shrug me off, dead?
DIO. 'Who knows? Perhaps to be alive is death'[3]
    (*Improvising equal nonsense*) and breath our bread and sleep a fleecy
    nap. 1481
PLU. Go in then, Dionysus, you and he. DIO. Why so?
PLU. You'll be my guests before you sail. DIO. That's fine,
god bless me, fine! I don't mind if I do.

    [1] From *Aeolus*.
    [2] Again from *Aeolus*, with one word-change, viz. 'audience' for 'doers'.
    [3] Euripides *Polyidus*; cf. 1082.

2

PLATO

Plato's discussions of poetry and rhetoric are numerous and have often been studied. For a recent, systematic treatment see P. Vicaire, *Platon: critique littéraire*, Paris, 1960.

A. RHAPSODES AND INSPIRATION

We give the *Ion* in full. It is in Plato's lighter vein: Socrates punctures the pretensions to knowledge of a professional reciter of epic, Ion of Ephesus, and in the process makes a number of points about the irrational nature of poetic inspiration and the weakness of the claim that the poets and their expositors can teach the arts of life.

Grube 48–9.

H. Flashar: *Der Dialog Ion als Zeugnis platonischer Philosophie*, Berlin, 1958.

'Welcome, Ion! Where have you arrived from? Have you been home to Ephesus?'

'No, Socrates; I've come from Epidaurus, from the Asclepicia.'[1]

'Oh, do the Epidaurians hold a competition for rhapsodes too in honour of the god?'

'Yes indeed, and for other musical arts.'

'Did you compete then? And how did you get on?'

'We won the first prize, Socrates.'

'Splendid! Mind we win the Panathenaea too!'

'God willing, we shall.'

'I have often envied you rhapsodes your profession, Ion. It is an enviable lot, to find it always professionally appropriate to be beautifully dressed and look as handsome as possible, and at the same time to find it essential to occupy oneself with so many good poets, and Homer above all, the best and divinest of all, and learn not only his words but his meaning. No one can be a good rhapsode who fails to understand what the poet says; the rhapsode has to be an interpreter of the poet's meaning, and this can't be done properly unless he understands what the poet says. It's all most enviable.'

'Quite right, Socrates. Anyway, that is what gives me most work in my profession, and I believe I can speak about Homer better than any man.

[1] The most celebrated festival of Asclepius in Greece was that at Epidaurus; games and musical contests formed a part of it from classical times. See E. J. and L. Edelstein, *Asclepius*, Baltimore, 1945, i. 313, ii. 208 ff.

Neither Metrodorus of Lampsacus nor Stesimbrotus of Thasos nor Glaucon nor anybody else has ever had so many fine thoughts to utter about Homer as I have.'[1]

'Splendid, Ion! I'm sure you won't grudge me a demonstration.'

'Well, Socrates, my embellishments of Homer really are worth hearing. I deserve a golden crown from the Homeridae,[2] I fancy.'

'I shall make leisure to hear you yet; but for the moment just tell me one thing. Are you good only at Homer, or at Hesiod and Archilochus too?'

531

'Only at Homer; I think that is quite enough.'

'But is there anything about which Homer and Hesiod say the same?'

'Many things, surely.'

'Then can you expound what Homer says about these things better than what Hesiod says?'

'Equally well, Socrates, as far as the things about which they both say the same are concerned.'

'And what about things where they don't say the same? For instance, Homer and Hesiod both speak of divination.'

'Yes.'

'Well, would you or a good diviner give a better explanation of the similarities and differences between what these two poets say about divination?'

'The diviner.'

'And if you were a diviner, would you not know how to expound the things which they say differently, if you were able to expound those of which they give a similar account?'

'Certainly I should.'

'Why then are you good at Homer but not at Hesiod or any other poet? Is it that Homer talks about different things from all other poets? Does he not for the most part talk of war, dealings of men—good and bad, laymen and craftsmen—with one another, the dealings of gods with one another and with men, the phenomena of the heavens, Hades, the genealogies of gods and heroes? These are the subjects of Homer's poetry, are they not?'

'Indeed, Socrates.'

'And what about other poets? Don't they handle the same subjects?'

'Yes, but not like Homer, Socrates.'

'Worse?'

---

[1] See R. Pfeiffer, *History of Classical Scholarship*, Oxford, 1968, p. 35. Metrodorus, a pupil of Anaxagoras, allegorized Homer; Stesimbrotus did not; nothing is known about Glaucon.

[2] A guild of reciters known in Chios by the sixth century and claiming (apparently) descent from Homer.

'Much.'

'Homer's better?'

'Yes, indeed.'

'My dear Ion, when many people speak about number, and one talks best, the good speaker can be recognized, can't he?'

'Yes.'

'By the same person who will recognize the bad speakers?'

'Yes.'

'In fact, by the possessor of the skill of arithmetic?'

'Yes.'

'Take another example. When a number of people discuss healthy food and one speaks best, will it be the same critic or a different one who will be able to recognize the best speaker and the worse?'

'The same, obviously.'

'Who? What is he called?'

'A doctor.'

'So to sum up, it will always be the same person who, in a given group of speakers, will know who is speaking well and who badly; if he doesn't 532 recognize the bad, he won't recognize the good either, so long as the subject is the same.'

'Yes.'

'Then the same man is clever at both tasks?'

'Yes.'

'Now you say that Homer and the other poets, including Hesiod and Archilochus, talk about the same subjects, but not all equally well?'

'Yes, and it's true.'

'Then if you know the good speaker, you will also know that the bad speakers are in fact worse.'

'So it would seem.'

'Then we shall not be wrong if we say that Ion is clever both about Homer and about other poets, since you admit yourself that the same person is an adequate judge of all who speak about the same subject, and that poets, generally speaking, all compose on the same subjects.'

'Then why is it, Socrates, that when someone talks about any other poet I don't attend and I can't contribute anything at all worth while— I just doze off—but as soon as someone mentions Homer, I wake up and attend and find I have something to say?'

'It's not hard to make a guess about that, my friend. It's plain to anyone that you are not capable of talking about Homer out of skill (*technē*) and knowledge; because, if you were, you would have been able to talk about all the other poets as well; the whole thing is poetry, isn't it?'

'Yes.'

'Then, when one takes some other complete art, the inquiry will take the same form, whatever the art? Do you want to understand what I mean, Ion?'

'Indeed I do, Socrates. I love listening to you clever people (*sophoi*).'

'I wish you would tell the truth, Ion; it's you rhapsodes and actors and those whose poems you recite who are clever; I simply tell the truth, like a plain man. To take the question I asked you just now; see how easy and unspecialized it is—anyone can understand the point—to see that when one takes any art as a whole the manner of inquiry is the same. For instance, take painting; it's an art as a whole, isn't it?'

'Yes.'

'And there are and have been many painters, good and bad?'

'Yes.'

'Well, have you ever seen anyone good at explaining what is well done and what badly in the work of Polygnotus[1] the son of Aglaophon, but 533 incapable of doing this for other painters? Anyone who dozes and is at a loss and can make no contribution when shown the work of other painters, but wakes up and attends and has something to say when he has to give an opinion about Polygnotus or some other one, individual painter?'

'Good gracious, no.'

'Take sculpture too. Have you ever seen anybody good at explaining the good things in Daedalus son of Metion or Epeus son of Panopeus or Theodorus of Samos[2] or some other one individual sculptor, but dozes and is at a loss and has nothing to say about the works of other sculptors?'

'No, I've never seen anyone like that either.'

'Nor yet, I imagine, have you ever seen, in connection with flute- or lyre-playing or singing to the lyre or being a rhapsode, anyone who is good at expounding Olympus or Thamyras or Orpheus or Phemius the rhapsode from Ithaca,[3] but at a loss about Ion of Ephesus, with no contribution to make as to what he recites well and what badly?'

'I can't oppose you, Socrates. But I do know that I speak about Homer better than anyone else, and I have much to say, and everyone says I am good; but not about the others. Please see what this can mean.'

'I do see, Ion, and I am going on to explain to you what I think it is.

'This ability of yours to speak well about Homer is, as I was saying just now, no art (*technē*). It is a divine force which moves you. It is like

---

[1] Of Thasos, active in Athens after the Persian wars; G. M. A. Richter, *Handbook of Greek Art*, London, 1959, p. 264.

[2] The first two are mythical; Theodorus was a gem-engraver of the sixth century B.C.

[3] Legendary figures: Phemius is from the *Odyssey* (1. 154 etc.).

the force in the stone Euripides calls a magnet, and most people "the Heraclean stone". This not only attracts iron rings, but induces in the rings the power to do the same themselves in turn—namely to attract other rings, so that sometimes a long chain of iron rings is formed, suspended from one another, all having the force derived from the stone. Thus the Muse herself makes people possessed, and from these possessed persons there hangs a chain of others, possessed with the same enthusiasm. All good epic poets produce all their beautiful poems not by art but because they are inspired and possessed. So too with good lyric poets: 534 just as Corybantic dancers[1] perform when they are not in their right mind, so the lyric poets compose these beautiful songs when they are not in their right mind; once involved in harmony and rhythm, they are in a state of possession and it is then—just as women draw honey and milk from the rivers when under Bacchic possession, but not when they are in their right mind—it is then that the lyric poets have the experience they describe to us. They say, you see, that it is from fountains flowing with honey, in groves and gardens of the Muses, that they cull, like bees, the songs they bring us; and they too do it on the wing. Now this is perfectly true: a poet is a light, winged, holy creature, and cannot compose until he is possessed and out of his mind, and his reason is no longer in him; no man can compose or prophesy so long as he has his reason. So, because it is not art but divine dispensation that enables them to compose poetry and say many fine things about the world, as you do about Homer, every individual poet can only compose well what the Muse has set him to do—one dithyrambs, one encomia, one hyporchemata,[2] one epic, one iambics. They are no good at anything else. This is because their utterances are the result not of art but of divine force. If they could utter on any one theme by art, they would also be able to do so on every other. This is why god takes away their senses and uses them as servants, as he does divine prophets and seers, so that we who hear may realize that it is not these persons, whose reason has left them, who are the speakers of such valuable words, but god who speaks and expresses himself to us through them. There is good evidence for this in Tynnichus of Chalcis, who never composed a poem worth remembering except the paean[3] which everybody sings, perhaps the most beautiful of all lyrics, a real 'windfall of the Muses', as he says himself. Herein god seems to me to have shown, to prevent us

[1] i.e. participants in an orgiastic ritual dance, which was believed to have therapeutic powers in some kinds of madness. See E. R. Dodds, *The Greeks and the Irrational*, University of California Press, 1951, p. 79.

[2] Dithyrambs were elaborate sung lyrics in various metres, sometimes of narrative content; encomia are songs of praise; hyporchemata are songs with a dance accompaniment (the word first occurs here, and exact definition is difficult).

[3] Strictly, a song in praise of Apollo.

being in any doubt, that these beautiful poems are not human and of men, but divine and of the gods, poets being merely *interpreters* of the gods, each possessed by his own peculiar god. To demonstrate this, the god deliberately sang the most beautiful song through the mouth of the 535 worst poet. Don't you think I'm right, Ion?'

'Indeed I do. You touch me in the heart, Socrates, by what you say, and I believe it is by a divine dispensation that good poets interpret these messages to us from the gods.'

'And you rhapsodes then interpret the messages of the poets?'

'That's right too.'

'So you are interpreters of interpreters?'

'Just so.'

'Well now, tell me this, Ion, and don't hide what I ask you. When you recite well and most amaze your audience—say when you sing Odysseus[1] leaping on the threshold, revealing himself to the suitors and pouring the arrows out at his feet, or Achilles[2] advancing against Hector, or some pathetic passage about Andromache or Hecuba or Priam—are you at that time in your right mind, or are you beside yourself? Does your mind imagine itself, in its state of enthusiasm, present at the actual events you describe—in Ithaca or at Troy or whatever the poem requires?'

'That's a very clear indication you've given me, Socrates; I'll tell you without concealment. When I recite a pathetic passage, my eyes fill with tears; when it is something alarming or terrifying, my hair stands on end in terror and my heart jumps.'

'Well, now, Ion: can we call a man sane who, when elaborately dressed and wearing a gold crown, and not having lost any of this finery, nevertheless breaks into tears at a sacrifice and festival, or feels frightened in the company of twenty thousand or so friendly persons, not one of whom is trying to rob him or do him any harm?'

'To tell you the truth, Socrates—no.'

'You know then that you people have the same effect on many of the spectators?'

'Certainly I do. I can see them from up on the platform, weeping and looking fierce and marvelling at the tale. Indeed, I am obliged to attend to them; for if I can set them crying, I shall laugh when I get my money, but if I make them laugh, I lose my money and it's I who'll be crying.'

'You know then that the spectator is the last of the rings which I described as taking their force from the Heraclean stone? You—the rhapsode or 536 the actor—are the middle link, and the poet himself is the first. Through all these, the god draws the human mind in any direction he wishes, hanging a chain of force from one to the other. Just as with the stone,

[1] *Odyssey* 22. 1 ff.   [2] *Iliad* 22. 312 ff.

there is a huge chain of dancers, producers, and under-producers, hanging sideways from the rings which hang down from the Muse. Poets are suspended from different Muses—we say "possessed by", but it is much the same thing—a matter of being held—and from this first set of rings, the poets, are suspended—or possessed—other persons, some from one and some from another, some from Orpheus, some from Musaeus—but most are possessed and held by Homer. You are one of these, Ion. You are possessed by Homer. When something by any other poet is performed, you fall asleep and have nothing to say, but the moment anyone utters a song of Homer, you wake up, your heart dances, and you have a lot to say; this is because your talk about Homer comes not from knowledge or art, but from divine dispensation and possession. Like the Corybantic dancers, who are keenly aware only of the tune that belongs to the god who possesses them and can dance and give utterance to this alone, taking no notice of others, so you, Ion, are ready enough when Homer is mentioned, but at a loss with everything else; and the reason for this, which is what you're asking, the reason why you are ready on the subject of Homer but not of the others, is that it is not art but divine dispensation that makes you a good encomiast of Homer.'

'You *do* speak well, Socrates; but I should be surprised if you were eloquent enough to persuade me that I am possessed and mad when I praise Homer. I don't believe you'd think so yourself if you heard me speaking about Homer.'

'I want to hear you very much, but not before you have answered one question.[1] Which of the subjects Homer speaks of do you speak well about? It can't be *all*, surely.'

'Every single one, Socrates.'

'But not surely about things which Homer speaks of but of which you are ignorant?'

'And what is there, pray, that Homer speaks of and I don't know?'

'Well, doesn't Homer often say a good deal about various arts? For 53? example, chariot-driving. If I can remember the lines, I'll say them.'

'No, I will: I remember.'

'Well, then, repeat what Nestor says to his son Antilochus, advising him to take care at the turn in the chariot race in honour of Patroclus.'[2]

> 'Lean over yourself in your polished chariot
> gently, to the left; goad on the right-hand horse,
> and let him have the reins.

---

[1] This passage marks the transition from the account Socrates has given of 'possession' to his demonstration of the falsity of the rhapsodes' claim to knowledge.

[2] *Iliad* 23. 335 ff.

> Let the left-hander graze the post,
> so the wheel-hub seems just to touch,
> but beware of hitting the stone.'

'That'll do. Now, Ion, who would know best whether Homer is right here—a doctor or a charioteer?'

'A charioteer, of course.'

'Because he possesses the art, or for some other reason?'

'Because he possesses the art.'

'Then god has granted every art the power of knowing some one thing? What we know by the pilot's craft, we shan't know by medicine, for instance.'

'Indeed not.'

'And what we know by medicine, we shan't know by carpentry.

'No.'

'And so with all other arts: what we know by one, we shan't know by another? But first answer me this: do you say there are *different* arts?'

'Yes.'

'When one is knowledge of one set of things, and another of another, I go by that, and call them different arts: is that what you do?'

'Yes.'

'Now if there were a science which dealt with one set of things, how could we say that there were two *different* sciences, at least if the same facts were to be learned from both? For example, I know that these fingers are five in number, and you know so too; and if I were to ask you whether you and I both knew this by the same art, namely arithmetic, or a different one, you would reply "by the same".'

'Yes.'

538   'Then tell me now what I was going to ask you just then. Do you think it applies to all arts that the same art must necessarily have knowledge of the same things, and a different art of different things?'

'Yes I do, Socrates.'

'Then anyone who doesn't possess a certain art will not be able to know properly the words or actions which belong to that art?'

'True.'

'Then consider the lines you recited. Will you or a charioteer know better whether Homer is right or not?'

'The charioteer.'

'Because you are a rhapsode, not a charioteer?'

'Yes.'

'And the rhapsode's art is different from that of the charioteer?'

'Yes.'

'Therefore, since it is different, it is knowledge concerned with different things?'

'Yes.'

'And what about the place where Homer says that Hecamede, Nestor's concubine, gave the wounded Machaon a draught to drink?—

> ... with Pramnian wine; and she grated goat's cheese upon it
> with a bronze grater; and an onion went with the drink?[1]

Is it the business of the rhapsode's art or that of the doctor to tell properly whether Homer is right?'

'The doctor's.'

'And when Homer says:[2]

> Like a lead weight she went to the bottom,
> that, mounted on the horn of an ox of the field,
> goes to bring trouble to the ravenous fish,

is it the business of the rhapsode's art or the fisherman's to judge the correctness of this?'

'The fisherman's, obviously, Socrates.'

'Then suppose you were to put a question to me in these terms: "Socrates, since you are discovering what there is in Homer which each of these arts ought to determine, go on now, please, to prophets and divination—of what ought the prophet to be able to judge the correctness or incorrectness?" See how readily I shall give you an answer. In the *Odyssey*, there is a lot of this: for instance the words of the Melampodid prophet Theoclymenus to the suitors:[3]

> Gentlemen, what's wrong? Your heads are covered in darkness   539
> and your face and your bodies:
> wailing I hear, and cheeks are wet with tears;
> the hall and the courtyard are full of ghosts
> hastening hellwards in the dark;
> the sun has gone from the sky and an evil gloom has come over
>   everything.

And there's a lot in the *Iliad*, too: for example, in the battle for the wall:[4]

> A bird came towards them as they made to cross,
> an eagle flying high, flanking the host on the left.
> He carried a huge snake in his claws,

---

[1] *Iliad* 11. 639 f.   [2] *Iliad* 24. 80 ff.
[3] *Odyssey* 20. 351 ff.   [4] *Iliad* 12. 200 ff.

> alive, still writhing—it had not yet forgotten its fight,
> for it bent back and bit the eagle by the neck,
> and he felt the pain and dropped it to the ground,
> dropped it in the middle of the army,
> and flew off screaming on the wind.

This and similar passages, I shall maintain, are for the prophet to examine and criticize.'

'You are quite right, Socrates.'

'Well, you say it's right too, Ion. Now what I want you to do for me is this: just as I picked out for you passages in the *Iliad* and the *Odyssey* which belong to the prophet, the doctor, and the fisherman, you pick out for me, since you know Homer better than I do, passages which belong to the rhapsode and his art—things which the rhapsode ought to be able to examine and criticize better than other people.'

'In my view, Socrates, that means everything.'

'That's *not* your view, Ion: or are you so forgetful? A rhapsode has no business being forgetful.'

540   'What am I forgetting?'

'Don't you remember that you said that the rhapsode's art was different from the charioteer's?'

'I remember.'

'And you admitted that, being different, it would have knowledge of different things?'

'Yes.'

'Then, on your view, the rhapsode and his art will not have knowledge of everything.'

'No; they will, Socrates, except perhaps for such exceptions.'

'And by "such exceptions" you mean the fields of other arts. But what *will* the rhapsode know, since it won't be everything?'

'I think it would be what a man *ought* to say, or a woman, or a slave, or a free man, or a subject or a ruler.'

'You mean that the rhapsode will know better than the pilot what the ruler of a ship ought to say in a storm at sea?'

'No; the pilot will know that better.'

'And the rhapsode will know better than the doctor what the ruler of a sick patient ought to say?'

'No.'

'He knows what a slave ought to say, does he?'

'Yes.'

'The rhapsode will know better than the cowherd, will he, what a slave cowherd ought to say to quieten his cattle when they are excited?'

'Oh no.'

'And what about what a woman woolworker ought to say about the treatment of wool?'

'Not that either.'

'But he will know what a man ought to say as a general exhorting his troops?'

'Yes; that's the sort of thing the rhapsode will know.'

'Then is the rhapsode's art the same as the general's?'

'Well, I should know what sort of thing a general ought to say.'

'Perhaps because you have the talents of a general, Ion. If you were both a horseman and a lyre-player, you would know good horsemanship from bad, but if I asked you which of your arts it was that enabled you to recognize good horsemanship, what would you answer?'

'The horseman's art.'

'And if you recognized good lyre-playing, that, you would admit, would have been by virtue of your being a lyre-player, not by virtue of your being a horseman?'

'Yes.'

'Then since you understand military matters, is this so because you have military talents or because you are a good rhapsode?'

'I don't think there's any difference.'

'What? No difference? Are the rhapsode's art and the general's one or two?'

'One, I believe.'

'Then the man who is a good rhapsode is in fact a good general'?

'Certainly, Socrates.'

'And the good general is a good rhapsode?'

'Well, no.'

'But the good rhapsode—you still think this?—is a good general?'

'Yes.'

'And you're the best rhapsode in Greece?'

'By a long way, Socrates.'

'Are you the best general in Greece, too, then?'

'Of course, Socrates, I've learned it from Homer.'

'Then why on earth, Ion, being the best rhapsode *and* the best general in Greece, do you go round performing as a rhapsode but not commanding as a general? Do you think Greece has need of a rhapsode with his gold crown but not of a general?'

'My city, Socrates, is under the government and military leadership of yours and needs no general, and your people and the Spartans would never elect me, for you think you are good enough yourselves.'

'My dear Ion, don't you know Apollodorus of Cyzicus?'

'Who do you mean?'

541

'The foreigner whom the Athenians have often elected general. And
there's Phanosthenes of Andros and Heraclides of Clazomenae, whom this
city advances to generalship and other offices, though they are foreigners,
because they have shown that they are men of worth. Won't it then elect
Ion of Ephesus general, and honour him, if *he* seems to be a man of worth?
Anyway, aren't you Ephesians Athenians by old tradition? Isn't Ephesus
a city as great as any? The fact is, Ion, that if you are right in saying
that your capacity for ḻraising Homer comes from art and knowledge,
you are not playing fair: you professed to know many fine things about
Homer, and you said you would demonstrate your knowledge, but now
you deceive me and are far from making the demonstration; why, you
won't even say what it is you're clever at, despite all my insistence, but
twist about and turn yourself into all sorts of shapes like a veritable
Proteus, until in the end you escape me altogether and turn up as
a general! Anything to avoid demonstrating how good your Homeric
542 scholarship is. As I say, if you are a man of art and are deceiving me with
your undertaking to give a demonstration about Homer, you are not
playing fair; but if you are no man of art, but are possessed by Homer
by some divine dispensation and say many fine things about the poet
without having any knowledge—this is the account I gave of you—then
you're not being unfair. So choose which you would rather be thought—
an unfair man or an inspired one.'

'That's a very unequal choice, Socrates; it's much more honourable
to be thought inspired.'

'Then, so far as I am concerned, the more honourable part is yours,
Ion; it is not art that makes you praise Homer as you do, but divine
inspiration.'

B. POETRY IN EDUCATION

In this first discussion in the *Republic* (2. 376–3. 398), Socrates is explaining to
Adimantus his ideas for the education of the 'guardians' of the new state. The
passage is mostly concerned with a critique of the moral values inculcated by
existing myth and poetry; there follow some suggestions of what poets ought to
do. After discussing content, Socrates goes on to form; this gives rise to a first
account of *mimēsis* (imitation).

Text and commentary: J. Adam, 1902.

Grube 50 ff.; Vicaire 41 ff.

There are many English translations: e.g. by F. M. Cornford, Oxford, 1941,
clear but abridged; and by H. D. P. Lee in the Penguin Classics.

THE PLACE OF FICTION IN EDUCATION

'Then what is this education? Or is it difficult to invent one any better than that which long ages have evolved? In other words, gymnastics for the body and "music" for the mind.'

'Indeed it is.'

'Then shall we begin with music before gymnastics?'

'Naturally.'

'And do you regard words (*logoi*) as part of music or not?'

'I do.'

'And there are two kinds of words, the true and the false (*pseudos*)?'

'Yes.'

'Education is in both kinds, but first in the false.'   377

'I don't understand what you mean.'

'Don't you understand that we first of all tell children fables? Now these are, taken over all, falsehood, though there are true things in them. And we give children fables before we give them physical exercises.'

'That's true.'

'Well, that's what I meant by saying that we must tackle music before gymnastics.'

'You were right.'

'Well, you know that the beginning is the biggest part of any work, especially where the young and tender are concerned; for that is the most malleable age, when any mark you want can best be stamped on the individual.'

'Exactly.'

'So shall we lightly allow our children to hear *any* fables, no matter who made them up, and to take them to heart, though they are in fact, generally speaking, contrary to the opinions we shall expect them to hold when they grow up?'

'We shan't allow that at all.'

'Then, it would seem, we must begin by controlling the fable-makers, and admit only the good fables they compose, not the bad. We shall then persuade nurses and mothers to tell children the admitted fables, and mould their minds with fable much more than they now mould their bodies with the hand. Most of the tales they tell now will have to be thrown out.'

'Which?'

'If we look at the big fables, we shall also see the little ones. Big and little need to be of the same type and have the same effect. Don't you agree?'

'Yes: but I don't see what you mean by the big ones.'

'Those that Hesiod and Homer told, and the other poets. For it's the poets who told men, and still tell them, the false stories they themselves compose.'

'What stories? And what fault do you find with them?'

'The fault one must find, first and foremost, especially when someone tells falsehoods wrongly.'

'But what is it?'

'Making bad verbal likenesses of gods and heroes—just like a painter making a picture unlike the object he wants to paint.'

'Well, it's certainly right to find fault with that sort of thing. But just what do we mean?'

'To begin with, the greatest falsehood, involving the greatest issues, was wrongly told by the person who said that Ouranos did what Hesiod said he did,[1] and that Kronos took his revenge upon him. What Kronos did and what happened to him at his son's hands is something I should not want to be told without precaution to the young and foolish, even if it had been true. If possible, it should have been veiled in silence; but if there had been great need to tell it, it should have been made a secret, for as small an audience as possible—and they should have had to sacrifice not a pig,[2] but some expensive and inaccessible victim, so that as few people as possible should hear the tale.'

'These stories are indeed difficult.'

'They are not to be repeated in our city, Adimantus. Nor is it to be said in a young man's hearing that if he committed the most outrageous crimes, or chastised an erring father by the direst means, he would be doing nothing remarkable, but only what the first and greatest of the gods have done.'

'I don't myself think that these are suitable stories.'

'It's the same with all the tales of how gods war, plot, and fight against gods—not that they're true anyway—if our future city-guardians are to believe that readiness to hate one another is the greatest scandal. Still less must they be told elaborate fables of battles of giants, and all the other various hostilities of gods and heroes towards their kith and kin. If we are somehow to convince them that no citizen has ever been the enemy of another, nor is it right that he should be, then *that* is the lesson that older men and women must impress on the children from the start, the lesson (more or less) that poets too must be forced to impress on the adult population. Hera tied up by her son, Hephaestus thrown out by his father because he was proposing to defend his mother against a beating, Homer's

---

[1] *Theogony* 137 ff., 453 ff. According to this primitive myth, Kronos castrated his father Ouranos and swallowed his children.

[2] The victim required of an initiate in the Eleusinian mysteries.

battles of gods—all this is inadmissible, whether it was composed allegorically (*en huponoiais*) or not. Young people can't distinguish the allegorical
from the non-allegorical, and what enters the mind at that age tends to
become indelible and irremovable. Hence the prime need to make sure
that what they first hear is devised as well as possible for the implanting
of virtue.'

'That makes sense. But if we were to be asked what these things are,
what the stories are, what should we say?'

ADMISSIBLE PATTERNS FOR TALES OF THE GODS

'You and I, Adimantus, are not poets, at the moment: we are founders 379
of a city. Founders have to know the patterns within which poets are to
be made to construct fables, and beyond which they must not be allowed
to go, but they don't have to make up fables themselves.'

'True enough: but just what *are* the patterns for an account of the gods?'

'Something like this, I fancy. God must always be represented as he is,
whether in epic or in lyric or in tragedy.'

'Yes indeed.'

'Now God is in truth good and must so be described.'

'Of course.'

'And nothing good is harmful, is it?'

'No.'

'Does the non-harmful harm?'

'No.'

'And does what doesn't harm do any evil?'

'No.'

'And what does no evil is cause of no evil?'

'Of course.'

'Now again. The good is useful?'

'Yes.'

'Therefore the cause of felicity?'

'Yes.'

'The good therefore is not the cause of everything, but only of what is
well.'

'Certainly.'

'God therefore, being good, cannot be responsible for everything, as is
the common opinion, but only of some few things in human life. There is
much for which he bears no responsibility. Our blessings are far fewer
than our troubles, and, while none but God is responsible for the blessings,
we must seek other causes for the troubles.'

'That seems perfectly right.'

'We must therefore not allow Homer or any other poet to make this foolish mistake about the gods, and to say that

> by Zeus's door stand two jars full of dooms,
> one good, one bad,[1]

and that if Zeus gives a man a mixture of the two,

> sometimes he is in trouble, sometimes in luck,

while if he gives him the one kind unmixed,

> grim famine drives that man over the earth.

Nor can we allow that Zeus is "steward of our goods and ills". Nor shall we approve anyone who says that the breach of the oaths and truce, committed by Pandarus, was due to the agency of Athena and Zeus[2]— or that the quarrel and judgement of the goddesses was the work of Zeus and Themis. Young people must not be allowed to be told, in Aeschylus' words, that

> god breeds a crime in men.
> when he would utterly overthrow a house.[3]

If a poet does write about the story of Niobe, or the House of Pelops, or Troy, or anything like that, then either he must be allowed to say that they are not the works of god, or if they are, he must concoct some such account as the one we are now seeking, and say that what god did was just and good, and the victims profited from their punishment. What the poet mustn't say is that god did it, and the victims were wretched. It is all right to explain that the wicked were wretched because they needed punishment, and profited from receiving that punishment at the god's hands. But that god, who is good, is the cause of evil to anyone is a proposition to be resisted at all costs. No one must say such a thing in the city, if it is to be well governed. No one must hear it said. This goes for young and old, for verse fables and prose. Such tales, if told, would be wicked, unprofitable and self-contradictory.'

'I shall vote with you for that law. I like it.'

'Then that's *one* of the laws and patterns relating to the gods, which speakers and poets will have to observe: god is responsible only for the good things.'

'That suffices.'

'What about the second one then? Do you think that god is a magician and appears, as it were deliberately, in different shapes at different times, sometimes in person, changing himself into many shapes, and sometimes

---

[1] *Iliad* 24. 527 ff.; cf. Plutarch (below, p. 523).   [2] *Iliad* 4. 69 ff.
[3] Aeschylus, fr. 156 Nauck.

deceiving us and making us think this of him? Or is he single and least likely of any being to depart from his own form?'

'I can't say, just at the moment.'

'Well. If he *were* to depart from his own form, must he not do so either by his own act or under the influence of another?'

'Yes.'

'But things which are in a very good condition are not changed or moved by other things. Consider the effect of food, drink, and exercise on bodies, or of exposure to sun and wind and other circumstances on plants; the healthiest and strongest are changed least.'

'Of course.'

'Then the mind which external happenings are least likely to disturb 381 and change is the bravest and wisest?'

'Yes.'

'And, similarly, manufactured tools, houses, and clothing are least altered by time and other circumstances if they are well constructed and in good condition?'

'Yes.'

'Then, in general, whatever is in a good condition, as a result of nature or art or both, admits the minimum change from external influence?'

'So it seems.'

'But god and what is god's is in every way exceedingly good?'

'Of course.'

'So from this point of view god can't have "many shapes"?'

'No.'

'But might he change and vary himself?'

'He must, if he varies at all.'

'Well, then, does he change himself for better or for worse?'

'For worse, inevitably, if he does vary: for we can't say that god is defective in beauty or goodness.'

'Quite right. And that being so, Adimantus, do you think any god, or man, would voluntarily make himself worse in any way?'

'Impossible.'

'Impossible therefore for god to want to vary himself. Every god, being exceedingly beautiful and good, remains always simply, so far as possible, in his own shape.'

'Necessarily so.'

'So let none of the poets tell us that

> in guise of foreign strangers
> gods visit cities in every manner of shape.[1]

[1] *Odyssey* 17. 485 f.

Let us have no tales against Proteus and Thetis; let us not have Hera brought in, in tragedy or any other poem, disguised as a priestess begging

to the life-giving children of Inachus, river of Argos.[1]

There are a lot of other false tales we must not hear. Mothers must not be persuaded by these people into frightening their children with horrid fables of how the gods go about at night in the shape of strangers of all kinds. We can't have them blaspheming the gods and making cowards of their boys at the same time!'

'No, they mustn't do that.'

'Can it be then that, though the gods themselves can't change, they make us think they appear in various guises, deceiving and bewitching us?'

'Maybe.'

'Indeed? Might a god want to give a false impression in word or deed by exhibiting a phantom?'

'I don't know.'

'You don't know that all gods and men abhor the true falsehood, if I may use such an expression?'

'What do you mean?'

'That no one deliberately wants to be false in the most important part of his being or in relation to the most important subjects. Everyone is afraid of having falsehood *there*.'

'I still don't understand.'

'Because you think I'm saying something grand. But all I'm saying is that everybody will refuse to continue or to be put into a state of falsehood, or to be ignorant, in relation to reality in the mind, or to have or acquire falsehood in that department. This is something they detest.'

'Indeed.'

'But it's the mental ignorance of the deceived that is rightly called, as I was saying, true falsehood. Verbal falsehood is a representation of the mental situation, a subsequent image, not real, undiluted falsehood. Agreed?'

'Yes.'

'So real falsehood is abhorred by men as well as by gods?'

'I think so.'

'What about verbal falsehood? When is it useful, and not deserving of detestation? Is it not useful in dealing with enemies, and, as a medicine, against some supposed friends, to deter them when they try to do something bad through madness or folly? Or again, falsehood can surely be made useful in mythology, such as we have been discussing, because we

---

[1] Aeschylus, fr. 168 Nauck.

don't know the truth about antiquity: what we do is to make the false-hood as like the truth as possible.'

'That's right.'

'Then in which of these ways is falsehood useful to god? Will he produce falsehoods of the likeness type because he doesn't know the past?'

'Ridiculous idea!'

'So there's no false poet in god?'

'No.'

'Will he lie then for fear of enemies?'

'Certainly not.'

'Or because of his friends' folly or madness?'

'No lunatic or fool is god's friend.'

'So god can have no reason for falsehood?'

'No.'

'So the superhuman and divine is altogether free from falsity?'

'Yes.'

'God, therefore, is simple and true in deed and word. He neither changes nor deceives in visions or words or significant signs, in waking or in sleep.'

'That is how it seems to me as I listen to you.'

383

'You agree, then, that this is the second pattern within which tales and poetry about gods are to be constructed: they are not wizards to change themselves nor do they trick us with falsehoods in word or deed.'

'Agreed.'

'There is much in Homer we must praise: but we shall not praise the dispatch of the Dream by Zeus to Agamemnon.[1] Nor, in Aeschylus, shall we praise the passage where Thetis tells of Apollo's song at her marriage:

> he hymned my happy children,
> a long and healthy life;
> he told it all, sang of god's love, my good fortune,
> heartening me, and I thought his holy lips,
> so skilled in prophecy, could speak no falsehood;
> but he who sang the hymn, he who was at the feast,
> he who said all this, he is my boy's killer.[2]

When a poet says things like this about gods, we shall be angry and shall not let his play be produced. Nor shall we allow teachers to use it for education, if our guardians are to be god-fearing and divine, in so far as human powers can be.'

'I agree completely with these patterns. I shall regard them as laws...'

'To conclude, then: men who are to honour the gods and their parents   3. 386

[1] *Iliad* 2. 1–34.   [2] Aeschylus, fr. 350 Nauck.

and set a high value on mutual friendship must keep to some such rules as these about what may and may not be listened to concerning the gods.'

'And I think our view is right.'

THE ENCOURAGEMENT OF BRAVERY

'But what about their being brave? Must we not also say things of a kind to make them unafraid of death? Or do you think a man can be brave if he has this fear in him?'

'I do not.'

'Do you think that anyone who believes that Hades exists and is terrible will be unafraid of death, or will prefer death in battle to defeat and slavery?'

'No.'

'We must therefore exercise control over these myths too, and ask those who essay them not to speak ill of Hades but to praise it: otherwise what they say will be neither true nor useful to future warriors.'

'Right.'

'So we shall delete all such passages, beginning with:

> Rather would I be bound to the soil, a thrall to another,
> to a poor man at that, with no land to his portion,
> than be king of all the nations of the dead . . .[1]

387 b We shall ask Homer and the other poets not to be angry if we strike out these and similar lines. Not that they're not poetical and pleasant hearing for the general public: indeed, the more poetical they are, the less they should be presented to boys and men who ought to be free, and more afraid of slavery than of death.'

'Certainly.' . . .

387 c 9 'The pattern to be followed in stories and poetry is therefore the opposite of these.'

'Clearly.'

'We shall therefore excise lamentations and expressions of pity by men of note.'

'Inevitably, if we excluded what we have already discussed.'

'Well, consider whether we shall be doing right or not. We say, I think, that the good man (epieikēs) will not think death a terrible thing for another good man, whose friend he is.'

'We do.'

---

[1] *Odyssey* 11. 489 ff. Other examples follow, but we omit them: *Il.* 20. 64, 23. 103; *Od.* 10. 495; *Il.* 16. 856, 23. 100; *Od.* 24. 6–9.

'So he won't lament for him as though something dreadful had happened to him.'

'No.'

'We also say that such a man is particularly self-sufficient for living a good life, and needs other people less than anyone does.'

'True.'

'So it's least dreadful for him to be deprived of a son or a brother or money or anything like that.'

'Yes.'

'So he grieves least, and endures most placidly, when such a disaster overtakes him.'

'Yes.'

'So we should be right to remove the laments of notable men, and give them to women—but not to good women—and to bad men, so that the guardians whom we claim to be educating are disgusted at the idea of doing likewise.'

'Right.'[1] . . .

'If our young men heard things like this in earnest and did not laugh 388 d at them as unworthy remarks, they would be most unlikely to think themselves, being but men, below this sort of thing, or to check themselves if it occurred to them to say or do anything of the kind. They would mourn and lament freely, without shame or restraint, at small accidents.'

'Very true.'

'But they ought not to do so, as our argument just now showed—and we ought to be convinced by it, until someone convinces us with a better one.'

'Indeed they ought not.'

LAUGHTER AND JEST

'Nor must they be fond of laughter. If you indulge a violent fit of laughter, you're looking for a violent change.'

'I agree.'

'So we mustn't allow anyone to represent serious men as overcome by laughter, much less gods.'

'Much less.'

'So, on your argument, we mustn't admit Homeric passages about the gods like

---

[1] Examples of laments of heroes and heroines follow, but are here omitted: *Il.* 24. 10, 22. 414, 18. 54, 22. 168, 16. 433.

then unquenchable laughter arose among the blessed gods,
as they saw Hephaestus bustling about the room.'¹

'Call it my argument if you like. Anyway, we mustn't admit that.'

'But we *must* attach great value to truth. If we were right just now, and falsehood is useless to gods and useful to men only as a remedy, it can be allowed only to doctors, not to the layman.'

'Clearly.'

'Rulers of the city, therefore, may, if anybody may, appropriately use falsehoods, because of enemies or fellow citizens, to help the city. No one else can be allowed to touch such things. For a private person to employ falsehood towards rulers like ours is wrong: it is the same mistake, only on a bigger scale, that a patient makes if he doesn't tell his doctor the truth about his physical condition, or an athlete his trainer, or a sailor if he doesn't give the helmsman a proper account of what he or his fellow sailors are doing.'

'True.'

[Plato goes on to deal similarly with the need for modest behaviour (*sōphrosunē*) and endurance. He concludes the section on the content of literature as follows:]

392 a   'In our attempt to define what kind of stories should be told, and what not, what class of story still remains? We have discussed gods, demigods and heroes, and Hades.'

'Yes.'

'The subject of men remains.'

'Clearly.'

'Well, we can't legislate for that at the moment.'

'Why not?'

'Because, I imagine, we shall say that poets and prose-writers make serious bad statements about men—that there are many unjust men who are happy and just men who are miserable, that secret wrongdoing is profitable, that justice is the good of others and our own loss—and so on. We shall have to forbid them to say this, and command them to compose songs and fables to the opposite effect.'

'I'm sure we shall.'

'Then if you agree I am right, shall I say you have agreed to what we have long been seeking?'

'Yes, that's right.'

'Then we shall come to our agreement that this is the sort of thing to be said about men only when we have discovered what justice is and what is its natural advantage to its possessor, whether or not he *appears* just.'

'True.'

¹ *Iliad* 1. 599.

MORAL ASPECTS OF THE CHOICE OF EXPRESSION

'So much for what is said (*logoi*). We must next consider its expression (*lexis*). When that is done we shall have covered the whole subject of what is to be said and how.'

'I don't understand what you mean.'

'You ought to; but perhaps you'll know better if I put it like this. Everything that fable-tellers or poets say is a narrative of past or present or future.'

'Of course.'

'And they execute it either by simple narrative or by narrative conveyed by imitation (*mimēsis*) or by both.'

'I should like a clearer account of that too, please.'

'I must be a ridiculously obscure teacher. I'll try to do what incompetent speakers do and show you what I mean by taking a little bit, and not the whole topic. Tell me: you know the beginning of the *Iliad*, where the poet says that Chryses asked Agamemnon to release his daughter, Agamemnon was angry, and Chryses, unsuccessful, cursed the Achaeans to the god?' 393

'I know.'

'Then you know that as far as the lines

> and he begged all the Achaeans,
> and especially the two Atridae, the generals of the host,[1]

the poet speaks in his own person, and does not try to turn our attention in another direction by pretending that someone else is speaking. But from this point on he speaks as though he were Chryses himself and tries to make us think that it is not Homer talking, but the old priest. And he does practically all the rest of the narrative in this way,[2] both the tale of Troy and the episodes in Ithaca and the whole *Odyssey*.'

'Yes.'

'Now it is narrative both when he makes the various speeches and in the passages between the speeches.'

'Of course.'

'But when he makes a speech pretending to be someone else, are we not to say that he is assimilating his expression as far as possible to the supposed speaker?'

'Certainly.'

'And to assimilate oneself in voice or gesture to another is to imitate him?'

---

[1] *Iliad* i. 15–16.
[2] i.e. in a combination of speeches with linking or introductory narrative.

'Yes.'

'So in this sort of thing Homer and the other poets are conveying their narrative by way of imitation (*mimēsis*)?'

'Yes.'

'Now if the poet never concealed himself, his whole poetry and narrative would be free of imitation. Don't say you don't understand again—I'll explain how it would be. If Homer, having said that Chryses came with his daughter's ransom to be a suppliant of the Achaeans, and particularly of the kings, had gone on not as Chryses but as Homer, it would have been pure narrative, not imitation. It would have gone something like this—I'll do it without metre, for I'm no poet. "The priest came and prayed that the gods might grant them to capture Troy and return home safely, if they accepted ransom, respected the god, and freed his daughter. Most of them respected his words and were ready to agree, but Agamemnon was angry, telling him to go away and never come back, lest his staff and the god's garlands might prove of no avail to him: before the daughter was freed, she would grow old in Argos with him. And he told the old man to be off and not stir up trouble, if he wanted to get home safe. Hearing this, Chryses was frightened and went silently away, but when he had left the camp he prayed long to Apollo, calling on him by his special names, reminding him and begging him, if he had ever given him before an acceptable gift in temple-building or sacrifice; in return for this, he prayed to him to avenge his tears on the Greeks with his arrows."—That's pure narrative without imitation.'

'I understand.'

'Then understand that the opposite happens when the poet removes the passages between the speeches and leaves just the exchange of conversation (*ta amoibaia*).'

'I see: that's what we have in tragedies.'

'Quite right. I think I'm making clear to you now what I couldn't before, namely that there is one kind of poetry and fable which entirely consists of imitation: this is tragedy and comedy, as you say; and there's another kind consisting of the poet's own report—you find this particularly in dithyrambs; while the mixture of the two exists in epic and in many other places, if you see what I mean.'

'Yes: I understand now what you meant then.'

'Remember also what we said even before that—that we've dealt with the question *what* to say, but have still to consider *how*.'

'I remember.'

'Well, what I meant was, that we must come to an understanding as to whether we are to allow our poets to narrate by imitation, or partly by imitation (and if so, what parts), or not to imitate at all.'

'I have an inkling that you are asking whether we should admit tragedy and comedy into the city or no.'

'Perhaps—or perhaps more than that. I don't know yet: we must go where the wind of the argument blows.'

'That's right.'

'Well then, consider whether our guardians ought to be imitative people or not. Or does this follow from our previous argument that an individual can do one thing well but is liable to fail in everything, so far as acquiring real note is concerned, if he tries to do many things?'

'Bound to follow.'

'Similarly with imitation—one individual can't imitate many things well, though he can one?'

'Yes.'

'So still less will one man be able to pursue some worthwhile pursuit and also imitate many things and be an imitator. Even apparently closely related imitations (*mimēmata*) cannot be practised well by the same 395 person—tragedy and comedy for example. You called these two imitations, didn't you?'

'Yes; and you're quite right, the same people can't do both.'

'Nor can people be both rhapsodes and actors.'

'True.'

'Nor even tragic actors and comic actors. All these things are imitations, aren't they?'

'Yes.'

'Now it seems to me as if human nature is specialized even more minutely than this. It is unable to imitate many things well, or to do well the things of which the imitations are likenesses.'

'True.'

'So if we are to preserve our first conclusion, that our guardians ought to be exempt from all other crafts and be craftsmen of freedom in the city, and perfect craftsmen, and ought to practise nothing that does not conduce to this end, they *must* not do or imitate anything else. If they do imitate, the subject of their imitation, from childhood onwards, must be what is appropriate to them: the brave, the self-controlled, the righteous, the free, and so on. They must neither display in action nor be good at imitating the illiberal, or any other disgraceful quality, lest the fruit of their imitation be the reality. Haven't you observed that imitations, if persisted in from childhood, settle into habits and fixed characteristics of body, voice, or mind?'

'I have indeed.'

'So we shan't allow those whom we profess to care for, and who we say ought to be brave men, to imitate a woman, young or old, in the act

of reviling her husband or boastfully competing with the gods, full of the
conceit of her own felicity, or possessed by misfortune or mourning or
lamentation. And as for illness, love, or childbirth—God forbid!'[1]

'Yes indeed.'

'Nor slaves, male or female, performing slavish tasks.'

'No.'

'Nor bad men, cowards, and people doing the opposite of what we have
just described, people abusing or ridiculing one another or using filthy
396 language, drunk or sober, or committing any of the other errors of word
or deed against self or others that such people incur. Nor must we allow
them to form the habit of likening themselves to madmen by word or
action. Of course they must be able to recognize mad or wicked men
or women—but they're not to do or imitate any of these things.'

'True.'

'Well then, what about smiths or other workmen doing their work, or
rowers in triremes or their officers? Is anything like this to be imitated?'

'How could it be? None of them is going to be allowed even to think
of these things.'

'Well, horses neighing? Bulls lowing? Rivers babbling? The roar of the
sea? Thunder? Are they to imitate this sort of thing?'[2]

'They have been forbidden to be mad or to make themselves like the
mad.'

'If I understand what you're saying, there is a kind of expression and
narrative which the really good man would use, if he had to say anything,
and there is another and very different kind which the person of opposite
breeding and education would consistently use for his narratives.'

'What are these kinds?'

'As it seems to me, the decent man, when he comes in his narrative to
the words or action of a good man, will want to report it by identifying
himself with that good man, and will not be ashamed of such imitation.
Especially will he imitate the good man secure and sane: less readily, the
good man tripped up by sickness, love, drink, or some other accident.
But when he comes to a man unworthy of himself, he will not want
seriously to liken himself to his own inferior, except momentarily, when
he's acting well. He will be ashamed. For one thing, he will have had
no practice in imitating such characters. For another, he will feel disgust
at modelling himself on, and inserting himself into, the patterns of the
inferior. He will have an intellectual contempt for them, except as a game.'

'Probably so.'

'He will therefore use the style of narration that we described in

---

[1] Plato is thinking of tragic heroines: Medea, Niobe, Phaedra.
[2] Cf. Plutarch, below, p. 514.

connection with Homer's epic. His expression will have elements both of imitation and of narrative, but with very little narrative to a long story. Right?'

'Yes: that must be the pattern of a speaker of this kind.'

'But consider the other kind. The worse he is, the readier he will be to imitate everything. He won't regard anything as beneath him. He will try to imitate everything, seriously and in public—even what we were speaking of just now, thunder and the noise of wind and hail, axle and pulley, the sound of trumpets, oboes, pipes, and all kinds of instruments, the cries of dogs, sheep, and birds. His expression will be entirely imitative, in voice and gesture—or at most it will have a little narration in it.' 397

'Necessarily so.'

'Then this is what I meant by the two kinds of expression.'

'I see.'

'In one of them, the variations are not great. If you give the expression its appropriate harmony and rhythm, a correct speaker is able to deliver the piece practically in one and the same harmony—the variations are small—and in very much the same rhythm.'

'Quite so.'

'The other performer's type, on the other hand, needs the very opposite —all harmonies and all rhythms—if it is to be delivered appropriately, because of the manifold forms of its variations.'

'Certainly.'

'Then all poets and speakers fall into one or other pattern of expression or into one arising from their combination of the two.'

'Inevitably.'

'What shall we do then? Shall we admit all these patterns into the city, or one or other unmixed, or the mixed one?'

'If my vote is allowed to prevail, the imitator of the good, unmixed.'

'But the mixed pattern is pleasing—while to children and their attendants and to the multitude it's the one that's opposite to your choice that gives by far the most pleasure.'

'Yes, it is.'

'But perhaps you would say it didn't suit our "republic", for we have no double or multiple men, because everybody performs one function.'

'Well, it doesn't suit.'

'So this is the only city where we shall find the cobbler a cobbler and not a ship's pilot as well, the farmer a farmer and not a juryman as well, and the man of war a man of war and not also a man of money.[1] Isn't it?'

'It is.'

---

[1] Plato is contrasting his city with democratic Athens, where just these combinations of roles were characteristic.

F

398   'Suppose then there arrived in our city a man who could make himself into anything by his own skill, and could imitate everything. Suppose he brought his poems and wanted to give a display. We should salute him as divine, wonderful, a pleasure-giver: but we should then say that there is no one of his sort in our city and it is not allowed that there should be. We should therefore pour ointment on his head, give him a garland of wool, and send him off elsewhere. Meanwhile we should employ the more austere and unpleasing poet and tale-teller, for use not pleasure: he would imitate the expression of the good man and tell his tales within the patterns for which we legislated at the beginning, when we were trying to educate the soldiers.'

'Indeed we should, if it were in our power.'

C. THE TRUE NATURE OF IMITATION

We turn to Book X of the *Republic*. Here Plato comes back to the subject of poetry in the light of the philosophical and psychological doctrines expounded in the middle books: the 'theory of forms' and the doctrine of the three elements of the soul (the reasoning, 'spirited', and 'desiring' elements). The result is a profounder account of the dangers inherent in *mimēsis*.

Socrates is here talking to Glaucon.

CONFIRMATION OF THE EXCLUSION OF POETRY

595   'There are many respects in which I feel convinced, when I reflect on it, that we founded our city rightly—and not least in this business of poetry.'

'In what way?'

'In our refusing to admit imitative poetry. It is even clearer, I think, that we ought not to admit it, now that we have distinguished the elements in the mind.'

'How so?'

'Between ourselves—and I know you're not going to denounce me to the writers of tragedy and all the other imitators—all this kind of thing is ruination to the listeners' minds, unless they are protected by the knowledge of what it really is.'

'What are you thinking of?'

'I shall have to be frank—though my lifelong liking and respect for Homer inhibits me, for he is the prime teacher and leader of all these fine folk. Still, persons mustn't be put before the truth. As I say, I shall have to be frank.'

'Indeed you will.'

'Listen then—or rather answer.'

'Ask away.'

THE REAL NATURE OF IMITATION

'Can you tell me what imitation in general is? I can't see myself what it means.'

'Then it's hardly likely that I should.'

'There would be nothing surprising if you did. Duller eyes often see sooner than sharp ones.'

'I dare say. But with you there I shouldn't be able even to want to speak if I have an idea. *You* try and see.'

'Would you like us to begin with our usual procedure? We are in the habit of assuming a "form" in relation to each group of particular objects to which we apply the same name.[1] Or do you not understand?'

'I understand.'

[On this assumed basis of the 'theory of forms' Plato develops the argument that there are, for instance, three beds: the 'idea' of bed, the actual bed, the image of a bed. The constructor of the first is God, of the second the bed-builder, of the third the painter, who is an imitator. So imitators— tragic poets, for instance—are 'third from the King and from truth' (597 e 7). We resume where the argument returns specifically to poetry.]

'We must now consider tragedy and its leader, Homer, in the light of 598 d this, for we hear it said by some that tragedians know all arts, all human affairs where vice and virtue are involved, and all divine things too: for, they say, the good poet must compose with knowledge if he is to compose well on any subject. We must therefore consider whether these people have fallen in with a set of imitators who have deceived them and have failed to realize that their works, which they see, are 'third removes' from 599 the reality and are easy to make even if you don't know the truth. They are images, not realities. Or do you think there is something in what they say, and good poets really do know about the things which ordinary people think they describe so well?'

'We must certainly go into this.'

'Do you think then that if anyone could make *both* the object of imitation *and* the image, he would let himself take image-construction seriously and make it the guiding principle in his life, as though it were the best thing he had?'

'No.'

'But if he was really knowledgeable about the things he imitates, he would take trouble over the real object rather than the imitation, and try to leave many beautiful objects behind as his memorial. He would rather be praised than compose the praises of others.'

[1] A reference to Plato's characteristic 'theory of forms': see e.g. R. S. Bluck, *Plato's Phaedo*, London, 1955, pp. 7 ff.

'Surely: the honour and the advantage are not comparable.'

'There are things we need not ask Homer or any other poet about. We need not ask whether, supposing one of them was a doctor and not an imitator of medical language, anyone is said to have been made healthy by a poet, old or new, as by Asclepius, or whether any poet has left pupils in medicine, as Asclepius left descendants.[1] Nor need we ask such questions about the other arts. We can let them be. But it's fair to ask about the grandest and most splendid subjects that Homer tries to speak of— wars, strategy, government, education. "Dear Homer," let us say, "if you are not at third remove from truth in the matter of goodness, an image-maker, an *imitator* as we defined it, but only at two removes, and if you have been able to know what pursuits make men better and worse in their private and public conduct—tell us what city was better governed because of you, as Sparta was because of Lycurgus, and many others, great and small, because of others? What city claims you as a good law-giver and its benefactor? Italy and Sicily claim Charondas, we claim Solon. Who claims you?" Will he be able to name anywhere?'

'I don't think so; at any rate nothing is said even by the Homeridae.'

600   'But is there record of any war in Homer's time which was well con-ducted thanks to his generalship or advice?'

'No.'

'Then are there many ingenious ideas for techniques or other activities reported of Homer as being a clever man in some craft? I am thinking of Thales of Miletus and Anacharsis the Scythian.'

'Nothing like that.'

'Well, if there is no public service, perhaps Homer is said to have guided the education of some privately—people who respected him for his company and handed down to posterity a Homeric Way of Life, as Pythagoras was respected in this way and his followers still speak of a Pythagorean life which distinguishes them from the rest of the world.'

'Nothing like that is reported. Indeed Creophylus, Homer's friend, may prove even more ridiculous in his education than in his name,[2] if what we are told about Homer is true. Homer is said to have been very much neglected by him in his lifetime.'

'So they say. But, Glaucon, do you think that if Homer had really been able to educate men and make them better—being capable of knowing about these things, not just imitating—he would have failed to acquire many friends and earn their respect and liking? Protagoras of Abdera, Prodicus of Ceos, and many others are able to convince their contem-poraries in private conversation that they will be incapable of managing house or city unless *they* take charge of their education. They earn such

---

[1] Cf. *Ion*, above, p. 39.   [2] 'Meat-stock.'

affection for this expertise that their friends almost carry them round on their heads. Now if Homer had been able to help men to acquire virtue, would his contemporaries have let him—and the same goes for Hesiod—wander round reciting poetry? Would they not have held on to him more eagerly than gold and forced him to stay at home with them? Failing that, wouldn't they have danced attendance wherever he went till they got enough education?'

'I think you're absolutely right, Socrates.'

'Shall we then put down all poets, from Homer onwards, as imitators of images of virtue and of all their other subjects, without any contact with the truth? As we were saying just now, the painter will make a semblance of a cobbler, though he knows nothing about cobbling, and neither do his public—they judge only by colours and shapes.'

'Yes.'

'Similarly, we can say that the poet with his words and phrases lays on the colours of every art, though all he understands of it is how to imitate it in such a way that other people like himself, judging by the words, think it all very fine if someone discusses cobbling or strategy or anything in metre, rhythm, and harmony. These have by their very nature such immense fascination. I imagine you know what the content of poetry amounts to, stripped of the colours of music, just on its own. You must have seen it.'

'I have.'

'It's like a pretty but not beautiful face, isn't it, when youth has departed from it?'

'Exactly.'

[Plato proceeds to distinguish three arts relating to any one subject: the art that uses it, the art that makes it, the art that imitates it. The imitator, he argues, will have no knowledge of the subject such as the others have. Poets merely imitate what the ignorant think about good and bad. A new and important argument begins at 602 c.]

THE PSYCHOLOGICAL EFFECTS OF IMITATION

'So this imitation relates to something three removes from truth, 602 c does it?'

'Yes.'

'Now what element in human nature does it affect?'

'What do you mean?'

'Something like this. The same size appears different according to whether it is seen close at hand or at a distance.'

'Yes.'

'A thing may seem straight or crooked according to whether it is seen in or out of water. Similarly with the concave and convex, because of visual error connected with colours. This is evidently a sort of total mental confusion: and it's this natural experience that perspective drawing exploits with its magic, and conjuring tricks too, and many other such devices.'

'True.'

'Now the best aid in all this is measurement, counting and weighing. These prevent the *apparently* bigger or smaller, heavier or more numerous, from prevailing in our minds, and make the calculating, measuring, and weighing element do so.'

'Just so.'

'Now this will be the work of the ratiocinative part of our mind.'

'It will.'

'Now it often happens that when this faculty has measured and indicates that A is bigger or smaller than B, or equal to it, it nevertheless finds contrary *appearances* at the same time about the same object.'

'Yes.'

'Now we said that the same thing cannot make contrary judgements at the same time about the same object.'

'And that was surely right.'

603 'Then the element of the mind that judges against the measurements is not the same as that which judges with them.'

'No.'

'But that which relies on measurement and calculation will be the best element of the mind.'

'Of course.'

'So its opponent will be one of the inferior elements.'

'Necessarily.'

'This is the agreement I was aiming at when I said that painting, and imitative art generally, accomplishes work that is far removed from truth and addresses itself to an element in us that is far removed from wisdom, becoming this element's friend and close associate for no good or honest purpose.'

'Quite so.'

'So the art of imitation is an inferior thing, its associate is inferior, and its products are inferior.'

'So it seems.'

'Does this apply only to visual imitation or also to auditory imitation —what we call poetry?'

'Probably to this too.'

'Then let us not simply trust the probability on the evidence of painting, but consider what mental element it is that poetical imitation consorts with. Is it good or bad?'

'We must indeed consider that.'

'Let us set the question out like this. Imitation imitates men performing actions[1] either forced or voluntary, and believing that they are either successful or not in these actions, and feeling pain or pleasure as a result of it all. Is there anything else?'

'No.'

'Now is a man in a state of concord with himself in all these circumstances? Or does he dissent and quarrel within himself in his actions as he did visually when he had contrary judgements at the same time about the same things? But I recall that we need not agree this point now, because we agreed earlier quite adequately that our minds are full of contradictions of this kind.'

'Quite rightly, too.'

'Yes: but I think we must now go into the point which we omitted then.'

'What is that?'

'We said that a good man who has, for example, lost a son or something else to which he attaches great value, will bear the disaster more easily than others.'[2]

'Yes.'

'Let us now consider whether he will feel no grief at all or, that being impossible, show moderation in his grief.'

'The second seems right.'

'Then tell me one thing more. Do you think he will resist and fight his grief more when he is seen by his peers, or when he is alone by himself in solitude?' 604

'When he's being seen, by a long way.'

'Yes: when he's alone, I imagine, he will allow himself to say many things he would be ashamed to be heard saying, and do many things he would not allow anyone to see him doing.'

'Yes.'

'Now the element that bids him resist is reason and law; that which pulls him towards the grief is the painful experience itself.'

'True.'

'And if there are contrary pulls in the man at the same time in regard to the same situation, we say that there must be two elements in him.'

'Of course.'

'One of which is ready to obey the law, wherever it gives guidance.'

---

[1] Cf. Aristotle, *Poetics* 1448[a]1 (below, p. 92).   [2] 387 d–e (above, p. 58).

'What do you mean?'

'The law says it is best to keep as quiet as possible in misfortune and not show distress. The good and the evil in such situations are not clear, nothing is gained for the future by indignation, no human affairs are worth great trouble, and, finally, grief prevents the arrival of what ought to be our most present help.'

'What do you mean by that?'

'Planning in relation to the event. We have to make the right move to respond to the throw of the dice, as it were, and do what reason dictates as best. If we fall down, we mustn't clap our hands to the hurt place and scream like babies, but accustom our mind to attend as quickly as it can to the healing and setting upright of the fallen and sick. Medicine must drown threnodies.'

'Certainly that is the right way to react to disasters.'

'So the best part of us wants to follow this reasoning.'

'Obviously.'

'And the element that encourages recollection of the trouble and lamentation, and is never sated with these, is irrational, inert, and associated with cowardice?'

'So we shall say.'

'Now the indignant element admits much varied imitation, while the quiet and sensible personality, always very much on the same level, is difficult to imitate—and difficult to detect if someone does try to imitate it, especially at a festival where miscellaneous multitudes throng into the theatre, for it's an imitation of an experience which is foreign to them.'

605   'Quite so.'

'So the imitative poet is obviously not made for this element in the mind—nor is his skill directed to please it, if he is to win popular renown—but for the indignant and variable personality, because it is easy to imitate.'

'Clearly.'

'So we can now properly take hold of him and place him as corresponding to the painter. He is like him in his inferiority with regard to truth, and also in his habitual association with an element of the mind which has the same characteristics, rather than with the best element. We should now be right not to admit him into a potentially well-governed city, because he rouses and feeds this part of the mind and by strengthening it destroys the rational part. It is like giving power to bad men in a city and handing it over to them, while ruining the better. The imitative poet, we shall say, produces a bad government in the individual mind, indulging the foolish element that cannot recognize greater and less but thinks the same thing one moment big, and the next little; he is an image-maker, far removed indeed from the truth.'

'Yes.'

'But we still haven't brought the greatest accusation against him. It is a terrible thought that he can ruin good men, apart from a very few.'

'But of course he can, if he does this.'

'Listen and think. When the best of us hear Homer or some other tragic poet imitating a hero in mourning, delivering a long speech of lamentation, singing, or beating his breast, you know how we feel pleasure and give ourselves up to it, how we follow in sympathy and praise the excellence of the poet who does this to us most effectively.'

'Of course I know.'

'But when we have some private bereavement, you notice how we pride ourselves on the opposite reaction—on keeping quiet and sticking it out—because this is a man's reaction, and the other, which we were praising just now, a woman's.'

'I notice that.'

'Is this approval proper? Is it right not to be disgusted, but to feel pleasure and give praise when you see a man whom you would be ashamed to be yourself?'   606

'Well, it's not reasonable.'

'No, especially if you look at it like this.'

'Like what?'

'The element which is forcibly restrained in our own misfortunes, starved of tears and the satisfaction of lamentation, though it naturally desires this, is the very element which is satisfied and given pleasure by the poets. In these circumstances, our best element, not being adequately trained by reason or habituation, relaxes its watch over this element of lamentation, because the sorrows it sees are others' sorrows and there seems no disgrace in praising and pitying a man who claims to be virtuous and is mourning out of season; indeed, the pleasure seems a positive gain, and we can't bear to reject the whole poem and so be deprived of it. Not many people can see that the consequences of others' experience invade one's own, because it is difficult to restrain pity in one's own misfortunes when it has grown strong on others'.'

'Very true.'

'Does not the same apply to the ridiculous? Suppose you enjoy in a comedy or a private conversation jokes you would be ashamed to make yourself, instead of disliking them as morally bad—aren't you doing the same thing as with the expressions of pity? You are releasing the element in you that likes jokes, and that you used to restrain by reason because you were afraid of a reputation for buffoonery. Without realizing it, you have made a big thing of it by your frequent indulgence in private conversation, with the result that you've become a comedian.'

'Quite so.'

'Poetical imitation in fact produces the same effect in regard to sex and anger and all the desires and pleasures and pains of the mind—and these, in our view, accompany every action. It waters them and nourishes them, when they ought to be dried up. It makes them our rulers, when they ought to be under control so that we can be better and happier people rather than worse and more miserable.'

'I cannot but agree.'

'So when you find admirers of Homer saying that he educated Greece and that for human management and education one ought to take him up and learn his lesson and direct one's whole life on his principles, you must be kind and polite to them—they are as good as they are able to be— and concede that Homer is the foremost and most poetical of the tragic poets; but you must be clear in your mind that the only poetry admissible in our city is hymns to the gods and encomia to good men. If you accept the "sweetened Muse" in lyric or epic, pleasure and pain will be enthroned in your city instead of law and the principle which the community accepts as best in any given situation.'

607

'True.'

'Well, these were the points that I wanted to recall to complete our justification for wishing to banish poetry from the city, such being its nature. The argument forced us. But let us say to her, lest she damn us as coarse and philistine, that there is an old quarrel between poetry and philosophy. I could quote a lot of passages for that: "the yapping bitch that barks at her master", "a great man amid the vanities of fools", "the rabble of know-all heads", "thin thinkers starve", and so on.[1] However, let us make it clear that if poetry for pleasure and imitation have any arguments to advance in favour of their presence in a well-governed city, we should be glad to welcome them back. We are conscious of their charms for us. But it would be wrong to betray what we believe to be the truth. Doesn't poetry charm you, especially when you see her in Homer?'

'Indeed she does.'

'So she deserves to return from exile, if she can make her defence in lyric or other metre?'

'Yes.'

'And we might also allow her defenders, who are lovers of poetry but not themselves poetical, to make a prose speech on her behalf, to show that she is not only pleasing but useful for government and human life; and we shall be glad to listen. After all, it will be our gain if she turns out useful as well as pleasing.'

'Certainly it will.'

---

[1] The source of these quotations is not known.

D. POETIC MADNESS

Plato's *Phaedrus* deals mainly with rhetoric; but it includes also this classic statement of the irrationality of the poet's urge (245 a).

Translation: R. Hackforth, Cambridge, 1952. Commentary: G. J. de Vries, Amsterdam, 1969.

See E. R. Dodds, *The Greeks and the Irrational*, chap. 3.

. . . Third[1] is the possession and madness of the Muses. Gripping the delicate and untouched mind, it rouses it to frenzy in songs and other poems, and, by its adornment of innumerable deeds of the ancients, it educates posterity. He who comes to poetry's door without the Muses' madness, convinced that art will make him an adequate poet, is without fulfilment himself, and his sane man's poetry vanishes before that of the insane.

E. RHETORIC, ACTUAL AND IDEAL

This part of Socrates' conversation with Phaedrus (266 d–274) contains both a critique of the existing art of rhetoric and some suggestions for an improvement on it. This is a late work of Plato (? 360–350 B.C.)—contemporary with early Demosthenes.

'. . . We must explain just what remains in rhetoric.'   266 d

'There's a great deal, Socrates, in the books that have been written on the art or science (*technē*) of speech.'

'I am glad you reminded me. There's something called a *prooemium*, to be spoken at the beginning—that's what you mean, isn't it—this sort of refinement in the art?'

'Yes.'

'And secondly there's "narration" (*diēgēsis*) and "evidence", thirdly "arguments" (*tekmēria*), fourthly "probabilities" (*eikota*). And the great word-contriver of Byzantium added "confirmation" and "supraconfirmation" (*pistōsis, epipistōsis*).'

'You mean the excellent Theodorus?'

'I do. And "refutation" and "counter-refutation" (*elenchos, epex-* 267 *elenchos*), to be used in accusation and defence. And don't we mention the admirable Euenos from Paros, the inventor of "subdemonstration" (*hupodēlōsis*) and "indirect laudation" (*parepainos*)? Some say he wrote "indirect invectives" (*parapsogoi*) in metre, for mnemonic reasons. He was a brilliant man. Are we to let Tisias and Gorgias sleep undisturbed? They saw that probabilities are more to be honoured than the truth; they make small seem great and great small through the force of words, old new and new old—and they discovered how to be brief or infinitely

---

[1] The first two 'useful madnesses' are those of prophecy and orgiastic religion.

lengthy on any subject. Prodicus heard me say this once, and he laughed and said *he'd* invented the art of right speech—and right meant moderate, neither brief nor lengthy.'

'Brilliant, Prodicus!'

'And not a word of Hippias? I suspect that visitor from Elis would have sided with Prodicus.'

'Certainly he would.'

'And how shall I tell of Polus' "word museums", *reduplication, maxims,* and *similes*? And what of the vocabulary of Licymnius, that he gave Polus as a present to enable him to produce fine writing?'

'Wasn't there something like that in Protagoras, Socrates?'

'Correct diction, yes, and many other splendid things. But it was the mighty man of Chalcedon[1] who learnt to control scientifically the woeful words of victims of age and poverty; and he was a remarkable man, too, at making many people angry at once, and then charming them (his own word) with his spells—not to speak of accusing and rebutting accusations from any quarter; he was famous at that. As to the end of the speech, they're all agreed—some call it a résumé (*epanodos*), some have another name for it.'

'You mean the recapitulation that reminds the audience at the end of what was said?'

'That's right. Now, if you've anything to say about the art of speech—'

'Only some small points, not worth mentioning.'

268 'Well, let's let them be, then, if they're only small points. Let's just look at these things in a good light to see what force they have derived from their art.'

'Immense force, Socrates, in big assemblies.'

'Yes, indeed. But see if you agree with me in finding them not of very close texture.'

'Explain.'

'Well, suppose someone went up to your friend Eryximachus[2] or his father Acumenus and said, "I know how to apply various things to the body to produce heat or cold, if I want, or to make a man vomit or be purged—all kinds of things like that. With this knowledge, I claim to be a medical man and to make others medical men by transmitting my knowledge to them." What would Eryximachus or Acumenus say?'

'They'd ask him if he also knew who should be treated, and when and to what extent.'

'Then suppose he replied, "No; but I expect my pupil to be able to do what you ask"?'

---

[1] Thrasymachus.   [2] A doctor—a character in Plato's *Symposium*.

'Then they'd say he was mad—he'd heard a reading from a book somewhere or had come across some medicines, and thought himself a doctor without any knowledge of the science.'

'Now suppose someone went up to Sophocles or Euripides and said he knew how to compose long speeches on small subjects and small speeches on big subjects, and speeches of pity, fear, or menace as he wished, and so on; and he thought that by teaching this he could transmit tragic poetry?'

'They would laugh at him, Socrates, if anyone supposed that tragedy was anything other than a combination of these elements formed in a way appropriate to them individually and to the whole.'

'No doubt, of course, they wouldn't be rude. If a musician meets a man who believes himself to know harmony because he knows how to make the highest and the lowest notes, he wouldn't say fiercely, "Fool, you're mad"; he'd give a gentler answer, being a musician, and say, "My friend, a potential musician must indeed know this, but there's nothing to prevent a person in your state of mind from being totally ignorant of harmony. You know the studies preliminary to harmony, but not harmony proper."'

'Quite right too.'

'So Sophocles might say that the person who was boasting to Euripides 26 and himself knew the preliminaries of tragedy, not tragedy; and Acumenus might similarly speak of the preliminaries of medicine, as distinct from medicine.'

'Certainly.'

'Now what about Adrastus of the honeyed voice—or Pericles for that matter? Suppose they heard us talking about our wonderful devices, *brachylogies* and *iconologies*, and all the other things we said we'd better look at "in a better light". Would they make rude remarks—as you and I were uncultivated enough to do—about writers and teachers of these techniques who claim that they are the "art of rhetoric"? Or would they, being wiser than we, reproach us too? I imagine them saying, "Phaedrus and Socrates, there's no need to be angry. If people who are ignorant of dialectic can't define rhetoric, they are to be excused. It is this disability that has led them to imagine that they possess rhetoric when all they have is the essential preliminary studies, and to think that by teaching these they've taught rhetoric, while their pupils ought to provide for themselves in their speeches the convincing use of each element and the composition of the whole; there's nothing to *this*, they believe."'

'I agree, Socrates. This probably is the state of the art which these people teach and write as rhetoric. I think you are right. But how can one acquire the art of the truly rhetorical and convincing?'

'The capacity to become an accomplished performer in court, Phaedrus, probably—perhaps *necessarily*—rests on the same conditions as everything else: if you are by nature of a rhetorical disposition, you will be a famous orator if you acquire also the knowledge and the practice. Without either of these, you will be defective in that department. As to the element of art, the right method doesn't seem to me to be the one by which Lysias and Thrasymachus proceed.'

'Then what is it?'

'It may be quite natural that Pericles was the most accomplished of all men in rhetoric.'

'Why?'

'Every great art needs a supplement of talk and speculation about 270 Nature. Sublimity and perfection seem to come from some such source. Pericles was not only well endowed by nature: he acquired new powers by associating with Anaxagoras, who was that sort of person, and thus filling himself with lofty speculations and arriving at the essence of Mind and Mindlessness[1]—a favourite subject of Anaxagoras—and then adopting for rhetorical purposes whatever in all this seemed appropriate.'

'What do you mean?'

'Rhetoric is like medicine, I imagine.'

'How?'

'Both require an analysis of their subject—body in one, mind (*psuchē*) in the other—if you're going to have a science, and not just knack and expertise, to help you in giving health and strength to the body by the application of drugs and food, and conviction and virtue to the mind by the application of words and proper habits.'

'That sounds plausible, Socrates.'

'Now do you think one can analyse the nature of mind properly apart from the nature of all things?'

'If we may believe Hippocrates the follower of Asclepius, not even body can be understood without this procedure.'

'And he's quite right too. Still, we mustn't simply trust Hippocrates, but see if the argument holds together.'

'Agreed.'

'Consider then what Hippocrates and reason say about nature. Have we not to ask the following questions about the nature of anything? One: is the subject about which we wish to acquire or impart science simple or complex? Two: if it is simple, what capacity has it for action in what direction, and for reaction to what stimulus? And if it is

---

[1] Anaxagoras' philosophical writings contained a famous account of the part played by Mind (*Nous*) in the creation and continuance of the universe. Pericles did indeed know Anaxagoras; but Plato's account of his debt to him is fantastic.

complex, how many parts has it, and what are the capacities for action
and reaction in each?'

'That's about right, Socrates.'

'Well, a procedure without this would be like a blind man's walk.
But the scientific inquirer can't be compared to the blind or the deaf.
If you are imparting rhetoric to anyone scientifically you'll obviously
have to explain to him carefully the nature of the thing to which he is to
apply his rhetoric. And that means the mind.'

'Yes.'

'Then that's where all the effort goes; it's conviction that he tries to 271
produce, isn't it?'

'Yes.'

'Then Thrasymachus, or anyone else who seriously imparts a science
of rhetoric, will first describe the mind with complete accuracy and make
it apparent whether it is a homogeneous whole or complex, like the body;
this is what we mean by "explaining a nature".'

'Quite so.'

'And, secondly, he will show how it acts and reacts in relation to other
things.'

'Of course.'

'And, thirdly, having classified the species of words and of the mind,
together with the ways they are affected (*pathēmata*), he will explain the
causes, fitting each species to each, and explain what kind of mind is
bound to be convinced or not convinced by particular kinds of words,
and why.'

'That would be excellent.'

'Neither this subject nor any other will ever be scientifically treated in
speech or writing, for display or delivery, in any other way. The present
writers of treatises on the science, whom you have heard, are dishonest;
they know all about the mind, but hide it. Let us therefore not allow that
they are writing scientifically, until they talk and write in this way.'

'What way?'

'It's not easy to put words to it. But I am prepared to explain how
one must write if it is to be as scientific as possible.'

'Do.'

'The power of speech is a charm for the mind (*psuchagōgia*), and the
potential orator must therefore know the kinds of mind there are. They
are such-and-such in number, and of such-and-such kinds. Men therefore are of various types. These distinguished, we proceed to distinguish
various kinds of words. We then say: men of type A are easily convinced
by words of type B, for reason C, of proposition D—and type E, for
reason F, is *not* so easily convinced. Having grasped this theory, one must

then see these things in practice, and be able to pick them up by quickness of perception. Otherwise, one doesn't know any more than the lectures one used to hear! Once able to explain what types of men are convinced by what types of argument—once able to point out to oneself by perception
272 in actual fact that "this is the man and this is the sort of character we were talking about—it's really here now, and I must apply argument X in *this* way to persuade them to Y"—once able to do this, given also the proper moments for speech and silence, and understanding when it is opportune and when inopportune to employ concision and "words of pity" and "exaggeration" and so on—then, and then only, one will have reached the perfection of art. If there is any defect in these respects in the speaker or teacher or writer, but he still claims science, the unbeliever wins! "Do you really think *that*?" our writer may object—"or is there some other way of understanding the notion of a science of speech?"'

'No other way possible, Socrates. But it's a big job.'

'Indeed it is. This is why we ought to turn all the arguments this way and that to see if there's any easier and shorter road. We don't want a long, rough journey for nothing, if a short, smooth one will do. Do try and recollect if you have heard Lysias or anyone else say anything helpful.'

'I can *try*, but I haven't anything in mind at the moment.'

'Would you like me, then, to repeat something I heard from the experts in these matters?'

'Of course.'

'Even the wolf's cause ought to be presented, as they say, Phaedrus.'

'Well, present it.'

'They say there is no need to make such a grand business of it, or go such a roundabout way. As we said at the beginning of our discussion, the potential good orator need have nothing to do with truth in regard to just or good actions—or men, whether good by nature or by education. Nobody worries about these things in law-courts. They are concerned with persuasiveness—and this means probability, which *is* the scientific speaker's proper study. Both in prosecutions and in defences, there are times when one ought not to tell the truth, if it's not probable, but rather what is probable. Probability is always to be pursued, and you can say good-bye to truth. It's probability, which runs through a speech from
273 beginning to end, that constitutes the whole subject of the science.'

'Indeed, Socrates, that is exactly what those who claim to understand the science of speech say. I remember we touched on this before; it's a big subject for those concerned.'

'Well, you've studied Tisias himself pretty thoroughly; so let Tisias tell us whether he means by probability anything other than "what most people believe".'

'He can't.'

'This clever and scientific discovery, it seems, led him to write that if a weak but brave man beat up a hefty coward, stealing his cloak or something, and was brought into court, neither party ought to tell the truth. The coward ought to say he wasn't beaten up by the brave man alone, and the other ought then to prove that there were only the two of them, and then use the argument "Look at him and look at me; how could I have tackled him?" The other man, of course, won't admit his own cowardice; he'll try some other lies, which will soon give his opponent a chance to refute it. "Scientific" advice is all about this sort of thing, isn't it, Phaedrus?'

'It is indeed.'

'Ah me, it's a fearfully recondite science that Tisias discovered, or whoever it was and whatever he likes to be called. But ought we, or ought we not, to say to him—'

'What were you thinking of?'

'This. "Tisias, we have been saying for some time, before you came in, that this probability generally arises through similarity to the truth, and we argued a little while ago that in everything it's the man who knows the truth who best knows how to find similarities. So, while we'd give a hearing to anything *else* you say about the science of words, as to this, we'll abide by our discussion. Without enumerating the natures of the potential audience, and being able to divide things according to their kinds and grasp each under a single form, no one can attain science in words, so far as human capacities go. And this is unattainable without much labour, which the good man ought not to undertake for the sake of speech and action in human relationships, but only in order to be able to speak and act as far as he can in a manner pleasing to the gods. Wiser men than we, Tisias, say that the wise ought not to strive to please their fellow 274 slaves, except incidentally, but to please masters who are good and of good folk. So don't wonder if the way round is long; the object is a great one, on a different scale from what you imagine . . ."'

F. REAL AND ASSUMED TASTES

We append three short passages from Plato's last work, the *Laws*, in which he modifies or expands upon points made in the *Republic*. The first is from Book II, 655 c–656 a.

Vicaire 66 ff.; Grube 61 ff.; G. R. Morrow, *Plato's Cretan City*, Princeton, 1960.

Translation: A. E. Taylor, London, 1934; T. J. Saunders, London (Penguin), 1970.

Athenian. Now another point. Do we all enjoy all dances alike, or is this far from true?

Clinias. As far from true as anything can be.

Athenian. Then what do we say can have led us into error? Is it that the same things are not beautiful to us all? Or only that the same things don't seem beautiful? No one, surely, will say that the dances of vice are lovelier than those of virtue, or that he himself enjoys the figures of wickedness, though others like some very different Muse. Yet most people say that musical correctness (*orthotēs*) consists in giving pleasure to the mind. This idea, however, is intolerable and impious. It's the other that is more likely to be the cause of our error.

Clinias. What do you mean?

Athenian. Dancing is an imitation of manners, involved in actions and fortunes of every kind. The personages do everything by character and imitation. Consequently, whatever is said, sung or performed in any way to accord with a man's manner, be it natural or habitual, that he inevitably enjoys, commends, and calls beautiful. Those who find it contrary to their nature, ways, or habits, can neither enjoy it nor praise it, but call it ugly. People whose natures are right and habits wrong, or habits right and natures wrong, give their praises in a way contrary to their pleasures; they say things are pleasant but bad, and are ashamed to put their bodies through such movements in front of people they believe to be wise, or to sing and give the impression they seriously think the song beautiful—though privately they enjoy it.

G. PLEASURE AS A CRITERION—BUT WHOSE PLEASURE?

From the same book (658 a–659 c).

'Now suppose someone proposed a competition without saying whether it was gymnastic, musical, or equestrian, but just assembled the whole population and offered a prize, for whoso wished to come forward to compete in pleasure—the prize being for the man who delighted the audience most. There would be no limitation on how he should do it . . . What do we think would happen as a result of such a proclamation.'

'In what respect?'

'Well, someone might perform a rhapsody, like Homer, someone a piece of lyre-music, others a tragedy or a comedy, and I dare say some character would expect to win with a conjuring show. But can we say who would justly win out of these innumerable and various performers?'

'What an odd question! How could anyone answer with knowledge without hearing—without in fact having heard all the competitors himself?'

'Well? Would you like me to give you your odd answer?'

'Of course.'

'If the little children were the judges, they will award it to the conjurer, won't they?'

'Yes, of course.'

'If it's the bigger boys, it'll be the comedian; the educated women, the young lads, and perhaps the general multitude, will be for the tragedy.'

'I dare say.'

'And it'll be we old men who will give the palm for pleasure to a rhapsode who's given a good performance of the *Iliad* or *Odyssey* or some piece of Hesiod. Who then will have rightly won—that's the next question, isn't it?'

'Yes.'

'Now it's plain that you and I *have* to say that the competitors chosen by our contemporaries are the right winners. For our habits are, we generally suppose, much the best of any today in all cities, and indeed everywhere.'

'Well?'

'I am in agreement myself with the majority, so far as to say that music should be judged by pleasure—but not by the pleasure of all and sundry. The most beautiful Muse, for me, is that which gives pleasure to the best and best-educated, and especially that which pleases a single judge, outstanding for virtue and education. This is why we say the judges of these competitors need virtue; they must have something of all wisdom, and especially of courage. The true judge must not learn from the audience, and be thrown off his balance by the noise of the multitude and his own lack of training; nor must he, when he makes his judgement, give a soft and insincere one out of cowardice and unmanliness, lying with those very lips with which he called on the gods when he began giving his judgement! The judge is there, properly speaking, as a teacher of the audience, not as their pupil; he is to oppose those who offer the spectators pleasure wrongly or improperly. Under the old Greek law this was allowable. The present Italian and Sicilian practice of handing over to the mass of spectators and deciding the winner by a show of hands has corrupted the poets, because they regard the vulgar pleasures of their judges as a standard and let the audience be their teachers. It has also corrupted the audience's own pleasures, because, when they ought to put their pleasure on a higher level by hearing things above the level of their own character, they in fact experience the opposite—and by their own action at that.'

H. CAUSES OF DECLINE

Finally (3. 700 a–701 b), a short passage on a theme much canvassed in later times. Vicaire 69.

'. . . Under our old laws, the people was not the master in certain fields, but in a sense was voluntarily enslaved to the laws.'

'What laws?'

'Firstly, those relating to the music of that period. I want to explain from the beginning the growth of the life of licence. In those days, our music was divided according to genres and forms. One kind of song was prayers to the gods—these were called *hymns*; another kind, opposite to this, was what might best have been called *dirges*; then there were *paeans* and *dithyrambs*—these concerned with the birth of Dionysus. They actually used the word *nomoi* (laws) also for a sort of tune, and added the adjective "citharoedic". With these and other similar distinctions firmly established it was impossible to use one type of song for the purposes of another. The authority to decide and judge and fine the disobedient was not a hiss or a raucous shout from the mob, as it is today, nor the hand-clapping that nowadays awards praise. The educated were determined to listen in silence all through; the children, their attendants, and the multitude were kept in order by the rod. The mass of the people was thus willing to be controlled in an orderly way, and did not venture to give a noisy judgement. But as time went on, tasteless lawlessness was initiated by poets who were poetical enough by nature but ignorant of the due and right rules of the Muse, frenzied and indecently possessed by pleasure; they mixed dirges and hymns, paeans and dithyrambs, made the lyre mimic the flute, and generally confused everything; their folly led them to the false conclusion that there was no correctness (*orthotēs*) in music, but it is judged most correctly by the pleasure of the enjoyer, whether he be good or bad . . . Hence audiences became vocal, and imagined they understood beauty and ugliness in the Muses. Instead of an aristocracy, a vile theatrocracy arose. If it had only been a democracy of decent men, it wouldn't have been so bad.'

3

ARISTOTLE

BIBLIOGRAPHY

Poetics

Aristotle *Poetics*: Introduction, Commentary, and Appendixes by D. W. Lucas, Oxford, 1968 (this, the most recent commentary, itself contains a useful brief bibliography).

H. House, *Aristotle's Poetics*, London, 1956.

The translation of T. S. Dorsch in the Penguin volume *Classical Literary Criticism*, 1965, is valuable.

Rhetoric

E. M. Cope, *An Introduction to Aristotle's Rhetoric*, London and Cambridge, 1867.

—— *The Rhetoric of Aristotle with a Commentary*, revised by J. E. Sandys, 3 vols., Cambridge, 1877.

J. H. Freese, *Aristotle: The 'Art' of Rhetoric* (Loeb), London, 1926.

A. POETICS

INTRODUCTION

Aristotle's *Poetics* is probably the most important single book that has ever been written about poetry, both for what it says and for what it has been taken to say. Various factors make it a work singularly easy to misinterpret, and the misinterpretations have been just as seminal in the development of aesthetic theory and, at some periods, of poetry itself as a correct understanding of it.

The factors that make for misunderstanding are worth listing, if only for monitory purposes: (1) Aristotle's thought, though generally exquisitely lucid, is never easy and never slack; it is therefore as hard for a person who knows Greek to follow him as it is for a person who knows English to follow Hume. (2) Some accidental features of its composition or its transmission have made the *Poetics* one of his most compressed and elliptical works; the contrast with the comparatively open texture of the *Rhetoric*, for instance, is marked. (3) Aristotle presupposed in his audience an acquaintance not only with the doctrines of the *Ethics* and *Politics* but also with the central concepts of his logical and metaphysical theories (cf. below, pp. 98 n. 4, 99 n. 1, 101 n. 3, 106 n. 1). (4) The *Poetics* envisages a variety of different interests in literature, the politician's, the poet's, the critic's; but the book is not written primarily for any of these, but rather for the philosopher. In other words, it is neither principally a defence of poetry, nor a treatise on how to write it, nor an enunciation of principles of literary criticism, though it has elements of all these; it is first and foremost a work of aesthetic theory, and interpretations that under-stress this fact inevitably lead to distortion.

ARISTOTLE'S THEORY OF AESTHETIC PLEASURE

Aristotle had a quite coherent theory of the nature of our pleasure in art. It starts from simple principles and ramifies everywhere; it explains his preferences in literature and it is the antithesis of Plato's, though it accepts some of the same presuppositions.

The basic premiss of Aristotle's aesthetic theory is stated in c. 4 of the *Poetics* and several times in the *Rhetoric* (below, pp. 94, 134, 150): it is that by and large human beings positively enjoy learning or understanding or realizing things.[1] Our desire to understand things is a natural desire like hunger, and its satisfaction is pleasurable, a 'restoration to a natural state', like eating (below, p. 134). Our pleasure in art is a branch of this pleasure; the poet or the orator or the painter makes us see or understand things that we did not see before, and particularly he points out the relations and similarities between different things, enables us to say, in Aristotle's phrase, 'this is that' (below, pp. 94, 134, 150).

This basic foundation of aesthetic pleasure explains many of Aristotle's further requirements in art. First and foremost, it justifies the general Greek belief, which Aristotle accepted and elaborately defends, that art is essentially 'representational', i.e. that *mimēsis* is necessary to it.[2] Aristotle takes the relation between *mimēsis* and *mathēsis* to be a close one, both at the simplest level, where 'we make our first steps in learning through *mimēsis*' (below, p. 94) and at the infinitely more sophisticated one where the tragic poet makes 'general statements' analogous to those of the moral philosopher. At the lowest level *mimēsis* is what Plato asserted it was at any level, mere copying, a parrot act that can be performed without any real knowledge of the act or object copied; even here, however, Aristotle implies that though we may not have knowledge before we engage in *mimēsis* we acquire knowledge by engaging in it. And at the higher level the tragic poet, presenting individually characterized people in specific situations, makes us aware of moral facts and moral possibilities relevant to more than the situation he envisages.

If *mimēsis* is to produce the sort of realization that Aristotle demands of art at its best, a prime requirement is obviously truth. A poem or play that operates in the realm of fantasy can charm and rouse wonder, and Aristotle is as susceptible as anyone to the enchantment of the fantastic in Homer (below, pp. 125 f.). Yet his judgement is against fantasy and given in favour of the more

[1] These are different possible translations of *mathēsis* and the associated verb *manthanein*.

[2] Once at any rate, in an interesting passage of the *Philebus* (51 b–e), Plato does question the necessity of *mimēsis* to aesthetic pleasure; but in general he, like Aristotle, accepts the general Greek assumption that our pleasure in art is principally pleasure in *mimēsis*.

rigorous causal chain of tragedy,[1] which, because it is presented to the senses and not just to the feebler imagination, cannot afford to follow epic into the area of the marvellous and the irrational.

Yet the realization must be a sudden one too, and for this the prime requirement is surprise. A play whose plot, however truthful, is predictable will not give us the pleasure of sudden realization. This is the reason for Aristotle's insistence on the unexpected and a second reason for his preference for the complex form of tragedy, which is defined with reference to surprise turns (*peripeteiai*) and recognitions. It is juxtaposition that best makes us aware of opposites (below, pp. 138, 149, 167), and the sudden reversals of fortune in complex tragedy most powerfully bring home to us the truths that the poet is stating.

For both these reasons Aristotle regards complex tragedy as the *entelecheia* or full realization of the essential nature of poetry. It is the form that makes us realize most truth fastest, and therefore provides in greatest measure and concentration the pleasure that a work of art can provide. The same criteria are deployed not only to judge between or within literary kinds, but also in evaluating details of style, both in poetry and prose. It is the requirements of *mathēsis* that determine the high estimate Aristotle sets on metaphor (pp. 122, 150), on the periodic style (p. 148), on antithetical expression (pp. 149, 150 f., 154), on rhythm in prose (p. 146), on various forms of argument (p. 150).

THE DEFENCE OF TRAGEDY

Whatever may be true of other arts,[2] tragedy at any rate operates on a consciousness heightened by intense emotion, and specifically by the two emotions of fear and pity. The discussion of these two emotions in *Rhetoric* 2. 5 and 2. 9 shows them closely related; essentially they are roused by the same kind of situations, but fear is self-regarding and pity other-regarding. Aristotle's statement that tragedy arouses fear in the audience therefore implies that he takes for granted a remarkable degree of identification between the audience and the characters presented. No doubt the fear felt by the audience of tragedy does not cover the whole range of fear in ordinary life, but the flat statement of the *Rhetoric*[3] inescapably implies that Aristotle does not agree with Dr. Johnson's 'The truth is, the audience are always in their senses', much less with more recent aesthetic theories about the necessity of 'distancing'.

A by-product of the stimulation of these intense emotions is their *catharsis* (p. 97). This cryptic phrase has attracted more attention than it deserves, but the theory concealed by it is nevertheless important. Plato had attacked *mimēsis*, and particularly tragedy, on two counts, the first that it does not present us with truth (above, pp. 66 ff.), the second that it stimulates emotions that a

---

[1] The topic is developed in *Poetics*, cc. 7–9, below, pp. 100 ff.

[2] It is never made quite clear whether or not epic also operates by rousing the same emotions as tragedy.

[3] 1382[b]30 ff. 'No one feels fear if he thinks nothing is likely to happen to him, or fear of things he does not think would happen to him or of people he does not think likely to harm him, or at the time when he does not anticipate harm.'

good man tries to suppress (above, pp. 69 ff.). Aristotle's answer to the first charge is to be found in the *mathēsis* doctrine, and especially in c. 9 of the *Poetics*: Plato had claimed that an instance of *mimēsis* has less reality than an individual particular, which in turn has less reality than the *idea*. Aristotle replies that the statements of the poet, so far from being inferior to statements of particulars, are more comprehensive and more philosophical (below, p. 102); if he were thinking in Platonic terms this would amount to saying that the object of *mimēsis* is not the particular but the *idea*. Of course he does not say any such thing, as he did not believe in substantive *ideai*; but the implication was drawn by later Platonists.[1] The answer to Plato's second charge is contained in the reference to *catharsis*.[2]

Some light is thrown on the concept of *catharsis* by the passage cited from the *Politics* (below, pp. 132 ff.). But that passage is also in some respects misleading, as there Aristotle is talking from the point of view of the legislator and educationalist and discussing the uses of various kinds of music. In the *Poetics* he is indeed talking at the legislator, but not from his point of view, and he can be content with a more purely defensive position. As against Plato he only has to show that tragedy's stimulation of the emotions is not in fact undesirable and may indeed be beneficial.

The passage, unprovided with the explanation promised in the *Politics*, has provoked the most various interpretations. The most promising line is that put forward by House, op. cit., pp. 100 ff.; he takes *catharsis* in its medical sense of the production of a 'mean', and interprets the concept of 'mean' in Aristotle's own sense. When we consider what degree of emotion is 'undue', we take into account not merely the quantity of emotion but its object and its circumstances (*Nic. Eth.* 1106^{b}18 ff. 'One can feel fear, confidence, desire, anger, pity . . . both too much and too little, and in both cases wrongly; but the mean is attained when we feel them at the right time, at the right objects, towards the right people, for the right reason, in the right way'). Aristotle's answer to Plato, so maddeningly undeveloped, seems to be that tragedy presents us with objects (great and good men suffering terrible fortunes) that are proportioned to the degree of emotion they arouse. So far from encouraging a vicious indulgence in emotion on any and every occasion, tragedy gives us an imaginative apprehension of a degree of suffering normally beyond our ken. We need not suppose that Aristotle has romantic expectations about the educative power of tragedy; of course one perception of the mean is not enough to make a virtuous man. Yet any perception of the mean helps one to right feeling and right behaviour, and that is so far, so good.

It is important that the concept of *catharsis* does not commit Aristotle to either of two erroneous aesthetic positions common both in antiquity and later times. *Catharsis* is not something the tragic poet aims to produce. His aim is

---

[1] Cicero, *Orator* 8 ff., Plotinus 5. 8. 1.

[2] It certainly required a reply and in the *Poetics* gets no other. This is a main reason for rejecting the interpretation of *catharsis* recently proposed by L. Golden, *Transactions of the American Philological Association*, 93, 1962, 55 ff. (reiterated in the commentary of Golden and Hardison); cf. also *Classical Philology* 64, 1969, 145 ff.

defined below (p. 108) as 'to produce the pleasure springing from pity and fear via *mimēsis*'. *Catharsis* is a therapeutic by-product, not something the poet either does or should intend. But just as Aristotle can therefore avoid the Scylla of taking the poet to have a duty to improve his audience's morals, he equally shuns the Charybdis of denying that poetry has any moral effect. Tragedy is not trivial; it does alter our moral attitudes, and a legislator might well consider whether to do something about it. Aristotle is not however convinced that the legislator would be well advised to tell the poet what kind of poems to write.

THE TRANSLATION

Theories on how to translate the *Poetics* are almost as numerous as the actual translations. This translation is based on the single principle of trying to make coherent sense, of the material presented by tradition when one can make sense of it, of modern conjectures when one cannot. The attempt to express in English the logical relation between Aristotle's ideas inevitably leads to some camouflaging of the way he puts them, but is necessary to avoid the more damaging impression that Aristotle spoke a version of the higher Babu. If he arranges two nouns and two adjectives chiastically and says that the ridiculous is 'a blunder or ugliness that does not imply pain or cause damage', one should suppress this stylistic elegance in the interests of clarity. If he says 'On the one hand this and on the other hand that' and means, as Greeks did, 'Though this, nevertheless that' or alternatively 'Just as this, so also that', it is better to make him say in English what he means in Greek. If he wants to say 'anything' and has to use a word equally open to the translation 'everything', there is no reason to make him tell lies by putting the second into his mouth. He is not responsible for the fact that Greek is over-fond of the co-ordinate form of expression and sometimes uses one word for two different concepts. Anyone who understood his author would accept such principles of translation if he were dealing with, say, an orator; there is no sense in allowing a slavish adherence to the actual Greek words to obscure Aristotle's meaning in a way that would not be tolerable in a rendering of Demosthenes. On the other hand, I have tried to be very scrupulous in warning the reader by square brackets whenever I have added a phrase to show what I take to be the logical relation between sentences. The chapter and paragraph headings are mine.

Some constant technical terms are merely transliterated, like *peripeteia* or *pathos* (with its plural *pathē*); these are defined in the treatise itself and when used in the sense defined are left in their transliterated form. I have followed the same course with *mimēsis*, the central concept of the *Poetics*, which is too important to be rendered by an only roughly approximate English word. It is never defined and the range of ideas Aristotle uses it to cover is a shifting one; one sees better what they are if one comes to it with no English-based pre-conceptions.

In some other places, particularly those dealing with minute stylistic points, the Greek examples are left untranslated; we have no way, for instance, of showing in English the stylistic effect of what Aristotle calls a 'dialect term' (below p. 119). Merely to render it by a stronger, though current, English word undervalues the strangeness of the dialect term, while a scattering of occasional phrases from Lallans or Mummerset would not be, to English taste, agreeable.

CHAPTER I

THE PRELIMINARIES TO THE DEFINITION OF TRAGEDY

Contents

1447ᵃ The subject I wish us to discuss is poetry itself, its species with their
1 respective capabilities, the correct way of constructing plots so that the work turns out well, the number and nature of the constituent elements [of each species], and anything else in the same field of inquiry.

SECTION A. THE DIVISION *PER GENUS ET DIFFERENTIAM*

1. *The genus we are here concerned with stated*[1]

To follow the natural order and take first things first, epic and tragic poetry, comedy and dithyrambic, and most music for the flute or lyre are all, generally considered, varieties of *mimēsis*, differing from each other in three respects, the media, the objects, and the mode of *mimēsis*. ['Media' needs explaining]: in some cases where people, whether by technical rules or practised facility, produce various *mimēseis* by portraying things, the media are colours and shapes, while in others the medium is the voice;[2] similarly in the arts in question, taken collectively, the media of *mimēsis* are rhythm, speech, and harmony, either separately or in combination.

2. *The genus divided*

(a) ACCORDING TO DIFFERENCES OF MEDIA

(i) *Those which do not use speech*

For example, harmony and rhythm are the media of instrumental music,[3] rhythm alone without harmony the medium of dancing, as dancers

---

[1] The genus that Aristotle proceeds to divide is not, as one sometimes finds stated, *mimēsis* in general, but a variety of *mimēsis* defined by the media, '*mimēsis* in speech, harmony, and rhythm, separately or in combination'.

[2] The reference is to sounds, not necessarily articulate, made by the human vocal organs. Direct mimicry of the bird-call kind seems to be what Aristotle has in mind.

[3] Literally 'flute-playing and lyre-playing and any other arts that have the same capability, for example, playing the Pan-pipe'.

represent characters, passions,[1] and actions by rhythmic movement and postures.

(ii) *Those which do use speech (i.e. the poetic kinds)*[2]

The art that uses only speech by itself or verse [that is, rhythmical speech], the verses being homogeneous or of different kinds, has as yet 1447[b] no name;[3] for we have no common term to apply to the [prose] mimes of Sophron and Xenarchus and to the Socratic dialogues, nor any common term for *mimēseis* produced in verse, whether iambic trimeters or elegiacs or some other such metre. True, people do attach the making [that is the root of the word *poiētēs*] to the name of a metre and speak of elegiac-makers and hexameter-makers; they think, no doubt, that 'makers' is applied to poets not because they make *mimēseis* but as a general term meaning 'verse-makers', since they call 'poets' or 'makers' even those who publish a medical or scientific theory in verse. But [this is open to two objections]: (1) as Homer and Empedocles have nothing in common except their metre, the latter had better be called a scientific writer, not a poet, if we are to use 'poet' of the former; (2) similarly, if we suppose a man to make his *mimēsis* in a medley of all metres, as Chaeremon in fact did in the *Centaur*, a recitation-piece in all the various metres, we still have to call him a poet, a 'maker'.[4]

So much for the simpler kinds. Some use all the media mentioned, rhythm, song, and verse:[5] these are dithyrambic and nomic poetry,

[1] Others interpret this as the opposite of 'actions', i.e. 'things that happen to people'.

[2] The order of the following section suggests that here too Aristotle is using a not-*x*, *x* method of division, considering first the arts that do not use music and dancing and next those that do.

[3] Aristotle's complaint seems to be double, that the whole mimetic art that uses speech but not music and dancing has no name and that the two species, prose and verse composition, have no names. Lobel makes the sense tidier by conjecturing: 'The art that uses only speech by itself and that which uses verse . . . have as yet no names.'

[4] The point (a sophistical one) seems to be that both on Aristotle's criterion of *mimēsis* and on the ordinary language criterion of verse, Chaeremon belongs to the generic class 'poet', but that ordinary language can find no specific term for him parallel to 'hexameter-maker'. The other argument is no better, given Aristotle's own commendation of Empedocles in the *On the Poets* as 'Homeric and stylistically excellent, particularly in his use of metaphor'. In arguing for the necessity of the criterion of *mimēsis* Aristotle is not too particular about the weapons he uses.

[5] This is commonly equated with the 'rhythm, harmony, and speech' mentioned above; but Aristotle is here dealing with more complicated elements than in the original definition. By 'rhythm' here he means dancing, while 'song' is a combination of all three of the media isolated earlier, and verse a combination of rhythm and speech. The analysis really applies better to comedy and tragedy than it does to choral lyric, in which there is no distinction between 'song' and 'verse'; later in the *Poetics* 'verse' is used to refer to the dialogue scenes in tragedy as distinct from the choral 'songs'.

tragedy and comedy. But the two former use them all simultaneously, while the latter use different media in different parts. So much for the differentiae derived from the media.

(b) ACCORDING TO DIFFERENCES OF OBJECTS

1448ª   The objects of this *mimēsis* are people doing things,[1] and these people
2 [as represented] must necessarily be either good or bad, this being, generally speaking, the only line of divergence between characters, since differences of character just are differences in goodness and badness, or else they must be better than are found in the world or worse or just the same, as they are represented by the painters, Polygnotus portraying them as better, Pauson as worse, and Dionysius as they are;[2] clearly therefore each of the varieties of *mimēsis* in question will exhibit these differences, and one will be distinguishable from another in virtue of presenting things as different in this way.

These dissimilarities can in fact be found in dancing and instrumental music, and in the arts using speech and unaccompanied verse: Homer for instance represents people as better and Cleophon as they are, while Hegemon of Thasos, the inventor of parodies, and Nicochares, the author of the *Deiliad*, represent them as worse; the same is true of dithyrambs and nomes, where the *mimēsis* can differ as . . . ,[3] and as that of the Cyclopes does in Timotheus and Philoxenus; this is also the differentia that marks off tragedy from comedy, since the latter aims to represent people as worse, the former as better, than the men of the present day.

(c) ACCORDING TO DIFFERENCES OF MODE

3   There is still a third difference, the mode in which one represents each of these objects. For one can represent the same objects in the same media

   [1] Aristotle's word *prattontōn* means, for him, 'people performing responsible and morally characterizable actions'.
   [2] The second distinction is a refinement on the first, perhaps an afterthought. The translation 'better than are found in the world' is suggested by Dryden's classification of the subject-matter of comedy as 'such humours, adventures and designs as are to be found and met with in the world' (Preface to *An Evening's Love, or The Mock Astrologer*, 1671). Dryden of course is speaking of comedy as it descends from the post-Aristotelian New Comedy of Menander and his fellows, which claims to portray people 'as they are'; the comedy Aristotle is talking about is a comedy of caricature like Pauson's painting, and nearer to Dryden's 'Farce'. What Aristotle intended by 'better than are found in the world' is most usefully shown by *Nic. Eth.* 1145ª19 ff.: 'An excellence beyond the human scale, something heroic and divine, which may be illustrated by the phrase Homer makes Priam use of Hector to express his signal excellence, "He seemed the son of a god, not of a mortal man".' I owe this reference to Miss G. M. Matthews.
   [3] Text defective.

   (i) sometimes in narration and sometimes becoming someone else, as
     Homer does, or
   (ii) speaking in one's own person without change, or
   (iii) with all the people engaged in the *mimēsis* actually doing things.[1]

These three then, media, objects, and mode, are, as I said at the beginning, the differentiae of poetic *mimēsis*. So, if we use one of them [to
separate poets into classes], Sophocles will be in the same class as Homer,
since both represent people as good, and if we use another, he will be in
the same class as Aristophanes, since they both represent people as
actively doing things.

Digression on the etymological fancies of the Dorians[2]

Some people say that this verb *drān*, 'to do', is why plays are called
dramas, because such poets represent people as doing things; and this
is the ground on which the Dorians claim the invention of both tragedy
and comedy. Comedy is claimed by the Megarians, both by those of
mainland Greece, who say it arose when their democracy was established,[3]
and by those of [Megara Hyblaea in] Sicily, the home of Epicharmus,
who lived well before Chionides and Magnes.[4] Tragedy is claimed by some
of the Peloponnesians. In each case they found their claim on etymology:
they say that while they call outlying villages *kōmai*, the Athenians call
them *dēmoi*, and they take 'comedy' to be derived not from *kōmazein*, 'to
revel', but from the fact that the comic actors wandered among the
villages because driven in contempt from the city; and they say that they
use the word *drān* of doing, while the Athenians say *prattein*.

1448b

Conclusion

So much for the number and nature of the differentiae of poetic
mimēsis.

  [1] The Greek is perhaps defective and also admits the interpretation '(i) sometimes in
narration, either becoming someone else, as Homer does, or speaking in one's own
person without change, or (ii) with all the people . . .'. The threefold classification given
in the translation is in accordance with Plato's view (*Rep.* 392 d ff.); more important,
it agrees better with Aristotle's own insistence on the uniqueness of Homer (pp. 94 f.,
101 f., 123, 125 f.).
  [2] The position of this digression, carefully segregated from the following serious
discussion of the development of the poetic kinds, seems to show that Aristotle thought
little of the Dorian claims.
  [3] Early in the sixth century.
  [4] The first known poets of Attic comedy, very little later, in fact, than Epicharmus.

SECTION B. THE PROOF THAT THE KINDS WE ARE INTERESTED
IN DEFINING ARE EACH A COMPLETELY DEVELOPED AND
A SINGLE SPECIES

1. *The origins of poetry*

4   Poetry, I believe, has two over-all causes, both of them natural:

(*a*) *Mimēsis* is innate in human beings from childhood—indeed we
differ from the other animals in being most given to *mimēsis* and in making
our first steps in learning through it—and pleasure in instances of *mimēsis*
is equally general. This we can see from the facts: we enjoy looking at the
most exact portrayals of things we do not like to see in real life, the lowest
animals, for instance, or corpses. This is because not only philosophers,
but all men, enjoy getting to understand something, though it is true
that most people feel this pleasure only to a slight degree; therefore they
like to see these pictures, because in looking at them they come to understand something and can infer what each thing is, can say, for instance,
'This man in the picture is so-and-so'.[1] If you happen not to have seen
the original, the picture will not produce its pleasure *qua* instance of
mimēsis, but because of its technical finish or colour or for some such
other reason.

(*b*) As well as *mimēsis*, harmony and rhythm are natural to us, and verses
are obviously definite sections of rhythm.

2. *The development of pre-dramatic poetry*

These two were gradually developed by those who had most natural
gift for them. Poetry, arising from their improvisations, split up according
to the authors' divergent characters: the more dignified represented noble
actions and those of noble men, the less serious those of low-class people;
the one group produced at first invectives, the others songs praising gods
and men. We cannot name any author of a poem of the former kind before
Homer's time, though there were probably many of them, but from
Homer on we do find such poems—his own *Margites*, for instance, and
others of the kind. These introduced the metre that suited them, still
called 'iambic' (from *iambizein*, 'to lampoon'), because it was the metre of
their lampoons on each other. So some of the ancients produced heroic
[i.e. hexameter] verse and the others iambics.

As well as being the most creative poet of high actions,[2] his *mimēseis*

---

[1] The pleasure of understanding and realizing something is for Aristotle basic to
aesthetic pleasure; cf. the fuller discussion in *Rhet.* 1. 1371[a]21 ff. (below, p. 134) and
pp. 86 f.

[2] The translation is borrowed from Milton (*P.R.* 4. 266); the word is translated 'good'

in this kind being the only ones that are not only well done but essentially dramatic, Homer also first adumbrated the form of comedy by dramatizing the ridiculous instead of producing invectives; his *Margites* bears the same relation to comedy as the *Iliad* and *Odyssey* do to tragedy.[1]

On the subsequent appearance of tragedy and comedy, those whose natural bent made lampooners of them turned to comedy, while those naturally inclined to epic became tragedians, because the new forms were more ample and more highly esteemed than the old.

3. *The development of tragedy*

To inquire whether even tragedy [as distinct from epic] is sufficiently elaborated in its qualitative elements, judging it in itself and in its relation to the audience, is another story.[2] At any rate, after originating in the improvisations of the leaders of the dithyramb, as comedy did in those of the leaders of the phallic songs still customary in many Greek cities, tragedy gradually grew to maturity, as people developed the capacities they kept discovering in it, and after many changes it stopped altering, since it had attained its full growth. The main changes were:

(i) in the number of actors, raised from one to two by Aeschylus, who made the choral part less important and gave speech the leading role; Sophocles added a third—and also scene-painting;

(ii) in amplitude: as tragedy developed from the satyr-style, its plots were at first slight and its expression comical, and it was a long time before it acquired dignity;

(iii) in metre: the iambic trimeter replaced the trochaic tetrameter, which had been used before as suitable for a satyr-style poetry, that is, for productions involving more dancing; when verbal expression came to the fore, however, nature herself found the right metre, the iambic being the most speakable of all metres; this we can see from the fact that it is the one we most often produce accidentally in conversation, where

(for example, at p. 92) or 'noble' (p. 96) when used of persons. For the concept cf. p. 92, n. 2.

[1] Aristotle's unwillingness either to distort or accurately to report the facts of history produces in this section some embarrassment of expression, which has induced some editors to rearrange the argument in the form Aristotle would have given it if he had been unscrupulous. The series hymns–Homer–tragedy leads him to posit a similar series invectives–Homer–comedy. In fact the invention of the iambic trimeter was attributed to Homer in the *Margites*, and Archilochus, the great poet of invective, was later than Homer.

[2] Tragedy is more elaborated than epic, as it has more qualitative elements (p. 96). The 'other story' seems to be given by the deduction of the sufficiency of the qualitative elements of tragedy on pp. 97 f.

hexameters are rare and only occur when we depart from conversational tone;

(iv) in the increased number of episodes.

There is no need to say more of this or of the other developments that gave it beauty; it would take too long to go through them in detail.

4. *The development of comedy*

5 Comedy is, as I said, a *mimēsis* of people worse than are found in the world —'worse' in the particular sense of 'uglier', as the ridiculous is a species of ugliness; for what we find funny is a blunder that does no serious damage or an ugliness that does not imply pain, the funny face, for instance, being one that is ugly and distorted, but not with pain. While the changes and the authors of the changes in tragedy are known, the 1449ᵇ development of comedy is obscure because it was not at first taken seriously; the chorus, for instance, were for a long time volunteers, and not provided officially by the archon. The form was already partly fixed before the first recorded comic poets, and so we do not know who introduced masks, prologues, numerous actors, and so on; the making of plots, however, certainly came first from Sicily, Crates being the first Athenian to drop the lampoon form and construct generalized stories or plots.

SECTION C. APOLOGY FOR POSTPONING THE TREATMENT OF EPIC, IN DEFIANCE OF CHRONOLOGY

Epic, in so far as it is a sizeable[1] *mimēsis* in verse of noble personages, goes along with tragedy, but differs from it in using metre alone [without music] and in being in narrative form; it also differs in length, tragedy attempting so far as possible to keep to the limit of one revolution of the sun or not much more or less, while epic is unfixed in time. This differentiates them now, but at first tragic practice was the same as epic. Of their elements some are the same, some peculiar to tragedy, so that any judge of excellence in tragedy can judge of epic too, since tragedy has everything that epic has, while epic lacks some of tragedy's elements.

6 I shall deal later with the art of *mimēsis* in hexameters and with comedy; here I want to talk about tragedy, picking up the definition of its essential nature that results from what I have said.

---

[1] The text is corrupt and the 'sizeable' is a conjecture.

Chapter II

The Nature of Tragedy

Section A. The Nature of Tragedy According to the Category of Substance

Well then, a tragedy is a *mimēsis* of a high, complete action ('complete' in the sense that implies amplitude), in speech pleasurably enhanced, the different kinds [of enhancement] occurring in separate sections, in dramatic, not narrative form, effecting through pity and fear the *catharsis*[1] of such emotions. By 'speech pleasurably enhanced' I mean that involving rhythm and harmony or song, by 'the different kinds separately' that some parts are in verse alone and others in song.

Section B. The Nature of Tragedy According to the Category of Quality

1. *The deduction of the qualitative elements of tragedy*

One can deduce as necessary elements of tragedy (*a*) [from the mode] the designing of the spectacle, since the *mimēsis* is produced by people doing things; (*b*) [from the media] song-writing and verbal expression, the media of tragic *mimēsis*; by 'verbal expression' I mean the composition of the verse-parts,[2] while the meaning of 'song-writing' is obvious to anybody. [Others can be inferred from (*c*) the objects of the *mimēsis*:] A tragedy is a *mimēsis* of an action; action implies people engaged in it; these people must have some definite moral and intellectual qualities, since it is through a man's qualities that we characterize his actions,[3] 1450ᵃ and it is of course with reference to their actions that men are said to succeed or fail. We therefore have (i) the *mimēsis* of the action, the plot, by which I mean the ordering of the particular actions; (ii) [the *mimēsis* of] the moral characters of the personages, namely that [in the play] which makes us say that the agents have certain moral qualities; (iii) [the *mimēsis* of] their intellect, namely those parts [of the play] in which they demonstrate something in speech or deliver themselves of some general maxim.[4]

---

[1] Cf. below, pp. 132 ff.   [2] i.e. of the dialogue parts.

[3] The manuscripts add 'to explain actions we refer to the moral character and intellect of the person doing them'; this is sensible enough in itself, but it disrupts the sentence and is clearly an intrusive gloss to explain the preceding clause.

[4] Throughout the rest of the treatise '*mimēsis* of character' and '*mimēsis* of intellect' are used without square brackets to translate *ēthos* and *dianoia* in this technical sense.

So tragedy as a whole will necessarily have six elements, the possession of which makes tragedy qualitatively distinct [from other literary kinds]: they are plot, the *mimēsis* of character, verbal expression, the *mimēsis* of intellect, spectacle, and song-writing. The media of *mimēsis* are two, the mode one, the objects three, and there are no others. Not a few tragedians do in fact use these as qualitative elements; indeed virtually[1] every play has spectacle, the *mimēsis* of character, plot, verbal expression, song, and the *mimēsis* of intellect.

2. *The qualitative elements ranged in order of importance*

(*a*) THE ARGUMENTS FOR THE PRE-EMINENCE OF PLOT

The most important of these elements is the arrangement of the particular actions [as the following arguments show]:

(*a*) A tragedy is [by definition] a *mimēsis* not of people but of their actions and life. Both success and ill success are success and ill success in action—in other words the end and aim of human life[2] is doing something, not just being a certain sort of person; and though we consider people's characters in deciding what sort of persons they are, we call them successful or unsuccessful only with reference to their actions.[3] So far therefore from the persons in a play acting as they do in order to represent their characters, the *mimēsis* of their characters is only included along with and because of their actions. So the particular actions, the plot, are what the rest of the tragedy is there for,[4] and what the rest is there for is the most important.

---

[1] The manuscripts nonsensically attach this to 'Not a few'; the transposition was suggested by Bywater.

[2] Commonly assumed by the Greeks to be *eudaimonia*, an assumption that Aristotle accepts. The word is often rendered by 'happiness', here by 'success'.

[3] The content of this passage is Aristotelian, but the word for 'ill success' does not occur elsewhere in his works; other arguments urged against the passage are unconvincing, though there may be corruption in detail. Whether entirely written by Aristotle or embodying explanatory additions by somebody else, it is not out of harmony with the insistence (no doubt against some current opinion) on the primacy of plot over character.

[4] Sometimes misleadingly rendered as 'are what tragedy aims at'. But Aristotle is talking in terms of his own theory of explanation (traditionally called 'the doctrine of the four causes'); in this teleological explanations ('final causes') are of more than one kind. Though one sort of 'final cause' is the answer to the question 'What is the purpose of *x*?', another is the answer to the question 'For the sake of what in *x* is the rest of *x* there?'; to take a simple example, one 'final cause' of a knife is cutting, and another is the cutting edge. The argument here plainly shows that plot is the 'final cause' of tragedy in the second sense, not in the first. The purpose of tragedy is stated on p. 108, 'the poet's job is to produce the pleasure springing from pity and fear via *mimēsis*'.

(*b*) [By definition] a work could not be a tragedy if there were no action. But there could be a tragedy without *mimēsis* of character, and the tragedies of most of the moderns are in fact deficient in it; the same is true of many other poets, and of painters for that matter, of Zeuxis, for instance, in comparison with Polygnotus: the latter is good at depicting character, while Zeuxis' painting has no *mimēsis* of character to speak of.

(*c*) If you put down one after another speeches that depicted character, finely expressed and brilliant in the *mimēsis* of intellect, that would not do the job that, by definition, tragedy does do, while a tragedy with a plot, that is, with an ordered series of particular actions, though deficient in these other points, would do its job much better.

(*d*) The most attractive things in tragedy, *peripeteiai* and recognition scenes, are parts of the plot. (e. pertain to actions caf. chap. 11)

(*e*) Novices in poetry attain perfection in verbal expression and in the *mimēsis* of character much earlier than in the ordering of the particular actions; this is also true of almost all early poets.

(*b*) THE STATEMENT OF THE ORDER

The plot therefore is the principle, or one might say the principle of life,[1] in tragedy, while the *mimēsis* of character comes second in importance, a relation similar to one we find in painting, where the most beautiful colours, if smeared on at random, would give less pleasure than an un-coloured outline that was a picture of something. A tragedy, I repeat, is a *mimēsis* of an action, and it is only because of the action that it is a *mimēsis* of the people engaged in it. Third comes the *mimēsis* of their intellect, by which I mean their ability to say what the situation admits and requires; to do this in speeches is the job of political sense and rhetoric, since the older poets made their people speak as the former directs, while the moderns make them observe the rules of rhetoric. Of these two, the *mimēsis* of character is that [in the play] which makes plain the nature of the moral choices the personages make,[2] so that those speeches in which there is absolutely nothing that the speaker chooses and avoids involve no *mimēsis* of character. By '*mimēsis* of intellect' I mean those passages in which they prove that something is or is not the case or deliver themselves

1450^b

---

[1] The 'principle of life' renders *psychē* ('soul'), which stands to the living body in the same relation as plot to tragedy; it is 'what the rest is there for' as in argument (*a*), and it is what the living body essentially is as in argument (*b*). In traditional language it is both a 'final cause' and the 'formal cause'. Cf. *De Anima* 415^b8ff.

[2] After this the manuscripts add 'in cases in which it is not clear whether (?) he chooses or avoids', a corrupt anticipation of the following clause.

thought is to action what rhetoric and politics are to discourse of some general statement.[1] Fourth comes the expression of the spoken parts, by which I mean, as I said before, the expression of thought in words; the meaning is the same whether verse or prose is in question. Of the others, which are there to give pleasure, song-writing is the most important, while spectacle, though attractive, has least to do with art, with the art of poetry, that is; for a work is potentially a tragedy[2] even without public performance and players, and the art of the stage-designer contributes more to the perfection of spectacle than the poet's does.

3. *Closer analysis of plot*[3]

(*a*) THE ESSENTIAL CHARACTERISTICS OF A PLOT, WITH REFERENCE TO ITS DEFINITION AS THE *MIMĒSIS* OF A WHOLE ACTION[4]

(i) *The first implication of wholeness: order*

7 Now that these definitions are out of the way, I want to consider what the arrangement of the particular actions should be like, since that is the prime and most important element of tragedy.

Now, we have settled that a tragedy is a *mimēsis* of a complete, that is, of a whole action, 'whole' here implying some amplitude (there can be a whole without amplitude).

By 'whole' I mean 'with a beginning, a middle, and an end'. By 'beginning' [in this context] I mean 'that which is not necessarily the consequent of something else, but has some state or happening naturally consequent on it', by 'end' 'a state that is the necessary or usual consequent of something else, but has itself no such consequent', by 'middle' 'that which is consequent and has consequents'. Well-ordered plots, then, will exhibit these characteristics, and will not begin or end just anywhere.

---

[1] Cf. pp. 116 f.

[2] Others interpret 'a tragedy can do its job', making Aristotle say the same as in c. 26, pp. 131 f. But the point here seems a different one; though an actual, fully realized performance of a tragedy demands spectacle, the poet has done what he has to do when he has produced something that is potentially a tragedy. Its staging is not something that belongs to the poet's art.

[3] In this large and important section Aristotle is not yet talking about what is necessary for a good plot, a subject that he only begins to discuss on p. 106. He is continuing his analysis of the essential nature of tragedy by considering the minimum characteristics that a plot must have if it is not to be judged positively defective.

[4] It is perhaps worth pointing out that the four essential characteristics are not on a level, but that the first three are defined in terms of the last. The kind of order, the kind of amplitude, the kind of unity in question are all explained in terms that invoke probable or necessary connection.

(ii) *The second implication of wholeness: amplitude*

It is not enough for beauty that a thing, whether an animal or anything else composed of parts, should have those parts well-ordered; since beauty consists in amplitude as well as in order, the thing must also have amplitude—and not just any amplitude. Though a very small creature could not be beautiful, since our view loses all distinctness when it comes near to taking no perceptible time, an enormously ample one could not be beautiful either, since our view of it is not simultaneous, so that we 1451ᵃ lose the sense of its unity and wholeness as we look it over; imagine, for instance, an animal a thousand miles long. Animate and inanimate bodies, then, must have amplitude, but no more than can be taken in at one view; and similarly a plot must have extension, but no more than can be easily remembered. What is, for the poetic art, the limit of this extension? Certainly not that imposed by the contests and by perception[1]—if a hundred plays had to be performed during the festival, they would time the performances by the hour glass, †as they say once on another occasion . . .†[2] As the limit imposed by the actual nature of the thing, one may suggest 'the ampler the better, provided it remains clear as a whole', or, to give a rough specification, 'sufficient amplitude to allow a probable or necessary succession of particular actions to produce a change from bad to good or from good to bad fortune'.

(iii) *The third implication of wholeness: unity*

Unity of plot is not, as some think, achieved by writing about one man; 8 for just as the one substance admits innumerable incidental properties, which do not, some of them, make it a such-and-such,[3] so one man's actions are numerous and do not make up any single action. That is why I think the poets mistaken who have produced *Heracleids* or *Theseids* or other poems of the kind, in the belief that the plot would be one just because Heracles was one. Homer especially shows his superiority in taking a right view here—whether by art or nature: in writing a poem on Odysseus he did not introduce everything that was incidentally true of him, being wounded on Parnassus, for instance, or pretending to be mad at the mustering of the fleet, neither of which necessarily or probably

[1] The remark is puzzling, in view of the preceding discussion; if Aristotle means the perception of a particular audience, its power of attending to a play, the audience in question must at any rate be presumed defective (cf. perhaps p. 107 below).

[2] The text is corrupt and its reference uncertain.

[3] The interpretation is that of Vahlen and is the only one that does justice to the Greek. The analogy is drawn from logic. To give an example, some of the statements to be made about a coffee-pot will define it as a piece of crockery, those *plus* some more statements will define it as a coffee-pot; but a great many statements that are incidentally true of it will only detail its life history and not define it as a member of any species.

—also, poet makes a gen. statement not about a man qua (although he does not name) but a certain kind of man.

c.f. 9.*

implied the other at all; instead he composed the *Odyssey* about an action that is one in the sense I mean, and the same is true of the *Iliad*. In the other mimetic arts a *mimēsis* is one if it is a *mimēsis* of one object; and in the same way a plot, being a *mimēsis* of an action, should be a *mimēsis* of one action and that a whole one, with the different sections so arranged that the whole is disturbed by the transposition and destroyed by the removal of any one of them; for if it makes no visible difference whether a thing is there or not, that thing is no part of the whole.

(iv) *The fourth implication of wholeness: probable and necessary connection*

9   What I have said also makes plain that the poet's job is saying not what did happen but the sort of thing that would happen, that is, what can happen in a strictly probable or necessary sequence. The difference 1451ᵇ between the historian and the poet is not merely that one writes verse and the other prose—one could turn Herodotus' work into verse and it would be just as much history as before; the essential difference is that the one tells us what happened and the other the sort of thing that would happen. That is why poetry is at once more like philosophy and more worth while than history, since poetry tends to make general statements, while those of history are particular. A 'general statement' means [in this context] one that tells us what sort of man would, probably or necessarily, say or do what sort of thing, and this is what poetry aims at, though it attaches proper names; a particular statement on the other hand tells us what Alcibiades, for instance, did or what happened to him.[1]

That poetry does aim at generality has long been obvious in the case of comedy, where the poets make up the plot from a series of probable happenings and then give the persons any names they like, instead of writing about particular people as the lampooners did. In tragedy, however, they still stick to the actual names; this is because it is what is possible that arouses conviction, and while we do not without more ado believe that what never happened is possible, what did happen is clearly

---

[1] It is hard to be temperate in one's admiration for the intellectual power and refinement of analysis that Aristotle displays in this argument. One should remember that to the Greeks Oedipus was just as much a historical personage as Alcibiades. The distinction between what a poet means when he says 'X did such-and-such' and what an historian means when he makes an identical statement is not in itself obvious and was not grasped by most ancient historians. The historian must not suppress the fact that does not fit in, he must not bridge the gaps in his evidence with plausible conjecture presented as a statement of fact. The poet, on the other hand, cannot say anything that his audience will not take to be relevant to the picture they assume he is presenting, and this picture is an investigation of moral possibilities. Poetry is therefore like philosophy (or like science); its statements, though in form the same as the historians', are in fact taken to be statements of the greatest generality that its subject-matter allows.

possible, since it would not have happened if it were not. Though as a matter of fact, even in some tragedies most names are invented and only one or two well known: in Agathon's *Antheus*, for instance, the names as well as the events are made up, and yet it gives just as much pleasure. So one need not try to stick at any cost to the traditional stories, which are the subject of tragedies; indeed the attempt would be absurd, since even what is well known is well known only to a few, but gives general pleasure for all that.

It is obvious from all this that the poet should be considered a maker of plots, not of verses, since he is a poet *qua* maker of *mimēsis* and the objects of his *mimēsis* are actions.[1] Even if it is incidentally true that the plot he makes actually happened, that does not mean he is not its maker; for there is no reason why some things that actually happen should not be the sort of thing that would probably happen,[2] and it is in virtue of that aspect of them that he is their maker.

(v) *Plots that fail to exhibit the essential characteristics*

Of defective[3] plots or actions the worst are the episodic, those, I mean, in which the succession of the episodes is neither probable nor necessary; bad poets make these on their own account, good ones because of the judges;[4] for in aiming at success in the competition and stretching the plot more than it can bear they often have to distort the natural order.   1452ª

(*b*) A FIFTH REQUIREMENT, SUGGESTED BY THE MENTION OF PITY AND FEAR IN THE DEFINITION: SURPRISE

Tragedy is a *mimēsis* not only of a complete action, but also of things arousing pity and fear, emotions most likely to be stirred when things happen unexpectedly but because of each other (this arouses more surprise than mere chance events, since even chance events seem more marvellous when they look as if they were meant to happen—take the case of the statue of Mitys in Argos killing Mitys' murderer by falling on

---

[1] It is sometimes obscured that Aristotle's purpose here and on p. 91 above is not to deny the necessity of verse to poetry (though he might have done, if pushed), but to assert the necessity of *mimēsis*.

[2] The manuscripts add 'and that can happen', perhaps defensible as a piece of donnish humour, but suspect because it is absent from the Arabic version.

[3] This reading is due to conjecture; the manuscripts have 'Of simple plots . . .'. It is not a serious objection to this that we have not yet been introduced to the simple plot (below, p. 104); what does matter is that a reference to the simple plot is irrelevant in the context.

[4] Most manuscripts have 'because of the actors'; for the bad influence of the judges, cf. Plato's remark (above, pp. 83 f.).

him as he looked at it; for we do not think that things like this are merely random); so such plots[1] will necessarily be the best.

(c) THE SPECIES OF PLOT

10   Some plots are simple, some complex, since the actions of which the plots are *mimēseis* fall naturally into the same two classes. By 'simple action' I mean one that is continuous in the sense defined[2] and is a unity and where the change of fortune takes place without *peripeteia* or recognition, by 'complex' one where the change of fortune is accompanied by *peripeteia* or recognition or both. The *peripeteia* and recognition should arise just from the arrangement of the plot, so that it is necessary or probable that they should follow what went before; for there is a great difference between happening next and happening as a result.

(d) THE ELEMENTS OF PLOT

(i) *Peripeteia* (reversal)

11   A *peripeteia* occurs when the course of events takes a turn to the opposite in the way described,[3] the change being also probable or necessary in the way I said. For example, in the *Oedipus*, when the[4] man came and it seemed that he would comfort[5] Oedipus and free him from his fear about his mother, by revealing who he was he in fact did the opposite. Again in the *Lynceus*, Lynceus was being led off and it seemed that he would be put to death and that Danaus who was with him would kill him, but the earlier actions produced Danaus' death and Lynceus' release.

(ii) *Recognition*

Recognition is, as its name indicates, a change from ignorance to knowledge, tending either to affection or to enmity; it determines in the direction of good or ill fortune the fates of the people involved. The best sort of recognition is that accompanied by *peripeteia*, like that in the *Oedipus*.

---

[1] Those where things happen unexpectedly but because of each other.
[2] That is, one that has probable or necessary connection.
[3] That is, in a way involving surprise.
[4] The Corinthian shepherd.
[5] Or 'came with the intention of comforting'. The construction used is the same here and in the *Lynceus* example, where one can certainly say that it was not Lynceus' intention to be put to death. In view of this it is unnecessary to attribute to Aristotle the misstatement that the shepherd came with the intention of freeing Oedipus from his fear about his mother, or even with the expectation of doing so. The frustrated expectation seems to be felt not by the characters but by the audience, who are here, as on p. 103 above, taken not to be very familiar with the events of heroic legend.

There are of course other kinds of recognition. For a recognition of the sort described can be a recognition of inanimate objects, indeed of quite indifferent ones, and one can also recognize whether someone has committed an act or not. But the one mentioned has most to do with the plot, that is, most to do with the action; for a recognition accompanied by *peripeteia* in this way will involve either pity or fear, and tragedy is by definition a *mimēsis* of actions that rouse these emotions; it is moreover such recognitions that lead to good or bad fortune. 1452^b

Since recognition involves more than one person, in some cases only one person will recognize the other, when it is clear who the former is, and sometimes each has to recognize the other: Orestes, for example, recognized Iphigenia from her sending the letter, but a second recognition was necessary for her to recognize him.

(iii) *Pathos*

These then are two elements of the plot, and a third is *pathos*. I have dealt with the first two, *peripeteia* and recognition. A *pathos* is an act involving destruction or pain, for example deaths on stage and physical agonies and woundings and so on.

So much for the parts of tragedy that one ought to use as qualitative elements. 12

SECTION C. THE NATURE OF TRAGEDY ACCORDING TO THE CATEGORY OF QUANTITY

Now for the category of quantity and the quantitative divisions of a tragedy: they are prologue, episode, *exodos*, choral part, the last being divided into *parodos* and *stasimon*; the last two are common to all plays, while some have as well songs from the actors and *kommoi*.

The prologue is the complete section of a tragedy before the entrance of the chorus, an episode the complete section of a tragedy between complete choral odes, the *exodos* a complete section of a tragedy not followed by a choral ode. Of the choral part, the *parodos* is the first complete utterance of the chorus, a *stasimon* a choral song not using the anapaestic dimeter or trochaic tetrameter,[1] a *kommos* a lament shared by the chorus and the actors.

Having dealt beforehand with the parts of tragedy that one ought to

---

[1] The anapaestic dimeter is a marching metre, normal in chorus entries, the tetrameter a running metre appropriate to a hasty choral entry. Cf. A. M. Dale, *Collected Papers*, Cambridge, 1969, pp. 34 ff.

use as qualitative elements, I have now dealt with the category of quantity and the quantitative divisions of a tragedy.[1]

CHAPTER III

EXCELLENCE IN TRAGEDY

SECTION A. WITH RESPECT TO PLOT

13 What ought one to aim at and beware of in composing plots? And what is the source of the tragic effect? These are the questions that naturally follow from what I have now dealt with.

1. *Things to aim at and beware of*

Well, the arrangement of tragedy at its best should be complex, not simple, and it should also present a *mimēsis* of things that arouse fear and pity, as this is what is peculiar to the tragic *mimēsis*.

So it is clear that one should not show virtuous men passing from good to bad fortune, since this does not arouse fear or pity, but only a sense of outrage. Nor should one show bad men passing from bad to good fortune, as this is less tragic than anything, since it has none of the necessary 1453ᵃ requirements; it neither satisfies our human feeling nor arouses pity and fear. Nor should one show a quite wicked man passing from good to bad fortune; it is true that such an arrangement would satisfy our human feeling, but it would not arouse pity or fear, since the one is felt for someone who comes to grief without deserving it, and the other for someone like us (pity, that is, for the man who does not deserve his fate, and fear for someone like us); so this event will not arouse pity or fear. So we have left the man between these. He is one who is not pre-eminent in moral virtue, who passes to bad fortune not through vice or wickedness, but because of some piece of ignorance, and who is of high repute and great good fortune, like Oedipus and Thyestes and the splendid men of such families.[2]

[1] This sentence repeats almost exactly that at the beginning of the section, importing as well a late form not used by Aristotle; such a dreary piece of scholasticism is unlike him. The whole discussion of tragedy under the category of quantity has been challenged, and may be an interpolation. Yet it stands where it should stand, concluding the analysis of the nature of tragedy and preceding the consideration of its virtues, and though bald is not absurd in content. Of the ten categories that belong to the Aristotelian theory of predication, it is of course these three, substance, quality, and quantity, that provide the definition of a thing's essential nature; the other categories only state things that are incidentally true of it at a particular time and place.

[2] Aristotle's thought in this section is best illuminated by the discussion in *Rhetoric* 2. 9 of the emotions that expel pity, and particularly by the discussion of 'justified

So the good plot must have a single line of development, not a double one as some people say;[1] that line should go from good fortune to bad and not the other way round; the change should be produced not through wickedness, but through some large-scale piece of ignorance; the person ignorant should be the sort of man I have described—certainly not a worse man, though perhaps a better one.

This is borne out by the facts: at first the poets recounted any story that came to hand, but nowadays the best tragedies are about a few families only, for example, Alcmaeon, Oedipus, Orestes, Meleager, Thyestes, Telephus, and others whose lot it was to suffer or commit fearful acts.

Well then, the best tragedy, judged from the standpoint of the tragic art, comes from this sort of arrangement. That is why those who censure Euripides for doing this in his tragedies and making many of them end with disaster are making just the same mistake.[2] For this is correct in the way I said. The greatest proof of this is that on the stage and in the contests such plays are felt to be the most properly tragic, if they are well managed, and Euripides, even if he is a bad manager in the other points, is at any rate the most tragic of the poets.[3]

Second comes the sort of arrangement that some people say is the best: this is the one that has a double arrangement of the action like the *Odyssey*, and ends with opposite fortunes for the good and bad people. It is thought to be the best because of the weakness of the audiences; for the poets follow the lead of the spectators and make plays to their

indignation' (*nemesān*). This emotion has several aspects, pain at the undeserved misfortunes of the good, pain at the undeserved good fortune of the wicked, pleasure at the deserved misfortunes of the wicked; these three aspects correspond to the three cases that Aristotle here excludes. 'What satisfies our human feeling' (*to philanthrōpon*) seems here to be the opposite of 'the morally outraging' (*to miaron*).

Aristotle clearly has some difficulty in reconciling the need to avoid 'justified indignation' with the requirement that the characters of high poetry should be good. To do so he invokes *hamartia* as the cause of their misfortune. In the context two things are necessary, that the tragic figure should in some sense be responsible for his fate (to avoid the first case), and that his fate should nevertheless be worse than he deserves (to avoid the third case); that is, a *hamartia* here is 'a going wrong that is venial'. Other discussions (especially *Nic. Eth.* 3. 1–2) show that it is venial because the character did not know what he was doing; the same act done in full knowledge would be a crime. In the case of Oedipus, for instance, the *hamartia* is simply and solely the murder of Laius and the marriage with Jocasta, in ignorance of the fact that they were his parents. The Bradleyan notion popular among English critics that the *hamartia* is a fault of character is of course excluded by the description of the *hamartia* as large-scale; a large-scale fault of character is not, in Aristotle's view, venial.

[1] See below, n. 2.

[2] They make the same mistake as the 'some people' mentioned above and below, those who prefer a happy ending for the good.

[3] 'Most tragic' must mean 'best at arousing pity and fear'.

specifications. But this is not the pleasure proper to tragedy, but rather belongs to comedy; for in comedy those who are most bitter enemies throughout the plot, as it might be Orestes and Aegisthus,[1] are reconciled at the end and go off and nobody is killed by anybody.

2. *The source of the tragic effect*

1453[b]
14
Now though pity and fear can be elicited by the spectacle, they can also be elicited just by the arrangement of the particular actions [that make up the plot], and this is a prior consideration[2] and the sign of a better poet. For the plot ought to be so composed that even without seeing the action, a man who just hears what is going on shudders and feels pity because of what happens; this one would feel on hearing the plot of the *Oedipus*, for instance. But to produce this effect via the spectacle has less to do with the art of tragedy and needs external aids. To go further and use the spectacle to produce something that is merely monstrous, instead of something that rouses fear, is to depart entirely from tragedy. For one should look to tragedy for its own pleasure, not just any pleasure; and since the poet's job is to produce the pleasure springing from pity and fear via *mimēsis*, this clearly ought to be present in the elements of the action.

What sort of events, then, do seem apt to rouse fear, or [rather] pity? This is my next subject. In such actions, people must do something to those closely connected with them, or to enemies, or to people to whom they are indifferent. Now, if it is a case of two enemies, this arouses no particular pity, whether the one damages the other or only intends to; or at least, pity is felt only at the *pathos*[3] considered in itself. The same is true in the case when people are indifferent to each other. The cases we must look for are those where the *pathos* involves people closely connected, for instance where brother kills brother, son father, mother son, or son mother—or if not kills, then means to kill, or does some other act of the kind.

Well, one cannot interfere with the traditional stories, cannot, for instance, say that Clytaemestra was not killed by Orestes or Eriphyle by Alcmaeon; what one should do is invent for oneself and use the traditional material well. Let me explain more clearly what I mean by 'well'. One can make the act be committed as the ancient poets did, that is, with the

[1] In tragedy, naturally. Aristotle is denied his joke by those who either hunt solemnly for a comedy on the topic of Orestes and Aegisthus or take this to be a reference to a hypothetical third form of tragedy, with a happy ending for everybody.

[2] Prior both in time and in importance, as it belongs to the poetic art proper; the point is the same as that made about spectacle on p. 100 above.

[3] Cf. above, p. 105.

agents knowing and aware [whom they are damaging]; even Euripides has the example of Medea killing her children with full knowledge. [And they can have knowledge and not act].¹ Or they can commit the deed that rouses terror without knowing to whom they are doing it, and later recognize the connection, like Sophocles' Oedipus; this indeed happens outside the play, but we have examples in the tragedy itself, for example, Astydamas' *Alcmaeon* and Telegonus in the *Wounded Odysseus*.² Again, apart from these one might through ignorance intend to do something irreparable, and then recognize the victim-to-be before doing it. These are the only possible ways, as they must either do it or not, and in knowledge or ignorance.

The worst of these is to have the knowledge and the intention and then not do it; for this is both morally outraging and untragic—'untragic' because it involves no *pathos*. That is why nobody does behave in this 1454ᵃ way except very rarely, as Haemon, for example, means to kill Creon in the *Antigone*.³ The second worst is doing it: the better form of this is when the character does it in ignorance, and recognizes his victim afterwards; for this involves no feeling of outrage and the recognition produces lively surprise. But the best is the last, for example, the case in the *Cresphontes*⁴ where Merope means to kill her son and does not, but recognizes him instead, and the case involving brother and sister in the *Iphigenia in Tauris*; again in the *Helle* the son recognized his mother when on the point of giving her up.⁵

¹ In view of the last sentence of the paragraph this addition from the Arabic translation seems necessary.

² The *Odysseus Acanthoplex* of Sophocles.

³ The incident is not shown but described in three lines of Sophocles' messenger's speech (1232 ff.).

⁴ Of Euripides.

⁵ No amount of special pleading can do away with the fact that in commending this last case Aristotle is commending a situation that leads to a happy ending for the good. This passage is therefore in downright contradiction with the censure of the happy ending on pp. 107 f., and it is hardly possible to believe that it forms part of the same chain of thought. Moreover the next paragraph follows more happily on the words 'or if not kills, then means to kill, or does some other act of the kind' than it does on anything else in the section. Bywater is therefore probably right in taking the two paragraphs from 'Well, one cannot interfere . . .' to '. . . giving her up' to be a later addition made by Aristotle himself to his own text and enshrining a change of mind. He cannot be right about the reason for the change of mind, which he finds in Aristotle's 'somewhat tardy recognition of the necessity of avoiding' the morally outraging; the recognition is so far from tardy that it has dominated the discussion from the beginning of c. 13, and in any case the tragic situation where the deed is done in ignorance is expressly said to involve no feeling of outrage. There seems little to be done with the change of mind but to accept it. However surprising it may seem to people in full strength, Aristotle is not after all the only great man to pass in later years from a preference for tragedy to a preference for tragicomedy; Shakespeare and Sophocles are notable examples.

As I said before, this is why tragedies are about very few families. As it was not art but chance that led the poets in their search to the discovery of how to produce this effect in their plots, they have to go to the families in which such *pathē* occurred.

So much for the arrangement of the particular acts and the qualities required of plots.

SECTION B. WITH RESPECT TO CHARACTER

15 In the representation of character, there are four things that one ought to aim at:

(*a*) First and foremost, the characters represented should be morally good. The speech or action will involve *mimēsis* of character if it makes plain, as said before, the nature of the person's moral choice, and the character represented will be good if the choice is good. This is possible in each class: for example, a woman is good and so is a slave, though the one is perhaps inferior, and the other generally speaking low-grade.

(*b*) The characters represented should be suitable: for example, the character represented is brave,[1] but it is not suitable for a woman to be brave or clever in this way.[2]

(*c*) They should be life-like; this is different from the character's being good and suitable in the way I used 'suitable'.[3]

(*d*) They should be consistent: for even if the subject of the *mimēsis* is an inconsistent person, and that is the characteristic posited of him, still he ought to be consistently inconsistent.

An example of unnecessary badness of character is Menelaus in the *Orestes*,[4] of the unsuitable or inappropriate Odysseus' lament in the *Scylla*[5] and Melanippe's speech,[6] of the inconsistent Iphigenia in the *Iphigenia at Aulis*, as the girl who pleads for her life is quite different from the later one.

In the representation of character as well as in the chain of actions one ought always to look for the necessary or probable, so that it is

---

[1] And therefore meets the requirement of being morally good.

[2] Cf. *Politics* 1. 5, and 1277b21 ff., for the difference between the virtues of men and women, even when their virtues are called by the same name.

[3] It is not clear what Aristotle means by this requirement, especially as he either did not give or the tradition has lost the example of its violation.

[4] His cowardice in 682–715. Else rightly argues that this and the other examples given are, when we can check them, 'unnecessary' because they do not contribute to the action of the play, which would be unaffected whether they were there or not.

[5] The example does not come from tragedy, but from a dithyramb by Timotheus.

[6] In Euripides' *Melanippe the Wise Woman*.

necessary or probable that a person like this speaks or acts as he does, and necessary or probable that this happens after that. Clearly then, the dénouements of plots ought to arise just from the *mimēsis* of 1454ᵇ character,[1] and not from a contrivance, a *deus ex machina*, as in the *Medea* and in the events in the *Iliad* about the setting off.[2] The contrivance should be used instead for things outside the play, either all that happened beforehand that a human being could not know, or all that happens later and needs foretelling and reporting; for we attribute omniscience to the gods. In the particular actions themselves there should be nothing irrational, and if there is it should be outside the tragedy, like that of Sophocles' *Oedipus*.[3]

Since a tragedy is a *mimēsis* of people better than are found in the world, one ought to do the same as the good figure-painters; for they too give us the individual form, but though they make people lifelike they represent them as more beautiful than they are. Similarly the poet too in representing people as irascible and lazy and morally deficient in other ways like that, ought nevertheless to make them good, as Homer makes Achilles both good and an example of harsh self-will.[4]

One must watch out for all these points, and also for the errors against[5] the perceptions necessarily attending on the poetic art; for in these perceptions too one can often go wrong. But I have said enough about them in my published works.

DIGRESSION ON VARIOUS TOPICS OF INTEREST TO THE PRACTISING PLAYWRIGHT[6]

1. *Recognition*

I gave before the genus definition of recognition. Now for its species: 16
   (*a*) The first and least artistic (and the one most used because people

---

[1] This is the reading of the sixth-century Syriac translation and is the only one that allows all this chapter, apart from the last sentence (below, n. 5), to deal with character. The rest of the evidence for the text has 'should arise from the plot itself'. If this is right, we must suppose that the bundle of practical hints for playwrights that occupies chapters 16–18 and interrupts the orderly development of the treatise begins with this sentence, and not with the last sentence of c. 15 or the first of c. 16 (below, n. 6).

[2] Probably Athene's intervention at *Iliad* 2. 166 ff.

[3] Cf. below, p. 126.

[4] The last clause renders Lobel's conjecture.

[5] Or 'arising from'. The text and interpretation are uncertain. The sentence seems to have some relation to the discussion of poetic imagination on p. 113 below.

[6] The discussion of excellence in tragedy, which proceeds from plot (cc. 13–14) and character (c. 15) to the representation of intellect (c. 19) and verbal expression (cc. 19 ff.), is suspended, and we have three chapters which nobody would have planned to put where we find them, though they are indubitably Aristotelian.

can think of nothing better) is recognition by visible signs. These signs may be birthmarks, like 'the spear the earth-born bear' or stars like those Carcinus supposed in his *Thyestes*, or acquired after birth; there are two kinds of the latter, bodily ones like scars, or external ones, like necklaces and the recognition by means of the cradle in Sophocles' *Tyro*. Even such signs can be well or badly handled: for example, Odysseus' scar leads to his being recognized in one way by his nurse and in another by the swineherds; recognitions like the latter, which are just meant to convince [the other characters in the poem], are less artistic, and so are all others similarly contrived; those that spring from a *peripeteia*, like that in the Bath episode, are better.[1]

(*b*) The next are those manufactured by the poet: this makes them inartistic. An example is Orestes' making himself known in the *Iphigenia in Tauris*; for she herself was recognized by means of her letter, but Orestes says without more ado what the poet wants him to say, not what the plot demands. So this is quite near the previous fault, since it would have been possible for him to bring some tokens too. There is also the 'voice of the shuttle' in Sophocles' *Tereus*.[2]

(*c*) The third is by means of memory, that is, when one's awareness is
1455ª roused by seeing something: for example, in Dicaeogenes' *Cyprians*, he sees the picture and bursts into tears, and in the story of Alcinous Odysseus is reminded by listening to the harpist, and weeps; this leads to the recognition in each case.

(*d*) The fourth is recognition on the basis of reasoning: in the *Choephoroe*, for instance, we have the argument 'Somebody like me has come; nobody but Orestes is like me; so Orestes has come'.[3] Another example is the way the sophist Polyidus dealt with Iphigenia; it was natural, he thought, for Orestes to argue that his sister had been sacrificed and now it was his turn to be sacrificed. Another is in Theodectes' *Tydeus* to the effect that in coming to find his son he was losing his own life. Again, in the *Sons of Phineus*, when the women saw the place they inferred that they were destined to die there, since that was where they had been exposed.

There is also a composite kind involving a false inference on the part of the other character. An example of this is in *Odysseus the False Messenger*. For that Odysseus and only he can string the bow is something

---

[1] The Bath episode is the recognition by Eurycleia in *Odyssey* 19.

[2] Philomela told her story by weaving it, as her tongue had been cut out.

[3] Electra does not use this dubious bit of reasoning to help her recognize Orestes; he recognizes her because he hears her producing it in lines 164 ff. Her recognition of him is 'manufactured by the poet', i.e. he simply declares who he is (219) and also produces tokens (225 ff.: the lock fits the place on his head from which it was cut and he has a robe that Electra embroidered). Editors have failed to see this.

manufactured by the poet, and there is a hypothesis 'If he said that he would know the bow that he has not seen',[1] but to construct the plot so that it looks as if he will recognize him through this [false inference] is [the case of] paralogism [being described].[2]

(*e*) The best kind of all is that which arises from the actions alone, with the surprise developing through a series of likelihoods; examples are that in Sophocles' *Oedipus* and Euripides' *Iphigenia in Tauris*; for it was likely that she would want to send a letter.[3] Only such recognitions are really free from manufactured signs and necklaces. The next best are those that come from reasoning.

2. *Poetic imagination*

In composing plots and working them out so far as verbal expression 17 goes, the poet should, more than anything else, put things before his eyes, as he then sees the events most vividly as if he were actually present, and can therefore find what is appropriate and be aware of the opposite. The censure on Carcinus is an indication of this: that was a matter of Amphiaraus' coming from the temple, which would have escaped notice if it had not been seen, but fell flat on the stage, because the audience made a fuss about it. So far as possible one should also work it out with the appropriate figures.[4] For given the same natural endowment, people who actually feel passion are the most convincing; that is, the person who most realistically expresses distress is the person in distress and the same is true of a person in a temper. That is why poetry is the work of a genius rather than of a madman; for the genius is by nature adaptable, while the madman is degenerate.[5]

---

[1] Taking this to be a hypothesis entertained by one of the characters and meaning 'If he truly says that he will recognize the bow that he has not, since his arrival in Ithaca, seen', one can see that the character might falsely infer 'He is Odysseus'. The false inference is the fallacy of inferring the antecedent from the consequent; below, p. 126.

[2] Text and interpretation are a matter of speculation. The false inference might be made by the audience instead of by another character, and we do not know whether the work discussed is a play or the relevant part of the *Odyssey*.

[3] *Iph. Taur.* 725–803.

[4] i.e. of speech and thought. Others interpret 'gestures'.

[5] The manuscripts have 'That is why poetry is the work of a genius or of a madman', in conjunction with which the next clause must be interpreted 'for the genius is by nature adaptable, while the madman is beside himself'; if this is right Aristotle is placidly assenting *en passant* to Plato's account of poetic *mania* (above, p. 75), though that account can hardly be reconciled with the demands he himself makes on the poet in this discussion. This attitude is, to say the least, less to be expected than that of tacit dissent from a Platonic paradox. The pseudo-Aristotelian *Problems* (954) implies that both madmen and geniuses share the temperament later called 'melancholy adust', but that in

Whether the argument of a play is pre-existent or whether one is
1455ᵇ inventing it oneself, one should set it out in general terms, and only
then make it into episodes and extend it. By 'setting it out in general
terms' I mean, to take the case of the *Iphigenia in Tauris*: [before the
action proper begins] a girl was sacrificed and disappeared without the
sacrificers knowing what had happened to her, and she was settled in
another country where there was a law that one sacrificed strangers to
the goddess; she was installed as priestess of this rite; [then in the action
proper] it came about later that the priestess's brother arrived (that he
came because of an oracle and his purpose in coming are things outside
the action); anyway he came and was captured and when on the point
of being sacrificed disclosed himself, either as in Euripides' poem or
as in Polyidus,[1] saying, that is, as was natural, that it turned out that he
was destined to be sacrificed as well as his sister; and this recognition
produced his rescue. After this one should come to adding the names
and making the episodes. Take care that the episodes are relevant; for
example, in the case of Orestes in the *Iphigenia* such episodes are the fit
of madness that led to his capture, and his escape through being purified.

In plays episodes are brief, but epic uses them to increase its length.
The *Odyssey*, for instance, has a very brief argument: [as preliminary to
the action] a man is away from home for many years and jealously
watched by Poseidon and has lost his followers; moreover at home his
affairs are such that his property is being wasted by suitors and plots
laid against his son; [and in the action proper] he comes home in dire
distress and after disclosing himself makes an attack and destroys his
enemies without being killed himself. This is what is proper to the
action; the rest of the poem is episodes.

the genius 'the excessive heat has sunk to a moderate amount'; it also contains the significant remark that 'Maracus the Syracusan was *even* a better poet when he was mad',
an example so remote from the main stream of poetry and so cautious in expression that
it is clear that the author of the *Problems*, at any rate, did not think poetic *mania* very
common. The manuscript tradition has been challenged by three people in whose
company it is a comfort to be, Castelvetro, Dryden, and Tyrwhitt; there is also a passage
in which Coleridge, though without reference to Aristotle, fascinatingly makes the same
point (*Table Talk*, May 1, 1833):

' "Great wits are sure to madness near allied" says Dryden, and true so far as this,
that genius of the highest kind implies an unusual intensity of the modifying power,
which, detached from the discriminative and reproductive power, might conjure a
plaited straw into a royal diadem: but it would be at least as true, that great genius is
most alien from madness, yea, divided from it by an impassable mountain,—namely,
the activity of thought and vivacity of the accumulative memory, which are no less
essential constituents of "great wit".'

[1] Above, p. 112. Aristotle's expression here rather implies that Polyidus produced
this criticism in a poem, not in a critical work, i.e. that he made his criticism by managing
the recognition differently.

3. *Complication and dénouement* (desis *and* lusis)

Part of every tragedy is the complication, part the dénouement: the 18
preliminaries and often some of the action proper are the complication,
the rest the dénouement. By 'complication' I mean the section from the
beginning to the last point before he begins to change to good or bad
fortune, by 'dénouement' the part from the beginning of the change to
the end; for example, in Theodectes' *Lynceus* the complication is made
up of the preliminaries, the kidnapping of the child and their being
found out, the dénouement is everything from the capital charge to
the end.

4. *The species of tragedy*

Tragedy has four species,[1] the complicated, whose entire nature depends
on *peripeteia* and recognition, the tragedy of *pathos*, for example those
about Aias and Ixion, the tragedy of character, for example the *Phthiotides*   1456ᵃ
and the *Peleus*, while the fourth is spectacle,[2] like the *Phorcides* and
Prometheus and any set in hell.

Preferably, of course, one should try to have all four, but if not, to
have the most important and as many as may be, especially given the way
people criticize poets nowadays; for since there have been poets good in
each kind, they demand that a poet should all by himself surpass the
peculiar excellence of each of them. It is fair too to say that tragedies are
the same or different principally on the basis of their plots, that is, when
they have the same complication and dénouement. Many can manage the
first but not the second, but one should always be master of both.

5. *The selection of tragic material*

One ought to remember what I have often said and not make an epic
body of material into a tragedy (by 'epic' I mean one containing many
stories), as if, for instance, one were to compose a play on the whole story
of the *Iliad*. For in epic because of its length the parts can have a size
that suits them, whereas in plays things turn out quite contrary to what
one expected. We can find a proof of this in the poets who have dealt
with the whole of the sack of Troy and not with a part of it as Euripides
did, or with the story of Niobe and not in the way Aeschylus did; such

---

[1] The manuscripts add 'for that was the number of the elements mentioned', a
statement that has no possible reference; if Aristotle made it, he had forgotten his own
analysis.

[2] The reading is uncertain.

poets are either hissed off the stage or do badly in the contest—even Agathon was hissed off just for this reason.

6. *The element of surprise*

In *peripeteiai* and also in simple plots poets aim at the effects they want by means of surprise,[1] as surprise is tragic and satisfies our human feeling.[2] This happens when a clever scoundrel is deceived, like Sisyphus, and a courageous wrongdoer worsted. For this is not only surprising but likely in the way described by Agathon, when he said it is likely that many things should happen contrary to likelihood.

7. *The treatment of the chorus*

One should regard the chorus too as one of the actors, and as a part of the whole and taking part in the action; that is, one should follow Sophocles' practice rather than Euripides'. In poets apart from these,[3] the songs have no more to do with the plot than with some quite other tragedy; this is why they [nowadays] sing interpolated songs (the first who began this practice was Agathon). But it is absurd, for there is no difference between singing interpolated songs and transferring a speech or a whole episode from one play to another.

SECTION C. WITH RESPECT TO THE *MIMĒSIS* OF INTELLECT[4]

19 As I have dealt with the other qualitative elements, I now have to talk about the representation of intellect and about verbal expression. The representation of intellect we may take to be covered by the *Rhetoric*; for it does belong rather to that inquiry. What is involved in the representation of intellect is every effect to be produced by speech. Its sections are proof and disproof, rousing emotion (pity, fear, anger, and so on), making a 1456ᵇ thing look important or unimportant.[5] Clearly in the plot too one ought

---

[1] The manuscripts have 'to a surprising degree'; the translation is of Castelvetro's conjecture.

[2] Above, pp. 106 f.

[3] To a modern reader the failure to take Aeschylus into account is notable. One may remark also that Aeschylus is thought to have composed a trilogy on the main action of the *Iliad* (*Myrmidons*, *Nereids*, *Phrygians*), something derisively mentioned only as an absurd possibility on p. 115 above.

[4] At this point the main line of the argument is resumed (above, p. 111 n. 6).

[5] Except on p. 99 above, Aristotle in c. 6 confined the *mimēsis* of intellect to the speeches containing demonstrative arguments and general maxims. Here he includes

to proceed from just these same main heads, when one needs to produce an effect of pity or fear, likelihood or importance. There is some difference, though; in the action these should be obvious without one's being told, whereas the other effects should be produced in words by the person using them and should result from his words, as the speaker would be quite unnecessary if the desired result were obvious without his saying anything.

SECTION D. WITH RESPECT TO VERBAL EXPRESSION

1. *Exclusion of subjects that fall under delivery*

So far as verbal expression goes, one branch of inquiry is that into the forms of speech. Knowledge of this really falls under the study of delivery and is the province of the expert in that subject. I mean such questions as 'What is a command, a wish, a statement, a threat, a question, an answer?' and so on. A poet's knowledge or ignorance in this sphere does not leave him open to any critical censure worth bothering about. For anyone would think pretty trivial the fault censured by Protagoras, when he says: 'Homer thinks he is beginning with a prayer and in fact uses a command, when he says, "Sing of the wrath, goddess", since to tell somebody to do something or not is a command.' So let us leave that alone, since it belongs to another field and not to poetry.

2. *The grammatical basis of the discussion*

Verbal expression as a whole has the following parts: element, syllable, 20 linking word, articulatory word, noun, verb, termination, statement.

An element is an indivisible sound, not any sound, but that capable of producing intelligible utterance; for some animals produce indivisible sounds, which I do not, however, call elements. This class has three subdivisions, sounded, half-sounded, and soundless.[1] A sounded element is that which has an audible sound without any contact occurring. A half-sounded element is one that produces an audible sound when contact

the use that the characters make of persuasive language more widely defined. The negatives 'disproof' and 'unimportant' and the varieties of emotions mentioned show that in this sentence he is speaking of the effect the characters in a play have on each other. The next sentence seems a rather casual addition, pointing out that the poet in composing his plot and aiming to produce a certain effect on his audience draws on the same sources of argument as he makes his characters use.

[1] In modern terminology: vowels, fricatives, and stops.

does occur: such are *s* and *r*. A soundless element is one where contact occurs without the element itself having any audible sound, though it is audible when combined with elements that have audible sound: such are *g* and *d*. The elements in these three classes can be further classified, according to the shape of the mouth, the place of contact, rough or smooth breathing, length or shortness of quantity, and accent, acute, grave, or intermediate. One can investigate the subject further in works on metric.

A syllable is a composite non-significant sound made up of a voiceless element and one with voice: *gr*, for example, is a syllable by itself without *a*, and also if *a* is added to make *gra*.[1] But the investigation of this too is a matter of metric. (*phonetics*)

1457[a]   A linking word is (*a*) a non-significant sound which neither prevents nor produces the formation from a number of sounds of one significant utterance; it ought not to stand alone at the beginning of a statement: examples are *men*, *toi*, *dē*, *de* [the linking particles]; (*b*) a non-significant sound that naturally produces from a plurality of sounds that nevertheless signify one thing a single significant utterance: examples are *amphi*, *peri*, and the rest [of the prepositions].[2]

An articulatory word (*arthron*) is a non-significant sound that indicates the beginning or end or dividing point of a statement; it is naturally put at either end (?) of a statement or in the middle.[3]

A noun is a composite significant sound with no temporality, and made up of parts not in themselves significant. For in compound words we do not take the parts to be significant in themselves; in *Theodorus*, for example, the *dōron* has no significance.

A verb is a composite significant sound with temporality, and, like a noun, is made up of parts not in themselves significant; by 'with temporality' I mean that, while 'man' and 'white' do not signify when, 'walks' and 'walked' do signify present and past time respectively.

Termination is the part of a noun or verb that signifies case and number and also the part concerned with delivery, for example, question and command: 'Did he walk?' and 'Walk' show terminations of the verb under the sections of this class.

A statement is a composite significant sound whose separate parts are themselves significant; I give this definition because not every statement is made up of nouns and verbs—the definition of man, for instance;[4]

---

[1] Cf. *CR* N.S.20, 1970, 179.

[2] Text very uncertain: we follow Bywater's conjectures and transpositions.

[3] Aristotle probably means co-ordinating and subordinating conjunctions—he does not mean the article, though the same term is used for this in later grammatical terminology.

[4] In statements like 'Man is a featherless biped' Greek can omit the copula; the definition of 'statement' corrects one given by Plato.

one can, that is, have a statement with no verb, but it will always have a significant part.[1] A statement is one statement in two senses: (*a*) as signifying one thing, (*b*) by being composed of a plurality of statements: the *Iliad*, for example, is one as being composite, and the definition of man as signifying one thing.

3. *Different ways of classifying nouns*[2]

The species of nouns are: (*a*) simple: by this I mean 'not composed of 21 significant parts', for example, 'earth'; (*b*) double: this has two varieties. (i) composed of a significant element and a non-significant element [e.g. prepositional compounds]; one must qualify this by saying that they are not significant and non-significant in the word;[3] (ii) composed of significant elements; (*c*) possible species are also triple, quadruple, and indeed multiple, like most aggrandized words,[4] 'Hermocaicoxanthus' . . .   1457[b]

Nouns may also be divided into standard terms, dialect terms, metaphorical terms, decorative terms,[5] neologisms, lengthened words, shortened words, altered words.

By 'standard term' I mean that used by any society.

By 'dialect term' I mean one used by another people. The same word can obviously be both a standard term and a dialect term, though not in the same society: *sigunon* is a standard term in Cyprus, a dialect term in Athens.

A 'metaphorical term' involves the transferred use of a term that properly belongs to something else; the transference can be from genus to species, from species to genus, from species to species, or analogical.

---

[1] The manuscripts add the lunatic and irrelevant clause 'for example, "Cleon" in "Cleon is walking".'

[2] To avoid repetition, Aristotle's discussion of poetical style covers more than tragedy, dealing as well with choral lyric and with epic. The compound words discussed in the first classification are particularly suitable to choral lyric, while many of the decorative elements in the second classification are epic rather than tragic.

[3] Above, p. 118. The qualification must also be extended to variety (ii).

[4] The Arabic translation has 'Massiliote words', for which editors have a strange affection, though they admit that the 'most' then becomes nonsensical; it also suggests that our text is defective after 'Hermocaicoxanthus'.

[5] Unlike the other terms in the list, this is not defined and discussed below. A papyrus fragment of a work perhaps written by Theophrastus seems to deal with ornamental epithets ('blazing steel', 'bright gold') after a discussion of metaphor akin to ours. Others have thought of synonymous terms and have tried to provide the treatment of 'decorative terms' from fr. 3: 'Aristotle says in his *Poetics* that things are synonymous if they have more than one name but the same definition, that is, things that have several names, for example, *lōpion* and *himation* and *phāros* (all words for "cloak").'

By 'from genus to species' I mean, for example, 'Here my ship is still',[1] as lying at anchor is a species of being still. By 'from species to genus', 'Odysseus conferred ten thousand benefits',[2] as 'ten thousand' is a specific example of plurality and he uses this instead of 'many'. By 'species to species', 'drawing the life with the bronze' and 'cutting off [the water] with the unwearying bronze';[3] in these examples 'drawing' is used for 'cutting off' and 'cutting off' for 'drawing', and both are species of the genus 'removing'. By 'analogical' I mean where the second term is related to the first as the fourth is to the third; for then the poet will use the fourth to mean the second and vice versa. And sometimes they add the term relative to the one replaced: I mean, for example, the cup is related to Dionysus as the shield is to Ares; so the poet will call the cup 'Dionysus' shield' and the shield 'Ares' cup';[4] again old age is to life what evening is to day, and so he will call evening 'the old age of the day' or use Empedocles' phrase,[5] and call old age 'the evening of life' or 'the sunset of life'.[6] Sometimes one of the four related terms has no word to express it, but it can be expressed through a comparison; for example, scattering seed is called 'sowing', but there is no term for the scattering of light by the sun; but as this is related to the sun as sowing is to the scatterer of seed, we have the expression 'sowing the god-created flame'.[7] There is yet another form of analogical metaphor: this is the use of the transferred term coupled with the denial of one of its implications, for example, calling the shield 'the wineless cup' instead of 'Ares' cup'.

Neologisms are terms not in use at all, but invented by the poet himself; some are thought to be of this kind, for example, *ernuges* for 'horns' and *arētēr* for 'priest'.[8]

1458ª   A 'lengthened word' is one using a longer vowel than is usual, or an extra syllable: an example of the former is *polēos* for *polĕōs*, and of the second *Pēlēïadeō* for *Pēleidou*.[9]

A 'shortened word' is one where something is removed from it, for example, *krī* for *krithē*, *dō* for *dōma*, and *ops* for *opsis* . . .

---

[1] Homer, *Odyssey* 1. 185.
[2] Homer, *Iliad* 2. 272.
[3] Both examples are assigned to Empedocles (frr. 138, 143); the reference in the second is to a bronze bucket.
[4] Timotheus, *PMG* 797; 'Dionysus' shield' may well be Aristotle's own invention.
[5] The reference to Empedocles may be misplaced or corrupt; it seems likely that he is responsible for one of the metaphors in this group.
[6] Plato, *Laws* 770 a.
[7] The phrase might come from choral lyric or from a tragic chorus.
[8] The latter is used three times by Homer.
[9] The terms in this and the following two sections are epic. To explain them nowadays we invoke comparative philology, but Aristotle thinks of poetic licence.

An 'altered word' is one where part of the ordinary term is left, and something made up is added, like *dexiteron* for *dexion* . . .[1]

4. *Excellence in poetic style*

[In poetry] verbal expression is good if it is clear without being mean.[2] 22
The clearest is of course that made up of standard words, but it is mean: an example is the poetry of Cleophon and Sthenelus. The style that uses strange expressions is solemn and out of the ordinary; by 'strange expressions' I mean dialect terms, metaphor, lengthening, and everything over and above standard words. But if anyone made an entire poem like this, it would be either a riddle or gibberish, a riddle if it were entirely metaphorical, gibberish if all composed of dialect terms. For it is the nature of a riddle that one states facts by linking impossibilities together (of course, one cannot do this by putting the actual words for things together, but one can if one uses metaphor), for example 'I saw a man welding bronze on a man with fire'[3] and so on. And a poem wholly made up of dialect terms is gibberish. So there ought to be a sort of admixture of these, as the one element will prevent the style from being ordinary and mean, that is, dialect, metaphor, decorative terms, and the other species I mentioned, while standard terms will make it clear.

Quite a large contribution to a style both clear and out of the ordinary 1458b
is made by lengthenings, shortenings, and alterations of words. For because it is other than standard, being unusual, it will produce an effect of being out of the ordinary; at the same time, it will be clear because of its element of the usual. So there is something incorrect in the censure of those who blame this sort of style and mock at Homer, in the way the elder Euclides did, when he said it was easy to be a poet if one were allowed to lengthen things as much as one liked . . .[4] Of course it is absurd to be found obviously using this sort of thing; but all the kinds demand a due measure, as one could also use metaphors and dialect words and so on in an inappropriate and deliberately ridiculous way and produce the same result. If one wants to see how important it is to use them suitably one should take epic verses and put ordinary words into them. In all cases, dialect, metaphor, and so on, if one substituted the

---

[1] After this the manuscripts add a section on the division of nouns into masculine, feminine, and neuter. This is untrue, fatuous, and irrelevant; it is impossible to believe that it is the work of the same man who produced the penetrating linguistic analysis of pp. 117 ff. above, and it is accordingly omitted here.

[2] Contrast the definition of excellence in prose style, below, p. 137.

[3] Cf. below, p. 139.

[4] Aristotle here quotes two hexameters in which Euclides parodied Homer's occasional irrational lengthening of short syllables.

standard word, one would easily see the truth of what I am saying. For example, Aeschylus and Euripides produced the same iambic line,[1] with the change of a single word, as Euripides put a dialect term for the standard word, and so produced a beautiful line instead of an unimpressive one; for Aeschylus in his *Philoctetes* said 'The canker that eats the flesh of my foot', while Euripides substituted *thoinātai* for [the standard verb] *esthiei*. Again, take the line 'being little (*oligos*) and no worth (*outidanos*) and hideous (*aeikēs*)' and substitute the standard words *mikros*, *asthenikos*, *aeidēs*;[2] and for 'putting down a poor (*aeikelion*) chair and little (*oligēn*) table'[3] put *mochthēron* (poor) and *mikran* (little);[4] and for *ēïones boöösin*[5] ('the shores shout') put *ēïones krazousin*.[6]

Ariphrades mocked the tragedians as well for using expressions that 1459ᵃ nobody would use in conversation . . .[7] Wrongly, for all such expressions, because not standard, produce a stylistic effect of being out of the ordinary; but Ariphrades did not know that.

It is extremely important to use in the proper place each of the kinds I have mentioned,[8] but by far the most important is to be good at metaphor. For this is the only one that cannot be learnt from anyone else,[9] and it is a sign of natural genius, as to be good at metaphor is to perceive resemblances. Of nouns, compounds best suit dithyrambs, dialect words hexameter verse, and metaphors iambic verse.[10] Though in hexameters all the kinds are useful, in iambics, because they most closely represent actual speech, the most suitable are those that one would also use in prose speeches, that is, standard words, metaphors, and decorative terms.[11]

So much for tragedy and *mimēsis* via action.

---

[1] Aeschylus, fr. 253; Euripides, fr. 792.

[2] Homer, *Odyssey* 9. 515. *oligos* in the sense of 'small' is here regarded as a dialect term; in Attic it means 'few'. *outidanos* does not belong to prose at all, while *asthenikos* is decidedly prosaic as most of the words terminating in -*ikos* were not only of recent formation, but associated with philosophical and scientific discourse. *aeidēs* also seems to be used only by philosophers and medical writers.

[3] Homer, *Odyssey* 20. 259.

[4] *mochthēros*, in the sense of 'distressed' or 'distressful' or as a term of moral condemnation, does belong to high poetry; but its use of things like chairs, to signify that they are 'in a bad way', is confined to Attic colloquial speech.

[5] Homer, *Iliad* 17. 265.

[6] *krazein* of human bawling is no more or less prosaic than *boän*, with which indeed it is sometimes linked as a synonym by the orators; but *boöösin* is a 'lengthened' word, for which Attic would use *boösin*.

[7] Aristotle adds examples: archaic forms of pronouns, anastrophe of prepositions (i.e. placing them *after* their nouns).

[8] The manuscripts add 'and (? both) compound words and dialect terms'. This seems to be a foolish interpolation from the context immediately below.

[9] Cf. below, p. 138.   [10] The metre of tragic dialogue.

[11] Cf. above, p. 119; below, pp. 136 ff.

CHAPTER IV

EPIC

SECTION A. THE SIMILARITIES BETWEEN EPIC AND TRAGEDY

1. *The need for unity*

Now for the narrative art that uses verse as its medium of *mimēsis*. 23 Clearly one should compose the plots here to be dramatic, just as in the case of tragedies, that is, about one whole or complete action with a beginning, middle parts,[1] and end, so that it produces its proper pleasure like a single whole living creature. Its plots should not be like histories; for in histories it is necessary to give a report of a single period, not of a unified action, that is, one must say whatever was the case in that period about one man or more; and each of these things may have a quite casual interrelation. For just as, if one thinks of the same time, we have the battle of Salamis and the battle of Himera against the Carthaginians not directed to achieve any identical purpose, so in consecutive times one thing sometimes happens after another without any common purpose being achieved by them. Most epic poets do make plots like histories. So in this respect too Homer is marvellous in the way already described, in that he did not undertake to make a whole poem of the war either,[2] even though it had a beginning and an end. For the plot would have been too large and not easy to see as a whole, or if it had been kept to a moderate length it would have been tangled because of the variety of events. As it is he takes one part and uses many others as episodes, for example, the catalogue of the ships and the other episodes with which he breaks the uniformity of his poem. But the rest make a poem about one man or one period of time,[3] like the poet of the *Cypria* or the *Little Iliad*. That is why 1459ᵇ the *Iliad* and *Odyssey* have matter only for one tragedy or only for two,[4] whereas there is matter for many in the *Cypria*, and in the *Little Iliad* for

---

[1] The plural, as distinct from the 'middle' of tragedy (above, p. 100), allows for epic's greater extension.

[2] In the *Iliad*; there seems to be a reference back to the discussion of the unity of the *Odyssey* on pp. 101 f. 'Whole' here as there implies 'unified'.

[3] The manuscripts add 'that is (? and) about one action with many parts'; this is very like the description of the *Iliad* and the *Odyssey* themselves that Aristotle gives below, p. 132. Moreover, if we believe that we know anything at all about the poems of the epic cycle, it is hard to credit that Aristotle ever allowed that their ramshackle structures dealt with 'one action', however polymerous.

[4] The reference is to the principal action of the poems, not to the episodes, like that of Bellerophon, which provided material for more tragedies; for the neglect of Aeschylus, cf. above, p. 116 n. 3.

more than eight, for example, *The Adjudgement of the Arms*, *Philoctetes*, *Neoptolemus*, *Eurypylus*, *Odysseus as a Beggar*, *The Laconian Women*, *The Sack of Troy*, *The Departure*, plus the *Sinon* and the *Trojan Women*.[1]

2. *The species of epic*

24 Moreover, epic must have the same species as tragedy, that is, must be simple[2] or complex, a story of character or one of *pathos*. ⟦And the elements are the same except for music and spectacle.⟧ And it needs *peripeteiai* and recognitions and *pathē*. ⟦Moreover its *mimēsis* of intellect and its verbal expression should be good.⟧ All of these Homer was the first to use and his use of them is exemplary. For in the case of each of the poems, the composition of the *Iliad* is simple and full of *pathos*, that of the *Odyssey* complex, as there are recognitions throughout, and full of character. ⟦And in addition he is pre-eminent in his verbal expression and *mimēsis* of intellect.⟧[3]

SECTION B. THE DIFFERENCES BETWEEN EPIC
AND TRAGEDY

Epic differs from tragedy in the length of its plot and in its metre.

1. *Length*

The above mentioned limit of length[4] is an adequate guide: that is, one should be able to get a synoptic view of the beginning and the end. This will be the case if the poems are shorter than those of the ancients,[5] and about as long as the number of tragedies offered at one sitting.

Epic has a peculiar characteristic in that its size can be considerably

---

[1] Probably not everything in this list is due to Aristotle.

[2] Cf. above, p. 115. 'Simple' here corresponds to what should probably be 'spectacle' there.

[3] F. Solmsen, *CQ* 29, 1935, 195, was probably correct in arguing that a series of remarks about the qualitative parts (here enclosed in double brackets) has been superimposed on a straightforward discussion of the species of epic. Whether he is right in believing that these inane interruptions are later additions by Aristotle himself is another matter.

[4] Above, p. 101.

[5] The phrase delicately veils the name of Homer, the only one of the older epic poets to produce very long compositions. The limit suggested by Aristotle is virtually that observed by Apollonius Rhodius; Virgil decided that he needed more room to deploy a heroic theme.

further extended; for though in tragedy it is impossible to represent many parts as at the moment of their occurrence, since one can only represent the part on the stage and involving the actors, in epic, because it is narrative, one can tell of many things as at the moment of their accomplishment, and these if they are relevant make the poem more impressive. So it has this advantage in the direction of grandeur and variety for the hearer and in being constructed with dissimilar episodes. For it is similarity and the satiety it soon produces that make tragedies fail.

2. *Metre*

The heroic verse was found suitable from experience. For if anyone were to make a narrative *mimēsis* in any other metre or in many metres, it would be obviously unsuitable, as the heroic metre is the steadiest and most weighty of all (which is why it is most ready to admit dialect terms and metaphors); for the narrative *mimēsis* has itself a sort of abundance in comparison with the others. The iambic trimeter and trochaic tetrameter are metres of movement, one of the dance, the other of action. It 1460ª would be even stranger if one mixed them like Chaeremon. That is why no one has composed a long composition except in heroic verse; instead, nature herself teaches people to choose the metre appropriate to the composition in the way I said.

SECTION C. THE SPECIAL MERITS OF HOMER

Homer especially deserves praise as the only epic poet to realize what the epic poet should do in his own person, that is, say as little as possible, since it is not in virtue of speaking in his own person that he is a maker of *mimēsis*. Other poets are personally engaged throughout, and only rarely use *mimēsis*; but Homer after a brief preface at once brings on a man or woman or other characterized person, none of them characterless, but all full of character.[1]

Though one ought of course to aim at surprise in tragedy too, epic is more tolerant of the prime source of surprise, the irrational, because one is not looking at the person doing the action. For the account of the pursuit of Hector would seem ludicrous on the stage, with the Greeks standing

---

[1] The doctrine in this section seems at variance with the view that plain narrative is a variety of *mimēsis* (above, p. 93). The same sort of exaggeration of the small part played in Homer by direct narration seems to occur in Plato, *Republic* 393 a (above, p. 61).

still and not pursuing him, and Achilles refusing their help;[1] but in epic one does not notice it. And surprise gives pleasure, as we can see from the fact that we all make additions when telling a story, and take it that we are giving pleasure. Now it was Homer who taught other poets the proper way to tell lies, that is, by using paralogism. For people think that if, whenever one thing is true or happens, another thing is true or happens, then if the second is true, the first is true or happens; but this is not so. That is why, if the first is false, but if it were true something else must be true or happen, one should add the second; for because we know that the second is true, our soul falsely infers that the first is also true. The thing in the Bath scene is an example of this.[2]

One ought to prefer likely impossibilities to unconvincing possibilities and not compose one's argument of irrational parts. Preferably there should be no irrationality at all, and if there is it should be outside the plot; the *Oedipus*, for example, has this sort of irrationality in his not knowing how Laius died.[3] It should not be inside the plot like the messengers from the Pythian games in the *Electra*[4] or the man who went speechless from Tegea to Mysia in the *Mysians*.[5] So it is absurd to say that otherwise the plot would have been ruined, as one should not compose them to be like this in the first place. If one does put in an irrationality and it is apparent that it could be dealt with more rationally, it is absurd as well. For it is clear that even the irrationalities in the *Odyssey* 1460ᵇ about his being put ashore on Ithaca would have been intolerable if produced by a bad poet;[6] but as it is Homer completely disguises the flavour of absurdity by his other excellences. It is in the parts that involve no action and no *mimēsis* of character or intellect that one should be most elaborate in verbal expression; when character and intellect are being represented too brilliant a style often conceals them.

[1] Homer, *Iliad* 22. 131 ff.
[2] The reference is to Homer, *Odyssey* 19. 220 ff. where Penelope infers from Odysseus' account of the clothes he wore in Crete that he had met Odysseus there. The instance is not particularly to the point, as it involves a false inference made by one character about another, whereas the context is talking about how the poet misleads his hearers.
[3] It may be remarked that Sophocles seems to have been aware of this irrationality, and to have tried to palliate it by attributing to the royal house of Thebes and to the chorus an instinctive distaste for the public discussion of unpleasant subjects (91 f. Creon, 637 f. Jocasta, 678 f., 685 f. the chorus).
[4] Sophocles, *Electra* 680 ff. The irrationality may lie in the anachronism.
[5] Of Aeschylus or Sophocles.
[6] Homer, *Odyssey* 13. 113 ff.

SECTION D. CRITICISMS OF HOMER AND HOW TO ANSWER
THEM[1]

1. *The bases of the answers*

The next subject is questions about what is said and the answers to them.
How many species do they fall under and what are the species? If we
look at the matter as follows the answer will be clear.

(*a*) Since the poet produces *mimēseis*, just like a painter or other visual
artist, the object of his *mimēsis* must always be one of three things, that
is, what was or is, what is commonly said and thought to be the case, and
what should be the case.

(*b*) The narration of these involves verbal expression, including the
use of dialect terms and metaphor and many abnormal elements of expression, as these are licences we allow to poets.

(*c*) Further, correctness in poetry is not the same thing as correctness
in morals,[2] nor yet is it the same as correctness in any other art. Faults
that are relevant to the art of poetry itself are of two kinds, one involving
its essential nature, and the other incidental. If the poet is incapable of
representing what he set out to represent, this is an error involving the
essential nature of poetry. If the error arises through the poet's setting
out to represent something incorrectly, for example, representing a horse
with both its right legs forward,[3] and this is the reason why we find
in the poem either a mistake with reference to any particular art (for
example, medicine or some other art) or, more generally, any other impossibility, this does not involve the essential nature of poetry.[4]

So one should use these principles in examining and answering the
questions raised.

2. *The twelve sorts of answer*

(*a*) ANSWERS DERIVED FROM BASIS (*c*)

Let us take first of all the errors that involve the art of poetry itself:

1. If the poem contains[, for instance,] an impossibility,[5] that is a
fault; but it is all right if the poem thereby achieves what it aims at (what

---

[1] This discussion is extremely difficult and compressed, presumably because it is
an epitome of the four books that Aristotle wrote on *Homeric Problems*.

[2] This curt phrase is a very important part of Aristotle's answer to Plato.

[3] Photography has shown that horses do sometimes employ this gait.

[4] The English reader may recall the justified censure of Milton's botany in *Lycidas*.

[5] It is important to realize that though Aristotle takes an impossibility as an example,
he could equally well have chosen something irrational, morally damaging, or self-
contradictory (below, p. 131).

it aims at I have already discussed), that is, if in this way the surprise produced either by that particular passage or by another is more striking. An example is the pursuit of Hector. However, if it was possible for the aim to be attained either more or no less without any error in the art [essentially] concerned, it is not all right; for, if possible, there should be no error at all.

2. Secondarily, one should consider whether the error involves the essential nature of poetry or something incidental, as it is a lesser fault not to know that a hind has no antlers than to paint it in a way that is not adequate to *mimēsis*.

(b) ANSWERS DERIVED FROM BASIS (a)[1]

3. In answer to the charge of not being true, one can say, 'But perhaps it is as it should be': Sophocles, for example, said that he represented people as they should be, and Euripides as they are; this is the answer.

4. If it is neither true nor as it should be, one can reply, 'But it is what people say'. An example of this is the treatment of the gods: for this, perhaps, is neither a better thing to say nor a true one, but instead the facts are perhaps as Xenophanes saw them;[2] but anyhow that is what people say.

5. Again, if the reply that it is better is not open, the answer can be, 'It used to be so'; an example here is the remark about weapons, 'Their spears stood upright on their butt-ends';[3] that was the custom then, as it still is among the Illyrians.

6. Then there is the question whether someone's statement or action is good or not. Here one should not look just at what is said or done in considering whether it is good or bad, but should also take into account the person who says or does it, asking to whom he said or did it, when, with what, and for what motive. Was it, for instance, to produce a greater good or avert a greater evil?

(c) ANSWERS DERIVED FROM BASIS (b)[4]

Some objections should be answered by considering the expressions used:

---

[1] The first three answers here are various ways of dealing with the charge that what is said is not true, the fourth with the charge that what is said is not as it should be, i.e. is morally damaging.

[2] Above, p. 4.   [3] Homer, *Iliad* 10. 152.

[4] The charges answered are, as one would expect, of very diverse kinds; answer (7), for instance, copes first with a supposed irrationality, then with a supposed self-contradiction ('How could Dolon run fast if he was deformed?'), then with something supposed morally damaging.

1461ª

7. A dialect word may be involved: for example, in 'First it attacked the mules',[1] it may be that *ouréas* means 'sentinels', not 'mules'; and in the case of Dolon 'whose form (*eidos*) was not good',[2] he means he had an ugly face, not a distorted body, since the Cretans use *eueides* to mean 'having a handsome face'; again, in 'make the mixture *zōroteron*', this word means, not 'stronger' with the implication that they were wine-bibbers, but 'faster'.[3]

8. Some expressions are metaphorical. For example, in 'The rest of gods and men slept the night long',[4] where he says at the same time 'when he looked toward the plain of Troy, he marvelled at the din of flutes and pipes',[5] 'all' is used metaphorically for 'many', as totality is a species of plurality. Similarly 'The pole star alone has no contact with the Ocean'[6] is also metaphorical; for 'alone' is put for 'best known'.

9. The answer may be to change the accents and breathing: such a solution was given by Hippias of Thasos in suggesting the imperatival infinitive *didómen* for *didomen* in 'and *we grant* him the achievement of glory',[7] and the negative *ou* for the partitive *hou* in '*part of it* is rotted by the rain'.[8]

10. Some may be answered by a change of punctuation, for example, Empedocles' 'at once things became mortal which had been used to be immortal, and things unmixed formerly mixed'.[9]

11. Another reply is that the expression is ambiguous, for example, in 'more of the night was past than two thirds; the third was left';[10] here *pleō*, 'more', is ambiguous [and may mean 'full'].

12. Some things are a matter of usage. We call wine and water 'wine', and by analogy with this Homer says 'greaves of new-forged tin'.[11] And we call iron-workers 'bronze-smiths', and on the analogy of this Ganymede is said to pour wine for Zeus,[12] though gods do not drink wine; this could also be explained as an analogical metaphor.

---

[1] Homer, *Iliad* 1. 50.

[2] Ibid. 10. 316.

[3] Ibid. 9. 202.

[4] Ibid. 10. 1 f., 2. 1 f.

[5] Ibid. 10. 11–13.

[6] Ibid. 18. 489, *Odyssey* 5. 275; Aristotle gives this and some other of the quotations in this section in a much abbreviated form.

[7] Homer, *Iliad* 21. 297 and perhaps in Aristotle's text of *Iliad* 2. 15.

[8] Ibid. 23. 328.

[9] Fr. 35. 14 f. Aristotle means that one should take 'formerly' with 'unmixed' instead of with 'mixed'.

[10] Homer, *Iliad* 10. 251 ff.

[11] Ibid. 21. 592; 'tin' is used for 'bronze', an alloy containing it.

[12] Ibid. 20. 234.

3. *Summary*

In fact, whenever a word is thought to signify something involving a contradiction, we ought to consider how many meanings the word might have in the phrase in question; for example, in 'by it the bronze spear was stayed',[1] in how many senses is it possible to take 'was stayed by it', and is it by taking it in this sense or in that sense that one would be 1461[b] going most contrary to the practice described by Glaucon, when he said that some people make irrational assumptions about a thing and, having passed this vote of censure all by themselves, make an inference from it and blame the poet as if he had said what they think he did, if what he says contradicts what they imagine. This has happened in the argument about Icarius. They think he was a Spartan and therefore say it is absurd that Telemachus did not meet him when he went to Sparta. But the facts may be as stated by the Cephallenians; they say that Odysseus took his wife from among them and that his father-in-law was Icadius, not Icarius; so probably the criticism rests on a mistake.

Generally speaking, one should answer a charge that a thing is impossible by a reference to the demands of poetry (1), or to the fact that it is better so (3) or commonly thought to be so (4). By 'the demands of poetry' I mean that a convincing impossibility is preferable to something unconvincing, however possible; again it is perhaps impossible for people to be as beautiful as Zeuxis painted them, but it is better so, as the ideal should surpass reality.

A charge of irrationality should be dealt with by reference to what is commonly said (4). That is one answer. Another is that on some occasions it is not irrational, as it is likely that things happen even contrary to likelihood.[2]

A charge of self-contradiction one should consider on the same basis as refutations in argument, asking, that is, whether it is itself the same, and related to the same thing, and used in the same sense, so that it is the poet himself who is contradicting either what he himself says or what a sensible man assumes.

A charge of irrationality or of representing wickedness is justified if there is no necessity for the irrationality or moral wickedness and no use is made of it. An example of the former is Euripides' treatment of Aegeus [in the *Medea*], of the latter his treatment of Menelaus in the *Orestes*.[3]

---

[1] Homer, *Iliad* 20. 272; the problem is how the layer of gold stopped the spear when it passed the layers of bronze.

[2] Above, p. 116. The figures in round brackets in this and the preceding paragraph refer to the relevant 'answers'.

[3] Above, p. 110.

Well then, people produce censures under five heads, claiming that things are impossible, irrational, morally dangerous, self-contradictory, or contrary to technical correctness.[1] The answers to them are on the basis of the points enumerated: they are twelve in number.

SECTION E. EPIC AND TRAGEDY

Which is better, the epic or the tragic *mimēsis*? This is a question one 26 might raise.

1. *The statement of the opponents of tragedy*[2]

Now if whichever is less vulgar is superior, and the less vulgar in any area is what is directed towards a superior audience, it is quite obvious that the one prepared to represent just anything is vulgar. For on the assumption that the audience will not grasp what is meant unless the performer underlines it, they go in for a variety of movements, like bad flute-players rolling about if they have to represent a discus, or dragging the chorus-leader up and down when they play Scylla. Now this is what tragedy is like, resembling in this the later actors, as their predecessors thought of them. For Mynniscus called Callipides an ape, meaning that he went too far, and people thought the same about Pindarus; their 1462[a] relation to their own predecessors is the same as that of tragedy as a whole to epic. Epic, they say, is directed to a cultivated audience which does not need gesture, tragedy to a low-class one; so if it is vulgar, it must obviously be worse.

2. *The arguments for tragedy*

We may say first and foremost that this charge is directed against the art of the performer, not that of the poet, since one can be over-elaborate and over-emphatic in reciting epic as well, like Sosistratus, and in a singing contest, like Mnasitheus of Opus. Moreover not all movement is disreputable, given that not all dancing is disreputable either, but only the movement of low-class people; this censure was made against Callipides and others, on the ground that they represent women of no repute. Again, tragedy produces its effect even without movement, just as epic

[1] i.e. involving ignorance of, for instance, botany or zoology; cf. above, p. 127. An offence against 'the art of poetry itself' would be an indefensible example of one of the other four.

[2] The position here stated is largely that formulated by Plato: see the criticism of *mimēsis* in the Republic (above, pp. 61 ff.).

does; for a reading[1] makes its nature quite clear. So if it is superior in all other respects, this charge will not necessarily lie.[2]

Again, tragedy has everything that epic has (it can even use its metre), and moreover has a considerable addition in the music and the spectacle, which produce pleasure in a most vividly perceptible way.

Moreover, it has vividness when read as well as when performed.

1462^b   Again, it takes less space to attain the end of its *mimēsis*; this is an advantage because what comes thick and fast gives more pleasure than something diluted by a large admixture of time—think, for instance, of the effect if someone put Sophocles' *Oedipus* into as many lines as the *Iliad*.

Again, the *mimēsis* of the epic poets is less unified, as we can see from the fact that any epic *mimēsis* provides matter for several tragedies. The result of this is that if they do make a single plot, it either appears curtailed, when it is only briefly indicated, or follows the lead of its lengthy metre and becomes dilute; I mean here the poem made up of several actions, in the way in which the *Iliad* has many such parts and also the *Odyssey*, and these parts have extension in themselves (and yet these two poems are as admirably composed as can be and are, so far as possible, the *mimēsis* of a single action).

If tragedy is superior in all these respects and also in artistic effectiveness (for these arts should produce not just any pleasure, but the one we have discussed),[3] it would obviously be superior to epic as it is more successful in attaining what it aims at.

So much for tragedy and epic, their nature, the number and differences of their qualitative elements and quantitative parts, the reasons for success and failure in them, and criticisms of them and how to answer them.

B. CATHARSIS
(*Politics* 1341^b32 ff.)

In the absence of better evidence, this passage must be taken as determinant of the meaning of *catharsis* in the *Poetics* as well; and in speaking of pity and fear Aristotle certainly seems to have tragedy in mind rather than just music. *Catharsis* therefore operates by rousing to a high pitch an emotion to which people are, either morbidly or to some degree, prone; the intensification of emotion produces a relief from it. Nevertheless, music is not quite on all fours with tragedy: its place in therapeutic practice was established; more important, though the Greeks regarded music as more 'programmatic' than we do, it is

---

[1] Cf. below, p. 143.

[2] The three arguments in this paragraph are defensive; the rest state positive advantages of tragedy.

[3] Cf. above, pp. 86 f. The *catharsis* of pity and fear could hardly stand at the point where it does in the definition of tragedy if Aristotle thought it characteristic of epic too.

still not the case that music makes 'general statements' of the kind that tragedy makes. Music stirs the audience up, tragedy presents it with something to get stirred up about. The physiological manifestations of the resulting emotion may be the same, but the psychological attitude will be other; as Aristotle remarks (*De anima* 403ª29 ff.), one needs to know both. Some caution is therefore necessary in applying the notion of musical *catharsis* to tragedy.

We accept the classification of tunes made by some of the philosophers when they say that some are relevant to character, some to action, and some to high excitement,[1] and also that each of these has a particular musical mode naturally related to it. We also say that we should use music for several beneficial purposes, not just one, for example, for the education of the young and for *catharsis* (the meaning of *catharsis* I leave unexpressed at the moment and shall explain more clearly in the *Poetics*), and thirdly for entertainment, for relaxation and relief from tense effort. These premisses obviously imply that we should use all the modes, but not all in the same way; instead, we should use for education those relevant to character, while when we are listening to others performing the best are those relevant to action and high excitement. For the emotions that violently affect some minds are present to all, though with differences of degree, pity and fear, for instance, and also high excitement, as this too is a disturbance to which some are morbidly subject. We see the effect of sacred music on the latter when they use the tunes that produce frenzy and are thereby restored to health, finding, as it were, cure and *catharsis*;[2] the same effect will necessarily follow in the case of those over-inclined to pity, fear, and other emotions, in the proportion appropriate to each individual, that is, they all get a sort of *catharsis*, a relief accompanied by pleasure. Similarly, cathartic melodies give people[3] a harmless enjoyment.

So we should allow the competitors who go in for the music appropriate to the theatre[4] to use such modes and melodies. Since the audience is diverse, some free-born and educated, others vulgar, artisans, labourers, and so on, the latter too should have contests, shows, and the like for relaxation. And just as their souls are warped from the natural state, so there are deviations from the modes and high-strung melodies with smaller intervals than normal, and what produces pleasure in any set of people is what they find naturally akin to them; so we should allow the contestants to use such music to such an audience. For the education of the

[1] These are *enthousiastika*; cf. p. 146 n. 3.
[2] For the homoeopathic use of music in curing madness, cf. E. R. Dodds, *The Greeks and the Irrational*, pp. 77 ff.
[3] Presumably those without the morbid tendency to emotion felt by the people mentioned in the previous sentence.
[4] Such music belongs to dithyrambs and nomes as well as to the drama.

young, however, as said above, we should use the melodies and modes
relevant to character.

C. THE ORIGINS OF AESTHETIC PLEASURE
(*Rhetoric* 1, 1371ª21–1371ᵇ25)

Again, generally speaking, understanding and wondering give pleasure, as
wondering involves a desire to understand, so that a thing that rouses
wonder is a thing in connection with which we feel desire, while understanding implies a restoration to a natural state . . .[1] Now since both
understanding and wondering give pleasure, the things that rouse them
must also give pleasure, an example of *mimēsis*, for instance, as painting
and statuary and poetry do, and in general any instance of successful
mimēsis, even if its object does not itself give pleasure. For the pleasure
is not just pleasure in the object; instead there is an inference that 'This is
that', so that the result is our coming to understand something. The same
is true of sudden changes of fortune[2] and hairbreadth escapes from danger,
as all such things rouse wonder.[3]

D. PROSE STYLE
(*Rhetoric* 3)

Book 3 of the *Rhetoric* is a kind of appendix to what Aristotle regarded as his
principal contribution to the art, the analysis of rhetorical argument and of
psychology. It is more open and much more richly provided with examples than
the *Poetics*, and can much more easily be left to speak for itself. Our headings are
designed merely to make obvious a structure that is in any case pretty per-
spicuous, and the notes to provide a minimum of background information.

PREFACE TO THE DISCUSSION OF VERBAL EXPRESSION AND ARRANGEMENT

1403ᵇ There are three things that need to be treated in discussing speaking,
1 the sources of convincing arguments, their verbal expression, and the
proper arrangement of the parts of the speech.[4] I have dealt with con-

---

[1] Cf. above, p. 86.
[2] The word used is *peripeteiai*, but it does not seem here to have its technical sense
(above, p. 104).
[3] The verb *thaumazein*, here translated 'wonder', can also be used of surprise; cf.
above, p. 87.
[4] Standard rhetorical theory added two others, memory and delivery. Aristotle says
nothing of memory and confines to the preface of this book the brief remarks he has to
make on delivery.

vincing arguments, stating the number of their sources (three), and what they are, and why there are no others (the reason is that in all cases people feel conviction either because they are affected in some particular way themselves, or because they suppose the speaker to have some particular character, or because they are offered demonstrative proof); I have also dealt with the proper sources of rhetorical inferences (*enthumēmata*), some of which are specific and some commonplaces. The next subject to be discussed is expression. This is necessary because it is not enough to know what to say; one must also say it in the right way, and this does a good deal towards giving a speech its particular character.

The first subject that people investigated was naturally what came naturally first, the sources of convincingness in what is being talked about; next came how to express and arrange them; there is a third which is powerfully effective but has not yet been seriously treated, the subject of delivery. Even in relation to tragic acting and to epic recitation it was a long time before it came to the fore, as the poets themselves acted their own tragedies at first. Now clearly there is something of this kind in the study of oratory as well as in the study of poetry, where it has been treated by Glaucon of Teos among others. This study is about the proper use of the voice (loud, soft, and moderate, to express individual emotions), the proper use of accents (acute, grave, and circumflex), and the rhythms appropriate to different things. These are the three subjects they investigate, loudness, harmony, and rhythm. Generally speaking it is actors good at delivery who win prizes in the dramatic contests, and nowadays the actors have more influence there than the poets; the same is true of political contests, because of the low character of the citizens.[1] But, as I said, there is no treatise on the subject (naturally enough, as even the study of verbal expression made a late appearance) and it[2] is thought   1404^a vulgar, and rightly so. Still, as the whole study of rhetoric is directed towards producing belief,[3] we should attend to it on the assumption that it is necessary even if not strictly proper. Of course the proper thing is not to bother about anything in speaking except the avoidance of giving either pain or pleasure; for the proper thing is to use no weapons other than the actual facts, so that everything except demonstrative proof is superfluous. Nevertheless, it is, as I said, very effective because of the low character of the auditor.

Now the study of verbal expression has some minimal necessity in all forms of instruction, as it makes some difference to clarity of exposition whether one says a thing in this way or that, though not all that much

---

[1] This is a conjecture; the manuscripts have 'of the political institutions'.

[2] The reference in the rest of this paragraph is to delivery, not verbal expression.

[3] That is, not knowledge.

difference, since all this is mere presentation and directed at the hearer; that is why nobody tries to teach geometry in a rhetorical fashion. Now whenever you find successful expression it will have the same effect as delivery; there has been a little systematic discussion of it, for example by Thrasymachus in his *Eleoi*.[1] And whereas delivery is a matter of natural endowment rather than of technique, the study of verbal expression is a technical one. So people who are powerful in this field also win prizes, just like the speakers who rely on delivery; for the written speeches are more efficacious because of their expression than because of their thought.[2]

CHAPTER I

VERBAL EXPRESSION[3]

SECTION A. THE ORIGINS AND NATURE OF PROSE STYLE

Now the first originators [of style] were naturally the poets, as words[4] are imitative of things and the voice is the most imitative of all our organs (hence the development of the various arts of epic recitation, acting, and others). Since the poets, because what they said was naïve, were held to have earned their repute by the way they said it, [prose] style was at first poetical, for instance, that of Gorgias; and even today the majority of the uneducated think such speakers the best. This is wrong, the style of oratory being different from that of poetry, as the facts show; for the tragedians no longer use it in the same way either, and just as they changed from the trochaic tetrameter to the iambic trimeter because this is of all metres the one most like prose, they have also given up words unfamiliar in ordinary usage, which were used for decorative effect by the earlier tragedians and are still used by hexameter poets. So it is absurd to imitate the poets, when they themselves no longer follow the former style. Clearly then we need not concern ourselves in detail with every

[1] Presumably a work on the production of pathetic effects.

[2] The paragraph is rather incoherent, and bears some signs of incomplete revision; it seems, for instance, to have two starting-points ('Now the study . . .' and 'Now whenever . . .'). Cope's note, which has misled translators, suggests that the subject of the second sentence is 'oratorical delivery' and that the word here translated 'delivery' means 'acting'; but this interpretation imports even more confusion into the paragraph.

[3] The word *lexis* is the active abstract noun derived from *legein* 'to speak'. In the following discussion it is sometimes translated 'verbal expression' or just 'expression', sometimes 'style', and occasionally 'the way they said them' or some such phrase.

[4] The word used is *onomata* 'names', which in its stricter use (as in c. 2 or on p. 118 in the *Poetics*) means 'nouns and adjectives'.

aspect of style, but only with what belongs to the sort of style we mean; the other has been discussed in the *Poetics*.

So much for that inquiry. Now let us define the excellence of prose 1404ᵇ style as being clear (for as speech indicates something, it will not do its 2 job if it does not make that thing clear) and neither mean nor too elevated for its purpose, but appropriate;¹ for a poetical style is perhaps not mean, but it is not appropriate to prose. Now among nouns and verbs those that produce clarity are the standard ones (*kuria*), whereas the others described in the *Poetics*² make the style decorated and not mean; departure from the ordinary makes it look more dignified, as men have the same reaction to style as they do when comparing strangers with fellow citizens. That is why one should make one's style something out of the ordinary; men feel wonder at what is not to hand, and what rouses wonder gives pleasure.³ Now in verse many things produce this effect and in verse they are suitable, because the subject-matter and the persons involved are more out of the ordinary, but prose has much more restricted resources, as its theme is less grand. (Even in poetry it would be inappropriate to put fine language into the mouth of a slave or a boy or to use it of trivial subjects; even there propriety demands a lowering as well as a heightening of tone.) That is why one should not produce this effect obviously, but should give the impression that one is speaking naturally, not artificially. Naturalness is convincing, artificiality the reverse; people think they are being got at and take offence, as they do at blended wines. One should aim at the effect attained by Theodorus' voice in comparison with other actors'; his seems to belong to the character, theirs to be imposed on it.⁴ Artifice is successfully concealed when one carefully chooses words from ordinary speech and puts them together; this Euripides does and he was the first to show how.⁵

SECTION B. THE RESOURCES OF PROSE STYLE

1. *Their nature and proper use*

The components of a speech are nouns and verbs, and the nouns are classifiable in the way investigated in the *Poetics*. Of the classes there

---

¹ Contrast the excellence of poetic style 'to be clear and not mean' (p. 121).
² Cf. pp. 119 ff.   ³ Cf. p. 134.
⁴ Cf. Proust on the acting of Berma: 'I could not even, as I could with her companions, distinguish in her diction and in her playing intelligent intonations, beautiful gestures. I listened to her as though I were reading *Phèdre*, or as though Phaedra herself had at that moment uttered the words that I was hearing, without its appearing that Berma's talent had added anything at all to them.'
⁵ Cf. 'Longinus', below, p. 498.

mentioned, there are very few times or places where it is right to use dialect words, compounds, and neologisms (I shall say where later, and the reason has already been given: they involve too great a departure from the appropriate); the only ones that are really useful for prose are standard proper words and metaphor. This is shown by the fact that they are the only ones everybody uses; everyone talks in metaphor and standard proper words, so that clearly if one does this well, the result will be out of the ordinary and yet not obvious, and it will be clear. And this is what we said was excellence in oratorical style.[1]

1405ª The definition of each of these, the enumeration of the species of
  3 metaphor, and the statement that the latter is most effective both in poetry and in prose, is to be found, as I said, in the *Poetics*; one should take all the more pains with metaphors in prose, because it has fewer resources than verse. It is metaphor more than anything that provides clarity, pleasure, and the unusual; moreover one cannot learn metaphor from anyone else. One's use both of epithets[2] and of metaphors should be appropriate. This is secured by using the right analogy; otherwise it will seem inappropriate, as opposites show up most when juxtaposed. Instead, one should consider, given that a scarlet cloak suits a youth, what suits an old man (it is not the same dress), and if one wants to make something look finer, one should derive one's metaphor from what is best in the same genus, and if one intends blame, from the worse. For instance, since opposites belong to the same genus, to say that a beggar is praying or that someone praying is begging, both being varieties of requesting, is doing what I describe. Another instance is Iphicrates' calling Callias a mendicant priest instead of a torch-carrier, to which Callias rejoined that Iphicrates could not have been initiated, as otherwise he would have called him a torch-carrier, not a mendicant priest (both offices are religious, but one is honourable, the other disreputable). Similarly someone called actors Dionysus' hangers-on, while they refer to themselves as artists (both of these are metaphors, one derogatory, the other the reverse), and pirates nowadays call themselves 'providers'. That is why one can say that a wrongdoer errs and the man in error does wrong, and use both 'takes' and 'plunders' of a thief. But Telephus' phrase in Euripides,

lord of the oar, landing in Mysia,[3]

---

[1] After this the manuscripts add: 'The sophist can use homonyms, as these are his instruments in cheating, the poet synonyms, I mean words both standard and synonymous, like *poreuesthai* and *badizein*; both these are standard and synonymous with each other' (they mean 'go'). This sentence is pointless in the context, laboured and tiresome in expression, and introduces a different classification from the one in the *Poetics*. It is tempting to regard it as an interpolation.

[2] Cf. below, p. 139 n. 3.   [3] Fr. 705.

is inappropriate because 'lord' is too grand for the subject; so the artifice is not concealed. There is also a fault in the syllables, if they do not express an agreeable sound; for instance, Dionysius Chalcus in his elegies calls poetry 'Calliope's scream' because both are vocal sounds, but the metaphor is a bad one because of the non-significant sounds.[1]

Moreover metaphors should not be far-fetched; instead one should derive them from things of the same genus or species so as to give to things that have no name one that will be obviously akin as soon as it is said, as in the celebrated riddle

I saw a man weld bronze on a man with fire;

1405[b]

what is happening has no name, but both are a sort of application and so he used 'welding' of the application of the cup.[2] Generally indeed one can derive good metaphors from good riddles, as metaphors do pose riddles, so that the metaphor [borrowed from a riddle] is clearly successful.

The sources from which one derives metaphors should also be beautiful. Beauty of words depends partly, as Licymnius says, on their sounds or on the object signified, and so does ugliness. There is also a third possibility, which answers a sophistic argument: it is not the case that, as Bryson says, nobody uses indecent words since the meaning is the same whether you say this or that; this is false, because one word is more standard than another and more like the object and more akin, by virtue of putting the thing spoken of before one's eyes. Moreover the thing is not regarded in the same light when one indicates it by this word rather than that, so that in this respect too one must take one word to be more beautiful or uglier than the other; both of them signify the beautiful or ugly thing, but not *qua* beautiful or ugly, or if they do, they express the beauty or ugliness in greater or less degree. One must then derive metaphors from sources that are beautiful either because of their sound or because of what they can signify or because of the appeal to the eyes or some other sense. It makes a difference whether one says 'rosy-fingered dawn' in preference to 'scarlet-fingered' or, worse still, 'red-fingered'.

Similarly in the case of epithets,[3] the qualities attributed can be derived from a bad or ugly source, like 'matricide', or from a nobler one, like 'father's avenger';[4] so too Simonides, when offered a small fee by the victor in the mule-race, refused to write a poem on the ground that he felt distaste at writing for mules, but when given an acceptable fee, wrote

Hail, daughters of the tempest-footed mares,

[1] The text is corrupt and the drift of the second criticism uncertain.
[2] The reference is to medical 'cupping'. Cf. below, p. 192.
[3] Epithets are 'accessory expressions'; the word covers genitival and other qualifications as well as adjectives; cf. the examples on pp. 140 f. below.
[4] The examples are from Eur. *Orestes* 1587–8.

though they were of course the asses' daughters too.[1] One can also use diminutives [for the same purpose]; a diminutive is what diminishes both evil and good, as, for instance, in Aristophanes' jests in the *Babylonians*, where he uses diminutive forms for 'gold-piece', 'cloak', 'abuse', and 'disease'. One should be careful and keep an eye on the right proportion in both [epithets and diminutives].

2. *Misuse of stylistic resources*

3 Bathetic lapses[2] are found in four stylistic features:

(i) The first is in the use of compounds, like Lycophron's 'many-countenanced heaven of high-peaked earth' and 'narrow-pathed shore', or Gorgias' 'beggarly-muse-flatterers false-swearing against one true-swearing', or Alcidamas' 'his soul swelling with wrath, fire-coloured his visage' and his saying he had thought their zeal would be 'achievement-bringing', and making persuasion in speeches 'achievement-bringing', and the sea's foundation 'indigo-coloured'; all these appear poetical because of the compounding.

(ii) The second reason for failure is the use of dialect words . . .[3]

(iii) A third is in the use of epithets that are too long, unseasonable, or over-frequent; though it is appropriate in poetry to talk of 'white milk', some things of this kind are inappropriate in prose, while others, if used to satiety, convict the work of being manifestly poetry. For though one should use the latter kind because they transform the usual and make the style out of the ordinary, one should aim at a mean since the result can be much worse than speaking haphazard; the latter misses excellence, but the former can incur failure. That is why Alcidamas' works fall flat; for he uses his epithets not as a seasoning but as the main dish, since they are so frequent, grandiose, and obtrusive. For example, he says not 'sweat' but 'damp sweat', not 'to the Isthmia' but 'to the gathering at the Isthmia', not 'laws' but 'laws that are kings of cities', not 'at a run' but 'with his soul's impulse arace', and 'taking over' not 'learning's shrine' but 'nature's shrine of learning', and 'his soul's anxiety glowering', and 'artificer' not 'of favour' but 'of a whole people's favour', and 'dispenser of the hearers' pleasure', and not 'with branches' but 'with the branches

---

[1] The point is clearer in Greek, where the standard term for mules is 'half-asses'.

[2] *Psuchra*. 'Bathos' is not an ancient critical term, but belongs to the English eighteenth century (cf. 'Longinus' 4, below, pp. 464 f.). The concept however is very like that which the Greeks expressed by *psuchros* and the Romans by 'frigidus' and which is often translated 'frigid' (cf. Demetrius 114, below, p. 194). The term is used of things that 'fall flat', 'do not come off', like bad jokes or, as here, unsuccessful attempts at elevation.

[3] Aristotle gives several examples of the use in prose of words belonging to high poetry. Cf. the discussion in the *Poetics*, above, pp. 121 f.

1406ᵃ

of the wood he concealed . . .', and 'he clothed' not 'his body' but 'his body's shame', and 'the desire of his soul counter-imitative' (this is compound as well as an epithet, so that the result is a piece of poetry), and 'the excess of depravity so beyond all bounds'. So by speaking in poetical style such people produce ridiculous and bathetic results because of the lack of propriety, while their garrulousness makes for lack of clarity; for whenever a speaker piles more on someone who already understands, he destroys the clarity of his expression by obscuring it. In ordinary life people use compounds when the thing referred to has no name and the compounding is easy, as in *chronotribein*, 'passing time'; but if this is done 1406^b much, the result is altogether poetical. That is why the compounded style is most useful to dithyrambic poets, as they make a great deal of din, dialect words to hexameter poets, as the epic is grand and domineering, and metaphor to iambic poets (it is metaphor that they use nowadays, as I said before).[1]

(iv) A fourth kind of failure is in metaphor. Metaphors, too, can be inappropriate, some because they are ludicrous (comic poets also use metaphors), some because they are too grand and tragic; they are also unclear if far-fetched, like Gorgias' 'affairs pale and bloodless', 'you sowed this in baseness and reaped it in misery' (this is too poetical). The same is true of Alcidamas' calling philosophy 'an outpost to assail the law' and the *Odyssey* 'a fair mirror of human life' and 'not employing any such toy in his poetry'; all these are unconvincing for the reasons given. But Gorgias' remark to the swallow when she flew overhead and dropped on him is in fine tragic style; he said 'Shame, Philomela!' It was no disgrace to a bird to do it, but it would be shocking if a girl did. There is elegance in his reproaching her by calling her what she was, not what she is.

3. *Eikones*[2]

The *eikōn*[3] is also a metaphor, as there is only a slight difference; for when 4 he says 'Like a lion he leapt upon him' it is an *eikōn*, while 'A lion, he leapt upon him' is a metaphor (because both are brave he[4] metaphorically called Achilles a lion). The *eikōn* can be used in prose, but only rarely, as

---

[1] Cf. above, p. 122.

[2] One would expect this section to come earlier, as part of the discussion of the resources of prose, not to follow the treatment of their misuse.

[3] Conventionally rendered 'simile', which suits the initial description well enough. But the statement that the *eikōn* is a possible metaphor if used without the reason for the comparison being stated suggests a more elaborate form, which appears in many of the examples, 'X is like Y; for Y is A and so is X'. But cf. M. H. McCall, *Ancient Rhetorical Theories of Simile and Comparison* (Harvard, 1969), pp. 32 ff.

[4] Homer (*Iliad* 22. 164).

it is poetical. They should be derived from the same sources as metaphors, since they are really metaphors, apart from the difference mentioned.

An example of an *eikōn* is Androtion's remark against Idrieus, 'He is like unchained curs; they rush at people and bite, and Idrieus grew tyrannical once freed from his chains'. There is also Theodamas' comparison of Archidamus to a Euxenus ignorant of geometry, which is analogical, as Euxenus will be an Archidamus with knowledge of geometry. So too in Plato's *Republic* the comparison of those who strip the dead with curs that bite the stone but do not touch the thrower, and of the people in a democracy with a sturdy but rather deaf ship's captain, and 1407ᵃ of the poets' verses with those who have the bloom of youth without beauty; for when the boys have lost their bloom or the verses are broken up, they no longer look the same.[1] And Pericles' saying of the Samians 'They are like children, who wail as they take the sop', and of the Boeotians 'They are like holm-oaks; just as the oaks are cut down by themselves, the Boeotians are ruined by intestine wars'.[2] And Demosthenes' saying of the people that they were like sea-sick passengers.[3] And Democrates' comparison of politicians with nurses who swallow the sop they chew, and smear the baby with the spittle.[4] And Antisthenes' comparison of the thin Cephisodotus with frankincense, because he gave pleasure by wasting away. One can produce all these either as *eikones* or as metaphors; so any such comparisons that have won favour when stated as metaphors will clearly be [possible] *eikones* as well, and *eikones* [possible] metaphors if used without the reason being given. One should always give the analogical metaphor reciprocity, so that it is applicable to either of the things of the same genus; for instance, if the cup is Dionysus' shield, it is also appropriate for the shield to be called Ares' cup.[5]

5   So much for the elements of which a speech is composed.

SECTION C. THE ESSENTIAL CHARACTERISTICS AND VIRTUES
OF PROSE STYLE[6]

1. *Correctness*

The first requirement of style is speaking pure Greek. This consists in five things:

[1] Pl. *Rep.* 469 d, 488 a, 601 b; Aristotle has misremembered the second example.

[2] The comparison involves an ironical twist, as the first statement is like our 'They are real heart-of-oak', and the *eikōn* therefore seems laudatory at first, and then turns out not to be.

[3] If the Demosthenes referred to is the orator, this is Aristotle's only reference to him.

[4] Nurses chewed the baby's food to soften it.   [5] Cf. above, p. 120.

[6] Cf. the statement (derived from Theophrastus) of the four requirements of prose style in Cicero, below, p. 241.

(i) The first is in the use of particles, giving them in sequence in their natural order, in the way some of them require; for instance, 'Now . . .' and 'Now I . . .' require 'but . . .' and 'but he . . .'[1] One should duly produce the second while the first is still in mind, and not append it at too great a distance, nor put another particle before the one needed, as this is very rarely suitable. 'Now I, when he had spoken (for Cleon came with both demands and entreaties), set off with them as company.' Here many particles are interpolated before the 'but he . . .' demanded by the 'Now I . . .'; if there is a long interval before the 'set off', the result is unclear.[2] One element, then, is the correct use of particles.

(ii) The second is the use of particular terms and not inclusive ones.

(iii) The third is the use of unambiguous terms, unless of course one intends the opposite effect, as people do when they have nothing to say, but pretend they have; such persons do use ambiguous expressions in verse, Empedocles, for example. This long circumlocution imposes on the hearers, who are affected in the same way as the majority are by fortune-tellers; when they speak ambiguously, people nod solemn assent ('Croesus by crossing the Halys will destroy a great empire'). And because it involves less error fortune-tellers use generic descriptions of what is being discussed; one would be more likely to succeed in playing 'odd and even' if one said 'Odd' or 'Even' and not how many the other player had, and similarly with saying an event will occur rather than when it will occur; that is why oracle-mongers never define the when. All these are akin to one another, so that, unless for some such purpose, one should avoid them. 1407^b

(iv) The fourth is the correct use of Protagoras' classification of nouns into masculine, feminine, and things; these must also properly and duly correspond.

(v) The fifth is the correct use of number.[3]

2. Clarity

Generally speaking, a written work should be easy to read aloud[4] and to deliver, which is really the same thing. This is impaired by a superfluity

---

[1] The Greek *men . . . de*: the commonest particles to indicate an adversative relationship between two statements.

[2] If the text is right, Aristotle himself has not succeeded in making it clear whether he approves or disapproves of the example he has constructed. Perhaps he wrote: 'Here *not* many . . .; but if . . .'

[3] Aristotle gives examples of the last two classes, which there is no point in translating into an uninflected language.

[4] The first person of whom we are told explicitly that he read without sound is St. Ambrose (Aug. *Conf.* 6. 3).

of particles or in works not easy to punctuate, like those of Heraclitus. Punctuating Heraclitus is hard work because it is not clear whether something is to be taken with what precedes or what follows, as, for example, at the beginning of his treatise, where he says, 'This truth which is constant ever misunderstood by men' and it is not clear to which phrase one should attach the 'ever'. Another thing that produces solecism is not giving the due accompaniment, I mean if you link [to two terms] one that does not suit both; for instance, 'seeing' is not appropriate to both sound and colour, while 'perceiving' is. It is also unclear if you do not make a full statement beforehand when you mean to interpolate many things in between, like saying 'I intended after a discussion with him about this and that and in these terms to set out', rather than 'I intended to set out after a discussion with him', and then 'This and that took place and in these terms'.[1]

3. *Pomp*[2]

6 Pomp of style is aided by the following means:

(i) The use of a definition instead of a word, saying, for instance, not 'circle' but 'the surface with a circumference equidistant from its centre'; concision results from the opposite, using a word instead of a definition.

(ii) When something is ugly or lacking in propriety, then if the ugliness is in the definition one should use the word, if in the word use the definition.

(iii) Representing things by metaphor and epithets, while taking care to avoid the poetical.

(iv) Using the plural for the singular, as the poets do; for even when there is only one harbour they still say 'to the Achaean harbours' and 'Here are the many-leaved folds of the tablet'.[3]

(v) Not combining [two words with one article], but giving each its own . . .[4]; for concision one should do the opposite.

(vi) Using particle linkings; for concision one should not use particles, but not write asyndetically either. Examples are 'having gone and had a discussion', 'having gone I had a discussion'.[5]

1408ᵃ (vii) One can also use Antimachus' trick of describing a thing by qualities it does not have (so he says of Teumessus 'There is a little windless hill'); this gives limitless possibilities of amplification. One can also use this 'It does not have so and so' of things good and bad, in

---

[1] The 'and then' is normally taken to be part of the example.
[2] *Onkos*.   [3] Eur. *Iph. Taur.* 727.
[4] Aristotle gives a simple example of a common idiom.
[5] It is far from clear what these are examples of.

whichever direction it is serviceable; this is the source of the poetical phrases like 'stringless' or 'lyreless music'. The poets give things such privative epithets, a practice that finds favour when used in analogical metaphors, saying, for instance, that the trumpet gives forth a lyreless music.

4. *Propriety*

There are three conditions for propriety: that the style be capable of 7 expressing emotion and of expressing character, and that it be proportioned to its subject-matter. Proportion consists in not talking in an off-hand way about subjects that require pomp nor in a grand style about trivial subjects, and in not attaching a decorative epithet to a trivial word; otherwise the result seems a piece of comedy as in Cleophon, whose expression in some cases was very much in the style of 'Lady fig'.

By 'capable of expressing emotion', I mean that if an outrage is being described the style should be that of an angry man, if impious and shameful acts, that of a person feeling disgust and reluctant even to describe them, if praiseworthy, that one should speak admiringly, if pitiable, miserably and so on. A fact is made more credible by the style that belongs to it; for our mind assumes that a man is speaking with genuine feeling and falsely infers that the feeling is roused by the events described, so that people think the facts are what the speaker says, even if they are not. Moreover the hearer always feels in sympathy with the person who expresses emotion, even if he says nothing of substance; that is why many speakers try to stun the audience with din.

One can express character too by this indication by signs, when the suitable indication goes with the relevant class and disposition. By 'class' here I mean, for example, determination by age or sex or nationality, while I confine 'disposition' to those that make us say that in his life a man has such and such a character; of course not every disposition helps to characterize a life. Well then, if a speaker uses the words adapted to his disposition he will express his character; a rustic and an educated man would not use the same terms or in the same way.

The hearers are also affected by the trick that the speech-writers use *ad nauseam*, 'Who does not know?' and 'Everyone knows'. The hearer assents in shame, so that he can share this universal knowledge.

Seasonable and unseasonable use is something common to all the 1408b kinds. The cure for every excess is the one constantly used, of reproaching oneself; this is thought to be all right, since the speaker is aware of what he is doing. Moreover one should not use all the elements of a proportion at once, as the hearer is less aware of what is happening if one does not;

I mean, for example, if the words are harsh, you should not also employ a voice and a facial expression to suit, as otherwise it is obvious what is going on in each case. But if one is one thing and one another, this secures the same effect without being obvious. So if one says soft things in a harsh tone and harsh ones softly, it is unconvincing.[1]

Compound words and plurality of epithets and terms out of the ordinary best suit the speaker who is expressing emotion; one forgives an angry man for saying that an evil is 'heaven-high' or 'monstrous',[2] and also a speaker who already has a grip on his audience and has filled them with high excitement[3] by encomium or invective or anger or love, as Isocrates too does in the *Panegyricus* at the end . . .[4] People do voice such expressions when excited, so that an audience in the same state will obviously find them acceptable. That is why I said they suit poetry, as it involves such high excitement. One should use them therefore either in the circumstances described or ironically, as Gorgias did or as in the *Phaedrus*.[5]

SECTION D. PROSE RHYTHM

8 The form of expression should be neither metrical nor unrhythmical. The former is unconvincing because it seems artificial, and it is also distracting because it makes one attend to the similarity and wonder when it will recur, just as children anticipate the answer to the herald's cry 'Whom does the freedman choose as his patron?' with 'Cleon'. On the other hand, the unrhythmical is indefinite, whereas the form should be defined, though not metrically, because the indefinite gives no pleasure and is hard to recognize. In every case it is number that gives definition, and number in the context of verbal expression is rhythm, of which verses (*metra*) are sections. That is why a speech should have rhythm, though not metre, as that would make it a piece of poetry. The rhythm moreover should not be too precise, and this is achieved by restricting its use.

Of the various rhythms the dactylic is grand but lacks the conversational tone, while the iambic is the rhythm of ordinary speech (which is why in conversation people utter more iambic trimeters than any other

---

[1] So the manuscripts: but interpretation is difficult. Thurot conjectured 'convincing', but the advice still seems quaint.

[2] The Greek word is one of the dialect terms censured on p. 140 above.

[3] This idea is expressed by the verb *enthousiazein*, which in earlier writers is used of divinely inspired excitement, as in the *Ion*, pp. 42 ff. above. In Aristotle the word has no such religious overtones and seems quite conventional.

[4] Aristotle misquotes some elevated phrases.

[5] 231 d, 241 e.

metre), whereas one needs grandeur and an effect higher than usual. The trochaic is too appropriate to the comic dance, as one can see from the tetrameter, which is a bustling rhythm. So we are left with the paean, 1409ᵃ which people have used from the time of Thrasymachus, though they were not able to describe it. The paean is a third rhythm, related to those mentioned, as it has the ratio of 3:2, while of the others the dactylic is 1 : 1, the iambic and trochaic 2 : 1; 1½ : 1 is related to these and is the ratio of the paean.¹ So the others should be left alone for the reasons given and also because they have fixed verse forms,² while the paean should be accepted, as it is the only one of the rhythms mentioned that has no fixed verse form and is therefore least obvious. Now at the moment people use the same form of paean both at the beginning of a sentence and at the end, but the end should be different from the beginning. There are two kinds of paean that are opposites, and one of them is suitable at the beginning, where people do in fact use it; this is the one with its first syllable long and the other three short.³ The reverse form is that which starts with three shorts and ends with a long.³ This makes a suitable end, as a short ending, being incomplete, makes the rhythm look maimed. Instead one should cut the sentence off with a long and make the ending clear not with the scribe's help, using a punctuation mark, but by means of the rhythm.⁴

So much for the subject of the necessity to prose of agreeable rhythm, and what rhythms are agreeable and how they are constructed.

SECTION E. THE LOOSE AND THE PERIODIC STYLES⁵

The style will inevitably be either strung together (*eiromenē*) and made one by connection, like the preludes in dithyrambs, or neatly ended like the antistrophes of the ancient choral lyrists. The strung-together style

---

¹ In measuring the quantity of syllables, a long syllable is taken to be equivalent to two shorts; thus the long of the dactylic or anapaestic foot (−∪∪, ∪∪−) exactly balances the two shorts, that is, they are in a 1 : 1 ratio, while the iambic and trochaic (∪−, −∪) have a 1 : 2 or 2 : 1 ratio. The long of the paean (−∪∪∪, ∪∪∪−) is 2 to its 3 short syllables, which gives a ratio midway between the 1 : 1 of the dactyl and the 2 : 1 of the iambic and trochaic.

² i.e. they are organized in trimeters, tetrameters, hexameters, and so on.

³ We omit Aristotle's examples.

⁴ Whether or not for Aristotle's mathematical reason, ancient prose did increasingly take as its basic rhythmical unit the cretic (−∪−), of which the paeans are resolved forms. There is not however much sign that writers took to heart the advice to begin with a first paean and end with a fourth, though there is again an increasing dislike for a short syllable ending.

⁵ Cf. Demetrius 1 ff., below, p. 173.

is the ancient one[1] (it was universally practised formerly, but rarely nowadays); by 'strung-together' I mean that the sentence has no end prescribed by its own structure, unless the thing being talked of is finished with. It is disagreeable because of its lack of definition, as everyone wants to have the end in view. That is why runners only pant hard and relax when they pass the goal; they do not flag earlier because they can see the end in front of them. Such, then, is the strung-together style.

By 'neatly-ended' I mean the periodic style. By 'period' I mean an expression that has a beginning and end determined by its own structure and a length that can be seen as a whole. This gives pleasure and is easy to grasp. It gives pleasure because it is the opposite of the indefinite and because the hearer constantly thinks that he has got hold of something and that something has been made definite for him, whereas not being able to foresee or finish something off is disagreeable; it is easy to grasp because it is easily remembered, the reason for this being that the periodic style involves number, which is of all things the easiest to remember. That is why everyone can remember verses better than pell-mell phrases; verses have number to measure them. The period should also be completed along with the thought and not cut up like Sophocles' lines[2]—

> This land is Calydon. Of Pelops' isle . . .

Such a division can lead one to suppose what is contrary to fact, in this case, for example, that Calydon is in the Peloponnese.

The period is of two kinds, that composed of *cōla* and the simple one. By 'that composed of *cōla*' I mean the one that is completely finished off and has its parts distinct and can be uttered without exhausting the breath, not with a stop at an arbitrary point as in the period cited, but as a whole (by '*cōlon*' I mean one of the two parts of the period), while by 'simple' I mean that which has only one *cōlon*. Both the *cōla* and the periods should be neither curtailed nor over-long. Shortness makes the hearer often stumble; it is inevitable, when he is still making for a distant point and for the limit that he defines for himself and then is pulled into reverse because the *cōlon* or period comes to an end, that he should as it were stumble because of the check. Excessive length on the other hand makes him feel left

---

[1] The manuscripts add 'This is the setting-forth of the inquiries of Herodotus of Thurii', a misquotation of the opening phrase of Herodotus, which disrupts the sentence and is not even an example of the 'strung-together' style, though that is frequent in Herodotus.

[2] Actually Euripides (fr. 515). The next line may be rendered:

> The adverse shore confronts its fertile plains.

But the two lines could also be translated:

> This land is Calydon in Pelops' isle,
> With fertile plains upon the adverse shore.

behind, just as those who only turn when they have passed the limit leave behind the people they are walking with; similarly periods that are too long become a speech in themselves and are like a dithyrambic prelude. The result is like what Democritus of Chios mocked at in Melanippides, who composed preludes instead of antistrophic works:

In working woe to another a man works woe to himself;
and a long trailing prelude is worst for the poet's self.[1]

One can say the same of periods with over-long *cōla*. Those where the *cōla* are too short are not periods at all; and consequently they send the hearer flying headlong.

The expression composed of *cōla* has two species, the divided and the antithetical; an example of a divided one is 'I have often marvelled at the men by whom assemblies are constituted and athletic games instituted'; ᵃ1410 while the antithetical is that in which in the pair of clauses either opposite answers opposite or one word serves as a bridge between the opposites. Examples are: 'They benefited both those who stayed at home and those who went out; for the latter they acquired more than they had at home, for the former they left their possessions at home adequate' (staying at home is opposed to going out, more to adequate); 'so that both those who needed money and those who wanted enjoyment' (enjoyment is opposed to acquisition). And again: 'It often happens in these affairs that the sensible fail and the senseless succeed', 'Then and there they were deemed worthy of the prize of valour, and not long after they acquired the empire of the sea', 'to sail over the land, to march over the sea, by bridging the Hellespont and channelling through Athos', 'and though by nature they are citizens, by law they are deprived of citizenship', 'some of them wretchedly perished, some were disgracefully saved', 'and as private citizens to use barbarians as slaves, but as a state allow many of their allies to be enslaved [to barbarians]', 'either to have in life or to leave at death'.[2] And what someone said in court against Pitholaus and Lycophron: 'while at home they sold you, and when they came to you they bought you'. All these produce the effect described. Such a form of expression gives pleasure because opposites are easiest to recognize (and even easier when put beside each other), and because it is like a piece of reasoning; for refutation involves bringing together opposite conclusions.[3]

---

[1] A parody of Hesiod, *Works and Days* 265 f.

[2] The above examples in this paragraph are all quotations or misquotations from Isocrates' *Panegyricus*.

[3] Or, 'refutation involves inferring opposite conclusions'. Aristotle seems to be referring to the form of refutation in which a respondent can be shown that his premises

[There follows a short section, mainly made up of examples, on *parisosis* (equal *cōla*) and similar figures: we resume where the next topic begins.]

SECTION F. WIT[1]

1410^b Now that we have got clear descriptions of all this, the next thing to
  10   discuss is the source of witty expressions that are well thought of. Though
       producing them is a task for the person of natural talent or practised skill,
       showing how to is a proper subject for this inquiry. So let us say what
       they are and list them, taking this as our starting-point: anybody natur-
       ally enjoys understanding something easily,[2] and as words signify some-
       thing those that produce understanding in us give most pleasure. Now
       as we are unfamiliar with dialect words and know standard terms already,
       it is metaphor that most produces this effect; for when he[3] calls old age
       stubble, he makes us understand and realize something via their generic
       similarity, as both are past their prime. The poets' *eikones*[4] also produce
       the same effect, and therefore, when successful, give an impression of wit.
       The *eikōn*, as I said before, is a metaphor with a difference in the way of
       setting it out; that is why it gives less pleasure, because it is more long-
       winded, and it does not say that this is that, so that our soul does not
       even inquire whether it is. So necessarily wit will be found in expressions
       and inferences that produce immediate understanding. That is why
       people think nothing of superficial inferences (those, I mean, that are
       obvious to anybody and are found without investigation), nor of those
       that we do not understand when they are expressed, but admire those
       whose force we realize the moment they are uttered, even though we had
       no notion of them before, or those where the understanding lags only a
       little behind; this produces a sort of sudden realization which is absent
       in the other two cases. Well then, so far as the sense is concerned, people
       think well of the sort of inferences described. In the expression of them a

are in conflict by deriving from them directly contradictory conclusions, rather than a
situation where one speaker says A and the other arrives at the conclusion not-A.

[1] *asteia*, in Latin *urbane dicta*. 'Wit' is unfortunately devalued in modern English;
it is used here in the hope that its older usage will carry over. The concept that Aristotle is
deploying is very like 'wit' in the two aspects that Dr. Johnson suggests in the *Life of
Cowley*: 'If by a more noble and more adequate conception that be considered as wit
which is at once natural and new, that which, though not obvious, is, upon its first
production, acknowledged to be just; if it be that which he that never found it wonders
how he missed . . . But wit, abstracted from its effects upon the hearer, may be more
rigorously and philosophically considered as a kind of *discordia concors*; a combination
of dissimilar images, or discovery of occult resemblances in things apparently unlike.'

[2] Cf. the discussion on p. 134 above.
[3] Homer (*Od.* 14. 214); cf. p. 141, n. 4 above.
[4] Cf. above pp. 141 f.

similar effect is produced by the form of the statement, if it is put antithetically, as in 'and they thought a peace all others shared a war directed
against their own interests'[1] (war is opposed to peace), and also by the
individual words if they involve metaphor, and a metaphor neither far-
fetched, as that makes it hard to see the two things together, nor superficial, as that leaves us unaffected. The expression should also bring things
before our eyes,[2] as we should see them as happening rather than likely
to happen. So one should aim at these three things, antithesis, metaphor,
[an impression of] activity.

Of the four kinds of metaphor[3] the most highly thought of is the ana-   1411ª
logical. So Pericles said that the young men lost in the war had vanished
from the city as if one were to take the spring from the year. Leptines
said of the Spartans, that they would not let Greece lose one of her two
eyes. Cephisodotus, when Chares was eager to pass his audit[4] about the
Olynthian war, complained that he was choking the people to suffocation
in trying to pass his audit. And when urging the Athenians to take provisions and proceed to Euboea, he said they should march to Miltiades'
decree.[5] Iphicrates, when the Athenians made a truce with Epidaurus
and the coastal area, complained that they had filched the travel-rations
of the war. Pitholaus called the state-trireme the people's cudgel, and
Sestos the corn-booth of the Piraeus. Pericles urged them to remove
Aegina, the eyesore of the Piraeus. Moerocles said he was no worse than
a prominent citizen he named, as the latter played the scoundrel at
33 per cent, while he himself was content with 10. And Anaxandrides'
line about daughters being past the time for marriage:

> My girls are in arrears for marriage now.

And Polyeuctus' phrase of a paralytic called Speusippus, that he could
not keep quiet though ill luck had locked him in a pillory of disease. And
Cephisodotus called the warships gaily painted millstones, and the Cynic[6]
said the cookshops were the mess-halls of Athens.[7] And Aesion that they
had poured the city down the drain of Sicily; this is both metaphorical
and vivid. And 'so that all Greece cried out' is also a kind of metaphor
and vivid. And as Cephisodotus urged them to beware of meeting in too

---

[1] Isocrates, *Philippus* 73.
[2] The phrase 'before our eyes' develops some curious syntactic usages later in the
book and will sometimes be translated 'vividness' or 'vivid presentation'.
[3] Cf. above, pp. 119 f.
[4] Athenian magistrates had to submit an account of their tenure of office and persuade
the people to accept it.
[5] As at the time of Marathon. One should perhaps accept Victorius's conjecture 'to
proceed to Euboea and get their provisions there'.
[6] Diogenes.   [7] Mess-halls were a Spartan institution.

many mobs.[1] And Isocrates of those who rushed together for the festivals. And as in the *Funeral Speech*,[2] that it was right that at the tomb of those who died at Salamis Greece should cut her hair in mourning, as her freedom was buried with their valour; if he had just said it was right to weep because their valour was buried with them, that would be a metaphor and vivid, but 'her freedom with their valour' involves a sort of antithesis. And in Iphicrates' phrase 'The path of my words lies through the midst of Chares' deeds' there is an analogical metaphor, and the 'through the midst' is vivid. And saying one is inviting dangers to help out dangers is vivid and a metaphor. And Lycoleon on Chabrias, 'not even feeling awe at the symbol of his supplication, the bronze statue'; that was a metaphor at the moment, though not for ever, but it is always vivid; for it is when he is in danger that the statue supplicates, the 'inanimate animated', the memorial of the city's achievements.[3] And 'practising poor-spiritedness with all his might';[4] 'practising' implies trying to increase something. And 'the god kindled intelligence as a light in the soul'; both make things clear. 'We do not put a truce to wars, but merely adjourn them';[5] both involve the future, adjournment and a peace of this kind. And saying that a treaty is a much finer trophy than those set up in war, because the latter are for trivial achievements and a single success, while the former celebrates success in the whole war;[6] here both are signs of victory. And 'cities pay a heavy reckoning to men's censure'; 'reckoning' is a punishment imposed by law.

11   So much for the fact that witty expressions are derived from analogical metaphor and from vivid presentation. The next thing to discuss is the meaning of 'vivid presentation', and what one does to secure this effect. Well then, I say it is produced by all expressions that signify activity; for example, to say that a good man is 'four-square'[7] is a metaphor, both being perfect, but does not signify activity. But 'with the prime of his manhood in bloom'[8] is [an expression of] activity, and so is 'but you, like a free-ranging creature', and in 'and then the Greeks darting on'[9] the 'darting on' is both expressive of activity and a metaphor, as it indicates speed. And Homer's frequent practice of attributing life to inanimate things via

---

[1] Used instead of 'assemblies'.
[2] Ps.-Lys. 2. 60; in fact, and more plausibly, the reference is to the Athenian dead at Aegospotami, not at Salamis.
[3] The statue, of a hoplite with spear protruded and his shield resting on the left knee, commemorated an exploit of Chabrias' in 378 B.C. It is not clear how much of the last clause is a quotation from Lycoleon, nor what precisely Aristotle is saying.
[4] Isocrates, *Panegyricus* 151.   [5] Ibid. 172.   [6] Ibid. 180.
[7] Simonides, fr. 542. 3.
[8] Isocrates, *Philippus* 10; the next example is from *Philippus* 127.
[9] Eur. *Iphigenia in Aulis* 80.

metaphor. In all such cases the expression finds favour because it produces [the impression of] activity, for example, 'once more the unmanageable boulder rolled down to the plain'[1] and 'the arrow flew'[2] and 'eager to hit its mark'[3] and 'they stuck in the ground longing for their fill of flesh'[4] and 'the spear rushed through his breast, quivering with eagerness'.[5] In all these cases they seem to be active because animate, as 'being insolent' and 'quivering with eagerness' and the rest are [expressions of] activity.[6] He has attached them to the objects via analogical metaphor, since the boulder is to Sisyphus as the insolent man is to the object of his insolence. He does the same with inanimate things in the *eikones* that find favour, 'arched, foam-crested, some first, then others after them';[7] he makes them all moving and living, and activity is a species of motion.

One should, as I said before, derive metaphors from things that are akin and not obvious, just as in philosophy it is the keen-witted man who can see the similarity in things remote from each other, like Archytas' saying that an arbitrator was the same as an altar, as both were the refuge of the ill-used. Or if one were to say that an anchor and a crane-sling are the same, as they are the same something but differ in that one goes down, and the other goes up. And 'levelling' used of political societies is the same concept applied to very different objects, namely, equality to surface and to power.

Most witty expressions depend not only on metaphor but on rousing a false expectation, as that makes it more obvious that one has learnt something because of the contrariety, and our soul seems to say 'How true, and I missed it!' And witty apophthegms are derived from not meaning what one says, like Stesichorus' 'The cicadas will sing to themselves from the ground'.[8] And good riddles give pleasure for the same reason that they involve both realization and metaphor. And so does saying something

1412ᵃ

---

[1] Hom. *Od.* 11. 598. Cf. below, p. 336.   [2] Hom. *Il.* 13. 587.
[3] Ibid. 4. 126.   [4] Ibid. 11. 574.   [5] Ibid. 15. 542.
[6] One may contrast with Aristotle's praise the condemnation of Ruskin in his essay on the Pathetic Fallacy (*Modern Painters* iii, pt. 4, § 6): 'Now we are in the habit of considering this fallacy as eminently a character of poetical description, and the temper of mind in which we allow it as one eminently poetical, because passionate. But, I believe, if we look well into the matter, that we shall find the greatest poets do not often admit this kind of falseness—that it is only the second order of poets who much delight in it'; (§ 11) 'it is one of the signs of the highest power in a writer to check all such habits of thought, and to keep his eyes fixed firmly on the *pure fact*, out of which if any feeling comes to him or his reader, he knows it must be a true one.'
[7] Hom. *Il.* 13. 799.
[8] Aristotle's manuscripts almost all offer the reflexive, which gives the threat two points, that the trees will be cut down and the people massacred; the scholiast and Demetrius (below, p. 192) have 'will sing to them'. Aristotle cites the saying also in Book 2 (1395ᵃ2) with no pronoun at all.

strange, to use Theodorus' phrase; this happens when the phrase is unexpected and, in his words, 'not in line with our previous opinion', but is instead like the parodic turns in jokes (the same effect is produced by puns, as they also cheat expectation) and in verse lines, as they too do not run in the way the hearer assumed ('he went on his way and beneath his feet were chilblains', when the hearer expected 'sandals'). Such a turn should be obvious the moment it is uttered.

[We omit a section on puns and the like, again mainly composed of examples, some of which are unintelligible.]

1412^{b}21   These expressions are all of the same kind; but the more succinctly and antithetically they are expressed, the better thought of they are. The reason is that we understand better because of the antithesis and faster because of the brevity. It should always have as well correct expression of its personal application, if what is said is to be both true and free of superficiality;[1] an expression can have one of these qualities[2] without the other, like 'One should die without doing wrong', 'The deserving man should marry the deserving woman'. But there is no wit unless both qualities are present, 'It is right to die when it is not right for one to die'.[3] The more of the qualities described an expression has the wittier it will appear, I mean, if the terms are metaphorical and the metaphor is of a particular kind and there is antithesis and *parisōsis*, and an expression of activity.

As I said above, the *eikones* that are well thought of are also metaphors in a way, as they always involve two terms, like analogical metaphors; for
1413^a instance, to use our ordinary example, 'the shield is Ares' cup' and 'the bow is a lyre without strings'.[4] When they speak in this way the expression is not simple, like calling the bow a lyre or the shield a cup. And they produce *eikones* in the same way, for instance likening a flute-player to an ape, a short-sighted man to a lamp with water dripping on it, because both blink. Excellence in them demands metaphor; one can produce an *eikōn* comparing the shield to Ares' cup and ruins to the rags of a house,[5] and Niceratus can be called 'a Philoctetes bitten by Pratys', as in Thrasymachus' *eikōn* when he saw Niceratus after his defeat by Pratys in the citharoedic contest, still dishevelled and unwashed. Such comparisons

---

[1] The text here is uncertain.
[2] i.e. truth and freedom from superficiality.
[3] In the section omitted Aristotle cited a line of Anaxandrides, 'It is fine to die before doing what rightly merits death', which he said was equivalent to the formulation given here.
[4] Theognis, *trag*. I, above, p. 120.
[5] The opposite comparison of rags to 'ruins of clothes' occurs in *trag. adesp.* 7, Eur. *Tro.* 1025.

earn poets the most hisses when they fail and the most applause when they succeed, I mean, when they make them correspond:

His legs are curly like parsley-leaves.[1]
Like Philammon at close quarters with the punch-ball.[2]

All such expressions are *eikones*. And I have said often already that *eikones* are metaphors.

Proverbs are also metaphors, of the species to species kind.[3] For instance, if a man calls in another expecting to benefit and is then hurt, he says 'Like the Carpathian with the rabbit',[4] as each of them has suffered the fate described. Well then, the sources of witty expression and the reasons why they are sources have been just about dealt with. Hyperboles of the kind that are well thought of are also metaphors, for instance, of the man with the black eye, 'You would have thought he was a basket of mulberries'; the black eye *is* red, but the expression is very extreme. The 'Just like such and such' is really a hyperbole with a different form of expression: 'like Philammon at close quarters with the punch-ball', 'You would have thought he was Philammon fighting with the punch-ball', 'His legs are curly like parsley-leaves', 'You would have thought his legs not legs but parsley, they were so curly'. Hyperboles are juvenile, as they indicate vehemence. That is why they are most used by people in a temper: 'Not if he were to give me gifts as many as the sand and dust. I shall not marry the daughter of Agamemnon, Atreus' son, not if she vies in beauty with golden Aphrodite and in handiwork with Athena.'[5] That is why 1413 such expression is inappropriate in the mouth of an older man.

SECTION G. THE VARIOUS KINDS OF STYLE

One must not forget that different styles are suitable for different kinds 12 of discourse. The styles of written composition and extemporary debate are not the same, and [within the latter] the style of political debate is different from that of the law-courts. One needs to know both; capability in debate is knowing how to express oneself in Greek, and the other means you are not compelled to be silent if you want to impart your ideas to the rest of the world, a fate suffered by those who do not know how to produce written compositions. The written style is the most finished, the style of debate that most capable of being delivered (the latter has two species, one expressive of character, the other of emotion); that is why actors eagerly seek for plays in this style and poets for such actors, while the

---

[1] *Com. adesp.* 208.   [2] *Com. adesp.* 207.   [3] Cf. p. 120 above.
[4] 'Like the Australians and the rabbit' would make the same point nowadays.
[5] Hom. *Il.* 9. 385 ff. At this point the manuscripts add: 'Its use is very frequent in Attic orators'.

poets who can be read are continually in our hands, like Chaeremon (he is as finished as a writer of speeches) and Licymnius among the dithyrambic poets. When the two sorts are put side by side the speeches of the writers seem too constrained in actual delivery, while those of the extemporary speakers, which were admirable when delivered, seem unprofessional when one takes them up to read. The reason is that it[1] is suitable in real debate; this is also why, when delivery is removed, the features adapted for delivery seem inane because they are not producing their proper effect, things, for instance, like asyndeta and frequent repetitions of the same idea, which are rightly disapproved of in the written style but not in that of debate, and are in fact used by the orators, as such a style is adapted for delivery. In repeating the same idea one should use variation, since this paves the way for the form of delivery, as in 'He is the one who robbed you, he is the one who cheated you, he the one who finally attempted to betray you', or as the actor Philemon did in Anaxandrides' *Old Men's Madness*,[2] whenever he said 'Rhadamanthys and Palamedes', and the 'I' in the prologue of the *Devotees*;[3] if one does not deliver such things expressively, one would be like a man who had swallowed a poker. The same is true of asyndeta, 'I came, I approached him, I besought him'; one needs to deliver this expressively and not give it a uniform vehemence and a uniform expression of character as if one were saying only one thing. There is moreover a special feature of asyndeta, that many things are taken to be said in the time it would take to say one, since connection makes a unity out of plurality, so that its removal obviously turns a unit into a plurality. It therefore gives an effect of magnification:[4] 'I came, I spoke to him, I besought him' (this seems a lot of things), 'he contemned everything I said'.[5] This is what Homer aims to do with his

> Nireus from Syme . . .
> Nireus son of Aglaia . . .
> Nireus the most beautiful . . .[6]

If one says a lot about a thing, one must speak of it more than once; so if one speaks of it more than once, one is taken to be saying a lot about it. So Homer here has magnified Nireus, though mentioning him only once, because we make the false inference, and has made us remember him though he says nothing at all about him later in the poem.

The style adapted to public assemblies is throughout like outline painting, since the more numerous the crowd, the further the individuals

1414ᵃ

---

[1] If the text is right the 'it' must be something like 'such a style'.
[2] *Com.* 2. 138 f. K.   [3] Also by Anaxandrides, ibid. 140.
[4] *Auxēsis.*   [5] The text is uncertain.   [6] Hom. *Il.* 2. 671 ff.

stand away from the picture. That is why in both cases exact finish is superfluous and indeed produces an inferior impression. The style of the law-courts is more finished, and most of all the style that depends on a single judge, as it least admits the arts of the speaker; it is easier here to keep in one view what is relevant to the case and what not, and as there is no public debate, the judgement is unimpeded. That is why the same speakers do not find favour in all three kinds; instead, whenever delivery is most in point, finish is least required. And this is the case where we need a voice and most of all where we need a loud voice.

Well then, the style of epideictic speeches is best adapted to writing, as its function is to be read, and next to it comes the style of the courts. It is superfluous to go in for further distinctions about style and say, for instance, that it should give pleasure and be magnificent. Why that rather than temperate or liberal or endowed with any other moral virtue? The qualities described above will obviously make it give pleasure, if excellence of style has been rightly defined. What else is the point of its being clear and not mean but appropriate? If one is garrulous one is not clear, and nor is one if one is over-concise, so that the mean between these is obviously suitable. The things described will make it give pleasure if they are well-blended, the usual and the out-of-the-ordinary, and rhythm, and the convincingness produced by propriety. So much for style, both the general discussion common to all kinds and the particular description of each.

Chapter II. Arrangement

Section A. The essential parts of a speech: arguments against the current over-elaborate terminology

The remaining subject is arrangement. There are two [real] parts of a speech: one must necessarily state what one is talking about, and then prove it. That is why it is impossible to make the statement and not proceed to proof, or to prove one's case without making the preliminary statement, since anyone producing proofs is trying to prove something, and anyone who makes a preliminary statement makes it with a view to proving it. These two parts are the preliminary setting-out and the argument, analogous to the division [in dialectic] between stating the problem and giving a demonstrative proof. The current method of division is ludicrous [for several reasons]:

(i) Narration belongs only to speeches in the courts, while epideictic

and political oratory cannot possibly admit a narration of the kind they
1414ᵇ describe, nor yet the arguments directed against one's rival litigant.

(ii) Demonstrative arguments cannot admit a peroration.[1]

(iii) The proem and the comparison of opposite positions and the
review occur in political oratory only where there is an opposing speech
(for that matter, accusation and defence also occur there, but not in so
far as it is political advice).

(iv) Moreover the peroration does not belong even to forensic oratory
as a whole, for instance, if the speech is short and the subject easily
remembered; for its effect is to remove the [impression made by] length.

So the necessary sections are the setting-forth and the argument. These
are the parts that characterize a speech, while the maximum is proem,
setting-forth, argument, peroration; arguments against the other litigant
are part of the argument, while comparison of opposite positions is an
amplification of the arguments for one's case, so that it too is part of the
argument, as the person who does it is trying to prove something. But
this is not true of the proem or the peroration, as that serves instead as a
reminder. If one goes in for divisions of the fashionable kind, as in Theodorus and his school, one will get narrative as one thing and supplementary narrative as another, and preliminary narrative and refutation
and supplementary refutation.[2] But one should state a species and use a
differentia when assigning names; otherwise the result is inane chatter
of the kind Licymnius produces in his treatise, using words like 'on-
wafting' and 'off-wandering' and 'branches'.

SECTION B. THE PROEM

14 Well then, a proem is the beginning of a speech, corresponding to the
prologue in poetry and the prelude in flute-playing; all these are beginnings and pave the way for what is to come.

1. *The proem in epideictic oratory*

The flute-prelude is like the proem of epideictic speeches. Flautists play
their best piece first and then link it to the theme, and one should write
in the same way in epideictic speeches, saying straight away whatever
one likes and then entering on the theme and linking it up. This is in fact
what they all do; an example is the proem of Isocrates' *Helen*, where the
eristics[3] have nothing to do with Helen. It is suitable for the speaker even

---

[1] Interpretation uncertain.
[2] Cf. Pl. *Phaedr.* 266 d–267 a.
[3] Isocrates begins with an attack on 'eristic' logicians.

to go off on an alien topic and for the speech not to seem all of one kind. The opening words of epideictic proems concern praise or blame, as in Gorgias' *Olympic*, 'There are many reasons, fellow Greeks, for admiring . . .' (he goes on to praise the organizers of the festal assemblies, whereas Isocrates[1] blames them for honouring only physical excellence and not establishing any prize for the intelligent); or they can start with advice (for example, that one should honour the good, which is why the speaker is praising Aristides, or one should honour those who are neither highly reputed nor base, but are good without being noticed, like Priam's son Paris, who is giving the advice);[2] they can also take their start from forensic proems, that is, be directed to conciliating the hearer, if the speech 1415ᵃ is about something surprising or difficult or trite, so as to win pardon as in Choerilus'

Now that all is assigned.[3]

Well then, the proems of epideictic speeches start from the topics mentioned, praise, blame, suasion, dissuasion, and appeal to the hearer; the opening themes may be either alien from or akin to the speech.

2. *The proem in forensic oratory*

As for the proem of the forensic speech, one should take it to have the same point as prologues in plays and proems in epics. The proems of dithyrambs are like those of epideictic speeches ('Because of you and your gifts or should I call them spoils?'), whereas in prologues and in epic there is an indication of what is to be said, so that the hearers can know beforehand what the work is about and the mind not be kept in suspense, since what is undefined makes the attention wander. So the speaker who as it were puts the beginning in the hearer's hand makes him hold fast and follow what is said. That is why we have

> Sing of the wrath, goddess . . .[4]
> Tell me of the man, Muse . . .[5]
> Tell me another story, how from the Asian land there came to Europe a great war . . .[6]

And the tragedians similarly tell what the play is about, if not at once as Euripides does, still somewhere in the prologue, like Sophocles' 'My

---

[1] *Panegyricus* 1 f.

[2] If this interpretation is right, this defence of Paris, which Aristotle also mentions several times in Book 2, was put into his own mouth, and is the earliest known example of a form of declamation that later became common.

[3] An epic poet who wrote on the Persian wars and used this phrase to excuse the novelty; for this sentiment, cf. Virg. *Georg.* 3. 4.

[4] Hom. *Il.* 1. 1.   [5] Hom. *Od.* 1. 1.   [6] Choerilus.

father was Polybus';[1] the same is true of comedy. So the most necessary and the characteristic function of the proem is telling what the speech is aiming at (which is why one need not use a proem if that is clear and the subject a small one).

The other general heads that they use [in proems] are 'remedies' and common to other parts of the speech. Remedies of this kind take their starting-point from the speaker, the hearer, the subject-matter, or the adversary. In the case of oneself and the adversary it is a matter of doing away with prejudice or creating it. The method is not similar: if one is defending oneself one answers the prejudice first, while if one is accusing another one attacks him in the peroration, for the obvious reason that in defence, if one is going to put oneself across, one must get rid of obstacles and therefore deal first with prejudice, whereas in rousing prejudice one should do it in the peroration, so that the audience remembers it better. Remedies directed at the hearer start from making him well-disposed or angry, and sometimes attentive or the reverse; it is not always useful to make him attentive, which is why many speakers try to divert him to laughter. So far as his being disposed to learn goes, everything produces that result if one wants it, including giving an impression of virtue, since people 1415^b do pay special attention to the virtuous. The things people attend to are important ones, and ones that concern them or surprise them or give them pleasure; that is why one should try to produce the notion that one's speech deals with matters of this kind, while if one wants them inattentive, one should suggest that the matter is trivial, of no interest to them, and painful. One should be aware that all such things are alien to the speech proper, as they are directed at a low-class hearer who listens to what does not concern the real subject-matter; if he is of a different kind one does not need a proem, except to state the subject in a summary form, so that the body can have a head. Moreover securing the audience's attention is something common to all parts of the speech, if it is required at all; there is nowhere they are less likely to relax than at the beginning, so that it is ridiculous to put it at the beginning, that is, at the point where everybody listens most attentively anyway. Instead, whenever the right moment comes, one should say, 'And listen carefully to what I say; it concerns you just as much as me', and 'I shall tell you something more dreadful and more surprising than you have ever heard'. This is the same as what Prodicus said, that whenever his audience showed signs of nodding off, he threw in a bit of the fifty-drachmae

---

[1] It is not easy to believe that Aristotle so far forgot the *Oedipus Tyrannus* as to attribute line 774 to the prologue. Ross conjectures 'if not at once as Euripides does in the prologue, still somewhere or other . . .'; but this will hardly do in a context talking of prologues.

course. It is obviously directed at the hearer not *qua* hearer [of the speech proper], since everyone uses the proem when they are trying to rouse prejudice or remove alarm ('Lord, I shall not tell you that with haste . . .'[1] and 'Why this proem?').[2] Similarly with those who have or think they have a bad case; they think it better to spend their speech on any subject rather than the facts of the case. That is why slaves do not answer the question asked but beat about the bush and produce a long proem. The sources of conciliating goodwill have already been stated,[3] and everything else of the same kind. 'Let the Phaeacians befriend me and pity me when I come to them' is a good saying; so one should aim at these two things.

In epideictic speeches one should make the hearer feel that he too is being praised, either himself or his family or his pursuits or something or other; there is truth in Socrates' remark in the *Epitaphios*[4] that it is not hard to praise Athenians among Athenians, though it is among Spartans.

3. *The proem in political oratory*

The proems of political oratory are derived from those of forensic oratory. Of its own nature it needs the proem hardly at all, since the audience knows what the speech is about and the facts require no proem unless because of oneself and opposing speakers, or if the audience assumes the matter to be of greater or less importance than you want it to, so that one has to rouse or dilute prejudice or heighten or diminish the importance of the subject. These are the reasons for needing a proem, or else for decorative effect, since it appears off-hand not to have one. 1416ª An example is Gorgias' encomium on the Eleans; that begins without any prelude or preliminary sparring with 'Elis, blessed city'.

4. *Prejudice*[5]

On the question of prejudice, one subject is the means of doing away 15 with a damaging assumption (it makes no difference whether someone has voiced it or not, so that this is a general description). Another topic is how to deal with the things one contests, by denying either that they are the case or that they are injurious or injurious to him, or saying that they are not so important as he says, or not a wrong or not a substantial

---

[1] The watchman's opening words in Soph. *Ant.* 223.
[2] Eur. *Iph. Taur.* 1162.   [3] Book 2, c. 4.
[4] Plato, *Menexenus* 235 d.
[5] This development, prompted by the mention of prejudice in § 2 above, is not altogether tidily worked in.

one, or not disgraceful or not a substantial disgrace. These are the sort of things that are contested, as by Iphicrates against Nausicrates; he admitted that he had done what his opponent said and that he had inflicted injury, but denied inflicting wrong. Or when one has done wrong one can try to compensate for it, by saying that if it was an injury it was nevertheless noble, if painful, yet beneficial or something else of the kind. Another topic is that it was done in error or by ill chance or under constraint; so Sophocles said that he was trembling not, as his adversary said, so as to be thought old, but because he could not help it; it was not of intent that he was eighty. One can also compensate by stating the expected result, that he meant to do not injury but something else, and did not do what he is accused of, as the injury was incidental ('It would be fair to hate me if I had intended this result of my action'). Another topic arises if the accuser himself or someone connected with him has been involved in the same charge, either now or formerly. Another, if others are involved in it who are agreed to be innocent, for example, 'If X is an adulterer because he dresses neatly, so must Y be'. Another, if someone else or the accuser himself has roused unfair prejudice against others, or if, without such an attack, others were exposed to the same suspicion as you are now, and were later shown to be innocent. Another from retorting the attack on one's accuser, and saying that it would be absurd to trust his words when his character is distrusted. Another, if there has been a previous decision, as in Euripides' reply to Hygiaenon in the exchange case, when he accused him of impiety for saying

My tongue has sworn, my mind remains unsworn;[1]

he retorted that it was not fair of Hygiaenon to bring judgements from the Dionysiac contest into court, as he had given account of his words there, or would do so if Hygiaenon wanted to accuse him. Another from the accusation of arousing prejudice, with the arguments that it is monstrous, that it introduces judgements about irrelevant matters, that it does not 1416ᵇ show confidence in the facts. Both accuser and defender can use the topic of tokens, as in the *Teucer*[2] Odysseus argues that Teucer was related to Priam, whose sister Hesione was, Teucer that his father Telamon was hostile to Priam and that he himself had not denounced the spies. Another is open to the attacker, praising the trivial at great length and blaming a substantial fault concisely, or setting forth many good qualities in his opponent and blaming just one, the one being that which really furthers the charge; such topics are the most skilful and most unfair, as they try to damage the good qualities by mixing them up with the bad. Another topic common to both accuser and defender is that of motive, as the

[1] *Hippolytus* 608.   [2] Of Sophocles.

same act can be done for different reasons; the accuser should disparage
the act by taking the worse motive, while the defender should take the
better, saying, for example, that Diomede chose Odysseus because he
was the bravest, whereas the accuser says that this was not the reason
but that he was the only Greek whose rivalry Diomede did not fear,
taking him to be a coward. So much for unfair prejudice.   16

SECTION C. THE NARRATIVE

1. *The narrative in epideictic oratory*

Narration in epideictic speeches should be not consecutive but divided.
The reason is that one has to report the achievements on which the speech
is based, since the speech is a composite unity, part of which does not
involve technical skill, as the speaker is in no way responsible for the
achievements, and part of which does, that is, showing that something is
the case, if it is hard to believe, or that it has some particular quality or
importance, or doing all these at once. One's narration should sometimes
be broken up, as displaying things consecutively is hard on the memory;
the achievements that show his courage are different from those that
show his wisdom or justice. And this sort of speech is less complicated,
whereas a differently constructed one is elaborate and not plain enough.
One should merely remind people of well-known achievements; that is
why people need no narration if you mean, for instance, to praise Achilles,
as everyone knows his achievements, and one should just use them; but
one does need a narration in praising Critias, as not many know about
him . . .[1]

2. *The narrative in forensic oratory*

. . . As things are they absurdly say that the narration should be swift.
In fact, there is point here too in what the man said to the baker when he
asked whether he should knead the dough hard or soft, 'Why, can't you
do it just right?' One should not make one's narration long-winded,
any more than one's proem or the statement of one's arguments; there
too excellence does not consist in speed or concision but in a due length,
that is, in saying enough to explain the facts, or to make the hearer take   1417ᵃ
it that the act, the damage, the injury did happen and was as important
as you wish to convey, while the opponent needs to do the opposite.
Along with the narration one should tell everything that helps to give an

[1] Several sentences have been lost at this point.

impression of one's own merits (for example, 'I tried to restrain him, by reiterating what was fair, from leaving his children in the lurch') or of your opponent's demerits ('And he answered that wherever he was himself, he could get other children', as Herodotus says the mutinous Egyptians replied). One should also add what gives pleasure to the jury. In defence the narration is less extensive, as one's retort is that it did not happen or was not a damage or not an injury or not so important, so that one need not waste time on what is agreed, unless something contributes to the desired aim, for example, if you admit the deed but claim it was not an injury. One should also tell of things as past, unless they tend to rouse pity or indignation when represented as actually going on; examples are the story told to Alcinous, which is retold to Penelope in sixty lines, and Phayllus' treatment of the epic cycle, and the prologue to the *Oeneus*.[1]

The narrative should be expressive of character, and will be so if we know what produces this effect. One thing is what reveals moral purpose; the character is of some particular kind because the purpose is of a particular kind, and the purpose is of a particular kind because of the end one aims at. That is why mathematical treatises do not express character, as they do not indicate moral purpose, not having any particular motive, whereas the Socratic dialogues do, as this is the sort of subject they are talking about. Other things indicative of character are the concomitants of different sorts of character, like for instance, 'He went on walking as he spoke', an act that shows insolence and boorishness of character. And not giving the impression of speaking from the intellect as people do nowadays, but from moral purpose ('I wanted it, and indeed had purposed it; but even if I gained nothing by it, it was better'; this shows both a prudent and a good man, as a prudent man pursues advantage and a good man what is honourable). And if the thing is hard to believe one should add the reason, as Sophocles does; an example is Antigone's saying that she cared more for her brother than for husband and children, as she could have more children if she lost them, 'But with my mother and father in Hades no other brother could be born for me'.[2] If you cannot give a reason, you should say you know what you are saying is hard to believe, but that is just how you naturally are, since people disbelieve that men willingly do anything except what is to their advantage. Part of your narrative should also employ such elements of emotional significance as the natural and known concomitants of an emotion and particular characteristics of yourself or your adversary ('He went off, giving me a 1417b   scowl', and what Aeschines said about Cratylus, 'furiously hissing and

---

[1] These seem to be cited as summary narratives of past events, suitable models for cases that do not demand a more elaborate and impassioned account.
[2] *Antigone* 909 ff.

waving his arms'); such things are convincing because they are known tokens of the unknown. One can derive many such indications from Homer, 'So he spoke, and the old woman threw her hands over her face';[1] people beginning to weep do cover their eyes. And introduce yourself at once as having a certain character so that the audience can contemplate you as such, and do the same with your adversary, but without being obvious. It is easy to do, as you can see from people who tell us stories, who give us an impression even of people we know nothing about. There are many places where narration is in point, and sometimes it is not in point at the beginning.

3. *The narrative in political oratory*

In political oratory narration has very little place, as no one uses narration of the future; but if there is narration, it should tell what has happened, so that people can deliberate better about the future for being reminded of the past, or by way of rousing prejudice or praising merit; but in this the speaker is not doing the job of giving political advice. If it is hard to believe, one should both promise and state the explanation at once and set it out with any details they want, as for instance Carcinus' Jocasta in the *Oedipus* keeps making promises when questioned by the man who is looking for her son, and like Sophocles' Haemon.[2]

SECTION D. THE ARGUMENTS

1. *Arguing a positive case*[3]

One's arguments should be demonstrative, and the demonstration should 17 bear on the point at issue, of which there are four kinds; for instance, if one disputes the actual occurrence of the event, one should direct one's demonstration to deciding this, if its being a damage, to this, and similarly to showing that it is not so important or not an injury, in the same way as if the occurrence of the event were in question. One should be aware that it is only in this last case that one or other of the contestants must necessarily be a scoundrel, since ignorance cannot be responsible for the dispute as it might be if they disputed about whether or not it was an injury; so one must spend time in this case, but need not in the others. In epideictic speeches one's method of amplification should usually be

---

[1] *Odyssey* 19. 361.
[2] The point of this reference is quite obscure.
[3] The main lines of this section are fairly clear, but it seems to degenerate into a rag-bag of assorted notes at the end.

stating that things are honourable and beneficial, as the facts should be taken on trust; there are a few occasions when one offers demonstrative proof of them, when they are hard to believe or someone else is supposed responsible for them. In political oratory one might dispute that something will be the case, or grant that it will be the case if they do what one's opponent recommends and argue that it will be injurious or not useful or not so important.

1418ª One should also keep an eye out for any lies that do not concern the fact in dispute, as they are indications that he is lying in other things as well. Examples belong more to political oratory, inferences to forensic, as the former concerns the future and so necessarily cites examples from the past, while the latter deals with things that are or are not the case, where there is more possibility of demonstrative proof and necessary statements, as past statements are necessarily true. One should not state one's inferences one after another but mix them up [with other things]; otherwise they damage each other, as there is also a quantitative limit ('My friend, since you have said as much as a sensible man would'; 'as much' he says, not 'what'). And one should not look for inferences about everything; otherwise you will end up like some philosophers, who arrive at conclusions better known and more convincing than the premisses they start from. And when you try to produce an impression of emotion do not employ an inference (it will either expel the emotion or itself be stated to no purpose, as simultaneous movements operate against each other and either destroy or weaken each other's effect). Similarly, when the statement is expressive of character one should not look for an inference at the same time, as demonstrative proof does not imply character or moral purpose. Instead one should use general reflections both in the narrative and in the argument, as they do express character ('And I gave it, though I well knew one should not be over-trusting') and can also be used for emotional effect ('And I do not regret it, despite the injury done me; he has the profit, but I have the advantage of acting rightly').

Political oratory is more difficult than forensic, reasonably enough, since it concerns the future and forensic oratory the past, which is already known even to prophets, as Epimenides the Cretan said (he did not produce divination about the future, but only about things past but lost in obscurity). Another reason is that the law provides the first premiss in forensic argument, and given the starting-point it is easier to find a demonstrative proof. Moreover, political oratory does not offer many chances of wasting time, in talking, for example, against one's adversary or about oneself or producing emotional effects; indeed it offers less than any other kind, unless it departs from its proper nature. So if one is short of matter one should do what the speakers at Athens do and also Isocrates;

in giving political advice he produces an accusation, of the Spartans, for instance, in the *Panegyricus*,[1] of Chares in the speech *On the Alliance*.[2] In epideictic oratory one should divide the speech into acts by laudations as Isocrates does; he is perpetually introducing some person or other. And what Gorgias said, that he was never at a loss for something to say, comes to the same; if his subject is Achilles, he praises his father, his grandfather, his divine great-grandfather, and also courage, which produces such and such effects or is a quality of such and such a kind.

When one has demonstrative arguments one should display one's character as well as produce arguments, while if you have no inferences to produce, you should just express character; and indeed it is more suitable to a good man to give an impression of virtue than produce a speech exactly argued.

1418[b]

Of inferences those that refute find more favour than those that prove something, because those that produce refutation more clearly show syllogistic reasoning, since opposites are better recognized when set beside each other.

2. *Refutation*

The refutation of one's adversary is not a separate element; to refute some of his case by producing a contrary proposition, some by reasoning, is part of the argument. Both in political and in forensic oratory one should, if one is the opening speaker, state one's own arguments first, and later meet the opponent's arguments by refutation, i.e. by pulling them to pieces before he produces them. If the opposition is very diversified, you should begin with the opponent's case, as Callistratus did in the Messenian assembly; he stated his own case only after destroying beforehand the arguments they were going to use. If one speaks second, one should deal first with the opponent's case, refuting it and producing counter-reasonings, most especially if it has found favour; the mind refuses a welcome to a man against whom prejudice has been created, and similarly to an argument, if the opponent is thought to have spoken well. So one should make room in the hearer for the speech that is to come, and this you will do if you destroy the arguments against you; that is why one should try to make one's own case convincing only after combating all or the most important or the most favourably received or the most easily refuted on the other side ('First I shall speak in the goddesses' defence; I think that Hera . . .';[3] with these words she attacked first the silliest opposing argument).

So much for arguments.

[1] §§ 110 ff.   [2] *De Pace* 27.   [3] Eur. *Troades* 969 f.

3. Character[1]

So far as character goes, it is invidious, long-winded, or open to contradiction to say some things about oneself, and abusive or boorish to say some things about other people; one should therefore ascribe them to another speaker, as Isocrates does in the *Philip*[2] and the *Antidosis*,[3] and as Archilochus[4] does in invective, where he makes the father speak of his daughter in the lampoon beginning 'Nothing is unexpected, nothing one would take one's oath will not happen', and introduces the carpenter Charon in that beginning 'Not Gyges' wealth for me'. Similarly Sophocles' Haemon defends Antigone against his father by citing other speakers.[5]

One should also occasionally change the form of one's inferences and express them as general maxims, for example, 'Men of sense should make peace when they are successful, as that would bring them the greatest gains' (in the form of an inference this would be 'If one should make peace when the peace would be most useful and bring most gain, one should make it when one is successful').

4. Interrogation

18   As for interrogation, the most advantageous occasion for its use is when
1419ᵃ your opponent has stated one [of two contradictory propositions], so
that with one further question an absurdity will result. For instance, when Pericles questioned Lampon about initiation into the rites of Demeter and Lampon said it was impossible for the uninitiated to be told, Pericles asked if he knew them himself, and when he said yes, continued 'And how, when you are not initiated?' The second best is when one premiss of an inference is obvious and it is clear that he will grant the other if questioned; one should ask him about the one premiss and not proceed to a question about the obvious one, but simply state the conclusion. An example is Socrates' question when Meletus denied that he recognized gods but said that he spoke of a *daimonion*; he asked whether the *daimones* were either children of gods or something divine, and when he said 'Yes', went on, 'Well, is there anyone who thinks there are children of gods but no gods?'[6] A third case is where one means to show that one's opponent is saying something self-contradictory or paradoxical. A fourth where he can resolve the difficulty only by a sophistic answer; if he gives such a reply, like 'It is and it isn't', 'Sometimes yes, sometimes no', or 'In some ways yes, in some ways no', the audience shout him down and

---

[1] This and the following two sections are appendices to the discussion of argument.
[2] 4 ff., 23.   [3] 141 ff.   [4] Frs. 74 and 22 Diehl.
[5] *Antigone* 688 ff.   [6] Plato, *Apology* 27 d.

think he is at a loss. Otherwise do not attempt it, as if he resists you will be thought to have been defeated, since one cannot ask many questions because of the feebleness of the audience. That is why one should try to make one's inferences, too, as compact as possible.

In answering, you should meet ambiguous questions with a developed distinction, not a concise one, and deal with supposed contradictions by producing the solution straight away in your reply, before he asks the next question and proceeds to the conclusion, as it is quite easy in some cases to foresee what he will say. Both this and the forms of solution are clear to us from the *Topics*. And when he draws the conclusion, if he puts it in the form of a question, one should give the explanation, as Sophocles did when Pisander asked if he, like the other *probouloi*, had assented to the establishment of the Four Hundred. 'Yes', he said. 'Well then, did you think this wrong?' 'Yes.' 'So you committed this wrong act?' 'Yes, as there was no better one possible.' Or like the Spartan being examined on his ephorate and asked if he thought the condemnation of his colleagues had been fair: 'Yes', he replied. 'Did you concur in their actions?' 'Yes.' 'Then would it not be fair to condemn you too?' 'Certainly not', he said. 'They did it for bribes, I because I thought it best.' That is why one should not ask another question after stating the con- 1419ᵇ clusion nor put the conclusion itself in the form of a question, unless there is a tremendous surplus of truth on your side.

5. Jokes

So far as jokes go, they are thought to have some use in actual debate, and Gorgias rightly said that one should ruin one's opponent's seriousness with laughter and his laughter with seriousness. Jokes are to be found classified in the *Poetics*,[1] some of them suitable for a gentleman, some not, so that one can choose what suits one. Irony is more gentlemanly than buffoonery, as the ironical man makes a jest for his own amusement, the buffoon for another's.

SECTION E. THE EPILOGUE

The epilogue is composed of four elements: they are making the hearer 19 well-disposed towards oneself and the contrary towards one's opponent, amplification and belittling, rousing emotion in the hearer, recapitulating. It is natural that one should first prove one's own truth and one's opponent's falsehood, and then go on to praise, blame, and hammer the point

---

[1] In the lost second book.

home. [In the first of the four] one should aim at one of two things, being thought good by this jury or being thought good without qualification (and also at making your opponent seem bad to them or bad without qualification). The sources from which one can produce this impression have been stated, that is, the topics basic to producing an impression of goodness or badness. The next thing, when the proof is over, is naturally amplification or belittling, since the facts must be admitted before one can assign a particular importance to them, just as bodily growth is growth from what was there before. The sources of amplification and belittling have also been stated previously. After this, when it is clear what the facts are and how important, is the time to produce emotion in the hearer. These emotions are pity, indignation, anger, hatred, envy, emulation, quarrelsomeness. The sources of these have also been previously described, so that the remaining subject is the recapitulation. The suitable place for this is not the proem, as usually but wrongly recommended (we are urged to be repetitive there so as to make the hearer receptive). Well now, in the proem one should state the subject, so as to make the hearer aware what his decision is about, and in the epilogue the various proofs of it, in a summary way. The starting-point is that one has performed what one promised, and so one must say what and why. This is sometimes based on a comparison with your adversary. One can compare what both have said on the same subject, either directly ('But he said this about that, while I said this other thing and for the following reasons'), or ironically 1420ª ('He said this, I that' and 'What would he have done if he had proved this rather than that?'), or in question form ('Well then, what has been proved?' or 'What has *he* proved?'). Either then one can do it this way via comparison or in the natural order as it was said, recapitulating one's own argument and in turn, if one likes, stating separately what one's opponent said. As the ending of the speech an asyndeton is suitable, something to finish off the speech, not make another one: 'I have said my say, you have heard it all, it is in your hands, give your judgements.'

4

DEMETRIUS *ON STYLE*

INTRODUCTION

(i) ANALYSIS

On Style may be summarized as follows:

1–35:[1] the structure of sentences—clauses and periods.
36–304: the four styles, each followed by a brief account of its corresponding faulty style:

Each style is analysed under the same three headings of diction, word-arrangement, and subject-matter; additional topics then follow. In the grand style, for example, we find grandeur from arrangement, subject-matter, and diction in 38–102, extra topics in 103–13. Similarly in the plain style the analysis under these three headings in 190–208 is followed by the accounts of vividness, persuasiveness, and the style of letters in 209–35, and in the forceful style subject-matter, composition, and diction in 240–76 are followed by a series of topics, for example, oblique allusion and the three categories of style in 287–98. The one exception is the elegant style: ostensibly we find the three headings of diction (137–55), subject-matter (156–62), and arrangement (179–85) but in 136 and 156 only two headings are recognized and the account of diction includes topics from arrangement (e.g. figures of speech in 140–1). The style is logically analysed as follows:

  (i) 128–35: the forms of charm.
  (ii) 136–62: the sources of charm: style and subject-matter.
(iii) 163–85: additional topics, of which the last is elegant arrangement—as if it had not been realized that arrangement had already been discussed with diction.

    This irregular structure is partly a result of the fact that the elegant style

---

[1] The numbering is sixteenth-century. In the translation these numbers appear in the margin, the paragraphing and sub-titling are the translator's.

contains two concepts, graceful charm and witty charm, partly of the adoption not only of material from a work on wit but the traditional twofold classification of wit under style and content (e.g. Cicero, *de Oratore* 2. 248).

(ii) AUTHORSHIP AND DATE

The author is unknown. We must reject the medieval attribution to Demetrius of Phaleron on grounds of chronology and style, but the author may well have been called Demetrius: it was a common name and would readily be associated with its most famous literary holder, Demetrius of Phaleron. Alternatively *On Style* was anonymous and ascribed to Demetrius of Phaleron because of its Peripatetic sympathies.

This sympathy for the Peripatetic school is the only probable fact we have about the author. The only authorities named are either Peripatetics (Aristotle, Theophrastus, and Praxiphanes) or unknown critics cited in connection with Aristotle (Archedemus in 34, Artemon in 223). Aristotle's influence is also frequent without direct acknowledgement: for example, the choice of the term 'frigid' in preference to the regular 'tumid' or 'swollen' to describe the fault adjacent to grandeur derives from *Rhetoric* 3. 38 (above, p. 140).

The date is uncertain and the subject of much controversy. Since there is no extant reference to the work in other writers before the fourth century A.D., we have to rely on internal evidence; but early material does not prove an early date because of the strong conservative tendency in rhetoric and in handbooks generally. There is the added complication that handbooks were open to later insertions or modifications, so that one part suggesting a late date need not necessarily prove that the work as a whole is also late. In its present form, however, *On Style* cannot be earlier than 275 B.C. (see especially the mention of the Sotadean metre in 189) and almost certainly precedes Dionysius of Halicarnassus, since it is a natural inference from 179 that Demetrius did not know of Dionysius' account of elegant word-arrangement. A date earlier than the first century A.D. also fits the subsidiary role played by Demosthenes, the supreme model in all styles of writing in critics like Dionysius but virtually confined in Demetrius to the forceful style of oratorical attack. More precise dating is probably impossible but the first century B.C. is, I think, at least consistent with the evidence of language and style.

(iii) MERITS AND DEFECTS

This unpretentious handbook can make no claim to originality but possesses much interest. It preserves much material not otherwise known to us, for example, the basic scheme of four styles. A system of three styles, grand, plain, and middle or flowery,[1] was more common, and though there are occasional references to other systems, *On Style* is the only practical illustration of this variety. More important perhaps, Demetrius gives us the only detailed and

[1] See below, pp. 240 ff.

systematic account of these styles still extant. Again, he is one of our few sources on wit and laughter and his account of letter-writing in 223–35 is especially valuable as an aid to understanding a minor but interesting genre of ancient literature.

The author has also some perhaps more positive merits. His comments are generally sensible and show sensitivity to the Greek language, for example his account of letters and the use of poetic vocabulary in 113–14. His style is admittedly plain and matter-of-fact, reminiscent of the schoolroom in its frequent summarizing and occasional repetitions; but there are no arid lists of stylistic devices such as figures of speech and the style is enlivened by short analogies such as the fine reference to the Mysteries in 101 (compare, for example, 58, 62, and 108) and proverbs (e.g. 28, 112, 119, and 297). In particular he illustrates his comments with frequent and usually apt examples from a strikingly wide range of authors, both verse and prose; these examples are then frequently rewritten by Demetrius to reinforce his argument. He is, moreover, not primarily interested in oratory, unlike so many other extant accounts—indeed he even shows an engaging interest in strictly irrelevant subjects, as in the Egyptians' songs in 71, musical words in 176–7, and dramatic technique in 195. In short, he is not an original thinker like Aristotle but neither is he a mere dry rhetorician.

Editions

L. Radermacher (text, notes), Teubner, 1901, reprinted 1966.
W. Rhys Roberts (text, translation, notes), Cambridge, 1902.

T. A. Moxon (translation), Everyman library, London, 1934.
G. M. A. Grube (translation, useful introduction), Toronto, 1961.
D. M. Schenkeveld, *Studies in Demetrius on Style*, Amsterdam, 1964 (includes a recent bibliography).
G. M. A. Grube, *The Greek and Roman Critics*, London, 1965, pp. 110–21.

ON STYLE

THE STRUCTURE OF SENTENCES: CLAUSES

Just as poetry is divided by metres such as the short metres,[1] hexameters,   1 and the like, prose is divided and articulated by what are called clauses (*cōla*). These may be said to offer rests for both the speaker and the subject itself and set frequent bounds to the discourse, which would otherwise prove long and unending and simply run the speaker out of breath. It is the function of these clauses to mark the conclusion   2 of a thought, sometimes a whole thought, as in the opening words of

---

[1] *Hemimetra*: I take this as meaning, e.g., the short epodic metres of Archilochus (cf. 5), but text and interpretation have been questioned.

Hecataeus' history, 'Hecataeus of Miletus relates as follows', where a complete thought is comprised in one complete clause and both come to an end together. In other cases the clause does not constitute a complete thought but only a part which is itself complete. For if it is of some length a complete thought may contain parts which are themselves complete, just as an arm is itself a complete whole but has parts which are also complete, such as the fingers and forearm (for each of these parts has

3 its own contour and component parts). Take, for example, the beginning of Xenophon's *Anabasis*: 'Darius and Parysatis had sons, the elder Artaxerxes, the younger Cyrus.' This is all one complete thought but its two clauses are each a part of it and each brings to a conclusion a thought which forms a distinct unit: in the case of 'Darius and Parysatis had sons' the thought that Darius and Parysatis had children has its own completeness, and the same is true of the second clause, 'the elder Artaxerxes, the younger Cyrus'. I hold, then, that a clause will in all circumstances comprise a thought, either a complete thought or a complete part of one.

4 Clauses should not be made very long, since the sentence then lacks due measure and is hard to follow. Even poetry only very exceptionally exceeds the length of the hexameter: for it would be ridiculous if metre lacked due measure and at the end of a line we had forgotten when it began. Long clauses, then, are unsuitable in prose because they lack due measure, but the same is true of short clauses, since the sentences become what is called arid, as in the following example: 'Life is short, art long, time fleeting.'[1] The sentence seems abrupt and fragmented and makes a

5 poor impression because all its parts are small. Yet sometimes a long clause is in place, for example to describe grand themes such as Plato's 'For all this universe is sometimes escorted and helped to revolve on its course by the god himself'.[2] The elevation of the passage matches the length of the clause. It is also for this reason of length that the hexameter is called the heroic metre and is suitable for heroes. It would not be fitting to write Homer's *Iliad* in the short metres of Archilochus, such as 'sorrowful staff' and 'who stole your wits?', nor yet in those of Anacreon, as in 'bring water, bring wine, lad':[3] that rhythm suits to perfection a drunken old man, but not a hero in battle.

6 Just as we have seen how a long clause may sometimes be suitable, there may also be occasions for a short one, for example when our subject is small, as in Xenophon's description of the Greeks' arrival at the river

---

[1] Hippocrates, *Aphorism* I. 1. The sentence continues on the same lines: 'experience dangerous, judgement difficult'.

[2] Plato, *Politicus* 269 c.

[3] Archilochus, frr. 89 and 94 Bergk; Anacreon, *Poetae Melici Graeci* 396 Page.

Teleboas:[1] 'It was not large, beautiful though.' The short, broken rhythm mirrors the river's smallness and charm. If he had expanded the sentence to say 'in size it fell short of most other rivers but in beauty it surpassed them all', he would have shown bad judgement and the passage would have become what is called frigid—but we must discuss frigidity later.[2] Short clauses may also be used in the forceful style, since much expressed 7 briefly gives added force and pungency. This forcefulness is the reason why the Spartans use words sparingly. Commands too are succinct and concise and every master is monosyllabic to his slave, whereas supplications and laments are prolix and Homer describes the Prayers[3] as lame and wrinkled because of their slowness, that is to say their loquacity; old men are similarly loquacious because they are frail. An example of such 8 brevity is 'Sparta to Philip: Dionysius in Corinth'.[4] This compressed message is much more forceful than if the Spartans had expanded it and said: 'Though Dionysius was once, like you, a great tyrant, he is now living as a private citizen in Corinth.' Set out in full it no longer resembles a threat but a piece of narrative and suggests an author imparting information, not instilling fear. The amplification weakens the vigour and strength of the passage and, just as wild beasts coil themselves before they attack, the spoken word should also draw itself taut to form a sort of coil for forceful impact.

This kind of brevity in sentences is called a phrase[5] and a phrase is 9 defined as being shorter than a clause, as in the above example, 'Dionysius in Corinth', and the maxims of the sages, 'know yourself' and 'follow god'. Brevity fits proverbs and adages and it shows considerable skill to compress much meaning into a few words, just as seeds contain the potentiality of whole trees. Express a maxim at length and it becomes instead a mere statement and empty rhetoric.

THE STRUCTURE OF SENTENCES: PERIODS

From the combination of such clauses and phrases are formed what are 10 called periods. A period is a combination of clauses and phrases which has brought the underlying thought to a conclusion with a neatly turned ending, as in this example: 'It was especially because I thought it in the interest of the state for the law to be repealed and secondly because of

---

[1] *Anabasis* 4. 4. 3. The same point is made in 121 below.
[2] See 114 ff. on the frigid style.
[3] *Iliad* 9. 502 ff.
[4] Cf. 102 below. Dionysius became tyrant of Syracuse in 367 B.C.
[5] 'Phrase' is an inadequate rendering of the Greek 'komma', which, like the clause, refers to a complete thought.

Chabrias' son that I have agreed to be, to the best of my ability, my clients' advocate.'[1] This period, formed from three clauses, has a sort of twist and concentration at the end. This is Aristotle's definition of the period: 'A period is a sentence with a beginning and end'[2]—a very good and appropriate definition. For by saying 'period' we immediately imply that it has a beginning, will have an ending, and is hurrying to a definite goal, just like runners when the race has begun, since from the beginning of the race they too have the goal in view.[3] Hence the term 'period', an image from paths which form a circle or ring. More generally, the period is but a certain kind of word-arrangement, as we see if a sentence expressed in periodic form is broken up and given a different arrangement: the content remains the same but the period will cease to exist. Suppose we turned round the period cited above from Demosthenes and said: 'I shall be my clients' advocate, Athenians; for the son of Chabrias is dear to me, and much dearer still is the state, whose interests it is right for me to defend.' The period is now lost.

12   The origin of the period is as follows. One kind of style is called the neatly-ended style, such as the wholly periodic style found in the rhetorical artifices of Isocrates' school, Gorgias, and Alcidamas, where period succeeds period no less regularly than the hexameters in the poetry of Homer. The other style is called the disjointed style and consists of loosely related clauses with little interlocking, as in Hecataeus, most of Herodotus, and all the early writers generally. Take this example: 'Hecataeus of Miletus relates as follows. I write of these things as I believe them to be true. For the stories of the Greeks are, it seems to me, both many and absurd.' The clauses seem to be piled one on top of the other and thrown together without any integration and interdependence and they do not

13   give the mutual support found in periods. Periodic clauses are in fact like stones which uphold rounded domes by their mutual support and dependence, while the clauses of the disconnected style resemble stones which are merely thrown down near one another and not fitted together.

14   It is this characteristic which gives early style the sharp outlines and neatness of early statues, when sculptors strove for compactness and spareness, while later style corresponds to the works of Phidias in the

15   combination of nobility and finish.[4] I myself consider that speech should be neither wholly a string of periods, as in Gorgias, nor wholly discon-

---

[1] Demosthenes, *Against Leptines* 1. The passage recurs in 20.

[2] Aristotle, *Rhetoric* 3. 9, 1409^{a}35: see above, p. 148.

[3] In the *diaulos* or two-lap race the runner ran back from the end of the first lap towards the starting-point again. The comparison is particularly apt since the Greek word 'periodos' means literally 'a path brought round'.

[4] For the rare chronological comparison to sculpture compare Cicero, *Brutus* 70 and Quint. 12. 10. 1–9 (below, pp. 404–6).

nected, as in the early writers, but a combination of the two. Then it will have both artistic finish and simplicity and from the presence of both it will be pleasing, neither too rude nor too artificial. As for those who use periods uninterruptedly, even their own heads reel and they seem intoxicated, while the audience feels nauseated by the implausibility and finds the end of each sentence so inevitable that they sometimes forestall them by shouting it aloud.

The smaller periods consist of two clauses, the longest of four. Anything beyond four would exceed the proper proportions of the period. There are also some of three clauses, while some have only one and are called simple periods. Whenever a clause has some length and a twist at the end, it becomes a single-clause period, as in this example, 'The results of the inquiries of Herodotus of Halicarnassus are here set forth',[1] or again 'Clear language brings great illumination to the hearer's mind'. Both characteristics of the simple period are essential, length and the twist at the end; one alone is not enough. In compound periods the last clause should be longer and, as it were, envelop and encompass the others.[2] Then the period will be grand and stately, since it ends on a long, stately clause; otherwise it is abrupt and seems to limp. Here is an example: 'Nobility lies not in noble words but in following noble words with deeds.'[3]

There are three forms of period, the historical, the dialogue, and the rhetorical. The historical is neither too well-rounded nor too loose but between the two, so that it does not seem rhetorical and unconvincing because of its rounding but has the dignity suitable for history from its simplicity, as in the sentence 'Darius and Parysatis' down to 'the younger Cyrus',[4] where the closing phrase seems to halt on a firmly secured and safe ending. The rhetorical period has a taut, circular form, requiring a firm utterance and gestures which are in accordance with the rounded structure, as in the sentence: 'It was especially because I thought it in the interest of the state for the law to be repealed and secondly because of Chabrias' son that I have agreed to be, to the best of my ability, my clients' advocate.'[5] From almost its very beginning such a period has a tautness which suggests that it will not run on to end simply. The dialogue period is one which is still looser and simpler than the historical period and is scarcely seen to be a period, as in the following example: 'I went down to the Piraeus yesterday with Glaucon, the son of Ariston, partly to offer

16

17

18

19

20

21

---

[1] Herodotus 1. 1. The author of the second example is unknown.

[2] A principle quite commonly followed in ancient prose, especially in 'tricolon crescendo', where three clauses appear with increasing length.

[3] Author unknown.   [4] Cf. above, 3.

[5] Demosthenes 20. 1. Cf. above, 10.

prayers to the goddess, but partly also because I wanted to watch the ceremony to see how they would conduct it, since this was its first celebration.'[1] The clauses have been thrown one on top of the other, as in the disconnected style, and when we stop at the end we barely realize that the sentence is a period. The dialogue period should be written in a manner midway between the disjointed and neatly-ended styles, forming a combination which draws from both. These, then, are the three forms of period.

ANTITHESIS AND SIMILARITY IN CLAUSES

22 Periods are also formed from clauses in antithesis. These may be antithetical either in content, as in 'sailing over the land and marching over the sea',[2] or in two respects, content and language, as in the case of this 23 same period. There are also clauses with purely verbal antithesis, as in this comparison of Helen to Heracles: 'For the one he created a life full of labour and danger, in the other he formed a beauty surrounded by admiration and strife.'[3] There is antithesis of article to article, connective to connective, like to like throughout, with correspondence of 'created' to 'formed', 'labour' to 'admiration', 'danger' to 'strife', in fact like matches 24 like at every point. We also find clauses which are not antithetical but have an apparent antithesis because they are shaped in an antithetical pattern, as in the playful words of the poet Epicharmus:

Now I was in their house, now in their company.[4]

The same idea is expressed twice and there is no real contrast, but the structure of the sentence, with its imitation of an antithesis, looks like an attempt to mislead; but perhaps Epicharmus used this antithetical form for its ludicrous effect and to ridicule the rhetoricians.

25 There are also closely similar clauses, some with the similarity at the beginning, as in

Presents could buy them, prayers could move them,[5]

others at the end, as at the beginning of the *Panegyricus*: 'I have often marvelled at the men by whom assemblies are constituted and athletic games instituted.'[6] Another form of similarity is the isocolon, where two clauses have the same number of syllables, as in Thucydides: 'Neither

---

[1] The opening words of Plato's *Republic*. Cf. Dionysius, below, p. 341.
[2] Isocrates, *Panegyricus* 89.
[3] Isocrates, *Praise of Helen* 17.   [4] Fr. 147 Kaibel.
[5] Homer, *Iliad* 9. 526.
[6] Isocrates, *Panegyricus* 1. Cf. above, p. 149.

did those questioned disclaim the deed nor did those concerned to know censure it.'¹ This, then, is isocolon. Homoeoteleuton occurs in clauses 26 with similar endings, either of the same word, as in 'When he was alive you would speak of him slightingly, now that he is dead you write of him slightingly',² or of the same final syllable, as in the *Panegyricus* passage above.

The use of such clauses is risky. They do not suit forceful speech, since 27 the artifice and premeditation destroy any forcefulness, as is clear from this example in Theopompus' invective against the friends of Philip: 'Slayers of men by nature, sleeping with men by habit, they were called his men but were really his women.'³ The balanced structure and antithesis destroy the forcefulness by their misplaced artifice. Anger has no need of artifice and the style of such invectives should seem spontaneous and natural. But if, as I have shown, such clauses do not suit forceful 28 speech, they are also alien to the expression of the passionate or milder emotions.⁴ Strong passion is essentially simple and unaffected, and the same is true of the milder emotions. Take the passage from Aristotle's *On Justice* where the speaker grieves for the city of Athens.⁵ If he were to say 'What city did they ever take from the enemy as great as their own city which they had lost?', he would have spoken with passion and grief. But if he used balanced clauses to say 'What city of the enemy had they constrained as great as their own which they had not retained?', he will assuredly excite neither passion nor pity but what are called tears of laughter. In fact the proverb, 'to jest among mourners', sums up such misapplied artifice in emotional contexts. Yet sometimes these devices 29 are useful, as in Aristotle: 'I went from Athens to Stagira because of the great king and from Stagira to Athens because of the great winter.'⁶ If you remove the second 'great', you will also remove the charm. Such clauses may also contribute towards a nobility of expression, as do many antitheses in Gorgias and Isocrates. So much, then, on similar clauses.

DIFFERENCE BETWEEN PERIOD AND ENTHYMEME

The enthymeme differs from the period in that the period is a rounded 30 form of sentence-structure (hence its name), whereas it is the content which gives the enthymeme its function and existence. The period may give rounded form to an enthymeme just as it can to any subject but the enthymeme is a thought which draws a conclusion either from a

---

¹ Thuc. I. 5.   ² Author unknown. It recurs in 211.
³ Fr. 249 Mueller. Compare 75 and 240.
⁴ *Pathos* and *ēthos*: compare Quint. 6. 2. 8 ff.   ⁵ Fr. 82 Rose
⁶ Cf. 154 below. Aristotle, fr. 669 Rose.

31 contradiction or in the form of a logical consequence.[1] In proof of this assertion, if you broke up the structure of an enthymeme, you would destroy any periodic form but the enthymeme remains untouched. Suppose, for example, we broke up this enthymeme of Demosthenes: 'Just as you would not have sponsored this bill if any of them had been convicted, no one else will in the future if you are convicted now.'[2] Let us break it up: 'Do not be lenient to sponsors of unconstitutional bills; for if they were always stopped, the defendant would not be sponsoring this bill now, nor will anyone else sponsor them in the future if he is convicted now.' Here the circular form of the period is broken up but the enthymeme

32 remains as it was. In general terms, the enthymeme is a rhetorical syllogism, whereas the period is not a form of argumentation but merely a particular sentence-structure. We also use periods in all the sections of a speech, for example in introductions, but we do not use enthymemes everywhere. The enthymeme is, as it were, an additional comment, the period is simply a form of words. The former is a sort of imperfect

33 syllogism, the latter involves no syllogism, perfect or imperfect. The enthymeme has the accidental property of being a period if it is expressed in periodic form but it is not itself a period, just as a white building has the accidental property of whiteness but buildings are not always white. This concludes my discussion of the difference between the enthymeme and the period.

ADDITIONAL COMMENT ON ARISTOTLE'S DEFINITION OF THE CLAUSE

34 This is Aristotle's definition of a clause: 'A clause is one of the two parts of a period.' He then adds: 'There is also the simple period.'[3] By 'one of the two parts' in his definition he clearly signifies a period of only two clauses. Archedemus[4] combined Aristotle's definition and additional comment to produce a clearer and more correct definition: 'A clause is

35 either a simple period or part of a composite period.' I have explained the simple period already; but in saying 'part of a composite period' it would seem that Archedemus does not limit the period to two clauses but allows three or more. I have given my views on the proper limits of the period: let us now turn to describe the types of style.

---

[1] On the two types of enthymeme compare Aristotle, *Rhetoric* 2. 22, 1396^{b}25 and Quint. 5. 14. 4. The first refutes the opponent, the second proves something from agreed premisses.

[2] *Against Aristocrates* 99.

[3] *Rhetoric* 3. 9, 1409^{b}16: cf. above, p. 148.

[4] No identification is possible.

THE FOUR STYLES

There are four primary styles, plain, grand, elegant, and forceful. There 36
are also styles formed from combinations of these, though not every
combination is possible: the elegant style combines with the plain and the
grand, likewise the forceful with the same two, but—the one exception—a
mixture of the grand and plain styles is impossible, since the two stand,
as it were, diametrically opposed to each other in permanent conflict.
This is in fact why some people claim that only these two styles exist
and that the other two are contained within them; for they classify the
elegant under the plain style and the forceful under the grand on the
grounds that the elegant style involves an element of triviality and
daintiness, the forceful style weight and majesty. But this line of argument 37
is absurd. It ignores the fact that, with the exception of the two extremes
already mentioned, every combination of styles is possible. In the epic
poetry of Homer, for example, and the prose of Plato, Xenophon, Herodotus, and many other authors there is a considerable element of grandeur
but also a considerable element of forcefulness and charm. We must, then,
recognize our original number of four styles, each with an appropriate
form of expression which I shall now describe.

THE GRAND STYLE, BEGINNING WITH WORD-ARRANGEMENT: RHYTHM, CLAUSES, PERIODS, HARSH JUXTAPOSITION, WORD-ORDER

I shall begin with grandeur, the quality which men now term true 38
eloquence. Grandeur springs from three sources, thought, diction, and
appropriate word-arrangement. In arrangement grandeur is, as Aristotle[1]
says, given by the use of paeonic rhythm. There are two kinds of paeon,
the initial paeon formed by one long syllable followed by three shorts
(e.g. *ērxătŏ dě*)[2] and, the reverse of this, the final paeon formed by three
short syllables and one long (e.g. *Ărăbĭā*). In the clauses of the grand style 39
the initial type of paeon should stand at the beginning, the terminal type
later, as in this example from Thucydides:

$$- \cup \cup \cup \qquad\qquad \cup\cup\cup -$$

ērxato de to kakon ex Aithiopias.[3]

Why did Aristotle give this advice? Simply because a note of grandeur
should be struck immediately at the very beginning of the clause and again

---

[1] *Rhetoric* 3. 8, especially 1408ᵇ32 ff. (above, p. 146).
[2] Thuc. 2. 48, 'it originated'.
[3] Thuc. 2. 48, 'the disease originated in Ethiopia'.

at the end, as is the case if we begin and end on a long syllable. For a long syllable is of its nature imposing. Put at the beginning it has an immediate impact, while at the end it leaves the reader with an impression of grandeur. We all remember particularly what comes first or last and are moved by it, while the intervening part has less force and is, as it 40 were, dimmed and outshone. This is evident in the case of Thucydides, where it is almost entirely the use of heavy rhythms which lends him grandeur throughout and, although he has grandeur of every kind, it is perhaps on his arrangement alone or for the most part that his greatest distinction depends.

41   We should, however, bear in mind that, even if we cannot give the beginning and end of our clauses initial and final paeons respectively in their exact form, we should at any rate make our sentences roughly paeonic, for example by beginning and ending with more than one long syllable. It would seem that this is what Aristotle himself intends and that he described the two kinds of paeon in technical language merely for the sake of exactitude. This is why Theophrastus can set down the following clause as an example of grandeur:

$$- \ - \ \smile\smile\smile \ -\smile\smile \ -\smile\smile \ \smile\smile\smile \ - \ -$$
tōn men peri ta mēdenos axia philosophountōn.[1]

It does not consist of paeons in the exact sense but is roughly paeonic.

The reason why the paeon should be adopted in prose is the element of safety provided by its mixture of long and short syllables. The long syllable 42 lends grandeur, the shorts suitability for prose. If we look at the other rhythms, the heroic rhythm is dignified but too sonorous for prose and not only an unsuitable rhythm but no rhythm at all when it has only long syllables,[2] as in *hēkōn hēmōn eīs tēn chōrān* ['arrived inside our land'], where the accumulation of long syllables goes beyond the limits of prose. 43 The iambic rhythm is undistinguished and like our everyday speech—in fact many people use iambics unconsciously in conversation. The paeon, however, forms a happy mean between the two with its elements of both. This, then, is how paeonic rhythm should be used in passages of grandeur.

44   Long clauses also create grandeur, as in 'Thucydides the Athenian composed this history of the war between the Peloponnesians and Athenians' and 'The results of the inquiries of Herodotus of Halicarnassus are here set forth'.[3] To stop abruptly on a short clause undermines the dignity of a passage, even if there is grandeur in the underlying thought and diction.

[1] 'Those who philosophize about trivialities.'
[2] Text uncertain. The example recurs, in longer form, in 117. The author is unknown.
[3] The opening words of the histories of Thucydides and Herodotus respectively.

Sentences formed with a periodic structure are also impressive, as in 45
Thucydides: 'The river Achelous, which flows from Mount Pindus
through Dolopia and the territory of the Agrianians and Amphilochians
and passes inland by the city of Stratus before running into the sea at
Oeniadae and surrounding the city with marshes, because of its volume
of water makes it impossible to start military operations in winter.'[1] The
grandeur derives entirely from the periodic structure and the fact that it
scarcely allows Thucydides or the reader to pause. If you were to break 46
it up and rewrite it as follows: 'The river Achelous flows from Mount
Pindus and has its outlet into the sea at Oeniadae, but before this outlet it
transforms the plain of Oeniadae into a marsh, with the result that the
water forms a protection and barrier against winter invasions from their
enemies'—rewritten in this form the passage will have many pauses but
the grandeur will be lost. In fact, just as frequent halts make a long 47
journey short, while deserted roads even over a short distance have an
illusion of length, exactly the same illusion is produced in sentences.

Another frequent source of grandeur is harsh-sounding juxtaposition, 48
as in

Aias d' ho megas aien ep' Hektori khalkokorustē,[2]
'Ajax, strong in might, aimed always at Hector of the bronze helmet.'

In other respects the clashing letters are perhaps discordant but they
bring out extraordinarily well the hero's might. Smoothness and euphony
have little place in the grand style, except very occasionally, and Thucydides almost without exception avoids a smooth, even flow of words and
always seems rather to stumble along, like men negotiating rough paths,
as in this example: 'The year, it was agreed, from all other illness was,
as it happened, free.'[3] It would be easier and more euphonious to say
'happened to be free' but the grandeur would be lost. Harsh word- 49
arrangement creates in fact the same effect of grandeur as intrinsically
harsh words such as 'shrieking' instead of 'calling' and 'bursting forth'
instead of 'moving along', the sort of words which Thucydides uses,
accommodating the words to his arrangement and the arrangement to
his words.

The order of the words should be such that the less vivid come first, 50
the more vivid second and last. Then the first word will sound vivid to us
but the next still more vivid, whereas on the opposite order we would
seem to lose strength and fall away, as it were, from strength to weakness.
Here is an example from Plato: 'When a man lets music sway him and 51
stream through his ears.' The second verb is much more vivid than the

---

[1] Thuc. 2. 102. Cf. 202.   [2] Homer, *Iliad* 16. 358. Cf. 105.
[3] Thuc. 2. 49.

first. Again, in the same passage: 'Yet, when the stream of music is not restrained but bewitches him, after that point his spirit melts and spills forth.'[1] Here 'spills forth' is stronger than 'melts' and closer to poetry. If Plato had put it first, 'melts' in second position would have seemed rather weak. Homer similarly heightens the hyperbole continually in his
52 account of the Cyclops and seems to climb ever higher:

> He did not resemble
> men who eat bread, but a wooded peak,

one which is, furthermore, a high mountain, towering above its neighbours.[2] The grandeur of each successive part is overtaken by something still greater.

CONNECTIVES

53 Connective particles such as *men* and *de*[3] should not answer each other too exactly. Exactitude is petty and we should cultivate instead a certain negligence, such as we find in this passage of Antiphon: 'The island *on the one hand* which we inhabit is visibly *on the one hand* high and rugged even from a distance, its productive *on the one hand* and arable area is small, its unproductive area *on the other hand* large for such a small
54 island.'[4] Here one *de* answers three instances of *men*. Often too a chain of connectives exalts even small things, for example the names of the Boeotian towns in Homer: of no account and unimpressive in themselves, they take on weight and grandeur from a great chain of connectives, as in:

> *and* Schoenus *and* Scolus *and* mountainous Eteonus.[5]

55 Expletive particles should not be used as empty fillers and, as it were, alien growths or extra chippings to fill cracks, though this is the aimless manner in which some people use 'indeed' and 'now', but only if they
56 increase the grandeur of what is being said, as in Plato's 'And indeed mighty Zeus in heaven' and Homer's

> But when indeed they came to the ford of the fair-flowing river.[6]

By forming a fresh start and wrenching what follows away from what precedes, the particle has created a stately effect, since many fresh starts achieve dignity. If Homer had said:

> But when they reached the ford of the river,

---

[1] *Republic* 411 a–b.   [2] *Odyssey* 9. 190–2.
[3] i.e. 'on the one hand' (*men*) and 'but on the other hand' (*de*).
[4] Fr. 50 Blass.   [5] *Iliad* 2. 497.
[6] Plato, *Phaedrus* 246 e and Homer, *Iliad* 14. 433 (also 21. 1).

the sentence would have seemed insignificant and a mere continuation
of the preceding narrative.

A particle may often be used to express emotion, as in Calypso's words 57
to Odysseus:

> ˙ Descendant of Zeus, son of Laertes, guileful Odysseus,
> so it is indeed your wish to return to your own dear country?[1]

If you remove the particle, you will also remove the feeling of emotion.
In general, as Praxiphanes[2] says, such particles were used to represent
moanings and groans and, just as we all see the function of 'ah! ah!' and
'alas!', in exactly the same way, he says, in Homer's

> And now upon their laments[3]

the 'now' was appropriate for laments because it creates the effect of an
interjection of woe. Those, however, he continues, who use particles 58
aimlessly are like actors who aimlessly insert this or that interjection, as if
one were to say:

> This land is Calydon and Pelops' realm, alas!
> beholds its fertile plains across the straits, ah! ah![4]

If the 'alas!' and 'ah! ah!' are redundant there, the same is true if we
pointlessly insert particles everywhere.

FIGURES OF SPEECH

This, then, is how particles give grandeur from arrangement. Figures 59
of speech are also a form of arrangement, since the expression of the
same idea twice, whether by repetition, anaphora, or anthypallage, implies
a rearrangement or change of word-order. We must, then, assign the
appropriate figures to each style, beginning with our immediate concern,
the grand style. First, anthypallage, as in Homer's 60

> The two rocks, one of them reaches up to the broad heaven.[5]

The unusual case gives far more stateliness than if he had said

> Of the two rocks one reaches up to the broad heaven.

This would have been banal; everything banal is trivial and as a result
fails to arouse wonder. Consider Nireus: he is himself unimportant, his 61

---

[1] *Odyssey* 5. 203–4.
[2] The text of this sentence is corrupt but the general sense seems clear.
[3] e.g. *Iliad* 23. 154.
[4] Euripides, *Meleager*, fr. 515 Nauck.
[5] *Odyssey* 12. 73.

contingent still less important (three ships and a few men); but he and his contingent are magnified and multiplied by Homer's use of the combined two figures of anaphora and asyndeton:

> Nireus brought three ships,
> Nireus son of Aglaia,
> Nireus the most beautiful of men.[1]

The anaphora of the repeated Nireus and the asyndeton give the impression of a mighty contingent, though he has only two or three ships, 62 and, although Nireus is named only once in the course of the action, we remember him as vividly as Achilles and Odysseus, whose names recur in almost every line. The reason is the force of the figure of speech: if Homer had said

> Nireus son of Aglaia brought three ships from Syme,

it would have been as if he had never mentioned him. This deceptive effect in literature is comparable to the arrangement of a few dishes at a banquet to seem many.

63 Often, however, it is polysyndeton, the opposite of asyndeton, which is more conducive to grandeur, as in this sentence, 'There marched together Greeks and Carians and Lycians and Pamphylians and Phrygians',[2] where the use of the same connective suggests an army of infinite 64 size. On the other hand, the absence of the connective 'and' makes Homer's 'arched, foam-crested'[3] more imposing than if he had said 'arched and foam-crested'.

65 Grandeur from figures is also obtained from a change to a different construction, as in Thucydides: 'The first to step on the gangway, he both fainted and, as he fell on the outrigger, his shield was dropped.'[4] This is far more imposing than if he had continued his construction to say 'and fell on the outrigger and dropped his shield'.

66 Repetition too can sometimes achieve grandeur, as in Herodotus: 'In some parts of the Caucasus there were vast serpents, vast and numerous.'[5] The repetition of 'vast' lends dignity to the sentence.

67 Figures should not, however, occur too frequently or they reveal a lack of taste and are obtrusive. Look rather at the early writers, who use

---

[1] *Iliad* 2. 671–3. Cf. Arist. *Rhet*. 3. 12, 1414ª2 ff.; above, p. 156.
[2] Author unknown.
[3] *Iliad* 13. 799. Cf. 81.
[4] Thuc. 4. 12.
[5] The passage does not occur in our texts of Herodotus. Either Demetrius has misattributed the passage or we should read Herodorus, a less famous early historian.

many figures in their works but because they distribute them with tact seem more natural than those who avoid them.

HIATUS

The subject of hiatus has produced varying opinions. Isocrates and his 68 followers deliberately avoided it, others used it indiscriminately at every opportunity. The proper course is not to make our sentences too resonant by a random and indiscriminate use of hiatus (that simply wrenches and jerks the words asunder) nor to pursue only an unbroken continuity, since the sentence will then perhaps run more smoothly but will be less musical and completely monotonous because it will have lost the melodious euphony which hiatus gives. We should bear in mind, first of all, that 69 even common usage, whose chief aim is euphony, admits words with internal hiatus, such as *Aiakos* and *chiōn*,[1] and even forms many words like *Aiaiē* and *Euios*[2] which have only vowels but are no less euphonious than any others and perhaps even more melodious. Then in poetry we 70 find forms where the vowels are deliberately resolved and juxtaposed, for example *ēelios*, which is more melodious than *hēlios*, and likewise *oreōn* instead of *orōn*.[3] The resolution and hiatus add the suggestion of a song. We also find many words which would sound harsher if the vowels were run together but are melodious if they remain apart and stand in hiatus, as in *kala estin*:[4] if you run the vowels together to say *kal' estin*, the phrase will sound harsher and more banal. Again, in Egypt the priests even chant 71 hymns to the gods in which they sound each of the seven vowels in turn, and men listen to the sound of these letters in preference to the flute or lyre because of their euphony. If we remove the hiatus, we simply lose entirely the hymns' melody and music. But perhaps now is not the time to enlarge on this topic.

In the grand style the appropriate form of hiatus to use is the juxta- 72 position of the same two long vowels, as in *lāan anō ōtheske*,[5] where the hiatus makes the line ponderous and reproduces the stone's resistance and the force needed to push it up. Similar examples occur in Thucydides . . .[6] The juxtaposition of different vowels also produces grandeur, with the 73 added merit of variety from the diversity of sound, as in *ēōs* and still

---

[1] i.e. 'Aeacus' and 'snow'.

[2] i.e. Aeaea, the name of an island, and Euius, an epithet of Bacchus.

[3] 'Sun' (*hēlios*) and 'mountains' (*orōn*).

[4] 'They are beautiful.'

[5] Homer, *Odyssey* 11. 596. 'He pushed the stone upwards.' Cf. the discussion of the passage by Dionysius, below pp. 335 ff.

[6] We omit two examples, one between two long vowels and one between two diphthongs.

more *hoiēn*,[1] where the change of vowels is accompanied by the transition
74 from aspirated to unaspirated sound. As a result it has many elements of
dissimilarity. In songs too trills are sung on one single long vowel, a song
within a song one might say: hiatus, then, between the same two long
vowels will compose a small part of a song or a trill. Here I conclude my
account of hiatus and the whole topic of grandeur in word-arrangement.

GRANDEUR FROM SUBJECT-MATTER

75 Grandeur also derives from the nature of the subject-matter, for example
an important and famous battle on land or sea or the theme of the heavens
or of earth. If we listen to a dignified subject we immediately suppose
that the speaker is using a dignified style—but we are deceived. We must
consider not the content but the manner of its expression. It is perfectly
possible to speak on dignified themes in an undignified manner and
produce a style inappropriate to the subject. This is why we find some
writers like Theopompus who are thought forceful but merely express
76 forceful themes in an unforceful style. The painter Nicias[2] used to say
that it was, to look no further, an important part of the painter's art to
choose a distinguished subject and not to fritter away his skill on tiny
things like little birds or flowers but to take cavalry or naval battles where
he could portray horses in many different poses—galloping, rearing,
stumbling to their knees—and many riders hurling javelins or thrown
to the ground. He thought that the theme itself was as integral a part of the
painter's art as the plot is part of the poet's. It is not surprising, then, if
grandeur results in prose also from the choice of dignified subject.

GRANDEUR FROM DICTION, BEGINNING WITH METAPHOR
AND SIMILE

77 In this style the diction should be ornate, distinctive, and unusual. It will
then have dignity, whereas normal, ordinary diction has clarity but is
78 plain and cheap. Pride of place belongs to metaphors, since these make
the greatest contribution of charm and grandeur to prose, but they must
not occur too frequently or we find ourselves writing dithyrambic poetry
instead of prose, and they should not be far-fetched but derived from a
related analogy in a similar field. For instance, there is a similarity between

---

[1] i.e. 'dawn' (*ēōs*) and 'such' (*hoiēn*).
[2] Athenian painter of the second half of the fourth century. For his choice of theme
compare the famous Alexander mosaic in the House of the Faun at Pompeii, a copy of a
fourth-century original.

a general, pilot, and charioteer, since they all control something, and we may safely call a general 'pilot of the state' or conversely a pilot 'charioteer of the ship'. Not all metaphors, however, have this reciprocal quality: 79 Homer could call the lower slope of Mount Ida its 'foot' but never a man's foot his 'lower slope'.

If a metaphor seems risky, turn it into a simile (*eikasia*). Then it will 80 be safer. A simile is an extended metaphor. For example, take the words 'Then the orator Python rushed in spate against you'[1] and expand them to say 'Then the orator Python rushed, as it were, in spate against you': the passage has become a simile and acquired safety, while the original version was a metaphor and more risky. This is why Plato's use of metaphor in preference to simile is thought a tricky procedure; Xenophon, however, prefers similes.

Aristotle considers the best metaphor to be what is called the active 81 metaphor,[2] where inanimate objects are presented as if they were animate, as in the description of an arrow 'sharp-pointed, eager to hit its mark in the crowd' and waves 'arched, foam-crested'.[3] All such terms as 'foam-crested' and 'eager' imply the activities of living creatures.

Some ideas are expressed more clearly and properly in metaphors than 82 if the proper terms were used. Take 'The battle shuddered';[4] no version using only proper terms could have greater truth or clarity. By 'shuddering battle' Homer has expressed the movement of the spears and their low, continuous sound—and at the same time he has also made use of the active metaphor we have just discussed, since he speaks of the battle shuddering like a living creature.

It must not be forgotten, however, that some metaphors create a loss 83 of dignity rather than grandeur, even when the metaphor is intended to give dignity as in:

All around the great heaven trumpeted.[5]

Homer should not have likened the sound of the heaven to the sound of a trumpet—unless perhaps he can be defended on the grounds that the great heaven resounded as it would if the whole heaven were a sounding trumpet. Let us find, then, a second example of a metaphor which creates 84 loss of dignity instead of grandeur, bearing in mind that metaphors should compare small to great, not the reverse. Take Xenophon's passage: 'When, during their march a part of the phalanx surged out.'[6] He has

[1] Demosthenes, *On the Crown* 136. Cf. 272.
[2] *Rhetoric* 3. 11, 1411^b32 ff. above, p. 152.
[3] Homer, *Iliad* 4. 126 and 13. 799. Cf. 64.
[4] Homer, *Iliad* 13. 339.
[5] Ibid. 21. 388. Cf. 'Longinus' (below, p. 469), Pliny (below, p. 430).
[6] *Anabasis* 1. 8. 18.

compared a falling out of rank to the surging waves and rightly applied the metaphor, but if anyone were to reverse the analogy and speak of waves falling out of rank, perhaps the metaphor would not even be appropriate, certainly it is utterly devoid of dignity.

85 Some people make a metaphor safe by adding an epithet if they think it too bold. Theognis, for example, applies the phrase 'lyre without strings'[1] to a bow in his description of a man shooting: to call a bow a lyre is bold but the epithet 'without strings' makes it safe.

86 Usage is our guide in everything but particularly in the case of metaphors. Almost every expression in common use involves a metaphor but we do not notice because they are safe metaphors, such as 'clear voice', 'keen man', 'rough character', 'lengthy speaker', and all the other instances where the metaphor is applied so aptly that it seems the proper

87 term. This, then, is my criterion for metaphors in prose, usage as established by art or nature. Usage has in fact taken over some metaphors so successfully that we no longer feel the lack of a proper term and the metaphor is firmly established as the proper term, for example 'the eye

88 of the vine' and suchlike expressions. Note, however, that when 'sphondulos', 'kleis', and 'ktenes' are applied to parts of the body,[2] these terms are not being used metaphorically from analogy but because of their physical resemblance to a spindle-weight, key, and comb respectively.

89 When we turn a metaphor into a simile in the way I described, we should aim at conciseness and add no more than 'like'. Otherwise it will be a poetic comparison instead of a simile, as in Xenophon's 'like a valiant hound which recklessly attacks a boar'[3] and 'like a horse let loose which

90 prances and cavorts over the plain'.[4] These no longer resemble similes but poetic comparisons, which should not be used lightly in prose but only with the greatest care. So much, then, for an outline sketch on the subject of metaphor.

COMPOUND WORDS

91 We should also use compound words, not dithyrambic formations such as 'divinely-portented wanderings' or 'the flame-speared army of the stars'[5] but those resembling compounds sanctioned by usage. To speak generally, in fact, I consider usage the only criterion in forming words,

---

[1] *Poetae Melici Graeci* 951 Page. He is probably the tragic poet of that name ridiculed by Aristophanes.

[2] viz. vertebra, collar-bone, and back of the hand.

[3] *Cyropaedia* 1. 4. 21.

[4] Author unknown: but cf. *Iliad* 6. 506 ff.

[5] Of unknown authorship. See *Poetae Melici Graeci* 962 Page.

and it gives us 'lawgivers', 'master-builders', and many other formations which we may safely copy. A compound word will not only have variety 92 and grandeur from the fact that it is a compound but also conciseness. A whole phrase will be replaced by one word, for instance 'supplies of corn' by 'corn-convoy', a much more impressive expression—though sometimes it may be more impressive to reverse the process and turn a word into a phrase, for example 'convoy of corn' instead of 'corn-convoy'. Another instance of a word replacing a phrase may be taken from 93 Xenophon: 'It was possible to catch a wild ass only if the horsemen were spaced out and hunted in relays.'[1] From the single word 'relays' we understand that some gave chase from behind, others rode forward to meet them, so that the ass was intercepted between the two. Finally, we should not use compound words in profusion or we transgress the limits of prose.

NEOLOGISMS

Critics define neologisms as words which imitate the sound of an emotion 94 or action, for example 'hissed' and 'lapping'.[2] Such words create grandeur 95 on account of their resemblance to inarticulate sounds and in particular from their strangeness, since the neologist does not use existing words but ones which are now appearing for the first time. It also shows cleverness to create a new form and, as it were, a new usage. In fact, in coining such words he resembles the original creators of language.

We[3] must aim primarily at clarity and natural Greek elements in 96 forming new words and secondly at achieving forms analogous to existing words, so that we may not seem to speak the barbarous Greek of Phrygians and Scythians. Such a neologism must be either a completely new form, 97 as, for example, when a writer called the drums and other accompaniments of the eunuch priests their 'effeminacies' and Aristotle invented 'elephantist',[4] or an existing form given a secondary meaning, as, for example, when a writer called a man who was rowing his craft a 'craftsman' and Aristotle called the man who lived alone by himself an 'autite'.[5] On the same lines Xenophon says 'The army rang out',[6] deriving the 98

[1] *Anabasis* 1. 5. 2.
[2] Homer, *Odyssey* 9. 394 and *Iliad* 16. 161. Cf. 220.
[3] The transition to derivative neologisms is harsh. If we compare the unwarranted 'as I said' in 98, it is attractive to assume a lacuna here: e.g. 'There are also derivative neologisms. Like all neologisms they carry risks, even for poets.'
[4] Author unknown and Aristotle, *History of Animals* 497[b]28.
[5] Author unknown and Aristotle, fr. 668 Rose. Elsewhere the latter example refers to home-made wine. The point is hard to make in English: 'selfish' is a possible rendering, if we suppose it might bear two meanings. Cf. 144 below.
[6] *Anabasis* 5. 2. 14.

meaning from their continuous ringing cheers. Neologism is, however, as I said, a risky procedure even for poets.

Again, a compound word will be a species of neologism, since a compound obviously derives from parts already in existence.

ALLEGORY

99 Allegory is yet another source of grandeur, especially when it has the function of a threat, as in Dionysius' warning: 'The cicadas will sing to
100 them from the ground.'[1] If he had said openly that he would cut down the trees of Locris, he would have seemed hot-tempered and negligible; as it is, he has used an allegory to veil his meaning. For what is implied is always more fearsome, since people imagine varying interpretations, whereas anything clear and explicit is likely to meet the scorn given to
101 men who have been stripped. This is why the Mysteries are expressed through allegories, to arouse fear and awe—the very reason why they are celebrated in darkness and at night. Allegory may indeed be regarded
102 as a sort of darkness and night. We should, however, take care not to accumulate allegories or our words turn into a dark riddle, as in the description of the doctor's cupping-glass:

I saw a man weld bronze on a man with fire.[2]

The Spartans too would often use allegory to arouse fear, as in their answer to Philip, 'Dionysius in Corinth',[3] and many similar threats.

FURTHER DISCUSSION OF WORD-ARRANGEMENT

103 In some cases brevity, especially aposiopesis, creates grandeur, since some things are more impressive if they are not openly expressed but merely implied; in other cases it has a trivial effect, just as its opposite, repetition, may give dignity, as in Xenophon: 'The chariots rushed along, some of them right through their allies, others right through the enemy.'[4] This version is much more impressive than if he had said 'right through
104 both allies and enemy'. Often too an oblique construction is more impressive than a straightforward one, for example 'The aim was one of charging and hacking a path through the ranks of the Greeks'[5] instead
105 of 'They intended to charge and hack a path through'. Contributory

---

[1] The warning is attributed to Stesichorus by Aristotle (*Rhetoric* 1395^{a}1-2 and 1412^{a}23-4).

[2] Cleobulina, fr. 1 Bergk. Cf. above, p. 139.   [3] Cf. 9 above.

[4] *Anabasis* 1. 8. 20.   [5] Xenophon, *Anabasis* 1. 8. 10.

factors are the verbal assonance and the obviously harsh sound. For harshness often gives weight, as in:

Ajax (*Aias*), strong in might, aimed always (*aien*) at Hector,[1]

where the clash of the two sounds is a more effective indication of Ajax' might than his shield of seven bulls' hides.

THE EPIPHONEME

What is called the epiphoneme may be defined as added ornamentation 106 and is the highest form of grandeur in prose. Language is in part functional, in part ornamental. The following is functional:

> like the hyacinth which the shepherds on the hills
> trample underfoot.[2]

Then we have a decorative ornamentation:

> and on the ground the purple flower . . .

Here it is obvious that the epiphoneme gives added ornamentation and beauty to the preceding words. Homer's poetry is full of examples, as in: 107

> Out of the smoke I rescued them, for they seemed no longer
> as they once were, when Odysseus went to Troy and left them behind.
> A god, moreover, put this still greater anxiety in my heart,
> that under the effects of wine you might turn to quarrelling
> and wound one another.[3]

Then he adds an epiphoneme:

> for iron of itself draws a man on to fight.

To speak generally, the epiphoneme resembles conspicuous displays of 108 wealth like cornices, triglyphs, and broad bands of purple:[4] for it is itself a sort of verbal mark of wealth.

The enthymeme might be considered a form of epiphoneme, but, even 109 if it does come last in the manner of an epiphoneme, it is not one, since it is used for proof, not ornamentation. Similarly, a maxim might seem 110 an appended epiphoneme but, even if it does sometimes have the final

[1] Cf. 48 above.
[2] Sappho, fr. 105 (c) Lobel–Page.
[3] *Odyssey* 19. 7–13.
[4] Most probably broad bands of paint, for example on the plain surfaces of the metopes or along the cornice.

position of the epiphoneme, it too is not one, since it is frequently put
111 first. Again, in the line

Fool! he was not fated to escape his harsh doom[1]

there is no epiphoneme. It is neither additional nor a decorative ornamentation and bears no resemblance to an epiphoneme but only to an address
or rebuke.

112 Poetical language in prose also gives grandeur—as is clear, in the words
of the proverb, even to the blind. Some writers, however, imitate the
poets quite openly, or rather they do not imitate but plagiarize, as is
113 Herodotus' practice. Contrast Thucydides: even if he adopts words from
poets, he makes them his own by using them in his own individual way.
In his description of Crete, for instance,

There lies the land of Crete, in the midst of the wine-dark sea,
beautiful, fertile, sea-girt,[2]

Homer had used 'sea-girt' for its dignity; Thucydides, on the other hand,
thought it right for the Sicilians to unite because their land was one
single sea-girt area,[3] but, although he has used the same words, 'land' to
describe an island and 'sea-girt', he seems to be saying something quite
different, because he is using them not for any dignity of style but as
arguments in favour of unity. Here I conclude my account of grandeur.

THE FRIGID STYLE[4]

114 Each style has an adjacent fault in the same way that there are adjacent
good and bad qualities in the field of ethics, such as courage and rashness
or reverence and shame. The first to be discussed will be the neighbour
of the grand style. Its name is the frigid style, and frigidity is defined by
Theophrastus as that which exceeds the proper expression, as in

A cup unbased cannot be tabled,[5]

instead of 'A cup which has no base cannot be placed on a table'. The
115 slight nature of the subject does not allow such an ornate style. Like
grandeur, frigidity springs from three sources: first the thought, as in
one account of the Cyclops hurling a rock at Odysseus' ship: 'As the rock
sped on its way, goats were grazing on it.'[6] This is frigid because the

---

[1] Homer, *Iliad* 12. 113.   [2] *Odyssey* 19. 172–3.
[3] Thuc. 4. 64.
[4] The use of the word *psuchros* to describe the fault of excessive grandeur is as odd in
Greek as 'frigid' in English. Demetrius' use derives from Aristotle, *Rhetoric* 3. 3,
1405[b]35 ff.: see note on this passage, where we use 'bathetic' for *psuchros* (above, p. 140).
[5] Sophocles, *Triptolemus*, fr. 554 Nauck.   [6] Author unknown.

thought is extravagant and an impossible exaggeration. In diction Aris- 116
totle[1] recognizes four forms . . .

[Brief lacuna which included the first two forms, glosses—i.e. dialectal or
rare words—and epithets.]

. . . as in Alcidamas' 'damp sweat'; thirdly compounds, if the compounding
produces dithyrambic formations like 'lone-wandering' or any other
excessively ornate word; and finally metaphors, as in 'The situation was
trembling and pale'.[2] These, then, are the four kinds of frigid diction.
In word-arrangement there is frigidity if the sentence lacks good rhythm 117
and is unrhythmical because all its syllables are long, as in this example:
'arrived inside our land, with all our state expectant'.[3] The series of long
syllables is unsuitable for prose and too bold. It is also frigid to use a 118
series of metrical phrases, as some writers do, since the regularity obtrudes.
Verse in prose is out of place and as frigid as lines in verse with excess
syllables. To sum up, frigidity is akin to boastfulness. The boaster lays 119
claim to what he does not have as though he did, and the author who
adorns a trivial subject with dignified language may be regarded as a man
boasting of what are really trivialities. The proverbial 'dressed up pestle'
exactly describes such misuse of elevated style upon trivialities.

Some critics, however, think it proper to use dignified language of 120
trivial circumstances and consider it a mark of exceeding skill. For myself
I do not disapprove of the rhetorician Polycrates[4] when he adorns his
eulogy of [. . .] as if he were an Agamemnon, with antithesis, metaphor,
and all the other stylistic embellishments of eulogy: he was writing in
jest, not in earnest, and the very ornateness of the style is part of the jest.
Let jesting, then, be permitted, I say, but propriety must always be preserved, that is to say, the style must be appropriate, plain for a trivial
subject, dignified for a dignified subject. Take Xenophon's description 121
of the beautiful little river Teleboas: 'This was a river which was not
large, beautiful though.'[5] The brevity of the clauses and the ending upon
a 'though' all but bring the little river before our eyes. Contrast another
writer's description of a river like the Teleboas: 'Its source lies in the
hills of Laurium and it disembogues into the sea.'[6] The style conjures up
the cataracts of the Nile or the mouth of the Danube. All such inappropriate grandeur is called frigidity.

There is, however, another way in which we may magnify trifles, yet 122

---

[1] Aristotle's account in *Rhetoric* 3. 3 (above, p. 140) allows us to fill the lacuna.
[2] Gorgias, fr. B. 16 Diels.   [3] Cf. 42 above.
[4] A fourth-century Athenian, noted for his paradoxical eulogies. The name of the
person praised has been lost—perhaps Thersites or Busiris.
[5] *Anabasis* 4. 4. 3. Cf. 6 above.   [6] Author unknown.

it is not inappropriate and sometimes a necessity. For example, we may wish to exaggerate a general's minor victory into a great victory, or we may wish to praise the Spartan ephor who flogged a man for playing ball with extra flourishes alien to the Spartan tradition. This misdeed taken by itself sounds venial, but we can dwell upon its consequences, pointing out that any leniency towards minor faults of character opens the way to more serious ones and that punishment should be directed against minor rather than serious offences; we may also adduce the proverb 'the beginning is half the whole' as an apt description of this slight fault or even assert
123 that no fault is slight. It is on these lines, then, that we may exaggerate a small success without fear of impropriety, and just as a great deed can often be usefully disparaged, a minor one can conversely be magnified.

124 The device most inherently frigid is hyperbole. It takes three forms, depending on whether it asserts a likeness, as in 'like the winds in speed',[1] or a superiority, as in 'whiter than snow',[2] or an outright impossibility,
125 as in 'her head reached up to meet the sky'.[3] Of course every hyperbole involves an impossibility—there is nothing whiter than snow, nothing like the winds in speed—but this third kind is specifically called the impossible. It is in fact precisely because of their element of impossibility that
126 every hyperbole is thought especially prone to be frigid. It is also the chief reason why the comic poets use hyperbole, since the impossible is a source of laughter, as in one writer's exaggerated account of the Persians' gluttony, 'they excreted whole plains', and 'they carried oxen in their
127 jaws'.[4] Of the same nature are the phrases 'balder than the blue sky' and 'healthier than a pumpkin'. Sappho's 'more golden than gold',[5] however, may be a hyperbole and impossibility but she draws charm, not frigidity, from this very impossibility. We may indeed give especial praise to the divine Sappho for the way in which she has used to charming effect a device which is of its nature dangerous and hard to use successfully.

THE ELEGANT STYLE

128 Here I conclude my account of frigidity and hyperbole and turn to discuss the elegant style, the style of charm and light pleasantries. Some forms of charm are more stately and dignified, those associated with poetry, others are more lowly and more suited to comedy, akin to gibes and found in such writers as Aristophanes, Sophron, and Lysias. If we consider such witticisms as Lysias' comment on an old woman, 'It would

---

[1] Homer, *Iliad* 10. 437.   [2] Ibid.   [3] Ibid. 4. 443.
[4] Unknown authors. The first may be a paraphrase of Aristophanes, *Acharnians* 82. The second reappears in 161.
[5] Sophron, frr. 108 and 34 Kaibel, Sappho, fr. 156 Lobel–Page. All recur in 162.

be easier to count her teeth than her fingers', and 'He has made off with as
many drachmas as he deserved strokes of the whip',[1] they are indistinguishable from gibes and close to the laughter of buffoonery. On the other 129
hand, Homer's lines,[2]

> The nymphs
> played at her side, and Leto rejoiced in her heart

and

> She was easily pre-eminent, though all were beautiful,

show what we call the dignified or stately kind of charm. Homer also uses 130
pleasantries on occasion to add force and expressiveness and the very
jesting makes him more fearsome. He seems to have been the first to
discover forceful pleasantries, as in the gift of hospitality offered by that
most repulsive character, the Cyclops:

> I shall eat No-man last, after the others.[3]

Nothing expresses his monstrous nature as vividly as this witticism, not
even when he devours two of Odysseus' companions, nor the huge door
of his cave, nor his mighty club. Xenophon too adopts this device and 131
derives forcefulness from pleasantries, as in the case of the armed dancing-
girl: when a Greek was asked by a Paphlagonian whether their women
too went on campaigns, he replied: 'Yes, and it was the women who
routed the king.'[4] The witticism is forceful on two scores, the implication
that the women who accompanied them were not ordinary women but
Amazons and the sneer that the king was so weak that he was put to
flight by women.

These, then, are the varieties and characteristics of charm. Some 132
derive from the content, such as gardens of the nymphs, wedding-songs,
loves, all the poetry of Sappho. Even if handled by a Hipponax[5] such
themes retain their charm and are intrinsically gay. No one could sing
a wedding-song in wrath or achieve a style able to turn Cupid into a
Fury or a giant, or laughter into tears. But if some themes have their own 133
charm, the style can lend added charm, as in Homer:

> As when the daughter of Pandareus, the auburn nightingale,
> warbles her sweet song in the first days of spring.[6]

---

[1] Frr. 1. 5 and 275 Sauppe.
[2] *Odyssey* 6. 105–6 and 108. Homer compares Nausicaa among her handmaidens to
Artemis among the nymphs.
[3] *Odyssey* 9. 369. Cf. 152 below.
[4] *Anabasis* 6. 1. 12–13.
[5] Sixth century B.C., notorious for his invective poetry.
[6] *Odyssey* 19. 518–19.

The nightingale is a charming bird and spring is always a charming thought but the style has greatly heightened the beauty by the added charm of 'auburn' and the personification of a bird as a daughter of
134 Pandareus. Both are the poet's own contributions. Often too a subject which is essentially unattractive and grim may acquire gaiety from the writer's treatment. This skill seems to be found first in Xenophon. His subject was a stern and grim character, the Persian Aglaitadas, yet he
135 created laughter with a charming jest: 'It is easier to strike fire from you than laughter.'[1] This kind of charm has the most powerful effect and more than any other depends on the writer, since he takes a subject like Aglaitadas which is essentially grim and hostile to charm and shows that it is possible to make jests even from unpromising material, just as one may be cooled by warmth and warmed by cold.
136   We have now indicated the forms of charm and the ways in which they appear. Now we shall indicate their sources. We have already seen that charm derives from style and content and we shall treat the sources under these two headings, beginning with style.

CHARM FROM STYLE, BEGINNING WITH BREVITY, WORD-ORDER, AND FIGURES OF SPEECH

137 First we have charm from brevity, where an idea which would become unattractive under detailed treatment derives charm from a passing mention, as in Xenophon: ' "This man has in fact no claim to be Greek, for I saw him with both ears pierced like a Lydian"—and this was so.'[2] The brevity of the final 'and this was so' creates charm, while a longer version, 'What he had said was true; they were obviously pierced', would
138 have replaced the charm with a bald narrative. Again, we may often contrive a charming effect by combining two ideas in one, as in one writer's description of the sleeping Amazon: 'Her bow lay strung, her quiver full, her shield beside her head; but they do not loosen their girdles.'[3] The same words indicate the regular custom about the girdle and the fact that she had not loosened her girdle, two points in one. The brevity is elegant.
139   A second source is word-order, since a final position lends some words a charm which they lack if put in the beginning or middle. Here is an example from Xenophon on Cyrus: 'He gave him gifts, a horse, a robe, a necklace, and a promise against further ravaging of his country.'[4] The last gift, the promise against further ravaging, creates charm from its

---

[1] *Cyropaedia* 2. 2. 15.   [2] *Anabasis* 3. 1. 31.
[3] Author unknown.   [4] *Anabasis* 1. 2. 27.

strangeness and peculiarity. The final position is responsible: reverse the order, for example 'He gave him gifts, a promise against further ravaging of his country, a horse, a robe, and a necklace', and there would be no charm; as it is, he begins with the conventional gifts and adds at the end the one which is strange and unusual. Hence the charming effect.

The charm derived from the use of figures of speech is self-evident 140 and is found above all in Sappho, as in her use of repetition, for example when a bride addresses her virginity,

> Virginity, virginity, where have you gone, deserting me?

and her virginity replies, using the same figure,

> Never again shall I come to you, never again shall I come.[1]

The idea would have less charm if it were expressed only once, without the figure of speech. It is true that repetition seems to have been invented rather as a means of lending forcefulness, but Sappho makes even the most forceful turns of style contribute charm. Sometimes she derives 141 charm from anaphora, as in her address to the evening-star:

Evening-star, you bring everything home,
you bring the sheep, you bring the goat, you bring the child to the mother.[2]

Here again there is charm, the result of the repetition of 'you bring' at the beginning of successive clauses. Many other examples could be 142 adduced.

CHARM FROM SINGLE WORDS

There are also examples from single words, for instance metaphor, as in this passage on the cicada:

> From under its wings
> it lets its shrill song flow forth, whenever the blazing . . .;[3]

or compound words of a dithyrambic nature, such as 143

> Pluto, lord of the black-winged . . .[4]

—but these are more especially the playful oddities of comedy and satyr-plays. There may also be charm from a word associated with a particular 144

---

[1] Fr. 114 Lobel–Page. [2] Fr. 104 (a) Lobel–Page.
[3] Alcaeus, fr. Z. 23 Lobel–Page. The end of the quotation is deeply corrupt.
[4] Author unknown. The rest of the quotation is deeply corrupt and it is uncertain whether it is from lyric or comedy. See *Poetae Melici Graeci* 963 Page and *Supplementum Comicum, Frag. Adesp.* 1 Demianczuk.

author,[1] as in Aristotle, 'The more lonesome I am, the fonder I have become of stories', or from a neologism, as in the same sentence, 'The more lonesome and "autite" I am, the fonder I have become of stories'. Here 'lonesome' is rare outside Aristotle,[1] while 'autite' is a neo-
145 logism from 'auto-'. Again, many words derive charm from a particular application, as in the remark, 'This bird is a flatterer and rogue',[2] where the charm lies in the mockery of the bird as if it were a man and the consequent use of words not normally applied to birds.

CHARM FROM COMPARISON, RECANTATION, PARODY, ALLEGORY, SIMILAR CLAUSES, AND VEILED ACCUSATIONS

146 Such are the sources of charm from single words. We may also derive charm from comparisons, as in Sappho's description of a tall, handsome man:

> pre-eminent, like the Lesbian singer among strangers.[3]

Here the comparison has resulted in charm, not the grandeur which could have been achieved by the choice of a more poetical comparison, for example 'pre-eminent, like the moon among the stars' or 'like the sun in
147 brightness'. Sophron too derives charm from this source, for example: 'See how many leaves and twigs the boys shower on the men, in just the way they say, my dear, the Trojans hurled mud at Ajax.'[4] This comparison is charming, because it makes fun of the Trojans as if they were children.

148   There is also a source which Sappho has made peculiarly her own, recantation. She says something, then recants and, as it were, changes her mind, as in this example:

> Raise the hall
> high, you builders.
> The bridegroom is entering, the equal of Ares,
> taller by far than a tall man.[5]

She seems to check herself, conscious of using an impossible exaggeration
149 since no one is the equal of Ares. Similar is this passage in Telemachus:[6] 'Two dogs were tethered in front of the court and I can even tell you the dogs' names—but why should I wish to give their names?' The writer has wittily changed his mind in the middle and suppressed their names.

---

[1] Or 'from a colloquial word' . . . 'is colloquial'. The fragment (668 Rose) is cited in 97 and is a probable interpolation in 164.
[2] Author unknown.   [3] Fr. 106 Lobel–Page.
[4] Fr. 32 Kaibel.   [5] Fr. 111 Lobel–Page.
[6] Unknown: name may be corrupt. But possibly a version of the *Odyssey* story is meant: we may recall Eumaeus' dogs (for the relevant passage see below, p. 324).

There is also charm in parodying someone else's line, for example 150 Aristophanes mocks Zeus somewhere for failing to cast his thunderbolts against the wicked:

But he strikes his own temple and 'Sunium, headland of Athens'.[1]

It is as though it were no longer Zeus but Homer and Homer's line which find ridicule, and this increases the charm.

Again, some allegories have a piquant flavour, as in 'Delphians, your 151 bitch is with child'[2] or Sophron's description of old men: 'Here I too sit at anchor with you, white-haired like myself, waiting to set sail on the sea; for men of our age are ready to lift anchor.' He also has an allegory on the subject of women, using the imagery of fish: 'Razor-fish, oysters with soft flesh, delicacies for widows.'[3] But comparisons like this last example are gross and suitable only for mimes.

Charm also springs from the unexpected, as in the Cyclops' words 152 that he would eat No-man last[4] (for neither Odysseus nor the reader had expected such a token of hospitality) or in Aristophanes' mockery of Socrates:

He melted the wax, then took a pair of compasses
and in the wrestling school—he stole a cloak.[5]

In this example there are, however, two sources of charm: the last com- 153 ment is not only unexpected, it does not even cohere with what precedes. This sort of incoherence is called *double-entendre*[6] and may be illustrated from the speech of Bulias in Sophron (none of his remarks cohere together) and the prologue of Menander's *Woman of Messenia*.

Similar clauses are another frequent source of charm, as in Aristotle: 154 'I went from Athens to Stagira because of the great king and from Stagira to Athens because of the great winter.'[7] The fact that both clauses have the same ending lends charm and, if you delete 'great' from either clause, you will also remove the charm.

Veiled accusations can sometimes seem charming, as in Xenophon's 155 account of how Heraclides, one of Seuthes' followers, approaches each of the dinner-guests in turn and urges him to give what he can to Seuthes.[8] The request has a sort of charm and is at the same time a veiled accusation.

---

[1] *Clouds* 401, with parody of *Odyssey* 3. 278.
[2] Author unknown and interpretation uncertain.
[3] Frr. 52 and 24 Kaibel.
[4] Homer, *Odyssey* 9. 369. Cf. 130.   [5] *Clouds* 149 and 178-9.
[6] At first hearing there is a surface meaning but it does not make sense and we look for the underlying real meaning. We have no details on either of the two examples (Sophron, fr. 109 Kaibel; Menander, fr. 268 Koerte).
[7] Fr. 669 Rose. Cf. 29.   [8] *Anabasis* 7. 3. 15 ff.

CHARM FROM CONTENT: PROVERBS, FABLES, MISTAKEN
FEARS, COMPARISONS, AND HYPERBOLES

156 So much, then, on the number and sources of charm derived from style. In content we derive charm from proverbs, since they are of their nature charming. In Sophron, for example, we find 'Epioles who choked his father' and, in another passage, 'he deduced the lion from the claw', 'he scraped the ladle', and 'he split cummin'.[1] He amasses charm by having two or three proverbs in quick succession and we can almost make a
157 complete collection of all proverbs from his dramas. Aptly introduced fables are also charming. Some are traditional, such as Aristotle's comment on the story that the eagle dies of hunger because its beak becomes bent: 'and it suffers this fate because once, when it was a man, it injured
158 a guest'.[2] This is a traditional and familiar fable. There are also many fables which we invent to match and suit the context, like one writer's novel addition to the story that the cat grows fat and thin in sympathy with the phases of the moon: 'hence the story that the moon is the cat's mother.'[3] There is not only charm from the novelty, the story that the moon is the cat's mother is itself attractive.

159 Relief from fear[4] is another frequent source of charm, when a man is needlessly afraid, for example when he mistakes a strap for a snake or a stove for a hole in the ground—but these mistakes are essentially more
160 suited to comedy. Comparisons are yet another source, if you compare a cock to a Persian[5] because its crest stands upright—or to a king because it is purple or because we jump up when a cock crows, just as we do when
161 a king calls. But comic charm derives especially from hyperbole, since every hyperbole involves an impossibility.[6] For example, Aristophanes exaggerates the gluttony of the Persians,

> They roasted oxen, not bread, in the ovens,[7]

and another writer of the Thracians, 'Medoces their king would carry
162 a whole ox in his jaw'.[8] There are other examples of the same kind, 'healthier than a pumpkin', 'balder than the blue sky', and Sappho's

> More melodious by far than a lyre,
> more golden than gold.[9]

The charm of all such examples derives from hyperbole.

[1] Frr. 68 and 110 Kaibel. The meaning of the first is obscure.
[2] *History of Animals* 619[a]16.
[3] Author unknown.   [4] Text uncertain.
[5] Aristophanes, *Birds* 486–7 and 490. In fact only the king in Persia wore his tiara upright.
[6] The impossible is a regular source of laughter.
[7] Aristophanes, *Acharnians* 85–6.   [8] Author unknown. Cf. 126.
[9] Sophron, frr. 108 and 34 Kaibel; Sappho, fr. 156 Lobel–Page. Cf. 127.

THE DIFFERENCES BETWEEN LAUGHTER AND CHARM

Comic laughter and graceful charm differ. They differ, first of all, in their 163
material. Gardens of the nymphs and loves are material for charm but
do not provoke laughter, unlike Irus and Thersites [1] who do. The difference, then, is as great as that between Thersites and Cupid. They also 164
differ in language: charm welcomes stylistic adornment and beautiful
words, the richest source of charm, as in

> The many-garlanded earth was carpeted with flowers

and 'auburn nightingale',[2] whereas laughter is not merely content to use
commonplace, ordinary words [3] but is actually destroyed by stylistic 165
adornment and becomes grotesque. Charm, then, may be adorned without
offence [4] but to elaborate upon a subject for laughter is tantamount to
beautifying an ape. It is for this reason that Sappho uses beautiful, 166
melodious words when she speaks of beauty or loves, spring and the
halcyon. Every beautiful word is woven into her poems and some are
even her own creation. But her style changes when she mocks the boorish 167
bridegroom and the doorkeeper of the bridal chamber: then she departs
from poetic language to use very ordinary and pedestrian words and we
feel readier to recite these poems in a conversational tone than to sing
them, and they would not fit the accompaniment of chorus and lyre—
unless of course you can imagine a chorus which merely recites. But the 168
most fundamental difference lies in their aims: the elegant and comic
writers have different aims, the former to delight us, the latter to make
us laugh. Their results are similarly different, since the one arouses
laughter, the other praise. Different too are their spheres of action: in 169
some genres, the satyr-play and comedy, we need both laughter and
charm, whereas tragedy makes frequent use of charm but laughter is
its enemy. No one could even conceive of a mirthful tragedy: he would
simply produce a satyr-play.

JESTS AND GIBES, SUITABLE AND UNSUITABLE

Even sensible men will sometimes make jests, on appropriate occasions 170
such as banquets and parties and in rebuking the dissolute, for example

---

[1] Irus, the beggar in Homer, *Odyssey* 18, and Thersites, ugliest of the Greeks in the
Iliad.

[2] Author unknown (*Poetae Melici Graeci* 964(a) Page) and Homer, *Odyssey* 19. 518,
already quoted in 133.

[3] I delete the example, Aristotle, fr. 668 Rose, quoted in 144, since it has charm and
does not illustrate the crude laughter of comedy.

[4] Text uncertain.

the beggar's bag of Telauges [1] and Crates' poetry [2]—or one might read a praise of lentil-soup to a gathering of gourmets. This is the sort of procedure associated with the Cynics, for such jests usurp the function
171 of moral anecdotes and maxims. A man's jests are also an indication of his character, revealing either humour or a lack of good manners, as in the case of the man who held out the wine which had been poured into his cup and said 'Peleus instead of Oeneus'.[3] The punning substitution and the air of premeditation indicate a character with no taste or breeding.

172 To turn to gibes,[4] some are harmlessly witty comparisons. Examples of this kind will be 'Egyptian clematis' to describe a tall, swarthy man and 'sea-sheep' to describe a fool at sea. This kind will be used, but we will avoid any others as coarse abuse.

BEAUTIFUL WORDS

173 Charm is also created by the use of what are called beautiful words. This is Theophrastus' definition: 'There is beauty in a word if it is attractive
174 to the ear or eye or has inherent nobility from its meaning.' Attractive to the eye are such expressions as 'rose-coloured' and 'flower-laden meadow' (for whatever delights the eye retains its beauty when we hear about it) and attractive to the ear are 'Callistratus' and 'Annoon', where
175 there is resonance in the double 'll' and 'nn'; it is also for the sake of euphony that Attic writers generally add 'n' in forms like *Dēmosthenēn* and *Sōkratēn*.[5] Nobility from meaning is exemplified by 'our ancestors' instead of 'the ancients': 'our ancestors' is more distinguished.

176 Musicians classify words as smooth, rough, well-proportioned, and weighty. A smooth word consists wholly or largely of vowels, for example '*Aiās*', whereas '*bebrōkë*'[6] is a rough word—in fact the sound of this particular rough word reflects its meaning. The well-proportioned

---

[1] A Pythagorean ascetic, contemporary with Socrates and mocked by Aeschines of Sphettus (see 291).

[2] *c.* 365–285 B.C.; a Cynic philosopher, whose parodies include a praise of lentil-soup, the diet of the poor.

[3] Peleus and Oeneus, the names of famous heroes, are made to pun on *pēlos* (mud or wine-lees) and *oinos* (wine).

[4] The text of this section is partly corrupt. The clematis is a tall plant, Egyptians dark—hence the man is tall and dark; the sheep was proverbially silly—hence this man is as silly as a sheep when he is at sea. The gibes are clever because there was in fact an Egyptian clematis (not a tall plant) and a fish called a sheep.

[5] Outside Attic the accusative of Demosthenes and Socrates was *Dēmosthenē* and *Sōkratē*.

[6] 'Devoured.'

word has elements of both and is in sound an equal admixture of rough and smooth. The weighty word has three characteristics, breadth, length, 177 and a resonant enunciation,[1] as in *brontā* instead of *brontē*,[2] where the first syllable has roughness and the long Doric 'a' of the second gives not only length but breadth. The Dorians broaden all their vowels—hence the fact that comedy was not written in Doric but in the sharp sounds of Attic. The Attic dialect has a terseness and everyday air which make it suitable for the wit of comedy. This disquisition has been an irrelevant 178 digression but of the various kinds of words we should use only smooth words in view of their elegance.

ELEGANT ARRANGEMENT

Elegance also derives from the arrangement of words, but it is not an easy 179 subject to discuss, since no earlier critic has treated elegant arrangement. I must, however, attempt it as best I can. It seems, then, that pleasure 180 and charm will result if we construct our sentences from metres, either whole or half lines, but so that the metres do not obtrude as such in continuous speech and we detect them only if you separate and analyse each different part. There will be the same charm even if the rhythm is 181 only roughly metrical. The charm from this kind of pleasing arrangement steals upon us imperceptibly and is the form prevalent in the Peripatetics, and in Plato, Xenophon, and Herodotus; it seems that it is also frequent in Demosthenes, but Thucydides avoids it. It might be 182 illustrated by the following example from Dicaearchus: *en Eleā tēs Italiās, presbutēn ēdē tēn hēlikiān onta*.[3] The ends of the two clauses are roughly metrical but the metre is hidden by the unbroken continuity in the flow of words. This gives considerable charm. Again, Plato often derives 183 elegance from rhythm alone by using long clauses which avoid harsh-sounding juxtapositions and a succession of long syllables (for the former characterizes the plain and forceful styles, long syllables the grand style). Each clause seems to glide smoothly into the next and they are neither completely metrical nor unmetrical, for example his description of music beginning 'we were saying a moment ago'[4] . . .

---

[1] One can linger on the sounds, producing a sort of recitative. Cf. Quint. 1. 11. 6.

[2] 'Thunder'; *brontē* is the regular form outside Doric.

[3] Fr. 39 Wehrli: i.e. 'at Elea in Italy, an old man already in years'. Dicaearchus was a Peripatetic, pupil of Aristotle and contemporary with Theophrastus.

[4] Plato, *Republic* 411 a. I omit 184 and 185, which contain further examples from *Republic* 399 d.

THE AFFECTED STYLE

186 So much, then, on the appearance of elegance in arrangement, a difficult topic. I have now concluded my account of the elegant style and shown its elements and sources. Just as the frigid style is the adjacent fault of the grand style, so there is an adjacent faulty perversion of the elegant style. I call it by that current catchword 'affected' (*kakozēlon*) and, like all the

187 others, it too springs from three sources. Affectation in thought is seen, for example, when one writer spoke of the Centaur being his own rider, and another writer, on the theme of Alexander considering whether to compete in the Olympic games, exclaimed: 'Alexander, run in your

188 mother's name.' It may also spring from diction, for instance 'The sweet-complexioned rose laughed', where the metaphorical use of 'laughed' is quite unsuitable and a sane man would not choose the compound 'sweet-complexioned' even in poetry, or, another example, 'The pine whistled

189 to the sound of the gentle breezes'.[1] So much, then, on diction. In arranging words it is affected to use rhythms which are anapaestic and resemble the dissolute and undignified metres, in particular the Sotadean on account of its effeminacy, as in

> *skēlas kaumati kalupson*

and

> *seiōn meliēn Pēliada dexion kat' ōmon*

instead of

> *seiōn Pēliadā meliēn kata dexion ōmon*.[2]

The line seems to have changed its nature, like the men in the legends who are turned into women. So much, then, on affectation.

THE PLAIN STYLE

190 In the case of the plain style we should perhaps choose trivial subjects of the kind appropriate to plain treatment, as in Lysias: 'I have a modest house on two floors, and the upper floor is exactly like the lower.'[3] The diction should be entirely ordinary and in everyday use, since anything

---

[1] Authors unknown. In the second example of 187, there is a pun on Olympias, the name of Alexander's mother.

[2] *Sotadea* 17 Powell ('having dried it, conceal it') and Sotades, fr. 4(a) Powell, a transposition of Homer, *Iliad* 22. 133 ('brandishing the Pelian ash-spear over his right shoulder').   [3] *Against Eratosthenes* 1.

ordinary is always more trivial, while words which are unusual and metaphorical create grandeur. Compound words are also to be avoided, since 191
they too are characteristic of the opposite style, as are neologisms and all
the other embellishments which produce grandeur. Above all, the plain
style should have clarity. This derives from several qualities, in the first 192
place from the use of ordinary words, secondly from connectives. Writing
which is unconnected and disjointed is utterly unclear, since the lack of
articulation obscures the beginning of each clause, as in Heraclitus, whose
lack of connectives is largely responsible for his reputation as a dark
riddler. This disconnected style is perhaps more suited to the immediacy 193
of debate. It is also called the dramatic style because the lack of connectives
stimulates dramatic delivery, whereas the written style is easier to read
because its parts are fitted together and, as it were, secured in place by
connectives. This is why actors like Menander, whose style for the
most part lacks connectives, but readers prefer Philemon.[1] To prove the 194
dramatic nature of unconnected clauses let us take this example:

I conceived you, I bore you, I nurse you, my dear.[2]

The lack of connectives will force even an unwilling reciter to give the
line a dramatic delivery: but if you insert connectives and say

I conceived you and I bore you and I nurse you,

the connectives will bring with them a great loss of emotion, and anything which lacks emotion gives no scope for dramatic delivery. Dramatic 195
technique includes other interesting factors. Euripides' Ion,[3] for example,
snatches his bow and threatens the swan which is fouling the statues:
here the actor is given a variety of movements, such as the run to his
bow, the face turned upwards to the sky as he addresses the swan and all
the other gestures which the dramatic nature of the scene demands. But
our present concern is not dramatic technique.

Clear writing should also avoid ambiguities and use the figure of 196
epanalepsis, the repetition of a connective in the course of a long sentence,
for example: '*Now* all Philip's actions, the subjection of Thrace, the capture of the Chersonese, the siege of Byzantium, the refusal to return
Amphipolis—*now* all these I shall pass over.'[4] The repetition of the connective may be said to remind us of the first words and re-establish us
at the beginning of the sentence. Again, we should often repeat ideas for 197
the sake of clarity, since greater charm than clarity results from brevity.

[1] Dramatist contemporary with Menander.
[2] Menander, fr. 685 Koerte.
[3] *Ion* 158 ff.   [4] Author unknown.

For just as we sometimes overlook men racing past us, a sentence too can rush along too quickly for comprehension.

198   The use of dependent constructions should also be avoided, because they lack clarity, as we see from the style of Philistus.[1] A briefer example of obscurity from a dependent construction may be found in Xenophon: 'He heard news of triremes sailing round from Ionia to Cilicia with Tamos on board and belonging to the Spartans and Cyrus himself.'[2] This could be expressed in the following straightforward construction: 'Triremes were expected in Cilicia, many of them Spartan but many of them Persian ships built by Cyrus for this very purpose. They were sailing from Ionia and the commander in charge was the Egyptian Tamos.' This version would perhaps be longer but certainly clearer.

199   As a general rule we must use the natural order of words, as in 'Epidamnus is a city on your right as you sail into the Ionian gulf'.[3] First the subject is mentioned, then the predicate (it is a city) and then the rest in due

200   order. The reverse order may also appear, for example 'There is a city Ephyra'.[4] We neither completely approve of the one nor disapprove of the

201   other: we are simply giving the natural way of ordering words. In narrative we must begin either with a nominative, 'Epidamnus is a city', or with an accusative, 'It is said the city Epidamnus . . .'[5] Use of other cases will result in obscurity and torture both speaker and reader.

202   Try also to avoid extremely long periods of the kind in this sentence: 'The Achelous, which flows from Mount Pindus and passes inland by the city of Stratus before running into the sea . . .'[6] Instead, make a break immediately and give the reader a rest: 'The Achelous flows from Mount Pindus and runs into the sea.' This version is much clearer, on the analogy of roads with many signposts and resting-places: the signposts act as guides, whereas a straight road without signposts, however short it is, seems aimless.

203   These are a few of the many remarks one might make on the subject of clarity. It is to be used particularly in the plain style.

[We omit 204–8, on word-arrangement in the plain style.]

VIVIDNESS

209   Vividness derives in the first place from accurate detail and the fact that no circumstance is omitted or deleted, as in the whole of Homer's simile beginning

---

[1] Historian c. 430–356 B.C.; his style imitated that of Thucydides: cf. Dionysius, *Letter to Pompey* 5.   [2] *Anabasis* 1. 2. 21.
[3] Thucydides 1. 24.   [4] Homer, *Iliad* 6. 152.
[5] In Greek an accusative and infinitive construction is a way of expressing indirect speech.   [6] Thucydides 2. 102. Cf. 45–7.

As when a man draws off water in a trench.[1]

It is vivid because all the details are included and nothing is left out. The 210 same applies to the chariot-race in honour of Patroclus, where Homer says

Their breath blew hot on Eumelus' back

and

They always seemed to be on the point of mounting his chariot.[2]

The whole passage is vivid because it includes all the race's usual and unusual features. One consequence is that it is often more vivid to repeat 211 an idea than to express it only once, for example 'When he was alive you would speak of him slightingly, now that he is dead you write of him slightingly',[3] where the repetition of 'slightingly' lends greater vividness to the reproach. Consider too the attack on Ctesias[4] for garrulous re- 212 petitions; the charge may often be justified but often his accusers are blind to his vividness. The repetition is there simply because it often produces a greater impact. This is true of the following example: 'When 213 Stryangaeus, a Mede, threw a Sacian woman down from her horse (the Sacian women fight like Amazons), he saw her grace and beauty and let her escape. Later, when peace was made, he fell in love with her but was repulsed. He decided to starve himself to death but first he wrote this letter of reproach: "I saved you, you were saved through me, yet I am dead through you."' Here a supporter of terse style might censure him 214 for a pointless repetition in 'I saved you' and 'you were saved through me', since both express the same idea. But if you remove either, you will also remove the vividness and the emotional impact of the vividness. Vividness is also present in the next sentence from the use of the past tense 'I am dead' instead of 'I am dying': put in the past it is more forceful than if it were still in the present or future. In fact, speaking generally, throughout 215 his writings this poet (for we may fairly call him a poet) has mastered the craftsmanship of vividness. Take this second example, remembering that 216 we should not tell bad news all at once but gradually, keeping the hearer in suspense and forcing him to share the anguish. This is what Ctesias does over the announcement of Cyrus' death. The messenger arrives but in the presence of Parysatis he does not immediately say that Cyrus is dead. That would be the proverbial bluntness of the Scythians. Instead he first announces Cyrus' victory. His mother rejoices and is deeply affected.

---

[1] *Iliad* 21. 257.　　　　　　　　　　　　[2] *Iliad* 23. 380 and 379.
[3] Author unknown. Cf. 26.
[4] Early fourth-century B.C. physician who wrote histories of Persia and India. The two examples which follow are frr. 27 and 42 Mueller.

Then she asks: 'How is the king?' He answers that he has fled. She remarks: 'Yes, for this he may hold Tissaphernes responsible.' Again she questions him: 'Where is Cyrus now?' The messenger replies: 'In the bivouac of the brave.' Little by little and step by step the truth is forced out until at last, to use the stock phrase, 'the news was broken'. By this delay Ctesias has very realistically and vividly brought out the messenger's unwillingness to announce the news and forced the reader to enter into the mother's anguish.

217   Vividness also springs from the mention of accompanying details, as in one writer's description of a farmer's walk: 'The crash of his feet heralded his approach from afar.'[1] 'Crash' suggests that the man is not
218 just walking but trampling the ground. Another example is Plato's description of Hippocrates: 'He blushed—for there was already a faint ray of light to let me see him.'[2] No one can fail to see the extreme vividness, the result of Plato's careful use of words and the recollection that Hippocrates had arrived during the night.

219   Harsh sounds are another frequent source, as in

> He dashed them down and out gushed their brains

and

> frequently upward and downward,[3]

where the sound mimics the jolty movement. In fact all mimicry is vivid.
220 Mimicry is the reason why onomatopoeia is vivid, as in 'lapping':[4] if Homer had said 'drinking', there would be no mimicry of the sound of dogs drinking and, as a result, no vividness. The juxtaposition with the next word, 'tongues', increases still more the vivid impression of the passage. So much, then, by way of a brief outline on the subject of vividness.

PERSUASIVENESS

221 Persuasiveness has two characteristics, clarity and ordinary language. Anything obscure and out of the ordinary is unconvincing. For persuasive effect, then, we must aim to avoid diction which is ornate and pretentious and arrange the words so that the sentence has a firm structure with no
222 attempt at rhythmical effects. In addition to these factors there is the point made by Theophrastus that not everything should be given lengthy treatment with full details but some points should be left for our hearer to grasp and infer for himself. If he infers what you have omitted, he no

---

[1] Author unknown.   [2] *Protagoras* 312 a.
[3] Homer, *Odyssey* 9. 290 and *Iliad* 23. 116.
[4] Homer, *Iliad* 16. 161. Cf. 94.

longer just listens to you but acts as your witness, one too who is pre-
disposed in your favour since he feels he has been intelligent and you
are the person who has given him this opportunity to exercise his intelligence. In fact, to tell your hearer everything as if he were a fool is to reveal
that you think him one.

THE STYLE OF LETTERS

Since the style of letters should also be plain, I shall turn to this topic. 223
Artemon,[1] the editor of Aristotle's letters, says that dialogue and letters
should be written in the same manner, since a letter may be regarded as one
of the two sides in a dialogue. His comment has some truth perhaps, but 224
not the whole truth. A letter should somehow be slightly more elaborately
written than a dialogue, because the latter aims at an effect of improvisa-
tion but the former is of its nature written and is sent as a sort of gift.
Who would ever talk to a friend in the way Aristotle writes to Antipater 225
to express sympathy for the old man in exile?—'If he wanders over all
the world, an exile with no prospect of return, clearly no reproach attaches
to men in his position if they wish to find a home in the kingdom of the
dead.'[2] A man who talked like that would seem to be declaiming, not
chatting.

Frequent disjointed sentences are also unsuitable in letters, since dis- 226
jointedness in written compositions destroys clarity and imitation of the
spoken word suits writing less than the immediacy of debate, as we see in
the *Euthydemus*: 'Who was that, Socrates, who was talking with you in
the Lyceum yesterday? There was certainly a large crowd standing round
you.' And a little further on: 'I thought he was from abroad, that man who
was talking with you. Who was he?'[3] All this kind of style in imitation
of the spoken word suits an actor but not the written nature of letters.

A letter should be very largely an expression of character, just like the 227
dialogue. Perhaps everyone reflects his own soul in writing a letter. It is
possible to discern a writer's character in every other form of literature
but in none so fully as in the letter.

The length of a letter should be moderate, as should its style. Any 228
which are too long and, furthermore, rather pompous in language can
assuredly never become letters but are monographs with the conventional
opening of a letter, as in the case of many of Plato's letters and that one of
Thucydides. The actual sentences should be rather loosely formed. It is 229
ridiculous to build periods as if you were writing a speech, not a letter.

---

[1] Date uncertain.   [2] Fr. 665 Rose.
[3] *Euthydemus* 271 a, at the beginning of the dialogue.

In fact such elaboration in letters is worse than merely ridiculous, it is also unfriendly, since friends should, in the words of the proverb, 'call a spade a spade'.

230   We should also recognize that it is not only a certain style but certain topics which suit letters. Let me quote Aristotle, who is admitted to be an especially felicitous writer of letters: 'I do not write to you on this: it
231 does not suit a letter.'[1] If anyone writes on logic or science in a letter, he is writing something but certainly not a letter. A letter aims to be a brief
232 token of friendship and handles simple topics in simple language. Its charm lies in the warmth of friendship it conveys and in its numerous proverbs. This is the only kind of wisdom a letter should have: for proverbs give popular sayings in everyday use. The man who is sententious and sermonizes seems to have lost the letter's air of a talk and mounted
233 the pulpit. Aristotle, however, can even use logical arguments sometimes in such a way that they are adapted to the letter. For example, he wants to prove that benefactors should help large and small towns alike: 'For the gods in both are equal and, since the graces are gods, you will lay up an equal store of grace in both.'[2] Here the point made suits a letter, as does the proof itself.
234   We sometimes write to cities and kings: give letters of this kind a slightly more elevated style, since we must also adapt ourselves to the character of the recipient, but not so elevated that the letter turns into a monograph, the fault of Aristotle's letters to Alexander and Plato's letter to the friends of Dion.
235   To summarize, the letter should derive its form of expression from a combination of two styles, the charming and the plain. So much, then, on the letter.

   [236–9, here omitted, illustrate the 'dry' style which is a perversion of the plain.]

THE FORCEFUL STYLE: SUBJECT-MATTER

240 We now come to forcefulness (*deinotēs*) and it will be clear from what has already been said that it too springs from the same three sources as all the preceding styles. There are some subjects which have an inherent forcefulness which makes even writers whose style is feeble seem forceful. When Theopompus, for example, speaks of the flute-girls of the Piraeus, the brothels, and the men playing the flute, singing, and dancing,[3] all

---

[1] Fr. 670 Rose.   [2] Fr. 656 Rose.
[3] Theopompus fr. 320 Mueller (115 *FGH* 290 Jacoby).

these ideas have such a forceful effect that his feeble style is overlooked and he is thought forceful.

[We omit 241–71, which deal with word-arrangements and figures appropriate to forcefulness.]

THE FORCEFUL STYLE: DICTION

We should use every kind of diction found in the grand style, only our aim will be different. Force can be achieved from metaphor, as in 'Python grew bold and rushed in full spate against you', and from simile, as in Demosthenes' words: 'This decree made the danger which then surrounded the city pass away like a cloud.'[1] Poetical comparisons, however, are disqualified by their length, as in 'like a valiant but inexperienced hound which recklessly attacks a boar':[2] beauty and precise detail characterize such images, whereas forcefulness requires pungent brevity and is like an exchange of blows. Again, compound words can give force, as we see from the many examples in current usage, for example 'looselivers', 'brainless',[3] and the like. Many such examples may be found in the orators. We should also attempt to find words in keeping with the thought. For example, a man acts with reprehensible violence: say 'he forced his way through'; or with open and reckless violence: say 'he cut and hacked his way through'; or with furtive secrecy: say 'he insinuated himself' or 'he stole his way through'.

[We omit 277–86, where other kinds of *deinotēs* are illustrated.]

OBLIQUE ALLUSIONS

What we call oblique allusion is used by modern orators in a ridiculous manner, with unseemly and obtrusive innuendo. True allusion has the two characteristics of propriety and wary circumspection. There is propriety when Plato, for example, wishes to censure Aristippus and Cleombrotus for feasting in luxury at Aegina during the many days of Socrates' imprisonment in Athens and not sailing across to their friend and teacher, a distance of under twenty-five miles. He does not give all these circumstances explicitly, for that would be open abuse, but tactfully implies them: Phaedo is asked who were with Socrates and names each in turn;

272
273
274
275
276
287
288

---

[1] Demosthenes, *On the Crown* 136 (cf. 80) and 188.
[2] Author unknown. Cf. 89.
[3] Literally 'thrown to the ground' (a common prostitute) and 'struck sideways' (a madman).

then he is further asked if Aristippus and Cleombrotus were also there and replies: 'No, they were in Aegina.'[1] The whole of what I have just said is expressed in the words, 'They were in Aegina', and the passage seems all the more forceful from the fact that it is the situation itself and not the writer's words which give the forceful effect. In this example of oblique censure Plato could perhaps have openly rebuked Aristippus and

289   his friends in perfect safety but we are often compelled to use an oblique approach when we are talking to a tyrant or some other domineering person whom we wish to reproach. For example, the Macedonian Craterus sat on a golden chair high above everyone else and received the embassies from Greece in a purple robe with insolent arrogance: Demetrius of Phaleron, however, countered with this oblique reproach: 'We too once received these men as envoys, Craterus here among them.'[2] The use of the

290   word 'here' indirectly indicates and rebukes all Craterus' insolence. The same tact is found in Plato's reply to Dionysius, who had broken and then repudiated a promise: 'I, Plato, have made no promise to you; but you— by heaven!'[3] Dionysius is convicted of breaking his promise, yet the

291   rebuke combines dignity with circumspection. On many occasions equivocation is also useful: if anyone wishes an example of hidden denunciation, Aeschines' treatment of Telauges[4] may be cited. Almost the entire narrative will leave the reader in doubt whether it is eulogy or derision. This kind of ambiguity is not irony but it creates an ironical effect.

292   Another form of oblique allusion is possible: since men and women in positions of power do not relish hearing of their own faults, we shall not warn them against their faults by any outright mention but either denounce others for similar behaviour—for example, in speaking to the tyrant Dionysius we shall censure the tyrant Phalaris for his cruelty—or praise men whose behaviour contrasts with that of Dionysius, for example Gelo and Hiero for proving fathers and teachers of Sicily; for the hearer is admonished without open censure, feels envious of Gelo's praises and

293   strives to achieve such praise for himself. Such guarded handling of tyrants is frequently required. Philip, for example, had only one eye and became angry at any mention of the Cyclops in his presence or even of the term 'eye' generally. Hermias, too, the ruler of Atarneus, was normally mild-tempered, we are told, but was sensitive to any mention of knife, surgery, or amputation: he was a eunuch. I have chosen these examples from a wish to single out the character of absolute rulers in particular, because there is especial need in their case for the guarded manner of

[1] *Phaedo* 59 c.   [2] Fr. 183 Wehrli.   [3] *Epistle* 7, 349 b.

[4] The text of this sentence is uncertain but the main point seems clear. Aeschines of Sphettus was a pupil of Socrates and wrote philosophical dialogues. Cf. 297.

speech called oblique allusion—though in fact important and powerful 294
democracies often require this kind of allusion as much as any tyrant,
for example the Athenian democracy in the time when it ruled Greece
and encouraged flatterers like Cleon and Cleophon. Flattery is shaming,
censure is dangerous, best is the middle course of oblique allusion.

Sometimes we will even praise a man who has been at fault, not for his 295
faults but for overcoming them. For example, we will tell a hot-tempered
man that he was praised yesterday for the mildness he showed to the
failings of such and such a person and that he is a model of behaviour for
the citizens around him. Everyone likes to be his own model and is eager
to add to his praises, or rather to win one consistent theme of praise.

In short, language is like a piece of wax which one man will shape into 296
a dog, another into an ox, and another into a horse. The same subject will
in one writer be phrased as a statement and assertion, for example: 'Men
leave their property to their children, yet they do not include in it the
knowledge of how to use the legacy.'[1] This form of remark is called
Aristippean. In another writer the idea will be phrased as a precept, the
form regular in Xenophon: 'You should not leave your property to your
children without including the knowledge of how to use it.' We also have 297
the form specifically called Socratic and considered the model of Aeschines and Plato in particular. Here our same example would be adapted
to become interrogative: 'My boy, how much property has your father
left you? A great deal, more than you can easily count?'—'A great deal,
Socrates.'—'Has he then also left you the knowledge of how to use it?'
Socrates unobtrusively drives the youth into a quandary, reminds him
that he lacks knowledge and urges him to find instruction. It is all done
with fine characterization and good taste and is far removed from the
proverbial Scythian bluntness. Such dialogues were very successful when 298
they were first invented, or rather people were struck with admiration for
their vivid realism and the nobility of the ideas they advocated. Let this,
then, suffice on the categories of speech and oblique allusions.

[We omit 299–304, which includes a short discussion of faults relating to
forcefulness.]

[1] Author unknown, conceivably Aristippus himself.

5

CICERO

Cicero, besides his life-long practice of oratory and literature, was always concerned with the theory that lay behind it; the list of his theoretical works begins with an immature handbook *On Invention*, dating from the 80s B.C., and passes through the dialogue *On the Orator* (55) to a series of shorter works written in the 40s. These later works reflect Cicero's standpoint in a controversy that had developed around the concepts of Atticism and Asianism in oratory; but that by no means limits their interest, and Cicero's theory shows at all periods of his development consistent enough attitudes to justify our abandoning the chronological order of his works in the interests of giving a clear over-all view. We begin therefore with an extract from the *Brutus* (46 B.C.; text by E. Malcovati (Teubner, 1965), complete translation by G. L. Hendrickson (Loeb); commentary by A. E. Douglas (Oxford, 1966)).

A. WHO SHOULD JUDGE ORATORS?

Brutus 183–200

183   Here Atticus said: 'How do you mean, both in your judgement and in everybody's? Does the judgement of the mob always coincide with that of the knowledgeable in the approval or disapproval of an orator? Or are some approved by the many, others by the experts?'

'You are right to ask, Atticus', I said, 'but you will hear an answer that perhaps may not be given the approval of everybody.'

184   'Does that worry you', he asked, 'if you manage to prove your point to Brutus here?'

'Atticus', I said, 'I should very much prefer this discussion on the approving and disapproving of the orator to please you and Brutus; my eloquence, however, I should wish to be approved by the people. For it follows that someone who speaks so as to win the approval of the many will win that of the connoisseur also. So long as I am capable of judgement, I shall be able to judge what is right or wrong in speaking. But an orator's quality will be realized from what he can *bring about* by his
185   oratory. There are in my opinion three things that oratory should bring about: the instruction of the hearer, his being given pleasure, his being strongly moved. It will be for the technical expert to judge what virtues in an orator cause each of these, and what faults mean that he fails to

attain them or even slips and falls in the attempt. But whether the orator succeeds or fails in making his audience feel the required emotions is normally judged by the applause of the mob and the approval of the people. And so there has never been a difference between the people and the experts on whether an orator was good or not. Or do you imagine 186 that, in the periods during which there flourished the orators I have mentioned,[1] there was not an identical ranking of orators in the judgement of the crowd and of the educated? If you asked the man in the street: "Who is the most eloquent man in the country?" he would answer either Antonius or Crassus, or he would hesitate between the two. Would nobody prefer to these Philippus, so agreeable, weighty, and witty an orator—one whom we ourselves, who are trying to apply some system to our weighing of these matters, claimed to be next in rank to the other two? Nobody surely; it is a mark of the top orator to be regarded as top orator by the people.

'If the flute-player Antigenidas said to a pupil who was a failure in 187 public "Play for me and the Muses", my advice to Brutus here when he speaks (as he often does) before a crowd is: "Play for me, my friend, and the people." Those who listen will feel the effect of your speech; *I* shall realize *why* that effect is produced. The orator's audience believes his words, thinks them true, assents, approves; his speech carries conviction; what more could the critic ask? A listening multitude is charmed and 188 allured by oratory, it is deluged with delight: what can the critic find fault with here? The crowd rejoices, grieves, laughs, cries, likes, dislikes, despises, envies, pities, feels shame, feels annoyance. It is angered and soothed, it hopes and fears. These effects take place according to the way in which the minds of those present are worked on by words, thoughts, and delivery. Why wait for the judgement of some expert? What the multitude approves must be approved by the expert too.

'Here is a final illustration of popular judgement—and there has never yet been any difference here between people and connoisseurs. There 189 have been many orators of various styles; yet who has been popularly reputed to excel without being approved by the expert as well? In our fathers' day either Antonius or Crassus would unquestionably have been the invariable choice of anyone free to select his advocate. Many other lawyers were practising; yet though someone might have doubted which of the two to choose, no one would have failed to choose one or the other. Again, in my youth, Cotta and Hortensius were pre-eminent: would anyone with a choice have preferred anybody else to these two?'

Then Brutus said: 'Why look elsewhere? What about you? We saw 190 what defendants preferred, and what Hortensius himself thought. When

[1] The *Brutus* consists largely of a roll-call of Roman orators down to Cicero's time.

he was splitting a case with you (I often used to be there) he would leave you the last speech, where oratory has most of its effect.'

'He did do that', I replied. 'It must have been his friendliness towards me that made him so generous. However, I don't know what the people think about *me*; but in the case of others, I am confident that those who have been popularly regarded as the most eloquent have been the most

191 highly regarded by the experts. Demosthenes could not have said what is attributed to the famous poet Antimachus. Once Antimachus got an audience together and began to read them a large volume of his (you know it). Everyone but Plato walked out as he read. "I shall go on reading all the same", he said. "For me Plato counts as a hundred thousand." And quite right too; for a poem, if abstruse, need move the enthusiasm only of the few. But a speech is meant for the people—and must win the approval of the crowd. And if Demosthenes were reduced to having Plato as his sole

192 audience, he would not be able to say a word. What could you do, Brutus, if you got abandoned by your audience as Curio once was by his?'

'To tell the truth', said he, 'I shouldn't be able to go on if I was abandoned by the audience, even in a case where my speech was wholly directed at the judge and not at the people at all.'

'That's how it is', I said. 'If a flute didn't give any sound when it was blown, the player would think it time to throw it away. And to the orator the people's ears are like a flute; if they don't receive what he blows in, or if the audience (like a horse) just doesn't *suit*—then it's no use persevering.

193 'However, there is this difference, that the mob sometimes approves an orator who doesn't deserve it—but it approves without applying any comparison. When it is pleased by a middling or even poor speaker, it contents itself with him and, not realizing that anything better is available, it gives its applause to what there is, whatever its quality. Even a second-rate orator, providing he has *something*, can hold the attention; for nothing so influences men's minds as arrangement and embellishment of style.'

[Cicero proceeds (194–8) to give the details of a case in which Quintus Scaevola and Lucius Crassus had been on opposing sides.]

198 'Now this ordinary critic of ours, having admired one of these two when heard by himself, might find himself laughing at his judgement when he heard the other; while an educated and knowledgeable hearer of Scaevola would sense that there was room for something richer and more ornate. But if both critics were to be consulted at the completion of the case as to which was the better orator, the judgement of the skilled man would surely not differ from that of the layman.

'Where then does the expert surpass the layman? In an important matter, 199
and one hard to achieve: for it *is* important to know how effects that
should be obtained by oratory, or at least must not be let slip, are in fact
achieved or lost. There is another superiority of skilled over unskilled
in that, when the people approve of two or more orators, the skilled critic
can tell what style is best. For what is not liked by the people cannot be
liked by the expert either. You can tell from the sound of the strings how
skilfully a lyre is being played; and you can tell from the emotions aroused
in the mind what the orator is doing by his playing on them. Thus 200
the skilled critic of oratory can often judge an orator in passing and
at a glance, without sitting by and listening carefully. He can see the
judges yawning, talking to a neighbour, sometimes even chatting in
groups, asking the time, calling for an adjournment: so he knows that in
that case there is no orator capable of bringing his oratory to bear on the
minds of judges like a hand to a lyre. But if he goes by and sees the judges
sitting up, wide-awake, proving by their very faces that they are getting
the point: if he sees them held in suspense by the speech like a bird by
music, or—most important of all—violently shaken by pity, anger, or some
other emotion: if he goes by, I say, and sees all this, even without hearing
anything he will judge that an orator is at work in that case and that the
orator's job is being done—or has already been completed.'

B. THE PROGRESS OF GREEK ORATORY

Also from *Brutus* (25–51); the rather repetitive and disorderly exposition is
Cicero's concession to the conventions of dialogue.

I said: 'It is not my intention here—nor is it necessary—to praise 25
eloquence, to describe the extent of its powers, and of the prestige it
brings to those who have attained to it. But one thing I will say without
hesitation: whether it is produced by art, by practice, or by nature,
eloquence is a uniquely difficult accomplishment. It is said to consist of
five elements:[1] and each of these is a great skill in itself. Thus it can be
imagined how powerful, and how difficult to reach, is this combination of
five major skills.

'Look, for example, at Greece: she was fired with enthusiasm for 26
eloquence, and has long excelled all her rivals in it; yet all her other
arts are longer established, and were discovered and even perfected well
before such effective and fluent oratory was developed. Now when I look at
Greece, Atticus, there particularly comes to my mind, with a sort of glow,
your favourite city Athens, where the orator first raised his head, and where

[1] Invention, arrangement, diction, memory, delivery.

27 speeches were first immortalized in the literary record. Yet before Pericles, some of whose works are extant in writing, and Thucydides, both of whom lived when Athens was adult, not adolescent, there is no written word that shows any degree of ornament, any sign of the orator, though there is certainly a tradition that the far earlier Pisistratus, together with Solon rather before him and Clisthenes after him, were, for their 28 times, powerful speakers. A number of years after that generation, as we can tell from Atticus' chronology,[1] came Themistocles, who is agreed to have stood out for wisdom and eloquence too; after him Pericles, a brilliant example of every virtue, earned nevertheless his highest fame in this field of oratory. It is known too that Cleon, at the same period, was, 29 though an obstreperous citizen, an eloquent speaker. More or less contemporary were Alcibiades, Critias, and Theramenes. The type of oratory that flourished at this time can be best judged from Thucydides, who lived at the same period. They were elevated in their vocabulary, close-packed in thought, brief, compressed, and sometimes, for that very reason, somewhat obscure.

30 'Now when it became known what influence careful and studied oratory could have, many teachers of the art of speaking suddenly sprang up. Gorgias of Leontini, Thrasymachus of Chalcedon, Protagoras of Abdera, Prodicus of Ceos, Hippias of Elis were in great repute; and many others at this period professed, arrogantly enough, their ability to teach how the weaker cause (as they put it) could by skill in oratory be made the 31 stronger. They found an opponent in Socrates, who used an acute method of disputation to reject their claims. His fruitful conversations gave rise to disciples of great learning; and it is at this time that the branch of philosophy that disputes about good and bad, about men's lives and ways, as opposed to the older type concerned with nature, is said to have been invented. This phenomenon lies outside my present subject: philosophers I must leave for another occasion; let us return to the orators from whom I have digressed.

32 'Now in the old age of the men I have just mentioned appeared Isocrates, whose home was open to all Greece as a sort of school and factory of oratory. He was himself a great orator and a consummate teacher, even though he avoided the glare of the courts and fostered indoors a glory that no one, in my judgement, has ever since equalled. He both wrote himself, much and brilliantly, and taught others; he excelled earlier orators in other ways but especially in that it was he who first realized that in prose too you must, while steering clear of verse, 33 preserve a certain measured rhythm. For before him there was no

---

[1] Atticus' *liber annalis*, the source of much of Cicero's chronological lore: cf. 39, 42; *Orator* 120.

structuring of words for effect, no rhythmic cadence—or, if there sometimes was, it was not clear that it had been purposely sought after: that
may be a compliment, but the fact remains that at that period such
occasional effects occurred naturally and by chance rather than by
systematic intention. For nature itself can express and round off a thought 34
in periodic form; and, when such a sentence is tightly organized with
words that fit, it generally also has a rhythmic ending as well. For our
ear by itself judges what sounds full, what hollow; and our breath by
a kind of natural law imposes an end on a period—for it is undignified
to be short of wind, let alone run out altogether.

'At this time, too, lived Lysias. To be sure, he did not himself play a 35
part in legal cases, but he was a writer of surpassing delicacy and elegance
(*subtilis atque elegans*), whom you could almost venture to call the perfect
orator. For the absolutely perfect orator, with virtually no deficiencies,
may easily be said to be Demosthenes. No acute, no (so to say) cunning or
clever line of argument could be found in the cases he dealt with but he
saw it. When he spoke, delicately, concisely, and to the point, nothing could
have been filed to greater perfection. When he spoke grandly, excitedly,
with every ornament of weighty word and weighty sentiment, nothing
could have been more sublime. Next to him come Hyperides, Aeschines, 36
Lycurgus, Dinarchus, Demades (who left no written speeches), and many
others—such was the fertility of that generation.

'In my view, it was only up to and including this period of oratory
that the juice and blood that gives a natural, not artificial bloom remained
untainted. For when they were old, they were succeeded by a young 37
man from Phaleron,[1] more learned than any of them, but formed in the
training ground rather than the battlefield. So it was that he delighted
the Athenians: he did not set them ablaze. For he had come out into the
sun and the dust not (as it were) from a soldier's tent, but from the shady
retreat of the scholarly Theophrastus. And it was Demetrius who first put 38
oratory on a new path, making it soft and languishing; he wished to seem
(as indeed he was) sweet rather than serious, and sweet with a sweetness
to permeate the mind rather than to break into it. Hence he left a memory
of prettiness, unlike Pericles, who, in the words of Eupolis, left a sting,
along with the pleasure, in the minds of those who heard him.[2]

'Thus you may see how, even in the very city where eloquence was born 39
and bred, it was a late arrival on the scene. There is no record of any
eloquent man before the time of Solon and Pisistratus. They may be old-
timers by Roman standards, but they can only be regarded as comparative youngsters in the history of Athens. They flourished in the reign of

[1] Demetrius.
[2] Eupolis, fr. 94 Kock: cf. Pliny, *ep.* 1. 20. 17 (below, p. 425).

Servius Tullius. But at that date Athens had already existed for far longer
than Rome has existed to-day. Of course, I am not doubting that speech
40 has always had great influence. Back in the times of Troy, Homer would
not have assigned so much praise to the oratory of Ulysses and Nestor
(the one, for him, had forcefulness, the other sweetness) unless there was
already prestige accorded to eloquence.[1] Nor, indeed, would the poet
himself have been so skilled in speaking—a real orator, in fact. His date is
uncertain, but he lived many years before Romulus: for he was clearly
not younger than the first Lycurgus, founder of the legally enforced
41 Spartan system of education. But it is in Pisistratus that application to
this art, and greater capacity for it, can be recognized. Themistocles was
a generation after him, very ancient by our standards, not very
old by Athenian. For he lived when Greece was dominant, while our
state had not long freed itself from the tyranny of the kings: the Volscan
war of such importance in which Coriolanus participated as an exile was
at about the same time as the Persian war, and the two great men suffered
42 similar fortunes. Both had been famous citizens. Both were unjustly
expelled by an ungrateful people, betook themselves to the enemy, and
stilled in death the enterprises which their anger prompted. You have
a different account of Coriolanus, Atticus: but you must allow me to
acquiesce in this manner of his dying rather than yours.'

Atticus laughed and said: 'It's your choice. It's granted that orators may
tell lies in historical matters in order to make a point more neatly.[2] Just
as you made up a story about Coriolanus, so Clitarchus and Stratocles
43 produced their fictions about Themistocles. Thucydides, an Athenian, of
the highest birth and office, and not much later in date, wrote that
Themistocles died merely from natural causes and was buried secretly in
Attica, adding a rumour that he committed suicide by poison. But the
other two say that Themistocles sacrificed a bull, caught the blood in a
bowl, drank it, and dropped dead. That, of course, was the sort of death
they could give a rhetorical and tragic gloss: the other ordinary kind left
no scope for decoration. So since it suits you that everything was parallel
in the cases of Themistocles and Coriolanus, you can take the bowl from
me too, and I'll give you the victim as well—let Coriolanus be a straightforward second Themistocles.'

44 'Well', I said, 'be it as you wish about *him*. And in future I shall touch
on history more cautiously when you are listening. I can compliment you
as being the most scrupulous of authorities on Roman history.

'However that may be, about that time Pericles, son of Xanthippus,

---

[1] *Iliad* 3. 221; 1. 247: cf. Pliny (below, p. 426); Quint. 12. 10. 64 (below, p. 414).
[2] The context of this famous remark should be closely examined by those who wish
to generalize on Cicero's view of history: see Douglas's note (and also p. 255 below)

whom I mentioned before, first brought training to bear. This did not then exist in the field of oratory, but Pericles was taught by the philosopher Anaxagoras,[1] and easily transferred the mental accomplishments acquired in recondite and abstruse matters to cases before courts and people. Athens was captivated by his charm, wondered at his fullness and facility, and feared the terrifying force of his eloquence.

'This was the generation that was the first, at Athens, to produce the 45 almost perfect orator. Ambition for eloquence is not normally born in those founding states and waging wars, or in men hampered and hamstrung by the rule of despots. Eloquence is the companion of peace, the friend of leisure, foster-child of a securely settled society. And so, as 46 Aristotle says,[2] it was when the tyrants had been got rid of in Sicily, and private property was being claimed back after a long interval by legal process, that (the Sicilian race being sharp-witted and naturally gifted for dispute) a handbook and rules for oratory were first composed, by the Sicilians Corax and Tisias; no one before that was accustomed to speak methodically and systematically, though many spoke with care and from a written text. Protagoras prepared written discussions of important matters, now called commonplaces. Gorgias did the same, composing 47 eulogies of and invectives against particular things, because he regarded it as especially the orator's job to be able to increase merit by praise and to depress it again by invective. Antiphon of Rhamnus had similar compositions written out. We have the excellent witness of Thucydides,[3] who heard the speech, that no one ever pleaded a capital case better than Antiphon did in his own defence.

'Lysias (still according to Aristotle) was at first a professor of the art of 48 oratory, but later, because Theodorus was subtler in theory (though thinner in his practice), Lysias began to write speeches for others, and abandoned theory. Similarly, Isocrates at first denied the existence of an art of speaking, though he made a practice of writing speeches for others to use in court. But after himself being frequently summoned to trial for alleged offences against the law forbidding legal malpractice, he stopped writing speeches for others, and devoted himself entirely to composing handbooks. Here you have the birth and origin of Greek oratory, long 49 ago by the standard of our history, but quite recently by theirs. For the city of Athens had many memorable feats, in war and peace, to its credit before it began to take delight in the accomplishment of oratory.

'Now this enthusiasm was peculiar to Athens, not shared with the whole of Greece. Who can tell of an Argive or Corinthian or Theban orator 50 at that period? Unless, that is, we may speculate about the literary

---

[1] Cf. Plato, *Phaedrus* 269 e (above, p. 78).
[2] In a lost work.   [3] 8. 68.

accomplishments of Epaminondas. And I have never heard of a Spartan orator to this day. Homer tells us that even Menelaus was a man of few words, though an agreeable speaker.[1] Now conciseness is sometimes, and in particular passages, a good thing; but in oratory as a whole it is without 51 merit. Outside Greece, however, there were great vogues for oratory; honour was heaped on skill in eloquence, making the name of orator illustrious. For, once it left the Piraeus, eloquence passed through all the islands and made itself so much at home throughout Asia that it became contaminated with the ways of foreigners,[2] lost the old health and soundness of the Attic style, and almost forgot how to speak. Hence we have the orators of Asia, by no means to be despised for their speed and fullness, but not concise enough and over-redundant. The Rhodians are sounder, and more like the Attic orators. But enough of the Greeks: perhaps even what I have said is unnecessary.'

C. CATO

In *Brutus* 61–76, Cicero, in the course of his survey of Latin orators, praises the elder Cato.

61 'Cethegus, then, was followed chronologically by Cato, who was consul 63 nine years after him[3]. . . Cato's speeches are hardly less numerous than those of the Attic Lysias, and *he* wrote very many (there is no doubt of his being Attic, by the way: he was certainly born and died in Athens, and did all his civic duties there, though Timaeus . . . claims him for Syracuse): and in a way there is a certain resemblance between the two authors.[4] They are both pointed, elegant, witty, brief. But the Greek is 64 happier in his reputation. He has a distinct set of enthusiastic admirers who pursue slimness rather than grossness. So long as health is unimpaired, they find positive pleasure in being thin. In Lysias, indeed, there are often muscles showing too, nothing could be stronger; but he is in general pretty spare. However: as I say, he has his admirers, who rejoice in his very slenderness.

65 But what orator of our time reads Cato? Who even knows him? Yet *what* a man he was! Forget about Cato the citizen, the senator, the general —we are looking at the orator now. Who is more weighty than he in panegyric, more savage in invective, more penetrating in thought, more

---

[1] *Iliad* 3. 213—a passage elsewhere quoted with the lines cited above, 40.
[2] Cf. the account of the origin of 'Asianism' in Quintilian 12. 10. 16 f. (below, p. 407).
[3] i.e. in 195 B.C.
[4] Echoes of the Atticist–Asianist controversy are audible here.

subtle in exposition and explanation? His speeches, more than a hundred and fifty that I have so far found and read, are stuffed with notable language and content. Pick out the passages deserving especial notice and praise: you will find all the qualities of an orator there. And as to the 66 *Origins*, what ornament, what brilliance of eloquence do *they* not possess?[1]

Cato lacks admirers, just as many centuries ago did Philistus of Syracuse and even Thucydides. *Their* brief sentences, sometimes not altogether lucid because of their brevity and extreme point, are eclipsed by the high elevation of Theopompus (as Lysias is by Demosthenes); similarly the loftier stylistic erections of those who succeeded him have got in the way of our appreciation of Cato's brilliance. But our critics are so blind 67 that, while on the Greek side they rejoice in antiquity and what they call 'Attic' slenderness (*subtilitas*), they don't even know it exists in Cato. They want to be like Hyperides and Lysias. Well and good: why not like Cato? They say they enjoy the Attic type. Very wise—would that 68 they did imitate the Attic orators, blood as well as bones! Still, it's pleasant that they even want to.

Why, then, are Lysias and Hyperides loved, while Cato gets utterly ignored? His language is rather dated, his vocabulary sometimes a little uncouth. That was how they spoke then. Change that (*he* could not, in his day); give him rhythm, arrange the words to fit better and (so to say) joint them together (something antiquity didn't achieve even in Greece): then you won't put anyone higher than Cato. The Greeks think language 69 is embellished if they use the deviations of words that are called tropes, and figures (*schēmata*) in thought and speech. It is hardly credible how frequently and how notably Cato employs these features. I am perfectly aware that he's not yet polished enough, that he leaves scope for the search for something more finished. Fair enough—he's so remote in comparison with our day that no writer's work that is at all worth reading exists from any earlier period. But antiquity enjoys greater repute in every other art than it does in oratory.

No one who is expert in such comparatively trivial matters fails to 70 realize that Canachus' statues are too rigid to be life-like, that Calamis' are stiff, but less so than Canachus'; that Myron's aren't yet sufficiently realistic, though undoubtedly to be described as beautiful; that Polyclitus' are more beautiful and by now positively perfect (or so *I* think). So too in painting. We praise Zeuxis, Polygnotus, Timanthes, and the shapes and lines produced by those who used no more than four colours. But in Aetion, Nicomachus, Protogenes, Apelles, everything is now perfect.[2] Perhaps the same is true generally: nothing is perfect the moment it is 71

---

[1] This was Cato's work on Roman history, beginning with Aeneas.
[2] For the analogy with painting and statuary cf. Quint. 12. 10. 3 (below, p. 5).

invented. There were undoubtedly poets before Homer, as you can tell from the songs sung in his poems at the feasts of the Phaeacians and the suitors.[1] And where have *our* old verses got to, the ones that

> once the Fauns and bards would sing,
> when ⟨none had scaled⟩ the Muses' heights?

There was no one keen on learned words before him, as the poet[2] says of himself—and though he boasts, he does not lie. That's how the facts stand. For the Latin *Odyssey*[3] is a sort of work of Daedalus, and the plays

75 of Livius aren't worth reading twice . . . If only the songs still existed, the ones that Cato records in the *Origins* as once being sung by the guests in turn at banquets many centuries before his day, in praise of famous men! However, like some work of Myron's, the *Punic War* of an author[4] whom Ennius counted among bards and Fauns does give pleasure.

76 Ennius may be—certainly is—better finished. But if he despised him as he pretends to he wouldn't leave out the bitterly fought first Punic war in his recital of every war in Roman history. And he says why he does it: 'Others have written the story in verse'[5]—and written it brilliantly indeed, even if less elegantly than you, Ennius: and you shouldn't dissent—you've taken over much from Naevius: that's what we'll say if you admit to it; if you deny it, it's a theft.[6]

D. ATTICUS ON CATO

Brutus 292–9

This answers Cicero's encomium.

292   Then Atticus said: 'I regard as witty and elegant the irony they say Socrates possessed, which he displays in the books by Plato, Xenophon, and Aeschines.[7] Only a man of taste and wit could, when wisdom is under discussion, disown it for himself while playfully attributing it to those who claim it: thus in Plato Socrates praises to the skies Protagoras, Hippias, Prodicus, Gorgias, and the rest, and pretends that he himself is ignorant of everything and quite naïve. This somehow *suits* Socrates, and I don't agree with Epicurus' condemnation of it.[8] But in history—which after all you were employing throughout your description

---

[1] e.g. *Odyssey* 1. 154, 8. 43.   [2] i.e. Ennius (*Annales* 214).
[3] By Livius Andronicus, in Saturnians.
[4] Naevius.   [5] Enn. *Annales* 213.
[6] Cf. 'Longinus' on 'theft' and 'borrowing' (below, p. 476).
[7] The Socratic, not the orator.
[8] For an Epicurean attack on Socrates, cf. Plutarch, *Against Colotes* 19–20.

of the individual orators—you may find that irony is as reprehensible as it is in the giving of evidence.'

'What is this leading up to?' I said. 'I don't understand.' 293

'You praised certain orators in such a way as perhaps to mislead the ignorant. At one point I could scarcely restrain my laughter, when you were comparing our Cato to the Attic Lysias; Cato—as no one denies— was a great man, no, a supreme and remarkable man. But an *orator*? Comparable to Lysias? A master of colourful oratory? A nice piece of irony if we were having a jest; but if we are in earnest, I think that we're on oath just as much as if we were giving evidence. I give credit to your 294 Cato as a citizen, a senator, a general, a man of surpassing foresight and industry, marked by every virtue. His speeches I give high marks—for his time. They have some sign of genius, but a quite unpolished and untutored genius. But as for the *Origins*: when you said they are full of every good oratorical quality, when you compared their author to Philistus and Thucydides, did you expect to persuade Brutus or me? Those are authors no Greek even can aspire to imitate; yet you match with them a man from Tusculum who hadn't even the first idea what it means to speak with fullness and elaboration!

'You praise Galba. If you do so because he was foremost of his age, 295 I agree—that is what we are told. But if you praise him as an orator, please give me his speeches (they *are* extant) and dare to say that you would wish Brutus here, whom you love more dearly than yourself, to speak in that manner. You approve Lepidus' speeches. Here I do agree a little, so long as you praise them as being antique. So too with Africanus, and Laelius—whose speech, according to you, is incomparably charming: incomparably 'august', you add, whatever that may be. You use as bait for us the name of a supremely important man, the undeniable virtues of a life lived with the utmost taste. Take all that away: that 'charming' speech becomes so humble that no one wants to look at it.

'I know Carbo ranked among the great orators. But it is in oratory as in 296 other things: what is for the moment unsurpassed tends to be praised, whatever its quality. I have the same to say about the Gracchi, though you said things about them with which I agree. I won't discuss the rest, but come straight to the men in whom you think eloquence has already reached its perfection—great orators beyond all question, Crassus and Antonius. I heard them speak, and I very much agree with you in your compliments to them, but not in the way you put them. You said that Crassus' speech for the *Lex Servilia* was your tutor, just as Lysippus said of Polyclitus' *Doryphorus*. This is pure irony. I shan't say why I think so: you would think I was flattering you. I won't, then, mention what you said of these 297 orators, of Cotta, Sulpicius, and, just now, of Caelius. These certainly were orators; how good and what sort is for you to decide. I'm less concerned about your heaping together all the meanest labourers in oratory to such an extent that I think some people might have wished to die in order to qualify as one of your list of orators.'

'You have started something', I said when he had finished, 'that could be discussed for a long while, worthy, in fact, of a whole new argument:
298 but *that* we must put off to another time. It would involve turning over the books of many orators, in particular Cato; and you would then realize that nothing was missing in his sketches except the bloom and colour of pigments that had not then been discovered. My judgement on that speech of Crassus' is that he himself could perhaps have written it better—but no one else. You shouldn't regard me as ironical in saying that it was my tutor. You apparently think better of such abilities as I now have. But when I was young I had nothing in Latin more worthy of
299 my imitation. And as to the fact that many names appeared on my list, the point was (as I said not long ago) that I wished it to be understood how few worthy of mention came to the front in a field where so many were so ambitious.'

E. THE NATURE OF ELOQUENCE

Our next extract (*de oratore* 1. 80–95: text by K. Kumaniecki, Teubner, 1969; translation by E. W. Sutton and H. Rackham, Loeb, 1942; commentary by A. S. Wilkins, Oxford, 1892) conveniently summarizes various Greek views on the nature and scope of eloquence: cf. Quintilian 2. 15–21. The dialogue is set in 91 B.C., and the speaker is the orator Antonius, whom Cicero represents as sceptical of the views of Crassus on the wide training of an orator.

80   'You carry conviction with me, Crassus. I have no doubt that the man who has taken in the method and essence of every department of know-
81 ledge and every art would be much richer in his powers of speech. But, first, that is a difficult thing to attain, especially in the sort of life we lead and amid the sort of business that occupies us. Again, there is the fear that we may get diverted from the normal custom and practice of speaking in the forum and before the people. The men[1] you have just described, however brilliantly and impressively they speak on nature or on human affairs, have, I think, a rather different manner of oratory. It is a bright and rich style, belonging rather to the gymnasium and the oil-jars than to the rough-and-tumble of court and politics.
82   'I came late to Greek literature, and only had a smattering of it. But when I was on my way to Cilicia as proconsul I was held up several days in Athens because of sailing delays. I had some scholars in my company

---

[1] Philosophers.

every day—more or less the people you just mentioned; and when it got about somehow that I (like you) tend to get involved in important law-suits, they all put forward for themselves their arguments on the function and method of the orator. Some of them, including the famous Mnesar- 83 chus, said that what we call orators are no more than odd-job men with quick and practised tongues. Only the wise man is an orator.[1] Eloquence itself (defined as the knowledge of speaking well) is one virtue; whoever possesses one virtue possesses all, and all are equal and on a par. Thus the eloquent man has all the virtues and is a wise man. But this was a dry and thorny argument that I found very repellent.

'Charmadas, however, was much more forthcoming on the same sub- 84 ject—not that he voiced his own opinion, it being the traditional custom of the Academy always to oppose everybody in an argument. But on this occasion he argued that those who are called rhetors and who teach the rules of oratory have no real knowledge. The only man capable of attaining any sort of ability at speaking is the man who has learned the discoveries of the philosophers.

'Opposition was expressed by some eloquent Athenian lawyers and 85 politicians, including that Menedemus who was recently my guest in Rome. Menedemus said that there exists a certain practical wisdom that func-tions in the discovery of methods of organizing and ruling states; where-upon that quick-witted and widely learned speaker,[2] who has such an extraordinary fund of varied information, was provoked to reply that every facet of this practical wisdom is to be looked for from philosophy. The provisions of states about religion, education, justice, endurance, temperance, moderation in everything, and all the other things in whose absence cities could not exist, at least in any good condition, are never found in the books of the rhetoricians. If in fact teachers of rhetoric 86 embrace within their art such an abundance of key matters, why are their books full of proems and epilogues and trivialities (that was the word he used) of this kind? Why can no word be found there of the organization of states, the codification of laws, equity, justice, good faith, the over-coming of desire, the shaping of morals? This same man kept making 87 fun of rhetoricians' precepts, demonstrating that rhetors are quite devoid of the practical wisdom they claim for themselves, and what is more are not even aware of the correct method of oratory itself. He regarded it as the hallmark of the orator to appear to the audience in the light he wishes (that is attained by living a respectable life—a subject ignored by teachers of rhetoric in their precepts) and further to ensure that his hearers feel the emotions he intends them to feel: and *that*, too, cannot come about

---

[1] The Stoic position. Cf. also Quintilian's view (12. 1. 1 ff., below, p. 417).
[2] Charmadas.

unless the speaker knows what methods and what style of oratory avail to sway the minds of men in each direction. Now these are matters hidden away deep in philosophy, an ocean into which these rhetors have never ventured a toe.

88 'Menedemus endeavoured to refute all this by instances rather than by arguments. He quoted from memory a good deal of first-rate quality from the speeches of Demosthenes, and showed that that speaker was not unskilled in using his oratory to move judges and people in any direction, and could thereby get effects that the other had asserted could not be

89 attained without philosophy. To this the reply was that there was no denying that Demosthenes possessed supreme practical wisdom and supreme powers of speech: but that whether he owed that to his natural ability or to the fact that (as was well known) he had been an ardent pupil of Plato, the question at issue concerned not the genius of Demosthenes but the teaching of the rhetors.

90 'Often this speaker went so far as to assert that there is no 'art' of speaking. He had arguments to prove this, such as that we are born with a natural ability to flatter those from whom we have to get something, and to menace and frighten our adversaries, to narrate an event, to prove a point or disprove an opposite contention, and, finally, to beg or complain—this being the full range of the orator's potentialities. Or he would argue, again, that it is habit and practice that sharpen intellect and spur on eloquence to greater fluency. He also had an abundance of illustrations

91 to offer. First, he said that, as it were on principle, no writer of an 'Art' has ever been even moderately eloquent—and he went back to one Corax and one Tisias, apparently the acknowledged inventors and originators of the technique. On the other hand, he named countless very eloquent men who never learnt the 'art' and took no trouble to get acquainted with it: among them he counted myself, perhaps for a joke, or perhaps because he really believed, from hearsay, that I belong in that company, having had no training and nevertheless (so he said) possessing some power of oratory. I was very ready to agree on the point that I had learnt nothing; on the other point, I thought he was making fun of me or else was himself mistaken.

92 'However, he said there is no art that is not made up of known and thoroughly understood facts, tending to a single end and never deceptive; on the other hand, everything that is treated by the orator is uncertain and doubtful: the speaker is not in full possession of it, the hearer is regarded as the recipient not of knowledge but of temporary opinion,

93 false or at the least obscure. Isn't that enough? This was how he purported to persuade me that there is no technique of oratory, and that no one can speak cleverly or fully unless he is acquainted with the doctrines of the

most learned philosophers. Charmadas here used to express the highest admiration of your gifts, Crassus—he said that while I was a very ready listener, you were a very doughty disputant.

'So it was that I was attracted by this same view, and went so far as to say, in a little book that slipped out and was read by people though I was unaware and even unwilling, that I had known a few accomplished speakers, but none yet who was eloquent. I defined an accomplished speaker as one who could speak with tolerable intelligence and clarity in the presence of second-rate men and keeping to the average view. An eloquent man, on the other hand, was one who could magnify and embellish whatever he wished in an extraordinary and splendid manner, containing in his mind and in his memory all the sources of everything relevant to oratory. That is something hard to attain for us, who plunged ourselves in a legal career before we got round to training. But it does not, let us assume, lie outside the bounds of possibility. For I—as far as my powers of augury allow and in view of the eminent talents I see in our race—do not despair that one day there will be a man[1] gifted with keener enthusiasm than ours is or has been, with more leisure and opportunity to learn in early life, with superior industry and ability to work hard; who, having devoted himself to listening and reading and writing, may prove to be the sort of orator we are looking for, one who deserves to be called not just a good speaker but truly eloquent: a man embodied, in my opinion, either here and now in Crassus, or in someone who shall have equal abilities but, having heard and read and written more than Crassus, may be able to add somewhat to Crassus' attainments.'

F. PHILOSOPHY AND ORATORY

In this extract (*de oratore* 1. 64–73) Crassus, to whom Cicero gives most of his own views, discusses the wide training that the properly qualified orator must have. It must include some philosophy. Cf. also *Orator* 113 ff. (below, p. 248).

'Hence, if one is to define comprehensively the whole and precise meaning of 'orator', one must say, I think, that he alone is worthy of this imposing name who—whatever turns up that has to be put over in speech—is capable of speaking wisely, with order and ornament, displaying a good memory and a certain impressiveness of delivery. If anybody thinks that I'm being too indefinite in putting 'whatever' into my definition—well, let him chop it and prune it as he will; but I shall still maintain this: an orator may be ignorant of the details of other arts and disciplines, and be conversant only with the techniques of debate and the practice of the

---

[1] Cicero was thinking of himself.

courts—but all the same, if he has to make a speech on these other matters, he, as being an orator, will speak far better than the actual exponents of the arts in question, once, of course, he has been briefed in the individual details by an expert.

66 'For example, if our friend Sulpicius has to speak on a military subject, he will make inquiries of our relation, Gaius Marius; and having got the information, he will deliver his speech in such a fashion that Marius himself will think that the orator is better acquainted with such things than the soldier. If it's a question of civil law, he will get in touch with you, Scaevola. You are a man experienced and adept in the legal matters that he will learn from you; yet he will surpass you by his technique of

67 oratory. If something turns up in which remarks have to be made on nature, on human vice, on desires, on moderation, on continence, on pain, or on death, he may perhaps, if he feels like it, go to Sextus Pompeius, the learned philosopher, though an orator ought to be acquainted with such things himself. In fact, this will be the outcome: whatever the orator learns, whoever he learns it from, he will speak on that matter more brilliantly than the man who gave him the information.

68 'But if I am any authority, philosophy being divided into three categories—the secrets of nature, the complications of dialectic, and the problems of morality—we may let two of these go as a concession to our laziness: but unless we cling fast to the third, which has always been the province of the orator, we shall be leaving him nothing in which he can

69 display his greatness. So the subject of ethics must be learnt through and through by the orator; as for the rest, if he doesn't learn them he'll be able to give them the embellishment of his oratory, when necessary, so long as he is briefed in them.

'Scholars agree that Aratus, a man ignorant of astronomy, succeeded in writing an excellent and brilliant poem on the heavens and the stars; Nicander of Colophon could hardly have been more remote from the countryside—but he wrote successfully on agricultural matters by virtue of a poet's abilities, not a farmer's. Why, then, should not an orator speak most eloquently on matters which he has learnt up for a particular

70 case and a particular time? In fact, the poet is next door to the orator. His metre ties him down rather more, and he's freer to use words as he will: but in many departments of embellishment he is his ally and equal —virtually the same, indeed, in one thing at least, that he sets no bounds to his prerogatives, to his freedom to wander where he likes with the same licence as the orator enjoys.

71 'You said, Scaevola, that there was one thing you wouldn't have tolerated if you hadn't been on my demesne[1]—my saying that the orator should be

---

[1] The scene of the dialogue is Crassus' villa at Tusculum.

fully trained in every type of speech and in every branch of human affairs. Well, I should not say that if I thought that *I* was the man I'm trying to portray to you. But, as Gaius Lucilius used to say (a man who had a bit 72 of a grudge against you, and so wasn't as much my friend as he would have wished—still, a learned and a very witty man), my view is that no one should be counted an orator unless he is highly polished in all liberal arts. Even if we are not employing them in a speech, it is quite clear and evident whether we are ignorant or educated in them: similarly, a ball- 73 player may not employ in a game the virtuosity characteristic of the gymnasium, but his very manner of moving shows whether he's trained or untrained; or take an artist—he may not actually be wielding a brush at a given moment, but it's not difficult to tell whether he knows how to paint or not. So in oratory—in court, popular assembly, or senate: even if the rest of the arts are not being employed particularly, nevertheless it's perfectly easy to see whether the speaker has merely done the rounds of the declaimers or comes to his oratory equipped with all the arts a gentleman should have mastered.'

G. WHICH PHILOSOPHICAL SECT SHOULD THE ORATOR CHOOSE?

Here too Crassus is the speaker (*de oratore* 3. 54–71).

'Antonius said that he had never yet seen anyone who spoke like that, 54 and that it was only to such orators that the name of 'eloquent' should be given. So you may take my advice and laugh to scorn all those who think they have, thanks to the precepts of the rhetors (as they are now called), acquired all possible powers of oratory, but who have in fact not managed to realize what part they have to play and what their profession is. For the true orator should have investigated, heard, read, discussed, treated, and mulled over everything in human life—for that is the field of an orator, and that is the material that is set before him. For eloquence is one of the 55 supreme virtues. Even though all the virtues are equal and level,[1] nevertheless some are more beautiful and glorious to the gaze, as is this attainment, which masters facts and verbally sets forth the thoughts and plans of the mind in such a way that it compels the hearer in the direction which it takes. And the greater this attainment is, the more important is it that it should coincide with probity and supreme wisdom.[2] If we pass on the capacity for oratory to persons without these virtues, we shall not be making orators but putting arms into the hands of the mad.

---

[1] A Stoic view: see above, p. 229.
[2] Cf. Quintilian's view of the orator, below, p. 417.

56   'As I say, this method of thought and expression, this faculty of speech, was called by the ancient Greeks 'wisdom'. Partaking of it we find men of the stamp of Lycurgus, Pittacus, Solon, and, among Romans of a like kind, people such as Coruncanius, Fabricius, Cato, and Scipio. Perhaps these Romans were not so well educated, but they had similar vigour of mind and similar principles. The same wisdom, allied however to a different approach to life, which made them pursue leisure and quiet, marked for example Pythagoras, Democritus, and Anaxagoras, who rather than rule states devoted themselves entirely to knowledge. This kind of life, because of its tranquillity and because knowledge itself is so uniquely agreeable

57   to man, appealed to more people than was convenient for states. Men of the highest talents devoted themselves to philosophy; the opportunity was excellent, their time unoccupied. Hence scholars with leisure and ability in abundance thought they must trouble themselves with research and investigation into far more things than was strictly necessary. The old training had been the teacher of right behaviour as well as right speech; and there was no separation in the instruction—the same men taught about life and about speaking, like Phoenix in Homer, who says that he was given by Peleus to his son Achilles as a companion in war in order to

58   make him 'a speaker of words and a doer of deeds'.[1] Now men who are used to incessant toil every day tend to resort to ball or dice or dominoes when the weather stops them working, or even devise some new leisure-time game for themselves. Similarly, those men, being outside public business (which they regarded as work) either because the times kept them out of it or because they gave themselves a voluntary holiday, devoted themselves completely to poetry or mathematics or music; while others, like the dialecticians, organized a new hobby for themselves, and spent all their time, indeed all their lives, in arts that had been discovered

59   merely to mould the minds of children to morality and virtue. But there were some, in fact many, who were famous in their city for an ambidexterous wisdom in both speech and action (which indeed are inseparable), for example, Themistocles, Pericles, and Theramenes, or else who, while not themselves politicians, nevertheless proposed to teach this same wisdom—like Gorgias, Thrasymachus, and Isocrates.

'Thus there could be found men who, though learned and able, shrank from politics and affairs on principle, and therefore harried and despised

60   the practice of oratory. Chief among these was Socrates, a man who on the evidence of every scholar and in the judgement of all Greece easily excelled in every department to which he turned, combining as he did wisdom, intelligence, charm, and cleverness with eloquence, variety, and copiousness. Men who dealt with, professed, and taught the subjects with

[1] *Iliad* 9. 443.

which we are now concerned were called by a single name: for all knowledge of the most important things, and exercise in them, was known as
philosophy. This common name Socrates snatched from its exponents.
In his discussions he separated the knowledge of wise thought and embellished expression, which are in fact inseparable. Socrates himself left no
written word behind him. But Plato's writings handed down to immortality his genius and his varied conversations. This was the origin of a 61
split, as it were, of tongue from brain, ridiculous indeed and inexpedient
and reprehensible, that meant that one set of men teach us to be
wise, another to speak. Many more or less sprang from Socrates. But because different people took different points away from his varied,
diverse, and wide-ranging discussions, there were born separate and
disparate families that disagreed among themselves, even though all
these philosophers wanted to be known as Socratics and thought of
themselves as such.

'First from Plato himself sprang Aristotle and Xenocrates, who took on 62
the names of Peripatetic and Academy respectively. Next, from Antisthenes, who had particularly liked the ideal of endurance and toughness
that he found in Socrates' conversation, arose the Cynics and later the
Stoics. Again, from Aristippus, who enjoyed rather the lighter discussions, flowed the Cyrenaic philosophy. Aristippus and his successors
defended their view openly; those who nowadays measure everything by
the standard of pleasure,[1] though more modest, can find no proper place
for the good, though they do not despise it: at the same time they cannot
convincingly defend the very pleasure to which they long to cling. There
have been other philosophic sects, more or less all claiming to be followers
of Socrates—the Eretrians, the Erillians, the Megarians, the Pyrrhonians.
But these have by now long been broken and extinguished by the forcible
arguments of the rest.

'But of those that remain, the philosophy which has undertaken to 63
defend pleasure, though it may seem true to some, is far removed
from the man we are looking for, the man we want to be adviser of the
people, leader of the state, first in authority and eloquence in senate,
popular assembly, and law court. I intend no harm to that philosophy;
it will not be banished from fields it desires—it will be able to stay peace-
ably in its gardens where it likes to be, and from which, lounging there
luxuriously and fastidiously, it summons us to leave the rostrum, the
courts, the senate-house—perhaps it is wise, especially as things now are.[2]
But I'm not at the moment asking which philosophy is the truest, but 64
which is most appropriate to the orator. So let us get rid of that lot without

[1] The Epicureans.
[2] Epicureans advocated withdrawal from public life.

any insult intended. They are good men, and, as they see it, happy. Let us only warn them to keep one doctrine quiet as though it were a sacred mystery, however true it is—that it's no duty of the wise man to take part in public life. If they persuade us and all the best citizens on this point, they won't be able to go on being leisured, which is their dearest wish.

65 'As for the Stoics, with whom I find no fault, I still send *them* away. I have no fear of their being offended: they don't know how to feel anger at all.[1] And I'm grateful to them for one thing: alone of all sects they have called eloquence a virtue and wisdom. But surely there is something in them that is repugnant to the orator we are equipping. For one thing, they say that all those who are not wise are slaves, robbers, enemies, madmen, and they deny that anyone *is* wise. It is very silly to entrust an assembly, a senate, or any gathering to a man who regards none of those present as sane, free, or in possession of citizen rights. Moreover, they

66 have a style of speech that may be subtle and is undoubtedly acute, but which, for an orator, is thin, unusual, repellent to the ears of the crowd, obscure, feeble, bare, and yet quite unsuitable for use before the ordinary mob. The Stoics have different concepts of good and bad from their fellow citizens—or indeed from all other nations. They have a different idea of honour, dishonour, reward, punishment. Whether they are right or wrong is irrelevant: if we follow them, we have no chance of getting anything over in a speech.

67 'There remain the Peripatetics and Academics. The Academics have one name but two views. Speusippus, Plato's nephew, and Xenocrates, Plato's pupil, together with Xenocrates' pupils Polemo and Crantor, did not differ greatly from Aristotle, a fellow pupil of Plato. Maybe they were not up to him in fullness and variety of expression. It was first of all Arcesilas, pupil of Polemo, who fastened on the point in the various Platonic writings and Socratic dialogues that there is nothing certain to be perceived by mind or senses. Arcesilas disposed of a wonderfully charming style. He despised every judgement made by mind or sense, and was the first to make a practice (though this was a very Socratic trait) of not stating his own view but arguing against the views expressed by others.

68 This was the source of the newer Academy, in which flourished Carneades, divinely gifted in quickness of wit and breadth of language. I got to know many of those who sat at his feet in Athens. But I can mention as the most distinguished authorities both my father-in-law Scaevola, who heard him in Rome when a young man, and Quintus Metellus, son of Lucius, my friend and a notable man, who used to say that when he was a youth he heard Carneades, already old, over a number of days in Athens.

69 'Thus, just as the ridge of the Apennines is a watershed for rivers, so

[1] The ideal Stoic felt no violent emotion.

separate streams of doctrine flowed from the single hill-crest of wisdom. The philosophers flowed down, as it were, into the upper Greek sea, one that welcomes with many ports;[1] but the orators into our lower Tuscan sea, crude, rocky, and hostile, where even Ulysses went astray. Hence, if we are content with the eloquence and the orator that knows 70 one must either deny a charge, or, if that is impossible, show that the deed was done rightly or by the fault of another or by another's wrong-doing or according to the law or not against the law or by mistake or through necessity, or is not to be called by the name used in the charge, or that the trial is not being held rightfully and legally:[2] if you think it enough to learn the teaching of the handbook-writers—expounded by Antonius much more colourfully and richly than *they* expound them: if you are content with this, together with the precepts you have asked me to explain, then you are excluding the orator from a great and unlimited field and forcing him into a distinctly narrow compass. But if you want 71 to follow in the footsteps of the old Pericles or Demosthenes (who is more familiar to us because of the abundance of his writings), if you have fallen in love with that brilliant and outstandingly beautiful ideal of the perfect orator—then you must take in the dialectical force either of Carneades or of Aristotle.'

H. 'ATTIC' ORATORY

In the 40s, Cicero found himself under attack from admirers of the orator Calvus, who regarded his elaborate and rhythmical oratory as turgid—the sort of thing one would associate with Asia Minor rather than with Attica. Cf. Tacitus, *Dialogus* 18 (below, p. 443); Quintilian 12. 10. 12–15 (below, p. 406). He replied in the *Brutus*, by showing himself as the culmination of the long development of Roman oratory, and also in the *Orator* (ed. P. Reis, 1932; O. Jahn–W. Kroll, 1913; J. E. Sandys, 1885), where he showed that Attic oratory covered a wider field than the plainness of Lysias, the principal hero of the 'Atticists'. We begin with *Orator* 22–32.

We see that there have been orators whose style combined ornament 22 and weight, dexterity and plainness. Would that we could find such a model among the Romans! It would be excellent to content ourselves

---

[1] i.e. the Adriatic.

[2] This alludes to the doctrine of *stasis* (Lat. *status*), much developed in Hellenistic times by Hermagoras and others; it was a set of rules intended to help the orator to think out and select the most telling and appropriate ways of treating his case.

23 with home-grown products and not have to look abroad. In the conversation recorded by me in the *Brutus*, I conceded a good deal to Roman writers, to encourage others or because I was enthusiastic for my fellow countrymen: but I remember, all the same, that I put Demosthenes on his own ahead of all rivals.[1] And it is Demosthenes that I should wish to identify with the ideal eloquence which I *feel* without myself having known it in anyone. No one has ever been more weighty than Demosthenes, cleverer or more self-controlled. My advice, therefore, to those whose ignorant views have been publicized—who want to be called 'Attic' or themselves claim to speak in the Attic manner—is that they should admire this man most of all: Athens herself was surely not more truly Attic. Thus they would learn what the 'Attic' is, and would measure eloquence

24 by his strength, not their own weakness. For, as it is, everyone gives praise to what he thinks his own imitation may perhaps attain. These people have the most admirable enthusiasm, but their taste is unstable; and I do not think it irrelevant to try to instruct them in the nature of the characteristic excellence of the Attic orators.

Orators have always had, to guide their eloquence, the good sense of their listeners. All who wish to be popular have regard to the taste of those who hear them; they mould and adapt themselves to it completely, and

25 to their will and nod. Hence Caria, Phrygia, and Mysia,[2] being far from cultured and far from elegant, took up a style of oratory that, in its richness and as it were fattiness, was suited to their ears. This style was never liked by their neighbours across the narrow stretch of sea, the Rhodians, still less by the mainland Greeks; and it was altogether rejected by the Athenians, whose taste was always so sensible and sure that they could listen to nothing that was corrupt or inelegant. Their scruples had to be' respected by the orator, who would not dare to introduce a word that was

26 unusual or objectionable. Hence the orator whom I have ranked above the rest, in far his best speech, that for Ctesiphon, began quietly, proceeded concisely in his argument about the laws, but then later, after gradually enflaming his hearers, spread himself boldly in the remainder of the speech once he saw that the jury were on fire. Yet this same Demosthenes, who carefully weighed the merits of every word, was criticized in some respects by Aeschines. Aeschines harried him, mockingly saying that his vocabulary was harsh, hateful, intolerable: he went so far as to call him a monster, asking whether these were words or wonders.[3] To

27 Aeschines, apparently, not even Demosthenes seemed to speak Attic. Of course, it is easy to pick on one, as it were, burning word, and make fun of it once the flames of emotion have died down. So Demosthenes made

---

[1] Cf. *Brutus* 35 (above, p. 221).   [2] Cf. Dionysius, below, p. 306.
[3] Aeschines, *Against Ctesiphon* 166; cf. Pliny, *epist.* 9. 26 (below, p. 430).

a joke of the matter when he came to reply; he said[1] that the fortunes of
Greece did not turn on whether he used this word or that, stretched his
hand in one direction or another. How, then, would a Mysian or Phrygian
have been received in Athens when even Demosthenes was criticized as
tasteless? When such a visitor began to chant in the Asiatic style, with a
low wailing voice, who would have put up with him? Who indeed would
not have asked for him to be put out?

Those, then, who adapt themselves to the keen and scrupulous ears of   28
the Attic audience are to be judged as speaking in the Attic manner.
There are many kinds of Attic orator: my opponents can conceive only of
one. They think that the uncultivated rough speaker—so long as he is
discriminating and pithy—is the only Attic orator. They are wrong in
thinking that he is the only one: they are right in thinking that he *is* Attic.
On their standard, if that is the only type of Atticism, not even Pericles   29
spoke in the Attic manner—and he was accorded the highest rank without question. If *he* had used the plain style he would never have been
said by the poet Aristophanes to 'lighten, thunder, and confound Greece'.[2]
That most pleasant and polished of writers, Lysias, may be agreed to
speak in the Attic manner—who could deny it?—so long as we understand
that what makes Lysias Attic is not that he is plain and unadorned, but
that he has nothing unusual or tasteless. But it must be an Attic quality
to speak ornately, weightily, copiously—otherwise neither Aeschines nor
Demosthenes is Attic.

And now we have people who claim to be Thucydideans; a new variety   30
of ignorance, this, and one we have not heard of before. For those who
follow Lysias are at least following a lawyer—not perhaps a grand and
noble one, but a careful and elegant speaker who would take his place
with distinction in legal cases. But Thucydides narrates history, wars, and
battles, weightily and excellently no doubt, but not in such a way that
anything can be transferred from him to public or legal oratory. Even
those well-known speeches of his have so many obscure and recondite
thoughts that they can scarcely be understood—perhaps the worst fault
of all in public oratory. Can men be so perverse as to feed on acorns after   31
the discovery of corn? Food could be improved thanks to the Athenians:[3]
why not oratory? And which of the Greek rhetoricians ever drew anything from Thucydides? 'But he has been praised by everyone.' Certainly
—as a narrator of events, sensible, austere, and serious: not as dealing
with cases in the courts but as relating wars in history books. He was   32
never counted as an orator, and if he had not written a history his name

[1] *On the Crown* 232.
[2] *Acharnians* 530 (cf. Pliny, *epist.* 1. 20. 19, below, p. 426).
[3] Grain having, according to legend, originated in Attica.

would not survive, however honoured and well-born he may have been. In any case, no one tries to imitate his austerity of words and sentiment: they think that they are genuine Thucydideses when they have said something broken and gaping—and they could have managed that even without a model. I have even come across people who wanted to be like Xenophon—a writer whose style is certainly sweeter than honey, but very far removed from the hurly-burly of the forum.

I. THE THREE STYLES AND THE PERFECT ORATOR

Here (*Orator* 75–121) we have a classic exposition of a central theme of ancient criticism: the types of style. Cf. the four types of Demetrius (above, chap. 4); the three-type scheme is much the commonest, and we shall see it in various guises in Quintilian and Dionysius.

75   Next must be investigated the mark and pattern of each type—a great and difficult task, as I have often said before. But I should have reflected what I was about at the time of embarkation; now I must set sail, wherever the winds take me.

THE PLAIN STYLE

First of all, I must sketch the man whom some regard as the only true
76 Attic orator. He is pitched in a low key and unpretentious, giving an appearance of using ordinary language, but in reality differing from the inexpert more than is commonly supposed. Hence those who hear him, however incapable of utterance themselves, are confident that they too could speak like that. Plainness of style may seem easily imitable in theory; in practice nothing could be more difficult. It has not a great deal of blood about it, but it must have a sort of sap to give it good health even if it lacks the greatest strength.

77   The plain orator must first be freed from the shackles of rhythm: for there are, as you know, certain rhythms used in oratory, to be dealt with later, which one must methodically keep to in another style but altogether ignore here. This must be quite unrhythmic, though not wandering; it should seem to walk freely, not stray at random. It should not trouble to (as it were) cement words to each other: hiatus, thanks to the juxtaposition of vowels, has something soothing about it, something that indicates a not unpleasant negligence on the part of a speaker more worried about
78 content than about phraseology. But other matters must be seen to, even though these two factors—periodic structure and the 'glueing' of words—are not enforced on this style. For even short and cut-up sentences are

not to be organized negligently: even negligence sometimes demands care. Just as some women are said to be prettier when not made-up—for it is *that* that suits them—so this plain style pleases despite its lack of decoration. There is something present in each case that adds beauty without becoming apparent.

Next, all obvious pearls of ornament, as it were, are to be removed: not even the curling-tongs are to be applied; all preparations giving artificial 79 red or white are to be banned; only elegance and neatness will remain. The language will be correct and Latin, clear and unambiguous; regard will be paid to what is fitting; and the only absentee will be what Theophrastus put fourth in his list of the virtues of oratory[1]—ornamentation, smooth and rich. There will be perceptive, close-packed thought, dug up from I don't know what hidden depths: and—the most important point in this style—a sparing use of the stock-in-trade of oratory. For we have in a 80 way our stock, consisting of ornaments, partly of matter, partly of words. Ornament of words is twofold, one kind of words taken separately, one of words in combination. In the former, standard words (*propria*) and words in common parlance are 'ornamental' when they sound best or best express the content. Among words that are in some way unnatural, we have words transferred and borrowed:[2] those new and made up by the author: and those ancient and out of use (though even these can be classed among standard words, except that we only rarely use them). On the other hand, words in combination are ornamental if they produce 81 a certain balance that would not remain if the words were altered while the thought stayed the same: ornaments of thought, which remain even if you change the wording, are doubtless very numerous, but only a few of them are conspicuous.

Thus our slender orator, while remaining elegant, will be shy of coining words, modest and sparing in metaphor, restrained in the use of old words and of the other ornaments, both of word and thought: though he will perhaps use comparatively frequently the type of metaphor most commonly found in all conversation, of town and country folk alike— for it's countrymen who say 'the vines are gemming', 'the fields are thirsty', 'the crops are cheerful', 'the corn is luxuriant'. Each of these is bold 82 enough, but in every case the comparison is very close, or, if a thing lacks a name of its own, it is obvious that the metaphor is used to get the meaning across, not for fun. The restrained type of orator will use this rather more freely than other ornaments, but not so lavishly as if he were employing the amplest style of oratory. And so the unfitting, whose nature can be deduced from its opposite, is obvious in this field also, in cases

---

[1] These four 'virtues' were: correctness, clarity, appropriateness, and 'ornamentation'.
[2] i.e. metaphor. Compare with all this *de oratore* 3. 155 (below, p. 258).

where a metaphor is too violent, and what would be suitable in another style is placed in the 'low' style.

83   But the neatness which decks out collocations of words with the decorations that the Greeks call *schēmata*, 'gestures', as it were, of speech (the same word that they use also of decorations of thought), will certainly find a place in the armoury of the fine-spun orator (rightly called Attic, though the term should not be restricted to him). But he will use it rather sparingly. It is just like the organization of dinner-parties: fighting shy of grandness, he will want to be thought to have good taste (*elegantia*) as well as leanings to economy. Hence, he will choose (*eliget*) what device

84   to use. And there are many things that *are* suited to the thriftiness practised by the orator of whom I am speaking. Certainly our acute speaker must avoid the devices I described earlier, such as balanced clauses of equal length, clauses with the same endings and the same cadences, and clever effects sought by mere change of a letter: for he must avoid being

85   clearly convicted of artificial symmetry and the pursuit of pleasure. Again, repetitions of words involving strain and noise will be alien to this orator's restraint. But other devices he will be able to use without discrimination, so long as he dismantles and splits up long periodic structures, and uses the most ordinary words, the most gentle metaphors. He will employ even decorations of thought, at least those that are not over-gaudy. He will not make the republic speak, or call up the dead from the underworld,[1] or pile many elements up and bind them within one period. These things are suited to stronger lungs, and are not to be expected or required of the

86   orator we are sketching. *He* will be subdued in voice and style alike. But many of those figures *will* be suitable even to the plain style, although it will make a rougher use of the same ornaments: that is the kind of character I am exhibiting. Add a delivery that is not tragic or stagy, that involves little movement of the body, but accomplishes much by facial expression —not the type by which people are said to grimace, but that by which they signify without affectation in what sense everything they say is to be understood.

87   On this type of oratory there will also be sprinkled jests, which have extreme effectiveness in speech.[2] There are two kinds, one humour, the other wit. Our orator will use both; but one will be appropriate in telling a story pleasantly, the other in projecting and dispatching something that causes laughter—and of *this* there is more than one variety: but that is

88   another matter. A word of warning: the orator will employ the laughable infrequently, so as not to behave like a buffoon, with no *double entendre*, so as not to descend to the level of a mime, without malice, so as not to

---

[1] As, e.g., in *pro Caelio*. Cf. Quint. 12. 10. 61 (below, p. 414).
[2] In general, see *de oratore* 2. 216 ff.; Quint. 6. 3; Demetrius (above, p. 203).

be impudent. He will not use it against misfortune (that would be cruel), or against crime (lest laughter take the place of hatred). He will use no jest that conflicts with his character or that of the judges or with the situation: that comes under the head of the unsuitable. He will also avoid 89 the prepared joke, one not made up on the spur of the moment but brought along from home—such usually fall flat. He will spare his friends and men of importance; he will steer clear of inflicting injuries that cannot be healed; he will hit only his opponents, and them not always, and not all of them or in every way. With these exceptions he will employ wit and humour in a manner that I have not observed among our latter-day Atticists—though it is in itself, without question, a highly Attic attribute.

This, in my view, is the outline of the restrained orator who is yet a 90 great and genuine Attic speaker. For whatever is witty or healthy in a speech is characteristic of Attic orators. Not all of *them* were humorous: Lysias and Hyperides are reputed tolerable in this respect, Demades supreme, Demosthenes inferior. In my view, nothing could be more urbane than Demosthenes; yet he was not so much witty (*dicax*) as humorous (*facetus*): wit requires the keener natural gift, humour the greater art.

THE MIDDLE STYLE

There is another type, richer and rather more robust than this plain one 91 I have been describing, but more restrained than the fullest, which I have yet to discuss. This type has a minimum of muscle, a maximum of sweetness. For it is fuller than our concise type, more restrained than the ornate and copious style. Here all stylistic ornaments are appropriate: for this 92 pattern of oratory has the greatest possible charm. Many have distinguished themselves in it in Greece, but in my view Demetrius of Phaleron surpasses the rest. His style flows gently and quietly, but it is brightened, as if by stars, by words transferred and altered. I mean (as often before) by the former those that are transferred by means of a similarity from one thing to another to give pleasure or to satisfy a lack: by 'altered' those in which another word is substituted for the correct one, meaning the same, but drawn from some associated idea. This, too, of course, is the 93 result of 'transferring'; but Ennius was using one sort of transference when he said: 'I am bereft of citadel and city', quite another when he made 'horrid Africa shake with terrible tumult'.[1] This last the rhetoricians call *hupallagē*, because (as it were) words are exchanged for words; grammarians use the term metonymy, because it is names that are

---

[1] *Andromache*, fr. 88; *Annales* 310.

94 transferred. Now Aristotle[1] ranges under 'transference' (i.e. metaphor) both these phenomena and also 'abuse'—his word is *katachrēsis*—as, for instance, when we say that a man's spirit is 'minute' rather than 'small': and we can 'abuse' words neighbouring on each other, if we need a word that pleases or is suitable.

When several metaphors have flowed on successively, a new sort of speech develops: this type the Greeks call allegory—a good enough name, but the better classification is to regard all these devices, as Aristotle does, under the genus 'metaphor'. Demetrius uses them frequently, and they are most agreeable. He has much metaphor—and no one has more

95 'alterations' (*immutationes*). Into this same style of oratory (I am still speaking of the moderate and blended kind) fall all figures of speech, and many too of thought. Here wide-ranging and learned disputations will be deployed, and commonplaces recited without heat. To sum up, orators of this kind generally emerge from the schools of philosophy; they will merit our admiration for their own sake, so long as we avoid open com-

96 parison with a stronger. The style is decorative, flowery, bright, and polished; all beauties of word and sentiment are interwoven here. The whole flowed from a sophistic fountain-head into the courts; but scorned by the plain orators, rejected by the weighty, it has come to rest, as I have described, in the middle.

THE GRAND STYLE

97 The third type of orator is the full, copious, weighty, and ornate. Here surely lies the most power. It is he whose splendour and fullness the world has so admired that it has suffered eloquence to prevail in our cities— meaning by eloquence the sort which is carried along with vast flow and sound, looked up to and wondered at by all, by all thought to be above their own powers of attainment. *This* eloquence has it in itself to manipulate minds, to move them in every way. Sometimes it breaks through into the feelings, sometimes insinuates itself. It sows new opinions, uproots old ones.

98 But there is a great difference between this style and those discussed above. The orator in the plain and sharp style who has striven to speak shrewdly and acutely, without higher pretensions, is a great orator, even if not the greatest, if he attains this one aim. He will be on safe ground; if he once gets a footing, he will never fall. The middle orator, whom I call moderate and temperate, so long as he does justice to his own aims, need not fear the doubtful and uncertain chances of oratory. Even if, as

[1] *Poetics* 21 (above, p. 119).

often happens, he does not always succeed, he will not be running a grave danger: he cannot fall far.[1] But the weighty, fierce, and burning orator, 99 whom we put first, deserves the greatest scorn if he is born to this style *alone*, and has practised and studied it and only it, without blending his fullness with the other two kinds. The restrained speaker is regarded as wise because he speaks acutely and with an expert's skill; the middle manner is thought pleasant; but the very full speaker, *if he is nothing else*, is scarcely to be regarded as sane. He who can say nothing quietly and gently, nothing that shows organization, precision, clarity, and wit (especially as cases are sometimes in part, sometimes wholly to be handled in these ways), looks like a madman raving in sane company, a drunk revelling among the sober, if he begins to set a subject alight for ears that he has not prepared in advance.

THE PERFECT ORATOR

Here, then, Brutus, we have the man we are looking for—but in our 100 minds only: for if I'd managed to get him in my clutches, not all his eloquence would persuade me to let him go. But all the same we have surely found the eloquent man whom Antonius never saw.[2] Who is he? I shall sum up briefly, then explain at length. That man is eloquent who can speak of humble things plainly, lofty things with gravity, middling things with the blended style. There never was such a man, you will say. Maybe not. I am talking of what I should like to see, not what I have seen: 101 which takes me back to that Platonic 'form' and 'pattern' of which I spoke earlier, and which we can have in our minds even if we do not see it. I am not seeking the eloquent *man*, or anything that is mortal and subject to decay, but the *quality* whose possessor is thereby eloquent— nothing else, in fact, but eloquence itself, which we can see only with the eye of the mind. To repeat: he will be eloquent who can speak of trivial things in a subdued manner, middling things in the blended style, great things with gravity.

ILLUSTRATIONS OF THE STYLES

My whole speech in defence of Caecina concerned the words of an 102 interdict; I used definition to unravel the complicated circumstances, I eulogized civil law, I interpreted ambiguous words. In my speech on the Manilian law, I had to polish up the image of Pompey: I used a temperate

---

[1] On the topic of 'danger' in oratory cf. Pliny, *epist.* 9. 26 (below, p. 429).
[2] *De oratore* 1. 94 (above, p. 231).

style to provide the polish. The whole prestige of the state was involved in
the case of Rabirius; hence I then blazed out with every means of ampli-
103 fication. But sometimes these elements have to be blended and varied.
Well, what type cannot be found in the seven books in which I accused
Verres? Or in my defences of Cluentius, of Cornelius, of many others? I
might have looked out examples, but they are well known—or inquirers
can choose them for themselves. There is no quality in any style of which
there is not, in my speeches, if not a consummate instance, at least an
104 attempt and adumbration. I do not attain my goal: I see what goal ought
to be set.

DEMOSTHENES

Now, in fact, I am speaking not of myself but of a quality; and here I
am so far from being an admirer of my own productions, I am so harsh
and critical, that Demosthenes himself doesn't satisfy me. He is uniquely
eminent in all branches of oratory: yet he doesn't always give my ears
what they expect, so greedily and consumingly do they often yearn after
105 some immeasurable and infinite perfection. But you got to know this
orator as a whole when you were in Athens, studying with his fervent
admirer Pammenes, and you have not given him up: on the other hand,
you make a practice of reading my work also; you surely must be in a
position to see that he achieves much, I try for much, that he can speak
in whatever way the case demands, I merely wish to. That great man
had great predecessors, and excellent orators contemporary with him.
That is less true of myself. It would have been a great achievement if I
could have reached the heights to which I aspired in a city in which, as
106 Antonius said, no eloquent man has been heard. Yet if Antonius did not
think Crassus or even himself eloquent, he would not have thought
Cotta or Sulpicius or Hortensius eloquent. For Cotta could say nothing
grandly, Sulpicius nothing gently, Hortensius little with weight. Their
predecessors, I mean Crassus and Antonius, were more suited to all the
branches.

CICERO'S YOUTH

The taste of the city, then, as I took it over, was hungry for this oratory
of many facets, that spreads with equal facility into every style, and I
turned the ears of Rome, in my earliest years, however slight my qualities
and achievements, to a quite extraordinary enthusiasm for this kind of
107 oratory. How great the applause when, as a youth, I spoke words on the

punishment of parricides[1] that only rather later did I begin to feel had not sufficiently come off the boil! 'For what is so common a boon as breath to the living, as earth to the dead, as the sea to the storm-tossed, as the shore to the ship-wrecked? *They* live, while they can—but cannot draw breath from the sky. They die, but their bones never touch the earth. They are tossed by the waves, but they are never washed by them. They are cast ashore at last—but find no rest in death even upon the rocks', and what follows.[2] Everything bears the mark of a young man, praised not for mature performance but for the hopes he aroused. In that vein, too, were words spoken in maturer years: 'The wife of her son-in-law, stepmother of her son, rival of her daughter.'[3]

But I wasn't carried away into making all my speeches sound like this. 108 Even that youthful copiousness has much that is subdued, even something a little more gay: witness the speeches for Cluentius and Cornelius and some others. For no orator, even in the leisure of Greece, has written so much as I—and my works have the variety which I am recommending. I should concede to Homer, Ennius, and the rest of the poets, particularly 109 the tragedians, that they need not everywhere use the same strained manner, that they should frequently vary it, and sometimes even descend to the normal everyday style of conversation: was I myself then never to leave the vehemence of my highest flights? But why bring up the inspired poets? I have seen actors at the very top of their profession who could not only acquit themselves well in the most dissimilar characters, while keeping to their own special field, but could do pretty well in tragedy, though specializing in comedy, or in comedy, though specializing in tragedy; was *I* not to strive for the like?

And when I say 'I', I mean *you*, Brutus. What was possible in me was 110 long ago complete. But will you go on delivering all your speeches in the same way? Will you reject one particular sort of case? Will you, within the same case, preserve a constantly animated tone with no variation? Demosthenes—you must, I imagine, admire *him*, for I saw a bronze of him among the statues of you and your family when I visited you in your villa at Tusculum—Demosthenes yields nothing in plainness to Lysias, nothing in sharpness and acumen to Hyperides, nothing in smoothness and brilliance of diction to Aeschines. Many of his speeches 111 are plain throughout, as for example that against Leptines. Many are wholly grand, as some of the *Philippics*. Many have variety, such as the speech against Aeschines on the misconduct of the embassy or against the same man on behalf of Ctesiphon. Again, he snatches at the middle style whenever he wishes, and, when he leaves the grandest, it is thither

---

[1] Parricides were tied up in sacks and thrown into the sea.
[2] *Pro Sex. Roscio Amerino* 72.   [3] *Pro Cluentio* 199.

that he prefers to resort. But he rouses applause and has most effect in his oratory when he is developing the grand passages.

112 But let us leave him for a while; we are investigating a type, not an individual: let us reveal the potentialities and nature of a *thing*—eloquence. But let us remember what I said before, that I shall say nothing in the way of precept, and shall behave like a critic, not a teacher. But I go the further in many points because I see that you won't be the only reader of these words (which are more familiar to you than to me, your apparent instructor): this book is bound to be publicized by your name being attached to it—if not by any merit of mine.

THE ATTAINMENTS OF THE PERFECT ORATOR

113 Now I think the perfectly eloquent man must not merely have his own peculiar capacity, for flowing and copious speech: he must also acquire a neighbouring branch of knowledge, namely logic. Of course, oratory is one thing, disputation another. Dialectic and rhetoric differ. But both are branches of discourse. To the logicians belongs the technique of dispute and argument; to the orators that of speech and ornamentation. Zeno, founder of Stoicism, used to use his hand to demonstrate the difference between these arts. Clenching his fist, he would say that logic was like *that*: relaxing and spreading the hand, that eloquence resembled the

114 palm, so. Even before that, Aristotle, at the start of his *Rhetoric*, said that that art was as it were the complement of logic: they differ (of course) because rhetoric is wider, dialectic more contracted. Therefore, I want my supreme orator to be familiar with every logical technique that may be applicable to oratory. You are an expert in this field, and will know that logic has been taught in two ways. Aristotle himself handed down very many precepts for argument, and later the so-called dialecticians[1]

115 produced many rather thorny rules. My view is that the aspirant for eloquence should not be altogether naïve in these matters, but should receive training either in the old doctrine of Aristotle or in the newer one of Chrysippus. He should know the force, nature, and types of words both in isolation and in combination; the various modes of assertion; the method of judging between truth and falsehood; what deduction should be made from each statement, what is consequent, what contrary; and —since many ambiguous statements are made—how each ambiguity should be analysed and resolved. These principles must be borne in mind by the orator, and they often come up; but on their own they are

[1] Especially the Stoic Chrysippus.

somewhat unattractive, and a certain stylistic polish must be brought to
their exposition.

In everything that is being put over methodically, one must first of all 116
decide what each thing *is*: unless the disputants agree on the nature of the
point in dispute, there can be no meaningful discussion and no conclusion. So we must often use words to give our view on a thing, and to
clear up obscure concepts by definition—definition being words that show
as briefly as possible the point at issue. Next, as you know, once the genus
of each thing has been expounded, we have to see what the species and
parts of that genus may be, so that our whole speech may be distributed
among them. Our candidate for eloquence, then, must have the capacity 117
to define: not indeed so briefly and narrowly as is usual in scholarly
disputation, but more clearly, more fully, and in a way more calculated
to suit the average taste and the intelligence of the populace. When
circumstances demand, he will also be able to divide a genus into determi-
nate species, so that none is omitted and none superfluous. It is not relevant here to say when he is to do this and how; as I said, I want to be a
judge, not a teacher.

Nor should he be equipped only by the logicians; he should be familiar 118
in theory with all the commonplaces of philosophy, and have handled
them in practice. Nothing concerning religion, death, piety, patriotism,
good, bad, virtue, vice, duty, pain, pleasure, passion, and error—things
that often come up in cases, but tend to get treated pretty sparsely—
nothing on these subjects can be said and discussed with weight, dignity,
and fullness without the knowledge I have spoken of.

I am still talking of the subject-matter of oratory, not actual style. For 119
I want our orator to have a topic, and one worthy of the learned, before he
gets round to considering what language he is to employ. And, to make
him grander and loftier, as I said of Pericles above, I want him to be
acquainted with science also. Surely he will be capable of feeling and
speaking everything more sublimely and more magnificently when he
returns to humanity from the heavens.

Having mastered the divine, I don't want him ignorant of human affairs 120
either. He must grasp civil law, which is needed every day in court.
Nothing could be more shaming than to take cases that turn on law when
you are ignorant of the laws and the civil code. He should also know of the
course of history and the past, particularly at Rome, but extending to
imperial peoples and famous kings. This task has been lightened by the
pains of my friend Atticus,[1] for he has brought into the compass of a
single book the history of seven hundred years, with no important omission,
in strict conformity to a stated chronological order. Not to know what

[1] See on *Brutus* 28 (above, p. 220).

happened before you were born is to be a child for ever. What is the life of man unless history binds it to the past? In any case, reference to antiquity and the putting forward of instances is not only pleasurable but a source 121 of authority and conviction in a speech. This will be the equipment with which he will come to court.

J. THE BEST TYPE OF ORATOR

De optimo genere oratorum

This little treatise is a preface to a Latin translation (not extant) of the speeches of Demosthenes and Aeschines for and against Ctesiphon. Argument and style seem inferior to Cicero's best, and there are some grounds for thinking the work spurious. Text: A. S. Wilkins, Oxford, 1903.

1 There are said to be *types* of orators, as of poets. This is wrong. Certainly there are a number of branches of poetry. There is tragic, comic, epic, and also melic and dithyrambic poetry, each with its own individual properties.[1] For instance, in tragedy the comic is a fault, and in comedy the tragic displeases: and of the other branches each has a definite sound, a
2 sort of tone of voice that experts can recognize. But if anyone marks off various types of orator—some grand or grave or full, others plain or fine-drawn or concise, others in between and as it were forming the mean— he is saying something about the individuals, little in the abstract. For in the abstract, we inquire what is *best*. In the case of an individual, we describe what *is*. Thus, we may, if we like, call Ennius the greatest epic poet, and Pacuvius the greatest tragedian, and Caecilius, perhaps, the
3 greatest comic writer. But I make no divisions of type among orators: I am looking for the perfect one. There is only one type of the perfect orator; those who do not belong to it do not differ from him in type (as Terence does from Accius): they are of the same type, but not equal in quality. For the best orator is the one who by his oratory instructs, pleases, and moves the minds of his audience. To instruct is a debt to be paid, to give pleasure a gratuity to confer, to rouse emotion a sheer necessity.
4 Now it must be agreed that orators differ in their ability in these fields. But this is a matter of degree, not of type. There is one thing that is perfect, and what comes next is what is most like the perfect. From this it is clear that what is most unlike the best is the worst.

Now since eloquence consists of words and thoughts, we must contrive, while speaking in a pure and correct manner (that is, in good Latin), to attain, besides that, choiceness of words, whether used metaphorically or not. Among non-metaphorical words, we must choose the most

[1] Text uncertain.

smart: in metaphorical language, we must not stray far from our comparison, but use borrowed terms with moderation. Of thoughts, there are 5 as many types as I said there were of qualities of oratory. To instruction belong pointed sentiments, to pleasure-giving brilliant ones, to emotional oratory high-sounding ones. There is also such a thing as verbal structure, which brings about two results, rhythm and smoothness, while thoughts have their own organization, an order adapted to the formulation of a proof. But of all these things there is one foundation—memory: and all are given lustre by delivery.

The man, therefore, in whom all these things combine in their highest 6 degrees will be the most perfect orator: the middling orator will have them in middling degrees, the worst orator in their lowest degree. But they will all be called orators, just as even bad painters are still called painters; they will differ from each other not in type but in capacity. And so there is no orator who would not wish to be like Demosthenes. But Menander did not wish to be like Homer: their types differed. This is not true of orators. Or rather, if it does happen that one orator pursues gravity but shuns subtlety, while another wishes to be acute rather than ornate, neither (you may be sure) is the best, though he may be fairly good; the type that is best is the one that has *all* good qualities.

I have said all this more concisely than the matter deserved; but to 7 have been fuller would not have suited my present object. There is one type; we are inquiring what sort of a type it is. It is the sort that flourished in Athens; it is the source of the glory of the Attic orators (which is familiar), and of their capacity (which is not). Many have seen one side of them—that they have nothing faulty. Few have seen the other—that they have many points to be praised. It is faulty in a sentiment if anything in it is absurd or irrelevant or unintelligent or insipid: in vocabulary if a word is low, vulgar, inapt, harsh, or far-fetched. These faults have been 8 avoided by virtually all who are numbered among the Attic or even speak Attic. But those whose strengths only go as far as this may certainly be regarded as fit and healthy—but only like wrestlers who may stroll about the gymnasium but cannot hope for Olympic medals. Our pattern should if possible be those who lack every fault, but are not content merely with good health (as it were) but go in search of strength, muscle, red blood, a certain attractiveness of complexion. If this is not possible, we should prefer to imitate those whose health is unaffected (the Attic characteristic) rather than those in whom copiousness is taken to a fault (many such have been produced by Asia). When we do this (if we *can* attain even that: for 9 it is a great achievement), let us, if possible, imitate Lysias and his plain oratory for preference. He is, in many passages, fairly lofty; but since he wrote most of his speeches on private issues, and those for the delivery of others and concerning trivial matters, he gives a rather jejune impression, for he purposely filed his speech down to the standards of unimportant cases. Someone who does this, but cannot be richer if he wishes to be, may be regarded as an orator no doubt, but a minor one. On the other hand, a great orator also often has to speak in that manner, where the type

10 of case suits it. Thus, Demosthenes certainly could speak in a lower key: Lysias *may* not have been able to speak in a higher one. But as for those who think that it would have been fitting for the speech for Milo to have been made (at a time when the army was in position in the forum and all the temples round about) in the same tone as if I had been speaking about a private case before a single judge: such people are measuring the force of eloquence by their own capabilities, not by its potentialities.

11   So, since the claims of various people have been bruited abroad—some saying that they themselves are 'Attic' speakers, some that no Roman speaks in the Attic manner—we may ignore the one group. The facts themselves make sufficient reply to them, for they are either not made advocates in court at all, or, if they are, meet with scornful laughter (if it was just laughter, well and good; *that* would be a characteristic of Attic orators). But as for those who want me to speak in the Attic manner, but confess that *they* are no orators—well, if they have keen ears and perceptive taste, they will get a hearing, just as in the judging of pictures even those who cannot paint are appealed to, so long as they have a certain

12 knack of criticism. But if what they call 'perception' is merely fastidiousness in listening, and if they are not ready to be pleased by anything lofty and splendid, let them say outright that they want something fine-drawn and polished, but despise the grand and ornate: but let them stop saying that the only Attic speakers are those who speak in this fine-drawn way—that is, 'dryly' and 'correctly'. It is the mark of Attic orators to speak fully and ornately and copiously as well as soundly. Is there any doubt about our answer to the question: do we want our oratory to be merely tolerable, or worthy of admiration into the bargain? We aren't now inquiring what it is to speak in the Attic manner, but what it is to

13 speak in the best way. From this an inference can be drawn: since, of the Greek orators, the most eminent were the Athenians, and since, of these, easily the best was Demosthenes, an imitator of *him* will speak both in the Attic and in the best possible manner. So that as the Attic orators are suggested as our patterns, speaking well is the same as speaking in the Attic way.

But since a great error has got abroad as to what that type of oratory *is*, I thought that I should undertake a labour useful to students, though not

14 necessary for myself. For I have translated the most renowned speeches of the two most eloquent speakers of Attica—Aeschines and Demosthenes:

these speeches they made on opposite sides of the same case. I have translated not as an interpreter but as an orator, preserving the sentiments and their forms (so to say, 'figures') from the original, but adapting the words to our own usage. I have not thought it necessary to translate word for word, but I have kept to the same kind of words, preserving their general meaning. I did not think I ought to count the words out one by one to the reader, but as it were to weigh them out. The result of my 15 labour will be that our countrymen may know what to ask of those who want to be known as Atticists, and understand by what (as it were) rule of speech they should measure them.

'But', you may say, 'Thucydides will be brought up. Some people admire *his* eloquence.' That is certainly proper; but it has nothing to do with the orator we are in search of. It is one thing to give a survey of historical facts by narration, quite another to use arguments to bring accusations or refute them; one thing to hold a hearer's attention while narrating, another to stir his emotions. 'But his style is so agreeable.' Better than Plato's? In any case, the orator we are searching for must deal 16 with legal issues in a style of oratory suitable for instructing, pleasing, and stirring emotion. Thus, if there is anyone who claims that he will plead cases in the forum in the Thucydidean style, he can have no notion of what goes on in legal and political affairs. If he merely wants to register admiration of Thucydides, he can add my vote to his.

Even Isocrates himself, Plato's virtual contemporary and the subject 17 of a warm encomium by that immortal author, through the mouth of Socrates in the *Phaedrus*[1]—a man whom all scholars have accepted to be a great orator: even Isocrates I do not put into this class. He has no experience of battlefield and cold steel. His oratory fences, with a wooden sword. To use a trivial analogy, I am introducing a very notable pair of gladiators: Aeschines, like Aeserninus in Lucilius' poem (no 'lout', however, but a keen and learned man), 'is matched with Pacideianus, far the best of all men born'.[2] Nothing nearer the gods could be imagined, I think, than that great orator.

This task of mine encounters two types of criticism. One is this: 18 'Didn't the Greeks do this better?' The counter-question is: 'Could *you* do anything better in Latin?' The other is: 'Why should I read these rather than the Greek originals?' Yet these same critics welcome Latin versions of the *Andria* and the *Synephebi*, no less than the *Andromache* or the *Antiope* or the *Epigoni*.[3] What is this distaste of theirs for orations translated from the Greek which doesn't apply to poetry?

---

[1] 278 e.   [2] Lucilius 149 f. Marx.
[3] Comedies by Terence and Caecilius, tragedies by Ennius, Pacuvius, and Accius. All versions of Greek originals.

19 But I must start on my task—once I have explained the case that was brought to judgement. There was a law in Athens 'that no one should decree that anyone be granted a crown during his magistracy before he has rendered account for his office': and another that 'those who are rewarded by the people should have that reward conferred in the popular assembly; those rewarded by the council should have the reward conferred in the council chamber'. Demosthenes was the official in charge of the renewing of the walls, and he renewed them at his own expense; Ctesiphon, therefore, moved a decree, though Demosthenes had not accounted for his office, that a golden crown should be given to him, that the conferment should take place at an assembly of the people in the theatre, which is not the place for lawful assemblies, and that the citation should read that he received the honour 'because of the virtue and bene-

20 volence which he displayed towards the Athenian people'. This Ctesiphon was accordingly brought to court by Aeschines on the grounds that he had illegally moved that a crown should be awarded without account being given for the magistracy and that it should be conferred in the theatre, and on the further ground that what he had stated about Demosthenes' virtue and benevolence was false, as he was in fact not a good man and had not deserved well of the city. The case itself is not in accordance with the forms of our legal system, but it is an important one. It involves acute interpretation of the law on both sides, and a comparison of services

21 to the state that is certainly weighty. Aeschines had himself been accused by Demosthenes, on a capital charge, of misconducting an embassy; he therefore had a motive: in order to avenge himself on his enemy, the trial would (under the name of Ctesiphon) in reality concern the actions and reputation of Demosthenes. For Aeschines did not say so much about the failure to account as about the charge that a wicked citizen had been praised as though he were an excellent one.

22 Aeschines sought to inflict this penalty on Ctesiphon four years before the death of Philip of Macedon. But the trial actually took place a few years later, when Alexander was already master of Asia—and it was a trial to which there is said to have been a rush from all over Greece.[1] What indeed could have been more worth seeing or hearing than the confrontation of the greatest orators in an important case—a contest carefully

23 prepared for and sharpened by personal enmity? If (as I hope) I succeed in reproducing their orations, using all their qualities (their thoughts and figures and order of subject-matter), and keeping to their words except where they conflict with our usage (they may not all be translated from the Greek, but I have striven that they should be of the same kind), there will be a standard to which the speeches of those who wish to speak

[1] It took place in 330 B.C.; Philip had died in 336.

in the Attic manner may be directed. That is enough about me. Let us at last hear Aeschines himself, speaking in Latin.

K. HISTORY

This extract (*de oratore* 2. 51–8) gives some of Cicero's views on the writing of history. Compare the beginning of *de legibus*, the famous letter to Lucceius (*ad fam.* 5. 12), and *Brutus* 42 (above, p. 222). See also below, chap. 13, for some Greek views on similar topics.

'Well, now,' said Antonius, 'what sort of orator, how great a stylist does 51 it take to write history?'

'If you mean history in the way the Greeks wrote it,' said Catulus, 'it takes a very great one. If you mean our sort, there's no need of an orator at all. It's enough not actually to be untruthful.'

'I must stop you despising our historians', said Antonius. 'The Greeks themselves wrote like our Cato, Pictor, and Piso at the start. History 52 meant merely the compiling of annals. It was for this purpose, in other words for the preservation of public records, that, from the beginning of Rome right up to the pontificate of Publius Mucius, the Pontifex Maximus used to commit to writing the complete history of each year. He made a fair copy, and put up the tablet in his residence so that it became public knowledge: even nowadays these are called the 'Great Annals'. This kind of writing was imitated by many who have eschewed ornament 53 and left mere records of dates, people, places, and events. Corresponding to many Greeks, including Pherecydes, Hellanicus, and Acusilas, we have on our side Cato, Pictor, and Piso; they had no notion of what goes to embellish a piece of writing—*that* is something quite recently introduced to Rome—and so long as they were understood, they had only one criterion for excellence in speech—brevity. A fine man, Coelius Anti- 54 pater, a friend of Crassus', made a little progress and gave history a louder voice. The rest were merely narrators of events: they did not make them attractive.'

'That is quite true', Catulus said. 'But even Antipater did not set off his history with varied colour, nor did he polish it with studied word-arrangement and a smooth even flow of language. Still, for a man neither learned nor particularly suited to oratory, he chiselled away as best he could. And, as you say, he did surpass his predecessors.'

Antonius replied: 'There is nothing the least surprising if history hasn't 55 yet been made brilliant in Latin. No Roman studies eloquence except to shine at the bar. It was different in Greece. Extremely eloquent men, far removed from the law, applied themselves to various important

subjects, and particularly to history. Herodotus, one knows, the first distinguished writer in this field, never touched a lawsuit at all, yet he's so eloquent that I get great pleasure from him—so far, that is, as I can
56 understand Greek. Later, Thucydides was (in my view) easily superior to any other manipulator of words. His material is so close-packed that he has almost as many ideas as words, and he's so exact and concise in language that one doesn't know whether to say that his material is made brilliant by its expression or the other way round. Yet not even he— statesman though he was—is recorded as having pleaded cases; and his actual history is said to have been composed at a time when he was outside politics and indeed in exile—something that tended to happen as a matter of course to the most honourable Athenians.
57 'Next came Philistus of Syracuse, a great friend of the tyrant Dionysius, who spent his leisure time writing history, in imitation particularly, I think, of Thucydides. After that, a very famous rhetorical factory (so to speak) produced two highly talented men, Theopompus and Ephorus, who turned to history on the encouragement of their teacher, Isocrates.
58 *They* never touched a case. Finally, even philosophy gave rise to historians, notably Xenophon, a follower of Socrates, and later Callisthenes, an Aristotelian and friend of Alexander. Callisthenes certainly was more or less a rhetorician. But Xenophon employed a gentler tone; he hadn't the orator's drive, and so was perhaps less forceful—but *I* think he was a bit more agreeable. Younger than all these was Timaeus. As far as I can judge, he was much the most learned, overflowing with information and unfailing in ideas. Nor was he unpolished in word-arrangement. He brought great eloquence to his writing—but no forensic experience.'

L. THE USE OF WORDS

Our final extract from Cicero (*de oratore* 3. 149–81) gives a sample of his efficiency in handling technical matters in a relaxed and interesting manner. Contrast *Orator* 80 ff., 92 ff. (above, p. 241). The speaker is again Crassus.

INDIVIDUAL WORDS

149 All speech, then, is the product of words. Let us consider how they are employed, first singly, then in combination: for words taken individually and in combination form two different kinds of ornamentation of speech. The words we use are either (1) those 'proper' to things, as it were their fixed names, coeval, almost, with them: or (2) those 'transferred', put where they do not really belong: or (3) those that result from our own innovation and creation.

As to 'proper' words, the orator attains distinction if he avoids the vulgar 150
and obsolete and employs those that are choice and bright and that have
something full and resonant about them. In this type, selection has to
be exercised, the decision being left to the judgement of the ear: here
good usage is of paramount importance. The ignorant tend to say 151
of orators: 'This man uses good words', 'So-and-so doesn't use good
words'. But this is something not to be judged on any system; it has to
be left to a certain innate sense. It is important here, though hardly a
matter for high praise, to be able to avoid faults; but the essential foundation is the ability to use good words and never run short of them. What 152
the orator himself is to build on this foundation, where he is to employ
his art, is, I think, the subject of my inquiry.

Now there are three things with regard to the individual word that the
orator may use to brighten and ornament his language: the unusual word,
the coined word, the 'transferred' word.

'UNUSUAL' WORDS

Unusual words are, in most cases, old ones, long obsolete in ordinary 153
everyday conversation. They are more freely available to poetic licence
than to us: all the same even in prose a poetic word may occasionally
supply dignity. I should not hesitate to say (as Coelius [1] did) *qua tempestate
Poenus in Italiam uenit* ('at which tide the Carthaginian came to Italy'),
or *proles* ('scion'), or *suboles* ('offspring'), or *effari* ('outspeak'), or *nuncu-
pare* ('clepe'); or, as you often do, Catulus, *non rebar* ('I did not deem')
or *ŏpinabar* ('methought'); or many other things which in their right
place often make oratory more grand and more archaic.

COINED WORDS

Words are *coined* when they are produced and invented by the speaker 154
himself. It may be that he links words together:

> I am terrified: fear out-breasts all my sense [2]

and

> His crafty-spoken malice you'd not want me . . . [3]

You will observe that the words 'out-breasts' and 'crafty-spoken' are

---

[1] i.e. the historian Coelius Antipater.   [2] Ennius, *Alcmeo*, fr. 2.
[3] *Trag. fr. incert.* 62 Ribbeck.

manufactured, rather than born, by the linking of words. But often words
are coined even without such conjunctions: e.g. 'that abandoned oldster',
'genital gods', 'incurve with richness of berries'.[1]

METAPHORS

155 The third method, involving *'transferring'* words, has wide ramifications.
It was the result of necessity imposed by shortage of vocabulary; but
it was made popular later by the agreeable charm it brought. Just as
clothes were originally invented to keep off the cold, but later began to
serve the purposes of bodily decoration and dignity as well, so transference
of words was instituted out of need but extended for pleasure. Even
rustics say: 'The vine is gemming', 'the grass is luxuriant', 'the crops are
happy'. When we use a metaphor to express something that it is difficult
to get over without it, our meaning is given clarity by the analogy intro-
156 duced. These metaphors, therefore, are a kind of borrowing; you take
from elsewhere what you have not got to hand. But there is a rather bolder
category of metaphors that are not a sign of lack of vocabulary, but bring
a positive splendour to the style. It is hardly necessary for me to explain
157 their origin or types. But metaphor is desirable when it makes a thing
more vivid, e.g.

> the sea bristles,
> the shadows mass, the blackness of night and clouds blinds,
> flame dazzles in the clouds, the sky shakes with thunder,
> hail with heavy rain falls sudden, headlong.
> All the winds burst forth, savage whirlwinds appear,
> the sea seethes with surge.[2]

Almost all of this is expressed in metaphor for the sake of vividness.
158   Another object of metaphor is to express the whole of some action or
intention. For instance, this description, by means of two metaphors, of
someone concealing his intentions:

> for he clothes himself in words, fences himself with guile.[3]

Sometimes, again, metaphors allow brevity: e.g. the well-known 'If a
weapon *fled* the hand'—the lack of intention in the discharge of the
weapon couldn't have been put over more briefly in non-metaphorical
terms than it has been here in a single metaphor.
159   While I am on this subject, I should say that it often surprises me that
everyone should find more pleasure in transferred 'alien' words than in

---

[1] *Trag. fr. incert.* 72.   [2] Pacuvius, *fr. incert.* 45.   [3] *Trag. fr. incert.* 61.

the 'proper' ones that really belong. Certainly, if something has no name proper to it (a 'sheet' in a boat; 'bond' as used of a transaction in law; 'parting' in the case of a wife), you are forced to take from elsewhere what you do not possess. Yet even where 'proper' words abound, men still take much greater pleasure in the 'alien' word, providing the metaphor is properly done. This, I believe, is either because it's a sign of cleverness to 160 pass over the obvious in favour of the far-fetched, or maybe because the listener, without actually straying, is led in his thought in a new direction —and this is a source of the greatest pleasure. Or perhaps it is because the situation and the whole analogy is embodied in a single word, or because every apt metaphor is directed to the senses, particularly that of sight, the keenest of all. Of course, phrases like 'a whiff of urbanity' or 'the 161 softness of humanity' or 'the roar of the sea' or 'the sweetness of a speech' draw on other senses. But those appealing to the sight are much sharper: they almost place within the mind's eye things that we cannot see and perceive in fact. For there is nothing in the world whose name we could not use of something else. From wherever you can draw a likeness (from everything, in fact) the single word that contains the likeness will bring the brilliance of metaphor to one's language.

Here the first thing to avoid is *lack* of likeness. Take 'the vast archways 162 of heaven'.[1] Ennius may (as we are told) have brought a sphere on to the stage; but there is no likeness to *an archway* in a sphere.

> Live, Ulysses, while you can:
> snatch with your eyes the last bright light.[2]

He didn't say 'seek' or 'take' (that would imply the taking of a little time, on the part of a man hoping to live longer), but 'snatch': the word is suited to what went before—'while you can'.

Second, one must make sure that the likeness is not too remote. For 163 'the Syrtes of his patrimony' I should rather say 'the rock', for 'the Charybdis of his wealth' rather 'the whirlpool'. The mind's eye is more easily carried to things seen than to things heard of.

The highest distinction here is that a metaphor should strike the senses. Accordingly, one should shun any indecency in the things to which the attention of the listener will be directed by one's analogy. I don't like it 164 to be said that the state was 'castrated' by the death of Africanus. I don't like Glaucia to be called 'the excrement of the senate-house'. However close the analogy may be, the thought raised by both likenesses is not pretty. I also dislike the metaphor to be too great for the subject ('the tempest of the revelry') or too trivial ('the revelry of the tempest'). I dislike

---

[1] Ennius, *trag. fr. incert.* 33.   [2] *Trag. fr. incert.* 29.

the metaphorical word being narrower than the 'proper' one would have
been:

> What is it, I beg you? Why do you shake your head
> at my approach?[1]

Better would be 'Why do you forbid, prohibit, deter': for *he* had said:

> Stay right there,
> lest my contagious shadow harm good men.

165   Also, if you are afraid that a metaphor may seem over-harsh, you may
often soften it by prefixing some phrase. For instance, if, in days gone by,
at the death of Marcus Cato someone had said that the senate was left
'orphan', it would be rather harsh. But if he said 'so to say, orphan', it
becomes rather milder. Indeed, a metaphor should be modest; it should
seem to have been escorted to the place of another, not to have burst in:
to have come on sufferance, not by force.

ALLEGORY

166 There is no more decorative means of employing individual words, none
that brings more lustre to a speech: for the off-shoot of metaphor which
involves a difference between what is said and what is understood does
not consist in the transference of *one* word, but in the knitting together
of a whole series of transferred words:

> I shall not allow myself, like the Argive fleet
> of old, to run a second time on the same rock.[2]

Or again:

> You are wrong, wrong. As you exult in your confidence
> the strong bridles of the law will restrain you,
> press you with the yoke of empire.[3]

167 In this type a similar circumstance is selected, and the words proper to
that circumstance are, as I have said, transferred to another, in succession.
This is a great ornament of style. But obscurity must be avoided: for it is
in this type that there arise what are called *riddles*. However, this is not
a device applied to single words, but to speech, that is, the combination
of words.

[1] Ennius, *Thyestes*, fr. 8.   [2] *Trag. fr. incert.* 74.
[3] *Trag. fr. incert.* 67.

METONYMY

There is no coining of words to be found in substitutions and inter-
changes such as

> Horrid Africa shakes with terrible tumult,[1]

in which 'Africa' is used of the Africans. This doesn't involve coining
a word (like 'the sea with its *rock-breaking* waves') or using a metaphor
('the sea is *softened*');[2] instead, one 'proper' word is exchanged for another,
for the sake of ornament:

> Cease, Rome, your enemies . . .[3]

and

> Witness are the great plains.[3]

This is an impressive device to give ornament to style, and is often to be
employed. In this category fall 'Mars, impartial in war', or the use of
Ceres for corn, *Liber* for wine, *Neptune* for the sea, *senate-house* for the
senate, *booths* for elections, *toga* for peace, *arms* and *weapons* for war.
Also under this head comes the use of names of virtues and vices in place   168
of their possessors: 'the house into which *luxury* burst' and 'where
avarice penetrated', or '*faith* was strong', '*justice* brought it about'.
Surely by now you can see the whole type: thanks to the modification
and alteration of a word, the same thing is given more ornate expression.

Neighbouring on these is the less decorative but not unimportant
device of letting part represent whole (as when we say *walls* or *roofs* for
buildings), or whole represent part (as when we call one squadron 'the
cavalry of the Roman people'), or one stand for many:

> But the Roman, though the deed was well done,
> trembled in his heart . . .;[4]

or many for one:

> We are Romans who were once of Rudiae;[5]

or however it may be, in the same category, that one looks not to the
literal but to the suggested meaning.

CATACHRESIS

Further, we often 'abuse' a word, not so elegantly as when we make a   169
metaphor of it, but all the same not always with impropriety, however

---

[1] Ennius, *Annales* 310.   [2] Pacuvius, *Chryses*, fr. 1.
[3] Ennius, *Scipio*, fr. 5.   [4] Ennius, *Annales* 547–8.
[5] Ibid. 377. The reference is to Ennius himself.

boldly we do it. Thus we say 'a *great* speech' for a long one, a 'minute mind' for a small one. But you must see that the use of interlinked metaphors (see above) is a matter of speech, not of the individual word; while the *exchanged* words, as I put it, and those that have to be understood differently from what they actually say, are in some sense 'transferred'.

170 So all the distinction to be won from individual words has three sources. The word may be old, though still tolerable to current idiom: it may be manufactured—by combination, or by coining (here again one must have regard to taste and idiom): or it may be 'transferred'—something above all that marks off and brightens speech as though with stars.

ARRANGEMENTS AND PATTERNS OF WORDS

171 I turn to *series of words*. This requires two things primarily: first, arrangement, then a certain shape and pattern.

Arrangement involves so ordering and positioning words that their joins should not be harsh or gaping but smooth and as it were cemented. On this matter, Lucilius,[1] who could do that sort of thing very urbanely, put the following pleasantries into the mouth of my father-in-law:

> How nicely his phrases are put together! All just like mosaic,
> skilfully arranged on a pavement, in wriggling inlays.

After this joke at the expense of Albucius, he laid into me too:

> My son-in-law is Crassus—so don't get too rhetorical.

Well? This Crassus, since you make use of his name, what does he do? Just that. Rather better, however, than Albucius, as Scaevola implied (and as I should hope). Still, he had his joke at me, as usual.

172 All the same, we cannot neglect this arranging of words. It makes language rhythmic, coherent, smooth, flowing. You will attain it if you so juxtapose the end of one word with the start of the next that there is neither harsh clash nor too wide a gulf.

RHYTHM

173 Following on this duty comes the *shaping and balancing* of words. Catulus here, I fear, may find this puerile. The old writers thought that we should bring a certain rhythm, almost amounting to verses, into our prose: and that speeches should have pauses (*clausulae*) dictated by the need to draw

---

[1] Fr. 84 Marx. The father-in-law was Scaevola. Albucius was a very philhellene orator of the second century B.C. See *Brutus* 131.

breath rather than by complete exhaustion, and marked not by scribes' punctuation but by the pattern of words and content. This is said to have been introduced first by Isocrates; as his pupil Naucrates writes, his aim was to shackle with rhythm, for the sake of the pleasure it gives our ears, the disorganized manner of speech employed by the ancients. For two **174** things, verse and melody, were devised by musicians, who at one time were identical with poets; their aim was pleasure: they intended, employing word-rhythm and musical measure, to defeat monotony by the delight afforded the ear. They thus thought that these two factors, modulation of the voice and rounding off of words, should, as far as the severity of prose allowed, be transferred to eloquence from poetry.

The key point here is that if the sequence of words causes the appear- **175** ance of verse in prose, there is something wrong: yet at the same time we want the sequence of words to end rhythmically, just as a verse does, tidily and completely. There is no one thing, out of so many, that more clearly marks off the orator from the man who is ignorant and unskilled in speaking than that the untutored pour out all they can shapelessly, letting breath, not technique, dictate the pauses in what they say: while the orator so binds his thought in words that he imposes on it a rhythm at once disciplined and free. Having bound it with balance and rhythm, **176** he relaxes and frees it by changes of order, ensuring that the words are neither subjected like verse to some particular rule nor so free as to wander at large.

How, then, shall we set about this important task, so as to feel confident that we can attain this faculty of rhythmic utterance? It is a thing that is essential rather than difficult, there being nothing more pliant, flexible, and amenable to your lead than speech. It is capable both of **177** producing verses and irregular rhythms and of giving rise to prose of various manners and types. Vocabulary for conversation and for high oratory is one and the same. There is no difference in the type employed for daily purposes and for the public arena. We have taken up the words that were lying in the common stock, and we mould and shape them to our whim as though they were the softest wax. Sometimes we are grave, sometimes plain, sometimes in between; accordingly our style of speech corresponds to our standpoint, and varies and alters to suit every pleasure of the ear and every emotion of the heart. Nature, astonishingly, has **178** made provision, in speech as in many spheres, that what possesses most utility should also have most dignity—and often most beauty as well. It is for the safety and happiness of all that we see the whole universe of nature to be what it is—the sky round, the earth at its centre, held in position by its own force and tendency, the sun revolving round it, approaching the winter solstice, then rising again gradually in the opposite

direction, the moon receiving the sun's light according as it approaches or recedes, the five planets keeping the same courses though at different
179 speeds and on different routes. These things are so ordered that the slightest change would bring about their disruption: so beautiful that no vision could conceivably be more splendid. Let your mind turn to the shape and form of man or even the other living things. You will find that no part of the body has been shaped without some compelling reason: that the whole is the perfect product not of chance but of art. Look at those trees. Their trunks, their branches, their leaves have no other purpose than to guard and preserve their nature: no part anywhere that is not beautiful.

180 Let us leave nature and turn to the arts. What is more essential in a ship than sides, holds, prow, poop, yard-arms, sails, masts? Yet these things are so good to look at that they might seem to have been invented with pleasure as well as safety in mind. Columns keep temples and porticoes up: yet they are as dignified as they are useful. The gables of the Capitol and the other temples were the device not of beauty but of necessity: it was first considered how water could flow off both parts of the roof; the dignity of the gables came second to the needs of the temple. Yet the outcome is that even if the Capitol were to be erected in heaven, where rain would be impossible, it might be thought to have no dignity if it had no gables.

181 We find the same in every department of oratory: utility and virtual necessity go hand in hand with charm and attractiveness. Failure and shortage of breath caused *clausulae* and pauses between words; that, once discovered, turns out to be so pleasant that even if someone were granted unfailing breath we should not want him to deliver words without a break. For what our ears find agreeable is what is not only tolerable but easily attainable by human lungs.

6

LATIN CRITICISM OF POETRY

We group here a number of Latin views of poetry, most of them written by poets themselves.

A. A POET DEFENDS HIMSELF

The first is from Terence's first play, *Andria* (166 B.C.). Terence used the prologues of his plays for literary polemic rather than simply for introducing the plot.

When your poet first applied his mind to writing, he thought his only business was to make sure his plays pleased the public. But he's realizing that things are turning out quite differently: he has to use all his time in his prologues not in describing the plot but in replying to the abuse of an ill-disposed old poet. Please listen to the complaint. Menander wrote an *Andria* and a *Perinthia*. Anyone who knows one of these plays well knows both; their plots are pretty similar—but they have different styles of language. Your poet agrees that he has transferred various things that fitted from the *Perinthia* to his *Andria* and used them for his own purposes. This is what people carp at—they claim that it's not right for plays to be 'contaminated'[1] in this way. Doesn't their understanding let them understand anything? When they accuse this poet, they accuse those he relies on as precedents—Naevius, Plautus, Ennius:[2] he would rather rival *their* negligence than these people's dim diligence. I suggest they keep quiet from now on, and stop their abuse if they don't want to hear their own faults rehearsed. Be kind, be fair, and judge: you may learn what hope there is—whether the comedies he writes in future are to be given a hearing, or hissed off the stage. (*Andria* 1–27)

More positive is Terence's claim to delicate comedy and pure language:

Be fair—give me permission to put across a quiet comedy in silence, so that we don't always have to have a Running Slave, an Angry Old Man, a Greedy Parasite, an Impudent Sycophant, a Miserly Pander [3]—all acted

---

[1] Disputed meaning; see *Fifty Years (and Twelve) of Classical Scholarship*, Blackwells, 1968, p. 305.

[2] i.e. the first great Roman dramatists, already thought of as classics.

[3] Stock characters of comedy: Terence claims more discriminating characterization, higher and less farcical comedy.

with the greatest noise and the maximum effort . . . In this play is uncorrupted language. Try out what my talents can do in both directions.

(*Heauton Timōroumenos* 35 ff.)

B. A DEFENCE OF SATIRE

Horace's satirical poems contain a good deal of comment on poetry. We begin
with two *sermones* (conversation-pieces), written in the 30s B.C., in which he
discusses the genre of satire. Many of the names used are fictional or unknown.

There are many editions: A. Palmer, London, 1883; E. C. Wickham, Oxford,
1891; A. Kiessling–R. Heinze–E. Burck, Leipzig, 1959. See also E. Fraenkel,
Horace, Oxford, 1957, 124 ff.; N. A. Rudd, *The Satires of Horace*, Cambridge,
1966, 86 ff. On satire see U. Knoche, *Die Römische Satire*², Göttingen, 1957.

Horace: *Satires* 1. 4

LUCILIUS

The poets Eupolis, Cratinus, and Aristophanes, and other writers of Old
Comedy, used great freedom in pillorying anyone worthy of being represented as a bad man and a thief, as an adulterer or murderer or some
other type of criminal. On them Lucilius is completely dependent; he
followed their footsteps, changing only their metres and rhythms; he was
witty, sharply discerning, tough in composing his verses—indeed he was
10 *that* to a fault: he would often take pride in dictating two hundred lines
in an hour, standing on one leg. He flowed along like a muddy river, and
there was much in him that cried out for deletion; he was garrulous, and
lazy in carrying the burden of writing.

THE CHARGE AGAINST THE SATIRIST

Writing *well*, that is: that he wrote a lot is irrelevant. Here's Crispinus
taking me on at long odds: 'Come on, if you like, pick up these tablets:
let's have a place, a time, umpires—let's see which of us can write more.'
The gods did well to give me a scanty and feeble talent that says little and
that rarely; *you* can behave, if you wish, like the air shut up inside a pair
20 of goat-skin bellows, labouring on until the fire softens the iron. Fannius
is a popular success—people bring him presents of bureaux and busts:

nobody reads *my* writings, and I don't like to give public recitations because some people aren't best pleased by this genre—after all, most of them deserve criticism. Choose someone out of a crowd: he's a victim of avarice or the unhappiness of ambition; one man is mad with love for married women, another for boys; one is dazzled by the gleam of silver— but Albius there is crazy over bronze; another trades from the lands of sunrise to the sunset warmth of the west—he's carried headlong from 30 one disaster to another like the dust in a whirlwind, dreading that he may lose something from his capital or fail to increase it. All such people fear poetry and hate poets. 'He has hay on his horns:[1] keep a long way away from him—so long as he can raise a laugh, he isn't concerned to spare any of his friends, or himself: he's agog that anything he smears down on paper as first thoughts should be read by every labourer coming back from bakery and vat, boys and old women alike.' Hey, listen to something on the other side.

HORACE IS NO POET

First of all, let me dissociate myself from the company of those I grant to be poets; you can't say it's enough merely to write in verse—you 40 shouldn't think anyone who, like me, writes something nearer to ordinary language, is a *poet*. Give the honour of *that* name to someone of genius, with inspired mind and resonant tongue. This is why some people have raised the question: 'Is Comedy poetry or not?' For its content and its language equally lack inspiration and force—it's mere conversation, except for the regular metre. 'But you get a father seething with rage because his spendthrift son is madly in love with a whore, and is refusing 50 an heiress, and disgracefully walks the streets before nightfall with torches, drunk.' But would Pomponius be let off lighter than that if his father were alive?[2] So it's not enough to write verses in ordinary words which, reduced to prose, you might hear on the lips of any angry father, just the same as a stage one. If you removed the beat and the fixed metre from what I'm writing now—or what Lucilius wrote in the past—and switched the order of words about, putting first later and last first, you wouldn't get the same result as if you broke up 'After loathsome Discord 60 shattered War's ironbound posts and doors'[3]—there you'd get the re- mains of a *poet*, albeit a dismembered one.

---

[1] Like a dangerous bull.
[2] i.e. the language of comedy, even in exalted scenes, rises to the heights only in the way that real speech may. For the context, cf. *The Art of Poetry* 92 ff. (below, p. 282).
[3] Lines of Ennius (*Annales* 266–7).

SATIRE UNJUSTLY SUSPECTED

So much for that. Another time I may inquire if satire is legitimate poetry
—now I merely ask whether this type of composition justly arouses
your suspicion. When fierce Sulcius and Caprius,[1] terribly hoarse,
summonses at the ready, stroll the streets, they strike fear into the hearts
of robbers. But if a man lives honestly and with clean hands he can despise
70 both. *You* may be like the robbers Caelius and Birrius: that doesn't make
me like Caprius and Sulcius. Why fear me? My books aren't to be found
in shops and stalls to be clutched by the sweaty hands of the mob—and
of Hermogenes Tigellius. I give recitations to no one except friends—
and I have to be forced to do that: and I give them not just anywhere or
in just anyone's presence. There are many who recite in mid forum, or in
the bath-house—the enclosed space gives an agreeable resonance to the
voice. This pleases empty-heads who don't stop to inquire whether they
mayn't be acting tactlessly and out of season.

THE REAL SNAKE IN THE GRASS

'You *like* hurting', someone says, 'and you do it with conscious malice.'
80 Where did you get *that* stone to cast at me? Who among those I have lived
with told you that story? A man who backbites a friend in his absence,
who doesn't defend him from another's criticism, who clutches at cheap
laughs and wants to be known as a wit, who can make up things he hasn't
seen, but cannot keep a secret—this is the viper, this is the one you should
beware of, citizen of Rome! You may often see a dinner-party, four
guests each on three couches: one of them makes it his business to find
something to sneer at in all those present, except the host—and him too
once he's tight, when truthful Bacchus opens up the secrets of the heart.
90 You hate vipers—yet you find such a man pleasant, urbane, frank. But
if I smile because Rufillus smells of lozenges, Gargonius of goat, can you
call me bitter and biting? If there's some mention in your hearing of the
thefts of Petillius Capitolinus, you may defend him as your custom
demands—'Capitolinus has been my companion and friend since boy-
hood, and he's done a great deal for me when I've asked him to, and I'm
delighted he's still safe and in Rome: all the same, I'm surprised that he
100 got off that charge.' *This* is the real venom, the straight smear. I promise—
if I ever promise anything faithfully about myself—that in the future as
in the past *that* vice will stay far from my pages and from my mind.

[1] Informers.

HORACE'S FATHER

If I should ever say anything a little too frankly, or a little too jokingly, you will concede me a point and forgive me: it was my father who accustomed me to avoid vices by putting a black mark against examples of them. If he was exhorting me to live carefully and frugally, contented with what he'd saved for me, he'd say: 'Don't you see what a bad time Albius' son has, and pauper Baius? They're an excellent warning to anyone not to squander his fortune.' When he steered me off sordid affairs with tarts: 'Don't be like Scetanus.' If he was discouraging me from chasing married women when I could find legitimate sex elsewhere: 'Trebonius got caught—and his reputation isn't pretty', he used to say. 'A philosopher will give the reasoning on what to pursue and what to avoid. It's enough for me if I can keep the old traditions up, and preserve your life and your good name while you're in need of a guardian. As soon as age has hardened your limbs and your character, you will swim without cork.' That was the way he shaped me as a boy with his advice. If he was ordering me to do something, he'd say: 'You have a precedent for doing this', and point out one of the judges. If he was forbidding me, 'You surely can't doubt that this is a dishonest and unprofitable thing to do when this or that man is in such bad odour?' Ailing gluttons are terrified by a neighbour's death and forced through reflection on mortality to go carefully: similarly reproaches cast at others often deter tender minds from wrong.

The result is that I am free of disastrous vices, though the prey of minor and venial faults. Perhaps even they have been diminished generously by long life, a frank friend, my own good sense; I don't leave myself alone when I'm in a litter or a portico. 'This thing is more honest: if I do this I shall lead a better life. In such-and-such a way I shall make myself agreeable to my friends. So-and-so was not wise to act like that: shall *I* ever unwittingly do something similar?' These are the thoughts I ponder, lips pursed: when I have a moment, I scribble in my notebook. Indeed, *that* is one of my 'minor faults': and if you won't concede me that one, a great band of poets would come to my rescue—we should outnumber you, and like Jews force you to conform with our company.

C. MORE ABOUT LUCILIUS AND SATIRE

Horace: *Satires* I. 10

All right, I said Lucilius' verses ran harshly. Lucilius' most stupid fan would agree with me. But on the same page you'll find compliments on

the man's rubbing the city down with a great deal of salt. If I concede that, I don't concede the rest—if I did, I should have to admire even the mimes of Laberius, think *them* beautiful poems. So it's not enough to split the hearer's mouth with a smile (though that's one point to watch):
10 you need conciseness, so that the thought runs free and doesn't bog itself down with words that tire the dulled ear: and you need a style now sad, now gay, keeping up the role sometimes of a declaimer or poet, sometimes of a wit who purposely spares his strength and tones down his efforts. Normally it's the joking, not the bitter word that hits the important nail on the head, hard and well. This was the principle of Old Comedy, and that's where we should follow it—though the pretty Hermogenes never read it, nor did the well-known ape whose learning extends only so far as reading Calvus and Catullus.[1]

MIXING GREEK AND LATIN

20 'But Lucilius mixed Greek and Latin words—there's a feat!' You're a bit slow, aren't you—that's no wonderful achievement: the Rhodian Pitholeon brought it off without even trying. 'But a style fitted up with both languages at once is sweeter, like a mixture of Chian and Falernian.' Well, I ask you—do you mean when you're writing verse, or when you've got to fight Petillius' case for him against the odds as well? I suppose while Pedius Publicola and Corvinus are content to sweat away at their briefs in Latin, you forget your country and your father and choose to
30 mix up foreign words with native ones, like the bilingual Apulians. When *I* was trying to write Greek verses, despite being born this side of the Tyrrhenian sea, Quirinus warned me off;[2] he appeared after midnight, when dreams are true, and said something like: 'Wanting to add to the ranks of the Greeks is madder than taking firewood into a forest.'

WHAT SUITED HORACE

Thus, while turgid Alpinus[3] is slitting Memnon's throat and muddying the sources of the Rhine, I play at *this*: pieces that will never resound in the temple in a competition judged by Tarpa, never return over and
40 over again for performance in the theatre. When it's a question of a slick

---

[1] Catullus and Calvus are the fashionable poets of the previous generation, rarely praised by the Augustans. We do not know who their 'ape' is.

[2] i.e. Romulus, warning the poet as (e.g.) Apollo does Virgil (*Ecl.* 6. 3 ff.).

[3] Cover-name for M. Furius Bibaculus, who wrote an *Aethiopis* (hence Memnon) and a poem on Caesar's wars in Gaul.

courtesan and the slave Davus tricking old man Chremes, Fundanius is
the one living writer who can turn out agreeable chatty plays. Pollio is the
one for singing of the deeds of royalty in trimeters. Varius briskly leads
epic to battle—no one like him. To Virgil the muses of the countryside
have granted a gentle and witty talent (*molle atque facetum*). *This* was
what *I* proved capable of writing—better than Varro Atacinus and some
others who have tried it unsuccessfully, but worse than the man[1] who
showed me the way: and I wouldn't venture to snatch from his head the
crown that he wears with such distinction.

FOR AND AGAINST LUCILIUS

But I said Lucilius flowed along muddily, often carrying along in his   50
stream more that should be cut out than should be left Well, here's a
question for you: do you find no fault, you learned man, with the great
Homer? Doesn't the level-tempered Lucilius want to change anything
in the tragedian Accius? Doesn't he smile at verses of Ennius that are
something less than dignified, without regarding himself as superior to
the poets he criticizes? What is there to prevent me too from asking, as
I read the writings of Lucilius, whether it was his own shortcomings, or
the shortcomings of his subject, that stopped him producing better-
finished, smoother verses—smoother, that is, than a man might turn out
if he's content just to make sure there are six feet a verse and normally   60
writes two hundred lines before supper and two hundred after it, with
the flood-like facility of Cassius Etruscus, who is reported to have been
cremated on a pyre consisting solely of his own books in their cases?
Right: Lucilius may be pleasant, witty, more refined than an illiterate
untouched by the Greek culture, than the multitudinous primitives. But
if fate had made him a contemporary of ours, he'd be cutting a lot out
of his own works, deleting everything that goes on after the point is made.   70
He'd be scratching his head as he wrote his verses, and biting his nails
to the quick.

PLEASING THE FEW

If you want to write something worth re-reading, keep the eraser busy;
forget the adulation of the many, and be happy to have a few readers.
You're not, I take it, insane enough to want your poems dictated in the
elementary schools? *I* am not. It's enough for me if knights applaud—as

[1] i.e. Lucilius.

the unperturbed Arbuscula said when she was hissed off the stage. She
ignored the others. And am I to be worried about the louse Pantilius,
or feel the pinch if Demetrius gibes at me when I'm not there to defend
80 myself? Do I mind if silly Fannius, boon companion of Hermogenes
Tigellius, wounds me? Plotius, Varius, Maecenas, Virgil, Valgius, Octa-
vius—it's *their* approval I want, and the praise of my friend Fuscus and
the two Visci. I'm not looking to my future when I name Pollio, and
Messalla and his brother, and Bibulus and Servius, and the candid Furnius,
and many others whom I do not mention, but don't forget either, for
they are friends, and friends of taste. I want my book to please *them*,
90 such as it is; and I should be sorry if they like it less than I hope they
may. Demetrius and Tigellius can go and wail among the desks of their
school-girls. Run, boy, be quick and make this the last line of my book.

D. A LETTER TO AUGUSTUS

Horace: *Epistles* 2. 1

We come now to a major work. Commentaries by E. C. Wickham (1891),
A. S. Wilkins (1885), Kiessling–Heinze–Burck (1959); see also E. Fraenkel,
Horace, pp. 383–99; G. W. Williams, *Tradition and Originality in Roman
Poetry*, Oxford, 1968, pp. 71–4.

PROOEMIUM

You have much important business to conduct with no one to help you,
defending Italy with arms, adorning her with virtue, chastening her with
laws; and I should thwart the public interest, Caesar, if I occupied your
time with a lengthy conversation. Romulus and father Liber, Castor and
Pollux, were all received into the temples of the gods after a life of tremendous deeds; but while they looked after the world and the human race,
settling bitter wars, allotting land, founding cities, they lamented that
their services were not matched by the popularity for which they hoped.
10 The hero[1] who crushed the dread Hydra, and quelled familiar monsters in
labours assigned by fate, likewise found that death is the only cure for
unpopularity. The man who is felt by inferior talents to weigh on them
arouses envy by his brilliance; once he is eclipsed, he will be loved. Yet it
is while you are still with us that we bestow on you honours that come
before the usual time; we set up altars that bind oaths by your divinity,
and acknowledge that nothing comparable has arisen before or will arise
again.

[1] Hercules.

THE CRAZE FOR THE OLD

<u>All the same</u>, this people of yours, wise and correct in preferring you to
all rulers, Roman or Greek, do not apply similar standards to other things: 20
they scorn and hate everything that is not removed from the world and
safely dead. They so favour the ancients that they have a tradition that
the Muses spoke, on the Alban Hill, the Tables[1] forbidding misdoing
that the decemvirs sanctioned, the royal treaties made on equal terms with
Gabii and the unyielding Sabines, the books of the Pontiffs,[2] and the aged
volumes of the prophets. The oldest writings of the Greeks are the best;
and if one weighs Roman writers in the same scale there is not much to   30
say. On that principle,[3] an olive could be argued to have no stone, a nut
no shell. We have reached the peak: therefore we paint and play the lyre
and wrestle better than the well-oiled Achaeans.

But if passage of time improves poems as it does wine, I have a question:
how many years will give value to a book? Should a writer dead for a
hundred years be registered under the perfect old or the worthless new?
Let us have a limit, to stop disputes: 'He is old and good who completes a
century.' What then of someone who died a month or a year later—where   40
will *he* come? Among the old poets, or those to be rejected alike by the
present and the future? 'Of course it will be right to place him among
the ancients, if he is a short month, or even a whole year, more recent.'
I follow up this concession, and gradually pluck the hairs from the horse's
tail, taking away one and then another until, baffled by the Fallacy of the
Diminishing Heap,[4] the searcher of annals, the man who judges quality
by age, the admirer of nothing that Death has not sanctified, is brought
to his knees.

Ennius is—so the critics say—wise, strong, a second Homer, and doesn't   50
much worry how the promises of his Pythagorean dreams turn out.[5]
Naevius is on our shelves and in our minds, almost undated. Such is the
sanctity of every old poem. When dispute arises who excels whom,
Pacuvius carries off the reputation of being an erudite oldster, Accius
a sublime one. The Roman dress of Afranius' comedies, they say, fitted
Menander's back. Plautus hurries along after the manner of the Sicilian

---

[1] The Twelve Tables, the earliest code of Roman law.
[2] Cf. Cicero, *de oratore* 2. 52 (above, p. 255).
[3] i.e. such analogical arguments could be used to lead to absurd conclusions. Olives
have no stones because nuts have none (so too nuts have no shells); we are supreme in the
arts because we are masters of the world.
[4] If I take things away one by one, when does it stop being a heap?
[5] i.e. his immortality is assured whether or not he was right in believing in Pythagorean
transmigration. Ennius began his *Annals* with a vision of Homer, whose reincarnation
he perhaps claimed to be.

60 Epicharmus. Caecilius excels in dignity, Terence in technique.[1] These are the poets Rome at the height of its power learns by heart, these it packs the narrow theatre to see. These are the poets it reckons up between the writer Livius ⟨Andronicus⟩ and our own day.

Sometimes the majority gets things right, sometimes it gets them wrong. If it admires and praises the old poets without allowing anything to excel or compare with them, it is mistaken. If it believes that they wrote some things over-archaically, a certain amount harshly, a great deal casually— then it has taste: it agrees with me—and Jupiter favours its judgement. I don't inveigh against Livius' poems or suppose that they should be 70 consigned to destruction (I remember Orbilius beating them into me when I was a boy). But I'm astonished they should be thought polished, beautiful and nearly perfect. Perhaps a fine word gleams out in them, or one or two verses more elegant than the rest; but it's wrong that this should support and sell the whole volume. I get annoyed to hear something criticized, not for being grossly and disagreeably put together, but for being recent: to see honour and glory sought for the ancients, not merely allowance made. Should I dare to express a doubt whether it's right for 80 the comedies of Atta to walk the stage amidst the flowers and the saffron, pretty well all respectable citizens shout that decency has died, because I venture to find fault with pieces that grave Aesopus and skilful Roscius played. Perhaps they think nothing good unless *they* liked it; or perhaps they regard it as embarrassing to follow the views of the young, and at their age to acknowledge that what they learned before their beards grew should be consigned to oblivion. Indeed, the encomiast of Numa's Saliar Hymn,[2] who understands it no more than I, though he would like to be thought the only person who follows it—such a man is not really keen on the buried geniuses he applauds, but merely likes attacking *our* handi- work. He is jealous: he hates us and our products.

THE GREEK ATTITUDE

90 But if the Greeks had hated novelty as much as we, what would exist now to be ranked as old? What would the public have to read and thumb, man by man? When Greece first laid aside her wars and began to be frivolous, slipping into vice as fortune smiled, she burned with favour now for athletes, now for horses, loved craftsmen in marble or ivory or bronze,

---

[1] A comprehensive list of the second-century poets. Afranius' *togatae* were comedies in Roman dress, as distinct from the Greek-dress *palliatae* of Plautus, Caecilius, and Terence.

[2] The archaic chant of the Salii, priests instituted by Numa, unintelligible to Horace's contemporaries.

gazed long and thoughtfully at paintings, enthused over flute-players and tragic actors. Like a little girl playing around her nurse's feet, she soon 100 had had enough, and abandoned what she had sought so greedily. What finds favour or disfavour that is not subject to change?[1] All this was the result of benign peace and favouring winds.

THE CRAZE FOR POETRY

At Rome it was for long usual, and agreeable, to get up early, open the house up, tell one's client his rights, lend (with due security) to respectable debtors, pass on to the young what one heard from the old about the increasing of one's property and the avoidance of damaging self-indulgence. Now the fickle people has changed: it has only one enthusiasm to excite it—writing. Boys and dignified fathers alike dine with leaves 110 in their hair, and dictate poetry. I swear I write no verse, but I'm a bigger liar than a Parthian: I get up before dawn, to call for pen, paper, desk.

One who knows nothing about ships hesitates to steer them. You don't venture to prescribe southernwood[2] to the sick unless you've been to medical school—doctors look after their own profession. Craftsmen ply crafts. But we all write poetry, taught and untaught alike.

THE POET HAS HIS USES

This is an aberration, a mild form of madness, but it has many advantages. Look at it this way. A poet's mentality will not readily prove avaricious. 120 He likes verses—that's his one hobby. He smiles at loss, escaped slaves, fires. He won't plot frauds against his partner or his ward. He lives on pulse and black bread. He's an inefficient and lazy soldier—but he has his uses to the city, if you will grant that great affairs are helped by small. It is the poet who gives shape to the pliant, stuttering lips of the young boy; even at this early stage, he is diverting his ears from obscenity: soon he is forming his character with friendly precept, suppressing cruelty and envy and anger. He relates good deeds, equips youth with familiar 130 instances, consoles the poor and the sick. Where would chaste boys and virgin girls learn their prayers if the muse had not provided us with poets? The choir asks for help from the gods, feels the divine presence: winningly, with the prayers it is taught, it implores rain from heaven, turns away plagues, wards off fearful dangers, wins peace and a fruitful year. It is poetry that placates the gods of heaven and underworld.[3]

[1] Misplaced—or interpolated—sentence.
[2] An aromatic shrub, *Artemisia abrotanum*, much in favour in ancient medicine.
[3] Cf. Horace's own Secular Hymn, composed for the games of 17 B.C.

THE DEVELOPMENT OF ROMAN POETRY

Primitive farmers, brave men whom a little made rich, used to appease
140 Earth with a pig, Silvanus with milk, their Genius [1] (who knows how
short life is) with flowers and wine at feast-time, when they had brought
the crops in and were relaxing body and mind (it's the prospect of an end
that makes the mind endure) in company with their loyal wives and the
sons who shared their labours. In this manner, the licentious Fescennines [2]
were discovered, that made verse dialogues the vehicle for rustic insult;
this freedom, handed down through the years, gave agreeable sport, until
the joking became savage, turned to open madness, and raced, menacing
150 and unpunished, through decent households. Those who were attacked
had something to cry about—a tooth that drew blood. But even those
unaffected began to worry about the situation in general. In fact a law
and penalties were provided, forbidding anyone to be savaged in a malicious poem. Men were given the cudgel to fear, and so they changed their
ways, and returned to innocent words and entertainment.

ROMAN DRAMA

Greece, now captive, took captive its wild conqueror, and introduced the
arts to rural Latium. The unprepossessing Saturnian [3] rhythm went out,
160 and elegance drove off venom. All the same, traces of the country long
remained, and they are there today. It was late in the day that the Roman
applied his intelligence to Greek literature; for it was in the lull after the
Punic Wars [4] that he began to inquire what use there might be in Sophocles
and Thespis and Aeschylus. He had a go himself too, seeing whether he
could make a decent translation, and wasn't displeased with the result,
thanks to a natural loftiness and bite. The spirit was tragic enough, the
innovations daring and felicitous; but in his ignorance he feared erasure,
and thought it shameful.

Comedy is thought to involve less sweat, seeing that it takes its material
170 from daily life. But it is more burdensome in that it receives less indulgence. See how badly Plautus maintains the character of a youth in love,
an economical father, a treacherous pimp—what a Dossennus [5] he is with

---

[1] i.e. the individual's tutelary spirit.

[2] 'Fescennine verses' were traditionally ribald lines sung at Roman weddings: cf.
Catullus 61. 120.

[3] The common verse of early Roman poetry. Specimens survive, but even whether it is
basically quantitative or accentual is still discussed.

[4] The Hannibalic war ended in 201 B.C.

[5] i.e. clown, dolt.

his greedy parasites, shuffling in his loose slippers across the stage. The author only wants money for his pocket—after that he doesn't care if the play flops or keeps its footing.

If it was Fame that carried the playwright to the stage in her airy chariot, he is deflated by an indifferent audience, encouraged by an attentive one. So small and light a thing is it that can overthrow or refresh a mind that is athirst for praise. Goodbye to the stage if a prize denied sends me home 180 thin, a prize won makes me fat! And often, if a poet *is* brave, he is disconcerted and put to flight by the fact that the majority (deficient, however, in rank and virtue), stupid, illiterate, ready to fight it out with any of their betters who differ from them, call for bears or boxers in the middle of the play. That's what the plebs enjoys. In fact, even the knights have now transferred all their pleasure from the ear to the shifting and empty delights of the eye. The curtain is up for four hours or more while 190 squadrons of horse and hordes of foot pour over the stage. Once-glorious kings are dragged by, hands pinioned; chariots, carriages, wagons, ships hurry on, carrying looted ivory and models of captured Corinth.[1] If Democritus were alive he'd laugh at the way the hybrid camelopard or the white elephant keeps the crowds riveted; he'd watch the populace more attentively than the actual spectacle, as being far more worthy of his gaze. As for the writers, he'd imagine they were telling their tale to a deaf ass: no voice could make itself heard above the clamour emitted by 200 our theatres. You might think it was the moaning of the Apulian forests or the Tuscan sea—such is the noise as they watch the show, the *objets d'art* and the exotic wealth: when an actor is smeared over with that, he only needs to stand on the stage and hands start to clap. 'Has he said anything yet?' 'No, nothing.' 'What's so popular, then?' 'Wool turned violet by the purple of Tarentum.'

THE POET WHO KEEPS AWAY FROM THE THEATRE

You mustn't suppose that I am being sparing in praise of things that I refuse to do because others do them well; the poet who tears my heart 210 with imaginary griefs, provokes it, soothes it, fills it with unreal fears—such a poet I regard as capable of a tight-rope act. He is like a magician, who can transport me now to Thebes, now to Athens. But please spare a modicum of attention for those who devote themselves to a reader rather than put up with the haughty scorn of a spectator: if, that is, you want to fill your library (a gift worthy of Apollo)[2] and spur on the poets to seek

---

[1] Or 'captured Corinthian bronzes'.
[2] The new library on the Palatine, built by Augustus.

green Helicon more diligently. We poets often do ourselves damage (this
120 is to take a sickle to my own vineyard) when we give you a book despite
your being worried or tired; when we get hurt if a friend ventures to find
fault with a single verse; when we come back unrequested to passages
we've already recited; when we lament that our labour is lost and the
fine craftsmanship unnoticed; when we hope that the day will come when
you're nice enough to send for us the moment you hear we're composing
and say to us: 'Write—and want for nothing.'

THE COURT POET

230 All the same, it's worth finding out what sort of priests should serve
virtue well-tried at home and abroad—for it's not something to be handed
over to an unworthy poet. The great king Alexander gave his favour to
the notorious Choerilus,[1] who repaid the royal gifts of gold pieces in verses
ill-born and inelegant. Black ink when handled leaves a disagreeable blot;
similarly writers often smear disgusting poems over fine deeds. All the
same, this king who so dearly bought such absurd poetry (improvident
man!) made an edict that he was to be painted by none but Apelles, and
240 that only Lysippus should cast statues to represent the martial features
of Alexander. He had, then, an acute taste in the visual arts—but summon
it to pronounce on books and poetry, and you'd swear he was a Boeotian,
born in a gross climate.[2]

But your judgement of your favourite poets, Virgil and Varius, has not
been disgraced by them, nor the gifts which they have received from you,
so much to your credit. And for portraying the character and mind of
famous men, the work of the poet is as satisfactory as the representation
250 of their features in bronze statues. I wouldn't choose these conversation
pieces that creep along the ground in preference to writing history, telling
of the lie of lands and the course of rivers, of mountain-top citadels and
foreign kingdoms, of wars won over all the world under your auspices,
of Janus, guardian of Peace, shut up behind his gates, of Rome a terror
to Parthia now that you are emperor—if, that is, my abilities measured
up to my desires. But your greatness will not tolerate a slight poem, and
260 I am ashamed to try a theme that my strength won't stand. Attentiveness
tends to be stupid and annoy the object of its attentions, particularly when
it uses verse and art to commend itself. What we admire and venerate

---

[1] Cf. *The Art of Poetry* 357 (below, p. 289).
[2] Athenian malice made the stupidity of Boeotians a byword cf. the proverbial
'Boeotian pig'.

is less likely to impress itself on our memory than the risible. I[1] don't care for attentions that annoy me. I don't ever want to be set up in wax, my face portrayed for the worse. I don't want to be celebrated in badly-turned verse: I'd only blush when I got such a coarse gift; and along with the writer, laid out in an open book-case, I'd be removed to the quarter where they sell perfumes and scent and pepper and everything else that 270 gets wrapped up in worthless literature.

E. *THE ART OF POETRY*

Horace: *Ars Poetica*

This is an even longer and more elaborate 'epistle'. Its raw material is more technical (Horace used the work of Neoptolemus of Parium and, at least indirectly, Aristotle's *Poetics*) but its humour and allusiveness make it clear that we have something far removed from a versified treatise. Leading themes, however, are easy to define, though in the poem they are bewilderingly interlaced: consistency, unity, propriety, the debt to Greece, the need for scrupulous technique, the still greater need for moral seriousness. The poet must be a committed artist. The mere eccentric is no use.

Many of the themes and illustrations are also to be found in the other literary epistles. But here the relevance to the Augustan situation is harder to see. In particular, why so much time on satyr-plays, a minor genre never successfully revived? Was there an idea of reviving them? Or did the satyr-play, as a cross between tragedy and comedy, have a special theoretical importance?

Grube 238 ff.; C. O. Brink, *Horace on Poetry* (vol. i, Prolegomena, Cambridge, 1963; vol. ii, Commentary, 1971). Williams, op. cit., 329 ff. Good (Victorian) verse translation by J. Conington; but note also Ben Jonson's version.

Brink's textual divisions pencilled in.

Unity and Art.

UNITY AND CONSISTENCY

Winsatt divisions

I

I Imagine a painter who wanted to combine a horse's neck with a human *I Poetry* head, and then clothe a miscellaneous collection of limbs with various kinds of feathers, so that what started out at the top as a beautiful woman ended in a hideously ugly fish. If you were invited, as friends, to the private view, could you help laughing? Let me tell you, my Piso friends, a book whose different features are made up at random like a sick man's dreams, with no unified form to have a head or a tail, is exactly like that picture.

'Painters and poets have always enjoyed recognized[2] rights to venture on what they will.' Yes, we know; indeed, we ask and grant this permission 10 turn and turn about. But it doesn't mean that fierce and gentle can be united, snakes paired with birds or lambs with tigers.

---

[1] Horace now puts himself in the position of Augustus, recipient of unwanted poetic attention.

[2] Or 'equal'.

Serious and ambitious designs often have a purple patch or two sewn on to them just to make a good show at a distance—a description of a grove and altar of Diana, the meanderings of a stream running through pleasant meads, the River Rhine, the rainbow: but the trouble is, it's not the place for them.

Maybe you know how to do a picture of a cypress tree? What's the good of that, if the man who is paying for the picture is a desperate ship-wrecked mariner swimming to safety? The job began as a wine-jar: the 20 wheel runs round—why is that a tub that's coming out? In short, let it be what you will, but let it be simple and unified.

↳ clear?

SKILL NEEDED TO AVOID FAULTS

diction

Most of us poets—father and worthy sons—are deceived by appearances of correctness. I try to be concise, but I become obscure; my aim is smoothness, but sinews and spirit fail; professions of grandeur end in bombast; the over-cautious who fear the storm creep along the ground. Similarly, the writer who wants to give fantastic variety to his single 30 theme paints a dolphin in his woods and a wild boar in his sea.[1] If art is wanting, the flight from blame leads to faults. The poorest smith near the School of Aemilius will reproduce nails and mimic soft hair in bronze, though he has no luck with the over-all effect of his work, because he won't know how to organize the whole. If I were anxious to put anything together, I would as soon be that man as I would live with a mis-shapen nose when my black eyes and black hair had made me a beauty.

✓ You writers must choose material equal to your powers. Consider long what your shoulders will bear and what they will refuse. The man who 40 chooses his subject with full control will not be abandoned by eloquence or lucidity of arrangement.

plot

II

As to arrangement: its excellence and charm, unless I'm very wrong, con-sist in saying at this moment what needs to be said at this moment, and post-poning and temporarily omitting a great many things. An author who has undertaken a poem must be choosy—cling to one point and spurn another.[2]

As to words: if you're delicate and cautious in arranging them, you will give distinction to your style if an ingenious combination makes a familiar word new. If it happens to be necessary to denote hidden mysteries by novel symbols, it will fall to you to invent terms the Cethegi 50 in their loin-cloths[3] never heard—and the permission will be granted if

[1] Note this use of the idea of faults related to particular virtues: cf. 'Longinus' 3. 3 ff. (below, p. 464).

[2] Bentley and others rearrange so that this sentence is taken differently: 'As to words: an author who has undertaken a poem should be delicate and cautious in arranging them, like one and spurn another.'   [3] i.e. primitive Romans.

you accept it modestly—and, moreover, your new and freshly invented words will receive credit, if sparingly derived from the Greek springs. Is the Roman to give Caecilius and Plautus privileges denied to Virgil and Varius? Why am I unpopular if I can make a few acquisitions, when the tongue of Cato and Ennius so enriched their native language and produced such a crop of new names for things?

FASHIONS IN WORDS

It always has been, and always will be, lawful to produce a word stamped with the current mark. As woods change in leaf as the seasons slide on, and the first leaves fall, so the old generation of words dies out, and the 60 newly born bloom and are strong like young men. We and our works are a debt owed to death. Here a land-locked sea protects fleets from the North wind—a royal achievement; here an old barren marsh where oars were plied feeds neighbouring cities and feels the weight of the plough; here again a river gives up a course that damaged the crops and learns a better way. But whatever they are, all mortal works will die; and still less can the glory and charm of words endure for a long life. Many words which have fallen will be born again, many now in repute will fall if usage[1] decrees: 70 for in her hand is the power and the law and the canon of speech.

METRE AND SUBJECT

Histories of kings and generals, dreadful wars: it was Homer who showed in what metre these could be narrated. Lines unequally yoked in pairs formed the setting first for lamentations, then for the expression of a vow fulfilled;[2] though who first sent these tiny 'elegies' into the world is a grammarians' quarrel and still *sub judice*. Madness armed Archilochus with its own iambus; that too was the foot that the comic sock and tragic 80 buskin held, because it was suitable for dialogue, able to subdue the shouts of the mob, and intended by nature for a life of action. To the lyre, the Muse granted the celebration of gods and the children of gods, victorious boxers, winning race-horses, young men's love, and generous wine. If I have neither the ability nor the knowledge to keep the duly assigned functions and tones of literature, why am I hailed as a poet? Why do I prefer to be ignorant than learn, out of sheer false shame? A comic subject will not be set out in tragic verse; likewise, the Banquet of Thyestes disdains being told in poetry of the private kind, that borders 90 on the comic stage. Everything must keep the appropriate place to which it was allotted.

[1] Or 'need'.
[2] Horace is thinking of inscriptions accompanying dedications to gods.

Nevertheless, comedy does sometimes raise her voice, and angry Chremes perorates with swelling eloquence. Often too Telephus and Peleus[1] in tragedy lament in prosaic language, when they are both poor exiles and throw away their bombast and words half a yard long, if they are anxious to touch the spectator's heart with their complaint.

EMOTION AND CHARACTER

It is not enough for poetry to be beautiful; it must also be pleasing and
100 lead the hearer's mind wherever it will. The human face smiles in sympathy with smilers and comes to the help of those that weep. If you want me to cry, mourn first yourself; *then* your misfortunes will hurt me, Telephus and Peleus. If your words are given you ineptly, I shall fall asleep or laugh. Sad words suit a mournful countenance, threatening words an angry one; sportive words are for the playful, serious for the grave. For nature first shapes us within for any state of fortune—gives us pleasure
110 or drives us to anger or casts us down to the ground with grievous sorrow and pains us—and then expresses the emotions through the medium of the tongue. If the words are out of tune with the speaker's fortunes, the knights and infantry of Rome will raise a cackle. It will make a lot of difference whether the speaker is a god or a hero, an old man of ripe years or a hot youth, an influential matron or a hard-working nurse, a travelling merchant or the tiller of a green farm, a Colchian or an Assyrian, one nurtured at Thebes or at Argos.

CHOICE AND HANDLING OF MYTH

Either follow tradition or invent a consistent story. If as a writer you are
120 representing Achilles with all his honours, let him be active, irascible, implacable, and fierce; let him say 'the laws are not for me' and set no limit to the claims that arms can make. Let Medea be proud and indomitable, Ino full of tears, Ixion treacherous, Io never at rest, Orestes full of gloom. On the other hand, if you are putting something untried on the stage and venturing to shape a new character, let it be maintained to the end as it began and be true to itself. It is hard to put generalities in an individual way: you do better to reduce the song of Troy to acts than
130 if you were the first to bring out something unknown and unsaid.[2] The

[1] Euripidean characters.
[2] i.e. to invent names and circumstances for a general theme is undesirable; if you object that the known myths are hackneyed, the remedy is in the treatment of them in a new way.

common stock will become your private property if you don't linger on
the broad and vulgar round, or anxiously render word for word, a loyal
interpreter, or again, in the process of imitation, find yourself in a tight
corner from which shame, or the rule of the craft, won't let you move; or,
once again, if you avoid a beginning like the cyclic poet—

> Of Priam's fortune will I sing, and war
> well known to fame.

If he opens his mouth as wide as that, how *can* the promiser bring forth
anything to match it? The mountains shall be in labour, and there shall
be born—a silly mouse. How much better was the way of that poet whose   140
every endeavour is to the point!

> Tell me, O Muse, of him who, after Troy
> had fallen, saw the manners and the towns
> of many men.[1]

His plan is not to turn fire to smoke, but smoke to light, so as to relate
magnificent wonders thereafter—Antiphates and the Cyclops, Scylla and
Charybdis.[2] *He* doesn't start the Return of Diomedes from the death of
Meleager, nor begin the Trojan war from the twin egg; he is always making
good speed towards the end of the story, and carries his hearer right into
the thick of it as though it were already known. He leaves out anything
which he thinks cannot be polished up satisfactorily by treatment, and   150
tells his fables and mixes truth with falsehood in such a way that the
middle squares with the beginning and the end with the middle.

Let me tell you what I and the public both want, if you're hoping for
an applauding audience that will wait for the curtain and keep its seat
until the epilogue-speaker says 'Pray clap your hands'. You must mark
the manners of each time of life, and assign the appropriate part to changing natures and ages.[3] The child, just able to repeat words and planting
his steps on the ground with confidence, is eager to play with his contemporaries, gets in and out of a temper without much cause, and changes   160
hour by hour. The beardless youth, his tutor at last out of the way, enjoys
his horses and dogs and the grass of the sunny Park. Moulded like wax
into vice, he is surly to would-be advisers, slow to provide for necessities,
prodigal of money, up in the air, eager, and quick to abandon the objects
of his sudden love. Soon interests change: the grown man's mind pursues
wealth and influential connections, is enslaved to honour, and avoids doing
anything he may soon be trying to change. Many distresses surround
the old man. He is acquisitive, and, poor man, daren't put his hand on

[1] *Odyssey* 1. 1 ff.   [2] The various tales in *Odyssey* 9–12.
[3] Cf. Aristotle, *Rhetoric* 2. 12 for the 'ages of man'.

170 what he has laid up; he is afraid to use it. He goes about his business
timidly and coldly, procrastinating, letting things drag on in hope, lazy
yet greedy of his future; he is awkward and grumbling, given to praising
the days when he was a boy and to criticizing and finding fault with his
juniors. Years as they come bring many blessings with them, and as they
go take many away. To save yourself giving a young man an old man's
role or a boy a grown man's, remember that your character should always
remain faithful to what is associated with his age and suits it.

SOME RULES FOR DRAMATISTS[1]

Actions may be either performed on the stage or reported when performed.
180 What comes in through the ear is less effective in stirring the mind than
what is put before our faithful eyes and told by the spectator to himself.
However, you are not to bring on to the stage events which ought to be
carried out within; you are to remove many things from sight, and let
them be related in due course by the eloquence of an eye-witness. Don't
let Medea murder the children before the people's gaze, or wicked Atreus
cook human offal in public, or Procne be metamorphosed into a bird or
Cadmus into a snake. Anything you show me like that earns my incredulity and disgust.
190 A play that wants to be in demand and to be revived must not be
shorter or longer than five acts.[2]
There should be no god to intervene, unless the problem merits such a
champion.
No fourth character should attempt to speak.
The chorus should play an actor's part, and do a man's duty.[3] It should
not sing between the acts anything which has no relevance to or cohesion
with the plot. It should side with the good and give them friendly counsel,
restrain the angry, and approve those who scruple to go astray. It should
praise a frugal table's fare, sound justice, law, and times of peace when the
200 town's gates stand open. It should keep secrets entrusted to it, and beg
and pray the gods that Fortune may return to the wretched and abandon
the proud.

DEVELOPMENT OF TRAGEDY

The flute used not to be, as it is now, bound with copper and a rival to
the trumpet. It was slight and simple, with few apertures, but serviceable

---

[1] Cf. Aristotle, *Poetics*, for many of these precepts.
[2] Not Aristotelian; but Menander seems normally to have composed his comedies in
five acts, separated by choral interludes.   [3] *Poetics* 18 (above, p. 116).

to accompany and aid the chorus and to fill with its music the still not too crowded benches, where a population of no great size gathered in numbers easily counted, honest and decent and modest. But when that same population won wars and began to extend its territory, when longer walls came to embrace the cities, and people indulged themselves on 210 holidays by drinking in the daytime, and nobody blamed them, then rhythm and tunes acquired greater licence. For what taste could the uneducated show, the holiday crowd of countrymen and townsmen, honest folk and rogues, all mixed up together? This is how the musician came to add movement and elaboration to his art, and to trail his robe as he roamed the stage. This is how even the austere lyre gained a stronger voice, while lofty eloquence produced strange utterance and thought that shrewdly grasped practical needs and prophesied the future grew indistinguishable from the oracles of Delphi.

SATYR-PLAYS[1]

The competitor in tragic poetry, who strove for a worthless goat, next 220 showed the rustic Satyrs, naked. Preserving his seriousness despite his keen wit, he made an attempt at a joke, because the audience, drunk and lawless at the end of the festival, had to be prevented from going away by tricks and pleasing innovations. But the way to recommend your laughing, joking satyrs, the way to turn seriousness to jest, is this: no god or hero you bring on the stage, if he was seen not long ago in royal gold and purple, must lower his language and move into a humble cottage; nor, on the other hand, must his efforts to get off the ground lead him to try to 230 grasp clouds and void. Tragedy does not deserve to blurt out trivial lines, but she will modestly consort a little with the forward satyrs, like a respectable lady dancing because she must on a feast day.

As a Satyr-writer, my Piso friends, I shall not limit my liking to plain and proper terms, nor yet try to be so different from the tone of tragedy that there is no difference between Davus talking or bold Pythias, when she's just tricked Simon out of a talent,[2] and Silenus, at once guardian and servant of the god he has brought up. I shall make up my poem of 240 known elements, so that anyone may hope to do the same, but he'll sweat and labour to no purpose when he ventures: such is the force of arrangement and combination, such the splendour that commonplace words

---

[1] These featured Silenus and satyrs in burlesque episodes of myth; style and metre were those of tragedy, not comedy. The piece was commonly performed as a fourth play after three tragedies. Euripides' *Cyclops* is the only complete extant example. Aristotle believed satyr-plays were at the origin of tragedy (above, p. 95); others, as Horace here, that they were a later refinement.

[2] Typical New Comedy names: slave, maid or prostitute, old man.

acquire. Your woodland Fauns, if you take my judgement, should beware
of behaving as if they were born at the street corner and were creatures of
the Forum—they shouldn't play the gallant in languishing verse or crack
dirty and disreputable jokes; possessors of horses or ancestors or property
take offence at this sort of thing and don't look kindly on work approved
250 by the fried-peas-and-nuts public, or give it the prize.

THE NEED FOR TECHNICAL PERFECTION

A long syllable following a short one makes an iambus.[1] He is a quick
foot; this is why he ordered iambic lines to be called trimeters, although
he was giving six beats to the line, and was the same in form from first to
last. Not all that long ago, wanting to fall rather more slowly and weightily
upon our ears, he admitted the stately spondees to family privileges—
what a comfortable, easy-going foot he is!—but without being quite so
complaisant as to give up the second and fourth positions in the line.
Rarely does he appear in Accius' noble trimeters, and his rarity in Ennius'
260 weighty lines as they fly out on the stage damns them with the shocking
accusation of hasty and careless craftsmanship—or else sheer ignorance of
the trade.

Of course, it's not every critic that notices lines that aren't tuneful,
and Roman poets have enjoyed undeserved licence. But does that entitle
me to make mistakes and scribble away carelessly? Or should I rather
expect everyone to see my mistakes, and so play safe and cautious,
keeping within the bounds of what I can hope to be pardoned for? In
that case, all I've done is to avoid blame; I have not deserved praise.

GREEK MODELS

270 Study Greek models night and day. Your ancestors praised Plautus' metre
and his humour. On both counts their admiration was too indulgent, not
to say childish, if it's true that you and I know how to distinguish a witless
jest from a subtle one and if we've skill in our fingers and ears to know
what sounds are permitted.

[1] Horace's main theme in what preceded was propriety; in the next section it is
perfection. He marks the transition by humorously giving some very elementary metrical
instruction. Greek trimeters have the basic scheme: ⌣−|⌣−|⌣−|⌣−|⌣−|⌣−, whereas
the corresponding old Latin *senarius* (Ennius, Accius) admits spondees (−−) also in the
second and fourth feet.

INVENTIVENESS OF THE GREEKS IN DRAMA

The hitherto unknown genre of the tragic Muse is said to be Thespis' invention; he is supposed to have carried on a cart verses to be sung and acted by performers whose faces were smeared with wine-lees. After him came Aeschylus, the inventor of the mask and splendid robe; he gave the stage a floor of modest boards, and taught the actors to talk big and give themselves height by their high boots. Next came Old Comedy, 280 much praised, though its liberty degenerated into vice and violence deserving restraint of law; the law was accepted, and the chorus fell silent, its right of shameful insult removed.

INVENTIVENESS OF THE ROMANS

Our poets have left nothing unattempted. Not the least part of their glory was won by venturing to abandon the footsteps of the Greeks and celebrate our own affairs; some produced historical plays, some comedies in Roman dress. Latium would have been as famous for literature as for valour and deeds of arms if the poets had not, one and all, been put off 290 by the labour and time of polishing their work. Children of Numa, show your disapproval of any poem which long time and much correction have not disciplined and smoothed ten times over, to satisfy the well-pared nail.

THE POET[1]

Democritus [2] thinks native talent a happier thing than poor, miserable art, and banishes sane poets from his Helicon. That's why so many don't bother to cut their nails or beard, but seek solitude and keep away from the bath. For a man is sure to win the reward and name of poet if he never lets barber Licinus get hold of that head that three Anticyras [3] won't make 300 sound. I'm a fool to purge my bile when spring comes round. I could write as good poetry as any; but nothing is worth that price, and so I'll play the part of the whetstone, that can sharpen the knife though it can't itself cut. In other words, without writing myself, I will teach function and duty—where the poet's resources come from, what nurtures and forms him, what is proper and what not, in what directions excellence and error lead.

[1] From this point, the poem turns to topics concerned with the poet himself: inspiration, moral knowledge, care for posterity, commitment. This main theme continues to the end.   [2] See above, p. 4.

[3] Hellebore, proverbially a cure for madness, came from Anticyra.

Wisdom is the starting-point and source of correct writing. Socratic
310 books will be able to point out to you your material, and once the material
is provided the words will follow willingly enough. If a man has learned
his duty to his country and his friends, the proper kind of love with which
parent, brother, and guest should be cherished, the functions of a senator
and a judge, the task of a general sent to the front—then he automatically
understands how to give each character its proper attributes. My advice
to the skilled imitator will be to keep his eye on the model of life and manners, and draw his speech living from there.
320 Sometimes a play devoid of charm, weight, and skill, but attractive
with its commonplaces and with the characters well drawn, gives the
people keener pleasure and keeps them in their seats more effectively than
lines empty of substance and harmonious trivialities.

GREEK AND ROMAN ATTITUDES

The Greeks have the gift of genius from the Muse, and the power of
well-rounded speech. They covet nothing but praise. Roman boys do
long sums and learn to divide their as into a hundred parts.[1]
'Young Albinus, subtract one uncia from a quincunx: what's left? . . .
You could have told me by now . . .'
'A triens.'
'Excellent. You'll be able to look after your affairs. Now add an uncia.
What is it now?'
'A semis.'
330 Once this rust and care for cash has tainted the soul, can we hope for
poems to be written that deserve preserving with cedar oil and keeping
safe in smooth cypress?
Poets aim either to do good or to give pleasure—or, thirdly, to say
things which are both (pleasing) and serviceable for life.
Whatever advice you give, be brief, so that the teachable mind can take
in your words quickly and retain them faithfully. Anything superfluous
overflows from the full mind.
Whatever you invent for pleasure, let it be near to truth. We don't
want a play to ask credence for anything it feels like, or draw a living
340 child from the ogress's belly after lunch. The ranks of elder citizens chase
things off the stage if there's no good meat in them, and the high-spirited
youngsters won't vote for dry poetry. The man who combines pleasure
with usefulness wins every suffrage, delighting the reader and also giving

---

[1] 12 unciae = 1 as; 5 unciae = quincunx; $\frac{1}{3}$ as = triens; $\frac{1}{2}$ as = semis.

him advice; this is the book that earns money for the Sosii,[1] goes overseas and gives your celebrated writer a long lease of fame.

However, there are some mistakes we are ready to forgive. The string doesn't always give the note that the hand and mind intended: it often returns a high note when you ask for a low. The bow won't always hit what it threatens to hit. But when most features of a poem are brilliant, I shan't be offended by a few blemishes thrown around by carelessness or human negligence. But what then? If a copyist goes on making the same mistake however much he is warned, he is not forgiven; if a lyre-player always gets the same note wrong, people laugh at him; so, in my estimation, if a poet fails to come off a good deal, he's another Choerilus, whom I admire with a smile if he's good two or three times. Why, I'm angry even if good Homer goes to sleep, though a doze is quite legitimate in a long piece of work.

→Poetry is like painting. Some attracts you more if you stand near, some if you're further off. One picture likes a dark place, one will need to be seen in the light, because it's not afraid of the critic's sharp judgement. One gives pleasure once, one will please if you look it over ten times.

Dear elder son of Piso, though your father's words are forming you in the right way and you have wisdom of your own besides, take this piece of advice away with you and remember it. In some things, a tolerable mediocrity is properly allowed. A mediocre lawyer or advocate is a long way from the distinction of learned Messalla and doesn't know as much as Aulus Cascellius, but he has his value. But neither men nor gods nor shop-fronts allow a poet to be mediocre. Just as music out of tune or thick ointment or Sardinian honey with your poppy gives offence at a nice dinner, because the meal could go on without them, so poetry, which was created and discovered for the pleasure of the mind, sinks right to the bottom the moment it declines a little from the top. The man who doesn't know how to play keeps away from the sporting gear in the park. The man who's never been taught ball or discus or hoop keeps quiet, so that the packed spectators can't get a free laugh. But the man who doesn't know how to make verses still has a go. Why shouldn't he? He's free, and of free birth, he's assessed at an equestrian property rate, and he's not got a fault in the world.

You will never do or say anything if Minerva is against you: your taste and intelligence guarantee us that. But if you do write something some day, let it find its way to critic Maecius' ears, and your father's, and mine, and be stored up for eight years in your notebooks at home. You will be able to erase what you haven't published; words once uttered forget the way home.

350

360

370

380

390

[1] Booksellers.

POETRY AND ITS SOCIAL USES AND VALUE

Orpheus, who was a holy man and the interpreter of the gods, deterred the men of the forests from killing and from disgusting kinds of food. This is why he was said to tame tigers and rabid lions. This too is why Amphion, the founder of the city of Thebes, was said to move rocks where he wished by the sound of the lyre and coaxing prayers.[1] In days of old, wisdom consisted in separating public property from private, the sacred from the secular, in checking promiscuity, in laying down rules for the married, in building cities, in inscribing laws on wooden tablets. And that is how honour and renown came to divine poets and poetry.

400 After them came the great Homer and Tyrtaeus, who sharpened masculine hearts for war by their verses. Oracles were uttered in verse. The path of life was pointed out in verse. Kings' favours were won by the Muses' tunes. Entertainment was found there also, and rest after long labour. So there is no call to be ashamed of the Muse with her skill on the lyre or of Apollo the singer.

ART AND NATURE

Do good poems come by nature or by art? This is a common question. For my part, I don't see what study can do without a rich vein of talent, nor what good can come of untrained genius. They need each other's

410 help and work together in friendship.[2] A boy who wants to reach the hoped-for goal in the race endures and does a lot, sweats and freezes, refrains from sex and wine. The clarinetist who is playing in honour of Apollo learns his lesson first and stands in awe of his master. But nowadays it's enough to say: 'I write marvellous poems. The itch take the hindmost! It's a disgrace for me to be left behind and admit I don't know something that, to be sure, I never learned.'

420 A poet who is rich in land and investments bids his flatterers 'come and better themselves'—just like an auctioneer collecting a crowd to buy his wares. But if he's a man who can set out a good dinner properly and go bail for a poor and impecunious client and get him out of a grim legal tangle, I shall be surprised if the lucky fellow knows how to distinguish a false friend from a true. If you have given a man a present, or if you want to, don't then lead him, full of joy, to your verses. He's bound to say 'Splendid, beautiful, just right'; he'll grow pale here, he'll drip dew

430 from loving eyes, he'll jump about, he'll beat the ground with his foot. Your mocker is more deeply stirred than your true admirer, just as hired

---

[1] Horace allegorizes the myths. For similar *exempla* (no allegory), cf. Aristophanes, *Frogs* 1030 ff. (above, p. 22).   [2] Cf. 'Longinus' 2 (below, p. 463).

mourners at a funeral say and do almost more than those who genuinely grieve. Kings are said to ply a man with many cups and test him with wine if they are trying to discover if he deserves their friendship. If you write poetry, the fox's hidden feelings will never escape you. If you read anything aloud to Quintilius, he'd say 'pray change that, and that'. You would say you couldn't do better, though you'd tried two or three times, to no purpose. Then he'd tell you to scratch it out and put the badly turned 440 lines back on the anvil. If you preferred defending your error to amending it, he wasted no more words or trouble on preventing you from loving yourself and your handiwork without competition. A wise and good man will censure flabby lines, reprehend harsh ones, put a black line with a stroke of the pen besides unpolished ones, prune pretentious ornaments, force you to shed light on obscurities, convict you of ambiguity, mark down what must be changed. He'll be an Aristarchus.[1] He won't say, 'Why should I offend a friend in trifles?' These trifles lead to 450 serious troubles, if once you are ridiculed and get a bad reception.

THE MAD POET

Men of sense are afraid to touch a mad poet and give him a wide berth. He's like a man suffering from a nasty itch, or the jaundice, or fanaticism, or Diana's wrath. Boys chase him and follow him round incautiously. And if, while he's belching out his lofty lines and wandering round, he happens to fall into a well or a pit, like a fowler intent on his birds, then, however long he shouts 'Help! Help! Fellow citizens, help!' there'll be no one to 460 bother to pick him up. And if anyone should trouble to help and let down a rope, my question will be, 'How do you know that he didn't throw himself down deliberately? Are you sure he wants to be saved?' And I shall tell the tale of the death of the Sicilian poet. Empedocles wanted to be regarded as an immortal god, and so he jumped, cool as you like, into burning Etna. Let poets have the right and privilege of death. To save a man against his will is the same as killing him. This isn't the only time he's done it. If he's pulled out now, he won't become human or lay aside his love of a notorious end.

It's far from clear *why* he keeps writing poetry. Has the villain pissed 470 on his father's ashes? Or disturbed the grim site of a lightning-strike? Anyway, he's raving, and his harsh readings put learned and unlearned alike to flight, like a bear that's broken the bars of his cage. If he catches anyone, he holds on and kills him with reading. He's a real leech that won't let go of the skin till it's full of blood.

[1] The great Alexandrian scholar marked spurious or doubtful lines in Homer with the sign which Horace here attributes to the good critic.

F. A POET'S AUTOBIOGRAPHY

In this and the next two sections we give extracts from the elegiac poems of Ovid, the greatest poet of the generation after Horace. The first passage (*Tristia* 4. 10. 1–64), like the second, was written in exile at Tomi on the Black Sea in the first decade of our era.

See, in general, L. P. Wilkinson, *Ovid Recalled*, Cambridge, 1955.

Listen, readers of the future, if you want to know who I was—the jesting author of light love poems whom you read. My birthplace is Sulmo, rich in cold streams, and ninety miles away from the City. Here I was raised: if you want to know the year, it was when both consuls met a like fate.[1] If it's of any note, I inherit my rank from distant forefathers: it wasn't merely a gift of fortune that made me Knight. I was not the first child—
10 I had an elder brother, born a twelve-month earlier. The same star shone on both our birthdays: there was one day to celebrate, with two cakes. It's one of the five feast-days of the warlike Minerva—the one that is first to get stained with blood in battle.[2]

Our education began while we were still young; thanks to our father's care, we went off to distinguished professional men in the city. My brother had an inclination towards oratory from a tender age; he was born to wield the stout weapons of the garrulous forum. But as for me, while I
20 was still a boy I enjoyed poetry, gift of the gods, and the Muse kept furtively luring me over to her department. My father often said: 'Why touch it? It's a useless pursuit. Homer himself had no money to leave in his will.' I was persuaded by what he said, left Helicon altogether, and had a go at writing prose. But what I tried to say proved to be verse— poetry came of its own accord and the rhythms fitted.[3]

Meanwhile, as the years glided by on silent foot, my brother and I put on the toga of a free man: the purple robe with the wide stripe went
30 over our shoulders.[4] And still our former interests remained. When my brother was twenty, he died, and I had to start getting used to doing without a half of myself. I took on the first honours my youth allowed; once I was one of the *tresviri*. There remained the senate; but I had my stripe narrowed: that was a load too great for my strength. My body wouldn't put up with the work, my mind was not suitable for it; I became a fugitive from tiresome ambition. And the Muses kept persuading me
40 to retreat to safety and quiet—which *my* judgement had always hankered

---

[1] Hirtius and Pansa in 43 B.C.   [2] i.e. 20 March: cf. *Fasti* 3. 809 ff.
[3] Cf. Seneca on Ovid's declamations: below, p. 358.
[4] Signifying preparation for a senatorial career. When Ovid took to a narrower stripe (below), he renounced these ambitions, and remained an *eques*.

after. I cultivated the acquaintance of poets of the day. Any available bard I regarded as a god. The older Macer often read me his lines on birds, on dangerous snakes, on herbal remedies. Propertius often recited his love poetry to me, as was the due of my comradeship with him. Ponticus (famous for epic) and Bassus (famous for iambics) were agreeable members of my circle. The musical Horace attracted my attention as he struck out his polished poems on an Italian lyre. Virgil I only saw; and 50 the greedy fates did not allow time for me to become a friend of Tibullus. Tibullus was Gallus' successor, Propertius Tibullus': I was fourth in order of time after these.

Just as I cultivated my elders, so younger men cultivated me, and my muse swiftly became famous. When I first read my youthful poems to the public, I had only shaved once or twice. Corinna[1]—it was not her real 60 name—had been sung all over town, and she it was who aroused my talents. I wrote a lot; what I thought faulty, I personally gave for correction to the flames. When I was going into exile, too, I burnt things that would have pleased: I was angry with my pursuit, and with my poetry.

[The rest of the poem is of less critical interest: it describes Ovid's wives, the death of his parents, and his own exile to Tomi.]

G. POETRY AND MORALITY

This apologia is from *Tristia* 2. 353 ff. Compare for the theme Pliny, *Epistles* 4. 14 (below, p. 428).

Believe me, my character is different from my poetry: my life is decent, my Muse sportive. A great part of my *œuvre* is untruthful fiction, allowing itself indulgences not permitted to its author. A book is not a revelation of the mind, but a respectable entertainment, that brings much with it fit to soothe the ear. Otherwise Accius would be a savage, Terence a diner-out, and narrators of fierce war warlike.

And I'm not the only composer of light verses—though I was the only 360 one to pay the penalty for composing a love poem. What was the lesson of the lyric Muse of the old man of Teos?[2] Surely it was sex—and a flood of wine? What did Lesbian Sappho instruct girls in but love? Nevertheless Sappho was safe—and so was he. Nor did it go hard with you, son of Battus,[3] for the constant declarations of love the reader finds in your verse. None of the charming Menander's plays ignores love—and 373 he is read by boys and girls. What else is the *Iliad* itself but the story of an adulteress who caused a fight between her lover and her husband?

---

[1] The 'heroine' of the *Amores*. [2] Anacreon. [3] Callimachus.

What is told in it before the story of the passion aroused by Briseis, and of how the seizure of the girl angered the chieftains? What is the *Odyssey* except the tale of a woman sought by a horde of suitors in the absence of her husband—all for love? No one but Homer tells the story of Venus and Mars getting tied up when their bodies were twined on an adulterous
380 couch. How would we know, if Homer did not tell us, that two goddesses[1] burned with love for their guest? Every genre of writing is surpassed in seriousness by tragedy—yet it too constantly involves love.

[Ovid proceeds to illustrate the place of love in tragedy.]

I should run out of time if I went all through the amours of tragedy: my book will scarcely find room even for a bare list of names. There is also
410 the kind of tragedy[2] that merges with pornographic humour, full of words that leave shame behind. Yet the author who made Achilles effeminate did not rue it—despite diminishing his brave deeds by his verses. Aristides associated with himself the vices of Miletus—yet Aristides was not banished from his city. Nor was Eubius, writer of an obscene story, who described how the seeds within mothers were destroyed. No exile either for the late author of *Sybaritica*, or for those who have revealed the details of their sex lives. Such things form part of the output of learned men,
420 and, thanks to our rulers,[3] have become common knowledge.

ROMAN EROTICA

Let me not be defended only by foreign aid: Roman literature, too, has much of a sportive kind. While Ennius sang gravely of war—Ennius, so talented yet so primitive; while Lucretius expounded the causes of darting fire, prophesying that the threefold structure of the world would fall: wanton Catullus frequently sang of the woman disguised under the name
430 of Lesbia. Not content with her, he publicized many affairs, confessing his own adulteries. Tiny Calvus had equal licence; he revealed his exploits in various metres. Cinna is their companion, and Anser, more lascivious than Cinna, and the light-weight compositions of Cornificius and Cato. What of the work of Ticidas and of Memmius, in whom things are called by their names—and the names have their shameful side? What of those who have a place in their books for the woman till recently disguised as Perilla (now we read of her under your name, Metellus).
440 The man who carried the Argo on to the waves of Phasis could not keep

---

[1] i.e. Circe and Calypso for Odysseus.
[2] i.e. Satyr plays (for which see Horace, *Ars* 220 ff.: above, p. 285).
[3] Who founded public libraries in Rome.

quiet about his amorous adventures.[1] Hortensius' poems are equally
wanton, and Servius'. Who would hesitate to follow in the footsteps of
such great men? Sisenna translated Aristides, and it did not go against
him to have inserted obscene jests in his story. Gallus was not reproached
for celebrating Lycoris, merely for not holding his tongue when drunk.
Tibullus finds it hard to believe his mistress' oath—because she disclaims
knowledge of him to her husband in just the same way. He, moreover,
confesses to teaching how to deceive guards, and says that he's now   450
unfortunate enough to be caught by his own wiles.[2] He recalls that often
he touched his mistress' hand on purpose while pretending to test her
ring and seal. He often spoke with nods and gestures (he says), and drew
silent marks on the round table. He describes how he gets rid of the marks
of love-bites with herbs. He begs the all too unaware husband to look
out for him too, and see that she strays less often. He knows who gets
barked at when he walks alone, to whom he coughs so often before the   460
closed gate, and gives many precepts for similar deceptions, tells how
wives can trick husbands. *He* came to no harm; Tibullus is read, and he
is in favour, and was known when you were already emperor. You will
find the same precepts in the pleasing Propertius: yet *he* was not marked
by the least stain. I am their successor, as my uprightness makes me keep
quiet about the names of distinguished living poets. I did not, I must
confess, feel any fear that, on a route where so many ships had sailed
before, one should be shipwrecked, when all the rest were safe.   470

[There have been, says Ovid, 'arts' on dicing, cosmetics, and other frivolous
subjects.]

MIMES ARE NOT CRITICIZED

I was deceived by these, and wrote cheerful poems: but a grim penalty
followed on my jests. Out of all the writers there have ever been I can
find none except myself whose Muse has destroyed him. What if I had
written mimes with obscene jokes, which always contain passages on
illicit sex: where the bedizened adulterer is constantly abroad, and the
clever wife tricks the stupid husband? These are watched by girls ready   500
to marry, by matrons, men and boys—and most of the senate attends.
It's not enough that their ears should be besmirched by unchaste language:
their eyes have to get used to seeing much that is improper. And when the
lover has found some new trick to deceive the husband, there is applause,

----

[1] Varro Atacinus.
[2] See Tibullus 1. 5, 1. 6. Ovid selects things comparable to what was complained of
in his own *Art of Love.*

and the prize is awarded amid great enthusiasm. The less edifying the piece, the more profitable to the poet: and the praetor has to pay a fat sum for all these crimes. Augustus, look at the accounts of the games you
510 support—you will find that you have paid a lot for much that is of just this character. You have watched such things often in person, often put the show on yourself (so affable is your greatness in every sphere); with those eyes that are at the service of the world you have viewed adultery on the stage—without getting upset. If it is all right to compose mimes that represent obscenities, my subject surely deserves a smaller penalty. Or is it that this kind of writing is made safe by the stage on which it is shown—is it the theatre that makes mime permissible? Well, my poems
520 too have often been danced before the people, and have often found a watcher even in you.

A PARALLEL FROM PAINTING

In our houses there are paintings of men long ago, bright from the artist's hand—but you may find in some corner a miniature representation of various methods of intercourse and sexual postures. Ajax, son of Telamon, sits there, his face showing his anger;[1] Medea, that barbarous mother, has her crime in her eyes: yet a dripping Venus dries her wet hair and is seen newly emerged from the waves that gave her birth.

OVID'S OWN FORTE

530 Others sing loudly of war and its array of gory weapons; some hymn your deeds, some those of your race. Nature, grudgingly, has confined *me* to a narrow space, and given my intellect but feeble strength. Yet even the fortunate author of the *Aeneid* you patronized takes his 'hero and his arms' to bed in Carthage; no part of the whole work is so eagerly read as the story of that illicit love. As a youth, he had used the bucolic metre to sing lightly of the ardour of Phyllis and Amaryllis. In my case too it is long
540 ago that I gave offence with that sort of writing: it is the punishment, not the offence, that is new; and I had published poetry when I passed your scrutiny so often, a knight *sans reproche*. Thus the poems which as a youth I unwarily supposed would do me no harm have harmed me now that I am old. A late penalty has afflicted an old book, and the punishment is far in time from what called it forth.

[1] Because of the awarding of Achilles' arms to Odysseus.

SOME MORE SERIOUS WORKS

And you shouldn't imagine that all my work is relaxed; I've often hoisted big sails on my boat. I wrote twelve books of *Fasti*,[1] each volume finishing at the end of a month. That, previously, was written in your name, dedicated to you: but my calamity cut it short. I have issued a book, royal in its tragic buskins, with the language that the gravity of tragedy demands.[2] And although I did not put the last touch to it, I have written of bodies changed to new appearances. If only you would relax your anger for a little while, and in a moment of ease ask to have a bit of that book read to you—the passage in which I speak of starting from the first origin of the world and tracing the story down to your own times, Caesar.[3] You will observe how much spirit you gave me, how enthusiastically I sing of you and yours.

I never attacked anyone in vicious poetry: my verses bring no charges.[4] I am straightforward, I shunned humour steeped in bile: no word is given a venomous jest. Out of so many thousands of Romans, when I have written so much, I shall be the only one harmed by my Muse. I do not expect any Roman to have rejoiced at my sad fate—I expect many to have grieved. I cannot believe that anyone spurned my prostrate body—if my fairness has earned any reward. May your majesty be dissuaded by these and other pleas, father of your country, its care and its shield! I do not ask to return to Italy—unless later, when you are overcome by the length of my punishment; I ask only a safer and a somewhat quieter exile—to make my penalty fit the crime.

H. IMMORTALITY THROUGH POETRY

Ovid: *Amores* 1. 15

Compare Theognis 237 ff. (above, p. 3) and Horace, *Odes* 4. 9. This is an early poem, published 16 B.C.

Why, mordant envy, reproach me with years passed in idleness? You say poetry is the product of a slothful character, and you object that I haven't, like my ancestors, passed my manhood in the pursuit of prizes amid the dust of war, that I don't learn off wordy laws or prostitute my voice in the thankless forum.

What you are looking for is perishable; *my* aim is everlasting fame, that I should be ever on the world's lips.[5] Homer will live so long as

---

[1] Only six books of this 'calendar' are extant.   [2] *Medea*, not extant.
[3] *Metamorphoses* 1. 1–4.   [4] Cf. Horace, *Satires* 1. 4 (above, p. 266).
[5] The phrase recalls Ennius' epitaph: 'I flit alive on the lips of men.'

10 Tenedos and Mount Ida stand, so long as Simois rolls its swift waters
down to the sea. The poet of Ascra[1] will live so long as the grape swells
for the vintage, so long as the corn falls beneath the curved sickle. Battus'
son will always be talked of throughout the world; he may not have
great natural talents—but his art is great. The buskin of Sophocles will
suffer no loss; Aratus will last as long as sun and moon. Menander will
survive for as long as the deceiving slave, the hard father, the shameless
bawd, the persuasive whore. Ennius, for all his lack of art, and Accius
20 of the spirited tongue have names that will never disappear. What age will
forget Varro,[2] the first ship, the golden fleece hunted by the hero Jason?
The poem of lofty Lucretius will perish only when one day brings the
destruction of the world.[3] Tityrus and the crops and the arms of Aeneas
will be read of while Rome is at the head of the world she triumphed over.
While there are still fire and bow to arm Cupid, elegant Tibullus' verses
will be learned. Gallus will be known to East and West alike, and with
30 Gallus his Lycoris.[4]

Thus, though rocks and the patient plough-share are worn away by
Time, poetry is deathless. To poetry must yield kings and the triumphs
of kings, the generous strand of gold-bearing Tagus. Let the mob admire
worthless things; to me let fair-haired Apollo serve cups full of the water
of Castalia: may I bind my hair with myrtle that fears the frost, and be
constantly read by the anxious lover. Envy battens on the living: after
death it is quiet, when everyone is protected by the honour he has merited.
So, when the last fires have eaten my body away, I shall yet live—and the
best part of me will survive.[5]

I. THE TRUE POET

Petronius 118

This is a rather later comment (we draw on Petronius again, below, p. 361); it
leads up, in the context, to an extract from an epic on the Civil War.

'Young men,' said Encolpius, 'many have been deceived by poetry.
Anyone who's fitted a verse out with feet, and woven a thought of some
delicacy into a period, imagines that he's straightway arrived in Helicon.
Thus, men tired out by the duties of the courts often betake themselves to
the tranquillity of poetry as to a safe haven, thinking it easier to construct
a poem than a *controversia* [6] decked out with vibrant little epigrams. But

---

[1] Hesiod.   [2] Varro Atacinus.   [3] Cf. Lucretius 5. 235 ff.
[4] Cf. Virgil, *Ecl*. 10.   [5] Cf. Horace, *Odes* 3. 30.
[6] A rhetorical exercise. Cf. below, p. 344.

the more noble spirit loves health: the mind cannot conceive or bring forth its offspring unless it is washed by a vast river of literature. One must shrink from all so to say cheapness of vocabulary, selecting words that are remote from the mob (your motto should be: "I hate the profane crowd and keep it at a distance").[1] Further, one must take care that the epigrams don't project obviously from the body of the work, but shine with a colour that is woven into the texture. Witness Homer, and the lyric poets, Roman Virgil and the studied felicity of Horace. The rest either didn't see the route that leads to poetry, or saw it but feared to tread it. Look at the immense theme of the civil wars. Whoever takes on that without being immersed in literature must falter beneath the load. Historical events are not the stuff of verses—that's much better dealt with by historians. Instead, the free spirit must be plunged in complexities of plot, divine machinery, and a torrent of mythological material. The result should be the prophecies of an inspired soul, not the exact testimony of a man on oath.'

[1] Horace, *Odes* 3. 1. 1.

7

GREEK AUGUSTANS

Most of this chapter is devoted to Dionysius of Halicarnassus; but we begin with an extract from Strabo's *Geography* (written *c*. A.D. 17)

A. AGAINST ERATOSTHENES' VIEW THAT POETRY IS ENTERTAINMENT

Strabo 1. 2. 3–9

This is a statement of the Stoic position about the didactic value of poetry, and an argument against the opinions of the great Alexandrian scholar and scientist, Eratosthenes (*c*. 275–194 B.C.). See Grube 127 f., R. Pfeiffer, *History of Classical Scholarship*, Oxford, 1968, 166 f.

1. 2. 3 Every poet, according to Eratosthenes, aims at entertainment (*psuchagōgia*), not instruction. The ancients held a different view. They regarded poetry as a sort of primary philosophy, which was supposed to introduce us to life from our childhood, and teach us about character, emotion, and action in a pleasurable way. My own school, the Stoics, actually said that only the wise man could be a poet. This is why Greek communities give children their first education through poetry, not for simple 'entertainment' of course, but for moral improvement. Even the musicians lay claim to this, when they teach plucking the strings with the fingers, or playing the lyre or *aulos*;[1] they are, as they say, educators and correctors of character. Nor is it only the Pythagoreans who can be heard asserting this; Aristoxenus says the same. Homer himself regards bards as moral guides—like the man who was set to guard Clytemnestra—

> whom, when he sailed for Troy,
> Atrides oft enjoined to watch his wife.

Aegisthus, let us recall, did not succeed in seducing Clytemnestra until he had 'taken the bard to a desert island and left him there'; then he

> took willingly home the willing lady.[2]

Quite apart from this, Eratosthenes contradicts himself. A little before the statement just quoted, at the beginning of his *Geography*, he says that everyone has always been ambitious to publish researches into this sort

---

[1] See below, p. 497.
[2] *Odyssey* 3. 267, f., 272.

of question. Homer, for example, found room in his poetry for what he had found out about Ethiopia and Egypt and Libya, and went into extraordinary detail on Greece and adjacent areas; in phrases like 'Thisbe of the many doves', 'grassy Haliartus', 'remote Anthedon', 'Lilaia by Cephissus' spring', there is not an epithet without point.[1] Well, is the poet who does this offering entertainment or instruction? Instruction, of course; but—Eratosthenes might answer—what does not fall within sense-experience is filled up, by Homer as by other poets, with fabulous wonders. If this is so, one ought to say that poets say some things for entertainment and some for instruction; Eratosthenes' conclusion, however, was that *everything* was for entertainment. He labours the point further, asking what it contributes to the excellence of a poet to have experience of many places or of generalship or farming or rhetoric or whatever it is that people have wanted to foist on him. To try to foist everything on him would be the act of a man whose zeal brings him to grief: as Hipparchus says, to hang every variety of learning and skill on the poet would be like hanging fruits it can't bear, apples and pears, on an Attic begging-bush (*eiresiōne*).[2] You may well be right about that, Eratosthenes. But it is *not* right to take away all that learning and prove poetry to be a mass of old wives' tales, in which any fiction suitable for entertainment is allowed. Is no contribution made towards the excellence of the poets' audiences? Surely listening to poets gives them a knowledge of many places, and of generalship and farming and rhetoric?

Homer certainly attributes all such knowledge to Odysseus, whom he   I. 2. 4
adorns above all men with every excellence. Odysseus

> saw the cities of many men, and knew their minds;[3]

Odysseus

> knew all manner of guile and cunning devices;[4]

Odysseus is the sacker of cities, the man who took Troy

> by counsel and words and guileful art.[5]

According to Diomedes,

> if he is with us, even from burning fire
> we'd both return.[6]

---

[1] Phrases from the 'Catalogue of Ships' in *Iliad* 2.
[2] A wreath with fruits on it, taken from door to door in begging-visits at harvest time.
[3] *Odyssey* 1. 3.   [4] *Iliad* 3. 202.
[5] A line quoted by other ancient authors but not in our texts of Homer: cf. Stobaeus
4. 13. 48 Hense.   [6] *Iliad* 10. 246.

And he prides himself on farming skills; on harvesting—

> in the meadow, if I had a curving sickle,
> and you had one just like it—[1]

and on ploughing—

> you'd see if I could cut a straight furrow.[2]

Nor does Homer think so much of all this without finding support in the whole educated world, which trusts his evidence as embodying right judgement on the great contribution to wisdom made by such experience.

I. 2. 5   Rhetoric is wisdom relating to words; Odysseus displays this throughout the poem—in the Testing, the Prayers, the Embassy, the passage where Antenor says:

> But when he let his great voice come up from his chest,
> and the words like winter snows,
> no man on earth could contend with Odysseus.[3]

Can one believe that a poet who can introduce characters delivering speeches, commanding armies, and performing other virtuous actions, is himself a humbug and a mountebank, capable only of bewitching and cajoling his audience without doing them good? Do we pretend that the excellence of a poet lies in anything but his skill to represent life by the medium of words? If this is so, how can he represent, if he is inexperienced in life and foolish? The goodness of a poet is not like that of a carpenter or a smith. Theirs has nothing grand or noble about it; the poet's is linked with the man's—one cannot be a good poet without first being a good man.

I. 2. 6   So to deny the poet rhetoric is wholly to disregard our argument. What is more a subject of rhetoric than diction (*phrasis*)? And what is more closely connected with poetry? And who is better at diction than Homer? 'But poetic diction is something different.' Yes, it is a different species: just as, within poetry, tragic diction differs from comic, and, within prose, historical diction differs from forensic. Speech must be a generic term, with metrical and prose speech as its species; and this surely cannot be so unless rhetorical speech also is generic, and also diction and excellence of speech.

In fact, prose speech of an elaborate kind is very much an imitation of poetical. Poetical elaboration came into the world first and won fame. Then writers like Cadmus, Pherecydes, and Hecataeus[4] imitated it, keeping all the poetical qualities except metre. Their successors further pruned away various poetic elements, and so brought prose down from

---

[1] *Odyssey* 18. 368 f.   [2] Ibid. 375.   [3] *Iliad* 3. 221.
[4] Early historians; cf. Hermogenes, below, p. 578.

the heights to its present level. Similarly, one might say that comedy took its form from tragedy and descended from tragic heights to its present 'prosaic' state (*logoeides*). The use by early writers of 'sing' for 'tell' (*phrazein*) is also evidence of the same point, that poetry was the fount and beginning of all elaborate diction and rhetoric. Poetry used music to help her in performances; this was song, *ōdē*, or lyrical verse—hence the suffix -*ody* in rhapsody, tragedy (*tragōdia*), comedy (*kōmōdia*). Hence, since 'to tell' (*phrazein*) was first used of poetical diction, and poetry was accompanied by song, they could use 'sing' in the same sense as 'tell'. Then, 'sing' being misused for prose, the catachresis extended to the other term also. The term 'pedestrian' (*pezos*)[1] for language without metre also betrays the descent from a height or a vehicle to the ground.

Homer does not, as Eratosthenes says, speak only of places near at hand or in Greece. He gives also much accurate information of remote places. He does indeed tell fables more than his successors, but they are not all just wild fantasies. They are allegories or fictions or sermons composed for instruction. This is especially so with the wanderings of Odysseus. Eratosthenes is sadly astray about this, when he tries to prove that Homer's interpreters and Homer himself are talking nonsense. This is worth a fuller discussion.

1. 2. 7

For one thing, myths have been accepted not only by poets but, even earlier, by cities and lawgivers, for their utility. They have observed what comes naturally to a reasoning animal. Man loves knowledge; the prelude to this is a love of fable. This is the area in which children begin to listen and increase their understanding. The reason is that fable is a novelty of a kind—it does not tell of the ordinary, but of something new; novelty and the previously unknown are pleasant; and this is what makes us fond of knowledge. The addition of the wonderful and marvellous intensifies the pleasure—and pleasure is the charm to make us learn. These enticements are necessary in the early stages; as the child grows older, and his mind strengthens and has no need of cajoling, he may be brought to the knowledge of real things. In a sense, all ordinary uneducated people are children, and love fable in the same way. Indeed, the same is true of the partly educated, who have little strength of reason and preserve their childhood habits.

1. 2. 8

The marvellous is both pleasing and frightening; both children and adults need both these elements. We impress on children pleasing stories to encourage them, frightening ones to deter them: Lamia, Gorgo, Ephialtes, Mormolyce are such bogies. Most adult citizens, too, are encouraged by pleasing myths, when they hear the poets relating heroic deeds of mythology—the Labours of Heracles or Theseus, or the honours

[1] Cf. below, p. 538.

given by the gods—or when they see paintings, statues, or sculptures representing such mythical dramas. Similarly, they are deterred by learning, by word or by visible images, of divine punishments, terrors, or threats, or even by coming to believe that people have encountered such things. A mob of women and common folk cannot be summoned to piety and holiness and belief by philosophical argument; superstition is the only means, and this involves fables and marvels. The thunderbolt, the aegis, the trident, the torches, the snakes, the thyrsus-lances, are fables, primitive theology. The founders of our societies, however, used these tales as bogies for infantile minds. This characteristic of mythology, and its value in the transition to communal and public life and the acquisition of genuine knowledge, led the ancients to continue elementary education right up to adult life. They thought that all ages could receive adequate moral training through poetry. It was only later that history and philosophy, as it now is, appeared on the scene. Philosophy has a small audience; it is poetry, and above all Homer's, that is useful to the multitude and can fill the theatres. The first historians and scientists, moreover, were mythographers.

I. 2. 9   It was because Homer regarded his fables as educative that he thought so much of truth, while also 'placing therein' some falsehoods.[1] The truth he himself accepted; the false he used to manage and command the multitude.

Like a man that covers silver with gold,[2]

Homer added fable to real events, embellishing and adorning his style, but looking to the same end as the historian or the dealer in facts. Thus he added fabulous elements to the real event of the Trojan war, and so also with Odysseus' wanderings. Idle fantasy on no foundation of fact is not in Homer's way. No doubt it occurs to one that lies are more convincing if truth is mixed with them; indeed Polybius says this in his attack on Odysseus' wanderings. The line

he told many lies, resembling truth,[3]

points the same way—*many* lies, not *all* lies, for if it had all been lies it could not have resembled truth. Homer therefore took his starting-points from history. Aeolus, they say, dominated the islands round Lipara; inhospitable Cyclopes and Laestrygones ruled the area of Etna and Leontini. Hence the straits were inaccessible in those days; Charybdis and Scyllaeum were haunts of pirates. We can give similar interpretations of Homer's other descriptions. He knew, for example, that the Cimmerians lived on the Cimmerian Bosphorus, in the northern darkness; so he

---

[1] *Iliad* 18. 541.   [2] *Odyssey* 6. 232.   [3] Ibid. 19. 203.

moved them to a dark place near Hades, relevant to the mythology of the
Wanderings. Proof that he knew of them is supplied by the chroniclers
who date the Cimmerian invasion in or a little before the time of Homer.[1]

*B. ROME AND THE CLASSICAL REVIVAL

Dionysius of Halicarnassus, *de antiquis oratoribus, praefatio*

Dionysius of Halicarnassus was in Rome by 30 B.C., and published his *Roman
Antiquities* 22 years later. As a historian he is learned but diffuse, writing in the
rhetorical tradition in a moderately classicizing style. As a critic he is the clearest
Greek exponent of Augustan attitudes to the past and confidence in progress.
Much of his writing is concerned with applying a rather mechanical system
of 'good qualities' (*aretai*) to the classical writers whom he holds up for imitation; but his careful historical scholarship and his fine ear for the effect
of words give his work considerable distinction.

Text: vols. 5 and 6 of the Teubner Dionysius contain the critical works
edited by H. Usener and L. Radermacher. There is no Loeb, nor any complete
English translation: but there are translations of *Three Literary Letters* and *On
Literary Composition* in the editions by W. Rhys Roberts, Cambridge, 1901,
1910.

See Grube 207 ff.; S. F. Bonner, *Dionysius of Halicarnassus*, Liverpool, 1939;
G. A. Kennedy, *The Art of Persuasion in Greece*, Princeton U.P., 1963, 337 ff.

Dionysius' ambitious treatise on the classical orators began with a Preface, from
which this extract (5. 3–6 Usener–Radermacher) is taken, in which he condemns
Hellenistic writing as 'Asianic' and associates the revival of a purer style with the
domination (and good taste) of the Romans. Cf. Cicero, *Orator* 22–32 (above,
p. 237); Quintilian 12. 10 (below, p. 407).

We have need to be deeply thankful, my good Ammaeus, to the age we
live in, for the improved practice of many arts, and especially for the
great progress in the skills of oratory. In the period preceding our own,
the old, philosophical rhetoric collapsed under the insults and grievous
injuries it was forced to endure. Its slow wasting and expiration may be
said to have begun with the death of Alexander of Macedon; by our
own age it had almost completely disappeared. In its place arose another
kind of rhetoric, intolerable in its melodramatic shamelessness, tasteless,
innocent of philosophy or any other liberal study. Unnoticed and undetected by the ignorant vulgar, this rhetoric not only enjoyed an abundance,

---

[1] The Cimmerians lived north of the Black Sea until about 700 B.C. Then, under
pressure from the Scythians, they invaded Asia Minor and penetrated to the Ionian
coast. This would be a late date for Homer.

luxury, and elegance unknown to its predecessor, but attached to itself the honours and political supremacies which belonged by right to its philosophical sister. With its crudeness and vulgarity, it ended by making Greece like the household of some desperate roué, where the decent, respectable wife sits powerless in her own home, while some nitwit of a girl, there only to ruin the property, thinks she has a right to rule the roost, and bullies the wife and treats her like dirt. Just so, in every city, even—worst of all—in the highly cultivated, the old, native Attic Muse was in disgrace, cast out from her inheritance, while another, sprung from some Asian sewer the other day—some Mysian or Phrygian or, God help us, Carian plague—claimed the right to govern the cities of Hellas, and, in her ignorance and madness, to drive out her sane, philosophical rival.

But it is not only just men, as Pindar says,[1] of whom 'time is the best preserver', but arts and pursuits and indeed all good things. Our own age is an illustration of this. Whether some god set it in train, or the revolution of nature itself recalled the old order, or human impulse guided multitudes to the same goal—whatever the cause, this generation has restored to the old, respectable rhetoric her just honour, and stopped the young fool enjoying a reputation which did not belong to her, and behaving extravagantly in another's house. Nor is the fact that men have *begun* to honour the better above the worse the only reason for praising this age and its philosophers. It is true of course that 'well begun is half done'; but the point is also that the change has been rapid and the progress great. Apart from some few cities in Asia, where ignorance makes good learning slow to penetrate, the liking for the vulgar, frigid, and tasteless in literature has ceased. Those who formerly took pride in such things are becoming ashamed and gradually deserting to the other side, apart from a few incurables, while recent beginners are despising that style and ridiculing the passion for it.

The cause and beginning of this great change lies in Rome. The mistress of the world makes all other cities look to her. Her own men of power, who govern their country on the highest moral principles, are men of education and fine judgement. The discipline they impose has strengthened the wiser elements of the community, and forced the foolish to learn sense. In consequence, many serious historical works are now being written, many elegant speeches published, while philosophical treatises which are far from contemptible, and many other excellent works, serious productions both of Romans and of Greeks, have appeared and will no doubt continue to appear. Such is the change in such a short time that it would not surprise me if the taste for the foolish style does not

[1] Fr. 159 Snell.

survive this one generation; when something once universal has been contracted to such small properties, the step to its total disappearance is no great one.

C. DEMOSTHENES

Dionysius' treatise on Demosthenes affords good instances of his critical methods. We give chs. 1–7, 8–22, 23, 32, with omissions.
   Text: 5. 127–252 Usener–Radermacher.
   See Grube 222 ff., Bonner 60 ff.

   [Dionysius has just quoted Thucydides 3. 82—the famous description of attitudes to be found in cities in a state of revolution. It is the most striking example of the elaborate contortions of Thucydides' more abstract style.]

Such was the abnormal, extraordinary, and elaborate language (*lexis*),   1 filled out with every adventitious ornament, of which Thucydides is the standard and model. None of his successors surpassed him or indeed adequately imitated him.

   The other manner—the plain, simple one, whose ornament and strength   2 are thought to lie in its resemblance to ordinary speech—has found many powerful champions among historians, philosophers, and orators. Genealogists, authors of local histories, physical scientists, and composers of moral dialogues, including the whole Socratic school apart from Plato,[1] as well as virtually all writers of deliberative or forensic speeches, belong to this persuasion. It was perfected and brought to the peak of its peculiar excellence by Lysias, the son of Cephalus, a contemporary of Gorgias and Thucydides. His intentions and abilities have been discussed in the preceding book, and there is no need to repeat the discussion here. Suffice it to say that these two writers span the entire scale of style, each having chosen and perfected with superhuman zeal one of the two extremes. Lysias' style is to Thucydides' in the field of oratorical language what the highest note is to the lowest in music. Thucydides' style has power to amaze, Lysias' to give pleasure.[2] The one can concentrate and make tense, the other can relax and give ease. The one rouses us to strong emotion (*pathos*), the other settles us in a calmer frame of mind (*ēthos*). To be forceful and compelling is a mark of Thucydides, as deceit and evasion are of Lysias. Innovation and audacity characterize the historian's style, safety and avoidance of risk the orator's . . . [Text defective] . . . Both styles are highly elaborate, and each has reached the perfection of

   [1] Because of Plato's grandeur.
   [2] For this contrast cf. (e.g.) 'Longinus' 1 (below, p. 462).

its peculiar elaboration; but the one tends to exaggerate, the other to minimize.   (pp. 130, 1–131, 17)

THE MIXED STYLE

3 The third species of style was the mixed one: a combination of the first two. The first to make this combination and to bring the style to its present degree of polish may have been Thrasymachus of Chalcedon, as Theophrastus says, or another; I cannot feel sure. However, it was the Athenian orator Isocrates and the Socratic philosopher Plato who adopted, developed, and virtually perfected it. Indeed, it would be very hard to find anyone, apart from Demosthenes, who has done more than these two writers either in the practice of useful and necessary qualities or in the display of fine writing and accessory forms of ornament. Thrasymachus' own style—supposing him to have been really the fountain-head of the 'middle style'—obviously has serious (and worthwhile) intentions; it is a successful mixture and possesses the usefulness of both. But his ability does not match his ambitions.   (p. 132, 3–18)

[Dionysius quotes a prooemium to prove his point (fr. B 1 Diels–Kranz). His criticism is too dependent on verbal effects to be given in English.]

ISOCRATES

4 I have previously discussed at greater length the style of Isocrates, a writer of very high repute in Greece who produced many excellent pieces of every type, though he never actually took part in any real case, private or public. However, there will be no harm in repeating the main points here.

Isocrates' style possesses the purity and precision of Lysias'; no archaic, newly-coined, or obscure words (*glōttēmatika*), only the commonest and most familiar. It has character, persuasiveness and charm, and avoids metaphorical language, just like Lysias'. At the same time, it possesses the grandeur, solemnity, and fine writing of Thucydides and Gorgias. To convey to the hearer whatever information is needed with perfect clarity, it employs the simple, unadorned Lysianic diction; to amaze by the splendour of words and invest subjects with grandeur and solemnity, it reproduces the extraneous ornamentation of the school of Gorgias. Sometimes indeed the elegance leads into error. This is true of the imitation of Gorgias' juvenile figures—excessive and inappropriate antitheses, parisoses, and the like form an ugly blemish on the magnificent surface—

and even more true of the pursuit of euphony and rhythmical elegance, in the care taken to avoid the clash of vowels and the use of harsh sounds. The periodic structure at which this kind of writing consistently aims is not rounded and concentrated, but drawn-out and broad, curving into many sinuosities like a meandering river. This results often in excessive length and lack of sincerity, emotion, and life—in short, a style better suited to panegyric than to the real conflicts of the courts. I shall give examples shortly, in the appropriate place.

PLATO'S STYLE

Plato's style, too, also aims at being a mixture of the two manners—the 5 lofty (*hupsēlos*) and the plain (*ischnos*)—as I said above; but it is not equally felicitous in both. When it studies to be plain, simple, and unaffected in diction, it is extraordinarily agreeable and winning. It is pure enough, and transparent, like the most pellucid of streams, careful and delicate as any of its rivals. It pursues normality of vocabulary, and clarity, disdaining all accessory ornamentation. The patina of the past spreads softly and unobtrusively over its surface; the fresh green bloom of the springtime burgeons in it. It is as though a fragrant breeze were blowing off some flowery meadow. The clear tone gives no hint of garrulity, the cleverness no hint of theatricality. But when—and this often happens— the style takes an uncontrollable plunge into fanciness and fine writing, great deterioration ensues. Charmless, incorrect, and coarse, compared with what it was, it now obscures and darkens what was plain, and drags out the meaning to vast length when it ought to have been concentrated in a few words. It spreads itself in tasteless periphrases, showing off a vain wealth of vocabulary and seeking novel, foreign, and archaic terms out of contempt for the literal and usual. Most of all is it at sea with tropes. Rich in epithets, it indulges in and out of season in metonymy, and its harsh metaphors fail to preserve the proper proportions between the terms. It wraps itself up in lots of long allegories, unending and untimely, and makes a childish parade, with no sense of occasion, of nauseating poetical, and more particularly Gorgianic, figures. In a word, as Deme-trius of Phaleron and many others have said before me—'it's not my story'—there is a lot of hocus-pocus in Plato in this sort of thing.

I should not like anyone to think that in saying this I condemn all 6 Plato's unusual or elaborate style. I should not wish to be so ignorant or insensitive as to hold such an opinion about so great a man. I am well aware that he has written much on many subjects which is splendid and admirable and the product of the highest abilities. What I want to show is that he makes this kind of mistake *in his elaborations*, and that he falls below his true level when he aims at the grand or unusual in diction; he excels himself, on the other hand, when he adopts a manner which is slight and precise and gives the impression of being artless, though in fact it has been worked over with simple and faultless artistry. His mistakes indeed (if he makes any) are insignificant and not worth complaining about; but I rather thought that so great a genius should have avoided any possibility of criticism.[1] As a matter of fact, his contemporaries (whom I need not name) find fault with him for the same reason. Indeed, he does it himself—a brilliant stroke; for he seems to have perceived his own lack of taste, and used the word 'dithyramb' of it—a true comment, but one I should have been ashamed to make here on my own. The reason for this decline, in my opinion, is that Plato was reared on Socratic dialogues, which are very slight and precise in style, but instead of sticking to them fell in love with the elaboration of Gorgias and Thucydides. It was therefore only to be expected that he should acquire some of the faults as well as the excellences which these writers' styles possess.

7   The example I offer of elevated language comes from one of Plato's most famous works—the dialogue in which Socrates sets forth speeches about Love to one of his friends, Phaedrus, after whom the book is named. The opening scene has great elegance and charm: 'Where are you going, Phaedrus, and where have you been?' 'I've been with Lysias, Socrates, Cephalus' son. And now I'm going for a walk outside the wall. I've been sitting down a long time there, since early morning.'[2] This style continues up to the reading of Lysias' speech and for some time thereafter. Then, like a gale suddenly springing up out of calm and settled weather, he throws his pure diction into turmoil, breaking into tasteless poeticism. 'Hither, ye clear-toned (*ligeiai*) Muses—be it for your song you are so called or for your Ligurian birth—come aid me in my tale.'[3]

Plato shall explain for himself that this is simply noise and dithyramb, a vast clatter of words with very little meaning. Even in his explanation of how *erōs* comes to be the name of the emotion, he uses this manner: 'When irrational desire, tending to pleasure in beauty and in desires akin to herself, overcomes the judgement that aims at good, the pull towards beauty of body is mightily (*errhōmenōs*) strengthened (*rhōstheisa*) and from this strength (*rhōme*) received the name *erōs*.'[4] But after a long passage of this sort of periphrasis, expressing something which could have been put adequately in a few words, Plato attacks his own bad taste: 'Listen to me quietly. This is a holy place, I fancy. Don't be surprised if I am often bewitched as the argument proceeds. My present utterance

---

[1] This type of attack is answered by 'Longinus' 32–6 (below, p. 491).
[2] *Phaedrus* 227 a.   [3] Ibid. 237 a.   [4] Ibid. 238 b.

is pretty dithyrambic.'[1] So there you are, most divine Plato; by 'none other than ourselves condemned',[2] we are convicted of being in love with the sound and fury of the dithyramb! (pp. 134, 8–141, 9)

[Dionysius illustrates his point further by a detailed discussion of *Phaedrus* 246 e, comparing it with a passage of Pindar (*Paean* 9, 1 ff.).]

DEMOSTHENES AND HIS MODELS

To avoid too long a discussion, I shall now leave Plato and proceed to 8 Demosthenes. It was in connection with him, after all, that I enumerated what I considered the most important types of style, and the chief practitioners in each. My list of writers was not exhaustive. Antiphon, Theodorus, Polycrates, Isaeus, Zoilus, Anaximenes, and their contemporaries had no special novelty or peculiarity, but devised their own styles out of these types and on these principles. Such was the state of oratorical style which Demosthenes inherited, such the changes it had undergone. Demosthenes, in succeeding these great predecessors, took no single style or writer as his model, because he thought them all incomplete and immature. Instead, he wove his own style out of an eclectic choice of the best and most serviceable qualities of them all. The result was a manner at once grand and simple, elaborate and un-elaborate, unusual and usual, panegyrical and realistic, severe and smiling, tense and relaxed, sweet and sharp, attractive in character (*ēthikē*) and forcible in emotion (*pathētikē*). He is like the mythical Proteus in the old poets, who could take on any shape effortlessly; and who indeed, one might plausibly conjecture, was not really a god or demigod deceiving men's eyes but a clever trick of speech in a wise man, always deceiving the ear—for it is impious to attribute low or indecent appearances to gods or demigods.

A study of my examples will show whether this view of Demosthenes— 9 namely that his style is a combination of every other type—is the correct one.

Consider first his modification of Thucydides' manner.

Men of Athens, many speeches are made virtually at every meeting of the assembly about what Philip, ever since he made peace, has been doing wrong, not only to you but to all Greece—and everyone, I am sure, would have said, even if their acts belie their words, that one ought to speak and act in such a way as to ensure that he is stopped and punished for his arrogance; and yet I see the situation has gone so

[1] Ibid. 238 d.   [2] Aeschylus, fr. 135 Nauck.

far, and is so far out of control, that I fear it may now be true to say,
however disagreeable, that if all the speakers had chosen to propose, and
all of you had chosen to vote for, the thing that was going to make
the situation the worst possible, it could not have been worse than it is.[1]

How do I think this style resembles that of Thucydides? In a feature
very distinctive of that writer: namely, that he does not express his
thoughts in a straightforward manner or simply and plainly, as others
do, but writes in a strange language, perverted from the usual and natural
to the unusual and unnatural. Let me explain further. Expressed simply
and straightforwardly the passage would have run: 'Men of Athens,
many speeches are made at almost every assembly about the wrong Philip
has done you and the other Greeks ever since he made the peace.' But
as it stands, (i) the use of 'virtually' instead of 'almost', (ii) the separation
of 'wrong' and 'Philip' so that the connection is completed only after a
long interval, and (iii) the phrase 'not only you but all Greece' for something which could have been expressed by a simple connective without
a negative—all this makes the language elaborate and abnormal. Similarly
with the following phrase. Expressed simply and without complexity
this would have run: 'And everybody says, even if some people's actions
belie their words, that one should say and do things which will ensure
that he is stopped and punished for his arrogance.' But the actual expression 'everyone, I am sure, would have said' abandons the direct
path of speech. 'I am sure' does not need to be inserted, and 'would have
said' for 'says' gives an impression not of simplicity of language but of
abnormality and elaboration.   (pp. 143, 1–146, 9)

> [Detailed discussion of further passages (*Philippics* 3. 13, *Midias* 69)
> follows. This is hardly intelligible except in Greek, as the argument hangs
> on points of word- and clause-order.]

9   There are innumerable such cases in Demosthenes, especially in the
speeches against Philip; indeed, there is no deliberative speech without
these characteristics except *On Halonnesos*,[2] and there is a good deal of
the same sort in the forensic speeches, at least those concerned with
public affairs. Indeed, this is the clearest diagnostic sign of Demosthenes'
style in these speeches and in the public harangues. One may of course
make mistakes of attribution because he employs this manner in differing
degrees according to the nature of the subject and the dignity of the
persons involved. This is only to be expected.

---

[1] *Philippics* 3. 1.
[2] [Demosthenes], *Oration* 7—not in fact by Demosthenes, but probably by Heges-
ippus, as some ancient scholars noted. Dionysius evidently thinks it genuine.

Let us now state the difference between Thucydides' style (*lexis*) and 10 that of Demosthenes formed on the same pattern (*charaktēr*). This is necessary for our argument.

It is certainly not a matter of quality. They are both trying to do the same thing, namely to vary normal usage and achieve special and unusual effects. It is rather a matter of quantity, and still more of occasion. Thucydides uses elaboration indiscriminately and is its servant rather than its master; he does not understand how to seize the opportunity for it neatly. This is often the source of his error. Hence the extreme effort for novelty makes his style obscure, and failure to recognize opportunities makes it unpleasing. Demosthenes, on the other hand, aims at giving enough and not too much; he calculates the right moment, and elaborates his style for use, not, merely, like the historian, to produce a beautiful object to preserve for ever. Thus without abandoning clarity— the first requisite of real-life oratory—he manages to give also the impression of being vigorous (*deinos*), which he is obviously most concerned to make.

Such are the effects Demosthenes attained from the elevated, elaborate, devious, abnormal style whose force lay entirely in its vigour, and from his imitation of the master of this manner, Thucydides.

(pp. 148, 3–149, 13)

[Dionysius now turns to the influence of Lysias and the plain style on Demosthenes. He quotes a lengthy narrative from Lysias (fr. 232 S.) and one from Demosthenes (54. 3–9). One could hardly tell, he says, who wrote which.]

What then is the difference? How can one tell, when Demosthenes 13 descends to the manner of bare necessity, in what way he is superior to Lysias in style? You expect the answer to this question too, of course.

There is, as I said, a sort of natural elegance and grace all over Lysias' writing, in which he excels every orator save Demosthenes. It carries him, like a southerly breeze, through his prooemium and narrative; but it becomes faint and weak when he gets to the arguments and proofs, and fails altogether in the emotional parts of the speech, having little tension (*tonos*) or strength. In Demosthenes, on the other hand, the tension is strong and the charm has its own momentum, so that in the latter his steady and measured movement makes him superior, while on the point of tension there is just no comparison.

I add a second observation which may help in recognizing Demosthenes' style when it comes down to bare bones like this. Even if it strips off novelty, wealth of vocabulary, and all accessory forms of ornament, it does not strip off grandeur or tension; this last is irremovable, whether it is in fact natural or acquired by practice, though of course it does admit moments both of relaxation and of added intensity as appropriate.

(pp. 157, 12–158, 10)

THE MIDDLE STYLE

14 Of the type of oratory which lies between the two extremes, which Demosthenes inherited in an imperfect state from Isocrates, his predecessor Thrasymachus, and Plato, and which he perfected to the limit of human capacity, many examples can be found in the speeches against Philip and the other public orations, but the most numerous and best instances are in the defence of Ctesiphon, the speech which in my opinion employs the finest and most controlled stylistic art. If I had time, I would set out the actual passages; but with many essential topics still to cover, I can do no more here than present a few brief examples, relying on my readers' knowledge.

For example, the following passage from the attack on Aeschines is in the middle style: 'It is always right, men of Athens, to hate and punish traitors and bribe-takers. On this occasion it is especially right and it will do a service to all mankind. A terrible and dire disease, men of Athens, has invaded Greece; it needs great good luck and great effort on your part . . .'[1]   (pp. 158, 13–159, 13)

15   This is the style ⟨I approve most⟩. If anyone cannot accept my reason for not putting Thucydides' extravagances and abnormalities first or regarding the sovereign virtue of style as lying in the thin conciseness of Lysias, here is my reply.

People who attend assemblies, courts, and other gatherings where public speaking is necessary are not all clever or exceptional or possessed of Thucydidean intelligence. Nor yet are they all plain folk with no experience of the art of noble speech. Some indeed have come in from work on their farms or at sea or from some artisan's trade, and these are certainly better pleased by a simpler and more everyday way of talking. Precision, special elegance, anything that sounds unusual or unfamiliar, annoys them and distresses their ears just as really unpleasant food or drink turns the stomach. Others are used to public life, they come from the squares and streets and have had a regular education. These cannot be addressed in the same way. They need elaborate, special, recherché language. Of course they are not as numerous as the others—they are a tiny fraction of the whole, as everybody knows—but they are not to be

---

[1] 19. 258. Other examples follow: 23. 65, 20. 68, 18. 60.

despised on that account. Now the speech that aims at the educated few will not be convincing to the ignorant majority, and the speech that pleases the multitude of ordinary folk will be despised by the more sophisticated. The speech that tries to win both audiences will be less likely to fail in its purpose. This means the style composed of the two extreme styles; and this is why I regard a style so constructed as the most moderate, and am particularly willing to accept writing that avoids the extremes of the two manners.

DEMOSTHENES' ADVANCE OVER ISOCRATES

I said at the beginning that in my opinion Isocrates and Plato, the principal exponents of this style, developed it to a very high standard, but did not perfect it. I undertook then to show that it was Demosthenes who completed the task. To this point I now proceed, putting forward passages of admitted excellence from both authors, and comparing them with passages of Demosthenes on the same themes, so that the intentions and abilities of the writers reveal themselves by the searching test of similar subjects.

First, Isocrates. Let us take a passage of acknowledged charm from the oration *On the Peace.*[1] Isocrates himself quotes the passage in the *Antidosis.* No doubt he was proud of it. It is a comparison between the political scene in olden days and the present time, between ancient and modern achievements. Isocrates approves the old and criticizes the new. He shows that the responsibility for the deterioration lies with the demagogues, who, instead of introducing good measures, proposed only what would give pleasure to the masses. The comparison is lengthy: I quote only the most important part.

What foreign visitor, not corrupted as we are but coming fresh to the situation, would not think us lunatic and insane? We take pride in the deeds of our ancestors and think it right to praise Athens for what she did in those days, yet we act ourselves not as they did, but in a quite opposite way. They fought the barbarians on behalf of Greece, we have brought men from Asia, where their living came from, to attack Greeks. They liberated and aided Greek cities and so were thought deserving of hegemony; we enslave and do the reverse of what they did, yet grow angry that we are refused the honour they enjoyed. How far we fall short in thought and deed of the men of those days! They found the courage to leave their home on behalf of the safety of Greece; they fought by land and sea, they triumphed. We are not even ready to court

[1] Isocrates 8. 41-50.

danger for our own greed, but seek universal rule without being prepared to serve as soldiers. We go to war against the whole world, but instead of disciplining ourselves for it we train a horde of refugees, deserters, and criminals who will join the other side the moment they are offered higher wages. And yet we love them very dearly: if our own children do wrong we should not want to suffer on their behalf, but if these creatures steal and murder and flout the laws and complaints fall upon us, we feel no anger—indeed we enjoy hearing that they have done this kind of thing. Such a pitch of folly we have reached that we go without our daily needs while endeavouring to maintain mercenaries, and distress and over-tax our own allies to pay these enemies of mankind their wages. The measure of our inferiority not only to those of our ancestors whose fame stood high, but to those who earned unpopularity too, is that they, when they resolved on war, though the acropolis was full of silver and gold, nevertheless thought it right to risk their own lives for their decisions, while we, impoverished and numerous as we are, hire our armies like the king of Persia. In those days, if we manned triremes, we embarked the foreigners and slaves as sailors, and sent citizens under arms; now we use the foreigners as soldiers and make the citizens row. Consequently, when we make a landing in enemy territory, the would-be masters of Greece disembark with their bench-cushions, while the characters I have been describing face the foe in arms.

But perhaps seeing domestic affairs well managed may give us confidence about the rest? But is not this the area where indignation is most in place? We claim to be indigenous, we say that this is the oldest city in Greece—and, when we ought to offer an example of good and orderly government, we in fact manage our affairs less efficiently and more confusedly than recent foundations. We take pride, and find cause for boasting, in being of better race than others—and yet we share our racial superiority with others more readily than the Triballoi or the Lucanians do their inferiority of race.

18   Such is what is reputed to be Isocrates' best manner. It deserves admiration on many counts. Exceptionally pure in vocabulary and precise in expression, it is lucid and normal and embraces all the excellences that most make for clarity of expression. Moreover, it possesses many of the accessory ornaments. It is elevated, serious, dignified, and at the same time pretty, pleasant, and elegant to an adequate degree—though not in this respect perfect, for there are many ways, and those not unimportant, in which it might be criticized as deficient. First, conciseness. In the search for clarity, this style often neglects moderation. One ought to think of both at once. Secondly, concentration. It is supine, sinuous,

over-abundant in thought, like the styles of the historians. The style of real-life oratory, on the other hand, must be well-turned, shapely, and free from loose folds.

Isocrates has other failings too. He lacks boldness in metaphorical ornament, fears the sound of his own voice, and has no powerful tones. Athletes of real-life eloquence need a strong grip and an inescapable hold. He is incapable of arousing in his audience the passions he wants. Often, he does not even want, because he is convinced that the orator has only to express good thoughts and good character. Both these, one must admit, he achieves. But the fact is that the most important thing for an orator who is to persuade a people or a court is to move the audience to emotion. Nor does he invariably achieve propriety, thanks to his theory that language ought always to be florid and ostentatious, pleasure being the all-important factor in literature. But not all subjects call for the same language; there is a vocabulary appropriate to the thought, just as there is clothing appropriate to the body. To charm the ear by constant selection of soft and euphonious words, to expect every sentence to end in a well-formed periodic harmony, and to adorn one's style with ostentatious figures, is not always a useful course. Epic poets, tragedians, and serious lyricists teach us this. To them, the gift of pleasure is less important than the gift of truth.

An examination of the passage just quoted will readily confirm whether 19 these reflections are correct and whether Isocrates really is deficient in these qualities.

To begin at the beginning: the first thought could have been expressed in a few words, but he lengthens it out by writing round and round it and saying the same thing two or three times over. In the first colon, 'what foreign visitor' includes the idea 'not corrupted as we are but coming fresh to the situation': the two expressions come to the same thing. Again, 'we take pride in the deeds of our ancestors' includes 'we think it right to praise Athens for what she did in those days': 'to take pride in' and 'praise' are one and the same. Yet again, 'we act not as they did' includes 'in a quite opposite way'; either of the two expressions would have done by itself. The two sentences in fact would have made a single period, briefer and more pleasing: 'What foreign visitor would not think us mad, taking pride as we do in the deeds of our ancestors, but acting in no way as they did?' Many such inessential supplementations are to be found, in almost every period, which detract from the moderation of the expression but add to the elegance of the period.

His style, then, is long-winded. How does it also come to be flaccid and ill-organized? 'They liberated and aided Greek cities and so were thought deserving of hegemony; we enslave and do the reverse of what they did, and yet grow angry that we are refused the honour they enjoyed.' These folds could be gathered in and the whole rounded off better thus: 'They liberated and preserved Greece and so advanced to hegemony; we enslave and destroy and yet grow angry if we do not win the same reward.' The following thought also is flatly expressed and ill-organized. 'How far we fall short in thought and deed of the men of those days! They found the courage to leave their home on behalf of the safety of Greece; they fought by land and sea; they triumphed.' This flaccidity could be given tension by saying: 'How inferior we are to our ancestors! They left their country to save Greece; they fought by land and sea, they triumphed.' One could find innumerable examples of this weakness too, for with few exceptions, where conciseness is the result of accident rather than of intention, all his writing is of this kind.

20   Where then does it lack tension and a firm hold? In the appending to the passage just quoted of the thought that follows: 'The measure of our inferiority . . . the king of Persia'. How could this have been put more compactly? 'But, though we are inferior to our ancestors in this respect, we may well be superior in others—not indeed to the famous among them —that is inconceivable—but to the disliked. Who does not know that they filled the acropolis with treasure, and, so far from *conveying* the common wealth to the enemy as pay, themselves contributed and on occasion served in person, while we, poor and numerous as we are, fight with mercenary forces like the king of Persia?'

The lack of life and emotion in his style, and its poor share of spirit— the most important quality of all in writing meant for real-life contests— need, I imagine, no special mention. Of the many possible examples, I content myself with a single thought. The antithesis just discussed is followed by another, in the passage: 'In those days . . . face the foe in arms'. I find no fault here with the writer's intention—the thought is a noble one and capable of rousing emotion—but I do criticize the smooth-ness and softness of the language. It ought to have been rough, sharp, delivering something like a blow in the face; instead it is fluid, even, gliding noiselessly through the ear like olive-oil, in the hope no doubt of charming and pleasing the hearer.

Then what about all those elaborate figures? Are they well fitted for battle? Do they enable the style to rouse the audience's emotions? Far from it. These puerile balances and frigid antitheses and so forth are the very things that most destroy the force of the style and disgust the ear. For example, in the passage under discussion, the whole subject is an antithesis, the individual thoughts are set out one against another, and each of the periods is antithetically constructed, so that the hearers become sated and disgusted. Let me explain. Both the beginnings and the continuations of each thought, period, and point made are of the form 'they ... we ...', 'those ... we ...', 'then ... now', 'on the one hand ... on the other hand'. This cycle continues from beginning to end. Alternations, variations, and elaborations of figures, designed to relieve the monotony of the thought, are nowhere to be found.

(pp. 160, 15–172, 3)

[For contrast, Dionysius quotes Demosthenes, *Third Olynthiac* 23–32, as an example of variety and energy.]

I shall describe what effect these two styles have on me personally; 21 but I suspect that what I feel is a universal experience and not one peculiar to myself.

When I read a speech of Isocrates, whether one of those written for 22 law-court or assembly, or one intended for a ceremonial occasion, I feel morally improved, and very stable and settled in mind; the effect is like that of hearing spondaic music or Dorian and enharmonic melodies.[1] But when I pick up a speech by Demosthenes, I feel inspired;[2] this way and that goes my mind, caught in the grip of a succession of emotions— incredulity, anxiety, fear, contempt, hatred, pity, favour, anger, jealousy, every passion that can dominate the human mind. I feel just like the initiates in the rites of the Great Mother or the Corybantes or some similar cult, who achieve all their varied visions by being affected by smells, if that is what it is, or sounds, or the spirit of the divinities. I have sometimes wondered what the audiences of those days must have felt when they heard Demosthenes speak. When we, who are so remote in time and not involved emotionally in the events, are so seduced and won over and made to go wherever the argument leads, what was the orator's effect on the Athenians and the other Greeks in the midst of their own real conflicts? He was the speaker, his the thoughts. He used his standing among them to emphasize his personal feeling and emotion. And he coloured and adorned everything by appropriate delivery—a sphere in which he was a superb practitioner, as is universally agreed and indeed is obvious from the passage cited above. No one could go through that piece as if it were merely attractive reading-matter. It teaches us itself how it ought to be delivered—with irony, anger, and indignation, frightening, cajoling, admonishing, exhorting, making the whole meaning plain by the manner of delivery. If the spirit enshrined in his books has such strength and is so seductive after so many years, it must indeed have been a supremely wonderful thing when the speeches were first given.

[1] i.e. solemn but not disturbing music.

[2] Plato (*Menexenus* 235 b) makes Socrates declare (ironically) that he feels a greater man for hearing the orators, and 'loses himself' for a few days.

DEMOSTHENES AND PLATO

23 But I must not allow prolonged discussion of these matters to compel me to omit any part of the subject which remains. I shall therefore now leave Isocrates and the style of his school, and turn to Plato. Here I shall state my opinion with frankness, neither adding to Plato's reputation nor subtracting from the truth. This course is particularly forced on me because some people claim him as the supreme master, among philosophers and orators, of the stylistic expression of his material, and urge us to regard him as the model and standard of a style at once pure and forceful. Indeed, I have heard it said that if the gods use the language of men, the king of the gods must talk like Plato. I shall answer these assumptions and extravagances with my natural sincerity and straightforwardness; they are the notions of half-educated persons who neither know nor are capable of understanding what noble writing really is.

Let me first explain how I think the examination ought to be made.

I am a great admirer of Plato's skill in the dialogues, especially in those where he maintains the Socratic manner, as in the *Philebus*.[1] But I have no liking for his tastelessness in handling accessory ornament, as I said before—and certainly none for the occasions when he embarks on oratorical subjects, and tries to compose an encomium, a censure, an accusation, or a defence. He is then a changed man and a disgrace to his philosophical standing. I have often thought of applying to these works the words of Homer's Zeus to Aphrodite:

> The works of war are not for you, my child—
> go and attend to the charming works of love.[2]

'The works of love' correspond to the Socratic dialogues. This present business shall be the concern of statesmen and orators. I am happy to make all scholars the impartial judges of my thesis—all, that is, except the ambitious who judge things by repute and not by fact. I could not approve the practice, which some pursue, of choosing the worst things out of his whole works and setting against them the best specimen of Demosthenes. The right procedure seemed rather to be to set side by side and judge the most celebrated passages of both writers. This is what I shall do. (pp. 176, 7–179, 23)

[Dionysius chooses, and analyses in some detail, a passage of *Menexenus*, which he takes as a serious piece of oratory, though Plato probably intended a parody of the customary Funeral Speeches on Athenian war-dead. The

[1] An odd choice. Though the subject is an ethical, and so characteristically Socratic, one, the style is contorted in the way that we find in other late dialogues.

[2] *Iliad* 5. 428 f.

criticism is in the same vein as the passage on Isocrates. For contrast,
Dionysius takes *On the Crown* 199–209. His general conclusion is as follows:]

CONCLUSION

Anyone of moderate literary sensibility, free from malice and con- [32]
tentiousness, must admit that the difference between these passages is as
great as that between arms used in war and those carried in processions,
between real objects and reflections, between bodies bred in sun and toil
and the physique of those who take their ease in the shade. Plato's style
aims at nothing but prettiness; hence its beauty is not genuine. Demosthenes' seeks only what conduces to utility and realism. Plato's style
could well be compared to a flowery field, with pleasant resting-places
and short-lived delights; Demosthenes' to a rich and fertile soil with no
lack of the necessities of life or of the superfluities that give pleasure. I
could easily enumerate the individual successes of the two and show the
superiority of Demosthenes not only in point of realism and suitability
for real-life contests (this does not need elaboration) but in the sphere of
metaphor, where Plato's skill is particularly praised. But I have many
possible topics before me, and postpone this one for a future occasion,
if time allows: I shall not hesitate to write a separate book on it.

(pp. 200, 21–201, 22)

D. *ON THE ARRANGEMENT OF WORDS*

De compositione verborum

This treatise (called conventionally *De compositione verborum*, and by W. Rhys
Roberts (ed. 1910) *On Literary Composition*) is Dionysius' most original work
not only in content but in its own noticeably mannered style. He distinguishes,
on the analogy of the 'three styles', three types of verbal structure—*harmoniai*
or *suntheseis*, the two terms being apparently synonyms. The following extracts
(1–13, 20, 21–68, with omissions) illustrate both his general principles and
(so far as it can be seen in an English version) his detailed criticism.

See Bonner 71 ff.; Grube 217 ff.; L. P. Wilkinson, *Golden Latin Artistry*,
Cambridge, 1962, 10, 22 ff., 39 ff. etc.

INTRODUCTION: THE VALUE AND DIFFICULTY OF
THE SUBJECT

'And this, my dear child, is *my* present to you',[1] as Helen says in Homer [1]
when she entertains Telemachus. This is your first birthday since you

---

[1] *Odyssey* 14. 125.

came to man's estate; and to me it is the happiest of days, and one that I delight to honour. It is no 'work of my hands' that I send you, as Helen said when she gave the boy the robe, nor is it only 'against the season of marriage' or a gift to give joy to a bride. It is the product and child of my studies and my brain, a possession and a thing of service against all the needs in life that involve speech. If I have any right understanding in the matter, nothing can be more necessary than my present undertaking, both to all students of practical oratory, of whatever age and disposition, and especially to you young beginners, my dear Metilius Rufus, son of my excellent and much respected friend.

The study of any kind of speech involves, one may say, two kinds of exercise, one concerning thought and the other concerning words. The former touches more on that department of rhetoric which deals with content, the latter on that which deals with language. Aspirants to eloquence necessarily pursue these two branches equally, but the knowledge which leads to content and good judgement regarding content is slow of acquisition and difficult for the young; indeed it cannot be expected of the beardless youth, because it belongs rather to the mature understanding, disciplined by later life, nurtured by long research into words and facts and by long experience of misfortune, both one's own and others'. Linguistic taste, on the other hand, blossoms in the young. Every youth's mind is excited by the charms of language and acquires irrational, almost inspirational, impulses in this direction. The first instruction and training needs therefore to be careful and intelligent, if the beginner is to be saved from uttering 'what words soever come to a blundering tongue'[1] and putting phrases together at random, and made both to select a pure and noble vocabulary and to deploy it by an arrangement which combines dignity with charm. It is on this subject, therefore, the first the young student should pursue, that I now 'send you a song for love',[2] a treatise on the arrangement of words. This is a topic which few of the older writers of textbooks on rhetoric or logic thought of discussing, and no one, I am sure, has yet discussed it adequately or worked it out in detail. If I have leisure, I will write you another book on word-selection, so that you may have a complete treatment of the department of rhetoric relating to language. Expect it this time next year, if the gods keep me safe and healthy—if indeed it is my destiny to enjoy these blessings. For the present, pray accept this work, which the promptings of providence put into my head to write.

Here, then, are the headings under which my discussion falls:

What is the nature of arrangement? Wherein lies its power? What

---

[1] Unknown lyric poet.   [2] Philoxenus, fr. 6 Bergk.

are its aims and how does it achieve them? What are the characteristics of each variety of it, and which (in my view) is the best?

What is that poetic quality, smooth on the tongue and sweet to the ear, which prose acquires as a result of arrangement? What, too, is the force in a poetical manner that imitates unaffected speech and achieves great success in the imitation?

By what practices can that quality and that force be attained? These, in broad outline, are the questions I wish to discuss. Now I begin.

Arrangement (*sunthesis*) is, as its name implies, a placing (*thesis*) of ² the parts of speech—what some call the elements of language—beside one another. Theodectes, Aristotle, and the philosophers of those days took the number of these parts of speech to be three: nouns, verbs, and conjunctions. Their successors, especially the leaders of the Stoic sect, made it up to four, separating 'articles' from 'conjunctions'. Subsequent writers distinguished 'appellatives' from 'substantive nouns' and so made five, while a sixth element was added by the distinction made by some between nouns and pronouns. The number has been multiplied: adverbs are distinguished from verbs, prepositions from articles, participles from appellatives, and so on. It would be a long story.[1]

Now it is the combination and juxtaposition of these primary parts of speech—three or four or however many there are—which produces what are called cola; the connection of these in turn completes the period; and periods make up the entire discourse. The function of arrangement is thus to place words properly in relation to each other, to give cola their appropriate connection, and to articulate the discourse properly in periods. It is the second main subject in order under the general head of language—word-selection comes first and has a natural priority—but the charm, conviction, and force which arrangement imparts are of considerably greater importance. Word-selection is a complex and extensive subject, much discussed by philosophers and orators; arrangement comes second, and has had nothing like so much discussion. Nevertheless, it should not be regarded as paradoxical that it possesses force and power enough to put all the works of the other into the shade. We must remember what happens in other spheres. In arts which require materials of different kinds and make a combined product of them—building, carpentry, embroidery, and the like—the capacities of arrangement come second in order to those of selection, but they have greater importance. It is not absurd that the same should be true of speech; however, there is no harm in offering evidence for this, so as not to appear to take disputable propositions for granted.

[1] For the development of grammar, see G. Murray, *Greek Studies*, Oxford, 1946, 171–91; Pfeiffer, *History of Classical Scholarship*, Oxford, 1968, esp. 203 ff., 272.

3　Every expression by which a thought is signified is either metrical
or unmetrical. Either kind, if given beautiful rhythmical form[1] (*harmonia*),
is able to beautify either metre or prose. Thrown out ignorantly and ran-
domly, either kind ruins even the value of the thought it expresses.

Many poets, many historians, philosophers and orators, have chosen
with care and taste beautiful words appropriate to their needs, but have
wasted their efforts by giving them a careless and tasteless rhythmical
form. Others, taking vulgar and contemptible words but arranging them
with charm and distinction, have invested their writing with great elegance.
The relation of arrangement to selection seems in a sense analogous to
that of words to thought. Just as there is no profit in a good idea unless
one gives it the setting of fine words, so it is no use finding pure and
elegant expressions unless one gives them the appropriate setting of
rhythmical form.

In order not to give the impression of putting forward statements
without demonstration, I will try to show by a practical example why I
am convinced that arrangement is a higher and more significant study than
selection. I shall offer a preliminary taste both of poetry and of prose.
Let us take Homer as our poet, and Herodotus as our prose-writer. They
offer material enough for forming an opinion about the rest.

Odysseus, in Homer, is lodging with the swineherd. He is about to
have breakfast, according to the old custom, around dawn. Telemachus
appears, returning from his visit to the Peloponnese. It is a scene of
ordinary life, beautifully expressed. The lines themselves will show where
the excellence of the style lies:[2]

> Meanwhile, in the hut, Odysseus and the swineherd made breakfast;
> it was dawn, and they lit the fire.
> They had sent out the herdsmen with the pigs to pasture.
> Now on Telemachus the noisy dogs fawned, they did not bark
> at his approach. Odysseus noticed the dogs whining,
> and there was a sound of footsteps.
> He spoke at once to Eumaeus, who was just by.
> 'Eumaeus, some friend must be coming
> or someone well-known; the dogs are not barking,
> they are whining, and I hear the sound of footsteps.'
> He had not finished speaking, when his own son stood at the door.
> Up leapt the swineherd, surprised; the bowl,
> in which he was mixing the bright wine, fell from his hands.
> He ran to meet his master.

[1] Or 'sound form', if 'rhythmical' narrows the meaning too much.
[2] *Odyssey* 16. 1–16.

He kissed him on the head, on both his eyes,
on both his hands. His tears fell warm and fast.

I am sure it would be universally acknowledged that this passage attracts
and charms the ear and is not inferior to the most agreeable piece of
poetry. But where does its persuasiveness lie? What makes the piece what
it is? Is it the selection of words or the arrangement? No one, I am
convinced, could attribute it to the former: the whole context is made up
of the most commonplace and undistinguished words, which any farmer
or seaman or artisan—anyone who took no trouble to speak well—might
have found ready to hand. Without the metre, they will seem poor and
unattractive; there are no fine metaphors, no hypallages, no catachreses,
no trope of any kind—and not even any obscure archaic words or foreign
or newly-coined terms. What alternative have we, then, but to attribute
the beauty of the piece to the arrangement? Homer, as everybody of
course knows, contains countless such examples. This one suffices for
the present occasion, since all we want is a reminder.

(pp. 3, 5–12, 3)

[Dionysius then gives a prose example, Herodotus 1. 8–10—the story of
Gyges and Candaules. He follows this with some poetical examples intended to show how a change of order will produce different rhythms and
effects. We omit this, as it is almost impossible to translate adequately and
because it adds little that is new to the argument.]

'ARRANGEMENT' IN PROSE: A NOVEL SUBJECT

To make it easier to see how prose can be affected, like verse, by a change
of arrangement, though the words remain the same, I will take the beginning of Herodotus' history, because many people know it well, changing
only the dialect:

Croesus was a Lydian by race, the son of Alyattes, and the ruler of tribes
west of the Halys, which flows from the south between Syria and Paphlagonia and debouches in the north in the sea called the Euxine.[1]

Change the rhythmical form, and the shape of the sentence will no longer
be sinuous and suitable to history, but in the direct manner of the law-
court:

Croesus was the son of Alyattes, by race a Lydian, and ruler of the west
of the Halys tribes: the Halys flowing from the south, between Syria and
Paphlagonia, into the sea called the Euxine debouches in the north.

[1] Herodotus 1. 6.

This style may be thought not very different from that of this passage of Thucydides:

> Epidamnus is a city on the right as you enter the Ionian gulf; neighbouring it are the Taulantioi, barbarians, an Illyrian tribe.[1]

Next I am going to change the same passage round and give it another shape. Thus:

> Of Alyattes, the son was Croesus, by race a Lydian, and west of Halys ruler of the tribes; the Halys from the south flowing between Syria and Paphlagonia towards the north debouches in the so-called Euxine Sea.

This is Hegesianic arrangement, cheap, vulgar, effeminate. Hegesias[2] is high priest of all this nonsense:

> After a good feast a good we celebrate again;
>
> From Magnesia I come, the great, a man of Sipylus;
>
> Not a small drop into the Thebans' water spat Dionysus; sweet it is, but makes men mad.

Let this suffice for examples. I think I have now made my point clear, that arrangement has a greater effect than word-selection. It would be fair to make a comparison with Homer's Athena, who made Odysseus look different on different occasions, now small and wrinkled and ugly

> like a poor beggar or an old man,[3]

now, after another touch from the same wand,

> taller and stronger to see; and from his head
> made thick locks tumble, like the hyacinth flower.[4]

Similarly arrangement, taking the same words, makes thoughts seem at one moment ugly, low, and beggarly, and at another lofty, rich, and beautiful. Skilful arrangement of words is, indeed, what most distinguishes poet from poet and orator from orator. The ancients, almost all of them, took great pains about this. This is why their poems and lyrics and prose are so beautiful. Of their successors, only a few took trouble; and in the end the subject fell into total neglect, and nobody thought it necessary or indeed contributory in any way to the beauty of writing. They therefore left behind them writings which no one can bear to read to the end. I am referring to Phylarchus, Douris, Polybius, Psaon, Demetrius of Callatis, Hieronymus, Antigonus, Heraclides, Hegesianax, and innumerable others.[5] If I mentioned all their names, 'the day would

---

[1] Thucydides 1. 24.   [2] Cf. 'Longinus' 3 (below, p. 464).
[3] *Odyssey* 16. 273.   [4] *Odyssey* 6. 230 ff.
[5] All Hellenistic writers; only Polybius survives in sufficient quantity for us to judge the grounds of Dionysius' opinion.

be too short'. And why be surprised at these, when professors of philosophy and writers of logic textbooks are so miserably inefficient at the arrangement of words that one is really ashamed to mention it? No need to go further for a sufficient instance than Chrysippus the Stoic. No one has given a better or more exact treatment of logic—nor written a book, a famous and distinguished book anyway, in a worse style. Yet some of these philosophers claim to take this subject seriously, as a necessary part of linguistic study, and have written handbooks on the combination of parts of speech; but they all strayed far from the truth and did not even dream of what it really is that makes arrangement agreeable and beautiful. When I resolved on putting this book together, I investigated previous researches, and especially those of the Stoic philosophers, knowing that they had devoted considerable thought to linguistic questions—one must give them their due. But I found no work by any author of any note, small or great, bearing on the subject I proposed; the two treatises of Chrysippus 'On the combination (*suntaxis*) of the parts of speech' are concerned not with rhetoric but with logic, as those who have read them know. They deal with the 'combination' of propositions, true and false, possible and impossible, admissible, variable, ambiguous, and so forth; they have no practical value for oratory, at least as far as elegance and beauty, the aims of word-arrangement, are concerned. I therefore abandoned this study, and began to inquire independently to see whether I could discover some natural starting-point, the best kind of first principle, it is generally believed, for any subject or inquiry. I had got hold of some observations and thought that things were going well, when I realized that the road was not leading me in the direction in which I started and in which I had to travel. I therefore desisted. But perhaps I had better touch on the inquiry I thus abandoned, and say why I did so, lest anyone should think that it is ignorance and not deliberate intention that leads me to pass it over.   (pp. 18, 3–23, 12)

[This false trail is the logical–syntactical determination of order: e.g. nouns before verbs because substance is logically prior to accident; adverbs after verbs. Dionysius shows that this principle does not stand up to test— sometimes a beautiful arrangement obeys these rules, but often it does not. He dismisses it, and comes to his main positive thesis.]

The science of arrangement has three functions: (i) to see what combinations produce a total character which is beautiful and agreeable; (ii) to know what configuration of each of the elements to be combined will improve the joint effect; (iii) to recognize and execute in an appropriate fashion any necessary modification of the original elements— 6 subtraction, addition, or alteration. Let me explain these three functions more clearly by means of the analogy of constructive arts which everyone understands—building, ship-construction, and the like. When a builder has provided himself with the material from which he is going to construct the house—stones, timber, tiles, and so on—he proceeds to put the house together. He first considers three problems: he sees what sorts of stone, timber, and brick must be fitted together, how each of them should be placed and on which side, and finally how to trim and shape anything which does not fit with ease, so as to make it do so. The shipbuilder does the same. Similarly, the good arranger of the parts of speech. First, he considers what verb, noun, or other part of speech is appropriately combined with what other, and how the combination can be made good or better (not every arrangement affects the ear in the same way). Secondly, he decides what forms of noun, verb, or other word will be more agreeable, or more appropriate to the subject. For example: in nouns, which will give the better over-all impression, singulars or plurals, nominatives or oblique cases? If some masculines can be turned into feminines, or feminines into masculines, or these genders into neuters, which is the best form? And so on. Similarly with verbs. Are active or passive forms better? In what moods—'verbal cases' some call them—should verbs be expressed in order to aquire the best position? What tense differences should they indicate? And so on, with the other natural modifications of verbs. (The same precautions should be taken with the other parts of speech also, but I do not want to go into detail.) Thirdly, he decides whether any selected verb or noun needs alteration of form to secure better sound or setting. This question is a rich one in poetry, but there is less to it in prose, though it does occur where opportunity allows.

(pp. 27, 18–29, 18)

[Examples follow: *toutonī*, the emphatic and deictic form, for *touton* ('this'); *katidōn* 'seeing' for the uncompounded *idōn*; and various other examples of changed or modified words.]

COLA

7   One branch of the science of arrangement is thus that which deals with the primary parts and elements of speech. There is also, as I said at the beginning, the theory of 'cola', which needs longer and more elaborate treatment. This is what I shall now attempt to expound in my own way.

Cola must be fitted together so as to appear germane and suited to one another. They must be shaped in the best possible way. They must, finally, be prepared beforehand where necessary by reduction, enlargement, or any modification of which they are susceptible. Experience teaches all this, for it often happens that a given colon, if placed before or after some other one, proves harmonious and dignified, whereas in any other company it is unpleasing and without dignity. An example will make this clearer. In the speech of the Plataeans in Thucydides there is a very prettily composed and emotionally charged passage which reads thus:

You, Lacedaemonians, our only hope, we fear you may not be firm.[1]

Now suppose one were to break up this combination and re-organize the cola thus:

You, Lacedaemonians, we fear you may not be firm, our only hope.

Does the charm or the emotion remain the same if the cola are arranged like this? Of course not!

[A further example—Demosthenes 18. 119—follows; the points made are hardly translatable.]

If this is the theory of the combination of cola, what about that of 8 their conformation? Not all thoughts admit the same kind of expression. We say some things as statements, some as questions, some as wishes or instructions, some in doubt, some as hypothetical, and so on; and we endeavour to form our words in a manner consequent on these differences. So there are many conformations (*schēmatismoi*) of speech, as there are of thought. They cannot be embraced under a few headings—indeed they may well be infinite in number. They require long discussion and profound investigation. Consequently, the same colon will have a different effect if it has a different conformation. I will illustrate this by an example. If Demosthenes[2] had said 'When I had spoken, I made the proposal; and when I had made it, I went on the embassy; and when I went, I convinced the Thebans', would it have been as effective as it is in its existing form? 'I did not speak and then make no proposal; nor propose and then go on no embassy; nor go and then not convince the Thebans.' To explain all the forms of which cola are capable would take a very long time. The above suffices as an introduction.

On the other hand, it does not take long to show that some cola admit 9 modifications—such as the addition of elements not necessary for the sense, or subtractions which make the meaning incomplete, and which poets and prose writers adopt solely for the sake of rhythmical form, to lend charm and beauty. Who would not agree that the following passage of Demosthenes is pleonastic in virtue of an unnecessary addition made

---

[1] Thucydides 3. 57.   [2] 18. 179.

for the sake of the rhythmical form? 'A man who schemes and intrigues to entrap me is at war with me, even if so far he isn't throwing spears or shooting arrows.'[1] Here 'shooting arrows' is added not out of necessity but to make the concluding colon, otherwise harsher and more disagreeable to the ear than it should be, pleasanter by the addition. Again, take Plato's period from his Funeral Speech: who would not admit that unnecessary redundancies of diction have contributed to it? 'For deeds well done, in words skilfully spoken, come remembrance and honour for the doers from the hearers.'[2] Here 'from the hearers' has no essential function; its purpose is to make the final colon equal in length and impact to the preceding one. Again, consider the famous tricolon in Aeschines: 'You call him against yourself, you call him against the laws, you call him against democracy.'[3] Is not this of the same type? Aeschines has divided into three cola what could have been put in one: 'You call him against yourself and the laws and democracy.' The words 'you call' are repeated not out of necessity but to make the rhythmical form (*harmonia*) more agreeable.

So much for additions to cola. What about curtailments? These occur when some essential point is going to cause pain and annoyance to the listener, while its removal makes the rhythm more pleasing. A metrical example may be taken from Sophocles:

> I close my eyes, I open them, I rise,
> More guarding than I'm guarded.[4]

Here the second line consists of two incomplete cola: the complete sense would be

> more guarding others myself than guarded by others.

This however would have been contrary to the rules of metre and would not have had the present charm. Now for a prose instance: 'That to deprive everyone of immunity in the course of accusing some is an unjust man's part—this I will pass over.'[5] Here each of the first two cola has been curtailed. The full expression would have been: 'That, to deprive everyone of immunity, even those who have a rightful claim, in the course of accusing some people as being unsuitable recipients of it, is an unjust man's part—this I will pass over.' But Demosthenes decided not to make more ado about the exactness of meaning of the cola than about the rhythm.

---

[1] Demosthenes 9. 17.   [2] Plato, *Menexenus* 236.
[3] Aeschines 3. 202.
[4] Sophocles, fr. 706 Nauck.   [5] Demosthenes 20. 2.

I should like to take the same principle as being true of what are called periods. Here too, prior and secondary periods must be arranged in their proper order, whenever periodic writing is in place—which is not always; and indeed, the question of when and to what extent periods should be used and when not, is also a topic in the science of arrangement.

Having settled these points, I come next to the question of the proper 10 aims of the student of good word-arrangement, and the principles on which these aims may be attained. In the most general terms, there seem to be two objects which composers, whether of verse or of prose, ought to have as their aim: pleasure and beauty. The ear seeks both of these, resembling in this respect the eye, which, in contemplating sculpture, painting, carving, or any other work of men's hands, finds satisfaction and has no further longings as soon as it discovers pleasure and beauty in them. Let no one think it a paradox that I make two separate aims, and separate pleasure from beauty—nor think it odd for me to regard a style as pleasurably but not beautifully organized, or vice versa. The real world produces such results, and there is nothing novel in my claim. The style of Thucydides, for instance, or that of Antiphon of Rhamnus, is arranged as beautifully as any—no one could find fault with them on this score— but not very pleasurably. On the other hand, the styles of Ctesias, the historian from Cnidos, and of the Socratic Xenophon, are pleasurably composed but not as beautifully as one might have wished. (I am speaking in broad terms, not absolutely, for Thucydides and Antiphon certainly contain examples of pleasurable arrangement, and Xenophon and Ctesias of beautiful.) Herodotus' arrangement possesses both qualities: it is both pleasurable and beautiful.

The four most important elements which make a style pleasurable and 11 beautiful are: melody, rhythm, variety, and the accompanying virtue of appropriateness. Under 'pleasurableness' I class: freshness, charm, euphony, sweetness, persuasiveness, and the like. Under 'beauty' I class: magnificence, weight, solemnity, dignity, the patina of age, and so on.[1] These seem to me to be the most important elements—the main headings, as it were. These, and perhaps no others, are the aims that all serious writers of verse or lyric or what is called 'pedestrian' speech set before themselves. Many good writers have excelled in one or both of these manners. It is not possible for me to give examples of them all here— it would waste the whole book. Moreover, if I am in duty bound to discuss some one of them, and evidence is to be required, another occasion will be more suitable—namely, when I come to outline the types (*charactères*) of rhythmic arrangements (*harmoniai*). For the moment, the

[1] This is an important list of qualities: compare the *ideai* of Hermogenes (below, p. 561).

above suffices. I return now to the distinction I made of pleasurable and beautiful arrangements, so that my argument may proceed, as they say, according to plan.

I said then that the ear is pleased by tunes, by rhythms, and finally by variations, and in each case by what is appropriate. Experience shall testify to the truth of my words; no one can find fault with a witness who agrees with our common feelings. Who indeed has not found himself affected and charmed by one style and unaffected by another, or soothed by one rhythm and exasperated by another? I sometime think, in a crowded theatre, packed with a miscellaneous and uneducated crowd, that I can see how we all have a natural affinity with melody and rhythm, because I notice a popular lyre-player howled down by the mob for striking a wrong note and ruining the piece, or an *aulos*-player of supreme skill at his instrument suffering the same fate for blowing an unresonant note or not closing his mouth and so producing a false note or being what is called out of tune. And yet if one asked a layman to take the instrument and perform one of the actions which he was blaming the musician for doing badly, he couldn't do it. Why? Because this is a matter of knowledge, which we do not all share, whereas the other is a feeling which nature imparts to all. I have noticed the same thing with regard to rhythms. Everyone becomes angry and uncomfortable when a step or movement or gesture is made with incorrect timing and the rhythm thereby obscured. It might be thought that, while melody and rhythm give pleasure and we are all bewitched by them, variations and propriety do not possess that degree of charm and grace and do not have the same effect on all ears. But this would be wrong; correctness in this field does charm us all, as incorrectness causes us distress. For proof of this, I draw attention to the fact that instrumental and vocal music and dancing, if successful in achieving charm at every point but lacking timely variation or erring in propriety, produce in the end a heavy, sated feeling or a disagreeable sense of the inappropriateness to the subject.

All this is no irrelevant comparison. The science of oratory is a sort of music which differs quantitatively not qualitatively from the vocal and instrumental kind; words too have their melody and rhythm, their variation and propriety, so that in oratory too the ear is delighted by melody, seduced by rhythm, gratified by variety, and everywhere seeks what properly belongs. It is simply a difference of degree.

(pp. 32, 6–40, 16)

[The following passage, on accent, is valuable for what it tells us of the nature of the Greek accent but very technical and of little interest for criticism.]

Not all elements of speech affect the ear in the same way, any more 12
than all visible objects affect the sense of vision similarly or all tasted
things the sense of taste, or in general all stimuli their appropriate sense.
Some sounds give a sweet effect, some a bitter, some a rough, some a
smooth, and so on. This is due to the nature of the letters of which speech
consists, which have many and various potentialities, and to the multifarious combinations of syllables. Since the elements of speech have this
important capacity, but their nature cannot be changed, the only resource
remaining is to obscure the untoward effects of some of them by mixing,
blending, and juxtaposing. Rough must be mixed with smooth, soft with
hard, euphonious with cacophonous, short with long, sounds easily
articulated with those that are more difficult, and so on. All these elements
must be combined as occasion demands. We must avoid a succession of
many short words—this fragments the auditory impression—or of too
many long ones. Words of similar accentuation or quantity should not be
juxtaposed. With nouns and adjectives, frequent changes of case are
desirable; if one case continues too long, it seriously offends the ear.
The monotony produced by the juxtaposition of many nouns or verbs or
other parts of speech must be broken up; we have to be on our guard
against satiety. Nor should we stay always with the same figure, but make
frequent changes, nor keep on introducing the same tropes, but vary
them; nor begin or end with the same words again and again beyond
all proper occasion.

I should not like to be thought to imply that the devices I recommend
will always produce pleasure, or their opposites annoyance. I am not such
a fool. I know that pleasure results on occasion both from repetition and
from the avoidance of repetition. All I say is that we should always look
for the proper occasion, because this is the best criterion of pleasure and
its opposite. Now no rhetorician or philosopher has so far laid down a
definite technique for 'occasion'; even Gorgias of Leontini, the first to
attempt the subject, wrote nothing worth reading about it. Nor indeed
is it the kind of thing to fall into the framework of a technique; 'occasion'
is something to be tracked down not by knowledge but by opinion. This
opinion is better acquired by those who have exercised themselves often
and on many subjects, and it only rarely and accidentally as it were falls
to the lot of those who do not bother with exercise.

I must now proceed to other points. A writer who aims at making a
pleasing impression on the ear by his word-arrangement must observe
certain principles. First, he must *either* combine together words which
are harmonious, rhythmical, and euphonious, and which lend sweetness
or softness or, more generally, comfort to the senses, *or* link words without
these characteristics to others which do have power to charm, so that the

grace of the latter puts the disagreeable quality of the former into the shade. Wise generals do something of the kind with armies—they let the strong conceal the weak, so that the whole force becomes serviceable. Secondly, sameness must be broken by timely variety; in all things variety is sweet. Finally—and most important—he must give his subject the type of structure (*harmonia*) appropriate to it.

There is no need, in my opinion, to feel shy of any noun or verb in common use, unless it is something which it would be shameful to mention. My view is that no part of speech signifying any object or action is too low or dirty or otherwise disagreeable to find some appropriate place in our writing.[1] Trust your word-arrangement, I would advise, and come out with your words bravely and confidently. You have plenty of models: Homer, in whom the most commonplace words can be found, Demosthenes, Herodotus, and so on; I shall mention them all later, and make the appropriate comments on each.

These few observations—many more might be made—must suffice as general indications on the pleasant kind of word-arrangement.

13   To proceed, then. If I were asked how, and on what principles, a *beautiful* structure might be produced, I should give the same answers as for the pleasant kind. The same factors go to the making of both— noble melody, dignified rhythm, splendid modulation (*metabolē*, 'variation'), propriety in all these respects. As there is a pleasant kind of diction, so there is a noble one; as there is a smooth rhythm, so there is a grand one; modulation confers both charm and tension; propriety, finally, has no characteristics at all if it does not possess a good share of the beautiful. All these considerations make me say that the beautiful in structure of language must be sought by the same means as the pleasing.

(pp. 43, 17–47, 22)

[Dionysius now proceeds to discuss the four main factors in turn. 'Melody' depends largely on the natural qualities of sounds and syllables. This discussion, and that of rhythm and 'modulation' or 'variety', are detailed, depending largely on untranslatable features of Greek onomatopoeic words and the like, and often unconvincing. Of interest in the history of linguistic theory, this section is of little critical significance. We resume at the point where Dionysius passes to *propriety* in this field.]

PROPRIETY

20   It remains to consider propriety. Propriety is a necessary concomitant to all the rest. Any work which is lacking herein, lacks, if not its whole

---

[1] Cf. Quintilian 10. 1. 9 (below, p. 381).

effect, at least the most important part of it. This is not the occasion for a discussion of the entire subject, which is a profound study needing lengthy exposition. I shall content myself with discussing what I can of this topic— not indeed the whole or the major part— so far as it concerns the field here under consideration.

It would be generally agreed that 'propriety' consists in what suits the persons or actions to be handled. Just as word-selection can be proper or improper to a subject, so surely can word-arrangement. Ordinary life gives evidence of this: when we are angry or pleased, sorrowful or afraid, or in any other troubled or emotional state, we employ a different word-arrangement from when we think that there is nothing to perturb or grieve us. It would be an interminable task to enumerate all the species of propriety, but I will make one point which is both the most readily made and the most general in application. When people report events of which they have been eye-witnesses, even though their state of mind does not change, they do not use the same word-arrangement for everything, but imitate what they are reporting even in the way they put words together; this is a natural instinct, not the result of effort. Observing this, the good poet or orator should imitate whatever he is speaking about not only in his selection of words but in his arrangement of them. Homer does this, superb genius that he is, despite the fact that he possesses only one metre and few rhythms; he is none the less always innovating and using his ingenuity within this field, so that we see the things happening as much as we hear them described. I will give a few instances out of the large number possible.

THE STONE OF SISYPHUS

In his story to the Phaeacians, Odysseus, after relating his own wanderings and his descent to Hades, comes to the visions of the horrors there. In this context, he relates the sufferings of Sisyphus, for whom, they say, the gods of the underworld ordained an end to labour when he succeeded in rolling a stone over a certain hill—this being, however, impossible, because the stone always fell back again whenever it got to the top. It is worth while noticing how he depicts this imitatively with the help of the actual arrangement of the words:

> kai mēn Sīsuphon eiseidon krater' alge' ekhonta,
> lāan bastazonta pelōrion amphoterēsin.
> ētoi ho men skēriptomenos khersin te posin te
> lāan anō ōtheske potī lophon.

And I saw Sisyphus too in great distress,
lifting a huge stone in his two hands;
and straining with his hands and feet
he pushed the stone up, up the hill.[1]

Here it is the arrangement which makes all the happenings clear—the weight of the stone, the laborious shifting of it from the ground, Sisyphus straining with his limbs and climbing the hill, the rock pushed up with difficulty. That is undeniable. But just how is each of these effects achieved? Not automatically or accidentally. First: in the two lines in which he is rolling the rock uphill, all the words except two are mono-syllables or disyllables. Second: in each of the two lines, the long syllables are half as many again as the short. Again: the joints between the words are set wide apart and there are perceptible intervals, resulting from the clash of vowels or the combination of semivowels and consonants. Moreover, the rhythms of which the whole composition is made are dactyls and spondees, the grandest of all and those with the broadest spread. What then is the effect of these various factors? The mono-syllables and disyllables, leaving as they do numerous intervals between one word and the next, reproduce the slowness of the work; the long syllables with their rests and impediments reproduce its resistance, heaviness, and difficulty; the gaps between words and the juxtaposition of harsh sounds reproduce the interruption and hesitations of the action, and the immensity of the labour; finally, the rhythms, with their impression of drawn-out length, represent the stretching limbs and straining apart of Sisyphus, and the resistance of the stone. That this is the work not of nature improvising but of art endeavouring to imitate events is shown by the ensuing lines. Homer does not use the same style for the return of the stone from the top and its rolling downhill; he speeds up and concentrates the arrangement of the words. Beginning in the old manner,

all' hote melloi
akron huperbaleein . . .

but when it was just
about to pass the top,

he then adds

tot' epistrepsaske krataiis;
autis epeita pedonde kulindeto lāas anaidēs,

then momentum took control,
and down to the bottom rattled the unmanageable boulder.

[1] *Odyssey* 11. 593 ff.

Does not the word-arrangement roll downhill with the weight of the rock —or rather, the speed of the narrative overtake the momentum of the stone? I believe it does. Once again—why? The answer is worth noticing. The line which represents the downward movement of the rock contains no monosyllabic, and only two disyllabic, words. This, in the first place, accelerates rather than extends the intervals. Further, of the seventeen syllables in the line, ten are short and only seven long and those not perfect ones: the expression is therefore inevitably contracted and compressed under the influence of the shortness of the syllables. Again, no word has any appreciable separation from the next: no vowel is in juxtaposition with another vowel, no semivowel or consonant with semivowel —and these are the features which roughen or break up word-structure. There is no perceptible interval, you see, if the words are not separated. Instead, they slide into one another to form a single movement; in a manner of speaking they all become a single word through the exact fitting of the joins. Most wonderful of all, no long rhythm—spondee or bacchius[1]—such as naturally falls into a heroic metre, is to be found in the line except at the end. The others are all dactyls—and even they have their irrational syllables so much accelerated that some hardly differ from trochees. There is nothing to hinder a composition made up of such elements from running smoothly and easily and flowingly.

Many similar examples could be cited from Homer. I content myself with these, to leave myself room for my remaining topics. The above remarks do, I believe, comprise the most important and essential points to be kept in mind by those who wish to produce pleasing or beautiful word-arrangement, either in poetry or in prose. What I could not set down—minor and more recondite matters, too numerous to be easily embraced in one work—I will communicate in the course of our daily exercises, when I will also adduce the evidence of many good poets, historians, and orators. For the moment, I confine myself to essentials of my promised plan which have so far been omitted. I shall consider what different types of word-arrangement there are, and what is the general character of each. I shall state what writers are supreme in each kind, and offer specimens. This done, I shall elucidate a problem commonly discussed—namely, what it is that makes prose seem like poetry though it remains prose in form, and what makes poetical expression resemble prose while it preserves the dignity of poetry: most good writers of prose or poetry have these qualities. I must try, therefore, to say what I think about this problem too.

But I begin with the first point.

[1] $--, \cup--.$

THE TYPES OF WORD-ARRANGEMENT

21 I certainly think that there *are* many specific differences in word-arrangement. They are not easily seen in a general view or enumerated with exactness. Indeed, every individual has his own particular quality of word-arrangement, as he has his particular quality of looks. Painting is not a bad analogy. People who paint pictures all use the same paints, but the mixtures they produce are quite different from one another. Similarly, in language, whether in poetry or not, we all use the same words, but we do not put them together in the same way.

The *generic* differences, however, number, in my opinion, only three. Call them what you please, when you have been told their characteristics and differences. I know no literal terms for them, and so treat them as having no proper names and call them instead by metaphorical ones: the dry or austere, the smooth, the well-tempered—though how this last comes into being I know not, 'my mind is divided to utter the truth'[1]: is it by deficiency in both extremes or by their combination? It is hard to make a safe guess here; perhaps therefore it is better to say that there are many intermediate terms formed by the relaxation or intensification of the extremes. In music, the middle note is equidistant from the top and the bottom, but in literature the middle style is not equidistant from the two extremes: it is distinguishable only roughly, as with crowds, heaps, and the like. This, however, is not the moment for this question: I must keep my promise, and discuss the particular kinds—not indeed saying all I could (that would be a long story) but making the most salient points.

AUSTERE ARRANGEMENT

22 The characteristics of the austere type of structure are the following. It requires that words should be securely positioned and given safe standing, so that each word can be seen all round, while the various parts keep a respectable distance from each other and are separated by perceptible intervals. It is no disadvantage either if the joints are frequently rough and awkward, like building stones laid together not properly squared or smoothed but unworked and improvised. It is often, moreover, given greater length by the use of big words that cover a lot of space, while contraction into a few syllables is thoroughly alien to it except under dire necessity.

So much for the aims and preferences of this manner in regard to words. They apply likewise to cola, where it also affects grand and

[1] Pindar, fr. 213 Snell.

dignified rhythms, and dislikes equalized or similar cola, or any that are slaves to inexorable rules, wanting only the noble, splendid, and free. It prefers the appearance of nature to that of art, the expression of emotion to that of character. As to periods, it has generally no desire to construct such as complete the sense within their own compass; if this should accidentally happen, it seeks to demonstrate its artlessness and simplicity by employing no additions unhelpful to the sense merely to complete the period, by making no attempt to secure striking or smooth clàusulae, no calculations to ensure that the period is the right length for the speaker's breath, and indeed no endeavour of any such kind. This type of structure has further characteristics of its own: it is flexible in the use of cases, varied in figures, has few conjunctions and no articles, often despises connection, is unpolished, grand, plain-spoken, unembellished, with archaism and the patina of age as its beauty. This type has had many devotees in poetry, history and oratory. Specially distinguished are Antimachus of Colophon and Empedocles the scientist in epic, Pindar in lyric, Aeschylus in tragedy, Thucydides in history, Antiphon in oratory.

(pp. 88, 1–98, 12)

SMOOTH ARRANGEMENT

The smooth type of arrangement, which I placed second, has the following characteristics. It does not seek 'all-round visibility' for every individual word, or a broad secure base for them all, or long intervals between them. Any effect of slowness or stability is alien. The aim is words in motion, words bearing down on one another, carried along on the stability afforded by their support of one another, like a perpetually flowing stream. This style likes the individual parts to merge into one another, to be woven together so as to appear as far as possible like one continuous utterance. This is achieved by exactly fitting joints which leave the intervals between the words imperceptible. It is like cloth finely woven together or pictures in which the light merges into the shade. All the words are expected to be euphonious, smooth, soft, virginal; it hates rough, recalcitrant syllables, and has a cautious attitude towards anything at all bold or risky.

Not satisfied with suitable joins and smooth connections between words, this manner aims also at a close interweaving of cola, the whole building up to a period. It limits the length of the colon—not too short, not unduly long—and of the period, which should be such that an adult man's breath can control it. It cannot tolerate non-periodic writing, a period not divided into cola, or a colon out of proportion. It employs rhythms that are not very long but medium or quite short. The ends of its periods must be rhythmical and precisely based. Connections between periods here are formed on the opposite principle from those between words: this type of writing merges words but distinguishes periods and tries to make *them* visible all round, as it were. Its favourite figures are not the more archaic or such as produce an impression of solemnity or weight or tension, but the luxurious and blandishing kind, full of deceptive and theatrical qualities. To put it more generally, this manner has in all important respects the opposite characteristics to the former; no more need be said.

It remains to enumerate its distinguished practitioners. Of epic writers, the finest exponent of this manner is, I think, Hesiod; of lyric poets Sappho, and then Anacreon and Simonides; among the tragic poets there is only Euripides; strictly speaking there is no historian, though Ephorus and Theopompus are nearer than most. Among orators, we have Isocrates.

(pp. 111, 18–114, 9)

[Examples again follow; the first is Sappho's ode to Aphrodite—the only extant complete poem of Sappho.]

THE MIXED STRUCTURE

24 The third kind of structure, midway between the two just mentioned, I call the mixed kind, for want of a proper and better name. It has no special form, but is a reasonable combination of the other two, a sort of selection of the best features of each. To my way of thinking, it deserves the first prize, because it is a mean—and excellence is a mean in life and actions too, according to Aristotle and his school—though it is to be seen, as I said above, in broad outline, not in detail, and has many specific differences. Its users do not all make the same thing out of it, but some stress some features and some others, intensifying or underplaying the same elements in different ways; its successful practitioners, despite differences of approach, have all profited. Towering above them all,

the source of all the rivers, seas, and springs,[1]

is, we must say, Homer. Every passage in him that one touches is exquisitely elaborated in both the austere and smooth manners. The others who have practised the same 'mean' are very much his inferiors, though well worth study in their own right. Stesichorus and Alcaeus are the lyric poets, Sophocles the tragedian, Herodotus the historian, Demosthenes the orator. Among the philosophers, in my estimation, are to be seen Demo-

[1] *Iliad* 21. 196 f.

critus, Plato, and Aristotle; it is impossible to find any who have combined styles more successfully than these.   (pp. 120, 11–121, 21)

IMPORTANCE OF THE SUBJECT

At this point I suspect an attack from persons who have had no general 25 education but practise the day-to-day part of rhetoric without method or system. They must be answered. We must not be thought to let the case go by default.

Now this is what they will say. 'Was Demosthenes such a poor drudge that whenever he wrote a speech he had to have measures and rhythms to apply, like a modeller, and tried to fit his cola to these patterns, turning his words up and down, and watching his quantities and pauses, his cases and conjugations, fussing about all the tiny modifications of which the parts of speech are capable? A man of that ability would be a fool to devote himself to trivial pedantry of that sort.' This kind of scoff and jeer is not hard to repulse. First, it would not be odd if a man whose reputation for eloquence transcended all his predecessors, and who was composing eternal works and submitting himself to the authority of all-testing time, should want to avoid adopting any word or fact rashly, and should pay great attention both to the arrangement of his thoughts and to beauty of expression—especially as his contemporaries were publishing works more like fine carving and engraving than writing. I mean the sophists Isocrates and Plato. Isocrates, to take the minimum estimate, spent ten years writing the *Panegyricus*, and Plato, in the course of his eighty years, never gave up combing and curling his dialogues, refashioning them in all kinds of ways. Every scholar knows the anecdotes of his industry, especially the story of the tablet found after his death containing the opening sentence of the *Republic*, with the words arranged in various ways: 'I went down yesterday to the Piraeus with Glaucon the son of Ariston.' What was odd then in Demosthenes' also taking thought for euphony, harmony, and the avoidance of random and unconsidered placings of word or thought? It seems to me much more appropriate for an orator composing public speeches as a permanent memorial of his ability to take care of the smallest detail, than for painters and engravers, displaying the skill and industry of their hands on perishable material, to expend their craftsmanship on veins and down and bloom and similar minutiae. These seem to me reasonable arguments; one might add that it was only to be expected that, as a young beginner, Demosthenes should have been careful in everything, so far as human endeavour could go, but that when long exercise had given mastery and shaped forms and models in his mind of everything he practised, he became able to produce his results with ease and as a matter of habit. The same sort of thing happens in other arts whose end is activity or creation of some kind. For example, skilled players of the lyre or harp or *aulos*, when they hear an unfamiliar tune, finger it out on their instruments with the speed of thought, with no trouble at all; but while they are still learning, it takes much time and trouble for them to grasp the force of the various notes. At that stage, their hands were not in the habit of performing what they were bidden. It was later, when long practice had established a habit as strong as nature, that they succeeded in their efforts. There is no need for other examples. One fact, that we all know, is enough to explode all the nonsense. When we learn our letters, we first learn their names, then their shapes and functions, then syllables and what happens to them, only then words and their accidents—lengthenings and shortenings, accents, and so on. Then, when we have acquired knowledge of these things, we begin to write and read, at first slowly and syllable by syllable; it takes a long time to form firm models in our minds, but when that has happened we do it easily, and run through any book presented to us accurately and speedily. We must suppose that word-arrangement and facility with cola develop in the same way in expert performers. It is no wonder if the inexpert and ignorant are surprised and incredulous if anyone achieves perfect control through his skill.

26   So much for the scoffers at technical advice. I come next to some remarks on lyrical and metrical arrangement having a close resemblance to prose. The first cause of this type (as of the unmetrical equivalent) is the way in which the *words* are made to fit, the second is the combination of the *cola*, the third the balance of the *periods*. Success in this department requires multifarious variety in the handling and joining of words and the construction of cola with divisions at the right intervals, not complete at the ends of lines but dividing the metre; the cola in fact must be unequal and heterogeneous, often contracted into shorter *commata*, while the periods, at least juxtaposed ones, must not be equal in length or similar in form; irregularity in rhythm and metre gives the closest approximation to prose. Composers of epic, iambic, and other homogeneous metres cannot divide their verses up by variety of metrical or rhythmical form, but have to keep always to the same pattern; lyric poets on the other hand are allowed to combine many metres or rhythms in one period. Single-metre composers, therefore, when they break up their lines by dividing them by cola in a variety of ways, disintegrate and destroy the exactness of the metre, and when they compose periods of varying length and form cause us to forget it altogether. The lyric poets on the other hand, with their polymetric strophes, effect heterogeneous and unequal divisions

of unequal and heterogeneous cola; these two features prevent us from getting a grip of any consistent rhythm, and this produces poetry with a great similarity to prose. Even if metaphorical, foreign, rare, and otherwise poetic words remain in the poem, there is still this resemblance.

I should not wish anyone to think me unaware that what is called 'prosiness' is generally supposed to be a fault, or convict me of ignorance because I regard a fault as a virtue in poetry or prose. I ask my critic to hear how I think good work can be distinguished from bad in this field also. As I understand it, one kind of prose writing is private—garrulous and trivial—and the other public, containing a large element of elaboration and art. When I find a poem resembling the garrulous and trivial type of prose, I put it down as ridiculous; if it resembles the elaborate and artistic, I think it deserves our attention and imitation. Now if these two types of prose had different names, the two types of poets which resemble them would have different names also. But in fact, the good and the worthless are both called prose, and it is therefore quite right to call poetry good if it resembles good prose and bad if it resembles bad, and not be disturbed by the identity of name. A similarity of name applied to two different things will not prevent us from seeing the nature of both.

(pp. 131, 14–138, 9)

8

DECLAMATION AND THE SENECAS

An important key to the understanding of Silver Latin is the educational practice of declamation. This was already known in Cicero's time (he practised the art himself in his later years), but, as public oratory lost much of its point in real life under the Empire, declaiming became something of an end in itself.

There were two types of declamation, *controversia* and *suasoria*. In the former, the declaimer spoke for prosecution or defence in a mock-legal case. In the *suasoria* he offered advice to a historical personage in a particular situation. Examples of both kinds survive in some quantity, in the works of the elder Seneca and in collections attributed to Quintilian. There are analogous things in Greek, mostly rather later. The subject has been treated by S. F. Bonner, *Roman Declamation*, Liverpool, 1949, with useful references to earlier literature.

A. DISPUTE ABOUT THE SON OF A MAN WHO EXPOSED A CHILD AND A WOMAN WHO WAS DIVORCED

We begin with a *controversia* (338) from a collection which has come down under the name of Quintilian (ed. C. Ritter, 1884). The author gives us a statement of the theme, advice on its treatment, and a 'model answer'. The traditional framework of the five divisions of a speech is clearly in evidence.

THEME

A man divorced his wife, by whom he had (apparently) a son, now a young man, and took another. There were constant quarrels between stepson and stepmother. Then a poor man began to claim the youth and call him his own son. The apparent father put the nurse to the torture. In the first inquisition she said the boy was the son of her master. At the second she said he had been exposed by the claimant: at this stage she died. The father is ready to yield the youth to the claimant; the divorced wife claims him for herself.

ADVICE ON PROEM AND EPILOGUE

A proem has its own particular form, rules, and manner. The form of narrative and that of commonplaces is quite alien to the proem. There is one part of a declamation, however, that it is often like—the epilogue.

The resemblance is that both tend to be outside the issue. The proem precedes the issue, while the epilogue is spoken when the issue has been dealt with. Moreover, both have the same object—to win over the judge. They differ, however, in that proems must ensure the attentiveness of the judge, while this part of the burden is not required of the epilogue, the speech being over. The epilogue may sometimes indulge in repetition, to refresh the memory of the judge. Thus at the start we ensure that the judge listens to everything, at the end that he remembers what he heard. Further, the epilogue attracts feelings towards the speaker. This is true of the proem also, but the end requires more rousing of pity and more freedom. The proem, though it has something to ask of the judge, should not tire him (nor indeed should the epilogue either)—for it is a very true saying that tears dry quickly.

Proems are to be drawn from *persons*, either our own or those of our opponents, or sometimes those of the judges themselves. From ours, to win favour, from our adversaries' to arouse the judges' hatred of those we are attacking. The persons of the judges rarely come up in school declamations, though often in the forum. Sometimes we may also speak about *facts*, for the reason that the *controversia* of the schools embraces everything that may happen in the forum, and in the forum the proem *is* sometimes drawn from facts, if one speech has already been made on each side and the judge already knows the case. Well then, we shall be right to do it: as also[1] both to narrate and, in the same declamation, to put forward replies even when we are on the side of the accuser—something that will never happen, to my mind, in the forum; there the first speaker, who puts forward the case, will not himself be able to reply to objections unless written evidence has been given by the other side and received by the court. To sum up, you must never make capital out of what the other side *may* be going to say—only out of what they *have* said.

Today we are not dealing with the dispute of this woman with her husband. You can't have a suit between someone who yields and someone who claims. The youth is claimed by the poor man; the father is ready to yield to him—but the mother is not.

THE DECLAMATION

Even if the dispute of the woman for whom I appear,[2] judges, were with this poor man, my party would be thought the weaker and the worthier

[1] The point is that in a first speech, for the accuser, narration is in place, but not replies to something said by the other side, for nothing will yet have been said, unless there is evidence in writing. Cf. Quint. 4. 2. 28–9, 5. 13. 50.

[2] The speaker is counsel for the first wife.

of assistance. For woman is in herself a feeble thing, and in this lady the natural weakness is greatly increased by the fact that she is no longer married. There is the further particular point in her case that what was formerly a safeguard has become a source of anxiety. Even if she had ceased to have a husband and had been driven from the house into which she came as a young bride, she would not seem quite helpless if she had her youthful son. But this very fact is in dispute, and at this moment can bring the mother nothing but worry.

Nevertheless, my contention is that she is not in dispute with the man you see across the court from me; the case is weighted against her by a profounder influence. This mother would be distinctly more fortunate if her husband had been content to yield his claim to the son; as it is, he has added weight to his evidence, and forced the wretched nurse, twice subjected to torture because she spoke the truth, to die—to our disadvantage. If her authority moves you, judges, I am content to make one point in the first part of my speech: her words are evidence on both sides.

NARRATION

But if in fact he wanted his son claimed rather than yielded, he would be adequately supported by the mere setting forth of the facts. For once upon a time he was anxious to have children. So he married, rejoiced at the prospect of imminent offspring, reared the baby, and brought it through to adolescence (quite far enough) with no doubts. The husband has suffered a great injury: I should be happier to attack the stepmother, judges. I know what it meant when she burst into the house of a man already old, a matrimonial home with a grown son in it: she knew that the house could be emptied. Do not inquire what her plans were, how she did it—alone.[1] She began to hate the boy at once—not merely with a hidden and secret passion, but openly quarrelling. This very fact, judges, can be taken as a vital proof:[2] she hated this youth as only a stepmother can.

He did not lack the outspokenness that confidence inspires; but no fault could be found in his way of life to justify his being disinherited. Accordingly she found a novel method of getting rid of him. First of all, this worthless individual,[3] ready to be bought to forward any dispute, bore witness against himself, saying he had exposed the child: doubtless so that this man should not need to be ashamed of being a bad father. I call

---

[1] Text and sense uncertain.
[2] i.e. that the boy was her husband's son by the previous wife.
[3] The poor man.

the gods, I call your sense of what is right, judges, to witness: this man, wanting to get rid of his son, did not think it enough to believe this man; he mutilated with all kinds of cruelty the unfortunate nurse—he hated her too. You ask why he did this: you will realize—when he tortures her the second time.

The first tortures had merely tired her, and her loyalty had remained constant, her words the same. She had made *her* blood *his* reproach. The torturer was recalled, the torments renewed. It was obvious to the wretched woman that she would be tortured for as long as she went on saying the same thing. I am not angry with her. So long as she had strength and breath, she resisted. She was not forced into lying until she was on the point of death. Her conqueror thought that *this* was the sole object of the tortures; he had no further doubts. I do not claim him (to speak mildly) for equal torments. But I do ask that this should be regarded as applying only to his own cause.[1]

PROOF

I claim the son for his mother against one who only lately began to claim him. First of all, judges, you will realize that no burden of proof rests on me. There has never been any doubt that the youth in question lived for many years with this man—years that carried him right up to an age of maturity. Shall I now add weaker points—that she married and was capable of conception? In fact, if she had not conceived, her husband would not have believed her.[2] The whole burden lies on the other side. My opponent must prove a lot—that he had a wife, that she conceived, bore— and bore a *son*, bore him at a time which fits in with the age of the boy in dispute: that he exposed him, that the exposed child lived, that he was taken up by the man from whom he claims the boy—or on the other hand was produced as her own by this woman, she being (as he asserts) sterile or having recently miscarried. You will not be able to say she was sterile—her husband did not think so. And it's not enough to *say* she lost her child: it has to be proved. We should make these demands, judges, if the case concerned a slave, or a sum of money; but you are trying to snatch a *son* from a *mother*, to tear out part of her womb. Against the groans of a mother, you are content to adduce the negligence of the other parent.

'What motive have I? Why am I claiming the child if he is not my own?' Without yet explaining why you are in this dispute,[3] I can say that your

---

[1] Meaning uncertain.   [2] i.e. on the legitimacy of the son.

[3] The explanation is the bargain struck between the father and the poor man, alluded to above.

contention makes no sense. If you have no motive for claiming another's son, *he* hasn't any for keeping another's son. Indeed, it is easier for a poor man to make this pretence. What difference does it make to your fortune whether you have an heir? But I shall explain the reason for your invention later; meanwhile, I want to discuss the material on which your case rests.

'I rely', he says, 'on the testimony of the man you say is the father.' Let us suppose that that is true: the father is only one man, he is angry, he is the husband of another woman. When I say 'one man', you should bear in mind people like Cato and Scipio and many other names glorious in our city.¹ When I say 'he is angry', remember not factual instances in this country so much as plays on the stage—remember how great an effect this emotion has had, how many it has driven off course like some tempest. When I say 'he is the husband of another woman', I say two things at once. He has a motive for harming the woman he divorced, and he has a motive for being of service to the woman he married. This is what I should say if the evidence *were* his. What does your witness say? That he knows something. I must next ask: how does he know? From the nurse. The evidence then is that of the nurse—not of the witness who believes her. Let us for the moment leave the husband—we shall bring him back in his place; let us speak of the nurse.

If she had lied from the start, I should venture to say of her yet more boldly what I venture to say of him: she is only one. As it is, there were two different examinations. Let us see which is more likely to have elicited the truth. Under torture she said the youth is your son. I want to give the evidence weight: it was an old woman who was tortured. Is not one examination enough for a woman, for an old one? You rack those already naturally failing limbs, you lacerate with your whips skin that already hardly holds together—then you say: 'You lie.' Can she lie for long against your wishes? Even when the strongest men are tortured, even when the spirited are subjected to the bitterest pain, it still makes a lot of difference what reply the torturer wants. She stuck it out, I don't say against fire, against whips: against *you*. Truth is the object of the examination so long as she hopes you are beaten if she tells the truth. But when you repeat the treatment, call back the executioner, what are you saying except: 'Torture her—till she lies?' You certainly won a great victory: you overcame an old woman. As the breath failed, a whisper escaped: 'Pity me. He is not yours. Spare me. I have told the truth.' Here, I imagine, the torturer was told to press on, and make sure that the result of the examination was the woman's dying while still saying this, while you were the victor, happily announcing to your adversary what you had

¹ The relevance of Cato and Scipio is unclear.

done. I ask you: when the same woman says different things under torture, isn't it obvious that the answer you wanted was the answer you believed?

EPILOGUE

What mortal does not see through the whole farce? Who fails to see the wiles of a stepmother, the bargain struck by an unfortunate old man? I shall have to pity him, even if it goes against me. You ask: why does he yield? For the same reason that he drove the mother of his grown-up son from his house, that he broke a long happy marriage, when nothing was said or suspected of his wife, that he brought a new bride to a bed still warm with the imprint of the former wife, that he would not even give his son the privilege of being defeated.[1] Surely we find quite different behaviour in those [2] who become parents by means of a passing pleasure, who are bound to their sons by ties that lie outside themselves. Quite different is the love of a mother, who brings before you the memory of ten months, the recollection of all those dangers and anxieties. Count this youth's years—it will seem brief enough a space; count all the days, every individual moment that has passed: *that* is the length of a mother's testimony. No pretence could last so long.

If the laws permitted, if you allowed, she would wish to be tortured, demand to be placed on the fire and torn with blows. What are you up to, woman? You are rash: you are a woman and an old one. You may perhaps endure the first torments: but pain will overcome, and you will give way to the final ones. A wonderful thing to say, judges: 'Let him torture me: I am the mother.' Quite different [3] is a nurse, a slave, tortured by her master. Well? When you devote your last breath to uttering these words, to whom are we to deliver the boy? Will you want him to return to this father—and to that stepmother?

B. CICERO DELIBERATES WHETHER TO BEG ANTONY'S PARDON

This is a *suasoria*; it comes from a collection made by the elder Seneca, as an old man, in the reign of Tiberius. (Edition of *suasoriae* only by W. A. Edward (1928), with commentary: texts of *suasoriae* and *controversiae* by H. J. Müller (1887), H. Bornecque (2nd edn. 1932).)

Seneca's practice is to quote notable passages from various declaimers' treatment of the same theme, not complete speeches.

---

[1] i.e. he didn't dispute the claim of the poor man.   [2] i.e. fathers.
[3] And less credible under torture.

The subject of this exercise (*suas.* 6) was a favourite one; Cicero is given advice on whether or not to try to beg his life from Antony after the proscription of 43 B.C. §§ 1–7 contain extracts from declamations: §§ 8–14 describe how various speakers arranged their arguments, with a few choice epigrams (*sententiae*).

QUINTUS HATERIUS[1]

1 Let posterity know that the republic could have been Antony's slave, Cicero could not. You will have to praise Antony:[2] on that theme words will fail Cicero himself. Believe me, however carefully you control yourself, Antony will do something that Cicero could not pass over in silence. You must understand, Cicero, that he is not saying: 'Ask to live', but 'Ask to be a slave'. But how will you be able to enter the senate as it now is, cruelly drained, dishonourably replenished? Will you want to enter a senate where you cannot see Pompey, Cato, the Luculli, Hortensius, Lentulus, and Marcellus—or your own friends, Hirtius and Pansa, consuls both? Cicero, what place for you in an age not your own? Our day is over.

2   Cato, in himself the ultimate pattern for life and death, preferred to die rather than to beg (and he would not have had to beg Antony): in hands clean to the last of his people's blood he took a sword to strike his holy breast. Scipio,[3] his sword plunged into his breast, heard soldiers who had embarked on his ship looking for the general. 'The general', he said, 'is well.' Defeated, he uttered the words of a victor. 'Milo', you once said,[4] 'forbids me to beg his judges.' Beg Antony if you will.

PORCIUS LATRO

3 So does Cicero at last speak without Antony being afraid? Does Antony at last speak so as to frighten Cicero? Sulla's thirst for civil bloodshed returns to the state. At the triumvirs' auction not Roman taxes but Roman deaths are for sale. A single notice surpasses in disaster Pharsalus, Munda, Mutina. The heads of consuls are weighed for gold. Your words, Cicero, are in place: 'What times! What morals!'[5] You will see those eyes burning with cruelty and pride. You will see that face—not of a man but of

---

[1] What is known about Haterius and the other Augustan declaimers may be found in Bonner, op. cit., or in H. Bornecque, *Les Déclamations et les déclamateurs d'après Sénèque le père*, Lille, 1902.

[2] i.e. if he spares you.

[3] Q. Metellus Scipio, Pompey's father-in-law, who died after being defeated at Thapsus.   [4] *Pro Milone* 92, 105.   [5] *In Catilinam* I. 2.

Civil War. You will see the throat down which the wealth of Pompey passed, that torso strong as a gladiator's. You will see that place on the tribunal which once the Master of the Horse, whom a belch would have disgraced, defiled with his vomit.[1] Will you fall suppliant at those knees and beg for mercy? Will you give that voice, to which the people owes its safety, words abject and flattering? You should be ashamed: even Verres under proscription died more bravely.

CLAUDIUS MARCELLUS AESERNINUS

Let Cato, whose death you praised, come before your mind. Is anything 4 worth being indebted to Antony for your life?

CESTIUS PIUS

If you have regard to the loss the people will feel, Cicero, you will die too soon whenever you perish; if to what you achieved, you have lived long enough; if to the insults of fortune and the present state of the republic, you have lived far too long; if to the immortality of your works, you will live for ever.

POMPEIUS SILO

You can see that it is best not to live—if it is Antony who permits you to live. Will you be silent when Antony proclaims proscriptions and tears the state to shreds? Will even your groans not be free? I should rather the Roman people missed Cicero dead than alive.

TRIARIUS

'What Charybdis is so voracious? I say Charybdis—which, if it existed, 5 was a single animal: the Ocean itself could scarcely have sucked down so many different things at one and the same time.'[2] Do you imagine that Cicero can be saved from the clutches of *this* monster's rage?

ARELLIUS FUSCUS SENIOR

We rush from war to war. Victors abroad, we are slaughtered at home. At home, an internal enemy battens on our blood. When Rome is in this

[1] Cf. *Philippic* 2. 63.   [2] Ibid. 2. 67.

plight, Cicero—who could think otherwise?—lives only under duress. You will plead with Antony, Cicero, to your discredit: you will plead in vain. No base grave will hide your body: your virtue will not end with your life. Memory, eternal guardian of human works, source of perpetual
6 life to great men, shall give you to all time, sanctified: only your body will perish—fragile, ephemeral, prey to all disease, vulnerable to chance, exposed to proscription. But your mind, that was drawn from divine origins, suffering no old age and no death, will be freed of the heavy bonds that link it to the body and fly back to its abode, to the stars to which it is akin. Yet, if we have regard to your age, to the number of your years (a number never reckoned by the brave), you have passed sixty. You have clearly lived too long if you die the survivor of the republic. We have seen civil arms raging over the world: after battles in Italy and at Pharsalus, Egypt drained the blood of Rome. What cause for resentment if Antony has the power over Cicero that a eunuch of Alexandria had over Pompey? This is the death that comes to those who take refuge with those unworthy of them.

CORNELIUS HISPANUS

7 He who merely followed your lead has been proscribed. The whole list is just a prelude to *your* death. One triumvir allows the proscription of a brother, one of an uncle: what hope have *you*? All these parricides have been committed for Cicero to die! Recall your defences, your patronage, your consulship—greatest of your services: now you can understand that Cicero can be forced to die—but not to beg.

ARGENTARIUS

The luxurious banquets of the triumvir kings are laid out, the kitchen equipped with the tribute of nations. Himself, weak with wine and sleep, he raises drooping eyes to the heads of the proscribed. In this strait it is not enough to say: 'Wicked man!'[1]

DIVISION OF THE ARGUMENTS

8 Latro divided the *suasoria* thus: even if you can win your life from Antony, it is not worth so much to ask for it. Then: you cannot win it. In the first

---

[1] *Philippic* 2. 77.

part, he put the argument that it is shameful for any Roman, let alone Cicero, to beg for life. In this passage he placed instances of men who had voluntarily accepted death. Then: for Cicero life will be worthless in future, harsher than death now that liberty has gone. Here, he described all the bitterness of the slavery to come. Then: the bargain will not be kept. Here, after saying: 'There will be something to offend Antony: a deed or a word, a silence or a look', he added an epigram: 'Or else you will content him!'[1]

Albucius' division was different. His first point was: Cicero must die, 9 even if no one proscribed him. Here came an invective against the period. Then: he must die willingly, since he had to die even if he were unwilling. The hatred he aroused had serious causes; the greatest reason for the proscription was Cicero himself. Albucius was the only declaimer who ventured to say that Antony was not Cicero's sole enemy. Here he spoke the epigram: 'If there is any of the triumvirs who does not hate you, he finds you a nuisance'—and another very popular one: 'Ask, Cicero: beg one that you may be the slave of three.'

Cestius' division was as follows: it is expedient for you to die; it is 10 right; it is necessary, so that you may complete your life free and with undiminished authority. He produced the daring epigram: 'Thus you may be numbered with Cato, who could not be a slave even though Antony was not yet master.' Marcellus' epigram on Cato was better: 'Is everything as topsy-turvy as the Roman people's fortunes that some-one should be deliberating whether it is better to live with Antony or die with Cato?' But—to return to Cestius' division. He said it was expedient for Cicero to die to avoid bodily torture. Cicero would have no straight-forward death if he fell into Antony's hands. In this part he described the insults, blows, and tortures to be inflicted on Cicero, and introduced a much praised epigram: 'Cicero, when you come before Antony you will beg—for death.'

Varius Geminus' division was like this: 'I should advise you, if you 11 had to do one or the other now—die or beg—to die rather than beg.' He included all the points covered by the others: adding, however, a third main heading—he exhorted Cicero to exile. There was Brutus, there was Cassius, there was Sextus Pompeius. And he added an epigram highly admired by Cassius Severus: 'Why do we give way? The republic too has its triumvirs.' Next, he reviewed the regions he could make for. Sicily had been avenged by Cicero, Cilicia excellently administered in his proconsulship, Achaea and Asia were well known from his student days, the kingdom of Deiotarus was bound to him by services rendered, Egypt remembered a benefit and felt repentant for a perfidy. But he

---

[1] Text uncertain.

advised him most pressingly to go to Asia and Macedonia and the camp of Brutus and Cassius. So it was that Cassius Severus used to say that while others declaimed, Varius Geminus gave living advice.

12 Not many declaimers pleaded on the other side. Nobody, almost, ventured to advise Cicero to beg Antony's pardon: they thought too well of Cicero's spirit. Varius Geminus, however, took the opposite side also, saying: 'I hope I can persuade my friend Cicero to wish to live. His high-sounding words—"death not premature to an ex-consul or grievous to a wise man"[1]—do not sway me. He is a private citizen now; I know his ways well—he will do it, he will beg. As for slavery, he will not refuse it. His neck is already worn by the yoke—Pompey and Caesar broke him in. You see before you an experienced slave.' And he said many other facetious things, as usual.

13 His division was: he will be able to beg pardon with honour and with success. In the former part, he placed the argument that it is not shameful for the defeated to ask mercy from a victorious fellow citizen. Here he recalled how many had implored Caesar, and he mentioned Ligarius. Then: it was quite fair for Cicero to make satisfaction, having been the first to proscribe Antony and proclaim him enemy: satisfaction always starts from the defendant; let him be bold—and ask. Then: he will be begging not on behalf of his life but on behalf of the republic; Cicero had lived long enough for himself, not long enough for the state. In the second part, he said that enemies are constantly won over; Cicero himself had been reconciled and had defended Vatinius and Gabinius at their trials.[2] Antony could more easily be won over because he was one of three: he would be concerned to prevent either of the others from snatching this splendid chance for clemency from him. Perhaps Antony was angry

14 because he had not thought it worth his while to beg him. Varius described the danger of flight, and added that wherever he went he would still be a slave, would have to put up either with the violence of Cassius, the hauteur of Brutus, or the stupidity of Pompeius.

C. DECLAMATION AND THE FORUM

The prefaces to Seneca's collection of *controversiae* are full of genuine and interesting criticism. We quote first the Preface to Book 3.

1 I know several cases of eloquent speakers who did not match up to their reputation when they declaimed. In the forum they spoke to the admiration of all who heard them, but as soon as they retreated to our private exercises they were deserted by their talents. This frequent

---

[1] *Cat.* 4. 3.   [2] Having previously prosecuted them.

occurrence I find as surprising as it is undeniable. And I remember that I once asked Cassius Severus why it was that his eloquence failed him in declamation.

A SKETCH OF AN ORATOR

Now in no one could the contrast have been more striking. His oratory 2 was strong, polished, full of striking ideas; no one was less tolerant of the superfluous in his pleading; there was no part that did not stand on its own feet, no place where the listener could afford to let his attention wander. Everything was relevant and pointful. No one better controlled the emotions of his audience. My friend Gallio truly said of him: 'When he spoke, he was a king on his throne, so religiously did everyone do what they were told. When he required it, they were angry. Everyone was afraid, while he was speaking, in case he should stop.' It is impossible 3 to judge him from his publications, though even there one may sense his eloquence; he was far better heard than read. It happens to almost everyone that they gain from being heard rather than read, but to a smaller degree: in him there was a vastly greater gulf.

First of all, the man was as impressive as the talent. His body was noticeably big, his voice both sweet and strong (an infrequent combination, this), while his delivery would have made any actor's reputation, without being at all reminiscent of an actor's. For—and this is perhaps the most 4 remarkable thing about him—the dignity which he lacked in his life he possessed in his speech. So long as he steered clear of jokes, his oratory was worthy of a censor. Again, what he actually said was better than what he wrote. A man of resource, talented rather than studious, he gave more pleasure by his improvisations than by his prepared version. He spoke better when in a temper, and hence men took great care not to interrupt him—he was the only one to benefit by any onslaught on him; chance 5 always served him better than preparation. All the same, this gift never enticed him into negligence. In one day he would not give more than two private speeches, one before, one after midday. In public cases, his limit was one a day. I don't know that he ever defended anyone except himself: the only dangers that gave him any scope were his own. He never 6 spoke without notes, and he was not content merely with the sort that contains the bare bones of the speech, but to a large extent the whole would be written out. In this text, he used to note even possibilities for wit. However, though he was not ready to set off without equipment, he was glad to lay it aside. When he had to speak extempore, he excelled himself, and it always paid him to find himself in a tight corner rather than to be prepared; all the more remarkable that he did not abandon his care, even though his daring was so successful.

7   So he had everything that could equip him to be a good declaimer: choice diction, neither common nor low; a style of oratory that was not relaxed or languid but burning and spirited; developments neither slow nor empty, but richer in content than words; and finally the painstaking approach which is so great a stand-by even for a mediocre talent. But when he declaimed he fell below his own level—and that of many others: so he rarely did declaim—and only when his friends insisted.

CASSIUS EXPLAINS

8   Now when I asked him why he was inferior in declamation, he replied: 'What surprises you in me happens to almost everybody. When has great genius (hardly my category, I know) ever shown itself in more than one field? Cicero lost his eloquence when he wrote poetry; Virgil's abundant talents deserted him in prose; Sallust's speeches are read only as a compliment to the author of the *Histories*; the speech of the eloquent Plato on behalf of Socrates is worthy neither of defender nor defendant.

9   'So too with bodies, whose strength is not suited to everything that strength can accomplish. One man is unequalled in wrestling; one excels at raising a heavy load; one will not let go what he has taken a grip on, and when he puts his hands to a runaway carriage they will keep their hold. Animals also: some dogs are good for hunting the boar, others the stag. Not all horses, however swift, have speed suitable for racing; some bear a

10   rider better, some a yoke. To take examples from my own vice: Pylades in comedy, Bathyllus in tragedy are quite unlike their normal selves. My namesake's feet are swift—everyone concedes that, some even criticize him for it—but his hands are slower.[1] Some fight better with fully-armed gladiators, others with the lighter equipped; some desire, others fear to be matched against a left-hander.

'As to oratory, the material may be the same, but the good arguer narrates carelessly; in another the development is inferior to the preliminaries. When my friend Passienus begins to speak, there is general flight after his proem—but we return in force for his epilogue: what comes

11   between is heard only by those who cannot avoid it. Is there anything odd in a man not declaiming as well as he pleads? Or in another not treating *suasoriae* so well as legal *controversiae*? Pompeius Silo, when he is seated, displays eloquence and education, and would be regarded as an orator if he got rid of his audience after his preamble. But he declaims so badly

---

[1] Presumably a boxer.

that it was right of me to wish for him "never to get up". Eloquence is a great and varied gift, and is never so indulgent as to attend one man without flaw; you are lucky if you are received into one part of it.

'However, I may be able to give you a reason peculiar to me. I am used [12] to keeping my eye on the judge, not the audience. I am used to replying to my opponents, not to myself. I avoid the superfluous as well as the contradictory. Everything is superfluous in a declamation: declamation is superfluous. I will tell you what I feel. When I speak in the forum, I am doing something. When I declaim (to use Censorinus' excellent phrase of zealous candidates for local office) I seem to be toiling in a dream. Again, [13] the two things are quite different: it is one thing to fight, quite another to shake your fist. The school has always been taken to be a sort of game, the forum as an arena—hence the word 'tiro' for the maiden speaker in the courts. Come on, bring your declaimers into senate and forum! With their surroundings they will change their character. They will be like bodies used to the closet and luxurious shade, unable to stand in the open and put up with rain and sun. They will scarcely know where they are: they are used to being eloquent at their own rating. There is no point in judging an [14] orator amid these childish pursuits. How could you test a helmsman on a fish-pond? I should take more pains in my defence (pleading that I am not born for such things) if I didn't know that Asinius Pollio, Messalla Corvinus, and Passienus (now our leading orator) are rated as declaimers below Cestius or Latro. Is this the fault of the speakers—or their hearers? [15] They are not worse speakers; the audience is judging by worse standards. It is boys, usually, or youths who throng the schools: and they prefer their Cestius to the eloquent men I mentioned—and they'd prefer him to Cicero if they didn't fear a stoning. They do prefer him to Cicero, in fact, in the one way open to them: they learn all Cestius' declamations. Cicero's speeches they do not read—except the ones to which Cestius has written replies.

MOCKERY OF CESTIUS

'I recall that I once went into his school when he was going to recite a [16] speech against Milo. Cestius, with his usual admiration for his own works, said: "If I were a Thracian, I should be Fusius. If I were a mime, I should be Bathyllus. If I were a horse, I should be Melissio." I couldn't contain my rage. I shouted: "If you were a drain, you'd be the Great Drain." Universal laughter. The scholastics looked at me to discover who this lout was. Cestius, who had taken on himself to reply to Cicero, could find nothing to reply to me, and he said he wouldn't go on if I didn't leave. I said I wouldn't leave the bath until I'd had my wash.

17 'After that, I resolved to revenge Cicero on Cestius, in the courts. Soon, I met him and summoned him before the praetor, and when I'd had enough of deriding and abusing him, I requested the praetor to admit a charge under the law on unspecified offences. Cestius was so worried that he asked for an adjournment. Next, I haled him off to a second praetor and accused him of ingratitude.[1] Finally, before the Urban Praetor, I requested a keeper for him. His friends, who had thronged to the spectacle, put in a word for him, and in response to them I said I should give no further trouble if he swore he was less eloquent than Cicero. But neither joke nor serious argument would induce him to that.

18 'I've told you this tale to show that declamations breed a virtually separate race of men. To be comparable with them, I need not more genius but less sense. So I can scarcely be persuaded to declaim: and when I am, it is only before my best friends.'

And so he did. His declamations were unequal, but what stood out in them were things that would have made any declamation look unequal. His rhythm was harsh, and avoided periodic structure. His epigrams were lively. But it would be unfair to judge him from the extracts that follow. They don't show him at his best; but they are what I best remember.

D. OVID IN THE SCHOOLS

From *Controversiae* 2. 2. 8–9, 12.

8 I remember this *controversia* being declaimed by Ovid at the school of the rhetor Arellius Fuscus, whose pupil he was. Ovid greatly admired Latro, though his style of speaking was quite different. Ovid had a polished, tasteful, and attractive talent. His oratory even then was no more than poetry without the verse. He had put his attendance at Latro's declamations to such good use that he transferred many of Latro's epigrams into his own verses. On the Judgement of Arms, Latro had said: 'Let us loose off the weapons at the enemy, then go and retrieve them.' Ovid wrote:

> Let the hero's arms be hurled amidst the foe:
> bid them retrieve them *thence*.[2]

And this was not the only idea that he borrowed from Latro's treatment of that *suasoria*. I recall Latro in a preamble saying something that the schoolboys learnt off as a sort of tag: 'Do you not see how a torch unmoved is dim, but shaken gives out its fires? Leisure softens men; iron

---

[1] Bonner, op. cit. 86–8, discusses the legal aspects of these charges.
[2] *Metamorphoses* 13. 121–2.

is worn down by disuse and gathers rust; sloth brings forgetfulness.'
Ovid wrote:

> I have seen the flames grow when a torch is shaken,
> but die again when no one brandishes it.[1]

Well, when he was a student, he was regarded as a good declaimer. At 9
least, he declaimed this *controversia* before Arellius Fuscus (in my opinion)
with particular skill, except that he ran through the commonplaces without any sort of order . . .

But Ovid rarely declaimed *controversiae*, and then only when they 12
involved portrayal of character. He was keener on *suasoriae*: he hated all
argumentation. He was not unduly free in his use of words except in
poetry, where he was well aware of his faults—and liked them. This is
clear from an incident when he was asked by his friends to get rid of three
of his verses; in exchange he asked that he should be allowed to make
an exception of three verses which they could not touch. This seemed a
fair condition. They wrote down privately the ones they wanted damned:
he wrote down the ones he wanted saved. Both sheets contained the same
verses. The first (according to an eyewitness, Albinovanus Pedo) was:

> half-bull man and half-man bull,[2]

the second:

> the freezing North wind and the unfreezing South.[3]

From which it is clear that this talented man lacked the will rather than
the taste to restrain the licence of his poetry. He used sometimes to say
that a face was all the more beautiful for a mole.

E. THE DECAY OF ORATORY

From the Preface to Book 1 of the *Controversiae*, §§ 6–10. A common first-
century theme: cf. Tacitus, *Dialogus* (below, p. 432); 'Longinus' 44 (below,
p. 501).

My boys, you are doing something necessary and useful in not being 6
satisfied with the models provided by your own day and wanting
to get to know those of the last generation.[4] For one thing, the more

---

[1] *Amores* 1. 2. 11–12.   [2] *Art of Love* 2. 24.
[3] *Amores* 2. 11. 10.
[4] Cf. on imitation Quint. 10. 2 (below, p. 400) and 'Longinus' (below, p. 475).

patterns you examine, the greater advantage to your eloquence. You should not imitate one man, however distinguished, for an imitator never comes up to the level of his model. This is the way things are; the copy always falls short of the original. Moreover, you can by these means judge how sharply standards are falling every day, how far some grudge on nature's part has sent eloquence downhill. Everything that Roman oratory has to match the arrogant Greeks (or even prefer to them)

7 reached its peak in Cicero's day: all the geniuses who have brought brilliance to our subject were born then. Since then things have got worse daily. Perhaps this is due to the luxury of the age (nothing is so fatal to talent as luxury); perhaps, as this great art became less prized, competitiveness transferred itself wholly to sordid affairs that bring great prestige and profit; perhaps it is just Fate, whose grim law is universal— things that get to the top sink back to the bottom faster than they

8 rose. Look how lazy and sleepy-minded our young men are; no one can stay awake at night to work at one honest pursuit. Sleep, languor, and an activity for evil that is more shameful than either have seized hold of their minds. Libidinous delight in song and dance transfixes these effeminates. Waving the hair, raising the tone of the voice till it is as caressing as a woman's, competing in bodily softness with women, beautifying themselves with indecent cosmetics—this is the pattern our youth set themselves!

9   Which of your contemporaries—quite apart from his talent and his studiousness—is enough of a man? Born feeble and spineless, they stay like that throughout their lives; enemies of others' chastity, careless of their own. God prevent *them* being blessed with eloquence—something for which I should have scant respect if it exercised no choice in those on whom it bestowed itself. That well-known saying of Cato was really an oracle—and you are wrong, my dear young men, if you fail to realize it. For surely an oracle is the divine will given human expression: and what high priest could the gods have found more holy than Marcus Cato, not so much to teach mankind as to abuse it? What, then, was it that he said?

10 'An orator, son Marcus, is a good man skilled in speaking.'[1] Go and look for orators among the smooth and hairless of today, men only in their lusts. As one would expect, they have models as depraved as their intellects. Who cares for his future renown? Who is made popular—I won't say by great qualities—but even by qualities that are his own? Undetected by a casual public, they can easily pass off as their own epigrams let drop by really eloquent speakers, constantly violating the holiness of an eloquence they cannot attain.

[1] Cf. Quint. 12. 1 (below, p. 417).

F. THE ABSURDITIES OF DECLAMATION

Complaints about the unreality and absurdity of declamations are common in the first century.[1] We give perhaps the most entertaining of such attacks: the first preserved passage of Petronius' *Satyricon* (1–4). This was written before A.D. 66. The narrator is Encolpius; Agamemnon is a rhetor.

Text: K. Müller, Munich, 1961. See J. P. Sullivan, *The Satyricon of Petronius: a Literary Study*, London, 1968.

'It must be the same sort of Fury that irritates the declaimers who shout: "These wounds I received for the freedom of all: this eye I forfeited for you. Give me a guide to lead me to my children; my knees are hamstrung and will not support my body." Even this would be bearable if it paved the way for aspirers to eloquence. As it is, their only profit from their inflated material, their empty clamour of epigram, is that when they get into court they think they've been deposited in another world. My view is that youths get exceedingly stupid in school, and this is because they neither hear nor see anything there that one is normally acquainted with, but only pirates in chains on the beach, tyrants writing edicts instructing sons to cut off their fathers' heads, oracles ordering that three or more virgins should be sacrificed to remedy a plague, honeyed balls of words, everything that's done or said coated with poppy-seed and sesame.

'Boys brought up amidst all this have as much chance of being sensible as the inhabitant of a kitchen has of smelling nice. Don't be offended if I say that it is you people, first and foremost, who have destroyed eloquence. By stirring up outrageous effects amid trivial and empty sounds, you have made the body of oratory effeminate and drooping. Youths weren't confined to declamation when Sophocles and Euripides found words they could not but use. The scholar in his shady retreat had not yet stamped out genius when Pindar and the nine lyricists hesitated to write in Homeric verse. And, to leave poets out of account, I am sure neither Plato nor Demosthenes got involved with this style of exercise. Grand and, so to say, respectable speech is not tainted or turgid: it abounds in a beauty that is natural. It is only recently that grotesque and windy loquacity has migrated from Asia to Athens, and infected students of high aspirations like some pestilential planet.[2] The pattern once become decadent, eloquence came to a halt, fell silent. Who after them reached the heights of Thucydides, the reputation of Hyperides? There was not so much as a poem of healthy complexion to shed its brilliance

---

[1] Cf. Tacitus, *Dialogus* 35 (below, p. 454).

[2] Cf. Dionysius (above, p. 306), Cicero, *Brutus* 51 (above, p. 224). Note the tendentious 'recently'—the change, if a real one, happened in Hellenistic times.

abroad; everything was fed on the same food, and could not reach the white hairs of old age. Painting suffered the same fate, too, once the daring Egyptians found a short-cut for *that* great art.

3   'Agamemnon wouldn't let me declaim in the colonnade any longer than he'd sweated it out in the school. "Young man," he said, "your conversation is of no vulgar stamp. What is rarest of all, you approve of good sense. So I shall not deprive you of the secrets of my trade. No wonder teachers go astray in these exercises; they think they must rave in the company of the mad. Unless they say the sort of things the youth will like, they will be left, as Cicero[1] put it, alone in the schools. Flatterers in search of a rich man's hospitality rehearse nothing more readily than what they suppose will be most acceptable to their hearer—they won't get what they're after without laying some ambush for the ear. So with the teacher of eloquence. Unless, like a fisherman, he arms his hook with the sort of bait he knows the fish will like, he's left stuck on his rock, with no chance of a catch.

4   "What are we to conclude? The parents are to blame: they don't want their sons to prosper under stern discipline. Like everything else, their young hopefuls are sacrificed to ambition. Again, in a hurry to reach their aims, they thrust still raw lads into the courts, and clothe new-born kids in eloquence—though proclaiming that nothing is more important. If they only allowed for gradations of study, so that the studious young could be immersed in serious reading, form their minds in the precepts of philosophy, strike out wantonnesses with a savage pen, listen long to favoured objects of their imitation, if they got used to the idea that nothing is splendid that boys enjoy—*then* the old great oratory would have its proper weight and dignity. As it is, the children play at school: when they are youths they get laughed at in the forum. Worse than either, the mistakes a man imbibed at school he is disinclined to admit to in his old age."

G. STYLES AND MORALS

This is the first of three extracts from the younger Seneca, the second son of the 'rhetor' on whom we have been drawing. These letters were written A.D. 62-4, and deal with a variety of problems, mostly in ethics. Edition: L. D. Reynolds, Oxford, 1965. Commentary on selected letters (including 40 and 114) by W. C. Summers, London, 1910.

This letter (114) was regarded by Eduard Norden as the most important document for the history of first-century prose. It is illuminating to compare Seneca's strictures on Maecenas with the views of contemporaries and successors

[1] *Pro Caelio* 41.

on Seneca himself: the Emperor Caligula called Seneca's works mere prize-day speeches, 'sand without lime'; Quintilian (10. 1. 125, below, p. 399) solemnly warns the young against the 'pleasing vices' of Seneca's style.

Why, you ask, have certain periods seen the appearance of a corrupt 1 style of speech? How is it that writers have veered into different sorts of fault—so that sometimes bombast has prevailed, sometimes emasculated song-like oratory? Why have bold extravagant ideas found favour at one time, at another abrupt dark sayings in which there was more to be understood than heard? Why was there a time when immoderate use was made of the privilege of metaphor? The answer lies in a common saying—one that is proverbial in Greek: 'As are men's lives, so is their speech.'

Now just as each man's actions are like his style of speaking, so style 2 in oratory sometimes apes the *mores* of society—if the community's standards have slipped and it has given itself over to dissoluteness. Abandoned speech is a sign of public luxury, so long, that is, as such speech is not confined to a few but is generally approved and accepted.

One's intellect and one's personality cannot have different com- 3 plexions. If the personality is healthy, if it is sedate, serious, and restrained, the intellect too is dry and sober. When the personality is corrupted, the intellect too is infected. If the personality is depressed, you can see the limbs dragging, the feet trailing. If the personality is effeminate, the softness is expressed in the very gait. If it is fierce and fiery, the step quickens. If it is mad—or, what is hardly different, angry—the body's movement is troubled: it is carried along willy-nilly. But surely this is even more the case with one's intellect, which is inextricably mixed with the mind—is formed by it, obeys it, looks to it for orders.

LIFE AND STYLE OF MAECENAS

How Maecenas lived is too well known for me to have to relate here how 4 he walked, how fastidious he was, how he longed to be seen, how he had no wish to hide his faults. So? Is not his style as lax as the man himself was abandoned? Aren't his words as conspicuous as his dress, his company, his house, his wife? He would have been a great genius if he had taken a straighter road, and not tried to avoid being understood, extending his dissoluteness to his style. The result is a drunkard's eloquence, complex, wandering, abandoned. What could be worse than these phrases? 5

'Water and woods on the bank leafy.'
'Furrow the bed with the boat, and by stirring the shallows move back the gardens.'

'Wrinkles his face with a wink to a lady, bills with his lips and sighing
begins, as the monarchs of the glade rut with neck adroop.'
'A conspiracy beyond redemption, they ferret out with feasting, batter
households with the bottle, demand death for hope.'
'Genius scarcely to be invoked on its own festal day.'
'Threads of slim candle and spluttering grain.'
'The fireside mother or wife drape.'[1]

6 When you read this, you are immediately struck that this is the man
who always walked the streets with his tunic loose (for even when he was
deputizing for the absent Augustus, it was an unbelted Maecenas that
gave the watchword for the day); who at the tribunal, at the rostrum, in
every public gathering could be seen with his head wrapped in his
cloak—only his ears sticking out—like nothing so much as a rich man's
runaway slave in a mime. This was the man who, when the civil wars
were raging at their worst, when the city was in arms and anxious, had
as his bodyguard two eunuchs—and they more men than he; the man
who married one wife—a thousand times.

7 These words so licentiously arranged, so negligently flung down, so
abnormally employed, show us that his character was no less strange,
depraved, and individual. The best thing we can say of him is that he was
kind; he spared the sword, abstained from blood-letting—only in his
licence did he show his possibilities. But this compliment is spoiled by
those portentous self-indulgences in his speech; it is clear that he was
8 soft, not gentle. From that labyrinthine arrangement, those words that
lie in wait to trip you, those extraordinary sentiments, often grand, but
emasculated even in the utterance, anyone can see the truth: too much
luck had turned his head.

9 This sometimes happens to a man, sometimes to an age. When pros-
perity has spread luxury far and wide, in the first place dress starts to
become more elaborate; then trouble is taken over furniture; then care is
lavished on the very houses, so that they extend freely into the country,
walls shining with imported marble, roofs brightened with gold, ceilings
and floors reflecting each other's brilliance. Then lavishness moves on to
food: compliments are sought for novelty of dish or change of the normal
order, the dessert placed first, hors-d'œuvres offered to the parting guest.

10 Once the mind has grown accustomed to despising the normal and feeling
that the usual is stale, it looks for novelty in speech too. Sometimes it
recalls old worn-out words and trots them out again; sometimes it mints
new ones or varies familiar ones; sometimes—as has been popular
recently—bold and frequent metaphor is regarded as smart.

---

[1] These examples are all very obscure, and the translation we offer is tentative.

There are some who cut short their sentences, and hope the effect will **11**
please if the thought remains in the air, challenging the hearer to distrust
its surface meaning; there are others who hold sentences up, and stretch
them out; there are yet others who don't just run into faults—that is
inevitable if your aims are high—but who love faults for their own sake.[1]

Thus, wherever you see that a corrupt style of speech finds favour,
you may be sure that morals too have gone astray. Luxury in feasting and
clothes are signs of an ailing society; so, too, licentious speech, where
widely spread, shows the degeneracy of the minds from which it proceeds.
You need not wonder at the acceptance of the corrupt by the intelligentsia **12**
as well as the mob; their only difference is in their togas, not in their
discernment. You may wonder more that faults find approval as well as
faulty works. One thing has always been true: no talent has merited
favour without allowance having to be made. Mention any man of high
reputation: I will tell you what his age had to forgive him, what it deliberately ignored in him. I can give examples of many who were not
harmed by their faults, some who were helped by them. I can mention
men of the highest fame, held up to us for our admiration, who would
be destroyed by being corrected. Vices and virtues are inextricably
linked: vices carry virtues along with them.

TYPES OF CORRUPT STYLE

Speech has no fixed rules: it is controlled by the usage of a country— **13**
and that never stays the same for long. Many hunt for words out of a
different century; theirs is Twelve-Table talk.[2] Gracchus and Crassus
and Curio are too smart, too new for them—they go back to Appius and
Coruncanius.[3] On the other hand, others want nothing that is not well-
worn by custom, and so fall into meanness. Both types are corrupt in **14**
different ways; no less, surely, than the practice of using only splendid,
resounding poetic words while avoiding ordinary everyday ones. One
man errs as much as the other; one is unduly elegant, the other unduly
negligent; one shaves even his legs, the other lets the hair grow under his
arms.

Let us pass to the rhythm of sentences. How many kinds of fault shall **15**
I produce here? Some want their structure broken and rough; if anything
comes out smoothly, they disturb it on purpose; they want no join to
lack its jolt; they think a sentence which strikes the ear by its lack of
symmetry to be virile and strong. Some go in for singing, not rhythm—

[1] Cf. the elder Seneca on Ovid (above, p. 359).
[2] i.e. the archaism of the primitive code of law.
[3] i.e. they go back beyond the pre-Ciceronian orators to very remote times.

such is the insinuation and smooth flow of their style. Then there is the
16 structure in which words are delayed: you have to wait for them—and
they scarcely arrive in time for the *clausula*. Or the kind that is slow to
reach an end, like Cicero's, gently sloping, softly restraining the hurrying
reader, never surprising in its customary metre.

There is a further fault in types of epigram—if they are trifling and
childish, or bold and daring beyond the bounds of decency: if they are
flowery and sickly-sweet, if they finish in a vacuum and have no effect
but of sound.

17 Faults like these are introduced by some individual who at a particular time dominates eloquence; others imitate them, and pass them
on one to another. Thus, when Sallust was at his height, smartness
consisted in the use of sentences cut short, unexpected halts, a dark
conciseness. Lucius Arruntius, a man of remarkable austerity, author
of a history of the Punic War, was a Sallustian—*that* was where he let
himself go. Sallust has: 'He made an army with silver'—that is, he raised
it by means of money.[1] Arruntius fell in love with this: he put it on every
page. At one point he said: 'They made a flight for our men'; at another:
'Hiero, king of Syracuse, made a war'; at another: 'This news made the
18 Panormitans yield to the Romans.' I only wanted to give you a taste;
the whole book is a patchwork of these expressions. What was rare in
Sallust becomes frequent in Arruntius—almost continuous. The reason
is clear: Sallust fell into such usages by chance, Arruntius went out to
look for them. You see what happens when a fault becomes a model.

19 Sallust said: 'When the seas wintered'; Arruntius in Book One of
the *Punic War* said: 'Suddenly the storm wintered.' And at another point,
where he wanted to say that the year was a cold one, he said: 'The
whole year wintered', and elsewhere: 'Then he sent off sixty merchant-
ships, lightly laden except for the soldiers and necessary crew, while the
north wind wintered.' He can't stop stuffing this word in everywhere.
Sallust says somewhere: 'While amid civil arms he sought fames for fairness and goodness.' Arruntius could not restrain himself from putting in
right away in the first book that there were great 'fames' about Regulus.

20 These faults, and ones like them, that imitation instils, are not signs of
luxury or a corrupted mind. You must judge a man's feelings from things
that truly belong to him, that are inborn; an angry man's speech is angry,
21 a disturbed man's unduly excited, a fastidious man's soft and fluid. Look
at the intention of those who pluck their beards or thin them, who shave
their lips close but leave the rest to grow, who wear cloaks of daring
colours, or transparent togas, who don't want to do anything that could
escape the attention of their fellow men: they are provoking them, in-

[1] This and the other passages from Sallust are from the lost *Histories*.

sisting on them taking notice, happy even to be criticized so long as they are not ignored. Such is the style of Maecenas and all the others whose fault is not due to chance but to their conscious will.

This arises from a great defect of character: when a man drinks wine, 22 his mind has to give way to the pressure, overthrown and betrayed, before his tongue starts to stammer; similarly, what I can only call drunkenness of style causes nobody trouble before the mind starts slipping. It is therefore the mind that needs treatment: it causes thoughts, produces words, it dictates to us our gait, countenances, dress. When it is healthy and sound, speech is strong too, tough and virile; if it is overthrown the rest follows its ruin. 'When the king is unharmed, all 23 have a common purpose; when he is lost, they break their faith.'[1] Our king is the mind; when it is unharmed the rest remain at their posts, obey, serve; when it totters a little, they begin to doubt. But when it has given way to pleasure, its skills and actions decay also, and all its impulses are enfeebled.

[The rest of the letter is not literary in interest; Seneca moralizes on cupidity.]

H. SPEED IN ORATORY

Seneca does not approve of too rapid delivery in philosophical lectures (*Epist.* 40. 11–14).

But there are some things, I think, more suitable or less suitable for 11 whole races as well. Among the Greeks this freedom[2] is tolerable; but the Romans are accustomed to punctuate even in writing. Our great Cicero, source of Roman eloquence, was an ambler. The Roman language is more watchful of itself; it examines itself, and is open to examination. Fabianus,[3] a man excellent in character and learning and also—a 12 secondary thing—in eloquence, used to argue readily rather than passionately. You could talk of his fluency rather than his speed. Speed I am prepared to tolerate in a wise man, but I don't demand it. So long as his speech issues unimpeded, I would rather it were brought forth deliberately than came pouring out.

Here is another reason to deter you from that disease. Speed is only 13 possible if you stop feeling shame; it involves growing a thick skin and failing to listen to your own words; unguarded flow of language carries with it much that you would wish to criticize. Speed, I say it again, cannot 14

---

[1] Virgil, *Georgics* 4. 212–13.   [2] i.e. to speak without pause, like Haterius.
[3] See the next extract.

come your way without harming your modesty. You need daily exercise for it, and concentration has to shift from matter to words. Even if they are available and can flow with no trouble on your part, words must be kept under control. A modest gait suits the wise man; so does a style that is concise and unadventurous. The sum total of my advice is: speak slowly.

I. THE STYLE FOR A PHILOSOPHER

In this letter (100) Seneca discusses Papirius Fabianus, an eloquent moralist of the early first century A.D.

1   You tell me you have devoured Papirius Fabianus' volumes on *Politics* —and that they disappointed you. You forget a philosopher is in question, and criticize his style. Suppose it is true, as you say, that he pours words out instead of aiming them. First, that pleases, in its way; writing that gently glides on has its individual charm: it makes a vast difference, I think, if it comes tumbling out or flows out smoothly. And here is another

2 great distinction: Fabianus, in my view, does not pour words away—he just pours them. His style is free, untroubled, yet flowing. It bears all over it the signs of lack of elaboration or over-long attention. Still, let us have it your way; it was character he was ordering, not words: he wrote this for the mind, not the ear.

3   Further, if he had spoken it himself, you would have had no time to scrutinize details: the whole would have swept you on. Generally what pleases heard at speed is less rewarding when pondered over. But it *is* a great thing to hold the gaze at a first glance, even if careful examination

4 will find something to condemn. If you ask me, it is better to sweep judgement off its feet than to win it over; and yet I know the latter is safer, I know he's promising himself a bolder effort in the future. Anxious writing does not suit the philosopher. If he fears for his words, how will

5 he ever be brave and firm, how will he ever put himself at risk? Fabianus was not careless in his style: he was free of care for it. You will, therefore, find nothing vulgar. His words are chosen without being hunted down. They are not, in the manner of the day, unnaturally placed or switched about; they are splendid—yet taken from the common stock. You have here upright and fine sentiments, not cramped into epigram but freely expanded. It remains to be seen what lacks concision, structure, the latest gloss: but when you look around at the whole, you will notice no

6 cramped nonsense. There may be no contrasted marble, no central heating, no pauper's cell, none of the other complications introduced by

the luxury for which simple elegance is not enough; but it is, as they say, a sound house.[1]

WORD-ARRANGEMENT

Moreover, there is no agreed view on word-arrangement. Some would like its roughness smoothed away; others are so keen on jagged edges that they purposely disarrange an order that chance had deployed too effeminately, and cut cadences short before they can answer to our expectation. Look at Cicero. His word-arrangement is homogeneous and bends its 7 steps gently and softly, though without any indecency. Yet that of Asinius Pollio is uneven, impetuous, liable to leave you where you least expect. In fact, in Cicero everything comes to a halt, in Pollio everything falls flat—except for a few passages confined to one definite pattern.

FABIANUS—AND HIS BETTERS

You go on to say that everything in Fabianus' books seems to you slight 8 and abject. In my judgement, that is not one of his faults. His work is not slight, but calm, shaped to an even and composed way of thinking: not low but flat. It lacks the vigour of oratory, and your favourite sudden and stimulating jabs of epigram. But you must surely see how elegant and decent is the whole effect. His style does not have dignity: it will confer dignity.

Bring forward conceivable superiors of Fabianus. There is Cicero, 9 who wrote almost as many books about philosophy as Fabianus. I concede that point—but to be inferior to the best does not automatically make a thing contemptible. There is Asinius Pollio. I concede that point: the reply is that in so important a matter to be third is to be outstanding. I can add Livy (for he wrote both professedly philosophical works and dialogues as much historical as philosophical): I make room for him also. Our man is defeated by three—the most eloquent: consider to how many he must be superior!

But he does not have everything. His style is elevated, but not auda- 10 cious: fluent, but not violent or torrential: pure but not clear. You say: 'One may look in vain for words that are harsh to combat vice, spirited to combat danger, proud to oppose fortune, abusive to oppose ambition. I want luxury reviled, lust disgraced, passion broken. There should be an element of oratorical savageness, tragic grandeur, comic delicacy.' You are asking him to labour over a tiny thing—words; *he* has devoted himself

---

[1] For this metaphor cf. Tacitus, *Dialogus* 22 (below, p. 446).

to the grandeur of his subject, unconsciously trailing his eloquence
11 behind him, like a shadow. No, the details will not be weighed and concentrated; not every word will provoke and prick. Many things will
emerge without making an impact; sometimes what is said will slip
casually by. Yet everything will be brightly lit, spacious without tedium.
One crowning achievement: he makes it clear that he meant what he
wrote. You cannot fail to notice that the point is that you are to know what
pleases him—not that h should please you. Everything aims at the reader's
improvement, at his moral welfare. Applause is not the goal.

12 That, I have no doubt, is the character of his writings—so far as my
recollection goes; I haven't got them in mind, and their tone remains
with me not familiarly through recent intercourse, but in a general
way, as happens with acquaintances from the past. Anyway, that is what
I thought of them when I sat at his feet: that they were full without
being solid, designed to uplift the right-minded youth and, without
making him despair of bettering them, summon him on to emulation—
surely the most effective method of exhortation. The man who makes
you want to imitate him while leaving you no hope of success is merely a
deterrent. But he had words in plenty; he did not try to make you admire
the detail, but he is splendid as a whole.

J. SENECA ON HIS PREDECESSORS

We conclude with a passage from Aulus Gellius (*Nights in Attica* 12. 2: ed.
P. K. Marshall, Oxford, 1968), which gives us both a judgement on Seneca
himself, written from the standpoint of the mid second century, and a report
on Seneca's own view of Cicero, Ennius, and Virgil.

1 Some think of Seneca as a singularly unhelpful writer whose books
there is no point in opening—his style being common and banal, the
content and thought either storming on foolishly and vacuously or
marked by a cheap lawyer's smartness, while his learning is regarded as
vulgar and plebeian, with no trace of older writings to give it attractiveness or weight. Others, again, while not denying that his language is not
elegant enough, say that he doesn't lack knowledge of the things he says,
and that the impressive severity he applies to the criticism of vice is not
2 disagreeable. I don't need to pass judgement on his talent and achievement in general; I put forward for consideration the nature of his own
judgements on Cicero, Ennius, and Virgil.
3 In the twenty-second book of the *Moral Epistles to Lucilius*, he
describes as quite ridiculous these verses of Ennius about the antique
Cethegus:

he once was called by the citizens
who lived then and passed their lives
the choice flower of the people, the marrow of Persuasion.[1]

He added on these same verses: 'I am surprised that men of great eloquence, 4
men devoted to Ennius, should have praised what is laughable as though
it were first-rate. At least, Cicero includes these among Ennius' good
lines'.

Of Cicero, too, he says: 'I am not surprised that there was a man 5
capable of writing these verses when there was one capable of praising
them: unless, perhaps, the great orator Cicero was pleading his own cause,
and wanted his own poetry to seem good.' Later he added this fatuous 6
comment: 'In Cicero himself you may find, even in his prose, indications
that he didn't waste the time he spent on reading Ennius.' He then puts 7
down what he criticizes as Ennian in Cicero, from *On the Republic*:
'Since Menelaus the Spartan had a certain sweet-speaking attractiveness',
and elsewhere: 'He cultivates brief-speaking in oratory.'[2] At this point 8
our trifler makes excuses for Cicero's mistakes: 'This was not the fault
of Cicero, but of his time. These things had to be said when those verses
found readers.' Then he adds that Cicero in fact inserted these words to 9
avoid being condemned for having too luxuriant and pretty a style.

In the same passage he says on Virgil: 'Our Virgil, too, put in some 10
harsh, monstrous, and over-long lines just so that a public steeped in
Ennius could find an element of archaism in a modern poem.'

I'm getting tired of Seneca's remarks. But I can't leave out some jokes 11
by this foolish and humourless man. 'There are some sentiments in
Quintus Ennius so grand that, though written when men smelled of the
goat, they may yet please when men smell of unguents.' And (after
criticizing those verses on Cethegus): 'Those who like verses of this kind
clearly admire beds made even by Sotericus.'

Obviously Seneca deserves to be read and studied by youth, if he com- 12
pares the splendour and attraction of the old style to the beds of
Sotericus—ones of no beauty, obsolete and scorned. All the same you 13
may hear people recalling some dicta of Seneca that *are* good, such as
what he said in criticism of a greedy avaricious money-grubber: 'What
difference does it make how much you have? What you do not have is
much more.' That is good, isn't it? But youth is so constituted that it 14
is less helped by good sayings than infected by bad—and much more so
if the worse predominate and some of the bad are used not to promote
some triviality but as advice in a crisis.

[1] Ennius, *Annales* 306.   [2] *De republica* 5. 11.

9

QUINTILIAN AND PLINY

QUINTILIAN

M. Fabius Quintilianus, of Spanish descent (as were the Senecas), had a long career as an imperially-favoured teacher of rhetoric in Rome. His great work, *Institutio Oratoria*, was written about A.D. 95. This 'education of an orator' covers the rhetorical training from the cradle to the grave.

Text: L. Radermacher, Leipzig, 1907, 1935; M. Winterbottom, Oxford, 1970.

Source-discussion and bibliography: J. Cousin, *Études sur Quintilien*, Paris, 1936; supplemented in *Lustrum* 7, 1962, 289 ff.

Loeb translation by H. E. Butler, London, 1921–2.

A. DECLAMATION AND REALITY

Our first extract (2. 10) gives Quintilian's views on the central feature of contemporary education, declamation: cf. Tacitus, *Dialogus* 35 (below, p. 454).

1 Once a boy has been well trained and sufficiently practised in these elementary exercises (which are not in themselves trivial, but rather the parts and so to say limbs of greater things), it will usually be time to approach deliberative and forensic topics. Before I get on to them, however, I must say a few words about the actual *raison d'être* of declamation —the most recently developed of all methods of training but far the most

2 useful. It contains within it virtually all the exercises I have mentioned, and gives the nearest approximation to reality; and so it has become prevalent to the extent that many people think it all that is needed to shape eloquence, there being no quality at least of continuous oratorical prose that is not found as well in this kind of preparation for oratory.

3 Thanks to its teachers it has now so degenerated that the licentious ignorance of declaimers has become one of the principal causes for the corruption of eloquence. But things that are naturally good can be put

4 to good use. We must ensure, then, that even fictitious topics should be as near as possible to real life, and that declamation, as far as may be, should follow the pattern of the speeches it was invented to train for.

5 For wizards and plagues and oracles and stepmothers crueller than those on the tragic stage and other still more fabulous phenomena will be

looked for in vain amid the stipulations and interdicts of the court.
Are we then never to permit youths to treat these unreal and indeed
poetic themes, giving them a chance to spread themselves and enjoy
their topic and as it were put on weight? That would indeed be best; but 6
at least let the themes be grand and even inflated without also being absurd
and laughable to the keen observer, so that, if we *are* to make this concession, the declaimer may sometimes stuff himself, so long as he realizes
that he must keep his fat down and be purged of any corrupt humours that
he accumulates if he wants to be strong and healthy (similarly, animals
swollen with green-stuffs are treated by blood-letting and can then get
back to foods that will keep them strong). Otherwise the emptiness of the 7
swelling will get shown up on his first attempt at any real-life contest.

Those who regard the whole business of declamation as utterly different
from forensic cases are surely blind even to the reason for the discovery
of this exercise. If it is not a preparation for the forum, it is mere his- 8
trionic display or crazy mouth-shooting. What is the point of 'preparing'
a judge who doesn't exist, narrating what all know to be false, elaborating
proofs for a case on which no one will pronounce? These are a waste of
time, but no more than that: it is sheer mockery, however, to feel emotion,
to be moved by anger or grief, if we're not as it were on manœuvres to
prepare us for the real battle and the serious fighting.

Is there, then, to be no difference between the legal manner of speaking 9
and this declamatory kind? None—if declamation aims solely at our
own improvement. I only wish that we could add to the rules the use of
proper names, and the occasional introduction of more complex *controversiae*, that would take longer to deliver. We ought to be less afraid
of ordinary words, and get used to putting in jokes. These are things that
show us up as tiros in the forum however practised we may have been in
other respects in the schoolroom. If, on the other hand, declamation is to 10
be aimed at display, we ought surely to go a little out of our way to please
the audience. For in speeches that are certainly to some extent 'real', 11
but are meant for pleasing the public (such as the panegyrics we read,
and the whole 'display' type) one is allowed to use more ornament, and
to acknowledge and even show off to an audience invited with that in
mind all the art that must generally in law-cases be kept hidden. So 12
declamation, as the mirror of suits and deliberations, must resemble
reality; but as having an element of display in it, it must take on a certain
brilliance.

This is the practice of comic actors, who don't speak quite as we do 13
normally (that would require no art), but don't, either, get too far away
from the natural, a fault that would destroy realism. Instead, they deck
out our ordinary habits of speech with a certain actors' gloss.

14   Even so, we shall be dogged by some disadvantages arising from our fictitious themes. In particular much in them is left uncertain, which can be taken as *we* decide: ages, wealth, children, parents, the strength
15 of cities, their laws and customs, etc. In fact, sometimes we actually draw arguments from loopholes in the themes set.

B. THE IMPORTANCE OF EXPRESSION

This passage (8 praef. 13–33) gives Quintilian's sane rejoinder to contemporary excesses of style; expression is important, but content more important still.

13 What follows demands more care and trouble. For from now on I shall be dealing with the technique of expression (*elocutio*), the most difficult department of oratory, as all orators agree. Marcus. Antonius,[1] whom I mentioned earlier, said he had seen many accomplished speakers, no eloquent ones; his view was that an accomplished orator is satisfied to say what he must, while the eloquent is characterized by speaking with
14 embellishment. Now if this quality had been found in no one up to that period, including even Crassus and Antonius himself, it is certain that its lack in all these orators was due to its extreme difficulty. Again, Cicero[2] regards 'invention' and arrangement as the mark of the man of sense, eloquence as the sign of the orator; and so he took particular trouble with his precepts in this department.
15   That he was right to do so is made plain by the very name of our topic. For to 'express' (*eloqui*) is to bring out and put over to the audience everything you have conceived in your mind: and without expression, whatever I have prescribed so far is empty and like a sheathed sword
16 stuck away in its scabbard. So this matter is particularly taught; no one can attain it without technique; and to it special attention must be paid. It is the object of training and of imitation, our preoccupation at every age. This is what makes orator excel orator, one type of oratory preferable
17 to another. For it isn't that the Asianists or any other type of 'corrupt' orator did not see what they should say or failed to arrange it: nor were those we call 'dry'[3] either stupid or blind in their conduct of their cases. The trouble was that the former lacked judgement and moderation in *expression*, the latter strength: from which we can see that the good and bad qualities of oratory lie in expression.
18   That does not mean that we should take trouble *only* about words:

---

[1] Cicero, *de oratore* 1. 94 (above, p. 231).   [2] *Orator* 44.
[3] i.e. the 'Atticists'.

and I must meet and resist those who are likely to seize on my admission as it were on the threshold, without letting me go further—I mean the people who neglect content, the sinews of a case, and grow old in an empty zeal for words. They do it for the sake of 'beauty', which can in my view be a most attractive feature in oratory—but only when it comes naturally, not when it is searched after. Healthy bodies, sound of blood 19 and strengthened by exercise, get their beauty from the same source as their strength—for they are of good complexion, spare, muscles showing. But suppose these bodies were to be plucked and rouged and effeminately prinked; they would become hideous just because of the trouble taken to make them beautiful. Legitimate and splendid dress gives a man 20 authority (as a Greek verse testifies); but when it is womanish and luxurious it does not beautify the body—it lays bare the mind. In the same way, the diaphanous and multi-coloured way of expression that some affect takes the manhood from the matter which they clothe in such verbal costume. Therefore I want care in words—but anxiety for content. For 21 generally the best words cling close to what we want to say, and are visible by their own light; yet we go in search of them, as though they were always hiding and secreting themselves. As a result, we never think they could be round about our subject: instead we look for them elsewhere, and when we find them we have to apply force to them. Elo- 22 quence is something to be approached in a loftier spirit: if it is strong all over, it will not think it part of its business to polish its nails and set its hair.

It generally happens, in fact, that oratory actually gets worse as a result of taking undue trouble for words. First of all, the best words are 23 the nearest, those that give a simple and realistic effect. Those that proclaim the labour spent on them, positively wanting to look artificial and contrived, attain no charm and lose all pretence to plausibility, quite apart from the fact that they envelop the meaning in shade and engulf it like corn under luxuriant weed. What can be said straightforwardly 24 our love of words makes us express periphrastically; we repeat what has been sufficiently said, weigh down with many words what would be clear with one, and often think it better to hint at things than to say them outright. Further, nothing but the figurative pleases now; there is no reputation for eloquence to be won by anything that another might have said. We borrow figures and metaphors from the most decadent of the poets, 25 and are apparently only geniuses if it needs genius to take our meaning. Yet Cicero's precept[1] was quite clear: in oratory the very worst fault is to shrink from ordinary language and normal idiom. But then Cicero is 26

[1] *De oratore* 1. 12. For contemporary views on Cicero, see Tacitus, *Dialogus* 18, 22 f. (below, p. 443).

'harsh' and 'unsophisticated'; we do better—we for whom everything that nature prescribed has grown stale, who look not for the ornamental but the meretricious: as if words had any value divorced from content. If we have to work all our lives to ensure that words are correct,[1] clear, ornamental, and fittingly arranged, we have lost all the fruits of our studies.

27 Yet you may see many stuck over individual words, both while in search of them and while weighing and measuring them.

Even if the object were that they could always use the best words, this lack of proportion would still be deplorable: it bridles the onward rush of oratory, and extinguishes the heat of imagination amid delay and diffi-

28 dence. For the orator who cannot with equanimity bear to waste a word is wretched and poverty-stricken. But in fact he will *not* lose a word if he learns the technique of expression, gets together a generous supply of words by wide and suitable reading, applies to them methodical arrangement, and finally strengthens the whole with a great deal of practice,

29 so that everything is constantly to hand and in view. The man who does this will find that content brings its words with it. But the prerequisite is study, together with abilities that are first acquired and then as it were put into reserve. That anxious care to search, evaluate, and compare is to be indulged while we are learning, not while we are speaking. Otherwise, just as those who have not amassed capital have to make a living from day to day, so in oratory those who have not laid in sufficient

30 store of words [2] will be in trouble; but if power of speech has been acquired in advance, the words will be at their posts, seeming not so much to respond when called upon as always to be attached to thoughts, following

31 them as a shadow follows a body. But to this very care there is a limit. When words are Latin, meaningful, ornate, and fittingly arranged, what more have we to strive for? Yet some make no end of quibbling: they linger over almost every syllable, and even when the best words have been found go on hunting for something more archaic, obscure, and unexpected, not realizing that content is the loser when it is the words

32 that are praised. Let us, then, take the greatest care in expression compatible with the principle that nothing is to be done for the sake of words —words having been introduced for the sake of content. And of words those are most to be commended that best express what we think and

33 have the effect that we desire on the minds of the judges. Such words cannot but produce diction that is both attractive and admirable—but not admirable in the sense that we 'admire' prodigies, and attractive with a charm that is not debased but allied to good reputation and dignity.

---

[1] Cf. below, 31. These are the four 'virtues' of style attributed to Theophrastus. Cf. Cicero, *Orator* 79 (above, p. 241).

[2] 'laid . . . words': this represents a conjectural supplement to the text.

C. READING IN THE SCHOOLS OF RHETORIC

In 1. 8, Quintilian discusses what the child should read in the school of the *grammaticus*: Homer, Virgil, tragedy, selected lyric (but no elegy), Menander. In this passage (2. 5) he prescribes reading for the next stage: the school of the *rhetor*.[1]

I shall discuss the technique of declamation a little later;[2] for the moment, **1** as I am dealing with the earliest stages of the rhetorical training, I should not, I think, omit to point out how much the rhetor will contribute to the progress of the learner if—just as the *grammatici* are expected to give expositions of the poets—he too sees that the pupils he has taken on are made to read history and especially oratory. I myself kept up this practice in the case of a few children whose age required it and whose parents regarded it as useful; but though my intentions even then were excellent, **2** I was hindered by two things: a long-established custom of teaching by other methods had hardened into a rule, and youths who were practically grown-up and had no need of this exercise insisted on attending. In any **3** case, even if I had made a new discovery too late to put it into practice in my own school, I should not be ashamed to make it a precept for the future. As it is, I know that this is practised by the Greeks—though rather by means of assistant teachers, because the rhetors think time would run short if they themselves should undertake to be always seeing individual pupils through their reading. Certainly the kind of exposé which aims at **4** ensuring that children can easily and accurately follow writing with their eyes, and even the type that gives the meaning of any unusual words that crop up, is to be regarded as far below what the rhetor can be expected to do. On the other hand, to point out good qualities in an author, **5** or if necessary bad ones, *is* highly appropriate to a rhetor's profession and his claim to be a teacher of eloquence: particularly as I am by no means asking him to go to the length of calling each pupil to his side and pandering to him in the reading of whatever book the pupil may care to choose. For it seems to be, as well as easier, also much more profitable **6** to impose silence and appoint, preferably in rotation, some one pupil as reader, so that they can get used at the same time to enunciation: then, after explaining the case to which the speech that is to be read **7** refers (thus promoting clearer understanding of what is said), to leave nothing untouched that can be remarked on as to content and style, making clear the technique of winning over the judge in the proem, the clarity, brevity, and plausibility of the narration, occasional scheming and

---

[1] See H.-I. Marrou, *Histoire de l'éducation dans l'antiquité*[6], Paris, 1965, 412 ff.
[2] In 2. 10 (above, p. 372).

8 hidden cunning (for in this matter the only skill is that which the skilful alone can fathom); then pointing out how methodical the division, how subtle and tight the arguments: how powerfully the orator arouses passion, how agreeably he soothes: his bitterness in insult, his wit in raillery: how he rules his hearers' emotions, bursting into their minds, moulding

9 them to his words; then explaining, as to style, which words are appropriate, ornamental, lofty: where the exaggeration is worthy of praise (together with its opposite), what beautiful metaphor, what figures of speech appear, what rhythms are smooth and squared off without losing their virility.

10 Nor is it without profit that even corrupt and faulty speeches (admired, nevertheless, by many, thanks to the decadence of our taste) should sometimes be read aloud, and that it should be pointed out how many things in them are inappropriate, obscure, inflated, undignified, sordid, wanton, and effeminate—things which are not only praised by many but, what

11 is worse, praised just because they are corrupt. For straightforward speech, expressed naturally, is regarded as having no element of genius, while we admire as more 'exquisite' things that in one way or another diverge from this standard. A parallel can be found in the fact that some people put a greater price on distorted or somehow monstrous bodies than

12 on those which have not forfeited a normal appearance, and that even those who really are attracted by beauty think that more of it attaches to the plucked and the pumiced, those who curl and pin up their hair and shine with a colour that is not their own, than could be bestowed by untouched nature—so that bodily beauty is made to appear the result of moral depravity.

13 The instructor should not only himself teach these things, but ask frequent questions and try out his pupils' taste. Hence, as they listen, they will be unable to lapse into inattention, and what is said will not go in at one ear and out at the other: and at the same time they will be being brought towards the required state of themselves understanding and making discoveries. For what else are we about in teaching than ensuring

14 that our pupils will not always require to be taught? I should venture to say that this kind of attention will contribute more to learners than all the handbooks of all the rhetors, which are doubtless very helpful but can hardly, with their broader scope, cover *all* the types of thing that

15 daily come to light. Similarly in military matters, there are handed down certain generalized precepts; but it will be more useful to know what method each general used, wisely or unwisely, in what kinds of circumstance, time, and place; for in pretty well everything precepts are less

16 important than practice. Are we to make the teacher declaim as a model for his pupils while denying that more would be provided by the reading

of Cicero and Demosthenes? Certainly, if a pupil makes a mistake in his declamation he can be put right for all to hear; but it would surely be more effective to put a written speech right—more agreeable, too, for everyone would rather hear another's faults being reproved than his own. There is a lot more I could say; but no one can be unaware of the 17 usefulness of what I recommend. It would not be disagreeable; let us hope that it will not be shirked.

If we can carry that point, a further, though easier, question will remain: 18 who should be read by beginners? Some have approved of the minor authors, because they thought it easier to understand them; others of the more flowery type, as being better adapted to nurturing the talents of the young. Personally, I should prefer the reading of the best authors 19 from the start (and indeed always), but the clearest and most accessible of the best: for instance, Livy rather than Sallust (even if Sallust is the greater historian: but to appreciate him requires a degree of attainment). Cicero, at least in my view, is liked by beginners also, and is sufficiently 20 accessible. He can be loved by his readers as well as useful to them. After that—in the words of Livy's precept—come the authors most like Cicero.

But two dangers I regard as particularly to be avoided by children. 21 On the one hand, excessive admiration for antiquity should not prompt the teacher to let their style harden by the reading of the Gracchi, Cato, and other similar authors. That will make them rough and stark; for they will be as yet unable to appreciate the strengths of those authors, and, restricting themselves to the imitation of their style (excellent, doubtless, for that period but alien to ours) they will—and this is the worst fault here—regard themselves as equals of the great. On the other hand, 22 pupils should not be allowed to fall victim to the blooms of the recent decadence and lull themselves in vicious pleasures, thus coming to an excessive admiration for that over-sweet style which is the more agreeable to the young mind because it is nearer its own level. Only when the 23 intellect is strong and finally out of danger should I recommend reading the old authors (and if we take from them their sturdy virile strength of genius and wipe off the grime of their untutored era we can make our elegance shine out the more brilliantly). The same applies to new authors: they too have many virtues—nature has not condemned us to slowness 24 of mind, it is merely that we have changed our manner of oratory and indulged ourselves more than we should. The orators of the past excelled us not so much in talent as in ideals. Thus we have much scope for selection, but we must take care not to allow what we select to be infected by the surrounding faults. But I have no reason to deny—indeed I assert 25 quite freely—that there have recently been and still are some orators whom we may imitate as a whole; but it isn't for everyone to decide who 26 these authors are. It is better to stick to earlier writers, because even error is safer in their company; I have recommended this delay in the reading of new authors just in order that imitation should not get ahead of judgement.

D. READING FOR THE ADVANCED STUDENT

In this ambitious survey (10. 1), Quintilian attempts to go through in detail the authors, both Greek and Latin, who will be 'particularly suitable to those proposing to become orators'. He meant the list to be used by older pupils who had finished the rhetorical course and wished to improve their control of vocabulary, figures, and word-arrangement. This famous passage must be read in the light of these specific intentions, which account for the sketchiness of some of the judgements, particularly those on types of poetry (e.g. the elegiac) that offered little to the speaker. The Greek material, at any rate, is for the most part not original: the fragments of Dionysius' *On Imitation* show many close verbal resemblances to Quintilian's judgements.

HOW TO ACQUIRE A HABIT OF FACILITY

1 But these precepts on style, though necessary for theoretical knowledge of oratory, are by no means sufficient to instil mastery of speaking unless they are reinforced by that stable facility in composition called by the Greeks *hexis*. I am aware that it is usual to ask the question whether it is writing or reading or speaking that contributes most to this ability; and I should have myself to consider this point carefully if we could in 2 fact rest content with any one of these methods. But they are actually so interconnected and inseparable that if any of them were left out time spent on the others would be wasted. Eloquence can never be mature and tough if it has not drawn strength from constant writing, and without the pattern supplied by reading effort devoted to writing will drift unguided. One may know how everything ought to be said, but unless one has one's eloquence always on the alert, ready for any emergency, 3 one will be like a miser brooding over buried treasure. Something may be an absolutely essential element in oratory, but that does not automatically make it of correspondingly great importance in the forming of an orator. Certainly speech comes before everything else—for it is in speaking that an orator's task lies; and it is obvious that it was from speech that the technique of oratory historically evolved, imitation coming next 4 and writing practice last of all. But though you cannot reach the heights unless you start from first principles, the first principles start to become of least importance as the training goes forward. But I am not talking here

about how an orator should be trained (I have already expressed myself on this topic enough—or at least as well as I could); now I am dealing with an athlete who has already learnt all the tricks from his teacher: by what kind of exercise is he to be prepared for combat? To apply the analogy: we have to do with someone who already knows how to find and arrange his material, and has learnt how to choose and dispose his words. Now we must show him how to do what he has learnt as well and as easily as possible.

ACCUMULATING VOCABULARY

It is surely beyond question that his task is to assemble (as it were) a 5 store of wealth that he can use whenever he needs it. This wealth consists of an abundance of matter and of words. But matter is individual 6 to each particular case, or, if common, common to only a few cases. Words have got to be made ready for all kinds of case. If they corresponded one-for-one to things, and varied with them, they would demand less trouble, for they would all present themselves immediately along with the matter. But some are more appropriate or more ornate or more significant or more euphonious than others; and so they have not only all to be known, but all to be ready and (so to say) on view, so that when they come under the critical inspection of the speaker he can easily choose the best among them. I observe that people are accustomed to learning off 7 synonyms by heart, so that one is sure to come to hand out of many— and also so that when one has been used and it becomes necessary to use it again in a short while, they can pick an alternative that means the same thing and avoid repetition. This is a childish and thankless task—and not particularly useful either. One merely accumulates a throng of words out of which one tends to grab at the most handy without discrimination.

We must, however, provide a supply of words without sacrificing 8 judgement; we have an orator's facility, not a huckster's volubility, in our sights. This we shall attain by reading the best and hearing the best; for by taking care to do that we shall learn not only the names for things but the most appropriate for a particular place. Oratory has room 9 for almost all words, except a few that are too indecent. Writers of iambic verses and Old Comedy may often win applause by using these; it is enough for us to concentrate on our own field. All words, with the exceptions of which I spoke, are somewhere or other the best. For sometimes one needs even low, vulgar words; words that would seem sordid in a brilliant context are the correct ones where the matter calls for them. If we want to get to know words—and not only their meanings but their 10 shapes and rhythmic values too, so that they fit in where we put them, there is only one means: much reading and listening. For it is by ear that we first pick up all speech. That is why those infants educated on royal orders by dumb nurses in the wilderness lacked the power of speech,

11 even though they did (we are told) utter a few words.[1] Now some words are such that they mean the same thing, though differing in their sounds, so that it makes no difference to the sense which you decide to use: e.g. *ensis* and *gladius* used of swords. Others, though when used in their primary sense they connote separate things, can be transferred figuratively from their own meanings to signify the same: e.g. 'steel' and 'blade'.

12 Indeed, by a device known as 'abuse' we can call murderers who have employed any sort of weapon *sicarii*.[2] Other things we can express by a circumlocution, involving more words than one (e.g. 'abundance of pressed milk'),[3] and many by a change in the form of the phrase: thus 'I know' may become 'I am not unaware' and 'it does not escape me' and 'it does not pass me by' and 'who does not know?' and 'no one

13 doubts'. But it is also possible to borrow from a neighbour. Often 'I understand' and 'I feel' and 'I see' mean the same as 'I know'. Rich abundance in such matters we shall obtain by reading, in such a way that we can use them not just as they come to hand but as they are appropriate.

14 For it is not always that these words perform the same function reciprocally. I can correctly say 'I see' about mental understanding, but I cannot say 'I understand' in connection with visual seeing. A 'blade'

15 can indicate a sword, but 'sword' does not connote 'blade'. This is the way to acquire a copious vocabulary. But we must not read and listen merely for the sake of words. For from these sources we get models of everything that I have been giving instruction in—and more efficacious they are too than the teachings of the textbooks: once, that is, the learner has come to be able to understand these models without any one pointing them out, and to proceed on his own feet. What the teacher recommended, the orator points out, in action.

READING AND LISTENING

16 Hearer and reader have different rewards. A speaker arouses the listener by his animation—he sets him on fire not by the shadow of things but by the things themselves. Everything lives and moves, and we receive his words as they (as it were) come newly to birth, with a sympathetic anxiety. We are moved not only by the way the judgement may go, but

---

[1] Herodotus (2. 2) tells how the children, thus brought up, uttered the word *bekos*, which turned out to be Phrygian for bread.

[2] i.e. 'dagger-men'.

[3] i.e. cheese (Virg. *Ecl.* 1. 81).

also by the danger run by the speakers. Everything combined goes to 17
impress us—voice, grace of gesture, and (perhaps the most powerful
factor in oratory) delivery adapted to the requirement of each particular
passage. When one reads one's judgement is more reliable, while, in a
listener, it is often led astray by partisanship or enthusiastic applause:
one is ashamed to dissent, and a sort of inarticulate shame inhibits us 18
from putting more confidence in our own taste, though in fact bad works
are liked by the majority, and invited audiences are ready to applaud even
things they don't like. Equally, on the other side, it often happens that 19
those whose taste is untrustworthy fail to do justice to the best works.
Reading is free; nor does it hurry by, like a constantly moving speech.
You can frequently go back if you are doubtful of a point or want to
impress it firmly on your memory. We must in fact go back; we must work
over our reading, and hand it on to our memory and our faculty for imitation not raw but softened and, so to say, masticated by constant iteration—
just as we don't swallow food until it has been chewed and almost lique-
fied for easier assimilation.

READING SPEECHES

For a good while only the best writers and the ones least liable to deceive 20
those who trust in them should be read. And it should be done carefully,
almost as carefully as writing. Everything should be scrutinized—but
not merely a little at a time; a book should be read right through, and
then taken up again from the beginning: especially a speech, whose good
points are often hidden, and even deliberately so. Often an orator plans 21
for the future, pretends, lays traps, says in the first part of his speech
things that will pay off at the end. Such passages, therefore, cannot be
properly appreciated in their immediate context, while we are still
unaware of their point, and we shall have to go back to them when we
are familiar with the whole. One most useful thing is to know the details 22
of the cases to which the speeches we are dealing with relate, and, where
possible, to read the pleas on both sides: for example, those of Demosthenes and Aeschines against each other,[1] Servius Sulpicius and Messalla
(the one for, the other against Aufidia), Pollio and Cassius at the trial of
Asprenas, and many others. Even if some do not appear to be evenly 23
matched, we are right to turn to them in search of an understanding of
the point at issue in the case—for instance, the speeches of Tubero
against Ligarius and of Hortensius for Verres when Cicero was on the

---

[1] The speeches *On the Crown* and *Against Ctesiphon*: cf. Cicero's (?) preface to the
Latin version of both, above, p. 250.

other side. Moreover, it will be profitable to know how two orators treated the same case. For Calidius too spoke on Cicero's house, and Brutus wrote, as an exercise, an oration in favour of Milo (Cornelius Celsus is
24 wrong to think that he actually delivered it in court). Pollio and Messalla defended the same clients, and in my childhood there circulated notable speeches in defence of Volusenus Catulus from the pens of Domitius Afer, Passienus Crispus, and Decimus Laelius. Nor should we, as we read, immediately assume that everything which great authors said must necessarily be perfect. Sometimes they slip, find their task too much for them, give their talents a field-day for fun. They are not always trying hard; sometimes they get tired—Demosthenes in Cicero's view sometimes nods off, and Horace thought that even of Homer himself.[1]
25 They are great, these authors, but they remain human; and it is the fate of those who regard everything they find in these writings as a stylistic law to find themselves imitating the inferior parts of their models (that being easier), and to regard themselves as strikingly similar to the great
26 if they attain to the faults displayed by the great. However, in judging such men, one must be modest and cautious, to avoid a pitfall fatal to many—condemnation of what they fail to understand. And if one must err in one direction, I should rather that readers of these authors liked everything than disliked much.

READING POETRY

27 Theophrastus says that much is contributed to an orator's training by reading poetry, and many follow this lead, reasonably enough: for the poets are a source of inspiration in subject, sublimity of language, range of emotion, appropriateness in depiction of character. In particular, minds deadened by the daily round of legal activity find especial refreshment in the attractions of poetry. Hence Cicero's view that we should take our
28 ease in reading of this sort.[2] But we must remember that an orator cannot follow poets through thick and thin; their liberty in use of language and their licence to employ figures are quite alien to him; the genre is designed for display; and besides the fact that it is in search of pleasure alone, and pursues it by the invention not only of falsities but even of impossibilities,
29 it is also aided by a special privilege. It is tied down to a definite and predetermined pattern of feet, and hence cannot always use the correct terminology; driven from the straight road it has necessarily to resort to byways of expression. It must not only change words, but extend,

---

[1] *The Art of Poetry* 359 (above, p. 289). For Cicero, see Plutarch, *Cicero* 24. 6.
[2] *Pro Archia* 12 (Cicero's defence of a poet-client).

shorten, transpose, and divide them. We, by contrast, are armed soldiers, standing in the front line, with important matters at stake and victory to strive for. But I should not wish the arms we use to be dirty, mouldy, and rusted. They should have the glint that brings terror to the beholder, the glint of steel that dazzles mind and sight at once, not the gleam of gold and silver which has nothing to do with war and is positively dangerous to its possessor.

READING HISTORY

History too can nourish the orator, with a rich and pleasant juice. But this also we must read in the knowledge that many of its good qualities must be avoided by the orator. It is very near poetry; in a manner of speaking it *is* a poem written in prose, composed for telling a story, not proving a case. The whole genre is designed not for practical effect and the contest of the moment, but for the enlightenment of posterity and the glory of the writer's genius. Thus it avoids monotony of narrative by using words a trifle remote from ordinary usage, and figures a shade free. So—as I have said before—we must not aim, when we speak in front of a preoccupied and often uneducated judge, at the brevity of Sallust, perfect as that is for the ears of the attentive and the learned. Equally, Livy's milky richness is not the style in which to bring a point home to someone who is looking for conviction, not for agreeable narration. Cicero, moreover, thinks that not even Thucydides or Xenophon are useful for an orator, though he feels that the one 'sounds for war' and that the Muses spoke with the other's lips.[1] We may sometimes use even the historians' brilliance in our digressions, so long as we bear in mind that in the crucial passages of a speech it is the strong arm of the soldier, not the bulging muscle of the athlete that is needed, and that the many-coloured coat assumed (it is said) by Demetrius of Phaleron is unsuitable for the dust of the forum. History has a further use—a very important one, though not relevant here—in its supply of knowledge of events and precedents: in these an orator must be well versed. He must not rely on his client to supply all the evidence; much he must provide for himself from his own carefully garnered knowledge of the past: that alone can escape the charge of prejudice and bias—hence its special authority.

READING PHILOSOPHY

We have to go to the philosophers for a great deal; this is the fault of the orators themselves in yielding to the philosophers the best part of

---

[1] *Orator* 39, 62.

their own field. For it is the philosophers who specialize in talk of justice, goodness, utility, and their opposites, and of theology: moreover, they argue keenly, and are particularly useful in preparing the budding orator
36 for questioning and cross-talk in court. But here too we must exercise judgement. We may sometimes be dealing with the same matters as philosophers; but we should not imagine that the same rules apply both to suits and to disputations, to forum and to lecture-hall, to moral precepts and to practical risks.

THE READING-LIST: INTRODUCTORY REMARKS

37 Doubtless many will expect me—since I judge reading so useful—to add to my book a list of those who should be read and assign each author his special virtue. But it would be an endless task to go through them all one
38 by one. Cicero in his *Brutus* spends thousands of lines merely on Roman orators, even though he keeps silent about all his surviving contemporaries except for Caesar and Marcellus. What limits could we set if we dealt with them, and their successors, and all the Greek orators, and the philo-
39 sophers, poets, and historians as well?[1] The safest course would be a brief dictum—like the well-known precept in Livy's letter to his son: 'Read Demosthenes and Cicero; then those who are most like Demosthenes and
40 Cicero.' And I cannot forbear to summarize my own judgement too: in my view few—perhaps none—can be found, among those who have worn well, who would not have something useful to offer to readers prepared to exercise judgement. Cicero admits that he was much helped
41 even by the oldest authors, who had natural talent but lacked art. I feel much the same about the moderns. Few can be found so mad as not to have some slight confidence in at least a part of their work, sufficient to give hope for its fame with posterity. And if anyone does lack this faith, it will be obvious within a line or two, and we shall leave him smartly
42 before our trial of him costs us too much time. But it is not the case that everything relevant to some department of knowledge is thereby suited also to forming style, which is my present topic.

But before I go on to individuals, I must say a little in general about
43 diversity of opinion. Some think that only the ancients should be read, and that only they have natural eloquence and true manly strength. Others are gratified by the latest panderings to wantonness, where everything
44 is aimed at tickling the palates of the uneducated mob. And of those who do want to follow a correct style of speaking, some think that health and true Atticism lie only in concise, plain language, as near as possible to

---

[1] 'poets . . . as well': this represents a conjectural supplement to the text.

everyday speech; others are attracted by a more exalted gift, more forceful and full of spirit. And there are not a few lovers of a calm, polished,
and sedate style. I shall have more to say about this variety when I come
to examine types of oratory.[1] Meanwhile, I shall merely touch briefly on
what a reader should look for, and where he should look for it, if he wants
to strengthen his faculty for oratory. I intend to pick out a few authors, 45
the most eminent. Students may easily judge who are the most like these;
so that nobody need complain that I have omitted his special favourites.
I admit that more writers are worth reading than those I shall name; but
now I intend to list the types of reading that I think particularly suited to
those proposing to become orators.

GREEK AUTHORS: HOMER

Well then: just as Aratus thinks that one should start with Zeus,[2] I 46
think our proper beginning is with Homer. He—rather as, in his own
words,[3] Ocean is the source of rivers and fountains—gave rise to all
departments of eloquence and provided them with a pattern. No one
could surpass his sublimity in great subjects or his aptness in small.
He combines luxuriance and concision, charm and gravity; he is a miracle
of copiousness as well as brevity, and he is outstanding in the qualities
of an orator as well as a poet. To leave aside his panegyrics, his exhorta- 47
tions, and his consolatory speeches, is it not clear that the ninth book[4]
containing the embassy to Achilles, or the quarrel between the leaders
in the first, or the opinions voiced in the second, lay bare for us all the
techniques of law-suit and political deliberation? No one is so uneducated 48
as to deny that this author had under his control all types of emotion,
whether gentle or violent. Indeed, by the openings of both his poems did
he not, in a very few lines—I can hardly say observe—did he not formulate
the rules to be followed in composing a proem? For he makes his listener
well-disposed to him by calling on the goddesses who, it was believed,
preside over poets: attentive by his mention of the greatness of the theme:
and open to instruction by his swift sketch of the plot. As for narrative, 49
who could conduct that more briefly than the author of the announcement of Patroclus' death?[5] Who more vividly than the narrator of the
war of Curetes and Aetoli?[6] And take the comparisons, amplifications,
instances, digressions, signs, and arguments, and the rest of the means
of proof and refutation—all these are so frequent that even writers of

---

[1] 12. 10 (below, p. 404).   [2] *Phaenomena* 1: 'Let us begin from Zeus.'
[3] *Iliad* 21. 196.   [4] The references in § 47 are all to the *Iliad*.
[5] *Iliad* 18. 18 ff.   [6] *Iliad* 9. 529 ff.

rhetorical handbooks look to this poet for very many of their examples
50 of these matters. Again, what peroration could ever be equal to Priam's
prayers to Achilles?[1] Surely in language, thought, figures, the organization
of his whole work, he passes the bounds of human genius. It takes a great
man to match up to his qualities—not by rivalling them (that would be
impossible) but by understanding them.

OTHER WRITERS IN HEXAMETERS

51 Homer left all others, in every kind of eloquence, far behind him: the
epic poets in particular, for where the matter is similar the comparison
52 can be pressed home most harshly. Hesiod rarely leaves the ground, and a
good deal of his space is occupied with lists of names; however, his
didactic reflections are of use, and one may approve his smooth wording
and structure. He gets the palm in the middle style.

53 In Antimachus, on the other hand, force, impressiveness, and distinction of style merit praise. The almost unanimous opinion of critics
gives him the second position; but he is deficient in emotion, charm,
arrangement—in technique generally: so that it is quite clear what a
difference there is between coming closest to first and being second.

54 Panyasis, a mixture of the last two, is judged to equal neither's virtues
in his style; but Hesiod he surpasses in subject-matter, Antimachus in
method of organization.

Apollonius [Rhodius] does not come into the classification drawn up
by the critics, for those judges of poets, Aristarchus and Aristophanes,
included no one of their own times. But it was no contemptible work that
55 he composed; it keeps a sort of sustained middle course. Aratus' subject
lacks movement—it has no variety, no emotion, no characters, no speeches:
but he is up to the task to which he thought himself equal. Theocritus in
his genre is wonderful; but that rustic and pastoral muse of his fights shy
even of the city—let alone the law-courts.

56 I seem to hear people pressing numerous names of poets on me from
all directions. Did not Pisandros well describe the deeds of Hercules?
Are we to say that Macer and Virgil were mistaken in their imitation of
Nicander? Are we to pass Euphorion by?—after all, unless Virgil had
thought he was good, he would never have mentioned in the *Eclogues*
'poems wrought in Chalcidian verse'.[2] Was Horace wrong to link the names
57 of Tyrtaeus and Homer?[3] The fact is that no one is so ignorant of poets
that he could not transfer to his book at least a library catalogue of their

---

[1] *Iliad* 24. 486 ff.
[2] *Ecl.* 10. 50. Euphorion came from Chalcis in Euboea.
[3] *The Art of Poetry* 402 (above, p. 290).

names. If I miss people out, that does not mean I have not heard of them
—or necessarily that I value them lightly: have I not already said that
everyone has something useful to give? But to those lesser poets we shall 58
return once our strength is complete and established. After all, at big
dinners we often find that when we are sated with the best food, the
variety provided by the less luxurious is welcome.

ELEGY, IAMBIC, AND LYRIC

It is then, too, that we shall have leisure to pick up elegy; here the leader
is Callimachus, while most agree that Philetas took second place. But 59
while we are in the process of acquiring the stable facility of which I
spoke, we must get used to the best; our minds must be formed, our style
developed, by much reading rather than the exploration of many authors.
On this principle, we shall say that, of the three writers of iambics marked
off by the judgement of Aristarchus, it is Archilochus who will be found
to have most relevance to *hexis*. He has the greatest force of style; his 60
reflections are at once powerful, concise, and vibrant, and he has a great
deal of blood and muscle: to such a degree that some people think that
it is not his genius but his subject-matter that prevents him from
leading the field.

Of the nine lyric poets, Pindar is far and away the best. He excels in 61
sublime grandeur of conception, in thought and figures. He has an unsurpassed supply of words and matter, a great flood of eloquence. And
Horace, for these reasons, was right to believe him inimitable.[1] The 62
strength of Stesichorus' genius is demonstrated, amongst other things,
by his material, for he sings of the greatest wars and the most famous
generals, measuring up to the burdens of epic poetry on a mere lyre.
For he can give characters their due weight in action and speech alike,
and he could be thought a potential rival of Homer had he preserved a
sense of proportion; but he is redundant and spreads himself—a fault,
without doubt, but a fault of a rich talent. A part of Alcaeus' *œuvre* 63
merits his being awarded a 'golden plectrum'[2]—the part in which he
attacked tyrants: here he has much to contribute to morals also. As to
his style, he is brief, lofty, careful, often similar to an orator. But he also
wrote trivia, and descended to erotica, though he was more suited to
higher themes. Simonides, otherwise a slender talent, can be praised for 64
his correctness of language and a certain charm; but his principal quality
lies in his power to arouse pity, so that some critics prefer him in this
respect to all other writers in the genre.

[1] *Odes* 4. 2. 1.   [2] *Ibid.* 2. 13. 26.

COMEDY AND TRAGEDY

65 Old Comedy is almost alone in preserving the genuine grace of the Attic tongue; moreover, it has a most eloquent freedom of speech: and if it is especially notable for its attacks on vices, it has a great deal of strength in other departments also. It is splendid, elegant, graceful; and nothing else after Homer (who, like Achilles,[1] must always be the exception) is 66 more like oratory, or more suitable for training orators. It has many exponents, but Aristophanes, Eupolis, and Cratinus stand out.

Tragedy was first brought to light by Aeschylus, lofty, impressive, and often grandiloquent even to a fault—but in many respects unformed and inharmonious. Hence the Athenians allowed later poets to correct his plays for competitive performance, and many won prizes in this manner. 67 Much greater brilliance was brought to this genre by Sophocles and Euripides: their styles are very different, and many have disputed which of the two is the better poet. This is irrelevant to my present purpose, and I leave the question unanswered. But all must agree that it is Euripides who will be far more useful to those who are preparing themselves for 68 speaking in court. His style is nearer the oratorical type (a point that is in fact criticized by those who find Sophocles' grave tragic resonance more lofty). He abounds in noteworthy thoughts, and in philosophical precept he is almost the equal of the philosophers themselves. In both speech and repartee he is comparable with any of those whose eloquence has been heard in the court-room. His command of all emotions, especially pathos, is remarkable.

69 Menander, as he frequently testifies, greatly admired Euripides; and he imitated him, though in a different genre. Menander himself, in my opinion, is the one poet who, if carefully studied, would be enough to give a pattern for everything that I have been recommending—such is the complete picture of life that he drew, such his richness of invention and his powers of expression, such his capacity for adaptation to all subjects, 70 characters, and emotions. And the critics who think that the speeches published under the name of Charisius were the work of Menander certainly have a point. But the proof of his rhetorical skill seems to me to lie far more in his own plays: all an orator's stock-in-trade is seen to perfection in the well-known trial scenes in the *Arbitration*,[2] the *Heiress*, and the *Locrians*, or the soliloquies in the *Timid Man*, the *Law-giver*, 71 and the *Changeling*. But I think that he has even more to offer to the declaimers, who have to assume many different characters to comply with the nature of *controversiae*—fathers, sons, bachelors, husbands, soldiers,

---

[1] *Iliad* 2. 673-4.
[2] *Epitrepontes* 42 ff.; of the scenes mentioned this alone survives.

countrymen, rich men, poor men, people angry, pleading, gentle, harsh: in all these types this poet preserves a wonderful trueness to life.[1] And 72 he has eclipsed the reputation of all other writers in that genre, putting them in the shade by his resplendent brilliance. All the same, there are other comic writers who can provide occasional passages worth excerpting, though you have to read them in an uncritical spirit; particularly Philemon, who was often preferred to Menander by their contemporaries —wrongly, though everyone agrees that he did deserve second place.

HISTORY

Many have written history with distinction, but no one doubts that two 73 are far ahead of the rest, different in qualities, but hardly to be distinguished in reputation. Thucydides is close-knit, concise, always pressing on. Herodotus is charming, clear, discursive. The one excels in strong, the other in calm emotions; the one in set speeches, the other in conversations; the one in force, the other in giving pleasure. Theopompus 74 ranks next to these, inferior to them as a historian, but more like an orator than either—and an orator indeed he was for a long time before he was persuaded to enter this new field. Philistus, too, deserves to be distinguished in the throng of later historians (however good they may be); he imitated Thucydides, and managed to be rather more lucid without attaining his force. Ephorus, as Isocrates thought, needs the spur. Clitarchus' talents are admired, his veracity impugned. Timagenes ap- 75 peared after a long gap, and is praiseworthy for this very achievement of restoring with new lustre a historical tradition that had lapsed. I have not forgotten Xenophon, but shall deal with him under philosophy.

ORATORY

There follows a great throng of orators, ten together produced at the 76 same time in Athens. Of them by far the first is Demosthenes: indeed, he is virtually a complete code of oratory. He has such force, such concentration, such nervous tension, such continuous point, such restraint of style, that you will not find anything lacking in him, or anything superfluous. Aeschines is fuller, more discursive, resembling a more elevated 77 speaker to the extent that he is less condensed—but it is more fat that he has, the muscles are less. Hyperides is eminently pleasant and sharp, more suitable for less important, not to say more trivial, cases. Lysias is 78 older than these, refined, elegant, the acme of perfection if it were enough

[1] Cf. Plutarch, below, p. 531.

for an orator to instruct. He has no hollowness, nothing exotic: but he
79 resembles a clear fountain rather than a great river. Isocrates' style of
oratory is different; he is flowery, pretty, more suited to the wrestling
ring than the battlefield. His aim was every possible beauty of style—
a reasonable pursuit, for he had equipped himself for the lecture-room,
not the law-court. He is facile in imagination, concerned for what is
right, and so careful in his word-arrangement that people even criticize
his minuteness.

80   In all these of whom I have spoken, the virtues mentioned are those I
think most important, but they are not the only ones: nor do I regard the
other orators as without importance. Even Demetrius of Phaleron, who
is said to have ushered in the decadence of oratory, must be admitted to
have had a great deal of talent and eloquence: and he is worth remembering
for the very fact that he is pretty well the last of the Attic school who
deserves the name of orator; and yet in the middle style of oratory which
he exploited Cicero prefers him to all his rivals.

PHILOSOPHY

81 As to philosophers, from whom Cicero[1] admits that he derived a good deal
of his eloquence, no one can doubt that Plato should be put first, whether
we are thinking of his acuteness in argument or of his divine and Homeric
gift of eloquence. He rises far above prose writing (what the Greek metaphor calls 'pedestrian'), and to me he seems to have been inspired by a
82 sort of Delphic oracle, that exalts him above merely human talent. I
hardly need to mention Xenophon's unlaboured charm—charm, however,
that no labour could equal: the Graces themselves might be thought to
have shaped his speech, and the praise given in Old Comedy to Pericles
could very properly be transferred to him—that on his lips sat some god-
83 dess of persuasion.[2] No need, either, to expatiate on the elegance of the
other philosophers of the Socratic school. As to Aristotle, I am undecided
what to regard as his salient virtue: his factual knowledge, his prolific
output, his pleasant style, his acute thought, or his variety of subject.
Theophrastus' divine brilliance of style is such that he is even said to
84 have taken his name from it.[3] The old Stoics paid less attention to eloquence. They spoke up for virtue, and showed their best side in arguing
and demonstrating their doctrines. But the acuteness of their argument is
not matched by any grandeur of style—something, of course, they were
not looking for.

[1] *Orator* 12.   [2] Eupolis, fr. 94 Kock.
[3] 'Theophrastus' might be supposed to mean 'of divine utterance'.

LATIN LITERATURE: HEXAMETER POETS

I must keep to the same order in dealing with Roman writers also. 85
With us Virgil—like Homer with the Greeks—may provide the most
auspicious opening; indeed, of all poets of that genre in either language
he undoubtedly comes nearest to Homer. To quote the answer which, as a 86
young man, I received when I asked Domitius Afer who he thought most
nearly approached Homer: 'Virgil comes second, and nearer first than
third.' Of course, we have to yield pride of place to Homer's superhuman
and immortal genius. But Virgil shows more care and pains for the very
reason that he had to work harder. And perhaps we make up by Virgil's
good general level for the inferiority our champion shows to Homer's
heights.

All the rest will be found to follow far behind. Macer and Lucretius 87
are worth reading—but not for any ability to provide the style that is
the stuff of eloquence; each shows elegance on his own subject, but the
one is unambitious, the other difficult. Varro Atacinus made his name as a
translator of another's work; he is not to be despised, but he is hardly
rich enough to increase an orator's powers. Ennius we must venerate as 88
we do groves whose age makes them holy, full of great old oaks that nowadays have less beauty than sanctity. Others are closer to us, and more
useful for the matter in question. Ovid is as frivolous in his hexameters
as elsewhere: he is too much in love with his own talents, but deserves
praise in parts. Cornelius Severus, even though a better versifier than 89
poet, could lay good claim to the second place if (as has been said) he had
completed his *Sicilian War* to the standard of his first book. Premature
death prevented Serranus coming to ripeness, but his youthful works show
outstanding gifts and a concern for stylistic purity especially admirable in
someone so young. We have recently had a great loss in Valerius Flaccus. 90
Saleius Bassus' genius was forceful and poetic, but he too did not have
long life in which to mature. Rabirius and Pedo are worth getting to know
if one has time to spare. Lucan is passionate, spirited, full of brilliant thoughts: indeed, to be frank, a better model for orators than poets.

PRAISE OF THE EMPEROR DOMITIAN

This is the extent of my list; for Germanicus Augustus was deflected 91
from the poetic studies he had embarked on by his responsibility for the
world: the gods clearly thought it not enough that he should merely be
the greatest of poets. But what could be more lofty, more learned, more
wholly outstanding than those works of his to which he had recourse when
as a young man he had handed the principate to another? Who is better

qualified to be a poet of war than one who wages it as he does? Whom would the goddesses who preside over literature listen to more sympathetically? To whom would his patron deity, Minerva, more readily 92 open the secrets of her art? Future centuries will tell of this more fully; for us now his poetic fame is eclipsed by the brilliance of his other qualities. Our duty, however, is to worship at the sacred shrines of literature; and you will bear with us, Caesar, if we do not pass this by in silence, and at least bear witness, in a line of Virgil, that 'the ivy creeps among your victory bays'.[1]

ELEGY, SATIRE, LYRIC

93 In elegiac verse, too, we can offer a challenge to the Greeks. The most brief and elegant exponent is in my opinion Tibullus; there are those who prefer Propertius. Ovid is less restrained than either, Gallus more harsh.

As for satire, it is completely our own. Lucilius was the first to win outstanding praise for it, and he still has admirers so devoted that they do not hesitate to class him above all other poets, not merely all other 94 satirists. I am as far from their view as from that of Horace,[2] who thinks that Lucilius 'flows along muddily' and that there are things in him that you could well be rid of. He has astonishing learning and outspokenness—and, as a result of that, acerbity: and a great deal of wit. Horace is much more concise and pure: unless I am biased by my love for him, he is the best. Persius won a good deal of genuine fame, despite writing only one book. There are brilliant satirists today, whose names will be celebrated in the future.

95 The other type of satire,[3] an earlier invention, was exploited by Terentius Varro, in his case with prose as well as a variety of metres. This most learned among Romans composed very many books of vast erudition. He was highly skilled in the Latin language and every aspect of antiquity, together with both Greek and Roman history; but he has more to offer to learning than to eloquence.

96 The iambus has not been much used by the Romans as a metre by itself, but rather with other sorts of line interposed. You may find instances of its bitter invective in Catullus, Bibaculus, and Horace (though in him short lines intervene). But of the lyric poets this same Horace is virtually the only one worth reading. He is lofty at times, full of gaiety and grace, varied in his use of figures, in his use of words most felicitously

---

[1] *Ecl.* 8. 13.   [2] *Sat.* 1. 4. 11 (above, p. 266).
[3] i.e. that developed by Ennius, with a variety of metres. Varro's 'Menippean satires' included also prose: compare the use of verse passages in a prose context in Petronius.

daring. If you want to add a second, it will be Caesius Bassus, whom we have only recently lost. But he is far surpassed by the genius of living writers.[1]

TRAGEDY AND COMEDY

Among writers of tragedy, Accius and Pacuvius are the most renowned 97 of the ancients for the high seriousness of their thought, their weighty language, and their impressive characters. They lack brilliance and the final touches in the polishing of their plays—but that may be thought to have been a deficiency of their age, not of themselves. Accius, however, is conceded to have more power, while critics who lay claim to learning would have us believe this is where Pacuvius excels. Varius' *Thyestes* 98 is comparable to any Greek tragedy. Ovid's *Medea* shows, in my view, what its author could have achieved if he had been ready to control his genius rather than pander to it. Of my contemporaries, far the best is Pomponius Secundus. Old men thought him not tragic enough, but they had to agree that he excelled in learning and brilliance.

In the field of comedy, we are at our lamest. Varro may say that the 99 Muses, in the view of Aelius Stilo, would have spoken in the language of Plautus if they had wished to talk Latin; the ancients may praise Caecilius; Terence's plays may be thought to have been the work of Scipio Africanus (they are certainly the most elegant examples of this genre, and would have had even more grace if they had been restricted to trimeters);[2] but despite all this it is a fleeting shadow that we attain to. Indeed I 100 think that the very language of Rome does not admit of the charm that is conceded to Attic speakers (and only to them, for even the Greeks could not attain to it in any other dialect of their language). Afranius excels in plays on Roman subjects. I wish that he had not spoiled his plots by introducing the sordid homosexual affairs that throw such light on his own habits.

HISTORY

But in history we do not need to yield to the Greeks. I should not be 101 afraid to match Sallust with Thucydides; and Herodotus should not be angry to find Livy put on a par with him. For Livy shows extraordinary grace and brilliant lucidity in narration, while in his speeches he is indescribably eloquent, so nicely is everything that is said adapted to

---

[1] Including Statius?

[2] i.e. had not used also the longer and more vivacious iambic and trochaic lines.

circumstances and character; and to put it mildly, no historian has better
102 judged his use of emotions, particularly the gentler ones. Hence, by quite
different qualities, he equalled the wonderful speed that we associate with
Sallust. It was, I think, an excellent dictum of Servilius Nonianus that
these two are on the same level rather than alike. Nonianus himself I
have heard recite; he was a man of splendid talents, full of pointed
103 reflection, but more diffuse than the dignity of history demands. That
dignity was excellently maintained, especially in the books on the German
war, by a slightly earlier writer, Aufidius Bassus, thanks to his style.[1]
He is deserving of approval in all respects, though in some points he
104 falls short of his own powers. There still survives, to the distinction of
our age, a writer[2] worthy of the attention of posterity. In the future he
will be named; now my readers will know who I mean. Cremutius' outspokenness, not unreasonably, has its admirers, though it has been docked
of the parts that it ruined him to have written: but you can detect his
splendidly exalted spirit and his daring thoughts even in what survives.
There are other good writers in this field, but I am only dipping into
each genre, not searching out whole libraries.

ORATORY

105 It is our orators, however, who in particular can put Latin eloquence
on a par with Greek: for I should happily pit Cicero against any Greek
writer whatever. I am not unaware of the battle I am provoking: though
I do not intend here to compare him with Demosthenes. Indeed, there is
no point in such a comparison, for I am in any case convinced that Demosthenes must be a primary subject for study—or rather for learning by
106 heart. Their virtues, I think, are most of them alike: their judgement,
arrangement, technique of division, preparation, and proof, everything in
fact that has to do with 'invention'. There *is* a certain difference of style.
One is closer-packed, the other more diffuse; one rounds his periods more
tightly, the other more spaciously. One fights all his battles by quickness
of wit, the other, often, adds brute strength. One permits of no abbrevi-
ation, the other of no expansion. Demosthenes is more studied, Cicero
107 more naturally gifted. In two matters of especial weight in emotional
oratory, wit and pathos, we Romans undoubtedly win. It may be that
Athenian customs denied Demosthenes his epilogues. But it is equally
true that the different genius of the Latin language handicaps *us* in
attaining effects that Attic audiences admire. There is no comparison
between the two in letters (which survive from both), or in dialogue

---

[1] Text uncertain.   [2] Perhaps Fabius Rusticus.

(not attempted by Demosthenes). But one point must be conceded: 108
Demosthenes came first, and he it was, to a large extent, who made Cicero
the great orator he was. For Cicero, in my opinion, devoted himself
entirely to the imitation of the Greeks. He reproduced the force of Demosthenes, the copiousness of Plato, the agreeable charm of Isocrates. But 109
he did not merely attain by study to the best points of each of his models;
his superhuman richness of genius produced from itself most, indeed all
of his virtues. He does not (to quote Pindar) 'collect the rain water',
but 'overflows with a vital torrent'.[1] He was born, by some gift of providence, as one in whom eloquence could try out her full strength. No one 110
can instruct more painstakingly, rouse emotion more forcefully. No one
was ever so pleasant to hear—so that even when he is wrenching something out of you, you believe that he is winning your willing consent:
and though he is sweeping the judges off their feet, *they* think they are
following without any constraint. In all that he says there is so much 111
authority that one feels ashamed to disagree. He brings to bear not the
partisan zeal of an advocate, but the reliability of witness or judge. What is
more, all these things, that an ordinary person could scarcely achieve
one at a time after the most laborious effort, flow out without trouble;
and that oratory, the fairest ever heard, nevertheless displays not only
perfect felicity but complete ease. It was, then, not undeservedly that 112
men of his day said that he was king in the courts—or that he has so made
his mark with posterity that 'Cicero' now is regarded not as the name of a
man but as the name of eloquence itself. This, then, should be the object
of our gaze, this the model we set ourselves. By this token a man shall
know that he has made progress—that he takes real pleasure in Cicero.

Asinius Pollio has great powers of invention, supreme (some think 113
excessive) diligence, tolerable judgement, and spirit: but he is so far
removed from the refined and agreeable Cicero that he might be thought
to be earlier by a century. Messalla is refined all right, and lucid, and (as
it were) shows his noble birth in his style: but he is inferior in vigour.

In Gaius Caesar, however, if he had devoted his attention solely to law- 114
suits, we should have an incontestable name to set against Cicero; such
are his force, pointedness, and vigour that it is clear that he spoke with the
same spirit with which he made war: and all this is given lustre by his
wonderful choiceness of language, on which he was so peculiarly keen.
In Caelius there is much talent, and, especially in accusation, much wit: 115
he deserved greater wisdom and a longer life. I have found those who
preferred Calvus to anyone else, others who agreed with Cicero[2] that by
excessive self-criticism he lost genuine full-bloodedness. All the same,
his style is grave, weighty, correct, and often forceful. But he was a

<hr>

[1] Fr. 287 Bowra.   [2] *Brutus* 283.

follower of the Attic orators; and his early death did him a disservice only if he would have added to his qualities, not if he would have pared them down.

116 Servius Sulpicius, too, won a not undeserved reputation, by three speeches only. Cassius Severus, if read with judgement, will give us much worthy of imitation. If he had added to the rest of his virtues a fit tone and gravity

117 of style, he would have to be ranked among the best. For he has a great deal of talent, astonishing tartness, and much wit; but he prized ill-temper before judgement. His humour may be bitter; but often the bitterness itself causes laughter.

118 There are many other eloquent men, for whom I have no space. Of my contemporaries, Domitius Afer and Julius Africanus are far the best. Afer is to be preferred for his use of words and his whole style of speaking; you would not hesitate to include him in the ranks of the ancients. Africanus is more vigorous, but he takes his care in choosing words too far, and his structure is sometimes diffuse, his metaphors too bold.

119 There have been distinguished talents even quite recently. Trachalus was often lofty and tolerably lucid. His aspirations, one could well believe, were of the highest. But he was better heard than read; vocal endowments, unparalleled in my experience, a delivery that would not have disgraced the stage, good looks—everything in fact that nature can give to an orator he had in full measure. There was Vibius Crispus, too, smooth, agreeable, born to please: better, however, in private cases than

120 public ones. If Julius Secundus had lived longer, he would surely have won the highest renown for oratory: he would have added, indeed he already was adding, to his other virtues what might be thought lacking in him—he would have become, that is, much more pugnacious, and

121 would have had more frequent regard to matter as opposed to style. Cut short as he was, he still can claim a distinguished position, such is his eloquence, his grace in putting over whatever he wishes, so clear, smooth, and attractive his style, such his correctness in the use of words, even those used figuratively, such his vividness even in expressions that go

122 near the brink of possibility. Later writers on oratory will have great scope for sincere praise of those who flourish today, when the highest talents give lustre to the courts. Those now mature are rivals of the ancients; and they are being imitated and followed by hard-working and aspiring young men.

PHILOSOPHY

123 There remain writers on philosophy—a genre in which Roman literature has so far produced few eloquent authors. Cicero, as everywhere else,

was in this genre too a rival of Plato. But Brutus—excellent here, and much more impressive than in his oratory—did not fall short of the importance of his subject. You may easily feel his sincerity. A very prolific writer was 124 Cornelius Celsus, follower of the Sextii, and not lacking in polish and refinement. Plautus, among the Stoics, is useful for his information. Among the Epicureans, a light-weight but not disagreeable authority is Catius.

SENECA

It is on purpose that I have put off mention of Seneca in every branch of 125 eloquence. For a false view has got around concerning me; I am supposed to condemn Seneca, and even hate him. This is the result of my attempt to recall a corrupted style of oratory, enervated by every vice, to more rigorous standards: and at the time when I did this, Seneca was virtually the only reading-matter of young men. I was not trying to reject him 126 altogether: but I was not prepared to have him preferred to his betters. *He* had never ceased to attack *them*: he knew that his own style was different from theirs, and lacked confidence that he could please those who liked them. But his admirers loved Seneca rather than imitated him; they fell as far short of him as he of the ancients—for to reach the level 127 of Seneca, or something near it, would be a laudable aim. But he was popular for his faults alone; everyone set himself to reproducing what he was capable of reproducing: and in boasting that they were speaking in the Senecan style his admirers slandered Seneca.

He had, in any case, many great qualities: a fluent and prolific talent, 128 much capacity for work, much knowledge (though he was sometimes misled by those to whom he had delegated research on various points). And he handled virtually every branch of study: we have from his hand 129 speeches,[1] poetry, letters, and dialogues. In philosophy he was careless, but excellent in his denunciation of vice. He has many brilliant reflections, and a great deal of what he wrote is worth reading for ethical reasons. But as far as his style goes, there is much that is corrupt, and particularly dangerous just because the constant faults are so attractive. You might 130 wish him to have written employing his own genius but someone else's judgement. If he had not scorned the straightforward and yearned for the corrupt, if he had not loved all his own work, if he had avoided breaking up his weighty pronouncements into the briefest possible epigrams, he would be approved by scholars generally, not merely by enthusiastic youth. Even as it is, he is to be recommended to those who are already 131

[1] None extant.

mature, toughened sufficiently in a more severe style—just for the reason that he puts the reader's judgement to the test, for and against him. As I have said, there is much to be praised, much even to be admired in him, so long as one takes the trouble to be selective—and would that he had done that himself! His genius was worthy of better aims: but what he aimed at he achieved.

E. IMITATION

Quintilian next proceeds (10. 2) to discuss imitation, which he obviously conceives as something much more than mechanical reproduction. Cf. 'Longinus' 13–14 (below, pp. 475–6).

1 From these authors, and others who may be worth reading, is to be derived a supply of words, varied figures of speech, and the principle of verbal arrangement: by them, too, the mind is to be directed towards examples of every good quality in writing—for there can be no doubt that a great part of art lies in *imitation*. Discovery clearly came first, and is of first importance. But it is none the less profitable to follow up other 2 people's successful discoveries. And every technique in life is founded on our natural desire to do ourselves what we approve in others. Hence children follow the shapes of letters to attain facility in writing; musicians look for a model to the voice of their instructors, painters to the works of their predecessors, countrymen to methods of growing that have been proved successful by experience. In fact, we can see that the rudiments of any kind of skill are shaped in accordance with an example set for it. 3 Certainly we must either be like or unlike those who excel. It is rarely that nature makes one man like another: but imitation often does. Yet this very principle, which makes every accomplishment so much easier for us than it was for men who had nothing to follow, is dangerous unless taken up cautiously and with judgement.

4 First of all, then, imitation by itself is not enough. It is the sign of a lazy mentality to be content with what has been discovered by others. What would have happened in those times which lacked models if men had thought that they should do and think nothing that they did not already 5 know? Obviously nothing would ever have been discovered. How, then, can it be wrong for *us* to discover something that did not exist before? Those untutored men of old were led by sheer natural talent to bring so much to fruition: are *we* not to be inspired to search by the very fact 6 that we know that those who have sought in the past have found? *They* had no teacher in anything, yet they handed down a great deal to posterity.

Can we not make use of our experience in one set of facts to dig out
another? Shall we have nothing except by someone else's courtesy—like
painters whose only ambition is to copy pictures by a process of guide-
lines and measurements? It is also shameful to be content merely to 7
reach the level of your model. For the same question arises—what would
have happened if nobody had ever done more than the man he was following? We should have nothing in poetry better than Livius Andronicus,
or in history to surpass the annals of the *pontifex maximus*.[1] We should still
be sailing about on rafts. There would be no pictures, except of the type
that traces out the shadow a body makes against the sun. And if you were 8
to make a general review, you would see that no art is as it was when it was
discovered, or has confined itself to its starting-place. The alternative is
to convict our times of a unique misfortune—it is only now that nothing
is growing. But nothing does grow by mere imitation.

Again, if it is wrong to add to one's predecessors' discoveries, how can 9
we hope for the 'perfect orator'? For among the orators whom so far we
know as the masters, no one has appeared who cannot be found lacking,
or open to criticism, in some respect or other. Even those who do not
intend to aim for the peaks ought to be rivals, not followers. The man 10
who struggles to overtake may perhaps manage to equal where he cannot
surpass. But no one can overtake someone if he thinks that he *must* follow
exactly in his footsteps; one who follows is necessarily always in the rear.
Moreover, it is often easier to achieve more than to achieve the same; an
exact replica is very difficult—indeed even nature herself has not contrived that things that look very similar and alike indeed should be incapable of being told apart by *some* difference. Again, something that is 11
like another thing must also be *less* than what it imitates, as a shadow is
less than a body, a picture than a face, an actor's representation than
true emotion. This is true also of speeches. Nature and real vitality lie
at the root of what we take as examples, but every imitation is a mere
artefact, accommodated to someone else's scheme. This is why declama- 12
tions have less blood and strength than speeches: in the latter the material
is real, in the former fictitious. Moreover, the greatest qualities of an
orator—talent, facility of discovery, force, fluency, everything that art
cannot supply—these things are not imitable. And so many people, 13
having extracted various words from speeches or a few fixed rhythms,
imagine that they have made a remarkable reproduction of what they
have read. But in fact words fall into disuse or come to popularity with
time, and custom gives the best rule for their use. They are not good or
bad by their own nature, for of themselves they are mere sounds, but
according as they are aptly and rightly positioned (or the opposite).

[1] Cf. Cicero, *de oratore* 2. 52 (above, p. 255).

Similarly, rhythmic structure must be adapted to the matter and win credit by its very variety.

14   Thus, every point concerning this branch of our studies is to be weighed with the most careful judgement. First of all, *whom* we should imitate, for there are many who have yearned to resemble the worst and most decadent authors. Then, in the authors we choose, what it is that we

15   should train ourselves to reproduce. For some faults find their way even into the great authors, to meet the disapproval of critics and even of other writers. If only people would improve their oratory by imitating what is good as much as they ruin it by imitating what is bad! Nor should those who have enough judgement to avoid faults be satisfied to produce a mirror-image of a good quality, giving, one might say, merely a veneer,

16   or those 'shapes'[1] said by Epicurus to flow off the surface of bodies. But that is what happens to those who have not seen deeply into good qualities, but have modelled themselves, as it were, on the first view of an orator's style. When their imitation has gone well, they are not very different from their model in vocabulary and rhythm: but they do not attain their force of speech and imagination. And generally they take a turn for the worse, and embrace the faults that lie so near good qualities. They become bombastic instead of grand, meagre instead of concise, rash instead of bold, affected instead of rich, jazzy instead of rhythmic,

17   careless instead of straightforward. Thus, those who have produced some frigid and empty piece of writing, without polish or structure, believe themselves the equals of the ancients; those who lack ornament and epigram rival the Attic orators; writers (we are asked to believe) who court obscurity by amputating their sentences are the superiors of Sallust and Thucydides; cheerless and jejune writers are rivals of Pollio, easy-going and limp ones, the moment they have fashioned some rather long period,

18   swear that Cicero would have put it thus. I have known some writers who imagined they had reproduced the style of that superhuman writer beautifully if they had put *esse videatur* at the end of their sentence.[2] Thus it is the first essential that everyone should understand what he is proposing to imitate, and should realize why it is good.

19   Next, in taking on a load, he should take account of his own strength. Some models a writer's weakness may fall short of; with some his utter unlikeness may clash. The slender talent should not wish to concentrate on the bold and the rugged. The strong but untamed talent will find that an enthusiasm for subtlety will destroy his strength, without enabling

---

[1] The *eidōla* that produced sense-perception in Epicurus' atomic theory were composed of a film of particles emitted from the surface of objects.

[2] A typical example of a favourite Ciceronian clausula: $-\cup\underset{\smile}{\smile}|--$, cretic (or paeon) + spondee. Cf. Tacitus, *Dialogus* 28 (below, p. 446).

him to reach the elegance he strives for. There is nothing more unbecoming than the unpolished handling of a delicate theme. Certainly in the 20 second book[1] I gave the teacher I was there instructing the duty of providing training that went wider than the things for which he saw an individual pupil might be most naturally suited. He has to nurture the good things he has found in each of them, but also, as far as possible, to add what is lacking and to correct and change other elements. He can do this because he is the ruler and indeed the moulder of another's intellect— to shape one's own nature is more difficult. All the same, not even the 21 teacher I was describing, however much he may wish his pupils to have all the right qualities in the highest degree possible, will trouble to try to make progress where he sees nature stand full in his path.

One thing to avoid (many fall into this trap) is thinking that we should imitate poets and historians in oratory, or orators and declaimers in poetry and history. Each genre has its own rules and proprieties. Comedy 22 does not rise high on tragic buskins, nor does tragedy stroll about in the slippers of comedy. All the same, every type of eloquence has something in common—and that is what we must imitate.

Those who have devoted themselves to one particular style find them- 23 selves afflicted by another trouble: if they have fallen in love with someone's harsh tone, they cannot get rid of it in cases of a gentle and relaxed type. If they approve of slenderness and agreeableness, they are unable to match up to the weight of the subject in tough and serious cases. For requirements differ not only from case to case, but even in different parts of the same case. Some things must be dealt with gently, some roughly: some excitedly, some calmly: some with an eye to instruction, some to emotion. All these things demand different methods. Thus, I should not 24 advise a student, either, to devote himself to one particular speaker as model in everything. Demosthenes is far the most perfect of the Greeks; he does most things better than anyone else could—but others may do the occasional thing better than he. Just because someone is most worthy of our imitation, we should not imitate him alone. Well, you may ask, 25 isn't it enough to say everything as Cicero said it? It would be enough for *me*, anyway—if I *could* reach his level in everything. But what harm can there be in adding, at certain points, Caesar's forcefulness, Caelius' pungency, Pollio's care, Calvus' taste? A prudent man should, if he can, 26 make his own what he sees to be best in every author; and, besides that, the matter is so difficult that, if we concentrate on one model alone, we shall be lucky to pick up even a part of his virtues. Thus, since it is scarcely given to man to reproduce in his entirety the orator he chooses as model, we should put before our eyes the good points of a number of

[1] 2. 8.

orators, so that one thing may stick from one source, one from another, and so that we can fit each in at the right place.

27   But imitation—I shall go on repeating this point—is not to be taken as being merely a matter of words. We must concentrate on the sense of fitness that those great men show in adapting themselves to circumstances and personalities: on their strategy, their arrangement, the way in which everything—even things that seem to be put in merely for entertainment —has victory as its aim. We should note what the proem is designed to do; what sort of tactics are adopted in the narration, and how various they are; what powers of proof and refutation are displayed, what skill in arousing all kinds of emotion; how even public popularity is turned to advantage (something that is honourable when it comes automatically

28   and unsought). If we see all this clearly, we shall be able truly to imitate. But he who can add his own qualities to these, supplying what was lacking in them, cutting out everything that may be superfluous—he will be the perfect orator we are looking for. He is capable of complete realization particularly at the present time, when so many more models of good oratory are available than were at hand for those who are, to date, the greatest. This will be *their* praise: that they surpassed their predecessors, and taught their successors.

F. TYPES OF ORATORY

Here (12. 10) Quintilian discusses different kinds of oratory. His remarks are by no means the stereotyped ones, and he has interesting things to say on the parallel with artistic progress, and on the contrast between the Greek and Latin languages. See R. G. Austin's edn. of Book 12, Oxford, 1948, 1965.

1   It remains for me to discuss types of oratory: this was the third topic I set myself in my original division, for I promised that I would talk of the art, the artist, and his product. The product both of rhetoric and of the orator is oratory, and, as I shall show, it has many forms, which differ much among themselves (though in all the art and the artist are found at work), not only in species, as statue differs from statue, picture from picture, one speech from another, but in type even, as Etruscan from

2   Greek statues, or an Asian orator from an Attic. Now all of these types of product that I speak of have their admirers as well as their exponents; and perfection in oratory and perhaps in any other art has not yet been attained not only because each orator has different strengths, but also because not everyone has preferred the same one kind, partly as a result of variation of time or place, partly because of individual tastes and aims.

THE DEVELOPMENT OF SCULPTURE AND PAINTING[1]

The first famous painters—the first, at least, whose works deserve looking 3 at not merely on account of their age—are said to have been Polygnotus and Aglaophon, whose simple use of colour still has admirers so enthusiastic as to prefer these crude pictures, mere shadows of the art that was to come, to the greatest of later artists: but this, I think, is merely a private bid to be taken for connoisseurs. After this, Zeuxis and Par- 4 rhasius, both of much the same period about the time of the Peloponnesian wars (we find in Xenophon[2] a conversation between Parrhasius and Socrates), added a great deal to the technique of painting; Zeuxis is said to have discovered the method of representing light and shade, Parrhasius to have brought new skill to the exploitation of outline. Zeuxis gave human 5 limbs more fullness, thinking that this gave increased nobility and distinction, and thereby following Homer (it is thought), who likes the strongest possible bodies, even in women. Parrhasius, however, was so universally definitive that they call him the lawgiver—everyone follows his authoritative representation of gods and heroes as though it were compulsory. Painting in particular flourished in the period of Philip 6 and right down to the successors of Alexander, though its qualities varied. Protogenes excels in care, Pamphilus and Melanthius in method, Antiphilus in facility, Theon of Samos in vividness of conception (the Greeks use the term *phantasia*),[3] Apelles in talent and the grace of which he is particularly proud. Euphranor is to be admired because, while being distinguished in the other honourable arts, he was at the same time an astonishing painter and sculptor.

A similar variety can be traced in statuary. Callon and Hegesias made 7 things that were rather harsh, very like Etruscan. Calamis' products were already less unbending, Myron's softer still. Polyclitus' had surpassing care and beauty; most yield him the palm, but, in order to have something to carp at, find in him a lack of weight. For, while giving an unrealistic 8 beauty to the human form, he is regarded as not having provided gods with their due of authority. Indeed, he is said to have avoided representing more advanced age, restricting his enterprise to smooth cheeks. What Polyclitus lacked, it is agreed that Phidias and Alcamenes possessed. But Phidias (so it is said) was more skilled at representing gods than men; 9 in ivory, however, he was far beyond any rival—even if he had done nothing except the Athena in Athens or the Olympian Zeus in Elis, whose beauty is thought even to have added something to the traditional

---

[1] See R. G. Austin's notes on this passage.
[2] *Memorabilia* 3. 10. 1.
[3] Cf. 'Longinus' 15, below, p. 477.

awe inspired by the god, so fully did the majesty of the piece come up to the majesty of its subject. It is claimed that Lysippus and Praxiteles best attained to realism; indeed Demetrius is criticized for over-indulgence in it, and he was certainly more keen on a likeness than on beauty.

DEVELOPMENT OF ORATORY

10 Now if you care to look at types in oratory, you may find almost as many kinds of talent as of human body. But there have been types of oratory that as a consequence of their period were rather rough, while nevertheless already displaying great vigour of genius. Here may be classed orators such as Laelius, Africanus, even Cato and Gracchus; these you might

11 call the Polygnotuses and the Callons. The middle class may be assigned to Lucius Crassus and Quintus Hortensius. After this we may allow to burst on us a great crop of more or less contemporary orators. Here we shall find the force of Caesar, the talent of Caelius, the subtlety of Calidius, the care of Pollio, the dignity of Messalla, the scrupulousness of Calvus, the weight of Brutus, the sharpness of Sulpicius, the bite of Cassius; add, among those recent enough for us to have seen ourselves, Seneca's flow, Africanus' power, Afer's sophistication, Crispus' sweetness, Tra-

12 chalus' voice-production, Secundus' elegance. But in Marcus Tullius we have someone not merely, as Euphranor was, outstanding in several types of art, but pre-eminent in all skills that are praised in any orator. Nevertheless, even in his own day, men dared to attack him as too inflated, an Asian, redundant, over-repetitious, occasionally humourless, and in his rhythms undisciplined, exuberant, and even (worst charge of all) too

13 effeminate to be a true man. And after his death in the triumvirs' pro-scriptions, when he could no longer answer back, he was the object of indiscriminate attacks from those who hated, envied, and rivalled him, and those who flattered the great ones of the day. But this man, who is today by some regarded as bare and dry, could give even his enemies no handle for criticism except for excessive floweriness and superfluity of gifts. Both charges are false; but we may grant that there was more

14 excuse for the lie in the latter case. But he was under especial pressure from those who wanted to be thought to be imitators of the Attic orators. This band of pseudo-initiates attacked him as a foreigner,[1] too little reverent, too little bound by their rules; their present-day representa-

15 tives are our dry, juiceless, bloodless speakers, the ones who cover their weaknesses with the description of 'health' (which is just the opposite); they cannot tolerate the sunshine, as it were, of a more brilliant onrush

---

[1] Cicero came from Arpinum, 70 miles from Rome.

of eloquence, and therefore they cower in the shade of a great name. Cicero has himself replied to them at length in many passages,[1] and I shall be safer to be brief on this topic.

ATTIC AND ASIAN

This division between Attic and Asian orators was an old one; the former 16 were regarded as brief and healthy, the latter tumid and empty; the former had nothing superfluous, the latter lacked in particular taste and moderation. Santra, amongst others, thinks that this came about because, as the Greek language gradually spread into the nearest Asian cities, their inhabitants were agog for eloquent utterance while they were not yet sufficiently skilled in ordinary language; thus they began to express by circumlocutions things that had their own special terms, and then proceeded to stick to this practice. My view, however, is that the difference 17 of speech was the result of the character of both speakers and hearers; the Attic people, smooth and correct, would put up with nothing empty or redundant, while the Asians, in general a more bombastic and boastful race, puffed themselves out with vainglory in oratory also. A third type, 18 the Rhodian, has been added by those who formulated this distinction, intending it to be a middle kind partaking of both the other two. The Rhodians are not concise in the Attic manner or wordy in the Asian, thereby revealing, besides a certain national characteristic of their race, the influence of a founder—Aeschines, who, having chosen this place for 19 his exile, brought there the literary interests of Athens, which, just as certain plants degenerate in new soils and climates, contaminated their Attic flavour with a foreign one. As a result, the Rhodians are thought of as rather slow and slack, though not without weight; they are like neither pure fountains nor muddy torrents: rather do they resemble calm meres.

TYPES OF ATTIC ORATOR

There is no room for doubt, then, that far the best type is the Attic. 20 Within this type, though there is a certain common element of concise and sharp tastefulness, we may distinguish many different kinds of talent. Thus, I think that a great mistake is made by those who regard the only 21 Attic orators as those who are plain, clear, pointed, but content with a certain economy of eloquence, always keeping their hand inside the cloak. Who will then count as this sort of Attic orator? Suppose it is Lysias (he is the standard fixed by admirers of the name of Attic, and by choosing him we may avoid the extreme of Coccus and Andocides): then I should 22

[1] Both the *Orator* and the *Brutus* are in effect a reply to the 'Atticists'.

want to ask whether Isocrates spoke in the Attic way. For nothing could be so different from Lysias. They will say no; yet Isocrates' school produced master-orators. Let us look for something a little nearer. Was Hyperides Attic? 'Surely.' But he was less austere than Lysias. I pass over many, such as Lycurgus, Aristogiton, and the earlier Isaeus and Antiphon, all of whom you might call similar to each other in genus but
23 different in species. What about Aeschines, whom I mentioned just now? Is he not broader and more daring and more lofty? Finally, what about Demosthenes? Did he not surpass all those plain and circumspect orators with his fire, sublimity, impetus, sophistication, and rhythm? Does he not have lofty commonplaces? Does he not gladly use figures?
24 Does he not shine with metaphor? He is not averse to using fictitious passages where he gives a voice to the silent; and that great oath by those who were killed defending their country at Marathon and Salamis[1] surely must make it clear that Plato was his teacher. (And I take it that we are not going to call Plato of all men an Asian; often he is comparable rather with divinely inspired poets.) Then there is Pericles. Shall we regard *him* as being slender like Lysias? After all the comic poets compare him to lightning flashes and thunder from heaven, even while they
25 abuse him.[2] There is no reason to think of the Attic savour as the prerogative of those who flow among pebbles in a slender rill, and imagine that it is only here that one can get a whiff of Attic thyme. I believe that such critics would be inclined to deny Attic nationality to any rich soil or fertile crop found in that country just because it gives back more seed than it received (with an allusion to Menander's jest about the exact-
26 ness with which Attica pays her debts).[3] Similarly if an orator were granted, in addition to the qualities which the supreme Demosthenes possessed, the one that, thanks to his own nature or the laws of his city, he lacked—more vigorous emotional appeal, would I hear people saying: 'Demosthenes was not like that'? If a passage were to run more rhythmically (perhaps that is impossible—but suppose it did), can't we count it as Attic? I suggest that these people should have a better opinion of the term, and come to believe that to speak in the Attic manner is to speak in the best manner.

LATIN AND GREEK CONTRASTED

27 I should be more sympathetic if it were Greeks who persisted in so perverse a view. But Latin eloquence, in my opinion, while it is similar

---

[1] *On the Crown*, 208. Cf. 'Longinus' 16, below, p. 480.
[2] Aristophanes, *Acharnians* 530 ff.
[3] *Georgos* (*The Farmer*) 35 ff.: Attica pays back exactly what is sown!

to Greek (and indeed altogether its pupil) in invention, arrangement, strategy, and all that sort of technique, can scarcely be in a position to imitate Greek in stylistic matters. For its sound makes it harsher straight away: we do not possess the most pleasant Greek letters. These are one vowel and one consonant,[1] unparalleled in their language for their sweet tone; we customarily borrow them whenever we use Greek words; and when this happens, speech instantly becomes somehow gayer and brightens up—as in words like 'Zephyros' and 'Zōpyros', which would produce a dull and outlandish effect if written out with our letters. But, to fill their gaps, as it were, up come two gloomy and spiky letters that Greek lacks. One, sixth in our alphabet, has to be blown out between one's teeth. In making this sound the voice is hardly human, or rather not a voice at all. Even when it gets a vowel next to it, it somehow quakes; but whenever it comes up against another consonant (as in the word I have just used, *frangit*), it becomes still more uncouth. (We are also dogged by the Aeolic letter;[2] we have indeed rejected its written form, but the force of it remains in *seruus* and *ceruus*.) The other letter, which also makes syllables harsh, is useful only for linking vowels following it, but is otherwise superfluous; we use this to write *equos* and *aequum*. These diphthongs, moreover, themselves produce a sound that is not heard in Greek and so cannot be written in their letters. We may add that Latin often ends words with that mooing letter *m* which is found at the close of no Greek word; they substitute for it the agreeable nu, a ringing sort of letter, particularly in the final position. We only very rarely put this last. Again, our syllables close in *b* and *d* to such harsh effect that many old writers, though not the ancients, tried to soften them, not only by saying *auersa* instead of *abuersa*, but also by adding the letter *s* (not a particularly nice sound in itself) to the *b* in the preposition *ab*. We also have a less agreeable system of accentuation, marred by a certain rigidity and also by lack of variety: the last syllable may never be given an acute or circumflex accent, but words always end in one or two graves. Hence, the Greek language is so much more pleasant than the Latin that when our poets want to make a poem agreeable they bedeck it with Greek names. More serious, many things lack terms, making metaphor or circumlocution inevitable; and even when things have been given names, our extreme poverty of vocabulary brings us back to the same expression time and again. The Greeks, however, have abundant words—and abundant dialects into the bargain.

28

29

30

31

32

33

34

---

[1] Upsilon (υ) and zeta (ζ).
[2] The digamma (ϝ), with the sound of our *w*, represented in Latin by consonantal *u* (cer*u*us).

HOW LATIN MUST FACE UP TO ITS DEFICIENCIES

35 Thus anyone who demands of the Latins the grace that characterizes the Attic tongue must provide us with an equally agreeable and rich language. If that is denied us, we shall have to go on fitting our thoughts to the words we have—taking care not to swamp slender subjects with words too rich (perhaps I had better say 'too strong') for them: for that

36 is the way to ruin both elements in the confusion. The less one's language helps one, the more one has to use one's material as one's weapon. We must search out lofty and varied sentiments, rouse every emotion, enliven our speech with sparkling metaphor. We cannot be so gracefully slender as the Greeks: let us be stronger. We are worsted in subtlety; let us prevail by weight. They have a better chance of finding the exact word;

37 let us vanquish by our fullness. Even lesser Greeks have their ports to shelter them; we generally sail under a greater spread of canvas. Let a stronger breeze billow out our sails. But we shall not always be traversing the open sea; sometimes we must follow the shore. The Greeks can approach it across the shallowest waters; I shall have to find something deeper—though not much deeper—to save my craft from going aground.

38 But, even though the Greeks produce these more plain and concise effects better, and we are inferior here, though only here (hence our inability to compete in comedy), we should not therefore abandon this side of oratory: rather we should exploit it as best we can. What we can do is to rival the Greeks in restraint and tastefulness of matter, while sprinkling on to our words from other sources the attractions that they do not in

39 themselves have. Cicero in his private speeches was surely pointed, exact, controlled; Marcus Calidius was noted for these qualities. Scipio, Laelius, and Cato showed in their actual language that they were the Roman equivalent of the Attic orators. What cannot be improved must needs suffice.

'NATURAL' ELOQUENCE

40 Again, some think no eloquence is natural unless it is as near as possible to ordinary language of the type we use when speaking to friends, wives, children, and slaves: language that is satisfied to get meaning over, and looks for nothing exotic or elaborate. Anything beyond that (they say) is affectation, ostentatious display of language, removed from reality, made up for the sake of the words it uses—though *their* natural function

41 is solely to play the servant to subject-matter. Similarly, the bodies of athletes may become stronger with exercise and dieting, but they are unnatural, and clash with normal human appearance. What is the point

(they add) of signifying things with periphrasis and metaphor—more words, that is, or words out of place—when everything has its proper name assigned to it? Their final contention is that the more antique an 42 orator, the more he spoke 'according to nature'. Later, orators began to resemble poets more and more, differing only in the degree in which they took fictions and abuses of language for virtues.

In this thesis there is some truth; and one would not depart as far as some do from primary and common words. But (as I have said when dis- 43 cussing rhythm) if someone manages to add something better to the indispensable minimum of expression, he should not have to face such criticisms. To my mind ordinary language has one 'nature', the speech of an eloquent man quite another. If an orator needed merely to point out facts, he would not trouble to go outside the straightforward meanings of words. But since he has to please, move, impel his audience into many different frames of mind, he will use the aids that are granted him—just as is straightforward speech—by nature. There is nothing unnatural, 44 after all, in hardening the arms by exercise, increasing one's strength, improving one's complexion. Hence, in every race, one man is accounted more fluent and agreeable in conversation than another (otherwise everyone would be equal and alike); in every race, the same men are capable of speaking differently on different subjects, and preserving differences of character. Thus, the more a man can bring about by speaking, the more he is speaking according to the 'nature' of eloquence.

CONCESSIONS TO THE AGE

So I am not too much in disagreement with those who think that the 45 temper of the age and men's tastes need some concession made to them when they demand something more polished and more emotional. I don't think an orator should be tied down to predecessors of Cato and the Gracchi, or even to those orators themselves. And Cicero's principle, I notice, was to give everything to the needs of his case—but a part to pleasure; he used to say that he had himself to consider also, but he was in fact considering his clients above all—the very fact that he was giving pleasure itself gave him an advantage. And to the pleasure *he* gave I 46 can personally see no possibility of addition—except that we have more epigrams in *our* speeches: something that need not harm the conduct of a case or our authority of language so long as these conceits are not frequent, continuous, and self-destructive. But if I make this concession, 47 I am not to be driven further. I will concede to the fashion that a toga need not be hairy, not that it should be silk: the hair doesn't have to be unbarbered, but it should not be trained into tiers and ringlets. I only add that unless your norm is luxury and lust, the better things really are the

48 more beautiful they look. These epigrams—*sententiae* as they are commonly called—were not used by the old orators, in particular the Greeks, though I find them in Cicero. But so long as they have content and are not simply redundant, and so long as they have a view to the winning of the case, they can hardly be denied to be useful. They strike the mind, and can frequently turn it at a single stroke; they stick just because they are brief, and they are persuasive because they are pleasurable.

WRITTEN SPEECHES AND SPOKEN SPEECHES

49 Yet there are those who feel that these more spirited conceits should be excluded from one's written text even if they allow them to be spoken. I cannot, then, neglect this topic [1] either. Very many scholars have thought there is one method for speaking, another for writing: and that that is why orators renowned for making speeches have in some cases left nothing to posterity and lasting literature—for example Pericles and Demades; on the other hand, others, such as Isocrates, have been excellent at com-

50 posing speeches but unequipped for delivering them. Further (this view holds) delivery usually needs more spirit, and rather more courting of pleasure (it being the uneducated whose minds have to be roused and won over); but something committed to paper and published as a model must be polished, filed, composed according to the rules, for it will come

51 into the hands of the learned and have artists to judge its art. In addition, well-known preceptors (subtle thinkers in their own view and others') have laid down that the instance (*paradeigma*) is more suitable for speech, the rhetorical syllogism (*enthumēma*) for writing. My own view is that it is one and the same thing to speak well and to write well: and a written speech is merely the record of a delivered speech. And so it must not have those virtues alone ... (*gap in the text*) and virtues, mark you, not faults— for I am well aware that sometimes the inexperienced like what is faulty. How, then, will they differ?

52 But if you were to grant me an audience of wise judges, I could prune quite a lot off the speeches not only of Cicero but even of the much sparer Demosthenes. For there would be no need to rouse any emotion, or provide pleasures to soothe the ear—even proems were thought by Aristotle [2] to be superfluous in such circumstances; these wise men would not be attracted by such devices—enough to describe the facts in exact

---

[1] Cf. Pliny, *epist.* 1. 20 (below, p. 424).
[2] *Rhetoric* 3. 14 (above, p. 160).

and clear language and draw out one's proofs. In fact, however, the judges 53
provided are the people or drawn from the people; those who will give
the verdict are often ill-educated, sometimes even rustics. We therefore
have to bring to bear everything that we think will aid us in carrying
our point. These things will be spoken when we are delivering a speech;
and they cannot be suppressed when we write out a speech, if in fact we
write in order to show how it should be spoken. Would Demosthenes or 54
Cicero have done badly to deliver their orations as they wrote them?
Have we, indeed, any way of knowing these distinguished speakers except
by their written texts? Now, did they deliver these speeches better or
worse than that? If worse, they should rather have spoken them as they
wrote them; if better, they should have written them as they spoke them.

Well then, is an orator always to deliver his speech just as he will 55
eventually write it? If possible, always. But there may be limits set by
the judge that embarrassingly shorten the actual speech, causing the
excision of much that could have been said: then the published text will
contain the lot. Again, certain things are said to suit the character of the
judges; they will not be handed down to posterity in that form—otherwise they might seem to reflect on the orator's standards rather than his
circumstances. In fact, it makes a great deal of difference *how* a judge is 56
prepared to listen. 'His very face is often the orator's guide', as Cicero
teaches us.[1] Hence the need to emphasize points that you realize are
popular, and to steer clear of what will not be well received. Even language
may be suited to make the judge take the point as easily as possible;
nor is this surprising, for variations have to be made even to suit the
character of witnesses. Compare the foresight of one who asked a rustic 57
witness whether he knew Amphion and received the answer 'no'. He
proceeded to ask the question again with no aspirate and the second
syllable of the name shortened:[2] in that guise the witness knew Amphion
very well. Circumstances of this kind will cause us sometimes to speak and
write differently—at times when it is impossible to speak as one would
write.

THE THREE STYLES[3]

There is another division—again tripartite—that is thought to mark off 58
from each other styles of speaking that are not faulty. One type is plain
(Greek *ischnon*): the second grand and strong (*hadron*). The third is
variously described as midway between the other two, or flowery (*an-
thēron*). The principle of these, roughly, is that the first undertakes the 59

---

[1] Not from any extant work.　　　　　　　　[2] i.e. Ampion, not Amp-hion.
[3] See, e.g., D. A. Russell, '*Longinus*', Oxford, 1964, xxxiv ff.

task of imparting information, the second of emotional appeal, and the third (whatever one calls it) of pleasing or, some say, conciliating. Giving information involves pointedness, conciliating requires gentleness, emotional appeal force. The technique of narration and proof will lie in the plain style; and this style is self-sufficient even without the other

60 virtues of speech. The middle style will have more frequent metaphors, more agreeable figures; its digressions will make it pleasant, it will be rhythmic, nicely epigrammatic, gentle like a river that is clear but over-

61 shadowed by green banks on either side. But the grand style is the sort of river that whirls rocks along, 'resents bridges',[1] makes its own banks; great and torrential, it will carry along even the judge who tries to stand up to it, forcing him to go where he is taken. Such an orator will raise the dead to speak (e.g. Appius Caecus),[2] and cause the state to cry aloud or sometimes (as in Cicero's case in the *Catilines*)[3] to converse with

62 him. He will lift the speech high by his amplifications, and launch into exaggeration ('What Charybdis was so voracious? . . . Even the ocean itself . . .' Even beginners are familiar with these brilliant passages).[4] He will come near to bringing the gods themselves down to meet and talk to him: 'You hills and groves of Alba, you uprooted altars of the Albans, companions and contemporaries of the shrines of the Roman people . . .'[5] He will inspire anger and pity; and as he speaks the judge will grow pale, weep, follow tamely as he is snatched in one direction after another by the whole gamut of emotion: he will not *ask* to be given the facts.

63 Thus if we had to choose one out of these three styles, who would hesitate to prefer this to the others? It is in general the most potent—and in particular it is adapted to the needs of the most important cases.

64 We have, here, the witness of Homer,[6] who provided Menelaus with an eloquence that was concise, pleasurable, correct (compare the phrase 'not missing the mark in words') and free of superfluities. These are the virtues of the first type. From the mouth of Nestor, said Homer, flowed speech 'sweeter than honey' (and no imaginable pleasure surpasses *that*). But when he had to represent the highest eloquence in the person of Ulysses, he gave him strength of voice and a force of oratory that in its

65 flow and onrush of words resembled the snows. No mortal, then, can compete with such an orator: men will look to him as a god.[7] This is the force and swiftness that Eupolis admires in Pericles, that Aristophanes compares to thunderbolts.[8] This is the capacity for real oratory.

---

[1] Virgil, *Aeneid* 8. 728. [2] In Cicero, *pro Caelio* 33.
[3] 1. 27. [4] Cic. *Philippics* 2. 67. [5] *Pro Milone* 85.
[6] *Iliad* 3. 214, 1. 249, 3. 221; cf. Pliny, *epist.* 1. 20. 22 (below, p. 426). Cf. Cicero, *Brutus* 40 (above, p. 222). [7] An allusion to *Odyssey* 8. 173.
[8] Cf. Pliny, *epist.* 1. 20. 17, 19 (below, p. 425).

But eloquence is not confined to these three forms. Just as there is a 66
third style between the slender and the strong, so there are gaps between
these three that are filled by styles blended between the styles on either
side. We may find something more full or more slender than the slender, 67
more relaxed or more vehement than the vehement. Similarly, the gentle
style may climb towards stronger things or sink to slenderer. Thus comes
about an almost infinite variety of types, which at least at some points
differ from each other. In just the same way, we learn as a general rule
that four winds blow from four points of the compass, whereas in fact
there are many winds in between these with different names, and some
are peculiar to certain regions or rivers. So, too, with musicians, who 68
have five notes on the lyre, but fill the spaces between these strings with a
great variety of notes, even filling in others among *those*: so that these
few intervals have many degrees.

ALL THE STYLES USEFUL

Eloquence, then, has many aspects. But it is stupid to ask to which the 69
orator should direct himself: every kind, if it is not faulty, has its use.
An orator cannot be said to have (to use the popular phrase) a 'style' of
oratory: he will use all the styles as necessary, varying them not only
according to the case but even to parts of the case. He will not speak in 70
the same ways in defence of a man on trial for his life, in a testamentary
case, on interdicts, securities, loans. He will also preserve the distinction
between speeches in senate and before the people and private delibera-
tions, altering much to suit persons, places, and times. But in one and the
same speech he will use one style to rouse, another to conciliate; he will
have different sources for inspiring anger and pity; he will employ one
technique for instruction, another for emotional appeal. He will not keep 71
to one tone in proem, narration, argument, digression, peroration. He
will speak gravely, austerely, spiritedly, vehemently, stirringly, fully,
pungently; he will speak agreeably, relaxedly, plainly, winningly, gently,
sweetly, briefly, wittily. He will not everywhere be the same, though he
will never fall below his own standards. Thus, he will speak effectively 72
and to good purpose (the main reason for the development of oratory);
and he will also win a reputation, among the populace as well as the
scholars.

MODERN EXCESSES

For it is a great fallacy to suppose that there is more popularity and 73
acclaim to be won by a faulty and decadent style of speech, that

cheerfully misuses words, revels in puerile conceits, puffs itself up with immoderate bombast, indulges in empty commonplaces, gleams with flowers that will fall at the lightest touch, regards hazardous expression as sublime expression, or raves under the guise of freedom of speech.

74 It is undeniable, and unsurprising, that this is popular with many. Any and every eloquence is an agreeable thing that finds much favour; every voice attracts minds with a pleasure that is only natural (hence the knots of listeners in the forum and on the ramparts). Every speaker reasonably

75 enough has a ready-made popular audience. But anything a little out of the way that falls on unpractised ears, whatever it is, so long as its hearers despair of producing such an effect themselves, arouses wonder. That is fair enough; even this is not easy. But such effects vanish and die away when compared with better things, just as dyed wool pleases when there is no purple by—'but if you compare it with Spartan purple, it is eclipsed

76 by the sight of something superior', as Ovid puts it.[1] But if you apply a more critical taste to these decadent phenomena (like sulphur to dyestuffs) they would lose the false colour by which they had deceived and pale into indescribable ugliness. These things shine only when the sun is hidden; just as in darkness certain tiny creatures give the impression of sparks. Many praise the bad; no one finds fault with the good.

'PERSEVERE'

77 All these things of which I have spoken the orator will carry out supremely well—and supremely easily. The highest force of oratory, the tongue men marvel at, is not constantly haunted by desperate worries; the true orator is not wasted and tormented by feverish juggling of words, nor does he pine away with the effort of weighing and fitting them together.

78 This brilliant, lofty, well-endowed speaker controls a wealth of eloquence that flows on all sides of him. When you have reached the top, you cease to struggle with the slope. The climber finds trouble on the lower stretches: the further you go, the gentler the gradient, the more fertile the soil.

79 And if you pass even beyond the gentler slopes, and persist in your endeavours, you will find fruits offering themselves to you without your labour, and everything coming automatically—though you have to pluck them daily, or they wither. But plenty requires moderation—without that nothing is praiseworthy or healthy: polish needs a manly

80 elegance, imagination judgement. The outcome will be the great, not the excessive, the lofty, not the precipitous, the bold, not the rash, the restrained, not the austere, the impressive, not the slow, the fertile, not

---

[1] In a lost hendecasyllabic poem.

the rank, the pleasant, not the luxurious, the grand, not the turgid.[1] It is the same with other qualities. The middle way is usually safest; the extreme on either side is a fault.

G. THE GOOD MAN SKILLED IN SPEAKING

Our final extract (from 12. 1) deals with a topic Quintilian thought of supreme importance. It puts forward his conviction that the orator must be a morally good man. He uses a phrase of the elder Cato—*vir bonus dicendi peritus*—but the conditions of the early empire (cf. Tacitus, *Dialogus* 12, below, p. 439, for the eloquence of professional informers) made the view still topical and piquant. At the same time, Quintilian's vision of the orator as a great political leader was altogether outdated—as Tacitus showed in the *Dialogus*.

Our orator then should be (as Marcus Cato defined him) 'a good man 1 skilled in speaking': but particularly a good man—for that is what Cato put first and what is naturally more desirable and more important. One reason is that if oratorical ability is added to the armoury of evil nothing would be more dangerous, whether publicly or privately, than eloquence, while I myself, who have tried, as far as man could, to contribute towards capacity for speaking, should deserve very ill of humanity in forging these weapons for the thief rather than for the soldier. And—to forget about 2 myself—nature would prove to have been no true parent but a mere stepmother in what is on the face of it her greatest favour to man, the one that marks us off from other animals, if she devised speech merely to be the ally of crime, the adversary of innocence, and the enemy of truth. It would have been better for men to be born speechless and altogether irrational than to turn the gifts of providence to the destruction of each other.

But my view goes further. I am not merely saying that the orator 3 ought to be a good man: I say too that he will not even become an orator unless he *is* a good man. Surely you would not regard intelligence as an attribute of those who prefer the worse way when the choice between honour and dishonour is placed before them? Or good sense when an unforeseen turn of events can land them in the direst punishments— those that their own bad consciences inflict, if not, as often happens, those exacted by the law as well. And if it is alike the saying of philosophers and 4 the constant belief of the lay that no one is bad unless he is also stupid, well, there will hardly be an orator who is stupid. Moreover, only a mind free of all faults can have the time even to study this most wonderful of

---

[1] For such relationships of faults and virtues, cf. (e.g.) Horace, *The Art of Poetry* (above, p. 280), 'Longinus' (below, p. 464).

subjects. First, the same breast cannot house good and bad at the same time, and to entertain the best and the worst thoughts simultaneously is as impossible for one mind as it is for the same man to be both good and
5 bad. Secondly, a mind fixed on so important a matter must be free of all cares, even innocent ones. Only thus, free and undivided, with nothing to distract it or lead it astray, will it be able to look firmly towards its objec-
6 tive. If excessive preoccupation with one's estates, extreme trouble taken over money, the pleasures of the hunt, days devoted to shows, can take much away from one's studies (time spent on anything else is lost to these), what can we suppose will be the effect of avarice, greed, and envy, which arouse uncontrollable thoughts, capable of disturbing even one's sleep
7 and dreams? Nothing is so busy, so various, so torn and mutilated by conflicting emotion, as the evil heart. When it is plotting, it is rent by hope, care, trouble; and even when it attains its wicked end, it is tortured by anxiety, remorse, the prospect of every sort of punishment. What place amidst all this for literature or any respectable pursuit? As little as for crops on land taken over by thorn and bramble.
8 Again, is not temperance necessary if the labours of study are to be borne? There is no prospect to be looked for from lust and luxury. Desire for praise is surely the major stimulus towards literary ambitions. But can we suppose the wicked are troubled about praise? And it is obvious that the greater part of oratory hinges on the treatment of the honest and the good, subjects on which the wicked and dishonest man will hardly speak worthily.
9 Finally, to by-pass most of this question, let us grant the impossible, that the best man and the worst have identical standards of ability, exercise, and training: which of the two will be called the better orator? Surely the one who is also the better man. The bad man and the perfect
10 orator, therefore, will never coincide. That which has something superior to it is not perfect.
But I don't want to be thought to be playing the Socratic game of making up replies to my own questions. Let us imagine someone so obstinate in his opposition to the truth as to venture to say that a bad man will be no worse an orator than the good man where ability, practice, and training
11 are equal; and let us refute this mad proposition too. Surely it cannot be denied that all oratory aims at making what it puts forward seem true and fair to the judge? Will it be the good man or the bad who will find it easier to produce such a conviction? The good man, too, will more
12 frequently say what is true and fair. But even if from time to time he is in honour bound (this can happen, as I shall soon show) to try to be misleading here, he must receive a more favourable hearing. Bad men, on the other hand, contemptuous of public opinion and ignorant of what is

right, sometimes lose their mask, and are led to shameless and immodest assertions. The result is an ugly obstinacy and vain trouble on points that 13 cannot be carried: in the courts, as in life, their ambitions are boundless. And it often happens that, even when they *are* speaking the truth, no one believes them: and an advocate bearing such a character is regarded as an indication of the weakness of the case.

Now to face the chorus of protest that I imagine will be raised. 'Was 14 Demosthenes, then, no orator?—yet we hear that he was a bad man. Wasn't Cicero?—yet many have found fault with his character.' What am I to do? My reply will involve me in much obloquy: let me first soothe my audience. I don't think Demosthenes' character so tainted that I can 15 believe all the charges heaped on him by his enemies. I read that his public policies were excellent, his death noble. As to Cicero, he clearly 16 was in no way deficient in the aspirations of a good citizen. Witness his noble consulship, the honest administration of his province and his declining of the vigintivirate:[1] while in the civil wars, the brunt of which was taken by his generation, neither hope nor fear diverted him from allying himself to the better side, that of the Republic. He is regarded as 17 rather cowardly by some; the best answer is his own: 'I am timid not in facing danger but in foreseeing it.' This he proved by the manner of his death: which he met in the noblest spirit. Perhaps these men lacked the 18 highest degree of virtue; but if anyone asks whether they were orators, I reply as the Stoics would reply if asked whether Zeno, Cleanthes, and Chrysippus himself were wise men: that they were good men, worthy of all respect, though they failed to realize the highest possibilities of man. Even Pythagoras preferred to be called a lover of wisdom rather than 19 (like his predecessors) a wise man.[2] But, keeping to ordinary ways of language, I have often said and shall say again that Cicero is the perfect orator, just as we commonly call our friends good and wise—attributes, strictly, only of the perfectly wise man. But when it is a matter of speaking correctly and according to the most rigorous standards of truth, I shall say, as Cicero himself said, that such an orator is still to seek. I claim that 20 Cicero stood at the very peak of eloquence; I can scarcely find anything that he lacks (though I might perhaps find something he would have pruned away: indeed, this is the general view of scholars, that he had many virtues and a few vices—while Cicero himself testifies[3] that he had to clamp down on much in his youthful extravagances). All the same, seeing that this by no means modest man never claimed the name of wise, and since he could undoubtedly have spoken better given a longer life and a period more suitable to calm composition, I am not being

---

[1] A place on a Caesarian land-commission offered him in 59 B.C.
[2] i.e. *philo-sophos*, not *sophos*.   [3] *Orator* 107 (above, p. 246).

grudging if I voice my belief that he failed to reach heights that no one
21 else has approached more closely. I could, if I felt differently, defend this
standpoint more stoutly and outspokenly. Marcus Antonius[1] claimed that
he had seen no eloquent man (a much lower thing), while Cicero himself
was still in search of the ideal and could only imagine it and represent it
to himself; am *I* then not to dare to say that in all the eternity of years
that remain it is impossible for something to turn up more perfect than
22 what has so far existed? I am not concerned with those who do not give
Cicero and Demosthenes their due even for their oratory—though in
fact Cicero himself regarded Demosthenes as not altogether perfect
(saying he sometimes nods),[2] a complaint made against Cicero by Brutus
and Calvus,[3] who criticized his word-arrangement to his face, and by
both the Asinii, who in several places attacked his oratorical faults in a positively hostile spirit.

23   Let us suppose what is in fact quite impossible, that some bad man has
been found who is supremely eloquent: I should nevertheless say that
he was no orator. Not all who are ready with their fists can be regarded
24 as brave; for bravery has no meaning unless virtue is present. Can we say
that an advocate for the defence has no need of a trustworthiness that
cannot be corrupted by avarice, deflected by prejudice, or broken by
fear? Shall we grant to a traitor, a turncoat, a conniver the sacred name of
orator? If even second-rate counsel are thought to do well to have what
is commonly called goodness, why should not the orator, possible though
25 not yet actual, be as perfect in character as in oratory? I am not training
up some court hack, some voice put out for hire, or (to avoid harsher
language) a not altogether useless advocate—'pleader', as they say: but
a man supremely endowed by nature, deeply imbued with all the fairest
arts, a crowning gift to humanity: a man such as the world has never seen,
however far back, unique and perfect in every way, with the finest thoughts
26 and the finest powers of expression. Only a small part of his energies will
be devoted to defending the innocent, crushing the crimes of the wicked,
standing up for the truth against calumny in financial cases. Our speaker
will be supreme in such matters too, but he will gain his brightest lustre
from higher things, the guiding of the counsels of the senate, the leading
of the people away from error and into better courses.

27   Did not Virgil invent a character like this—the man whom he represents controlling the rebellious mob when they are already hurling
brands and stones? 'Then if they catch sight of a man of authority and
virtue, they are silent and stand ears pricked.' Here, then, we have, before
all else, the *good* man. It is only after this that Virgil will proceed to add his

---

[1] Cf. on 8 pr. 13 (above, p. 374).   [2] Cf. 10. 1. 24 (above, p. 384).
[3] Tacitus, *Dialogus* 18 (below, p. 443).

skill in speech: 'with his words he rules their minds and soothes their hearts.'[1]

In war, too, this same orator I am forming will draw his material from 28 the heart of philosophical theory, should the soldiers need spurring on to battle. For how, as they go out to fight, are they to forget so many thronging fears of hardship, pain, and death itself, unless the place of those fears is taken by duty, bravery, and the vivid image of the Good? And surely these will be put over more persuasively by one who has 29 first persuaded himself. Hypocrisy, however well veiled, betrays itself; there is no eloquence so great that it does not stumble and come to a halt when the words are divorced from the feeling. But the bad man is bound 30 to speak against his feelings, while good men will never be short of good language or—for they will also be practical—of the ability to find good material. And such material, even if devoid of trappings, is sufficiently ornamented by its inherent qualities. Everything that is spoken honestly is spoken eloquently. Let us therefore while we are young—and indeed 31 at all ages, for no age is too late for good principles—strive with all our minds in this direction, and work towards these things. Perhaps we may even achieve them fully. Nature doesn't forbid the existence of the good man or the skilled speaker: why should not some one man attain both qualities? And why should not each of us hope to be that one man himself? If our powers are not up to that, we shall be the better for it in 32 both spheres however far we get. At least one thing should be banished far from our minds—the idea that eloquence, fairest thing of all, can be allied with vice. Power of speech falling to the lot of evil men must itself be judged an evil: for it makes those to whom it falls worse.

There will never be a shortage of those who prefer being eloquent to 33 being good; and I think I hear some people saying: 'What is the point of the well-developed technique in eloquence? Why have you gone on about 'colours' and the defence of difficult cases (even, to some extent, about admitting guilt) unless sometimes oratory can defeat the truth itself? Your good man only takes up good cases—and *they* are adequately defended by the truth even in the absence of training.' In replying to these 34 criticisms, I shall, as well as defending my own book, be touching also on the duty of a good man should circumstances lead him into pleading the cause of the guilty.

It is by no means unhelpful to discuss how speeches may sometimes be made in defence of untruth and even injustice, if only so that we can the more readily detect and refute them: if you know the diseases, you are in a better position to apply the remedies. The Academics, while 35 arguing against both sides, live according to one: and the Carneades who

[1] *Aeneid* 1. 151 ff.

is said to have been heard in Rome by the censor Cato inveighing against justice as powerfully as he had spoken on its behalf the day before, was himself a just man. But vice makes obvious the nature of its opposite, virtue; honesty becomes clearer as one observes the dishonest; and many things are shown to be good by their contraries. The orator, therefore, must be as acquainted with the intentions of his adversaries as a general with those of the enemy.

36 Again, expediency can even bring about what is at first view a hard saying, that a good man may sometimes, in defending his case, desire to conceal the truth from the judge. Some may be surprised that I put this view forward, though it is not mine specially, but that of those whom antiquity regarded as the most respectable teachers of wisdom; but my critics should bear in mind that there are many things that are good or bad 37 rather because of their motive than because of the actual deed. It is often a virtue to kill a man, sometimes glorious to slay one's children; still harsher-sounding actions are permissible should the common good demand. Therefore we should not have regard merely to the type of case the good man takes up, but also to why and with what motives he takes it.

38 First, everyone must grant me something that even the most rigorous Stoics concede, that the good man will at times go so far as to tell a lie, sometimes for fairly trivial reasons. Thus when children are ill we make up a great deal for their good, and promise much that we don't intend to do— 39 and still more if a brigand has to be diverted from murder or an enemy deceived for the safety of one's country. So something that on one occasion is reprehensible even in slaves on another may be praiseworthy in the Wise Man himself. If that is agreed, I can see many eventualities in which an orator would do well to take the sort of case he would have 40 declined in the absence of a good reason. I don't mean cases involving support for fathers, brothers, or friends in danger: I propose to follow sterner principles—though in fact considerable doubt arises when justice and natural affection come face to face. Let me leave no doubts. Suppose someone has plotted against a tyrant and is brought to trial for it: will the orator, as defined by me, refuse to ensure his safety—won't he rather, having once taken his case on, defend him with false arguments as readily 41 as someone who pleads a bad case before a jury? What if a judge is sure to condemn some good action unless we prove it was not performed? Will not the orator, even at the cost of deception, go to the help of a citizen who is praiseworthy as well as innocent? Suppose we know that something is in fact good, though inexpedient to the state owing to circumstances: shall we not use a technique of oratory that, though good, is 42 not unlike fraud? Again, undoubtedly, if criminals can somehow be reformed (as is agreed to be possible), it is in the state's interests that they

should be left unharmed rather than punished. Therefore, if the orator is convinced that a man answering to true charges will become good, will he not act to ensure his safety? Suppose a good general is faced by an 43 unanswerable accusation, and that without him the state could not defeat the enemy: the common good will surely call the orator to his aid. Certainly Fabricius, when war threatened, used his vote in public to elect to the consulship Cornelius Rufinus, knowing him to be an efficient general, though in other respects a bad citizen and his personal enemy. Some were surprised at this action, but Fabricius told them that he would rather be robbed by a citizen than sold by the enemy. So if he had been an orator, would he not have defended this same Rufinus even on an open-and-shut case of bribery? There are many possible parallels, 44 but one is enough. I am not proposing that the orator whom I am educating should act thus very often; my point is that if he is compelled to do so by the logic of events, he may so act without upsetting the definition of the orator as a good man skilled in speaking.

But it is essential to teach and learn how even awkward cases are to 45 be handled: often even the most respectable cases resemble the bad ones; often the innocent defendant is threatened by much that looks true, and so has to be defended in the same manner as if he were guilty. Indeed, there are innumerable points common to good and bad cases—witnesses, written evidence, suspicions, reputations. But the probable is proved or refuted just like the true. Oratory is to be adapted to circumstances; principle should stand firm.

H. PLINY'S *LETTERS*

The younger Pliny was a pupil of Quintilian. In his *Letters* he sometimes touches on literary themes, and often echoes his master. Text: R. A. B. Mynors, Oxford, 1963; commentary: A. N. Sherwin-White, Oxford, 1966; translation: Betty Radice, Penguin, 1963.

1. TO TACITUS: ON BREVITY (1. 20)

I frequently have arguments with a learned and experienced man who 1 likes nothing in the pleading of cases so much as brevity. Brevity, I 2 agree, should be maintained where the case allows; where it does not, it is mere treachery to one's client to neglect what ought to be said, or to touch only shortly and in passing on points that need to be pressed,

3 hammered home, and repeated. Most things gather weight and strength of a kind if they are given extended treatment. Speech is imprinted on the mind (like iron on the body) by slow degrees rather than at a single stroke.

4 Here my friend quotes authority at me, brandishes Lysias' speeches on the Greek side, on the Latin those of Cato and the Gracchi. Certainly many of these *are* brief and circumscribed. But I counter Lysias with Demosthenes, Aeschines, Hyperides, and many besides; while against the Gracchi and Cato I pit Pollio, Caesar, Caelius, and especially Cicero, whose best speech is said to be his longest. And indeed, like other good

5 things, a good book is better the larger it is. Observe how nothing rivals size for lending beauty to statues, portraits, pictures, and also men and many animals—trees too, so long as they are graceful. So with speeches; even the volumes that contain them gain a certain dignity and beauty from sheer bulk.

6 These, together with others to the same effect, are my habitual pleas; but he—slippery fellow that he is, never letting you get hold of him in argument—evades me by contending that these very orators on whose

7 speeches I rest my case in fact said less than they published.[1] I think the opposite. Witness many speeches from many hands, including Cicero's for Murena and Varenus, where we find a brief and bald sketch of certain charges indicated by mere headings: from which it is clear that he said

8 much that he left out on publication. Cicero, too, in his speech for Cluentius[2] says that he spoke the whole case through in person in accordance with tradition, and in that for Cornelius he says he took four days, so that we cannot refuse to believe that he spoke for several days (as he had to) rather diffusely, but afterwards cut down and revised his speech and confined it to the limits of one book, albeit a large one.

9 But a good spoken speech, it may be said, is one thing, a good written speech another. I know some think this, but I (perhaps wrongly) am convinced that it is possible for a speech to be good when spoken, bad when read: but that a good written speech must be good when delivered. For the written speech is the model and, as it were, archetype of the

10 spoken. And so in a good written speech there are always innumerable 'extemporary' devices to be found—and this is true even of speeches that we know were never actually delivered: for example, in one of the speeches against Verres:[3] 'Who was the artist? Who *was* he? Ah yes, thank you for reminding me—they said it was Polyclitus.' It follows that the most perfect delivered speech is the one that most faithfully reproduces the written: that is, so long as it is given a reasonable and proper

[1] Cf. Quint. 12. 10. 49 ff. (above, p. 412).
[2] *Pro Cluentio* 199. [3] 4. 5.

time for its delivery—and if that is denied it's no blame to the speaker, much to the judge.

This view of mine is supported by the laws, which grant very long 11 times for speeches, and thus encourage speakers not to be brief but full (that is, careful). And brevity cannot give full coverage except in the most restricted cases.

Let me add something I have learned from that excellent teacher, 12 experience.[1] I have often pleaded, often been a judge, often an adviser. People are influenced by different things, and often small things carry great ones with them. Men have differing tastes, differing attitudes. Hence judges who have heard the same case at the same time often reach different conclusions, sometimes the same ones for different motives.

Again, people tend to favour their own brain-child, clinging, in the 13 conviction that it is the strongest point, to something said by another but foreseen by themselves. Everybody, then, must be given something to hold on to, that they can recognize.

Regulus once said to me when we were both involved in the same case: 14 'You think that you have to go through everything in a case. I see the jugular at once, and press there.' Certainly he presses the point he has chosen—but he often gets his choice wrong. So I replied that it is con- 15 ceivable that what he thought to be the jugular should prove to be knee or heel. I on the other hand (I went on), who am incapable of identifying the throat, try everything, test everything, leave no stone unturned. In 16 farming I work trees as well as vines, and fields as well as trees; and in those fields I don't sow only spelt and wheat, but barley, beans, and other legumes as well. Similarly in a speech I scatter a lot of seeds pretty widely, so that I can collect up what comes to fruit. Judges are no less opaque, 17 uncertain and deceptive than weather and land.

I'm not forgetting that the great orator Pericles was complimented by Eupolis in the following terms:

> Apart from his swiftness
> Persuasion sat on his lips,
> such was his spell. And alone of orators
> he left his sting in those who heard him.[2]

But Pericles himself could not have commanded that persuasion or 18 exercised that spell by means of brevity or swiftness (or both, for they are different) without possessing the highest abilities also. Giving pleasure and influencing people requires much to be said, and time to say

[1] The point of this paragraph is that only a full speech can make the necessary appeal to different sorts of hearer and attitude.
[2] Fr. 94 Kock.

it; and the sting can only be left in the minds of the audience by someone who stabs, not pricks with a pin.

19   Or take what another comic poet wrote of the same Pericles:

He lightened, thundered, stirred up Greece.[1]

•   It is no amputated and crippled oratory but something wide and splendid and exalted that thunders, lightens, troubles and confuses everything around it.

20   'The middle way is best.' We all agree. But the middle way is abandoned as much by the orator who falls short of his theme as by the one who

21   goes too high for it: by the too-brief as well as the too-expansive. Thus you often hear, as well as 'immoderately and redundantly' the criticism 'baldly and weakly'. One is said to have exceeded his matter, another to have failed to match up to it. Both are faults, but one is the fault of weakness, one the fault of strength. And this latter may not be the fault of the more polished intellect, but it is the fault of the greater.

22   In saying this, I am not approving of the Homeric ⟨Thersites,⟩ who was 'immoderate in word', but the hero whose words were 'like the winter snows'. Not that I am not greatly pleased by the one who spoke 'little but very clearly'.[2] But if a choice is to be given us, I prefer the oratory that resembles the winter snows—by being, that is, dense, steady,

23   and abundant, divine and superhuman. 'But many prefer a shorter delivered speech.' Maybe—but they are the lazy: and it is absurd to revere their faddish sloth as the height of taste. If you take these people into account, better not just speak briefly—better not speak at all.

24   This is still my view, but I will change it if you disagree with me. But I do ask you to explain clearly *why* you disagree. I have a duty to yield to your authority, but I think it's better in so crucial a matter to be over-

25   come by reason rather than authority. If, however, you don't think me wrong, write to tell me so in as brief a letter as you like—but *do* write (you will be confirming my judgement). If I am mistaken, get a very long letter ready. Is not this bribery and corruption—to make you write a short letter if you agree with me, but a long one if you don't? Farewell.

2. TO CEREALIS: ON PUBLIC RECITALS (2. 19)

1   You advise me to recite my speech to a number of friends. I shall do it,
2   as you so advise, though with the gravest misgivings. I am well aware that speeches, when recited, lose all their impetus and warmth, almost their identity: for what normally sets them in a good light and brings them to

[1] Aristophanes, *Acharnians* 531.
[2] Cf. Quint. 12. 10. 64 (above, p. 414). Thersites is from *Iliad* 2. 212.

fever pitch is the throng of judges, the crowd of advocates, the excitement over the result, the fame of more than one of the speakers, the divided loyalties of the audience; add, too, the gesture and movement of the speaker, even his striding about and the way his body reacts vigorously to all his emotions. Thus those who deliver speeches sitting down, 3 though losing few of the advantages of the man who stands, are nevertheless thereby weakened and enfeebled. But reciters have the principal 4 aids of delivery, eyes and hands, shackled by the text. Hence quite naturally the attention of the audience relaxes, for it is attracted by no external lures, provoked by no stings.

Moreover, the speech I am talking about is combative, and pugnacious. 5 Again, it is inevitable that we should think that what we have taken trouble to write will take some trouble to listen to. Indeed, how few are the listeners 6 so high-minded as to take pleasure in the austere and concise rather than the charming and resonant! It is a shameful difference, but a real one, that (as often happens) the audience want one thing, the judges another, though a member of an audience really *ought* to be particularly moved by just those things that would most affect him if *he* were judge.

Maybe, however, despite these difficulties, this book will have the 7 advantage of novelty in its favour—novelty, that is, here: for the Greeks can show us something not wholly dissimilar (though applied in the other direction). They had a usage by which they confronted laws which they 8 regarded as contrary to earlier laws by a process of comparison. In rather the same way, I had to argue that what I was after was contained in the law on extortion by examining this law and some others. This is hardly calculated to win the ears of the ignorant, but its attraction to the learned should match its unpopularity with the lay. And if I do decide on a recita- 9 tion, I will get all the most erudite along. But please weigh again whether I *should* recite, putting all the arguments I have brought in the scales, and come to a conclusion that reason justifies. You are bound to provide reason: *I* shall be excused by my dependence on your judgement.   Farewell.

3. TO VOCONIUS ROMANUS: SENT WITH A COPY OF PLINY'S *PANEGYRIC*[1] (3. 13)

I have sent you my recent consular speech of thanks to our excellent emperor. 1 You asked for it, but I should have sent it even if you had not. I should 2 like you to take into account the difficulty of the subject as well as its attractions. In other speeches the reader is kept interested by the novelty

---

[1] Delivered by Pliny as consul before Trajan in A.D. 100.

alone; here everything is familiar, common property, everything has been said before. So the reader attends only to the style, leisurely and unmoved as he necessarily is: and when *only* style is under the critical 3 eye, it is more difficult to make it please. If only people would look at least at the arrangement, the transitions, the figures[1] as well! Brilliant content and impressive expression are sometimes within the capacities even of the uncivilized: only the expert can arrange with propriety and give variety to his figures. But one shouldn't always aim at the high-4 flown and the sublime. In a picture nothing sets off light so well as shade, 5 and similarly in a speech it is as fitting to relax as to strain. But I need hardly say this to someone so knowledgeable. This, rather: mark what you think needs correcting. I shall be more ready to believe you like the rest if you let me know there were some things you disliked.   Farewell.

4. TO PATERNUS: MORALITY IN POETRY (4. 14)

1 You are perhaps—as usual—demanding and expecting a speech from me: but I am exhibiting you some trivia of mine, part of an exotic and fanciful 2 stock. You will find with this letter my hendecasyllables—with which 3 I agreeably fill the time in my carriage or my bath or at meals. They are the vehicle of my humour, gaiety, love, pain, complaints, anger; they enable me to describe a thing, concisely or high-soundingly: and by this very variety I try to make sure that different tastes are served—and that something, maybe, finds favour with everyone.

4   Some things may appear a little *risqué*; but your learning will remind you that the great and distinguished men who have written similar poems have not fought shy even of the plainest language—let alone free-dom in subject-matter: and I have avoided such lengths not because I am more high-principled (how should I be?), but because I am more timid. 5 Anyway, I know that the truest principle for this genre is the one laid down by Catullus:[2]

> The good poet does well to be chaste
> himself: not, however, his verses—
> they have bite and brilliance only
> if they're relaxed and not too modest.

6   You may judge how highly I value your criticism from the fact that I wanted to let you ponder all my verses rather than praise a selection. And indeed even the neatest start looking less neat when they're all on a

---

[1] Or 'figuration'—i.e. the general way in which the thoughts are put, not in the narrower sense 'figures' of speech or thought.   [2] 16. 5–8.

level.[1] Besides, the wise and acute reader shouldn't compare different 7
poems, but weigh each for itself, not thinking it worse than another if it's
perfect of its own kind.

Enough. To use a long preface to excuse or commend one's indiscretions 8
is in itself hardly discreet. One proviso however: I am thinking of calling
these trifles of mine 'Hendecasyllables', thus referring to nothing except
the metre. You may call them epigrams or idylls or eclogues or (as many 9
do) *poematia*,[2] or anything else you like: I promise merely hendecasyllables.

You are a frank friend: please say to me about my book what you will 10
say to anyone else: no difficult request.[3] If this were my chief or only production, it might perhaps be hard to have to say: 'Look for something else
to do.' As it is, you can say, quite kindly and gently: 'You have other
things to do.' Farewell.

5. TO LUPERCUS: ON THE SUBLIME (9. 26)[4]

I once said of an orator of our time—a good sound one, but hardly lofty 1
and ornate enough—something that I think apt: 'He has no fault except
that he has no fault.' An orator ought to be roused and exalted, at times 2
even boil and get carried away: and he should often come near the edge,
precipices commonly lying near the heights. The flat route is safer, but
it is lower and duller. Runners slip more often than crawlers; but the
crawlers get no praise for failing to slip, and runners get some even if
they do. Eloquence thrives, like some other arts, on hazard as on nothing 3
else. You observe what applause greets tight-rope walkers on their way
up the wire when they seem to be all but falling off. Particular admiration 4
is the reward of the particularly unexpected, the particularly dangerous
and (as the Greeks put it more expressively) hazardous (*parabola*).
The qualities of a steersman show up by no means the same on a calm
as on a rough sea; in a calm he wins no admiration: unpraised, un-
honoured he makes his port. But when the sheets shriek, the mast
bends, the rudder groans—then he is famous and rivals the gods of the
ocean.

Why all this? Because you seem to have marked as turgid in my writings 5
some things I thought sublime: as outrageous what I thought daring: as

---

[1] i.e. if a selection is made containing only the best.
[2] i.e. 'little poems'.
[3] Cf. 'Longinus' 1 (below, p. 462) for this conventional request for frankness.
[4] The attitudes, and even some of the details, of this letter can be paralleled in
'Longinus'.

excessive what I thought full. But it's very important whether the
6 passages you mark are blameworthy or outstanding. Anyone can notice
something that sticks up and stands out; but it needs acute taste to decide
if it's excessive or grand, high or grotesque. To turn to Homer for preference: who can miss, one way or the other: 'all around the great heaven
trumpeted',[1] and 'his spear rested on a cloud', and all the part where 'the
7 seawave does not thunder so loud'?[2] But whether these are incredible
and empty passages or splendid superhuman ones requires the scales and
balance to decide. I don't mean that I have written or could ever write
anything comparable (I'm not so mad); I mean rather that the reins
should be kept loose on eloquence, that the natural impulses should not
be crippled by keeping them to too narrow a course.
8   'Orators have one set of rules, poets another.' As if Cicero were less
daring! Still, I will leave him out of account (I don't think there is any
dispute there). Let us take Demosthenes himself, the very pattern and
rule of the orator. Does he check and restrain himself when he says in a
famous passage: 'Filthy men, flatterers and devils'; or again: 'I did not
fortify the city with stones or brick . . .'; or just after that: 'Was it not to
make Euboea a sea-ward shield for Attica?';[3] or, in another speech:
'I think, men of Athens, that he by heaven is drunk with the vastness of
9 his acts.'[4] What could be more daring, again, than that long and fine
digression beginning 'For a disease . . .'?[5] What of another passage, shorter
than those but equally daring: 'Then I ⟨confronted⟩ Pytho in all his
pride, flowing down full on us'?[6] In the same rank: 'But when someone
grows powerful, as he has, on malevolent ambition, the first excuse, the
slightest false step customarily unseats and confounds all.'[7] Similarly:
'Roped off by every process of justice in the state'; and in the same speech:
'You, Aristogiton, threw away the pity they deserved—indeed, you utterly
destroyed it. Do not, then, think you can anchor in harbours that you
yourself have blocked and filled with obstructions.'[8] Before that he had
said: 'I see no spot where he can set foot, but everywhere cliffs, precipices,
chasms.' And again: 'I am afraid you may be thought to be tutoring each
new aspirant to vice in this city.' Or again: 'I do not imagine your ancestors built these law-courts for you to propagate such people in them.'
Even this was not enough; he also has: 'But if he is a trader and retailer
and trafficker in wickedness',[9] and many other such things—not to mention
what Aeschines[10] calls not words but wonders.

    [1] *Iliad* 21. 388: cf. 'Longinus' 9. 6 (below, p. 469); Demetrius 83 (above, p. 189).
    [2] *Iliad* 5. 356; 14. 394.
    [3] 18. 296, 299, 301. For the range of speeches cited, cf. Hermogenes (below,
pp. 561 ff.).   [4] *Philippics* 1. 49.   [5] 19. 259.   [6] 18. 136.
    [7] 2. 9.   [8] [25.] 28, 84.   [9] [25.] 76, 7, 48, 46.
    [10] *Against Ctesiphon* 167.

I have come up against an obstacle; you will say that here is Demo- 10
sthenes being criticized for these things. But observe the superiority of
the man who is criticized to the critic—and the superiority lies partly in
expressions like these: elsewhere we can glimpse his forcefulness—here
his grandeur shines out.

And did Aeschines himself avoid the 'faults' he found in Demosthenes? 11
'Gentlemen of Athens, the orator and the law must say the same thing;
but when the law speaks with one voice, the orator with another . . .'
Elsewhere: 'He can be seen throughout the bill . . .' And in yet another:
'But wait there in ambush and listen, and so drive him into words
that break the law.'[1] He liked this so much that he repeats it: 'But, as 12
in horse-races, drive him into the path of relevance.'[2] Then there is
something more brief and guarded: 'You open old sores, and care more
for your immediate words than for the safety of the state.' But this is
loftier: 'Will you not drive away one who is the common misfortune of
Greece? He sails through the state on a flood of words; will you not take
him and punish him as a pirate in public life?'[3]

I am sure that you will strike out with the same marks as the passages 13
I mentioned various expressions in this letter, like 'the rudder groans' and
'rivals the gods of the ocean': I know that in asking pardon for earlier
offences I have fallen into the very faults you pointed out. But strike
out as you will, so long as you fix a day now on which we can discuss all
my crimes in person. You shall make me cautious; or I shall make you
rash.   Farewell.

[1] Aeschines, *Against Ctesiphon* 16, 101, 206.
[2] *Against Timarchus* 176.   [3] *Against Ctesiphon* 208, 253.

10

TACITUS, *DIALOGUE ON ORATORS*

The dramatic date of this dialogue is under Vespasian, probably A.D. 74. But it was perhaps not written till after 100. In it, the historian Tacitus gives a different view of the state of eloquence from that of Quintilian; indeed, he may be answering Quintilian's lost work on the causes of the decay in eloquence. Quintilian. still looked for great oratory, and thought his kind of education might yet produce it. Tacitus shows that the times are unfavourable; his Maternus refutes both his Aper (the modern orator) and his Messalla (the admirer of the ancients). The *Dialogue* is a minor masterpiece of characterization. Style and form are modelled on Cicero's dialogues;[1] but the historian commands perspectives unusual in classical literary criticism.

Text: E. Köstermann, Leipzig, 1964. Commentaries: W. Peterson, Oxford, 1893; A. Gudeman, 2nd. edn., Leipzig, 1914. The best introduction to the problems of the work is in R. Syme, *Tacitus*, Oxford, 1958, 100 ff.

1 You often ask me, Justus Fabius, why, while earlier periods were brightened by the lustre and talent of so many outstanding orators, our own times should find themselves barren, bereft of distinction in eloquence—scarcely, indeed, even retaining the name 'orator'. We use the word now only of the old-timers; the accomplished speakers of our day are dubbed lawyers, advocates, attorneys—anything rather than orators.

To answer your question is to take up the burden of an important problem. It reflects on our abilities if we cannot reach the heights attained by our predecessors, and on our judgement if we do not wish to; in fact I should hardly venture on to this topic if I proposed to put forward my own views: actually, however, I have set myself to recount a conversation between men as eloquent as you may find nowadays, whom I heard discussing this very question when I was still quite young. So it's not talent I need, but power of memory. What I heard from these brilliant men they had thought out carefully, and they used considered language, each putting forward different though convincing reasons, and each marking them with the genuine stamp of his own personality and interests. My task now is to retrace what they said, altering no stage of the discussion, changing no argument, and keeping the same order that the disputants took. Nor, indeed, was there lacking someone on the other side,

---

1 The characters in both authors are historical—but little is known about Tacitus' figures apart from what we can learn from the dialogue itself.

ready to pour abuse and ridicule on the old days and back modern eloquence against the geniuses of the past.

The day before the discussion Curiatius Maternus had recited his 2 *Cato*, thus offending (it was said) the susceptibilities of powerful persons;[1] it was felt that in working out the plot of his tragedy he had forgotten his own situation and thought only of Cato's. The city was buzzing with the affair when Maternus had a visit from Marcus Aper and Julius Secundus, the most notable lawyers of the day—men whom I myself was engaged in following with all attention not only in the courts but even in their homes and whenever they made public appearances. For I was in love with my studies, and it was a sort of youthful passion that led me to hang on their lightest stories, their discussions, and their private oratorical exercises; though most people, it must be admitted, regarded them in a less flattering light—found Secundus halting, and thought that Aper had made his reputation by sheer natural force of intellect rather than by any systematic education. In fact, however, Secundus' style was clear, concise, and adequately fluent, while Aper by no means lacked learning—he wasn't without letters, he merely despised them, perhaps visualizing a greater reputation for hard work if his abilities stood in no apparent need of the support of extraneous techniques.

Thus it was that we three entered Maternus' room, to find him sitting 3 there holding the very book that he had read aloud the day before.

Secundus said: 'Maternus, don't the spiteful stories that are going around frighten you into loving this unpopular Cato of yours a little less? Or perhaps you've taken the book in hand to give it a thorough revision and cut out the parts that have given a handle to misrepresentation: so that *Cato* on publication may turn out, if not better, at least safer?'

'You will find in the book', he replied, 'what Maternus owed it to himself to put there—and you will recognize what you heard at the recitation. If Cato left anything out, Thyestes will repair the omission at the next recital. I've already got that tragedy organized in my mind—and I'm hurrying on the publication of *Cato* so that I can put that care aside and concentrate whole-heartedly on the new one.'

'You're never tired of these tragedies of yours', said Aper. 'You still neglect oratory and the law-courts, and spend all your time on Medea and now Thyestes, though you're constantly being summoned to the forum by your friends' cases and countless obligations to colonies and municipalities. You'd hardly have time for them even if you hadn't brought this new business on yourself of lumping in Domitius and Cato —Roman names and Roman episodes—with Greek mythology.'

---

[1] The story of the death of Cato naturally gave scope for anti-imperial sentiments.

4   'I should be more put off by your harshness', said Maternus, 'if our
continual differences of opinion hadn't turned virtually into a habit.
You keep harrying poets and hunting them down; *I* have a plea to sustain
every day—the defence of poetry against you: so much for my laziness
in advocacy. So I'm particularly glad we find ourselves provided with a
judge who can either forbid me writing my verses in future, or lend his
own authority to an old dream of mine—to abandon the niceties of the
law (I've sweated away quite enough at them) and devote myself to the
worship of an eloquence that better deserves my respect and reverence.'

5   'Before Aper rejects me as a judge', said Secundus, 'I shall do what
good honest judges always do—excuse themselves in cases where it's
clear that they have an interest on one side. Everybody knows that no one
is a closer friend and companion to me than Saleius Bassus, the best of
men and the most perfect of poets. If poetry is under attack, I can't
think of a more credit-worthy defendant.'

APER'S DEFENCE OF THE LEGAL PROFESSION

'Saleius Bassus', said Aper, 'can sleep undisturbed—and so can anyone
else who seeks a reputation for poetry because he is incapable of pleading
cases. I have found someone to judge this dispute; and I shan't allow
Maternus to shelter behind the protection of a crowd; I shall accuse him
alone—in this company—on the following count: he was born with an
orator's manly eloquence, that he could use to win friends and keep
them, form connections, put provinces in his debt; yet he neglects a study
that in our state is inconceivably more useful than any other, more pleasurable, more prestigious, more brilliantly productive of fame in Rome and
reputation empire-wide, even world-wide.

    'If we must put all our thoughts and actions to the test of utility,
what could be safer than to pursue an art that provides an unfailing weapon
to bring help to your friends, comfort to strangers, safety to the en-
dangered, and yet also strike terror into your enemies and detractors,
while you yourself remain calm behind a wall of perpetual power and
influence? When all is well, you see its power and usefulness in the refuge
and defence it provides for others; but if a note of personal danger
sounds, breast-plate and sword in battle are not a stronger defence than
eloquence to a defendant at risk—a weapon of offence and defence,
enabling you to assail your adversaries or to ward them off, in court or
senate or before the emperor. What could Eprius Marcellus use against a
hostile senate not long ago other than his own eloquence? *That* was the

threatening sword he wore when he parried the philosopher Helvidius, an eloquent speaker perhaps, but a crude tiro in a contest like that.[1] I don't need to say anything more on this count; I hardly think my friend Maternus will try to contradict me here.

'To pass to the pleasures of oratory. Its delights are not confined to 6 one particular moment—they are available almost daily, even hourly. What is more agreeable for a free-born gentleman, bred to appreciate something higher than vulgar pleasures, than to see his house always full, thronged with crowds of important persons: and to know that this popularity is a tribute paid not to his money or his childlessness or his job, but to *himself*? And indeed to be aware that very often the childless, the moneyed, and the powerful come to a mere poor youth to interest him in their own or their friends' troubles? Can huge riches and vast influence afford such pleasure as the sight of men, old and experienced, who bask in worldly prestige, having to confess, amid their material luxuries, that they lack the best thing of all? Think of the soberly-clad escort when you leave your house and walk the streets; the show you make on the public scene; the adoration displayed in the courts; the luxury of rising and taking up your position, the spectators silent, concentrating on you and you only! Think of the crowds gathering, pressing close to you, ready to feel any emotion the orator may assume!

'Those are the common-or-garden pleasures of oratory, ones that the most inexperienced eye can register; as for the more arcane delights, known only to orators themselves—these are the greater. If he is delivering a carefully rehearsed speech, the speaker's pleasure—like his words—has weight and lasting strength. If he has brought a new composition, hardly glanced at, he may feel a slight flutter of anxiety: but this very concern enhances his success, and adds to the joy success brings. But the highest pleasure by far is that of the extemporary speaker, daring and even rash in his invention. In the mind, as in the soil, other things may be sown and worked over for a long time—but it is the spontaneous growths that are more satisfying.

'I will make a personal confession. The day I received my stripe as a 7 senator, the day I won the quaestorship or tribunate or praetorship, despite being an unknown from a town which could offer me no advantages, was not more happy than the days I have been privileged to use what moderate ability I have as a speaker to get a defendant off, or plead some case successfully in the centumviral court,[2] or defend his

---

[1] A Stoic, praetor in A.D. 70, and outspoken in opposition to Vespasian, by whom he was ultimately exiled and executed.

[2] Where important civil suits were tried. See below, c. 38 (p. 457).

own procurators and freedmen before the emperor himself. On those occasions I feel that I am rising above tribunates and praetorships and consulships, that I possess something that, if it is not innate, cannot be granted by letters patent or supplied by influence. No art can give fame and prestige that could be compared with the glory accruing to an orator. Orators are well known in Rome—aren't they?—not only to the busy men of affairs, but to the idlest youth—at least any youth of character and ambition. Their names are the first that children are taught to utter: no one is more often pointed out and addressed by name in the street by ordinary people. Even visitors and foreigners have heard of them back in their municipalities and colonies: and as soon as they get to the city, they ask after them and are agog to recognize them.

8   'I would be prepared to say that Eprius Marcellus—whom I just mentioned—and Vibius Crispus (you see, I prefer up-to-date examples to far-off forgotten ones) are as great in the furthest corners of the world as at Capua and Vercellae, where I gather they were born. And this fame is the result not of Eprius' two millions, or Crispus' three, though one could argue that they attained this very wealth by their eloquence, but of that eloquence itself. Eloquence is something awesome and super-natural, and over the centuries it gives many instances of men reaching the heights by sheer natural ability; but the examples I have just given are not remote—we don't have to trust to hearsay, but can see them with our own eyes. The more humbly-born they were, and the more shameful the constricting poverty that surrounded their births, the more striking examples they present of the usefulness of oratory. Without advantage of birth or financial resources, neither principled, one of them even physically despicable, they have been the most powerful men in the country for many years; while it pleased them, they dominated the courts—now they dominate Caesar's intimate circle, carry all before them, and are regarded even by the emperor with respect as well as liking: for Vespasian, that decent and fair-minded old gentleman, knows perfectly well that his other 'friends' depend on things which they received from himself and which it is easy for him to accumulate and distribute to others; but that Marcellus and Crispus brought to their relationship with him something they did not receive from the emperor—and could not have received from anyone.

'It may seem trivial in this context of magnificence to mention por-traits, inscriptions, statues—but such things are not to be despised, any more than money, at which many rail, but not so many (you will find) turn up their noses. And it is these signs of fame and riches that we see thronging the homes of those who from their earliest youth have devoted themselves to law-courts and oratory.

APER ATTACKS POETRY

'As for poems and verses, on which Maternus wants to spend his whole 9
life—that was where all this started from—they win their authors no
respectable position and bring them no advantages; the pleasure they give
is fleeting, the fame empty and fruitless. Maternus' ears may reject this
and what I am going on to say: but what good is it to anybody if your
Agamemnons and Jasons wax eloquent? Does it mean that anyone can
return home successfully defended and in your debt? Does anyone escort
Saleius, our friend and excellent poet—most distinguished bard (is
that more impressive?)—or pay him visits or throng around him in
the street? If he himself, or a friend of his, or a relation gets into difficulty,
he will come running to Secundus here, or to you, Maternus—but not
in your capacity as poet, and not wanting you to write verses for him.
Verses Bassus can supply for himself—they grow in his garden, very
pretty and agreeable too: but the upshot of it all is that after burning the
midnight oil for a whole year, working all day and most of the night, and
contriving to knock together one volume, he has to go round begging and
canvassing to find someone who will condescend to listen to it—at a
price. He has to borrow a house and equip a recital-hall, hire seats and
distribute advertisements. And even if the recitation is a high success,
the praise he wins for it is the matter of a day or two, something plucked
in leaf or flower that cannot go on to give real tangible fruit; he gains no
'friendship', acquires no clients, leaves no grateful memory; the applause
is fleeting, the compliments empty, the pleasure swiftly gone. The other
day we thought Vespasian was being wonderfully and outstandingly
generous when he gave Bassus five thousand. Of course, it's nice to find
one's abilities paying off with the emperor; but it's even nicer, in a domestic emergency, to be able to look to oneself, draw on one's own resources,
test one's own generosity. And after all, if they want to produce anything
worthwhile, poets have to leave the society of their friends and the pleasures
of the city, throw up all their other responsibilities, and withdraw, as
they put it, 'to the woodland groves'—that is, to a life of solitude.

'They are enslaved to fame and reputation alone, and agree that this 10
is the only reward they get for their labours: but fame hardly attends
poets as assiduously as orators. Nobody knows the third-rate poet, few
the first-rate. Recitations, however successful,[1] are hardly ever reported
round the whole city, let alone the provinces of this great empire. Few
arrivals from Spain or Asia—to forget about my native Gaul—ask for
Saleius Bassus. And if anyone does, he passes on after seeing him once,
quite contented, just as if he'd viewed a picture or a statue.

[1] Text conjectural.

'I don't want you to think that I'm trying to turn away from poetry
those who have been denied a natural talent for oratory, if they can in
fact pass their spare time agreeably in this field and even make a bit of a
name. I regard all branches of eloquence as sacred and holy; not only
your tragic style and the thunder of epic, but pleasing lyrics, saucy
elegiacs, bitter iambics, playful epigrams, and all other types are to be
preferred to other artistic fields. My quarrel is with you personally,
Maternus; your constitution destines you for the heights of eloquence,
yet you prefer to wander below: you could reach the top, but you potter
over trivia. If you were Greek—for in Greece sport too is a respectable
career—and were fortunate enough to have the strength of a Nicostratus,
I shouldn't be content that your immense arms, obviously meant for
wrestling, should squander themselves on tossing light javelins and
discuses. In the same way now I can only summon you to leave your halls
and theatres and come to the forum, to lawsuits and real contests, especially as you can't take refuge in the plea which many shelter behind,
that poetry is less liable to offend than oratory. Your splendid natural
energy bubbles out, and you give offence—not for some personal friend,
but for Cato—which is more dangerous. *You* can't minimize the offence
by appealing to the ties of duty or an advocate's responsibilities or the
impulse of extemporary speech. You obviously took care to pick a character
that was notorious and would speak with authority. I can see a possible
reply—such a move brings immense applause, special praise in the
recital-hall, and soon a topic for all tongues. But that destroys the argument that a poet has a quiet, safe life. You are taking on an adversary
too big for you. *We* are satisfied to take up non-political disputes—and
ones of our own century: if it were ever necessary to offend great men
because a friend is on trial, our loyalty to him would be approved of, and
our freedom of speech excused.'

MATERNUS DEFENDS POETRY

11 Aper had said all this pretty pungently, as usual, and with a serious face.
Maternus was relaxed and smiling. 'I was getting ready,' he said, 'to
start accusing orators as thoroughly as Aper praised them; for I supposed
that he would pass on from his eulogy to a disparagement of poets and the
overthrow of the pursuit of poetry. But he has cunningly disarmed me by
allowing people who couldn't plead at the bar to write poetry. I may, with
an effort, be able to make some impression in law-cases; but it was by
reciting tragedy that I put myself on the road to fame, when, in Nero's

reign, I broke Vatinius' evil influence that was polluting even literature: and if I have any name or fame today, I think it's due to my poetry rather than my speeches. And now I've decided to disengage myself from work at the bar—I don't *want* the escorts and ceremonious departures and crowds of callers that you talk of, any more than the bronzes and portraits that have pushed their way into my house despite myself. Innocence is a better safeguard of a man's position than eloquence: no fears in *my* case that I may find myself speaking in the senate—except when someone else is in a fix.

'As for the woodland groves, and the solitary life Aper was jeering at, 12 they bring me such joy that I count it among the principal rewards of poetry that it is composed away from the bustle and the litigant at the door and the shabby and weeping defendants: the mind is free to withdraw to fresh innocent places, and enjoy a holy world. This is where true eloquence had its beginnings and its shrine—this the guise in which it first won over mortals and flowed into hearts still chaste and uncorrupted. This was the language of oracles. The profiteering and bloodstained eloquence of today is a new thing, born of evil habits and—as Aper said—a substitute for the sword. But the old happy and (as a poet may be allowed to put it) golden era had neither orators nor accusations, but it swarmed with inspired poets to sing of good deeds, not to defend bad ones. Nobody received greater fame or more reverent honour, either from the gods, whose oracles they passed on and whose feasts they attended (as the story goes), or from kings who were themselves sacred and descended from gods. We hear of no pleader then, but of Orpheus and Linus and, further back, Apollo himself. This may seem tendentious fiction: but you won't deny, Aper, that the fame of Homer with posterity doesn't yield to that of Demosthenes: the reputation of Euripides or Sophocles isn't narrower than Lysias' or Hyperides'. You will come across more people nowadays to carp at Cicero's reputation than at Virgil's: Ovid's *Medea* and Varius' *Thyestes* are more famous than any volume of Pollio or Messalla.[1]

'I have no worries about the contrast of the poet's lot, and his happy 13 relationship to the Muses, with the anxious troubled life of an orator. *They* may be brought by their struggles and their perils to the consulship; *I* prefer the quiet security of Virgil's retreat—and he didn't go without imperial favour or popular fame. You need only look at Augustus' letters, or remember the day when the people rose as one man in the theatre on hearing lines by Virgil quoted, and rapturously applauded the poet— who happened to be present as a spectator—as though he was Augustus himself. And in our time too Pomponius Secundus was every bit as respectable and lastingly famous as Domitius Afer.

[1] These famous Augustan plays are lost.

'What is there to envy in the fortunes of Crispus and Marcellus, on whom you want me to model myself? Is it the fear they feel or the fear they inspire? Is it that they are every day at the mercy of the importunate, who turn on them as soon as they get what they want? Or that they are fettered by every sort of obsequiousness, always too free for the emperor and too servile for us? How does all this give them supreme power? Freedmen have as much. I should prefer to be carried by Virgil's 'sweet Muses'[1] to their sacred haunts and fountains, far from troubles and cares and the daily compulsion to act against one's inclinations: and have no further truck with the mad slippery life of the forum, trembling and pale in the pursuit of fame. I don't want to be woken up by shouting clients or breathless freedmen, or worry so much about the future that I have to write safeguards into my will, or own more than I could safely leave to the heir I choose. For 'some day my hour too will come'—I trust the statue on my grave will be cheerful and garlanded, not sad and grim. No debates, no petitions about my memorial, please.'

ENTRY OF MESSALLA

14   Maternus, excited and even inspired, had scarcely stopped when Vipstanus Messalla entered the room. He realized from the intent expression on all their faces that a serious discussion was in progress, and he said: 'Have I come at a bad moment, and disturbed you in a private conversation on the preparation of some case?'

'Not at all, not at all', said Secundus. 'In fact, I wish you had come earlier. You would have had the pleasure of hearing the very detailed remarks of our friend Aper exhorting Maternus to turn all his attentions to lawsuits—and Maternus defending his poems in a brilliant speech: one—as was only right in a defence of poets—that was pretty bold and more poetic than oratorical.'

'I should have been infinitely delighted by such a debate,' said Messalla, 'and I'm pleased by the very fact that important people like you, the foremost orators of our age, should be prepared not to employ your gifts only on legal business and declamation practice, but to take up discussions of this kind. They feed the mind—and bring the most agreeable pleasures of learning and literature to yourselves, the disputants, and to all who hear of them. It is admirable that Secundus has written a life of Julius Africanus and given us the hope that he may produce more books like it; though less admirable that Aper hasn't yet deserted the exercises

---

[1] *Georgics* 2. 475.

of the schools, but prefers to spend his leisure as the new rhetoricians do, rather than as the old orators did.'

Aper said: 'You're always showing your admiration for the old and antique, Messalla, and laughing present-day pursuits to scorn. I've often heard you in this vein: forgetting your own eloquence, and your brother's,[1] and affirming that nobody nowadays is an orator—and particularly boldly because you don't fear to be called envious: the glory you deny to yourself others concede to you.'

'I don't repent of my words,' Messalla replied, 'and I don't believe Secundus or Maternus or even you, Aper, despite your occasional arguments to the contrary, really differ from me. I should like one of you to consent to investigate the causes of the infinite gulf between old and new, and expound them to me—for I often find myself reflecting on the problem. What consoles others only increases my puzzlement—I mean that the Greeks too have declined: there's a greater difference between Aeschines and Demosthenes on the one hand, and Nicetes Sacerdos[2] or any of the others who shake Ephesus and Mytilene with the shrieked applause of their pupils, than between Afer or Africanus or yourselves and Cicero or Asinius.'[3]

'It's a big question you bring up,' said Secundus, 'and one well worth discussing. But who is more qualified to take it up than you? You have supreme learning and outstanding powers, and you've taken trouble to consider the problem beforehand.'

Messalla said: 'I will tell you what I have thought—so long as I get you to agree in advance to help me in my speech.'

'I promise for both of us', said Maternus. 'Secundus and I will both take up the sections that we see you have left—not left *out*, but left to us. Aper is a habitual dissentient, as you said just now: and it's been obvious for some time that he's girding himself for the opposition, and won't easily put up with this alliance of ours in praise of the ancients.'

APER DEFENDS MODERN ORATORY

'No,' said Aper, 'I certainly shall not allow our own century to go unheard and undefended, and so be condemned by your conspiracy.

'My first question is this: who do you mean by "ancients"? What generation of orators do you mark off by this term? When I hear the word, I think of old-timers born long ago, and Ulysses and Nestor come into my mind—men living perhaps thirteen hundred years ago. But you

---

[1] M. Aquillius Regulus.   [2] A first-century Greek orator.
[3] i.e. Pollio, consul 40 B.C., a famous politician and literary man at the time of the beginnings of the principate.

bring up Demosthenes and Hyperides, who without a doubt flourished
under Philip and Alexander—and outlived both. So that little more than
three hundred years separate us from the age of Demosthenes. This may
seem a long time set against the frailty of human life. But it is very short
—merely yesterday—in comparison with the passage of the centuries and
the immeasurable past. Remember Cicero's *Hortensius*:[1] the true 'great'
year has passed when the same position of the stars in the heavens comes
round again—and this year embraces twelve thousand, nine hundred and
fifty-four of the years *we* speak of. If that is true, Demosthenes, your great
hero, whom you make out to be old and ancient, is in the same year—
and the same month—as us.

17   'Well, to pass to Latin authors. You don't, I suppose, usually class as
superior to present-day speakers Menenius Agrippa,[2] who really could
be counted an ancient—you mean Cicero, Caesar, Caelius, Calvus,
Brutus, Asinius, Messalla: but I don't see why you regard these as belonging to ancient times rather than our own. To take Cicero himself: he was
killed—as Tiro his freedman writes—on the seventh of December in
the consulship of Hirtius and Pansa, the year Augustus made himself
and Quintus Pedius suffect-consuls in place of Pansa and Hirtius. Reckon
fifty-six years for the deified Augustus' rule over the state: add Tiberius'
twenty-three, nearly four for Caligula, fourteen each for Claudius and
Nero, the one long year divided between Galba, Otho, and Vitellius, and
the six years that have so far passed in the present happy reign in which
Vespasian is protecting the country—that makes a hundred and twenty
years from the death of Cicero up to this year:[3] a single lifetime—for
I myself once saw a man in Britain who volunteered that he'd been present
at the battle in which they tried to keep Caesar from British shores and
drive him away when he invaded.[4] If this man who stood in arms against
Caesar had found his way to Rome because of captivity or his own choice
or some chance, he could perfectly well have heard speeches by Caesar
himself and by Cicero, and yet also attended orations given by us. At the
recent largess you yourselves saw plenty of old men who told how they
had received money once or twice from Augustus as well. The inference is
that they could have heard Corvinus and Asinius speaking: Corvinus
lasted till the middle of Augustus' principate, Asinius almost to the end
of it. You can't split up time like this, and go on using 'ancients' and 'old-
timers' of men whom the same hearers could have recognized and thus
joined to us in a single life-span.

---

[1] A lost 'exhortation to philosophy': a very famous and influential book; cf. St.
Augustine, *Confessions*, 3, 7.   [2] Cf. Livy 2. 32; a fifth-century figure!
[3] There is something wrong with the sum.
[4] Yet 97 years elapsed between Caesar's invasion and that under Aulus Plautius.

'This is all by way of preface, to show that any credit that may accrue 18
to their times from these famous orators is the common possession of all
—and more nearly available to us than to Servius Galba or Gaius Carbo
or others we could justly call ancients. *They* are uncouth, unpolished,
crude, coarse speakers—and your hero Calvus, or Caelius, or Cicero
himself would have done well not to imitate them at all. I want to take
a bolder and more daring line: but let it be said first that types and styles
of oratory vary with the period. Compared with the elder Cato, Gaius
Gracchus is fuller and richer: compared with Gracchus Crassus is more
refined and decorative: Cicero is more clear, witty, and sublime than
either—and Corvinus surpasses Cicero in gentleness and sweetness and
care in the use of words. I am not looking for the most eloquent among
them; I am for the moment content with proving that eloquence has no
single face. In those you call 'ancients', too, more than one type can be
discerned, and a thing isn't automatically worse because it's different.
But men are so jealous that the old always receives praise, the new scorn.
There have doubtless been those who admired Appius Caecus more than
Cato. It is beyond question that Cicero too had his critics, who found him
inflated, swollen, verbose, exuberant, redundant—and not 'Attic' enough.
You must have read Calvus' and Brutus' letters to Cicero: it's easy enough
to see from them that Cicero thought Calvus bloodless and dry, Brutus
flat and disjointed: and on the other hand Cicero was criticized by Calvus
as lax and spineless, and by Brutus—to use his own words—as "feeble and
hamstrung". If you ask me, *all* these criticisms were true; but I shall come
to individuals in a moment—meanwhile my business is with the general
trend.

'Admirers of antiquity tend to draw a firm line where it ends—at 19
Cassius Severus: him they make the scapegoat, asserting that he was the
first to stray from the old straight path of oratory. My contention is that
he changed to a new style by an intelligent act of judgement, and not
because of any lack of ability or education. He saw what I said just now
—that as times change and audiences vary, the style and appearance of
oratory must change too. The people in the old days were inexperienced
and ill-educated: they were quite ready to tolerate long speeches, cluttered
up with irrelevancies, and regarded it as a virtue if a speaker took all day.
Then there was applause for long introductions, and narratives delving
deep in the past, elaborate divisions put in merely for show, innumerable
interconnected arguments, and all the other items prescribed in the dry-
as-dust handbooks of Hermagoras and Apollodorus: as for anyone who
had an inkling of philosophy, and inserted a philosophic passage in his
speech, he was lauded to the skies. And no wonder: these things were new
then and unknown, and very few even of the orators themselves were

acquainted with rhetorical precept or philosophical dogma. But now that all this is commonplace, and scarcely anyone finds himself in the public seats who isn't at least a dabbler in these studies, if not an expert, one needs new and less obvious routes for eloquence to follow. Only so can an orator escape boring his hearers, especially where judges can decide on their own authority, not under a legal code, and can make their own provisions about the length of speeches, without having this dictated to them. They don't have to wait on the orator's pleasure until he cares to talk about the actual matter in hand: they often go out of their way to warn him and call him back when he digresses and affirm that they are in a hurry.

20 'Who nowadays would tolerate a proem on the bad health of the speaker—a normal theme for Corvinus? Who would wait while five volumes of speeches against Verres unrolled themselves? Who would endure the immense books on our shelves—the speech for Tullius or Caecina—all about objections and legal forms? Nowadays the judge is always ahead of the speaker, and he grows hostile unless he is lured on and seduced by fluent arguments, brilliant reflections, refined and colourful description. The crowds of by-standers, too, and spectators who casually drift in, have by now got used to demanding cheerful and agreeable oratory: they're no longer prepared to put up with gloom and unshaven antiquity in the courts any more than they would be to applaud the reproduction of Roscius' or Ambivius Turpio's gestures on the stage. Indeed youths still on the educational anvil, who pursue orators for their own scholastic advantage, want not only to listen, but to take something splendid and memorable back home with them. They swop things among themselves, often put them into letters back to their colonies and provinces—some short, sharp, brilliant epigram, or a passage resplendent with out-of-the-way poetic colouring. Yes, an orator now has to provide poetic beauty as well, not the Accius or Pacuvius variety, mildewed with age, but drawn from the shrines of Horace, Virgil, and Lucan. These are the ears and these the judgements that contemporary orators have to pander to—and it is for this reason that they have become more pretty and more ornate in style. And if our speeches do bring pleasure to their hearers, that doesn't make them any less effective: to think that would be as illogical as to suppose that modern temples are flimsier because they are bright with marble and brilliant with gold, rather than constructions of rough stone and unsightly tile.

21 'I tell you frankly that when I read some of the ancients, I can hardly suppress my laughter—and in some I can hardly stay awake. I don't mean the rank and file—Canutius, Attius, Furnius, Toranius, and other patients in the same hospital who enjoy desiccation and anaemia: but even Calvus,

who, I suppose, left twenty-one or so books behind him, comes up to the mark for me in hardly a single speech. I don't see any general dissent from this view. Very few read Calvus' speeches against Asitius or Drusus. Nevertheless all serious students have to reckon with the speeches against Vatinius, and particularly the second: it is brilliant in language and in content, and it was entirely suited to the tastes of the jury—so you can see that Calvus too realized where his style required improving; he didn't lack the desire to speak more loftily and with more refinement—only the talent and the strength. Again, it is just those speeches of Caelius in which we recognize modern colour and sublimity that please us, in whole or part. But his shabby language, disjointed rhythm, and lack of periodic structure are the symptoms of the old oratory; and no one, I think, can be such an antiquarian that he approves of the side of Caelius that is antique.

'We may surely agree that it was because of his multifarious cares and occupations that Caesar accomplished less in oratory than his miraculous talents suggested. Equally, we may leave Brutus to his philosophy—even his admirers confess that in his oratory he fell short of his reputation. I hardly suppose anyone still reads Caesar's *For Decius the Samnite* or Brutus' *For King Deiotarus* and all the other volumes of like flatness and tedium—except, perhaps, somebody who also admires their poetry. Yes, they did write poetry, and sent it to private collectors: they were no greater poets than Cicero, but they had more luck—fewer know about it. Asinius too—he was born more recently, but he looks to me like a fellow student of the Meneniuses and the Appiuses. He reproduced Pacuvius and Accius in his speeches as well as in his tragedies: such a hard dry writer is he.

'But oratory is like the human body—it is beautiful only when the veins don't stand out and the bones can't be counted; when good sound blood fills the limbs and pulses in the muscles. The sinews are covered in fine red flesh, and shown off by the attractive surface. I won't harry Corvinus: it wasn't his fault that he couldn't provide the brilliant luxuriance of our day. We can all see how far his mind and talent fell short of his judgement.

APER ON CICERO

'I come to Cicero. He had the same battle with his contemporaries as I 22 have with you. They admired the ancients, he preferred the eloquence of his own day. And there is nothing in which he outstripped the orators of that period more decisively than in his judgement. He was the first to *cultivate* oratory, the first to apply choice to words and artifice to structure.

He even attempted more flowery passages, and happened on a number of epigrams, at least in the speeches he wrote as an old man at the end of his life—after, that is, he had developed, and discovered by practice and experience what the best style was. For his early speeches have the faults of the ancients. He is slow in his proems, verbose in his narrative, lax in his digressions; he is slow to be moved, rarely catches fire; few sentences end neatly and with a punch. Nothing here to excerpt, nothing to take home—it's like a rough building, with a firm wall that will last but with no proper polish or splendour.

'I think of an orator as a family man of substance and taste: I don't want him to have a house that merely keeps wind and rain off, but one that catches the eye and pleases it. His furniture shouldn't be confined to necessities—he should have gold and jewels in his store, so that one enjoys frequently taking him down and admiring him. Some things are out of date and smelly—let them be kept out: we want no word tarnished with rust, no sentences put together in the slow sluggish manner of the annalists: he must avoid tasteless and disagreeable pleasantry, vary his structure, and use more than one kind of clausula.

23 'I have no wish to laugh at Cicero's "wheel of fortune"[1] and "boar-sauce"[2]—or the *esse videatur* which appears instead of an epigram at the end of every other sentence throughout his speeches.[3] I bring this up unwillingly, and I ignore many further instances that monopolize the admiration and even imitation of those who call themselves 'ancient' orators. No names—I am quite happy just to make the type clear. But in any case you can picture the people I mean: they read Lucilius in preference to Horace and Lucretius rather than Virgil; they find the eloquence of Aufidius Bassus and Servilius Nonianus tame in comparison with Sisenna's or Varro's; they scorn and even hate the model speeches published by rhetoricians—but admire Calvus'. These people go on chatting in front of the judge in the old style, but they have lost their audience's attention; the spectators don't bother to listen, and even the litigant can scarcely put up with them, so gloomy and unpolished are they. They may attain the healthiness they boast of, but they do so by starving, not by building up their strength. Even as far as the body is concerned, doctors hesitate to recommend a state of health that involves mental anxiety. It's not enough not to be unwell: I want a man to be strong, cheerful, and active. One who is praised only for his health is not far off illness.

---

[1] *In Pisonem* 22.
[2] Cf. *Verr.* 1. 1. 121: the Latin is a pun, and could also mean 'Verrine justice'.
[3] A form of the common cretic+spondee ($-\cup--$) clausula. Cf. Quint. 10. 2. 18 (above, p. 402).

'But you—my very eloquent friends—go on brightening this age of ours with beauty of speech as you can, and as you do. You, Messalla, I observe, choose out the brightest passages of the ancients for your imitation: and you, Maternus and Secundus, mix with your grave sentiments brilliant and refined language. Such is your choice of material, such your ordering of it, such your copiousness when the case demands, such your conciseness when the case permits, such your agreeable rhythm, such the clarity of your thought, such the vividness of the emotions you portray, such the discretion of your outspokenness, that even if the judgement of our own period is dulled by envy and jealousy, our descendants will surely speak the truth of you.'

MESSALLA REPLIES TO APER

After Aper's speech, Maternus said: 'One recognizes our friend Aper's force and ardour. What an irresistible torrent of eloquence he brought to the aid of our century! How fully, on how many fronts he harried the ancients! He showed not merely brilliance of inspiration, but learning and technique, borrowing from the ancients the weapons with which to go on and attack them. I trust, however, Messalla, that he hasn't put you off your promise. We aren't looking for a defender of the ancients—and despite his praise just now we don't put any of ourselves in the class of the men he attacked. Of course, he isn't being candid: it's an old trick, and one often used by our friends the philosophers, to take on oneself the role of opponent. So produce for us not so much a eulogy of the ancients —their fame is enough praise for them—as the reasons why we have lagged so far behind their standards of eloquence: particularly when chronology has proved that only a hundred and twenty years have passed since the death of Cicero.' 24

Then Messalla said: 'I shall follow the line you suggest, Maternus. There is certainly no need for a long refutation of Aper—indeed, his first point was in my view a verbal quibble: I mean, that it's improper to call men ancients who have quite certainly been dead a hundred years. I am not fighting about a word; he can call them ancients or elders or anything else he prefers, so long as it's granted that the oratory of those days was superior. And I'm not disposed to argue with the part where he came to grips with the problem and pronounced that you get more than one style of oratory even at the same time—let alone in different centuries. Now among the orators of Attica Demosthenes takes the crown, Aeschines and Hyperides and Lysias and Lycurgus are in next place: but it is that *period* which is by universal consent regarded as the peak. Similarly at 25

Rome Cicero outstripped all other eloquent speakers of his time, but Calvus and Asinius and Caesar and Caelius and Brutus are rightly regarded as superior to those who came before and after. It makes no difference that their species differ—the genus is the same. Calvus is more concise, Asinius more vigorous, Caesar more impressive, Caelius more bitter, Brutus more serious, Cicero more vehement and full and powerful than his contemporaries; but they all display the same *health* of eloquence: if you turn over all their books together, you can tell that, however much their talents differed, there is a certain similarity and kinship between their judgement and intentions. They carped at each other, to be sure— and there are traces of reciprocated malice in their letters; but that is a fault they were subject to as men, not as orators. Certainly Calvus, Asinius, and Cicero too were wont to envy and be jealous and to be afflicted by other human weaknesses; alone among them Brutus, I think, laid bare his inmost convictions with no malice or envy, but with simplicity and candour. It's hardly likely he could envy Cicero when he didn't (I think) envy even Caesar. As for Servius Galba and Gaius Laelius and other ancients that Aper couldn't stop chasing, the defence can be waived; I agree that their eloquence, still growing and adolescent, lacked much.

26   'But if we leave out of account supreme and perfect oratory, and look round for a style to choose, I should distinctly prefer Gaius Gracchus' impetuosity or Lucius Crassus' ripeness to Maecenas' curling-tongs[1] or Gallio's jingles: better clothe oratory in a hairy toga[2] than prink it out in gaudy and meretricious costumes. That sort of refinement doesn't suit oratory—or even a real man: I mean the sort many pleaders of our day so abuse that they come to reproduce the rhythms of the stage: language obscene, thoughts frivolous, rhythm licentious. Many people actually boast, as if it were a step towards fame and a sign of their genius, that their model speeches are sung or danced: it ought to be almost out of the question even to listen to talk like this. Hence the common remark— shameful and perverse though it is—that modern orators speak lasciviously, modern actors dance eloquently.

'I don't wish to deny that Cassius Severus—the only name Aper dared to mention—could be called an orator, if we compare him with his successors: though he has more bile than good red blood in the great majority of his speeches. He was the first to despise order in his material, to lay aside shame and modesty in language. He is inept even in the use of such arms as he does employ, often so eager to strike a blow that he loses his balance altogether. He doesn't fight—he brawls. But, as I say, compared

[1] Cf. Seneca, *epist.* 114 (above, pp. 363 ff.).
[2] Cf. Quint. 12. 10. 47 (above, p. 411).

with his successors he is superior by far to the others whom Aper couldn't bring himself to name or deploy in the battle—superior in variety of learning, wit, charm, and sheer strength.

'I was certainly expecting that Aper, having condemned Asinius, Caelius, and Calvus, would bring up a fresh division for us, and give even more names, or at least as many, so that we could find a pair for Cicero and Caesar and so on, one by one. As it is, he confines himself to criticizing the ancients by name—but hasn't dared to praise any of their successors except in a generalized manner. I suppose he was afraid that if he picked only a few out, he would offend many others. Every man jack of today's rhetoricians labours under the illusion that he can class himself Cicero's superior—though at the same time altogether inferior to Gabinianus. I shan't hesitate to name individuals; if I put forward examples, it becomes easier to see by what stages eloquence has been broken and enfeebled.'

'Spare us that', said Maternus. 'Just keep your promise. We don't need 27 a demonstration that the ancients are more eloquent—I for one am quite convinced of that: we're looking for the causes which you mentioned you frequently thought about. That of course was when you were in a quieter frame of mind a little while ago and hadn't been provoked by Aper's criticisms of your ancestors into getting angry with the oratory of today.'

'I haven't been provoked by Aper's point of view,' he said, 'and *you* mustn't be provoked if anything happens to grate on your ears. You know the rule of conversations of this kind: give your honest opinion and don't worry about giving offence.'

'Go on, then,' said Maternus, 'and since you speak of the ancients, employ the ancient habit of plain speaking—we've got even further away from that than from eloquence.'

Messalla went on: 'The causes you are looking for, Maternus, are by 28 no means abstruse—you and Secundus and Aper know them quite well, even if you have given me the role of expounding publicly things we all feel. Everybody knows that eloquence, and the other arts too, have declined from their old heights not for any lack of exponents, but because the young are lazy, their parents neglectful, their teachers ignorant—and because the old ways are forgotten. The rot started in Rome, then spread through Italy—and now is seeping into the provinces. You know better than I the situation there; I shall talk about the city, and its own individual and home-bred vices that are on hand to welcome a child as soon as he's born, and pile up as he grows older. First of all, I must say a few words about our ancestors' strict methods in the education and moulding of their children.

'In the old days everyone had his son—born in wedlock of a chaste mother—brought up not in the room of some hired nurse but on his mother's lap; and the mother's especial claim to praise was to look after her household and slave for her children. Or some older relation was selected, of tried and proved character, and the whole brood committed to her charge; in her presence it was not allowed to say anything that was shameful or do anything that was wrong. She brought an element of purity and modesty not only to their tasks and studies but to their games and relaxations as well. This is the way Cornelia, as is well known, took charge of the upbringing of the Gracchi, and educated these distinguished children; so Aurelia with Caesar, Atia with Augustus. The object of this austere training was that each child's nature, open, honest, untwisted by any vice, should immediately and whole-heartedly seize on good arts. And whether the child inclined to the army or to law or to eloquence he concentrated on that alone and made it his whole diet.

29   'But nowadays a child is delivered on birth to some Greek maid, who is helped by one or other of the slaves—and generally a quite worthless one at that, unfit for any serious duty. Their nursery stories and superstitions give the first colour to green and untrained minds. Nobody in the whole house cares what he does or says in the presence of the young master; even the parents don't trouble to get their little ones used to goodness and propriety—they substitute wantonness and pertness: hence very soon impudence creeps in, and contempt for one's own property and everyone else's. The peculiar and private vices of this city seem to be implanted in children while they're still in the womb, stage fever and enthusiasm for gladiators and race-horses. The mind gets taken over and besieged by these activities, and no room is left for better attainments. Do you often find people talking of anything else at home? All the youths are chatting about such things when we go into the lecture room. Even teachers have no more frequent topic of discussion with their pupils: indeed they attract students not by being disciplinarians or showing proof of their attainments, but by servile greetings and the enticements of flattery.

30   'I won't stop to discuss elementary education, though here too insufficient trouble is taken; not enough time is spent either on getting to know authors or studying history or acquiring knowledge of events, people, and times. They're all agog for the so-called rhetoricians. I shall shortly tell you when the profession was introduced into this city, and how it had no sort of standing in the eyes of our ancestors; but first let me draw your attention to the training that we know was undergone by those old orators: for their endless pains, their daily practice, their constant exercise in all kinds of study are mentioned in their own books.

'You will, of course, be acquainted with Cicero's *Brutus*, at the end of which, after his recital of the old orators one by one, he relates his own beginnings, the steps he took towards eloquence, what one may call his oratorical education. He relates how he studied civil law at the feet of Quintus Mucius and took a deep draught of all kinds of philosophy from the Academic Philo and the Stoic Diodotus. He was by no means content with the teachers to whom he had access in Rome, and so he traversed Greece and Asia also, in order to take in the widest variety of accomplish-ment. This, obviously, is why one can diagnose from Cicero's books that neither mathematics nor music nor grammar nor any other gentlemanly branch of knowledge fell outside his range. He was acquainted with the subtleties of dialectic, the practical teachings of ethics, and the physical causes and changes of events. This is the point I am making, my friends: that wonderful eloquence is the lavish overflow from great learning, wide skills, and universal knowledge. There is no narrow boundary circum-scribing oratorical potentiality and ability, as there is in other fields: he only is a true orator who can speak on any question brilliantly and splen-didly and persuasively, with equal regard for the importance of the subject, the circumstances of the time, and the pleasure of the audience.

'This was the conviction of those old-time orators. They realized that 31 it was therefore essential not to declaim in the rhetoricians' schools, not to exercise one's tongue and one's vocal chords in imaginary debates that have no sort of relation to reality, but to fill their minds with those high accomplishments that necessitate discussion of Good and Evil, Right and Wrong, Just and Unjust: this is the material that is the orator's stock-in-trade. In law-courts we are generally talking about equity, in delibera-tions about what is expedient, in eulogy about the Good. But often these distinctions are blurred: and no one can talk fluently and widely and elegantly on such topics unless he has acquainted himself with human nature, the power of virtue and the depravity of vice, and can understand the class of things that are neither virtue nor vice. Hence other advantages: the man who knows what anger is can more easily arouse or calm a judge's anger, and a knowledge of the nature of pity and the emotions by which it is aroused can enable one to move it more freely. If an orator is con-versant with these arts and this training, whether he has to speak to hostile or prejudiced or envious or morose or frightened men he will be able to feel his hearers' pulses, and proceed to adapt his speech as their characters require. He will have all the means available, stored up for every conceiv-able use. There are audiences with whom a concise, brief, one-argument-at-a-time style will carry more conviction; here a training in dialectic pays off. Others are pleased rather by oratory that is wordy, level, appealing to common feelings: to influence them we shall borrow from the Peripatetics commonplaces ready and available for any controversy.

The Academics will provide belligerence, Plato sublimity, Xenophon sweetness. An orator won't regard it as outside his province to bring into action good remarks even of Epicurus and Metrodorus, and employ them where appropriate. I am trying to model not a sage, or some disciple of the Stoics, but someone who must take a sip of all the arts, while draining only some of them down. So it was that the old orators included legal knowledge in their studies, and learnt the elements of grammar, music, and mathematics. Many of the cases one comes up against—indeed virtually all of them—require a knowledge of the law; and there are a large number that call for acquaintance with those other attainments, too.

32   'I don't want to hear the retort that it's enough for us to receive straight-forward special briefings as each occasion requires. First of all, we make different uses of our own and borrowed materials; it's obvious that it matters a lot if one owns what one puts on display or merely hires it. Moreover the very fact that we have wide knowledge of the arts lends us distinction even when we're on quite another tack—it stands out brilliantly when you least expect it. This is noticed by ordinary people as well as by a learned and observant listener; and their instantaneous praise means that they agree that here is a true orator, who has had a proper training and has gone through all the right hoops. Such a man cannot be, I maintain, and never has been anyone but somebody who goes into the forum armed with all the arts like a fully-equipped soldier striding into battle. But this point is so ignored by modern speakers that you may catch them in their cases uttering phrases with all the disgraceful and shaming faults of our every-day conversation. They have no knowledge of the laws, no acquaintance with decrees of the senate, no respect, even, for the Roman code; as for philosophy and the precepts of the wise they shudder at the very thought of them. They squeeze eloquence into a hand-ful of bright ideas and a narrow range of epigrams—dethroning it, one may say; for once it was the mistress of all the arts, and filled men's hearts with the beauty of its retinue. Now it is circumscribed and crippled, with no attendants and no respect shown it, without—I could almost say —any claim to breeding, and is learnt as though it were a mere low-class trade. This is, I think, the first and foremost cause for the extent to which we have fallen short of the old oratory.

'If you want witnesses, who better to call than Demosthenes among the Greeks, whom history relates to have been a most attentive student of Plato? And Cicero, I seem to remember, committed himself to the state-ment that anything he may have attained in eloquence he attained thanks not to the workshops of the rhetoricians but to the wide spaces of the Academy.[1] There are other reasons, weighty and important ones—but it's

[1] *Orator* 12.

only fair that *you* should expose them; I have done my job, and, according to my habit, offended quite enough people who, hearing my arguments, will certainly say that in praising the knowledge of law and philosophy as essential for an orator, I merely pander to my own foolish pursuits.'

Maternus said: 'Personally, I don't think you have yet completed the task 33 you undertook—indeed you seem merely to have begun it, and drawn a few preparatory lines and sketches. You've told us what arts the old orators were normally trained in, and you've contrasted our ignorance and sloth with their vigorous and fruitful studies. But I'm waiting for the rest: I've learnt what they knew—or what we don't know—but I want also to find out what exercises youths about to enter the forum generally used to strengthen and nourish their talents. Eloquence is a matter of art and knowledge—but far more of capacity and experience: you won't, I'm sure, dispute that, and I judge from the faces of our friends that they agree.'

Aper and Secundus assented, and Messalla made a sort of fresh start.

'I think I've given a sufficient exposition of the roots and beginnings of the old eloquence, showing you in what arts the ancient orators were normally trained and brought up: now for their exercises. Of course, there is exercise in the arts themselves; no one can grasp such recondite and varied matters unless theory is backed by practice, practice by capacity, capacity by actual experience. From which it can be inferred that there is no distinction between understanding what you are to express and expressing what you understood. This may seem a little obscure; but anyone who tries to separate theory and practice will at any rate concede that a mind that is full and trained in these arts comes much more prepared to those exercises that are characteristic of oratorical education.

'Well, in the time of our ancestors the youth who was preparing for the 34 forum and an oratorical career, after a thorough training at home and stuffed with desirable knowledge, was led off by his father or relations to an orator who held a high position in the state. He got used to following this man about, escorting him, being present at all his speeches in law-court or public assembly: he was on hand to listen to his legal cross-talk and observe his tiffs: he learnt to fight, you might say, in the battle-line. Hence vast experience, vast patience, and immense power of judgement came the way of youths right from the start. They studied in the full glare of daylight, amid actual crises where no one says anything stupid or inconsistent and gets away with it—he faces rejection by the judge, abuse from his adversaries, scorn even from his own supporters. Thus they straight away became imbued with an eloquence that was real and unspoilt. They might follow one man in particular, but they got to know all the advocates of the time in constant law-suits and actions. Moreover, they had a chance to observe the variations of public taste, and so easily discovered what in each man found favour or disfavour. Thus they had available a teacher—and a very good select one at that—who presented the actual face of eloquence to them, not a mere reflection: and opponents and rivals fighting with swords of steel, not of wood: and an auditorium never empty, never the same, consisting of hearers for and against them, with the result that nothing that was said, good or bad, could go unnoticed. For you know that really great and lasting distinction in oratory has its source as much in the benches opposite as in those on your side: there indeed it grows more firmly, and gains strength more surely. Under this sort of supervisor the youth of whom I am speaking—pupil of orators, spectator in the forum, follower of law-cases, trained and hardened in the experience of others, familiar with the laws from daily hearing of them, one to whom the faces of the judges did not seem strange—constantly observing the habits of assemblies, constantly aware of the taste of the people—such a man in prosecution or defence, from the start was by himself and alone equal to the demands of any case. Lucius Crassus prosecuted Gaius Carbo at eighteen, Caesar Dolabella at twenty, Asinius Pollio Gaius Cato at twenty-one, Calvus Vatinius when not much older—and those speeches we read even today with admiration.

35   'But now our poor young men are led off to the schools of the so-called rhetors. That these people emerged a little before the time of Cicero and displeased our ancestors is clear from the fact that they were ordered by the censors Crassus and Domitius to close—as Cicero says—their "schools for shamelessness".[1] But as I was saying: youths are led off to schools in which it is difficult to say what has the worst effect on their progress—the place, their fellow students, or the studies they go through. There is no respect in a place where no one not of equal ignorance ever goes; the other students are no help—boys among boys and youths among youths, they speak and are heard with equal irresponsibility; but the exercises themselves are to a large extent positively harmful.

'Two types of subject, of course, are dealt with in the rhetors' schools: *suasoriae* and *controversiae*. The former are regarded as much the less serious and as demanding less experience, and so they are assigned to the boys; but the older ones get the *controversiae*—God, how do I describe those! They are fantastically put together; and moreover these deliberately unreal subjects are treated with declamatory bombast. So it comes about that the most grandiose language is lavished on rewards for tyrannicides or choices by the raped or remedies for plague or adultery by matrons or

---

[1] *De oratore* 3. 94. This was in 92 B.C.

any of the other topics that come up daily in school, in the forum rarely or never: but when they come to speak before real judges. . .'[1]

'. . . consider the matter. He could utter nothing sordid, nothing low. 36 Great eloquence is like a flame: it needs fuel to feed it; it is roused by movement; and it brightens as it burns.

'It was the same principle in our city also that carried the oratory of the ancients to its heights. Modern orators have attained what influence they reasonably may in a settled, calm, and contented state; but *they* saw that they could reap advantages from the confusion and licence then prevailing; all was in turmoil, there was no single ruler, and an orator had prestige to the extent that he could carry a fickle people with him. Hence the continual passing of laws to win popular acclaim, hence the addresses by magistrates ready to spend pretty well all night on the rostrum, hence the prosecutions of leading men and the feuds handed down like family heirlooms, hence the quarrels of the great and the incessant rivalry of senate and people. These contributed to the dismemberment of the state: but they meant practice for the eloquence of those times and ensured that it was heaped with great rewards; the better at speaking one was, the more easily one could attain public office, the more when holding it one could outdistance one's colleagues, the more influence one could wield with leading men, the more authority in the senate, the more fame and glory with the public. These people were flooded with clients—even foreign nations counted as that; they were the object of respect from magistrates about to go to their provinces and of attentions from the same men on their return; they seemed to be at the beck and call of praetorships and consulships, and even when out of office they did not lack power, for their counsel and authority lent them control of senate and people alike. They had convinced themselves that no one could attain or preserve an outstanding and pre-eminent place in the city without eloquence. And no wonder, when they found themselves addressing the people even when they did not want to, when it was not enough just to give a brief explanation of your position in the senate, but you had to defend your opinion with all your powers of eloquence: when they regarded it as essential to reply in person if one was summoned to face some charge or calumny: when one had to give evidence at public trials not in absence or in writing, but present and personally. Eloquence was not just the route to the highest rewards—it was a vital necessity: it was splendid and glorious to be thought eloquent, and shameful to be called dumb and tongueless.

'So shame as much as reward urged them on, to avoid being petty 37 clients rather than patrons, to ensure that inherited connections did not pass to others, and that they did not, by a reputation for sloth and

---

[1] There is a lacuna here. When the text resumes, Maternus is the speaker.

incompetence, fail to achieve office—or come to grief in it when achieved. I don't know whether you have handled those old documents, still available in the libraries of antiquarians and just now being collected by Mucianus: eleven books of *Proceedings* and three of *Letters* have already come out, haven't they? Anyway from these you can judge that Pompey and Crassus excelled in oratorical talent as well as in military prowess; the Lentuli, Metelli, Luculli, Curios, and the other top people took a great deal of trouble over the same pursuits: no one in those days attained to great power without some eloquence.

'Remember too the distinction of the defendants and the importance of the cases, themselves a considerable spur to eloquence. For it makes a lot of difference whether you have to speak about a theft or a rule of procedure or an interdict—or about electoral bribery, the robbery of allies, and the slaughter of citizens. No doubt it is better that such things should not happen; no doubt the best state of affairs for a country is one in which we don't have to put up with such evils; but seeing that they *did* happen, they provided immense scope for eloquence. A talent swells with the size of the events it has to deal with; no one can produce a famous and notable oration unless he finds a case equal to his powers. Demosthenes is not famous, surely, for the speeches he wrote against his guardians, Cicero isn't a great orator because he defended Publius Quintius or Licinius Archias. It was Catiline, Milo, Verres, and Antony who covered him with glory. Don't think I'm saying that it was worth it that the state should produce such criminal citizens merely to give orators rich scope for their oratory. But, as I keep saying, let us remember the question under discussion, and realize that we are speaking of something that flourishes more easily in stormy and troubled times. It's better (everyone knows that) and more advantageous to enjoy peace than to be harassed by war: it remains true that wars produce more good fighters than peace. So it is with oratory. The more often it stands in the firing-line, the more knocks it gives and receives, the greater adversaries and the more bitter battles it takes on, the higher and more sublime it reigns, ennobled by those crises, in the mouths of men, who are so made that they desire safety but have a penchant for danger.

38   'I turn now to the shape and customs of the old law-courts. The present pattern is more convenient, but the forum in its old guise gave more practice to eloquence. No one then was forced to keep his speech down to a meagre ration of hours; there was free scope for postponements; every speaker fixed his own time-limit, and there was no limitation on the number of days or of advocates in attendance. Pompey, during his third consulship,[1] was the first to bring in restrictions and to put the bit on

---

[1] 52 B.C.

eloquence: all the same everything continued to be conducted in the forum and according to the laws and before the praetors. For the praetors presided over far greater cases then, as can most strikingly be seen from the fact that the centumviral cases, which now hold first place, were so overshadowed by the prestige of other courts that we now read no speech delivered before the Centumviri by Cicero, Caesar, Brutus, Caelius, Calvus, or any great orator—only the speeches of Asinius entitled *For the Heirs of Urbinia*: but *they* were delivered by Pollio as late as the middle of Augustus' reign, at a time when a long period of peace, continuous public calm, unbroken tranquillity in the senate, and particularly the restraining influence of the emperor had combined to pacify eloquence herself, like everything else.

'What I am going to say may perhaps seem ridiculously trivial, but I'll 39 say it all the same to get a laugh purposely. Don't we agree that eloquence has been brought into disrepute by those tight cloaks that enclose and fetter us when we chat away to the judges? Hasn't it been emasculated by the recital halls and public record offices where cases are now normally disposed of? Well-bred horses are proved by spacious race-tracks: and there is similarly a kind of unfenced field where orators must run free and unshackled if eloquence is not to be weakened and broken. We even find ourselves thwarted by the very trouble we take over careful style, because the judge often asks when you propose to begin—and you have to begin there, the moment he asks. Often the judge orders silence when proofs or evidence are being given. Only one or two people are present amidst all this, and matters proceed in a sort of vacuum. But what an orator needs is noise and applause, a theatre for his performance: the old orators had all that every day. An audience large (and well-bred too) packed the forum; clients, fellow tribesmen, municipal delegations, a good proportion of the population of Italy came to support defendants— for in many cases the Roman people believed that what was decided mattered to *them*. It is well known that when Gaius Cornelius, Marcus Scaurus, Titus Milo, Lucius Bestia, and Publius Vatinius were prosecuted and defended the whole state came running to listen: even the most tepid orator might have been excited and inflamed by the enthusiasm of the partisan public. And this is why, surely, these speeches are extant, and are so fine that their authors need cite no other evidence to be put in their true class.

'Moreover, the constant public assemblies, the opportunity to harass 40 any powerful man, the fact that vendettas could bring actual fame—for many eloquent speakers did not scruple to attack even Scipio, Sulla, or Pompey, and even actors[1] used their control of the public ear to assault

[1] Text doubtful.

grave personages (such is malice!)—all this made speakers eager, and gave the spur to oratory.

'It is no inert and passive thing I speak of, that rejoices in probity and modesty. The great and famous eloquence I have in mind is the nurseling of licence—which fools call liberty—and the companion of sedition: it unbridles and spurs on the people; it has no respect for persons, no proper dignity; it is insolent, rash, arrogant; in well-organized states it does not arise. What Spartan or Cretan orators have we heard of? Yet those states reputedly had the severest constitutions and the severest laws. We know of no eloquence that flourished among the Macedonians or Persians or any race that was content not to challenge its rulers. There were some Rhodian orators, and many Athenian ones—and in their cities everything was in the power of the people, everything under the control of the inexperienced: everyone, you might almost say, had a hand in everything. Our state, so long as it drifted, so long as it sapped itself by faction, dissension, and discord, so long as there was no peace in the forum, no agreement in the senate, no settled routine in the courts, no respect for superiors, no restriction imposed on magistrates, produced no doubt a stronger eloquence, just as an untilled field has some more luxuriant plants. But the eloquence of the Gracchi was not worth to the republic the price it had to pay—the laws of the Gracchi: and Cicero, by the end he met, bought his fame in eloquence at too high a cost.

41 'And what remains of the old forum only goes to prove that the state is not yet healed, not yet settled as we should wish. Who needs our advocacy except the guilty or the unfortunate? What town becomes our client unless it is harassed by a neighbouring people or by internal discord? Do we defend a province unless it has been despoiled and plundered? It would have been better not to have to complain than to have the complaint rectified. If a state in which no one committed any crime could be found, the orator would be superfluous amidst those innocent men, like a doctor among the healthy. And just as medicine has little practice and has made little progress in races that have the best health and the soundest constitutions, so among dutiful citizens ready to serve their ruler orators have less honour and a more obscure name. What need of long speeches in the senate? Our great men swiftly reach agreement. What need of constant harangues to the people? The deliberations of state are not left to the ignorant many—they are the duty of one man, the wisest. What need of prosecutions? Crime is rare and trivial. What need of long and unpopular defences? The clemency of the judge meets the defendants half way. Believe me, my excellent friends, who are as eloquent as our day requires: if you had been born in earlier ages and those men we so much admire had been born in our times, some god having suddenly switched round

your lives and periods, you would not have missed the highest distinction in eloquence—and they would not have failed to observe moderation. As it is, since no one can at the same time enjoy both great fame and great peace, let each group enjoy the blessings of his own age without carping at the other's.'

Maternus had finished. Messalla said: 'I should have liked to contradict 42 some things and hear more about others. But the day is over.'

'Let that be later on, as you like,' said Maternus, 'and if anything seemed obscure in what I said, we can discuss it again.'

And he got up, and embraced Aper, saying: 'I will tell on you to the poets, and Messalla will to the antiquarians.'

'And I will tell on both of you to the rhetoricians and the professors.'

They laughed; and we went our ways.

11

LONGINUS, *ON SUBLIMITY*

INTRODUCTION

(i) ANALYSIS

The single medieval manuscript on which our knowledge of 'Longinus' depends suffered damage before any of the extant copies of it were made: some pages fell out. Consequently, about a third of the book is lost (the seven *lacunae* are indicated in the translation). Though this robs us of much that would be of interest, it does not, except in one important particular, affect our understanding of the author's fairly simple plan.

The key to the book is in chapter 8; what precedes this is an extended introduction.

We may summarize the book as follows:

1–2: a formal Preface.
3–5: faults incident to the attempt to achieve 'sublimity'. (This helps to define the subject by contrast.)
6–7: some marks of true 'sublimity'.
  8: the five sources of 'sublimity':
    (i) The power of conceiving impressive thoughts (discussed in 9–15);
    (ii) strong emotion;
    (iii) certain kinds of figures of thought and speech (16–29);
    (iv) nobility of diction (30–8, 43);
    (v) 'Composition', i.e. word-order, rhythm, euphony (39–42).

(What has happened to (ii)? At the very end of the book (44. 12), we are told that a separate work on emotions is to follow. It seems most natural to conclude that the long lacuna in 9[1] contained a warning of this change of plan. Certain features both of the treatment of thought (9–15) and of later sections involve considerations of emotion, which is often mentioned and emphasized; it may be that the writer pointed this out also in the missing section.)

9–43: working out of the scheme (I have given more details in the headings of the translation; there is a good deal of unevenness in the scale of treatment).
  44: 'Appendix' on the causes of the current decline of literature.

[1] The chapter divisions are sixteenth-century, and are (as this example shows) perverse and unpractical. They will be found in the margin of the translation. My paragraphing and sub-titling are independent of them.

(ii) AUTHORSHIP

The author of *On Sublimity* is unknown. The manuscript attributes it in one place to 'Dionysius Longinus', in another to 'Dionysius or Longinus'. Modern scholars generally believe that this second version of the title is correct, and represents two guesses made in Byzantine times: the author was either the Augustan critic Dionysius of Halicarnassus or Cassius Longinus, a well-known statesman and critic of the third century A.D. This second view was universally held in the eighteenth century; it is eloquently developed (Longinus was a colourful, even heroic, figure) in Boileau's *Préface* and Gibbon's *Decline and Fall* (chap. xi). It has its recent defenders (G. Luck, *Arctos*, 1968); but the received opinion to-day is that we have to do with a book of the 1st cent. A.D. The sole argument for this—and it is a convincing one—is derived from the last chapter (44), in which the author discusses the relation between the decline of literature and the political change from republican to monarchical government. This topic occurs frequently in writers of the first century or so of the Roman principate—e.g. in the two Senecas and in Tacitus. It does not occur much after A.D. 100, and is inconceivable in the disturbances of the third century.

The only other probable conclusion about the author which can be drawn from the book—nothing is known about the Roman addressee, Postumius Terentianus—is that he was either a Jew or in contact with Jewish culture. This follows from his use (9. 9) of the opening sentences of Genesis as an example of sublimity. No other pagan writer uses the Bible like this. There are, moreover, several resemblances between the writer's language and thought and that of the Alexandrian Jew Philo (*c.* 30 B.C.–A.D. 45), but the attempts which are sometimes made to postulate a close connection (e.g. to say that the 'philosopher' of the last chapter is Philo) press the evidence too far.

The most we can safely say is that the book was written in the first century A.D., by a writer with both Roman and Jewish contacts.

Editions

W. Rhys Roberts (text, translation, notes), Cambridge, 1899, 1907.
D. A. Russell (text, commentary), Oxford, 1964.
(Both these books contain bibliographies.)

Older translations

N. Boileau-Despréaux, Paris, 1674, etc. (ed. Boudhors, 1942).
W. Smith, London, 1739, etc.

Influence

M. H. Abrams, *The Mirror and the Lamp*, New York, 1953.
S. H. Monk, *The Sublime*, New York, 1935.

ON SUBLIMITY

PREFACE

My dear Postumius Terentianus,

1. 1   You will recall that when we were reading together Caecilius' monograph *On Sublimity*, we felt that it was inadequate to its high subject, and failed to touch the essential points. Nor indeed did it appear to offer the reader much practical help, though this ought to be a writer's principal object. Two things are required of any textbook: first, that it should explain what its subject is; second, and more important, that it should explain how and by what methods we can achieve it. Caecilius tries at immense length to explain to us what sort of thing 'the sublime' is, as though we did not know; but he has somehow passed over as unnecessary the question how 2 we can develop our nature to some degree of greatness. However, we ought perhaps not so much to blame our author for what he has left out as to commend him for his originality and enthusiasm.

You have urged me to set down a few notes on sublimity for your own use. Let us then consider whether there is anything in my observations which may be thought useful to public men. You must help me, my friend, by giving your honest opinion in detail, as both your natural candour and your friendship with me require. It was well said that what man has in common with the gods is 'doing good and telling the truth'.

3   Your education dispenses me from any long preliminary definition. Sublimity is a kind of eminence or excellence of discourse. It is the source of the distinction of the very greatest poets and prose writers and 4 the means by which they have given eternal life to their own fame. For grandeur produces ecstasy rather than persuasion in the hearer; and the combination of wonder and astonishment always proves superior to the merely persuasive and pleasant. This is because persuasion is on the whole something we can control, whereas amazement and wonder exert invincible power and force and get the better of every hearer. Experience in invention and ability to order and arrange material cannot be detected in single passages; we begin to appreciate them only when we see the whole context. Sublimity, on the other hand, produced at the right moment, tears everything up like a whirlwind, and exhibits the orator's whole power at a single blow.

2. 1   Your own experience will lead you to these and similar considerations. The question from which I must begin is whether there is in fact an art of sublimity or profundity.[1] Some people think it is a complete mistake

----

[1] This is to translate *bathous*. The simple, eighteenth-century emendation *pathous* means 'emotion'. Boileau omits the word. The English word 'bathos' seems to have

to reduce things like this to technical rules. Greatness, the argument runs, is a natural product, and does not come by teaching. The only art is to be born like that. They believe moreover that natural products are very much weakened by being reduced to the bare bones of a textbook.

In my view, these arguments can be refuted by considering three 2 points:

(i) Though nature is on the whole a law unto herself in matters of emotion and elevation, she is not a random force and does not work altogether without method.

(ii) She is herself in every instance a first and primary element of creation, but it is method that is competent to provide and contribute quantities and appropriate occasions for everything, as well as perfect correctness in training and application.

(iii) Grandeur is particularly dangerous when left on its own, unaccompanied by knowledge, unsteadied, unballasted, abandoned to mere impulse and ignorant temerity. It often needs the curb as well as the spur.

What Demosthenes[1] said of life in general is true also of literature: 3 good fortune is the greatest of blessings, but good counsel comes next, and the lack of it destroys the other also. In literature, nature occupies the place of good fortune, and art that of good counsel. Most important of all, the very fact that some things in literature depend on nature alone can itself be learned only from art.

If the critic of students of this subject will bear these points in mind, he will, I believe, come to realize that the examination of the question before us is by no means useless or superfluous.

[Lacuna equivalent to about two of these printed pages]

FAULTS INCIDENT TO THE EFFORT TO ACHIEVE SUBLIMITY: TURGIDITY, PUERILITY, FALSE EMOTION, FRIGIDITY

> . . . restrain the oven's mighty glow. 3. 1
> For if I see but one beside his hearth,
> I'll thrust in just one tentacle of storm,
> and fire his roof and turn it all to cinders.
> I've not yet sung my proper song.[2]

This is not tragedy; it is a parody of the tragic manner—tentacles,

acquired its meaning from a misunderstanding of this passage; see Pope's *Peri Bathous or on the Art of Sinking* (1728).

[1] *Orations* 23. 113.

[2] Aeschylus, fr. 281 Nauck. The speaker is Boreas, the North Wind, who is enraged with King Erechtheus of Athens because he will not give him his daughter Orithyia. As the passage is incomplete, the point of some of the critical comment is lost.

vomiting to heaven, making Boreas a flute-player, and so on. The result is not impressiveness but turbid diction and confused imagery. If you examine the details closely, they gradually sink from the terrifying to the contemptible.

Now if untimely turgidity is unpardonable in tragedy, a genre which is naturally magniloquent and tolerant of bombast, it will scarcely be
2 appropriate in writing which has to do with real life. Hence the ridicule attaching to Gorgias of Leontini's 'Xerxes, the Persians' Zeus' and 'their living tombs, the vultures', or to various things in Callisthenes, where he has not so much risen to heights as been carried off his feet. Clitarchus is an even more striking example; he is an inflated writer, and, as Sophocles has it,

> blows at his tiny flute, the mouth-band off.[1]

Amphicrates, Hegesias, Matris—they are all the same. They often fancy themselves possessed when they are merely playing the fool.
3 Turgidity is a particularly hard fault to avoid, for it is one to which all who aim at greatness naturally incline, because they seek to escape the charge of weakness and aridity. They act on the principle that 'to slip
4 from a great prize is yet a noble fault'. In literature as in the body, puffy and false tumours are bad, and may well bring us to the opposite result from that which we expected. As the saying goes, there is nothing so dry as a man with dropsy.

While turgidity is an endeavour to go above the sublime, puerility[2] is the sheer opposite of greatness; it is a thoroughly low, mean, and ignoble vice. What do I mean by 'puerility'? A pedantic thought, so over-worked that it ends in frigidity. Writers slip into it through aiming at originality, artifice, and (above all) charm, and then coming to grief on the rocks of tawdriness and affectation.
5 A third kind of fault—what Theodorus called 'the pseudo-bacchanalian' —corresponds to these in the field of emotion. It consists of untimely or meaningless emotion where none is in place, or immoderate emotion where moderate is in place. Some people often get carried away, like drunkards, into emotions unconnected with the subject, which are simply their own pedantic invention. The audience feels nothing, so that they inevitably make an exhibition of themselves, parading their ecstasies before an audience which does not share them.

But I reserve the subject of emotion for another place,[3] returning mean-
4. 1 while to the second fault of those I mentioned: frigidity. This is a constant feature in Timaeus, who is in many ways a competent writer, not

---

[1] Fr. 701 Nauck.
[2] The context shows what is meant: the shallow pedantry of the immature.
[3] Presumably in the lost passage.

without the capacity for greatness on occasion, learned and original, but as unconscious of his own faults as he is censorious of others', and often falling into the grossest childishness through his passion for always starting exotic ideas. I will give one or two examples; Caecilius has already 2 cited most of those available.

(i) In praise of Alexander the Great, Timaeus writes: 'He conquered all Asia in fewer years than it took Isocrates to write the *Panegyricus* to advocate the Persian war.' What a splendid comparison this is—the Macedonian king and the sophist! On the same principle, the Lacedaemonians were very much less brave than Isocrates: it took them thirty years to capture Messene,[1] whereas he took only ten to write the *Panegyricus*!

(ii) Listen also to Timaeus' comment on the Athenians captured in 3 Sicily. 'They were punished for their impiety to Hermes and mutilation of his statues, and the main agent of their punishment was one who had a family connection with their victim, Hermocrates the son of Hermon.'[2] I cannot help wondering, my dear Terentianus, why he does not also write about the Tyrant Dionysius, 'Because he was impious towards Zeus and Heracles, Dion and Heraclides robbed him of his throne.'[3]

But why speak of Timaeus, when those heroes of letters, Xenophon 4 and Plato, for all that they were trained in Socrates' school, forget themselves sometimes for the sake of similar petty pleasures? Thus Xenophon writes in *The Constitution of the Lacedaemonians*: 'You could hear their voice less than the voice of stone statues, you could distract their eyes less than the eyes of bronze images; you would think them more bashful than the very maidens in the eyes.'[4] It would have been more in keeping with Amphicrates' manner than Xenophon's to speak of the pupils of our eyes as bashful maidens. And what an absurd misconception to think of everybody's pupils as bashful! The shamelessness of a person, we are told, appears nowhere so plainly as in the eyes. Remember the words Achilles uses to revile Agamemnon's violent temper: 'Drunken sot, with a dog's *eyes*!'[5] Timaeus, unable to keep his hands off stolen property, as it were, 5

---

[1] In the eighth century B.C. Our other sources make this war last twenty years; we do not know the source of the variant (assuming the text to be correct).

[2] The disastrous Athenian expedition against Syracuse (415–413 B.C.) had been preceded by a mysterious incident at Athens, in which the 'Hermae' in the city were mutilated one night.

[3] Dionysius II, expelled in 356. The name Dion is etymologically connected with Zeus (accusative *Dia*, genitive *Dios*).

[4] The word *korē* means both 'girl' and 'pupil'; Xenophon replaces it by *parthenos*, which means unambiguously 'maiden'.

[5] *Iliad* I. 225.—The text of this sentence in 'Longinus' is uncertain, but the general sense beyond doubt.

has not left the monopoly of this frigid conceit to Xenophon. He uses it in connection with Agathocles, who eloped with his cousin from the unveiling ceremony of her marriage to another: 'Who would have done this, if he had not had harlots in his eyes for pupils (*koras*)?'[1]

6 And what of Plato, the otherwise divine Plato? He wants to express the idea of writing-tablets. 'They shall write', he says, 'and deposit in the temples memorials of cypress.'[2] Again: 'As for walls, Megillus, I should concur with Sparta in letting walls sleep in the earth and not get up.'[3]

7 Herodotus' description[4] of beautiful women as 'pains on the eyes' is the same sort of thing, though it is to some extent excused by the fact that the speakers are barbarians and drunk—not that it is a good thing to make an exhibition of the triviality of one's mind to posterity, even through the mouths of characters like these.

5. 1 All such lapses from dignity arise in literature through a single cause: that desire for novelty of thought which is all the rage today. Evils often come from the same source as blessings; and so, since beauty of style, sublimity, and charm all conduce to successful writing, they are also causes and principles not only of success but of failure. Variation, hyperbole, and the use of plural for singular are like this too; I shall explain below the dangers which they involve.[5]

SOME MARKS OF TRUE SUBLIMITY

6. 1 At this stage, the question we must put to ourselves for discussion is how to avoid the faults which are so much tied up with sublimity. The answer, my friend, is: by first of all achieving a genuine understanding and appreciation of true sublimity. This is difficult; literary judgement comes only as the final product of long experience. However, for the purposes of instruction, I think we can say that an understanding of all this can be acquired. I approach the problem in this way:

7. 1 In ordinary life, nothing is truly great which it is great to despise; wealth, honour, reputation, absolute power—anything in short which has a lot of external trappings—can never seem supremely good to the wise man because it is no small good to despise them. People who could have these advantages if they chose but disdain them out of magnanimity are admired much more than those who actually possess them.[6] It is much the same with elevation in poetry and literature generally. We have to ask

---

[1] Agathocles was ruler of Syracuse from 317 to 287. The 'unveiling ceremony' was normally held on the third day after the marriage.   [2] *Laws* 741 c.
[3] *Laws* 778.d.
[4] Herodotus 5. 18.   [5] See chaps. 23 and 38.
[6] Compare Aristotle's 'magnanimous man': *Nicomachean Ethics* 4. 3.

ourselves whether any particular example does not give a show of grandeur which, for all its accidental trappings, will, when dissected, prove vain and hollow, the kind of thing which it does a man more honour to despise than to admire. It is our nature to be elevated and exalted by true sublimity. Filled with joy and pride, we come to believe we have created what we have only heard. When a man of sense and literary experience hears something many times over, and it fails to dispose his mind to greatness or to leave him with more to reflect upon than was contained in the mere words, but comes instead to seem valueless on repeated inspection, this is not true sublimity; it endures only for the moment of hearing. Real sublimity contains much food for reflection, is difficult or rather impossible to resist, and makes a strong and ineffaceable impression on the memory. In a word, reckon those things which please everybody all the time as genuinely and finely sublime. When people of different trainings, ways of life, tastes, ages, and manners all agree about something, the judgement and assent of so many distinct voices lends strength and irrefutability to the conviction that their admiration is rightly directed.

THE FIVE SOURCES OF SUBLIMITY; THE PLAN OF THE BOOK

There are, one may say, five most productive sources of sublimity. 8. 1
(Competence in speaking is assumed as a common foundation for all five; nothing is possible without it.)

(i) The first and most important is the power to conceive great thoughts; I defined this in my work on Xenophon.

(ii) The second is strong and inspired emotion. (These two sources are for the most part natural; the remaining three involve art.)

(iii) Certain kinds of figures. (These may be divided into figures of thought and figures of speech.)

(iv) Noble diction. This has as subdivisions choice of words and the use of metaphorical and artificial language.[1]

(v) Finally, to round off the whole list, dignified and elevated word-arrangement.

Let us now examine the points which come under each of these heads. 2

I must first observe, however, that Caecilius has omitted some of the five—emotion, for example. Now if he thought that sublimity and emotion were one and the same thing and always existed and developed together, he was wrong. Some emotions, such as pity, grief, and fear, are found divorced from sublimity and with a low effect. Conversely, sublimity often occurs apart from emotion. Of the innumerable

---

[1] Or 'and coined words'.

examples of this I select Homer's bold account of the Aloadae:

> Ossa upon Olympus they sought to heap; and on Ossa
> Pelion with its shaking forest, to make a path to heaven—

and the even more impressive sequel—

> and they would have finished their work . . .[1]

3 In orators, encomia and ceremonial or exhibition pieces always involve grandeur and sublimity, though they are generally devoid of emotion. Hence those orators who are best at conveying emotion are least good at encomia, and conversely the experts at encomia are not conveyers of emotion. On the other hand, if Caecilius thought that emotion had no 4 contribution to make to sublimity and therefore thought it not worth mentioning, he was again completely wrong. I should myself have no hesitation in saying that there is nothing so productive of grandeur as noble emotion in the right place. It inspires and possesses our words with a kind of madness and divine spirit.

(i) GREATNESS OF THOUGHT

9. 1 The first source, natural greatness, is the most important. Even if it is a matter of endowment rather than acquisition, we must, so far as is possible, develop our minds in the direction of greatness and make them always pregnant with noble thoughts. You ask how this can be done. 2 I wrote elsewhere something like this: 'Sublimity is the echo of a noble mind.' This is why a mere idea, without verbal expression, is sometimes admired for its nobility—just as Ajax's silence in the Vision of the Dead is grand and indeed more sublime than any words could have been.[2] 3 First then we must state where sublimity comes from: the orator must not have low or ignoble thoughts. Those whose thoughts and habits are trivial and servile all their lives cannot possibly produce anything admirable or worthy of eternity. Words will be great if thoughts are weighty. This is why splendid remarks come naturally to the proud; the man who, 4 when Parmenio said, 'I should have been content'. . .[3]

[Lacuna equivalent to about six pages.]

---

[1] *Odyssey* 11. 315-17.
[2] *Odyssey* 11. 563. Note that this is not an example, but a simile illustrating the point that ideas in themselves can be grand.
[3] Parmenio said to Alexander that if he were Alexander he would be content, and would not go on fighting. 'So would I, if I were Parmenio', replied Alexander.

SUCCESSFUL AND UNSUCCESSFUL WAYS OF REPRESENTING
SUPERNATURAL BEINGS AND OF EXCITING AWE

... the interval between earth and heaven. One might say that this is the 5 measure not so much of Strife as of Homer.[1]

Contrast the line about Darkness in Hesiod—if the *Shield* is by Hesiod:

Mucus dripped from her nostrils.[2]

This gives a repulsive picture, not one to excite awe. But how does Homer magnify the divine power?

As far as a man can peer through the mist,
sitting on watch, looking over the wine-dark sea,
so long is the stride of the gods' thundering horses.[3]

He uses a cosmic distance to measure their speed. This enormously impressive image would make anybody say, and with reason, that, if the horses of the gods took two strides like that, they would find there was not enough room in the world.

The imaginative pictures in the Battle of the Gods are also very remark- 6 able:

And the great heavens and Olympus trumpeted around them.
Aïdoneus, lord of the dead, was frightened in his depths;
and in fright he jumped from his throne, and shouted,
for fear the earth-shaker Poseidon might break through
the ground,
and gods and men might see
the foul and terrible halls, which even the gods detest.[4]

Do you see how the earth is torn from its foundations, Tartarus laid bare, and the whole universe overthrown and broken up, so that all things— Heaven and Hell, things mortal and things immortal—share the warfare 7 and the perils of that ancient battle? But, terrifying as all this is, it is blasphemous and indecent unless it is interpreted allegorically; in relating the gods' wounds, quarrels, revenges, tears, imprisonments, and manifold misfortunes, Homer, or so it seems to me, has done his best to make the men of the Trojan war gods, and the gods men. If men are unhappy, there is always death as a harbour in trouble; what he has done for his gods is to make them immortal indeed, but immortally miserable.

---

[1] The reference is to *Iliad* 4. 440 ff., where Strife is described as having her head in the sky and walking on the earth. 'Longinus' means that Homer too is a colossus of cosmic dimensions.

[2] *Shield of Heracles* 267.   [3] *Iliad* 5. 770–2.

[4] See *Iliad* 21. 388 and 20. 61 ff.

8   Much better than the Battle of the Gods are the passages which represent divinity as genuinely unsoiled and great and pure. The lines about Poseidon, much discussed by my predecessors, exemplify this:

> The high hills and the forest trembled,
> and the peaks and the city of Troy and the Achaean ships
> under the immortal feet of Poseidon as he went his way.
> He drove over the waves, and the sea-monsters gambolled around him,
> coming up everywhere out of the deep; they recognized their king.
> The sea parted in joy; and the horses flew onward.[1]

9   Similarly, the lawgiver of the Jews, no ordinary man—for he understood and expressed God's power in accordance with its worth—writes at the beginning of his *Laws*: 'God said'—now what?—'"Let there be light", and there was light; "Let there be earth", and there was earth.'[2]

10   Perhaps it will not be out of place, my friend, if I add a further Homeric example—from the human sphere this time—so that we can see how the poet is accustomed to enter into the greatness of his heroes. Darkness falls suddenly. Thickest night blinds the Greek army. Ajax is bewildered. 'O Father Zeus!', he cries,

> 'Deliver the sons of the Achaeans out of the mist,
> make the sky clear, and let us see;
> in the light—kill us.'[3]

The feeling here is genuinely Ajax's. He does not pray for life—that would be a request unworthy of a hero—but having no good use for his courage in the disabling darkness, and so angered at his inactivity in the battle, he prays for light, and quickly: he will at all costs find a shroud worthy of his valour, though Zeus be arrayed against him.

COMPARISON BETWEEN THE ILIAD AND THE ODYSSEY

11   In this passage, the gale of battle blows hard in Homer; he

> Rages like Ares, spear-brandishing, or the deadly fire
> raging in the mountains, in the thickets of the deep wood.
> Foam shows at his mouth.[4]

In the *Odyssey*, on the other hand—and there are many reasons for adding

---

[1] See *Iliad* 13. 18 ff., and 20. 60.

[2] Controversy about the genuineness of this reference to Genesis 1 has raged since the eighteenth century. For the influence of the reference on literary taste, see S. H. Monk, *The Sublime*, 33.   [3] *Iliad* 17. 645 ff.

[4] From *Iliad* 15. 605 ff.

this to our inquiry—he demonstrates that when a great mind begins to decline, a love of story-telling characterizes its old age. We can tell that 12 the *Odyssey* was his second work from various considerations, in particular from his insertion of the residue of the Trojan troubles in the poem in the form of episodes, and from the way in which he pays tribute of lamentation and pity to the heroes, treating them as persons long known. The *Odyssey* is simply an epilogue to the *Iliad*:

> There lies warlike Ajax, there Achilles,
> there Patroclus, the gods' peer as a counsellor,
> and there my own dear son.[1]

For the same reason, I maintain, he made the whole body of the *Iliad*, 13 which was written at the height of his powers, dramatic and exciting, whereas most of the *Odyssey* consists of narrative, which is a characteristic of old age. Homer in the *Odyssey* may be compared to the setting sun: the size remains without the force. He no longer sustains the tension as it was in the tale of Troy, nor that consistent level of elevation which never admitted any falling off. The outpouring of passions crowding one on another has gone; so has the versatility, the realism, the abundance of imagery taken from the life. We see greatness on the ebb. It is as though the Ocean were withdrawing into itself and flowing quietly in its own bed. Homer is lost in the realm of the fabulous and incredible. In saying 14 this, I have not forgotten the storms in the *Odyssey*, the story of Cyclops, and a few other episodes; I am speaking of old age—but it is the old age of a Homer. The point about all these stories is that the mythical element in them predominates over the realistic.

I digressed into this topic, as I said, to illustrate how easy it is for great genius to be perverted in decline into nonsense. I mean things like the story of the wineskin, the tale of the men kept as pigs in Circe's palace ('howling piglets', Zoilus called them), the feeding of Zeus by the doves (as though he were a chick in the nest), the ten days on the raft without food, and the improbabilities of the murder of the suitors.[2] What can we say of all this but that it really is 'the dreaming of a Zeus'?[3]

There is also a second reason for discussing the *Odyssey*. I want you 15 to understand that the decline of emotional power in great writers and poets turns to a capacity for depicting manners. The realistic description of Odysseus' household forms a kind of comedy of manners.

---

[1] Spoken by Nestor, *Odyssey* 3. 109 ff.
[2] For these various stories, see *Odyssey* 10. 17 ff., 10. 237 ff., 12. 447 ff., 22. 79 ff.
[3] Sense uncertain. Possibly the text is corrupt. 'A sick man's dream' has been suggested: cf. Horace, *The Art of Poetry*, above, p. 279.

SELECTION AND ORGANIZATION OF MATERIAL

10. 1 Now have we any other means of making our writing sublime? Every topic naturally includes certain elements which are inherent in its raw material. It follows that sublimity will be achieved if we consistently select the most important of these inherent features and learn to organize them as a unity by combining one with another. The first of these procedures attracts the reader by the selection of details, the second by the density of those selected.

Consider Sappho's treatment of the feelings involved in the madness of being in love. She uses the attendant circumstances and draws on real life at every point. And in what does she show her quality? In her skill in selecting the outstanding details and making a unity of them:

2   To me he seems a peer of the gods, the man who sits facing you
      and hears your sweet voice
         and lovely laughter; it flutters my heart in my breast. When I see
      you only for a moment, I cannot speak;
         my tongue is broken, a subtle fire runs under my skin; my eyes
      cannot see, my ears hum;
         cold sweat pours off me; shivering grips me all over; I am paler
      than grass; I seem near to dying;
         but all must be endured . . .[1]

3 Do you not admire the way in which she brings everything together— mind and body, hearing and tongue, eyes and skin? She seems to have lost them all, and to be looking for them as though they were external to her. She is cold and hot, mad and sane, frightened and near death, all by turns. The result is that we see in her not a single emotion, but a complex of emotions. Lovers experience all this; Sappho's excellence, as I have said, lies in her adoption and combination of the most striking details.

A similar point can be made about the descriptions of storms in Homer, **4** who always picks out the most terrifying aspects. The author of the *Arimaspea* on the other hand expects these lines to excite terror:

      This too is a great wonder to us in our hearts:
      there are men living on water, far from land, on the deep sea:

---

[1] See D. L. Page, *Sappho and Alcaeus*, Oxford, 1955, chap. 2, for this poem (= Sappho, fragment 31). Eighteenth-century translation by Ambrose Phillips, *Spectator* 229, with criticism by Addison; Romantic translation by W. Headlam, *Oxford Book of Greek Verse in Translation*, no. 141; recent version by Richmond Lattimore, *Greek Lyrics*, 2nd edn., Chicago, 1960, p. 39.

> miserable they are, for hard is their lot;
> they give their eyes to the stars, their lives to the sea;
> often they raise their hands in prayer to the gods,
> as their bowels heave in pain.[1]

Anyone can see that this is more polished than awe-inspiring. Now com- 5
pare it with Homer (I select one example out of many):

> He fell upon them as upon a swift ship falls a wave,
> huge, wind-reared by the clouds. The ship
> is curtained in foam, a hideous blast of wind
> roars in the sail. The sailors shudder in terror:
> they are carried away from under death, but only just.[2]

Aratus[3] tried to transfer the same thought: 6

> A little plank wards off Hades.

But this is smooth and unimpressive, not frightening. Moreover, by
saying 'a plank wards off Hades', he has got rid of the danger. The plank
does keep death away. Homer, on the other hand, does not banish the
cause of fear at a stroke; he gives a vivid picture of men, one might almost
say, facing death many times with every wave that comes. Notice also
the forced combination of naturally uncompoundable prepositions: *hupek*,
'from under'. Homer has tortured the words to correspond with the
emotion of the moment, and expressed the emotion magnificently by
thus crushing words together. He has in effect stamped the special
character of the danger on the diction: 'they are carried away from under
death'.

Compare Archilochus on the shipwreck, and Demosthenes on the 7
arrival of the news ('It was evening . . .').[4]

---

[1] From a lost poem attributed to Aristeas of Proconnesus, a prophet of Apollo said to
have travelled in Siberia in the seventh century B.C. The lines perhaps express the surprised comment of innocent continentals, deep in Asia, on the tales they have heard
about ships and seagoing.

[2] Ibid. 15. 624 ff.   [3] *Phaenomena* 299.

[4] The example from Archilochus cannot be certainly identified. That from Demosthenes (*On the Crown* 169) describes the alarm at Athens when news arrived of Philip's
occupation of Elatea (339 B.C.): 'It was evening when somebody brought the *prutaneis*
the news that Elatea was captured. Some of them got up in the middle of dinner and
began to drive the traders from the stalls in the *agora* and burn the wicker hurdles.
Others sent for the generals and gave instructions to the trumpeter. The town was full
of uproar.'

In short, one might say that these writers have taken only the very best pieces, polished them up and fitted them together. They have inserted nothing inflated, undignified, or pedantic. Such things ruin the whole effect, because they produce, as it were, gaps or crevices, and so spoil the impressive thoughts which have been built into a structure whose cohesion depends upon their mutual relations.[1]

AMPLIFICATION

11. 1 The quality called 'amplification' is connected with those we have been considering. It is found when the facts or the issues at stake allow many starts and pauses in each section. You wheel up one impressive unit after 2 another to give a series of increasing importance. There are innumerable varieties of amplification:[2] it may be produced by commonplaces, by exaggeration or intensification of facts or arguments, or by a build-up of action or emotion. The orator should realize, however, that none of these will have its full effect without sublimity. Passages expressing pity or disparagement are no doubt an exception; but in any other instance of amplification, if you take away the sublime element, you take the soul away from the body. Without the strengthening influence of the sublimity, the effective element in the whole loses all its vigour and solidity.

3 What is the difference between this precept and the point made above about the inclusion of vital details and their combination in a unity? What in general is the difference between amplification and sublimity? I must define my position briefly on these points, in order to make myself clear.

12. 1 I do not feel satisfied with the definition given by the rhetoricians: 'amplification is expression which adds grandeur to its subject'. This might just as well be a definition of sublimity or emotion or tropes. All these add grandeur of some kind. The difference lies, in my opinion, in the fact that sublimity depends on elevation, whereas amplification involves extension; sublimity exists often in a single thought, amplification cannot exist 2 without a certain quantity and superfluity. To give a general definition, amplification is an aggregation of all the details and topics which constitute a situation, strengthening the argument by dwelling on it; it differs from proof in that the latter demonstrates the point made . . .

[Lacuna equivalent to about two pages.]

---

[1] Text uncertain in detail; general sense clear.
[2] See Quint. 8. 4.

SAME GENERAL SUBJECT CONTINUED: A COMPARISON
BETWEEN PLATO AND DEMOSTHENES, WITH
A WORD ON CICERO

... spreads out richly in many directions into an open sea of grandeur. 3
Accordingly, Demosthenes, the more emotional of the two, displays in
abundance the fire and heat of passion, while Plato, consistently magnificent, solemn, and grand, is much less intense—without of course becoming
in the least frigid. These seem to me, my dear Terentianus—if a Greek 4
is allowed an opinion—to be also the differences between the grandeur of
Cicero and the grandeur of Demosthenes. Demosthenes has an abrupt
sublimity; Cicero spreads himself. Demosthenes burns and ravages; he has
violence, rapidity, strength, and force, and shows them in everything; he
can be compared to a thunderbolt or a flash of lightning. Cicero, on the
other hand, is like a spreading conflagration. He ranges everywhere and
rolls majestically on. His huge fires endure; they are renewed in various
forms from time to time and repeatedly fed with fresh fuel.—But this is 5
a comparison which your countrymen can make better than I.

Anyway, the place for the intense, Demosthenic kind of sublimity is in
indignant exaggeration, in violent emotion, and in general wherever the
hearer has to be struck with amazement. The place for expansiveness is
where he has to be deluged with words. This treatment is appropriate in
loci communes, epilogues, digressions, all descriptive and exhibition pieces,
historical or scientific topics, and many other departments.

To return to Plato, and the way in which he combines the 'soundless 13. 1
flow'[1] of his smooth style with grandeur. A passage of the *Republic*[2] you
have read makes the manner quite clear: 'Men without experience of
wisdom and virtue but always occupied with feasting and that kind
of thing naturally go downhill and wander through life on a low plane of
existence. They never look upwards to the truth and never rise, they never
taste certain or pure pleasure. Like cattle, they always look down, bowed
earthwards and tablewards; they feed and they breed, and their greediness
in these directions makes them kick and butt till they kill one another with
iron horns and hooves, because they can never be satisfied.'

IMITATION OF EARLIER WRITERS AS A MEANS TO SUBLIMITY

Plato, if we will read him with attention, illustrates yet another road to 2
sublimity, besides those we have discussed. This is the way of imitation
and emulation of great writers of the past. Here too, my friend, is an aim

---

[1] Plato, *Theaetetus* 144 b.   [2] *Republic* 9. 586 a (adapted).

to which we must hold fast. Many are possessed by a spirit not their own. It is like what we are told of the Pythia at Delphi: she is in contact with the tripod near the cleft in the ground which (so they say) exhales a divine vapour, and she is thereupon made pregnant by the supernatural power and forthwith prophesies as one inspired. Similarly, the genius of the ancients acts as a kind of oracular cavern, and effluences flow from it into the minds of their imitators. Even those previously not much inclined to prophesy become inspired and share the enthusiasm which comes from the great-

3 ness of others. Was Herodotus the only 'most Homeric' writer? Surely Stesichorus and Archilochus earned the name before him. So, more than any, did Plato, who diverted to himself countless rills from the Homeric spring. (If Ammonius had not selected and written up detailed examples of this, I might have had to prove the point myself.) In all this process

4 there is no plagiarism. It resembles rather the reproduction of good character in statues and works of art.[1] Plato could not have put such a brilliant finish on his philosophical doctrines or so often risen to poetical subjects and poetical language, if he had not tried, and tried whole-heartedly, to compete for the prize against Homer, like a young aspirant challenging an admired master. To break a lance in this way may well have been a brash and contentious thing to do, but the competition proved anything but valueless. As Hesiod says, 'this strife is good for men.'[2] Truly it is a noble contest and prize of honour, and one well worth winning, in which to be defeated by one's elders is itself no disgrace.

14. 1 We can apply this to ourselves. When we are working on something which needs loftiness of expression and greatness of thought, it is good to imagine how Homer would have said the same thing, or how Plato or Demosthenes or (in history) Thucydides would have invested it with sublimity. These great figures, presented to us as objects of emulation and, as it were, shining before our gaze, will somehow elevate our minds

2 to the greatness of which we form a mental image. They will be even more effective if we ask ourselves 'How would Homer or Demosthenes have reacted to what I am saying, if he had been here? What would his feelings have been?' It makes it a great occasion if you imagine such a jury or audience for your own speech, and pretend that you are answering for what you write before judges and witnesses of such heroic stature.

3 Even more stimulating is the further thought: 'How will posterity take what I am writing?' If a man is afraid of saying anything which will out-last his own life and age, the conceptions of his mind are bound to be incomplete and abortive; they will miscarry and never be brought to birth whole and perfect for the day of posthumous fame.

---

[1] Text uncertain: perhaps 'the reproduction of beauty of form . . .'
[2] *Works and Days* 24: healthy rivalry contrasted with the strife that produces war.

VISUALIZATION (*PHANTASIA*)

Another thing which is extremely productive of grandeur, magnificence **15. 1**
and urgency, my young friend, is visualization (*phantasia*). I use this word
for what some people call image-production. The term *phantasia* is used
generally for anything which in any way suggests a thought productive of
speech;[1] but the word has also come into fashion for the situation in
which enthusiasm and emotion make the speaker *see* what he is saying
and bring it *visually* before his audience. It will not escape you that **2**
rhetorical visualization has a different intention from that of the poets:
in poetry the aim is astonishment, in oratory it is clarity. Both, however,
seek emotion and excitement.

> Mother, I beg you, do not drive them at me,
> the women with the blood in their eyes and the snakes—
> they are here, they are here, jumping right up to me.[2]

Or again:

> O! O! She'll kill me. Where shall I escape?[3]

The poet himself saw the Erinyes, and has as good as made his audience
see what he imagined.

Now Euripides devotes most pains to producing a tragic effect with **3**
two emotions, madness and love. In these he is supremely successful. At
the same time, he does not lack the courage to attempt other types of
visualization. Though not formed by nature for grandeur, he often forces
himself to be tragic. When the moment for greatness comes, he (in
Homer's words)

> whips flank and buttocks with his tail
> and drives himself to fight.[4]

For example, here is Helios handing the reins to Phaethon:[5]   **4**

> 'Drive on, but do not enter Libyan air—
> it has no moisture in it, and will let
> your wheel fall through—'

[1] A Stoic definition.
[2] Euripides, *Orestes* 255-7. Orestes sees the Furies.
[3] Euripides, *Iphigenia in Tauris* 291. Again Orestes and the Furies.
[4] *Iliad* 20. 170.
[5] Fr. 779 Nauck. Euripides' lost *Phaethon* told the story of Phaethon's marriage and
how his mother Clymene revealed to him that Helios was his father; he then begs to be
allowed to drive the sun's chariot, and disaster follows. The passages quoted are probably
from a messenger's speech recounting Phaethon's fall.

and again:

> 'Steer towards the seven Pleiads.'
> The boy listened so far, then seized the reins,
> whipped up the winged team, and let them go.
> To heaven's expanse they flew.
> His father rode behind on Sirius,
> giving the boy advice: 'That's your way, there:
> turn here—turn here.'

May one not say that the writer's soul has mounted the chariot, has taken wing with the horses and shares the danger? Had it not been up among those heavenly bodies and moved in their courses, he could never have visualized such things.

Compare, too, his Cassandra:

> Ye Trojans, lovers of horses . . .[1]

5   Aeschylus, of course, ventures on the most heroic visualizations; he is like his own Seven against Thebes—

> Seven men of war, commanders of companies,
> killing a bull into a black-bound shield,
> dipping their hands in the bull's blood,
> took oath by Ares, by Enyo, by bloodthirsty Terror—

in a joint pledge of death in which they showed themselves no mercy. At the same time, he does sometimes leave his thoughts unworked, tangled and hard. The ambitious Euripides does not shirk even these risks. For example, there is in Aeschylus a remarkable description of the
6 palace of Lycurgus in its divine seizure at the moment of Dionysus' epiphany:

> the palace was possessed, the house went bacchanal.

Euripides expresses the same thought less harshly:

> the whole mountain went bacchanal with them.[2]

7   There is another magnificent visualization in Sophocles' account of

---

[1] Fr. 935 Nauck, perhaps from the *Alexandros*. As the context is lost, we do not know the point. Compare p. 473, n. 4 for a similar abridged quotation, where 'Longinus' assumes his readers to know the context.

[2] Aeschylus, fr. 58 Nauck; Euripides, *Bacchae* 726. Euripides makes the idea easier by adding the notion that the mountain *shared* the ecstasy of the bacchanals themselves.

Oedipus dying and giving himself burial to the accompaniment of a sign from heaven,[1] and in the appearance of Achilles over his tomb at the departure of the Greek fleet.[2] Simonides has perhaps described this scene more vividly than anyone else; but it is impossible to quote everything.

The poetical examples, as I said, have a quality of exaggeration which 8 belongs to fable and goes far beyond credibility. In an orator's visualizations, on the other hand, it is the element of fact and truth which makes for success; when the content of the passage is poetical and fabulous and does not shrink from any impossibility, the result is a shocking and outrageous abnormality. This is what happens with the shock orators of our own day; like tragic actors, these fine fellows *see* the Erinyes, and are incapable of understanding that when Orestes says

> Let me go; you are one of my Erinyes,
> you are hugging me tight, to throw me into Hell,[3]

he visualizes all this *because he is mad*.

What then is the effect of rhetorical visualization? There is much it can 9 do to bring urgency and passion into our words; but it is when it is closely involved with factual arguments that it enslaves the hearer as well as persuading him. 'Suppose you heard a shout this very moment outside the court, and someone said that the prison had been broken open and the prisoners had escaped—no one, young or old, would be so casual as not to give what help he could. And if someone then came forward and said "This is the man who let them out", our friend would never get a hearing; it would be the end of him.'[4] There is a similar instance in Hyperides' 10 defence of himself when he was on trial for the proposal to liberate the slaves which he put forward after the defeat.[5] 'It was not the proposer', he said, 'who drew up this decree: it was the battle of Chaeronea.' Here the orator uses a visualization actually in the moment of making his factual argument, with the result that his thought has taken him beyond the limits of mere persuasiveness. Now our natural instinct is, in all such cases, 11 to attend to the stronger influence, so that we are diverted from the demonstration to the astonishment caused by the visualization, which by its very brilliance conceals the factual aspect. This is a natural reaction: when two things are joined together, the stronger attracts to itself the force of the weaker.

[1] Closing scene of *Oedipus Coloneus*.
[2] Probably in the lost *Polyxena*. It is possible that something is lost between this sentence and the reference to Simonides.
[3] Euripides, *Orestes* 264-5.
[4] Demosthenes 24. 208.
[5] i.e. after Philip's victory at Chaeronea (338 B.C.). The speech is not extant.

12   This will suffice for an account of sublimity of thought produced by
greatness of mind, imitation, or visualization.[1]

(iii) FIGURES[2]: AN EXAMPLE TO ILLUSTRATE THE RIGHT USE OF FIGURES: THE 'OATH' IN 'ON THE CROWN'

16. 1   The next topic is that of figures. Properly handled, figures constitute, as
I said, no small part of sublimity. It would be a vast, or rather infinite,
labour to enumerate them all; what I shall do is to expound a few of those
which generate sublimity, simply in order to confirm my point.

2   Here is Demosthenes putting forward a demonstrative argument on
behalf of his policy.[3] What would have been the natural way to put it?
'You have not done wrong, you who fought for the liberty of Greece;
you have examples to prove this close at home: the men of Marathon, of
Salamis, of Plataea did not do wrong.' But instead of this he was suddenly
inspired to give voice to the oath by the heroes of Greece: 'By those who
risked their lives at Marathon, you have not done wrong!' Observe what
he effects by this single figure of conjuration, or 'apostrophe' as I call it
here. He deifies his audience's ancestors, suggesting that it is right to take
an oath by men who fell so bravely, as though they were gods. He inspires
the judges with the temper of those who risked their lives. He transforms
his demonstration into an extraordinary piece of sublimity and passion,
and into the convincingness of this unusual and amazing oath. At the
same time he injects into his hearers' minds a healing specific, so as to
lighten their hearts by these paeans of praise and make them as proud of
the battle with Philip as of the triumphs of Marathon and Salamis. In
short, the figure enables him to run away with his audience.

3   Now the origin of this oath is said to be in the lines of Eupolis:

By Marathon, by *my* battle,
no one shall grieve me and escape rejoicing.[4]

But the greatness depends not on the mere form of the oath, but on place,
manner, occasion, and purpose. In Eupolis, there is nothing but the oath;
he is speaking to the Athenians while their fortunes are still high and they
need no comfort; and instead of immortalizing the men in order to
engender in the audience a proper estimation of their valour, he wanders
away from the actual people who risked their lives to an inanimate object,
namely the battle. In Demosthenes, on the other hand, the oath is

---

[1] Note that this is not a complete summary of chaps. 9–15.
[2] The second 'source', emotion, does not appear in its expected place: see p. 460.
[3] The passage discussed is in 18. 208. Cf. below, p. 575.
[4] From the lost comedy *Demoi*. Eupolis parodies Euripides, *Medea* 395 ff.

addressed to a defeated nation, to make them no longer think of Chaeronea as a disaster. It embraces, as I said, a demonstration that they 'did no wrong', an illustrative example, a confirmation, an encomium, and an exhortation. Moreover, because he was faced with the possible objection 4 'your policies brought us to defeat—and yet you swear by victories!' he brings his thought back under control and makes it safe and unanswerable, showing that sobriety is needed even under the influence of inspiration: 'By those who *risked their lives* at Marathon, and *fought in the ships* at Salamis and Artemisium, and *formed the line* at Plataea!' He never says *conquered*; throughout he withholds the word for the final issue, because it was a happy issue, and the opposite to that of Chaeronea. From the same motives he forestalls his audience by adding immediately: 'all of whom were buried at the city's expense, Aeschines—all, not only the successful.'

THE RELATION BETWEEN FIGURES AND SUBLIMITY

At this point, my friend, I feel I ought not to pass over an observation of 17. 1 my own. It shall be very brief: figures are natural allies of sublimity and themselves profit wonderfully from the alliance. I will explain how this happens.

Playing tricks by means of figures is a peculiarly suspect procedure. It raises the suspicion of a trap, a deep design, a fallacy. It is to be avoided in addressing a judge who has power to decide, and especially in addressing tyrants, kings, governors, or anybody in a high place. Such a person immediately becomes angry if he is led astray like a foolish child by some skilful orator's figures. He takes the fallacy as indicating contempt for himself. He becomes like a wild animal. Even if he controls his temper, he is now completely conditioned against being convinced by what is said. A figure is therefore generally thought to be best when the fact that it is a figure is concealed.

Thus sublimity and emotion are a defence and a marvellous aid against 2 the suspicion which the use of figures engenders. The artifice of the trick is lost to sight in the surrounding brilliance of beauty and grandeur, and it escapes all suspicion. 'By the men of Marathon . . .' is proof enough. For how did Demosthenes conceal the figure in that passage? By sheer brilliance, of course. As fainter lights disappear when the sunshine surrounds them, so the sophisms of rhetoric are dimmed when they are enveloped in encircling grandeur. Something like this happens in painting: when light and shadow are juxtaposed in colours on the same plane, the light seems more prominent to the eye, and both stands out and actually appears much nearer. Similarly, in literature, emotional and sublime features seem closer to the mind's eye, both because of a certain natural kinship[1] and because of their brilliance. Consequently, they always show up above the figures, and overshadow and eclipse their artifice.

RHETORICAL QUESTIONS

18. 1   What are we to say of inquiries and questions? Should we not say that they increase the realism and vigour of the writing by the actual form of the figure?[2]

'Or—tell me—do you want to go round asking one another "Is there any news?"? What could be hotter news than that a Macedonian is conquering Greece? "Is Philip dead?" "No, but he's ill." What difference does it make to you? If anything happens to him, you will soon create another Philip.'[3]

Again: 'Let us sail to Macedonia. "Where shall we anchor?" says someone. The war itself will find out Philip's weak spots.'[4] Put in the straightforward form, this would have been quite insignificant; as it is, the impassioned rapidity of question and answer and the device of self-objection have made the remark, in virtue of its figurative form, not only 2 more sublime but more credible. For emotion carries us away more easily when it seems to be generated by the occasion rather than deliberately assumed by the speaker, and the self-directed question and its answer represent precisely this momentary quality of emotion. Just as people who are unexpectedly plied with questions become annoyed and reply to the point with vigour and exact truth, so the figure of question and answer arrests the hearer and cheats him into believing that all the points made were raised and are being put into words on the spur of the moment.

Again—this sentence in Herodotus is believed to be a particularly fine example of sublimity[5] . . .

[Lacuna equivalent to about two pages.]

ASYNDETON

19. 1   . . . the words tumble out without connection, in a kind of stream, almost getting ahead of the speaker: 'Engaging their shields, they pushed, fought, slew, died' (Xenophon).[6]

---

[1] See below, chap. 35.
[2] Notice that these remarks are themselves cast as rhetorical questions.
[3] Demosthenes 4. 10.   [4] Ibid. 44.
[5] *Perhaps* Herodotus 7. 21.   [6] *Hellenica* 4. 3. 19.

'We went as you told us, noble Odysseus, up the woods,   2
we saw a beautiful palace built in the glades',

says Homer's Eurylochus.[1]

Disconnected and yet hurried phrases convey the impression of an agitation which both obstructs the reader and drives him on. Such is the effect of Homer's asyndeta.

ASYNDETON COMBINED WITH ANAPHORA

The conjunction of several figures in one phrase also has a very stirring 20. 1 effect. Two or three may be joined together in a kind of team, jointly contributing strength, persuasiveness, charm. An example is the passage in *Against Midias*,[2] where asyndeton is combined with anaphora and vivid description. 'The aggressor would do many things—some of which his victim would not even be able to tell anyone else—with gesture, with look, with voice.' Then, to save the sentence from monotony and a 2 stationary effect—for this goes with inertia, whereas disorder goes with emotion, which is a disturbance and movement of the mind—he leaps immediately to fresh instances of asyndeton and epanaphora: 'With gesture, with look, with voice, when he insults, when he acts as an enemy, when he slaps the fellow, when he slaps him on the ears . . .' The orator is doing here exactly what the bully does—hitting the jury in the mind with blow after blow. Then he comes down with a fresh onslaught, like a 3 sudden squall: '. . . when he slaps the fellow, when he slaps him on the ears. That rouses a man, that makes him lose control, when he is not used to being insulted. No one could bring out the horror of such a moment by a mere report.' Here Demosthenes keeps up the natural effect of epanaphora and asyndeton by frequent variation. His order becomes disorderly, his disorder in turn acquires a certain order.

POLYSYNDETON

Now add the conjunctions, as Isocrates' school does. 'Again, one must 21. 1 not omit this point, that the aggressor would do many things, first with gesture, then with look, and finally with voice.' As you proceed with these insertions, it will become clear that the urgent and harsh character of the emotion loses its sting and becomes a spent fire as soon as you level it down to smoothness by the conjunctions. If you tie a runner's arms to his 2 side, you take away his speed; likewise, emotion frets at being impeded by

---

[1] *Odyssey* 10. 251–2.   [2] Demosthenes 21. 72.

conjunctions and other additions, because it loses the free abandon of its
movement and the sense of being, as it were, catapulted out.

HYPERBATON

22. 1 Hyperbaton belongs to the same general class. It is an arrangement of
words or thoughts which differs from the normal sequence . . .[1] It is a very
real mark of urgent emotion. People who in real life feel anger, fear, or
indignation, or are distracted by jealousy or some other emotion (it is
impossible to say how many emotions there are; they are without number),
often put one thing forward and then rush off to another, irrationally
inserting some remark, and then hark back again to their first point. They
seem to be blown this way and that by their excitement, as if by a veering
wind. They inflict innumerable variations on the expression, the thought,
and the natural sequence. Thus hyperbaton is a means by which, in the
best authors, imitation approaches the effect of nature. Art is perfect
when it looks like nature, nature is felicitous when it embraces concealed
art. Consider the words of Dionysius of Phocaea in Herodotus:[2] 'Now,
for our affairs are on the razor's edge, men of Ionia, whether we are to be
free or slaves—and worse than slaves, runaways—so if you will bear
hardships now, you will suffer temporarily but be able to overcome your
2 enemies.' The natural order of thought would have been: 'Men of Ionia,
now is the time for you to bear hardships, for our affairs are on the razor's
edge.' The speaker has displaced 'men of Ionia'; he begins with the cause
of fear, as though the alarm was so pressing that he did not even have
time to address the audience by name. He has also diverted the order of
thought. Before saying that they must suffer hardship themselves (that is
the gist of his exhortation), he first gives the reason why it is necessary,
by saying 'our affairs are on the razor's edge'. The result is that he seems
to be giving not a premeditated speech but one forced on him by the
circumstances.

3 It is even more characteristic of Thucydides to show ingenuity in
separating by transpositions even things which are by nature completely
unified and indivisible.

Demosthenes is less wilful in this than Thucydides, but no one uses
this kind of effect more lavishly. His transpositions produce not only
a great sense of urgency but the appearance of extemporization, as he
4 drags his hearers with him into the hazards of his long hyperbata. He
often holds in suspense the meaning which he set out to convey and,
introducing one extraneous item after another in an alien and unusual

---

[1] Probably a few words are missing here.   [2] 6. 11.

place before getting to the main point, throws the hearer into a panic lest the sentence collapse altogether, and forces him in his excitement to share the speaker's peril, before, at long last and beyond all expectation, appositely paying off at the end the long due conclusion; the very audacity and hazardousness of the hyperbata add to the astounding effect. There are so many examples that I forbear to give any.

CHANGES OF CASE, TENSE, PERSON, NUMBER, GENDER; PLURAL FOR SINGULAR AND SINGULAR FOR PLURAL

What is called polyptoton, like accumulation, variation, and climax, is, as you know, extremely effective and contributes both to ornament and to sublimity and emotion of every kind.[1]   23. 1

How do variations in case, tense, person, number, and gender diversify and stimulate the style? My answer to this is that, as regards variations of number, the lesser effect (though a real one) is produced by instances in which singular forms are seen on reflection to be plural in sense: 2

> The innumerable host
> were scattered over the sandy beach, and shouted.

More worthy of note are the examples in which plurals give a more grandiose effect, and court success by the sense of multitude expressed by the grammatical number. An example comes in Sophocles, where Oedipus says: 3

> Weddings, weddings
> you bred me and again released my seed,
> made fathers, brothers, children, blood of the kin,
> brides, wives, mothers—all
> the deeds most horrid ever seen in men.[2]

All this is about Oedipus on the one hand and Jocasta on the other, but the expansion of the number to the plural forms pluralizes the misfortunes also.

Another example is:

> Hectors and Sarpedons came forth.[3]

Another is the Platonic passage about the Athenians, which I have   4

---

[1] 'Polyptoton' is the occurrence of the same word in various inflexions. It is not certain whether 'Longinus' thinks of accumulation (*athroismos*), variation (*metabolē*), and climax as species of it or as distinct. For what the ancient rhetoricians called 'climax', compare Romans 5: 3, 8: 29–30.

[2] *Oedipus Tyrannus* 1403 ff.   [3] A line of an unknown tragedy.

quoted elsewhere:[1] 'No Pelopses or Cadmuses or Aegyptuses or Danauses or other barbarians by birth have settled among us; we are pure Greeks, with no barbarian blood', and so on. Such an agglomeration of names in crowds naturally makes the facts sound more impressive. But the practice is only to be followed when the subject admits amplification, abundance, hyperbole, or emotion—one or more of these. Only a sophist has bells on his harness wherever he goes.

24. 1 The contrary device—the contraction of plurals into singulars—also sometimes produces a sublime effect. 'The whole Peloponnese was divided.'[2] 'When Phrynichus produced *The Capture of Miletus* the theatre burst into tears' ('theatre' for 'spectators').[3] To compress the separate individuals into the corresponding unity produces a more solid effect.

2 The cause of the effect is the same in both cases. Where the nouns are singular, it is a mark of unexpected emotion to pluralize them.[4] Where they are plural, to unite the plurality under one well-sounding word is again surprising because of the opposite transformation of the facts.

VIVID PRESENT TENSE

25. 1 To represent past events as present is to turn a narrative into a thing of immediate urgency. 'A man who has fallen under Cyrus' horse and is being trampled strikes the horse in the belly with his sword. The horse, convulsed, shakes Cyrus off. He falls' (Xenophon).[5] This is common in Thucydides.

IMAGINARY SECOND PERSON

26. 1 Urgency may also be conveyed by the replacement of one grammatical person by another. It often gives the hearer the sense of being in the midst of the danger himself.

'You would say they were tireless, never wearied in war,
so eagerly they fought' (Homer).[6]

'May you never be drenched in the sea in that month!' (Aratus).[7]

---

[1] *Menexenus* 245 d. Not quoted in any other extant part of this book.
[2] Demosthenes 18. 18.   [3] Herodotus 6. 21.
[4] Or 'it is a mark of emotion to pluralize them unexpectedly'.
[5] *Cyropaedia* 7. 1. 37.   [6] *Iliad* 15. 697.
[7] *Phaenomena* 287.

'You will sail upstream from Elephantine, and then you will come to 2 a smooth plain. After crossing this, you will embark on another boat and sail for two days. Then you will come to a great city called Meroe' (Herodotus).[1]

Do you see, my friend, how he grips your mind and takes it on tour through all these places, making hearing as good as seeing? All such forms of expression, being directed to an actual person, bring the hearer into the presence of real events.

Moreover, if you speak as though to an individual and not to a large 3 company, you will affect him more and make him more attentive and excited, because the personal address stimulates:

> You could not tell with whom Tydides stood.[2]

LAPSES INTO DIRECT SPEECH

Sometimes a writer, in the course of a narrative in the third person, makes 27. 1 a sudden change and speaks in the person of his character. This kind of thing is an outburst of emotion.

> Hector shouted aloud to the Trojans
> to rush for the ships, and leave the spoils of the dead.
> 'If I see anyone away from the ships of his own accord,
> I will have him killed on the spot.'[3]

Here the poet has given the narrative to himself, as appropriate to him, and then suddenly and without warning has put the abrupt threat in the mouth of the angry prince. It would have been flat if he had added 'Hector said'. As it is, the change of construction is so sudden that it has outstripped its creator.

Hence the use of this figure is appropriate when the urgency of the 2 moment gives the writer no chance to delay, but forces on him an immediate change from one person to another. 'Ceyx was distressed at this, and ordered the children to depart. "For I am unable to help you. Go therefore to some other country, so as to save yourselves without harming me"' (Hecataeus).[4]

Somewhat different is the method by which Demosthenes in *Against* 3 *Aristogiton*[5] makes variation of person produce the effect of strong emotion and rapid change of tone: 'Will none of you be found to feel bile or anger at the violence of this shameless monster, who—you vile wretch, your right

---

[1] 2. 29.   [2] *Iliad* 5. 85.   [3] *Iliad* 15. 346.
[4] Fr. 30 Jacoby.   [5] 25. 27 (a spurious speech).

of free speech is barred not by gates and doors which can be opened, but . . .!' He makes the change before the sense is complete, and in effect divides a single thought between two persons in his passion ('who—you vile wretch . . .!'), as well as turning to Aristogiton and giving the impression of abandoning the course of his argument—with the sole result, so strong is the emotion, of giving it added intensity.

4 So also Penelope:

> Herald, why have the proud suitors sent you here?
> Is it to tell Odysseus' maidservants
> to stop their work and get dinner for them?
> After their wooing, may they never meet again!
> May this be their last dinner here—
> you who gather together so often and waste wealth,
> who never listened to your fathers when you were children
> and they told you what kind of man Odysseus was![1]

PERIPHRASIS

28. 1 No one, I fancy, would question the fact that periphrasis is a means to sublimity. As in music the melody is made sweeter by what is called the accompaniment, so periphrasis is often heard in concert with the plain words and enhances them with a new resonance. This is especially true if it contains nothing bombastic or tasteless but only what is pleasantly

2 blended. There is a sufficient example in Plato, at the beginning of the Funeral Speech:[2] 'These men have received their due, and having received it they go on their fated journey, escorted publicly by their country and privately each by his own kindred.' Plato here calls death a 'fated journey' and the bestowal of regular funeral rites a public escort by the country. This surely adds no inconsiderable impressiveness to the thought. He has lyricized the bare prose, enveloping it in the harmony of the beautiful periphrasis.

3 'You believe labour to be the guide to a pleasant life; you have gathered into your souls the noblest and most heroic of possessions: you enjoy being praised more than anything else in the world' (Xenophon).[3] In this passage 'you make labour the guide to a pleasant life' is put for 'you are willing to labour'. This and the other expansions invest the praise with a certain grandeur of conception.

4 Another example is the inimitable sentence of Herodotus: 'The goddess inflicted a feminine disease on the Scythians who plundered the temple.'[4]

---

[1] *Odyssey* 4. 681 ff.   [2] *Menexenus* 236 d.
[3] *Cyropaedia* 1. 5. 12.   [4] Herodotus 1. 105.

Periphrasis, however, is a particularly dangerous device if it is not used 29. 1
with moderation. It soon comes to be heavy and dull, smelling of empty
phrases and coarseness of fibre. This is why Plato—who is fond of the
figure and sometimes uses it unseasonably—is ridiculed for the sentence
in the *Laws*[1] which runs: 'Neither silvern wealth nor golden should be
permitted to establish itself in the city.' If he had wanted to prohibit
cattle, says the critic, he would have talked of 'ovine and bovine' wealth.

CONCLUSION OF THE SECTION ON FIGURES

So much, my dear Terentianus, by way of digression on the theory of the 2
use of those figures which conduce to sublimity. They all make style more
emotional and excited, <u>and emotion is as essential a part of sublimity as
characterization is of charm</u>.[2]

(iv) DICTION: GENERAL REMARKS

Thought and expression are of course very much involved with each other. 30. 1
We have therefore next to consider whether any topics still remain in the
field of diction. The choice of correct and magnificent words is a source of
immense power to entice and charm the hearer. This is something which
all orators and other writers cultivate intensely. It makes grandeur,
beauty, old-world charm, weight, force, strength, and a kind of lustre
bloom upon our words as upon beautiful statues; it gives things life and
makes them speak. But I suspect there is no need for me to make this
point; you know it well. It is indeed true that beautiful words are the 2
light that illuminates thought.

Magniloquence, however, is not always serviceable: to dress up trivial
material in grand and solemn language is like putting a huge tragic mask
on a little child. In poetry and history, however . . .

[Lacuna equivalent to about four pages.]

---

[1] 801 b.

[2] *'Pathos'* (emotion) characterizes truly 'sublime' writing; *'ēthos'* (realistic depiction
of manners or humours) belongs rather to lower, more human, and even comic, genres:
cf. the *Iliad–Odyssey* contrast, 9. 13–15. *'Hēdonē'* (pleasure, charm) is the typical aim
and effect of this second kind of literature. In terms of the 'three styles' (cf. above,
pp. 413 ff., etc.), it consorts with the 'smooth' style as pathos and sublimity do with the
lofty style.

USE OF EVERYDAY WORDS

31. 1 . . . and productive, as is Anacreon's 'I no longer turn my mind to the Thracian filly'.[1] Similarly, Theopompus' much-admired phrase seems to me to be particularly expressive because of the aptness of the analogy, though Caecilius manages to find fault with it: 'Philip was excellent at stomaching facts.' An idiomatic phrase is sometimes much more vivid than an ornament of speech, for it is immediately recognized from everyday experience, and the familiar is inevitably easier to credit. 'To stomach facts' is thus used vividly of a man who endures unpleasantness and **2** squalor patiently, and indeed with pleasure, for the sake of gain. There are similar things in Herodotus: 'Cleomenes in his madness cut his own flesh into little pieces with a knife till he had sliced himself to death', 'Pythes continued fighting on the ship until he was cut into joints.'[2] These phrases come within an inch of being vulgar, but they are so expressive that they avoid vulgarity.

METAPHORS

32. 1 As regards number of metaphors, Caecilius seems to agree with the propounders of the rule that not more than two or at most three may be used of the same subject. Here too Demosthenes is our canon. The right occasions are when emotions come flooding in and bring the multiplication **2** of metaphors with them as a necessary accompaniment. 'Vile flatterers, mutilators of their countries, who have given away liberty as a drinking present, first to Philip and now to Alexander, measuring happiness by the belly and the basest impulses, overthrowing liberty and freedom from despotism, which Greeks of old regarded as the canons and standards of the good.'[3] In this passage the orator's anger against traitors obscures the multiplicity of his metaphors.

3 This is why Aristotle and Theophrastus say that there are ways of softening bold metaphors—namely by saying 'as if', 'as it were', 'if I may put it so', or 'if we may venture on a bold expression'. Apology, they say, **4** is a remedy for audacity. I accept this doctrine, but I would add—and I said the same about figures—that strong and appropriate emotions and genuine sublimity are a specific palliative for multiplied or daring metaphors, because their nature is to sweep and drive all these other things along with the surging tide of their movement. Indeed it might be truer to

---

[1] Fr. 96 Bergk. 'Filly' is a probable, but not certain, supplement. The text here is uncertain. Perhaps: '. . . But not Anacreon's "I turn my mind . . .".'
[2] 6. 75, 7. 181.
[3] Demosthenes 18. 296.

say that they *demand* the hazardous. They never allow the hearer leisure to count the metaphors, because he too shares the speaker's enthusiasm.

At the same time, nothing gives distinction to commonplaces and descriptions so well as a continuous series of tropes. This is the medium *elevation* in which the description of man's bodily tabernacle is worked out so elaborately in Xenophon and yet more superlatively by Plato.[1] Thus Plato calls the head the 'citadel' of the body; the neck is an 'isthmus' constructed between the head and the chest; the vertebrae, he says, are fixed underneath 'like pivots'. Pleasure is a 'lure of evil' for mankind; the tongue is a 'taste-meter'. The heart is a 'knot of veins' and 'fountain of the blood that moves impetuously round', allocated to the 'guard-room'. The word he uses for the various passages of the canals is 'alleys'. 'Against the throbbing of the heart,' he continues, 'in the expectation of danger and in the excitation of anger, when it gets hot, they contrived a means of succour, implanting in us the lungs, soft, bloodless, and with cavities, a sort of cushion, so that when anger boils up in the heart, the latter's throbbing is against a yielding obstacle, so that it comes to no harm.' Again: he calls the seat of the desires 'the women's quarters', and the seat of anger 'the men's quarters'. The spleen is for him 'a napkin for the inner parts, which therefore grows big and festering through being filled with secretions'. 'And thereafter', he says again, 'they buried the whole under a canopy of flesh', putting the flesh on 'as a protection against dangers from without, like felting.' Blood he called 'fodder of the flesh'. For the purpose of nutrition, he says also, 'they irrigated the body, cutting channels as in gardens, so that the streams of the veins might flow as it were from an incoming stream, making the body an aqueduct'. Finally: when the end is at hand, the soul's 'ship's cables' are 'loosed', and she herself 'set free'.

The passage contains countless similar examples; but these are enough to make my point, namely that tropes are naturally grand, that metaphors conduce to sublimity, and that passages involving emotion and description are the most suitable field for them. At the same time, it is plain without my saying it that the use of tropes, like all other good things in literature, always tempts one to go too far. This is what people ridicule most in Plato, who is often carried away by a sort of literary madness into crude, harsh metaphors or allegorical fustian. 'It is not easy to understand that a city ought to be mixed like a bowl of wine, wherein the wine seethes with madness, but when chastened by another, sober god, and achieving a proper communion with him, produces a good and moderate drink.'[2]

---

[1] Xenophon, *Memorabilia* I. 4. 5 ff.; Plato, *Timaeus* 65 c–85 e ('Longinus' picks various details out of this long passage, and runs them together).

[2] *Laws* 773 c–d.

To call water 'a sober god', says the critic, and mixture 'chastening', is the language of a poet who is far from sober himself.

DIGRESSION: GENIUS VERSUS MEDIOCRITY

8 Faults of this kind formed the subject of Caecilius' attack in his book on Lysias, in which he had the audacity to declare Lysias in all respects superior to Plato. He has in fact given way without discrimination to two emotions: loving Lysias more deeply than he loves himself, he yet hates Plato with an even greater intensity. His motive, however, is desire to score a point, and his assumptions are not, as he believed, generally accepted. In preferring Lysias to Plato he thinks he is preferring a fault-less and pure writer to one who makes many mistakes. But the facts are far from supporting his view.

33. 1 Let us consider a really pure and correct writer. We have then to ask ourselves in general terms whether grandeur attended by some faults of execution is to be preferred, in prose or poetry, to a modest success of impeccable soundness. We must also ask whether the greater *number* of good qualities or the greater good qualities ought properly to win the literary prizes. These questions are relevant to a discussion of sublimity, and urgently require an answer.

2 I am certain in the first place that great geniuses are least 'pure'. Exactness in every detail involves a risk of meanness; with grandeur, as with great wealth, there ought to be something overlooked. It may also be inevitable that low or mediocre abilities should maintain themselves generally at a correct and safe level, simply because they take no risks and do not aim at the heights, whereas greatness, just because it is greatness, incurs danger.

3 I am aware also of a second point. All human affairs are, in the nature of things, better known on their worse side; the memory of mistakes is

4 ineffaceable, that of goodness is soon gone. I have myself cited not a few mistakes in Homer and other great writers, not because I take pleasure in their slips, but because I consider them not so much voluntary mistakes as oversights let fall at random through inattention and with the negli-gence of genius. I do, however, think that the greater good qualities, even if not consistently maintained, are always more likely to win the prize— if for no other reason, because of the greatness of spirit they reveal. Apollonius makes no mistakes in the *Argonautica*; Theocritus is very felicitous in the *Pastorals*, apart from a few passages not connected with

5 the theme; but would you rather be Homer or Apollonius? Is the Eratosthenes of that flawless little poem *Erigone* a greater poet than

Archilochus, with his abundant, uncontrolled flood, that bursting forth of the divine spirit which is so hard to bring under the rule of law? Take lyric poetry: would you rather be Bacchylides or Pindar? Take tragedy: would you rather be Ion of Chios or Sophocles? Ion and Bacchylides are impeccable, uniformly beautiful writers in the polished manner; but it is Pindar and Sophocles who sometimes set the world on fire with their vehemence, for all that their flame often goes out without reason and they collapse dismally. Indeed, no one in his senses would reckon all Ion's works put together as the equivalent of the one play *Oedipus*.

If good points were totted up, not judged by their real value, Hyperides 34. 1 would in every way surpass Demosthenes. He is more versatile,[1] and has more good qualities. He is second-best at everything, like a pentathlon competitor; always beaten by the others for first place, he remains the best of the non-specialists. In fact, he reproduces all the good features of 2 Demosthenes, except his word-arrangement, and also has for good measure the excellences and graces of Lysias. He knows how to talk simply where appropriate; he does not deliver himself of everything in the same tone, like Demosthenes. His expression of character has sweetness and delicacy. Urbanity, sophisticated sarcasm, good breeding, skill in handling irony, humour neither rude nor tasteless but flavoured with true Attic salt, an ingenuity in attack with a strong comic element and a sharp sting to its apt fun—all this produces inimitable charm. He has moreover great talents for exciting pity, and a remarkable facility for narrating myths with copiousness and developing general topics with fluency. For example, while his account of Leto is in his more poetic manner, his Funeral Speech is an unrivalled example of the epideictic style.[2] Demosthenes, by 3 contrast, has no sense of character. He lacks fluency, smoothness, and capacity for the epideictic manner; in fact he is practically without all the qualities I have been describing. When he forces himself to be funny or witty, he makes people laugh at him rather than with him. When he wants to come near to being charming, he is furthest removed from it. If he had tried to write the little speech on Phryne or that on Athenogenes,[3] he would have been an even better advertisement for Hyperides. Yet Hyperides' beauties, though numerous, are without grandeur: 'inert in 4 the heart of a sober man', they leave the hearer at peace. Nobody feels frightened reading Hyperides.

But when Demosthenes begins to speak, he concentrates in himself excellences finished to the highest perfection of his sublime genius—the

---

[1] Or perhaps 'fluent'.

[2] The speech (*Deliacus*) in which the myth of Leto was told is lost; the Funeral Speech is extant (*Oration* 2).

[3] The first is lost; the second is *Oration* 3 (5).

intensity of lofty speech, living emotions, abundance, acuteness, speed where speed is vital, all his unapproachable vehemence and power. He concentrates it all in himself—they are divine gifts, it is almost blasphemous to call them human—and so outpoints all his rivals, compensating with the beauties he has even for those which he lacks. The crash of his thunder, the brilliance of his lightning make all other orators, of all ages, insignificant. It would be easier to open your eyes to an approaching thunderbolt than to face up to his unremitting emotional blows.

35. 1   To return to Plato and Lysias, there is, as I said, a further difference between them. Lysias is much inferior not only in the importance of the good qualities concerned but in their number; and at the same time he exceeds Plato in the number of his failings even more than he falls short in his good qualities.

2   What then was the vision which inspired those divine writers who disdained exactness of detail and aimed at the greatest prizes in literature? Above all else, it was the understanding that nature made man to be no humble or lowly creature, but brought him into life and into the universe as into a great festival, to be both a spectator and an enthusiastic contestant in its competitions. She implanted in our minds from the start an irresistible desire for anything which is great and, in relation to ourselves, supernatural.

3   The universe therefore is not wide enough for the range of human speculation and intellect. Our thoughts often travel beyond the boundaries of our surroundings. If anyone wants to know what we were born for, let him look round at life and contemplate the splendour, grandeur, and

4   beauty in which it everywhere abounds. It is a natural inclination that leads us to admire not the little streams, however pellucid and however useful, but the Nile, the Danube, the Rhine, and above all the Ocean. Nor do we feel so much awe before the little flame we kindle, because it keeps its light clear and pure, as before the fires of heaven, though they are often obscured. We do not think our flame more worthy of admiration than the craters of Etna, whose eruptions bring up rocks and whole hills out of the depths, and sometimes pour forth rivers of the earth-born,

5   spontaneous fire. A single comment fits all these examples: the useful and necessary are readily available to man, it is the unusual that always excites our wonder.

36. 1   So when we come to great geniuses in literature—where, by contrast, grandeur is not divorced from service and utility—we have to conclude that such men, for all their faults, tower far above mortal stature. Other literary qualities prove their users to be human; sublimity raises us towards the spiritual greatness of god. Freedom from error does indeed

2   save us from blame, but it is only greatness that wins admiration. Need

I add that every one of those great men redeems all his mistakes many times over by a single sublime stroke? Finally, if you picked out and put together all the mistakes in Homer, Demosthenes, Plato, and all the other really great men, the total would be found to be a minute fraction of the successes which those heroic figures have to their credit. Posterity and human experience—judges whose sanity envy cannot question—place the crown of victory on their heads. They keep their prize irrevocably, and will do so

so long as waters flow and tall trees flourish.[1]

It has been remarked that 'the failed Colossus is no better than the Doryphorus of Polyclitus'.[2] There are many ways of answering this. We may say that accuracy is admired in art and grandeur in nature, and it is *by nature* that man is endowed with the power of speech; or again that statues are expected to represent the human form, whereas, as I said, something higher than human is sought in literature. 3

At this point I have a suggestion to make which takes us back to the beginning of the book. Impeccability is generally a product of art; erratic excellence comes from natural greatness; therefore, art must always come to the aid of nature, and the combination of the two may well be perfection. 4

It seemed necessary to settle this point for the sake of our inquiry; but everyone is at liberty to enjoy what he takes pleasure in. *thanks.*

SIMILES

We must now return to the main argument. Next to metaphors come comparisons and similes. The only difference is . . . 37. 1

[Lacuna equivalent to about two pages.]

HYPERBOLE

. . . such expressions as: 'Unless you've got your brains in your heels and are walking on them'.[3] The important thing to know is how far to push a given hyperbole; it sometimes destroys it to go too far; too much tension results in relaxation, and may indeed end in the contrary of the intended effect. Thus Isocrates' zeal for amplifying everything made him do a 38. 1 2

[1] 'Epigram on the tomb of Midas', ascribed to Homer: see Plato, *Phaedrus* 264 d.
[2] It is not certain whether 'Longinus' means the Colossus of Rhodes or some other large statue. For the Doryphorus, famous for its proportions, see, e.g., G. M. A. Richter, *Handbook of Greek Art*, Phaidon, 1959, 110.
[3] Demosthenes 7. 45—a speech generally thought to be spurious.

childish thing. The argument of his *Panegyricus* is that Athens surpasses Sparta in services to the Greek race. Right at the beginning we find the following:[1] 'Secondly, the power of speech is such that it can make great things lowly, give grandeur to the trivial, say what is old in a new fashion, and lend an appearance of antiquity to recent events.' Is Isocrates then about to reverse the positions of Athens and Sparta? The encomium on the power of speech is equivalent to an introduction recommending the

3 reader not to believe what he is told! I suspect that what we said of the best figures is true of the best hyperboles: they are those which avoid being seen for what they are. The desired effect is achieved when they are connected with some impressive circumstance and with moments of high emotion. Thucydides' account of those killed in Sicily is an example: 'The Syracusans came down and massacred them, especially those in the river. The water was stained; but despite the blood and the dirt, men continued to drink it, and many still fought for it.'[2] It is the intense emotion of the moment which makes it credible that dirt and blood should

4 still be fought for as drink. Herodotus has something similar about Thermopylae: 'Meanwhile though they defended themselves with swords (those who still had them), and with hands and mouths, the barbarians buried them with their missiles.'[3] What is meant by fighting armed men with mouths or being buried with missiles? Still, it is credible; for we form the impression that the hyperbole is a reasonable product of the situation, not that the situation has been chosen for the sake of the hyper-

5 bole. As I keep saying, acts and emotions which approach ecstasy provide a justification for, and an antidote to, any linguistic audacity. This is why comic hyperboles, for all their incredibility, are convincing because we laugh at them so much: 'He had a farm, but it didn't stretch as far as a Laconic letter.' Laughter is emotion in amusement (*hēdonē*).

6 There are hyperboles which belittle as well as those which exaggerate. Intensification is the factor common to the two species, vilification being in a sense an amplification of lowness.

(v) WORD-ARRANGEMENT OR COMPOSITION[4]

39. 1 There remains the fifth of the factors contributing to sublimity which we originally enumerated. This was a certain kind of composition or word-arrangement. Having set out my conclusions on this subject fully in two books, I shall here add only so much as is essential for our present subject.

[1] *Panegyricus* 6.   [2] Thucydides 7. 84.   [3] Herodotus 7. 225.
[4] Cf. in general Dionysius (above, pp. 321 ff.).

EFFECT OF RHYTHM

Harmony is a natural instrument not only of conviction and pleasure but also to a remarkable degree of grandeur and emotion. The *aulos*[1] [2] fills the audience with certain emotions and makes them somehow beside themselves and possessed. It sets a rhythm, it makes the hearer move to the rhythm and assimilate himself to the tune, 'untouched by the Muses though he be'.[2] The notes of the lyre, though they have no meaning, also, as you know, often cast a wonderful spell of harmony with their varied sounds and blended and mingled notes. Yet all these are but [3] spurious images and imitations of persuasion, not the genuine activities proper to human nature of which I spoke.[3] Composition, on the other hand, is a harmony of words, man's natural instrument, penetrating not only the ears but the very soul. It arouses all kinds of conceptions of words and thoughts and objects, beauty and melody—all things native and natural to mankind. The combination and variety of its sounds convey the speaker's emotions to the minds of those around him and make the hearers share them. It fits his great thoughts into a coherent structure by the way in which it builds up patterns of words. Shall we not then believe that by all these methods it bewitches us and elevates to grandeur, dignity, and sublimity both every thought which comes within its compass and ourselves as well, holding as it does complete domination over our minds? It is absurd to question facts so generally agreed. Experience is proof enough.

The idea which Demosthenes used in speaking of the decree[4] is reputed [4] very sublime, and is indeed splendid. 'This decree made the danger which then surrounded the city pass away like a cloud (*touto to psēphisma ton tote tē polei peristanta kindūnon parelthein epoiēsen hōsper nephos*).' But the effect depends as much on the harmony as on the thought. The whole passage is based on dactylic rhythms, and these are very noble and grand. (This is why they form the heroic, the noblest metre we know.) . . .

[A short phrase missing.]

. . . but make any change you like in the order:

touto to psēphisma hōsper nephos epoiēse ton tote kindūnon parelthein,

or cut off a syllable:

epoiēse parelthein hōs nephos.

You will immediately see how the harmony echoes the sublimity. The phrase *hōsper nephos* rests on its long first unit (– –) which measures four

---

[1] Oboe or clarinet rather than flute, though the word is often so translated. Cf. below, p. 541.   [2] Euripides, fr. 663 Nauck.
[3] Presumably in the work referred to in 39. 1.
[4] The decree making provision for war after Philip's occupation of Elatea.

shorts; the removal of a syllable (*hōs nephos*) at once curtails and mutilates the grand effect.

Now lengthen the phrase:

parelthein epoiēsen hōsperei nephos.

It still means the same, but the effect is different, because the sheer sublimity is broken up and undone by the breaking up of the run of long syllables at the end.

EFFECT OF PERIOD STRUCTURE

40. 1 I come now to a principle of particular importance for lending grandeur to our words. The beauty of the body depends on the way in which the limbs are joined together, each one when severed from the others having nothing remarkable about it, but the whole together forming a perfect unity. Similarly great thoughts which lack connection are themselves wasted and waste the total sublime effect, whereas if they co-operate to form a unity and are linked by the bonds of harmony, they come to life and speak just by virtue of the periodic structure. It is indeed generally true that, in periods, grandeur results from the total contribution of many elements.

2 I have shown elsewhere [1] that many poets and other writers who are not naturally sublime, and may indeed be quite unqualified for grandeur, and who use in general common and everyday words which carry with them no special effect, nevertheless acquire magnificence and splendour, and avoid being thought low or mean, solely by the way in which they arrange and fit together their words. Philistus, Aristophanes sometimes,

3 Euripides generally, are among the many examples. Thus Heracles says after the killing of the children:

I'm full of troubles, there's no room for more. [2]

This is a very ordinary remark, but it has become sublime, as the situation demands. [3] If you re-arrange it, it will become apparent that it is in the composition, not in the sense, that Euripides' greatness appears.

4 Dirce is being pulled about by the bull:

And where it could, it writhed and twisted round,
dragging at everything, rock, woman, oak,
juggling with them all. [4]

[1] Presumably in the two books on 'composition'.
[2] Euripides, *Hercules Furens* 1245.
[3] Or 'in accordance with its structure'.
[4] From Euripides' lost *Antiope* (fr. 221 Nauck). The Greek contains the words *perix helixas* and *petran drun*, and these are the effects to which the comment refers.

The conception is fine in itself, but it has been improved by the fact that the word-harmony is not hurried and does not run smoothly; the words are propped up by one another and rest on the intervals between them; set wide apart like that, they give the impression of solid strength.

FEATURES DESTRUCTIVE OF SUBLIMITY:
(1) BAD AND AFFECTED RHYTHM

Nothing is so damaging to a sublime effect as effeminate and agitated **41. 1** rhythm, pyrrhics ($\cup\cup$), trochees ($-\cup$ or $\cup\cup\cup$) and dichorei ($-\cup-\cup$); they turn into a regular jig. All the rhythmical elements immediately appear artificial and cheap, being constantly repeated in a monotonous fashion without the slightest emotional effect. Worst of all, just as songs distract **2** an audience from the action[1] and compel attention for themselves, so the rhythmical parts of speech produce on the hearer the effect not of speech but of rhythm, so that they foresee the coming endings and sometimes themselves beat time for the speaker and anticipate him in giving the step, just as in a dance.

(2) THE 'CHOPPED UP' STYLE

Phrases too closely knit[2] are also devoid of grandeur, as are those which **3** are chopped up into short elements consisting of short syllables, bolted together, as it were, and rough at the joins.

(3) EXCESSIVE BREVITY

Excessively cramped expression also does damage to sublimity. It **42. 1** cripples grandeur to compress it into too short a space. I do not mean proper compression, but cutting up into tiny pieces. Cramping mutilates sense; brevity gives directness. Conversely with fully extended expressions: anything developed at unseasonable length falls dead.[3]

(4) UNDIGNIFIED VOCABULARY

Lowness of diction also destroys grandeur. **43. 1**
    The description of the storm in Herodotus is magnificent in conception, but includes expressions which are below the dignity of the subject.[4]

[1] Of a play, presumably.
[2] Obscure: is this the same as the 'chopped up' manner or a separate fault?
[3] Again an obscure section, partly because 'Longinus' seems to intend it as an example of 'brevity'.   [4] Herodotus 7. 188, 191; 8. 13.

'The sea seethed' is one instance: the cacophony does much to dissipate the sublime effect. 'The wind slacked' is another example; yet another is the 'unpleasant end' which awaited those who were thrown against the wreckage. 'Slack' is an undignified, colloquial word; 'unpleasant' is inappropriate to such an experience.

2   Similarly, Theopompus first gives a magnificent setting to the descent of the Persian king on Egypt, and then ruins it all with a few words:[1]

'What city or nation in Asia did not send its embassy to the King? What thing of beauty or value, product of the earth or work of art, was not brought him as a gift? There were many precious coverlets and cloaks, purple, embroidered, and white; there were many gold tents fitted out with all necessities; there were many robes and beds of great price. There were silver vessels and worked gold, drinking cups and bowls, some studded with jewels, some elaborately and preciously wrought. Countless myriads of arms were there, Greek and barbarian. There were multitudes of pack animals and victims fattened for slaughter, many bushels of condiments, many bags and sacks and pots of onions and every other necessity. There was so much salt meat of every kind that travellers approaching from a distance mistook the huge heaps for cliffs or hills thrusting up from the plain.'

3   He passes from the sublime to the mean; the development of the scene should have been the other way round. By mixing up the bags and the condiments and the sacks in the splendid account of the whole expedition, he conjures up the vision of a kitchen. Suppose one actually had these beautiful objects before one's eyes, and then dumped some bags and sacks in the middle of the gold and jewelled bowls, the silver vessels, the gold tents, and the drinking-cups—the effect would be disgusting. It is the same with style: if you insert words like this when they are not wanted,

4   they make a blot on the context. It was open to Theopompus to give a general description of the 'hills' which he says were raised, and, having made this change,[2] to proceed to the rest of the preparations, mentioning camels and multitudes of beasts of burden carrying everything needed for luxury and pleasure of the table, or speaking of 'heaps of all kinds of seeds and everything that makes for fine cuisine and dainty living'. If he had wanted at all costs to make the king self-supporting,[3] he could have talked of 'all the refinements of *maîtres-d'hôtel* and chefs'.

5   It is wrong to descend, in a sublime passage, to the filthy and contemptible, unless we are absolutely compelled to do so. We ought to use words

---

[1] The passage is also quoted by Athenaeus (2, 67 f). 'Longinus' probably got it (like many of his quotations) from a collection of excerpts rather than from the original.

[2] Translation doubtful. Perhaps 'and then make a change of arrangement and proceed. . .'   [3] Text suspect.

worthy of things. We ought to imitate nature, who, in creating man, did not set our private parts or the excretions of our body in the face, but concealed them as well as she could, and, as Xenophon says,[1] made the channels of these organs as remote as possible, so as not to spoil the beauty of the creature as a whole.

CONCLUSION

There is no urgent need to enumerate in detail features which produce 6 a low effect. We have explained what makes style noble and sublime; the opposite qualities will obviously make it low and undignified.

APPENDIX: CAUSES OF THE DECLINE OF LITERATURE[2]

I shall not hesitate to add for your instruction, my dear Terentianus, one 44. 1 further topic, so as to clear up a question put to me the other day by one of the philosophers.

'I wonder,' he said, 'and so no doubt do many others, why it is that in our age there are minds which are strikingly persuasive and practical, shrewd, versatile, and well-endowed with the ability to write agreeably, but no sublime or really great minds, except perhaps here and there. There is a universal dearth of literature.

'Are we to believe', he went on, 'the common explanation that demo- 2 cracy nurtures greatness, and great writers flourished with democracy and died with it? Freedom, the argument goes, nourishes and encourages the thoughts of the great, as well as exciting their enthusiasm for rivalry with one another and their ambition for the prize. In addition the avail- 3 ability of political reward sharpens and polishes up orators' talents by giving them exercise; they shine forth, free in a free world. We of the present day, on the other hand,' he continued, 'seem to have learned in infancy to live under justified slavery, swathed round from our first tender thoughts in the same habits and customs, never allowed to taste that fair and fecund spring of literature, freedom. We end up as flatterers in the grand manner.'

He went on to say how the same argument explained why, unlike other 4 capacities, that of the orator could never belong to a slave.

---

[1] *Memorabilia* 1. 4. 6.
[2] It has been suggested that this chapter is out of place, and belongs after 15. 11. This is impossible to prove, but it is an ingenious solution to the problem of the book's arrangement.

'The inability to speak freely and the consciousness of being a prisoner at once assert themselves, battered into him as they have been by the 5 blows of habit. As Homer says,[1] "The day of slavery takes half one's manhood away". I don't know if it's true, but I understand that the cages in which dwarfs or Pygmies are kept not only prevent the growth of the prisoners but cripple them because of the fastening which constricts the body. One might describe all slavery, even the most justified,[2] as a cage for the soul, a universal prison.'

6 'My good friend,' I replied, 'it is easy to find fault with the present situation; indeed it is a human characteristic to do so. But I wonder whether what destroys great minds is not the peace of the world, but the unlimited war which lays hold on our desires, and all the passions which beset and ravage our modern life. Avarice, the insatiable disease from which we all suffer, and love of pleasure—these are our two slave-masters; or perhaps one should say that they sink our ship of life with all hands. Avarice is a mean disease; love of pleasure is base through and through.

7 I cannot see how we can honour, or rather deify, unlimited wealth as we do without admitting into our souls the evils which attach to it. When wealth is measureless and uncontrolled, extravagance comes with it, sticking close beside it, and, as they say, keeping step. The moment wealth opens the way into cities and houses, extravagance also enters and dwells therein. These evils then become chronic in people's lives, and, as the philosophers say,[3] nest and breed. They are soon busy producing offspring: greed, pride, and luxury are their all-too-legitimate children. If these offspring of wealth are allowed to mature, they breed in turn those inexorable tyrants of the soul, insolence, lawlessness, and shamelessness.

8 It is an inevitable process. Men will no longer open their eyes or give thought to their reputation with posterity. The ruin of their lives is gradually consummated in a cycle of such vices. Greatness of mind wanes, fades, and loses its attraction when men spend their admiration on their 9 mortal parts and neglect to develop the immortal. One who has been bribed to give a judgement will no longer be a free and sound judge of rightness and nobility. The corrupt man inevitably thinks his own side's claim just and fair. Yet nowadays bribery is the arbiter of the life and fortunes of every one of us—not to mention chasing after other people's deaths and conspiring about wills. We are all so enslaved by avarice that we buy the power of making profit out of everything at the price of our souls. Amid such pestilential corruption of human life, how can we expect

---

[1] *Odyssey* 17. 322–3.
[2] I translate as though the adjective *dikaios* meant the same as it does just above; but perhaps 'justly exercised', i.e. humane.
[3] Cf. Plato, *Republic* 9, 573 e.

that there should be left to us any free, uncorrupt judge of great things of permanent value? How can we hope not to lose our case to the corrupt practices of the love of gain?

'Perhaps people like us are better as subjects than given our freedom. 10 Greed would flood the world in woe, if it were really released and let out of the cage, to prey on its neighbours.'

Idleness, I went on to say, was the bane of present-day minds. We 11 all live with it. Our whole regime of effort and relaxation[1] is devoted to praise and pleasure, not to the useful results that deserve emulation and honour.

'Best to let these things be',[2] and proceed to our next subject. This was 12 emotion, to which we promised to devote a separate treatise. It occupies, as I said, a very important place among the constituents of literature in general, and sublimity in particular . . .

[A few words missing at the end.]

---

[1] Or 'all our effort and all that we undertake'.
[2] Euripides, *Electra* 379.

12

DIO CHRYSOSTOM AND PLUTARCH:
THE GREEK REVIVAL

A. PHILOCTETES IN THE TRAGEDIANS

Dio 'Chrysostom', a native of Prusa in Bithynia, was a successful sophist of the first century A.D. He is an elegant stylist, and a moralist of convincing earnestness and charm. See Sir S. Dill, *Roman Society from Nero to Marcus Aurelius*, London, 1905 (reprinted N.Y., 1956), 367–83, for a general account. His critical and aesthetic works (very few) are discussed by Grube 327 ff.

In *Oration* 52, a short informal speech, he compares the treatments of the story of Philoctetes and his bow by Aeschylus, Sophocles, and Euripides. Only Sophocles' play (the latest of the three) survives. See Jebb's edition of this, Introd., pp. xv ff., for a discussion of Dio's critique.

Dio's views sound conventional. His standpoint is very rhetorical, and the contrast he draws between Aeschylus and Euripides is essentially the one found in the *Frogs* (see above, pp. 8 ff.), applied almost *a priori* to these particular plays. Such comparisons (*sunkriseis*) were common stock in scholastic criticism; we may well owe to this taste the preservation of plays by all three tragedians on Orestes' vengeance on Clytemnestra.

I got up about an hour after daybreak, partly because I was unwell, and partly because the dawn air was cooler—more like autumn, though it was the middle of the summer. I attended to my toilet and said my prayers. Then I got into the carriage and took a number of turns on the racecourse, driving as gently and quietly as possible. I followed this up with a walk and a little rest; then I oiled myself and bathed and after a light meal began to read tragedies. They were all treatments of a single subject by the three great names, Aeschylus, Sophocles, and Euripides: the theft—or perhaps one should say violent robbery—of Philoctetes' bow. Anyway, Philoctetes is deprived of his weapon by Odysseus and himself taken to Troy, to a certain extent voluntarily, but with a degree of compulsion about it too, because he had been deprived of the weapon that gave him his livelihood on the island and confidence to face his disease, apart from being his claim to fame. I feasted on the performance, and reflected that if I had lived in Athens in those days I should not have been able to participate in a competition between these writers. Some indeed were present at competitions between the young Sophocles and the old Aeschylus, and again between Sophocles in his latter days and the young Euripides; but Euripides was altogether too late to encounter Aeschylus.

Moreover, they rarely if ever competed with plays on the same theme. So I thought I was much indulged, and had discovered a new way of consoling myself for being ill. I produced the plays for myself (in my mind's eye) very splendidly, and tried to give them my whole attention, like a judge òf the first tragic choruses. But had I been on oath, I could never have come to a decision. So far as I was concerned, none of them could have been beaten.

Aeschylus' grandeur and archaic splendour, and the originality of his thought and expression, seemed appropriate to tragedy and the antique manners of the heroes; it had nothing subtle, nothing facile, nothing undignified. Even his Odysseus, though shrewd and crafty for the times, was miles away from present-day standards of malevolence. He would seem an old-fashioned fellow indeed by the side of those who in our age claim to be simple and magnanimous. He did not need Athena to disguise him in order to prevent him from being recognized by Philoctetes, as Homer and (after him) Euripides have it. A hostile critic might perhaps say that Aeschylus was not concerned to make Philoctetes' failure to recognize Odysseus plausible. There is a possible defence, I think, against such an objection. The time was indeed perhaps not long enough for the features to fail to come to mind after a lapse of only ten years, but Philoctetes' illness and incapacity and the solitary life he had led so long also contribute to make the situation possible. Many people have suffered such a failure of memory as a result of illness or misfortune.

Nor did Aeschylus' chorus need to apologize, like that of Euripides. Both made up their choruses of inhabitants of Lemnos, but Euripides began by making them apologize for their neglect in not having come to see Philoctetes or given him any help for so many years, while Aeschylus simply brought the chorus on without comment. This is altogether simpler and more tragic, in contrast with Euripides' more sophisticated and painstaking treatment. If it had been possible to avoid every irrationality in tragedy, it might have been reasonable not to let this one pass either; but in fact poets often, for example, represent heralds as making several days' journey in one day. Secondly, it simply wasn't possible for none of the inhabitants of Lemnos to have approached Philoctetes or taken care of him. He could never have survived ten years without help. Probably therefore he did get some, but rarely and not on any great scale, and no one chose to receive him in their house and nurse him because of the unpleasant nature of his illness. Indeed Euripides himself introduces one Actor, a Lemnian, who visits Philoctetes as an acquaintance who has often met him. Nor do I think it right to find fault with Aeschylus' making Philoctetes relate to an apparently ignorant chorus his desertion by the Achaeans and his whole history. The unfortunate often recall their troubles and weary their listeners, who know it all well and don't want to hear it again, with their perpetual narrations. Again, Odysseus' deception of Philoctetes and the arguments by which he wins him are not only more respectable—suitable to a hero, not a Eurybatus or a Pataecion[1]—but also, as it seems to me, more convincing. What was the need of elaborate art and guile in dealing with a sick man—and an archer too, whose prowess was useless the moment one came near him? To relate the disasters of the Achaeans, the death of Agamemnon, the death of Odysseus for a shocking crime, and the total destruction of the army, was not only useful for cheering up Philoctetes and making him more willing to accept Odysseus' company, but also not implausible in view of the length of the campaign and the recent events consequent on the anger of Achilles, when Hector came near to burning the fleet.

Euripides' intelligence and care for every detail—nothing unconvincing or negligent is allowed to pass, and instead of bare facts he gives us the whole force of his eloquence—is the opposite of Aeschylus' simplicity. This is the style of the man of affairs and the orator; the reader can learn many valuable lessons from it. For example, Odysseus in the prologue is represented as revolving in his mind many rhetorically effective (*politika*) thoughts. He wonders about his own position. May he perhaps appear wise and intelligent to many people but in fact be the opposite? He could be living a secure, untroubled life—and here he is voluntarily involved in affairs and dangers! The cause, he says, is the ambition of talented and noble men; it is because they want reputation and fame among all mankind that they voluntarily undertake great and arduous tasks:

Nothing so vain as man was ever born.

Then he clearly and accurately explains the plot of the play, and why he has come to Lemnos. Athena has disguised him so that he shall not be recognized by Philoctetes when he meets him. (This is an imitation of Homer, who makes Athena disguise Odysseus when he meets various people, such as Eumaeus and Penelope).[2] He says an embassy is going to come from the Trojans to Philoctetes, to offer him the kingdom of Troy in exchange for his own services and those of his bow. This complicates the story, and affords a starting-point for a speech in which he shows himself resourceful and eloquent enough to stand comparison with anyone in developing the opposite position. Nor does he make Odysseus come alone; Diomedes is with him, another Homeric touch. In short, he shows throughout the play great intelligence and convincingness in incident, and wonderful, hardly credible, skill of language. The iambics are clear,

[1] Proverbial rogues: cf. Aeschines 3. 137, 189; Plato, *Protagoras* 327 d.
[2] Cf. *Odyssey* 13. 429 ff., 16. 172 ff.

natural, rhetorically effective. The lyrics afford not only pleasure but many exhortations to virtue.

Sophocles comes between the two. He possesses neither Aeschylus' originality and simplicity, nor the craftsmanship, shrewdness, and rhetorical effectiveness of Euripides. His verse is dignified and grand, tragic and euphonious to the highest degree, combining great charm with sublimity and dignity. At the same time, his management of the story is excellent and convincing. He makes Odysseus arrive with Neoptolemus because it was ordained that Troy should be captured by Neoptolemus and Philoctetes with the bow of Heracles, but conceal himself while sending Neoptolemus to Philoctetes, telling him what he must do. Moreover, the chorus is made up not, as in Aeschylus and Euripides, of natives, but of the crew of Odysseus' and Neoptolemus' ship. The characters are wonderfully dignified and gentlemanly. Odysseus is much gentler and more straightforward than in Euripides, Neoptolemus is simple and noble to excess, unwilling to win his point over Philoctetes by guile and deceit, but insisting on strength and openness, and afterwards, when Odysseus has persuaded him and he has deceived Philoctetes and got possession of the bow, unable to endure his victim's complaints and demands, and quite capable of giving him the bow back, despite Odysseus' appearance and attempt to stop him. Indeed, he does give it back in the end; and having done so then tries to persuade Philoctetes to go with him voluntarily to Troy. Philoctetes refuses to give way or comply, but begs Neoptolemus to take him home to Greece, as he had promised. The young man agrees and is ready to perform his promise, until Heracles appears and persuades Philoctetes to sail to Troy voluntarily. The lyrics are without the general reflections and exhortations to virtue which we saw in Euripides, but they possess extraordinary charm (*hēdonē*) and grandeur (*megaloprepeia*). It was not without cause that Aristophanes wrote:

He licked the lip of the jar, as it were, of honey-covered Sophocles.[1]

B. ON THE STUDY OF POETRY

Plutarch (cf. chap. 1, F, above) was roughly Dio's contemporary. He was born *c.* A.D. 45 and died *c.* 120. Moralist, philosopher, and biographer, he only occasionally touches on topics of literary criticism. His preoccupation with education is evident in all he wrote; he was a man of great learning and conventional views.

See R. H. Barrow, *Plutarch and his Times*, London, 1967; also D. A. Russell, *Greece & Rome*, 13 (1966), 139 ff. and 15 (1968), 130 ff.

[1] Fr. 581 Hall and Geldart.

Our first extract comprises the first part of an educational treatise entitled 'How young men should study poetry' (*De audiendis poetis* 1–8 = *Moralia* 14 d ff.), written in the tradition of the moralizing criticism of Plato's *Republic* (above, chap. 2, B). The ingenuity shown in explaining the poets in moral terms gives many insights into a kind of discussion of the standard classics which remained common throughout the Roman period. There are significant links between Plutarch's interpretations and those found in the scholia to Homer.

We have indicated the source of the quotations as far as they are known; but Plutarch drew many of them from existing collections, not from first-hand reading.

The text is in the first volume both of the Loeb and of the Teubner *Moralia*.

I

To Marcus Sedatius[1]

p. 14 d 'The nicest meat', said the poet Philoxenus,[2] 'is what is not meat, and the nicest fish is what is not fish.' Let us leave the discussion of this to the people who, in Cato's phrase, have more sensibility in their palates than in their heads. What is plain is that in philosophy very young students enjoy more what does not appear to be philosophical or serious; to this they are ready to submit and subject themselves. In going through not only Aesop's fables and tales from the poets but Heraclides' *Abaris* and Ariston's *Lycon*,[3] they take a passionate delight in the doctrines about the soul which are mixed with the mythology. Thus we must preserve the decency of the young not only in the pleasures of food and drink; more important, we must accustom them in their readings and lectures to make use of the pleasurable element sparingly, as a kind of sauce, and to pursue the profit and salvation that derives from it. Locked gates do not preserve a city if one door is open to let in the enemy; continence in other pleasures does not save a young man if he lets himself go inadvertently through the p. 15 pleasures of the ear. Indeed, the more firmly these delights take hold of the sensible and intelligent, the more they are overlooked and damage and destroy their host.

Now it is neither useful nor perhaps possible to keep boys of the age of my Soclaros or your Cleandros away from poetry. Let us therefore protect them. They need an escort in reading even more than they do in the street.

I have decided therefore to send you in written form the thoughts which came into my mind the other day when I had been talking about

---

[1] Not otherwise known.
[2] Probably Philoxenus of Leucas, author of a gastronomic poem.
[3] Two dialogues—popular philosophy with entertaining settings—by pupils of Aristotle.

poetry. If they strike you as equal to those prophylactics against drunkenness which people hang round themselves or take at drinking parties, share them with Cleandros and get a grip on his character. It is all the more amenable to the sort of thing we are speaking of because he is never slow but always so vigorous and alert.

In the polyp's head is good and bad:

it is nice to eat, but results in sleep disturbed by dreams, with confused and outlandish visions, or so they say. Similarly with poetry: it contains much that is pleasant and profitable to the young mind, but just as much that is confusing and misleading, if study is not properly directed. It can be said of poetry as of the land of Egypt:

> Many drugs it bears that are good, and many that are
> hurtful to its cultivators;[1]

> therein is love and desire and the intimacies
> that cheat and steal the hearts even of the wise.[2]

The deceitfulness of poetry does not affect the really stupid and foolish. This is why, when Simonides was asked: 'Why are the Thessalians the only people you do not deceive?', he replied: 'Because they are too ignorant to be deceived by me.' Similarly, Gorgias said that tragedy was 'a deceit in which the deceiver does his duty better than the non-deceiver, and the deceived is wiser than the undeceived'.[3]

What then ought we to do? Stop the young men's ears, like the Ithacan sailors', with some hard, insoluble wax, and force them to set sail with Epicurus, and steer clear of poetry?[4] Or fix and settle their judgment with rational arguments, not letting pleasure distract it into harm, and so protect them and guide them aright?

For not even the son of Dryas, mighty Lycurgus[5]

was a sane man, when, because many people were getting drunk and behaving badly in their cups, he went round cutting down vines, instead of bringing the water nearer and (to use Plato's expression) chastening a mad god with another and sober one.[6] Mixing destroys the harm in wine, but not its usefulness. Let us not therefore cut out or destroy the vine of the Muses. When unmixed pleasure makes its fabulous and theatrical elements wax wanton and luxuriant, blustering violently for reputation, let us take hold and prune and constrain: but when it touches poetry with its grace, and the sweet attractions of the style are fruitful and purposeful,

---

[1] *Odyssey* 4. 230.   [2] *Iliad* 14. 216.   [3] Cf. above, p. 6.
[4] 'Set sail and get away from education of every kind', said Epicurus (fr. 163 Usener).
[5] *Iliad* 6. 130.   [6] *Laws* 773 d.

let us introduce some admixture of philosophy. For just as mandragora planted beside vines and transmitting its qualities to the wine makes the effect on the drinker milder, so poetry, by taking some arguments from philosophy and combining them with an element of fable, makes learning easy and agreeable to young people. Future philosophers therefore must not avoid poetry. Rather should they be initiated into philosophy through it, becoming accustomed to seek and enjoy truth in pleasant surroundings

p. 16 —or to protest and be annoyed at the lack of it. This is the beginning of education, and

> work well begun is like to finish well

as Sophocles says.[1]

THE DECEITFULNESS OF POETRY

2 When we first introduce our young men to poetry, there is nothing they should have learned so thoroughly, nothing so readily springing to their mind, as the proverbial saying that

> poets tell many lies,

whether deliberate or not. The deliberate lies of the poets are due to their thinking truth drier than fiction, from the point of view of pleasure to the hearer and charm, which is what most of them aim at. Truth is real, and does not change course, however unpleasant the outcome. Fiction easily deviates and turns from the painful to the pleasant. Metre, trope, grand language, timely metaphor, harmony, and word-order possess nothing like the beguiling charm of a well-contrived plot. In painting, colour is more exciting than line because it is colour that represents flesh and deceives the eye; and similarly in poetry a convincing fiction produces admiration and satisfaction more than any device of metre or diction deficient in plot and story. This is why Socrates, the life-long striver for truth, found himself, when he set about composing poetry in obedience to a dream, no very convincing or gifted maker of lies; he therefore put Aesop's fables into verse, on the principle that where there is no fiction there is no poetry. For there can be sacrifices without dances and music, but poetry without plot and fiction is impossible. Empedocles, Parmenides, the *Theriaca* of Nicander, and the wise saws (*gnōmologiai*) of Theognis have borrowed from poetry the vehicle, as it were, of grandeur and metre, so as to avoid the pedestrian.[2]

---

[1] Fr. 747 Nauck.

[2] i.e. didactic poetry is not really poetry at all: cf. Arist. *Poetics* 1447^{b}16 ff. (above, p. 91).

Now consider any absurd or unpalatable statement, in poetry, about gods or demigods or virtue, put into the mouth of a man of distinction and reputation. The reader who accepts it as true is lost, and his judgement ruined. The reader who remembers and clearly bears in mind the magic of fiction that poetry possesses, and can say to it every time,

'You tricksy beast, more subtle than the lynx,[1]

why do you contract your brows in fun? Why do you pretend to teach when in fact you deceive?'—he will come to no harm and believe no evil. He will check himself when he feels afraid of Poseidon and dreads his bursting the earth open and laying Hades bare. He will hold himself back when he feels angry with Apollo on behalf of the first man among the Greeks—

he who sang the hymn, he who was at the feast,
he who said all this, he was the killer.[2]

He will stop weeping for the dead Achilles and Agamemnon in Hades, stretching out their feeble and powerless hands in their longing for life. Or if he is disturbed by their sufferings and drugged into submission, he will not hesitate to say to himself:

Make haste towards the light. Know all these things
to tell your wife hereafter.[3]

This is a neat touch of Homer's: the visit to Hades is aptly described as a tale for women because of its fabulous content.

VOLUNTARY AND INVOLUNTARY ERRORS OF POETS

So much for the poets' deliberate inventions. More often, however, it is not invention but false belief and opinion that produce the falsehood they then rub off on us. For example: Homer says of Zeus

He put in two dooms of death that lays men low,   p. 17
one for Achilles, one for Hector, tamer of horses;
he seized the middle, and poised it. Down went
    Hector's day of doom;
and he was away to Hades, and Phoebus Apollo
    abandoned him.[4]

And Aeschylus built a whole tragedy around the story, calling it 'The Weighing of the Souls', and presenting Thetis on one side of Zeus' scale and Eos on the other, praying on behalf of their sons as they fought.

[1] From an unknown tragedy (*Trag. adesp.* 349.)
[2] Cf. Plato, *Republic* 383 b (above, p. 57).
[3] *Odyssey* 11. 223.   [4] *Iliad* 22. 210.

Now this is plainly a myth or fiction constructed to please or astonish the hearer. By contrast,

> Zeus, who dispenses war among mankind,[1]

and

> God breeds a crime in men
> when he would utterly destroy a house,[2]

are written in accordance with the poets' own opinion and belief; they express and impart to us their own misconception and ignorance about the gods.

Again, few readers fail to realize that the portentous tales and descriptions found in accounts of Hades, where horrifying names are used to produce graphic images and pictures of burning rivers, savage places, and grim punishments, contain a large element of fable and falsehood—poison in the food as it were. Homer, Pindar, and Sophocles did not believe what they were saying when they wrote:

> whence the slow streams of murky night
> belch forth unending darkness;[3]

or

> and they passed by the streams of Ocean and the White Rock;[4]

or

> narrows of Hell, and ebb and flow of the abyss.[5]

But what they say in lamentation and fear of the pitifulness of death or the horror of going unburied comes from genuine feeling and the prejudices created by common opinion and error:

> Do not go away and leave me unwept and unburied;[6]

and

> The soul flew from the limbs and went down to Hades;
> lamenting its fate, leaving manhood and youth behind it;[7]

and

> Do not kill me untimely. Sweet is the light to see;
> do not force me to look on what lies under the ground.[8]

This is why they touch us more and disturb us, because we are filled with the emotion and weakness out of which they are spoken. To meet this danger, let us again ensure, right from the beginning, an insistence

---

[1] *Iliad* 4. 84.
[2] Cf. Plato, *Republic* 380 a (above, p. 54).
[3] Pindar, fr. 114 Bowra.
[4] *Odyssey* 24. 11.
[5] Sophocles, fr. 748.
[6] *Odyssey* 11. 72.
[7] *Iliad* 16. 856, 22. 362.
[8] Euripides, *Iphigenia at Aulis* 1218.

on the fact that poetry is *not* concerned with truth. Indeed, the truth about these matters is hard to track down or comprehend even for those whose only study is the knowledge and understanding of reality. They admit it themselves. Have ready Empedocles' words:

> not visible to men nor audible,
> nor to be grasped in the mind;[1]

and those of Xenophanes:

> the certainty no man has known or ever shall know
> about the gods and all the things I speak of.[2]

Remember Socrates' disavowal (in Plato) of knowledge of these things.[3] The young men will be less inclined to pay attention to the poets as sources of knowledge about these matters if they see the philosophers in a daze!

POETRY AS IMITATION

We shall keep our young student under control even better if, the moment ³ we introduce him to works of poetry, we indicate that poetry is an art of imitation, a capacity analogous to painting. He should of course be given the familiar dictum that 'poetry is speaking painting and painting silent poetry';[4] but in addition to this, let us explain that when we see a picture p. 18 of a lizard or a monkey or Thersites' face we feel pleasure and admiration not because it is beautiful but because it is *like*. In reality, ugliness cannot become beautiful, but imitation is commended if it achieves likeness, whether of a good or a bad object. Indeed, if it produces a beautiful image of an ugly thing, it fails to provide propriety or probability. Some painters do in fact represent disconcertingly odd events: Timomachus did a 'Medea killing her children', Theon an 'Orestes killing his mother', Parrhasius 'Odysseus feigning madness', while Chaerephanes depicted indecent intercourse of men and women. The young student must be educated especially in this kind of thing, and be taught that we praise not the action represented by the imitation but the art shown in the appropriate reproduction of the subject. Similarly, since poetry also often narrates by imitation wicked actions and bad emotions or traits of character, the young man must not necessarily accept admirable or successful work of this kind as true, or label it beautiful, but simply commend it as suitable

---

[1] Fr. 2 D–K.   [2] Fr. 34 D–K.   [3] *Phaedo* 96 b ff.
[4] Cf. chap. I, F (above, p. 5).

and appropriate to the subject. When we actually hear a pig grunt, a windlass rattle, the wind whistle or the sea roar, we feel annoyance and distress;[1] but if anyone mimics the noise convincingly, as Parmeno did the pig or Theodorus the windlass, we feel pleasure. We avoid a sick or ulcerated man as a disagreeable sight, but we enjoy looking at Aristophon's 'Philoctetes' or Silanion's 'Jocasta', which are made to resemble the sick and dying. Similarly, when the young man reads what Thersites the buffoon or Sisyphus the seducer or Batrachos the brothel-keeper is represented as saying or doing, he should be taught to praise the technique and skill of the imitation, but to censure and abuse the habits and activities represented. To imitate something beautiful is not the same thing as to imitate it beautifully. 'Beautifully' here means fittingly and suitably—and what is fitting and suitable to something ugly is ugly itself. Damonidas the cripple's shoes, which he prayed might fit the feet of the man who stole them, were poor shoes, but they fitted him. Similarly,

> If we *must* do wrong, it's best to do it
> to win a kingdom;

and

> Win a just man's repute, but act like one
> who will do anything for profit;

and

> The dowry's a talent. Not take it? Can I live
> if I disdain a talent? Shall I sleep
> if I let it go? Shall I not suffer in hell
> for blasphemy against a silver talent?—

all these remarks are wicked and false, but they are in character for Eteocles, Ixion, and an old moneylender.[2] If therefore we remind our children that the poets do not commend or approve this kind of thing but simply attribute queer and vicious words to vicious and queer characters, they will not be harmed by the poets' opinion. Indeed, the suspicion felt towards the character discredits the action and the speech as being the bad act or speech of a bad person. An example is Paris's going to bed with Helen after he ran away from the battle.[3] By representing no one else as going to bed with a woman in the daytime except the licentious adulterer, Homer obviously intends disgrace and blame to be attached to this kind of indulgence.

---

[1] Cf. Plato, *Republic* 396 a (above, p. 64).
[2] The first quotation is from Euripides, *Phoenissae* 524; the second must be from a tragedy (Euripides?) on Ixion (*trag. adesp.* 4), the third from a comedy (*com. adesp.* 117).
[3] *Iliad* 3. 380 ff.

HINTS TO BE TAKEN

Attention must be paid in this connection to any indication the poet gives 4
that he disapproves of what is being said. For example, Menander writes **p. 19**
in the prologue to *Thais*:

> Sing me a woman, O goddess, pert, pretty, persuasive,
> unfair, exclusive, demanding,
> loving nobody, but always pretending to love.[1]

Homer is best at this, because he gives advance discredit or recommendation to the bad or good things his characters say. For 'advance recommendation', compare:

> He spoke a sweet and shrewd word;[2]

or

> He stood by him, and restrained him with gentle words.[3]

In discrediting a remark in advance, Homer virtually gives a solemn warning not to use or attend to it, because it is outrageous and vicious. Thus, when he is about to relate Agamemnon's harsh treatment of the priest, he prefaces it by saying:

> But it did not satisfy Agamemnon, son of Atreus, in his heart,
> but he dismissed him evilly[4]—

that is to say, brutally, wantonly, and improperly. Similarly, he gives Achilles the harsh words

> drunken sot, with a dog's eyes and a hind's heart,[5]

only after stating his own judgement:

> Then Peleus' son again with grim words
> addressed Atrides: he had not yet ceased from his anger.[6]

For nothing said angrily and harshly is likely to be good.
Similarly also with actions:

> He spoke, and planned dire deeds on Hector,
> laying him out on his face by Patroclos' bier.[7]

And he also uses concluding lines to good effect, casting his own vote

---

[1] Menander, fr. 185 Körte.
[2] *Odyssey* 6. 148.
[3] *Iliad* 2. 189.
[4] Ibid. 1. 24.
[5] *Iliad* 1. 225; cf. 'Longinus' 4. 4, above, p. 465.
[6] *Iliad* 1. 223.
[7] Ibid. 23. 24.

as it were on what is said or done. Thus he makes the gods say of Ares'
adultery:

> Bad deeds do not prosper. The slow catches the swift.[1]

On Hector's pride and boasting, we have:

> So he spake, boasting; but Hera was indignant.[2]

And on Pandarus' archery:

> So spake Athena, and convinced the fool.[3]

Now these verbal assertions and opinions may be observed by any
attentive reader. But other lessons are supplied by the actual events
related. Euripides, for instance, is said to have answered critics who
attacked his Ixion as impious and vile by saying: 'But I didn't take him
off the stage until he was nailed to the wheel.' In Homer, this kind of
instruction is tacit; but it affords a useful kind of re-interpretation for the
most severely criticized myths. Some critics in fact have so forced and
perverted the meaning of these by using what used to be called *huponoia*[4]
and is now called allegory, as to interpret the revelation by Helios of
Ares' adultery with Aphrodite as meaning that the planet Mars in conjunction with the planet Venus produces adulterous births, which are
revealed by the return of the sun on his course to discover them; or
again, to interpret the way in which Hera beautified herself for Zeus,
and the magic of the cestus, as symbolizing a purification of the air coming
into proximity with the fiery element. As if Homer did not himself give
the solution of both these problems! In the story of Aphrodite, he in fact
teaches the attentive reader that poor music, bad songs, and speeches
with immoral themes produce dissolute character, unmanly life, and a race
of men content with luxury, softness, womanishness, and

p. 20   changes of clothes, hot baths, and bed.[5]

This is why he represents Odysseus as instructing the bard to

> change the tune, and sing the Making of the Horse[6]—

very properly suggesting that musicians and poets should take their
subjects from men of sense and wisdom. In the story of Hera, likewise,
he demonstrates that the sort of intercourse and pleasure between the
sexes that depends on drugs, magic, or deceit, is not only ephemeral,

---

[1] *Odyssey* 8. 329.   [2] *Iliad* 8. 198.   [3] Ibid. 4. 104.
[4] Cf. Plato, *Republic* 2. 378 d (above, p. 53).
[5] *Odyssey* 8. 249.   [6] Ibid. 492.

inconstant, and insecure, but turns to hostility and anger as soon as the effects of the pleasure fade. Zeus accordingly threatens Hera:

> So that you can see if love and bed avail you,
> the love you enjoyed when you came from the gods, and
> deceived me.[1]

If the description and representation of bad deeds includes as well the disgrace and damage which befalls the doers, it benefits rather than harms the audience. Philosophers use examples, admonishing and instructing from given facts, while poets do the same thing by inventing facts and spinning tales on their own. I am not sure whether Melanthius was joking or in earnest when he said that Athens was preserved by the dissidence and dissensions of the politicians, because they did not all lean to the same side of the boat, but their quarrels somehow counteracted their damaging effects.[2] But it is like that with poets: their differences among themselves produce compensating convictions and prevent any violent swing in a harmful direction. Sometimes, they themselves highlight the contradictions by putting opposing opinions side by side. We must then support the better side. For example:

> 'My child, the gods do often trip men up.'
> 'Yes, that's the easiest way—convict the gods';[3]

or

> 'Should you, but not they, glory in wealth of gold?'
> 'Stupid to be wealthy and know nothing else';[4]

or

> 'Why sacrifice, when you are going to die?'
> 'It's better; there's no hardship in piety.'[5]

The solutions of these problems are obvious if, as has been said, we direct the young by our critical judgement in the better direction.

HOW TO REFUTE THE POETS OUT OF THEIR OWN MOUTHS

Preposterous statements which are not immediately accounted for must be refuted by using contradictory statements made by the poet elsewhere, without showing anger with him or annoyance at remarks made not in earnest but humorously and in character. For example, we may answer

---

[1] *Iliad* 15. 32.
[2] It is not certain whether this Melanthius is a fifth-century tragedian or a later writer.   [3] Euripides, fr. 254 Nauck.   [4] Euripides, fr. 1069 Nauck.
[5] Unknown (*trag. adesp.*, fr. 350 Nauck).

Homer's episodes in which the gods are 'hurled down' by one another or wounded by men, or quarrel or are angry, by saying to the poet:

> You know a better tale than this [1]—

your thoughts and your words are much better elsewhere: for instance, 'the easy-living gods', or 'there the blessed gods have joy all their days', or 'such is the fate the gods give wretched men, to live in sorrow, while they themselves are carefree'. These are perfectly sane and truthful opinions about the gods; the other passages are inventions to amaze men.

Again, when Euripides says

> With many forms of trickery
> the gods, our masters, trip us up, [2]

it is not a bad answer to produce his own better line:

> If gods do ill, they are no gods. [3]

Pindar says cruelly and provocatively:

> Do anything to blot your enemy out. [4]

'But', we may reply, 'you say yourself

> A bitter end awaits unrighteous pleasure.' [5]

Sophocles says:

> Profit is sweet, even though it comes from falsehood. [6]

'But', we answer, 'we heard you say

> False words bear no fruit.' [7]

Similarly, in reply to the lines about wealth:

> For wealth is strong to travel
> on public and forbidden ground alike
> and places where the poor man, even if lucky,
> could never have his will; it makes the ugly
> look beautiful, the stumbling talker wise [8]—

one can cite many passages of Sophocles:

> Even the poor man can be held in honour, [9]

and

> no worse for being a beggar, if he's wise, [10]

---

[1] *Iliad* 7. 358. For the phrases quoted next, see *Iliad* 6. 138, *Odyssey* 6. 46, *Iliad* 24. 525.

[2] Euripides, fr. 972.   [3] Fr. 292.   [4] *Isthmian* 4. 52.
[5] Ibid. 7. 47.   [6] Sophocles, fr. 749.   [7] Fr. 750.
[8] Fr. 85.   [9] Fr. 751.   [10] Fr. 752.

p. 21

and

> What grace is there in much beauty
> if it is wicked intrigue
> that breeds prosperity of riches?[1]

Menander certainly encouraged and inflated the love of pleasure by the burning eroticism of the lines:

> All things that live and see our common sun
> are slaves to pleasure.[2]

But elsewhere he converts us and draws us towards the good, eradicating the wantonness of our wickedness with the words

> An ugly life is a disgrace, however pleasant.[3]

This is of course quite the opposite, and better and more useful.

ONE POET REFUTED BY ANOTHER

Consideration of juxtaposed opposites like this will either lead us to better views or at least destroy our belief in the worse. But if a poet does not himself provide a resolution of his absurdities, it is just as good to set against him the statements of other authorities of repute in order to turn the scale in the better direction. For example, Alexis disturbs some people when he says: 'The sensible man ought to collect pleasures. There are three that really contribute to life—food, drink, and sex. Everything else is an extra.'[4] To counter this, let us recall that Socrates said the opposite— namely, that bad men live to eat and drink and good men eat and drink to live. Again, against the saying

> Wickedness is no bad weapon against the wicked,

which in a sense invites us to make ourselves resemble them, we may adduce a remark of Diogenes: when he was asked how an enemy might be resisted, he replied 'by becoming a good man oneself'. Diogenes is also useful against Sophocles, who has made myriads despair by saying about the mysteries:

> Thrice blessed they who have beheld these rites
> before they go to Hades. They alone
> live there, the rest endure infinite ill.[5]

---

[1] Fr. 534.
[3] Fr. 756.
[4] Fr. 271 Kock.
[2] Menander, fr. 611.
[5] Fr. 753.

'What?' said Diogenes, 'will the thief Pataicion be better off than Epaminondas when he dies, just because he was initiated?'[1]

p. 22   Timotheus' hymn to Artemis, performed in the theatre, contained the
words:

> maddened maenad, raving ranting.[2]

'I wish you a daughter like that!' was Cinesias' impromptu retort.
  And there is a nice answer of Bion to Theognis' lines:

> Men beaten down by need can neither talk nor do;
> their tongues are tied.[3]

It runs: 'How do you manage to talk such rubbish to us when you're a
poor man yourself?'

5   Neither must we neglect opportunities for correction which arise out
of the context or associated remarks. The cantharis is deadly, but doctors
think its feet and wings valuable, and an antidote to its poison. Similarly,
in poetry, if some noun or verb in the context takes the edge off the compulsion we feel to interpret the passage in a bad sense, we should fasten
on to it and expound its implications. This is sometimes done with the
lines:

> This is the privilege of unhappy men,
> to crop their hair and let tears fall from their cheeks;[4]

and with the lines:

> Such is the fate the gods give wretched men,
> to live in sorrow.[5]

Homer does not mean here that the gods doom all men indiscriminately to
a life of sorrow, but only the foolish and thoughtless, whom he calls
'unhappy' and 'wretched' because of the miserable and pitiable state to
which their wickedness brings them.

SOME EDUCATIONAL USES OF PHILOLOGICAL KNOWLEDGE

6 Thus there is another way of removing the suspicions attaching to a piece
of poetry, and giving a better interpretation. This is based on the normal
use of words. The young student should be exercised in this more than
in the study of what are called 'glosses'.[6] The latter is indeed a scholarly

---

[1] Diogenes points out the immorality of saying that a ritual can give a rogue a better
hereafter than a hero.   [2] Timotheus, fr. 2 Page.
  [3] Theognis 177.   [4] *Odyssey* 4. 197.   [5] *Iliad* 24. 525.
  [6] Cf. *Poetics* 1457^{b}3 ff. (above, p. 119: 'dialect terms' there translates *glōssai*, here
rendered 'glosses').

pursuit, and it is nice to know that *rhigedanos* means 'doomed to a bad death' because *danos* is the Macedonian for death, or that the Aeolians say *kammoniē* for a victory produced by patience and endurance, or that the Dryopes call their daimones *popoi*.[1] The other however is genuinely valuable and essential.

If we are to profit from poetry and not be harmed by it, it is essential to understand how the poets use the names of the gods and of good and bad, what they mean by Fortune and Fate, whether these terms in their usage are univocal or equivocal, and so on and so forth. For example, the word *oikos* sometimes means 'house':

> to the high-roofed *oikos*;[2]

and sometimes property:

> my *oikos* is being eaten up.[3]

Biotos sometimes means life:

> and dark-haired Poseidon deadened the point of his spear,
> robbing him of *biotos*;[4]

and sometimes money:

> others consume my *biotos*.[5]

Similarly, *aluein* is used sometimes for being distressed or at a loss:

> He spoke, and she went away *distressed*, and greatly hurt;[6]

and sometimes for being exultant and joyful:

> Are you on *top of yourself* because you have beaten
> the beggar Irus?[7]

Thoazein means either 'to be moved', as in Euripides:

> a monster *moving* from the Atlantic deep;[8]

or 'to sit', as in Sophocles:

> Why *sit* you thus
> garlanded with suppliants' branches?[9]

It is also a neat trick to accommodate to the subject in hand the use of words which, as we learn from the grammarians, acquire a different force in different contexts. For example:

> Praise a small ship; load your cargo on a big one.[10]

---

[1] An explanation of the Homeric exclamation 'ō popoi'.
[2] *Odyssey* 5. 42.　　　　[3] Ibid. 4. 318.　　　　[4] *Iliad* 13. 562.
[5] *Odyssey* 13. 419.　　[6] *Iliad* 5. 352.　　　[7] *Odyssey* 18. 333-393.
[8] Fr. 145.　　　　　　　　　　　　　　　　[9] *Oedipus Tyrannus* 2.
[10] Hesiod, *Works and Days* 643.

The word *ainein* normally means 'praise' (like *epainein* which we now use similarly of refusal); compare the common phrases 'that's fine!' and 'how welcome!' which we use when we do not want or do not accept p. 23 something.[1] So some say that the adjective *epainē* applied to Persephone means 'she whom we seek to avert'.

This difference and distinction in words should be carefully observed in matters of greater consequence and seriousness. The instruction of the young student may begin with the names of the gods. These are used by the poets sometimes because they are thinking of the gods themselves but sometimes because (with no change of word) they are referring to certain forces which the gods give or over which they hold sway. For example, when Archilochus says in a prayer:

> O Lord Hephaestus, hear my prayer; be favourable to me and help me; and give whatever thou dost give,[2]

he is obviously appealing to the god himself. But when, in lamenting his sister's brother, who was lost at sea and unburied, he says that he could bear the trouble more easily

> if Hephaestus had worked on his head and lovely body, wrapped in clean clothing[3]—

he means fire, not the god of fire.

Again, when Euripides says in an oath

> by Zeus amid the stars, by bloody Ares,[4]

he means the gods themselves; but when Sophocles says:

> Ladies, Ares is blind and does not see; he grubs up trouble with a pig's snout,[5]

he means war; just as Homer means 'bronze' by Ares in the line:

> Sharp Ares spilt their dark blood by Scamander.[6]

There are many such examples. We should note particularly that the poets use the name 'Zeus' sometimes for the god, sometimes for fortune, often for destiny. When they say

> O father Zeus, who rulest from Ida,[7]

or

> O Zeus, who says he is wiser than thou?[8]

they mean the god in person. But when they give the name Zeus to the

---

[1] 'Merci' in refusal is a rough parallel to this usage.
[2] Archilochus, fr. 75 Diehl..   [3] Ibid. fr. 12.   [4] *Phoenissae* 1006.   [5] Fr. 754.
[6] *Iliad* 7. 329.   [7] Ibid. 3. 276.   [8] Unknown (*trag. adesp.* 351).

causes of all events and say that the wrath of Achilles 'hurled many valiant souls to Hades . . . and the plan of Zeus was fulfilled',[1] they mean destiny. The poet does not believe that the god plots evil for man; he is giving a correct indication of the necessity inherent in events: if nations, armies, or princes behave wisely, success and victory are guaranteed them; if, like the characters in the *Iliad*, they fall into passion and error, and differ and quarrel among themselves, they are fated to make a bad showing, suffer turmoil and confusion, and come to a bad end:

> fated it is that man shall reap
> from his bad plans a bad return.[2]

And, when Hesiod makes Prometheus advise Epimetheus,

> Never accept gifts
> from Zeus of Olympus; send them away,[3]

he is using the name Zeus for the power of fortune; it is the blessings of fortune that he calls 'gifts of Zeus'—wealth, marriage, office, all external goods, the possession of which is profitless to those who cannot use them well. This is why he thinks Epimetheus, a poor foolish creature, ought to be on his guard and cautious of good fortune, because he may be harmed and ruined by it.

Again, when he says

> Do not reproach a man with dire, killing poverty:
> it is the gift of the blessed immortals,[4]

he is calling the accident of fortune the gift of the gods, and saying that it p. 24 is wrong to reproach those who are poor through bad luck; it is need accompanied by idleness, softness, and extravagance that incurs shame and reproach. The actual word 'fortune' (*tuchē*) was not yet in use;[5] but the poets were aware of the strength and—to human calculation—unpredictability of the irregularly and indeterminately moving cause, and therefore used the names of the gods to describe it—just as we use the adjectives 'supernatural' and 'divine' of events, moral qualities, speeches, and men.

Many apparently outrageous statements about Zeus are to be corrected in this manner: e.g.

> By Zeus's door stand two jars full of dooms,
> one good, one bad;[6]

---

[1] *Iliad* 1. 3.　　　　　　　　　　　　[2] Unknown (*trag. adesp.* 352).
[3] *Works and Days* 86.　　　　　　　　[4] Ibid. 717.
[5] It was common doctrine (cf. Macrob. *Sat.* 5. 16) that Homer did not speak of 'fortune', though most later poets did.
[6] Cf. Plato, *Republic* 379 d (above, p. 54); Plutarch quotes from here, not directly from *Il.* 24. 527.

and

> Zeus, enthroned on high, has not ratified the oaths;
> he wishes both sides ill . . .;[1]

and

> For then the beginning of woe rolled on
> for Trojans and Greeks, through mighty Zeus' design.[2]

These passages are about Fortune or Fate—i.e. the element in causation unamenable to our calculations and in general outside our control. But where appropriateness, reason, and probability are present, we may suppose that the god himself is meant: e.g.

> The ranks of all the others he visited,
> but he avoided the troops of Aias son of Telamon;
> for Zeus was indignant when he fought a better man;[3]

and

> In great things, Zeus takes care for men;
> the lesser he leaves to other gods.[4]

Other words also deserve attention, for they suffer changes and variations at the hands of the poets in many different situations. 'Virtue' (*aretē*) is an example. Virtue not only makes men wise, just and good in word and deed, but also commonly invests them with fame and power. Accordingly, the poets treat reputation and power as virtue (compare the names of the trees 'olive' and 'beech' homonymously for their fruit). So when the poets say

> The gods have put sweat in the way of virtue,[5]

or

> Then by their virtue the Greeks broke the phalanx,[6]

or

> If we must die, it is honourable to die thus,
> bringing life to its close in virtue.[7]

the young student should realize immediately that this is said of the noblest and most divine quality in us, which we conceive as rightness of reason, excellence of our rational nature, and a consistent habit of soul. On the other hand, when he reads

> Zeus makes men's virtue wax and wane,[8]

---

[1] *Iliad* 7. 69.   [2] *Odyssey* 8. 81.   [3] *Iliad*. 11. 540.
[4] Unknown (*trag. adesp.* 353).   [5] Hesiod, *Works and Days* 289.
[6] *Iliad* 11. 90.   [7] Euripides, fr. 994.   [8] *Iliad* 20. 242.

or
>   Virtue and glory go with wealth,[1]

he must not sit back in wonder and amazement at the rich, as though virtue were something wealth could buy, nor must he think that the increase or diminution of his own virtue depends on fortune; he must realize that the poet has used 'virtue' in the sense of reputation, power, success, or the like.[2]

Similarly, by 'evil' (*kakotēs*), they sometimes mean, in the proper sense, vice or wickedness of soul: thus Hesiod:

>   Evil you can have in abundance.[3]

But sometimes they mean non-moral damage or misfortune: e.g. Homer's

>   For men grow old quickly in evil.[4]

Similarly, it would be self-deception to think that the poets mean 'happiness' in the philosophers' sense of 'complete possession or acquisition of good things' or 'perfection of life flowing smoothly in its natural tenour'. In fact they often (by catachresis) call the rich happy or blessed, and power or reputation happiness. Homer uses the words correctly in the line   p. 25

>   So I do not reign amid this wealth in happiness;[5]

so does Menander:

>   I have much property, all call me rich;
>   but no one calls me happy.[6]

But Euripides produces great muddle and confusion when he says:

>   I never want a happy life that's painful,[7]

and

>   Why honour tyranny, happy injustice?[8]—

unless, as I said, we follow the metaphors and catachreses carefully.

POETRY MUST REPRODUCE EVIL AND CONFLICT

Young men must be shown and reminded again and again that the imita-   7
tive purpose of poetry compels it to use its ornaments and splendours in handling the events and characters of its subject without abandoning the

---

[1] Hesiod, *Works and Days* 313.
[2] The argument anticipates a point often emphasized by modern scholars, that *aretē* in early literature is hardly moral at all, and means 'success' rather than 'virtue'.
[3] Hesiod, *Works and Days* 287.   [4] *Odyssey* 19. 360.   [5] Ibid. 4. 93.
[6] Fr. 612.   [7] *Medea* 603.   [8] *Phoenissae* 552.

likeness to reality, since the attraction of imitation lies in its convincing-ness. Any imitation therefore which is not utterly neglectful of truth inevitably reproduces the marks of vice and virtue along with the actions concerned. Homer's art, for example, will have no truck with the Stoic doctrine that virtue has nothing bad attaching to it and vice nothing good, the ignorant man being in error in everything and the good man univer-sally successful. That is what we are told in the schools; in real life, as Euripides says,

> good and bad are not to be found apart;
> there is a sort of mixture.[1]

And even apart from considerations of truth, poetry prefers if possible to use varied and diversified material: emotional effect, paradox, and surprise—prime sources of both wonder and charm—are given to myth by variety, whereas simplicity lacks both emotion and poetical effect. This is why poets do not represent the same people as always victorious, prosperous, or successful. Indeed, they do not even treat the gods, when involved in human affairs, as free from passion or error. This is to safe-guard the disturbing and exciting element in poetry from lapsing through the absence of danger and conflict.

8   This being so, we must ensure, when we introduce the young student to poetry, that he is free from the prejudice that these great and noble names were necessarily wise and upright men, excellent kings, and patterns of all virtue and right conduct. He will indeed come to harm if he thinks everything splendid and gapes in awe, never feeling annoyance at anything he reads and ignoring the protests of those who find fault with actions and words like

> O father Zeus, Athena, and Apollo,
> would that no Trojan alive might escape from death,
> and no Argive either, so long as you and I
> dodge the destruction, and break, alone, the holy ring-wall
>   of Troy;[2]

or

> I heard the piteous cry of Priam's daughter, Cassandra,
> whom treacherous Clytemnestra killed beside me;[3]

or

> To lie first with the concubine, to make her loathe the old man;
> I was persuaded, and I did it;[4]

[1] Fr. 21.   [2] *Iliad* 16. 97.
[3] *Odyssey* 11. 421.   [4] *Iliad* 9. 452.

or

> Father Zeus, no god is more baleful than thou . . .[1]

The young reader must not get into the habit of praising anything of this p. 26
kind, or displaying unscrupulous persuasiveness in devising excuses and
specious evasions for bad deeds. Poetry, he must realize, is an imitation of
the manners and lives of men, who are not perfect, pure, and irreproach-
able, but involved in passions, false opinions, and ignorance—though they
often indeed improve themselves through their natural goodness. This
kind of training and attitude in a young man exalted and inspired by good
words and actions and unreceptive of, and distressed by, bad ones, will
ensure that reading does no harm. The student who admires everything
and makes it his own, and whose judgement is ensnared by the heroic
names, will inadvertently fall victim to many faults: it would be like
imitating Plato's stoop or Aristotle's lisp. There is no need to be cowardly
about it, or shiver or fall down and worship in superstitious awe; we must
accustom ourselves to commenting with confidence, and saying 'wrong'
and 'inappropriate' as often as we say 'right' and 'appropriate'.

Consider for example the conduct of Achilles. He summons an assembly
when the soldiers are ill. It is his own military distinction and reputation,
of course, that particularly make him distressed at the lull in the fighting.
But he has medical knowledge and realizes, after the ninth day (the normal
crisis period), that the disease is no ordinary one and comes from no
common cause. He rises, and, instead of making a speech to the multitude,
addresses advice to the king:

> Son of Atreus, now I think we should turn and go home . . .[2]

This is correct, decent, appropriate behaviour. But when the seer
[Calchas] says he is afraid of the anger of the most powerful of the Greeks,
Achilles no longer behaves so well; he swears that no one shall lay hands
on Calchas while he lives, and adds 'even if you mean Agamemnon'.[3]
This displays neglect and contempt of the ruler. Then he becomes even
more furious and grabs his sword with intent to murder—a wrong action
from the point of view both of honour and of expediency. His repentance
follows:

> He thrust his great sword back into the scabbard
> and did not disobey Athene's words.[4]

It is quite right and proper that, unable to eradicate his anger altogether,
he controls it and subjects it to reason before doing anything irremediable.

[1] *Iliad* 3. 365.
[2] Ibid 1. 59. Note that Plato also (above, p. 61) chooses the beginning of the *Iliad*, as
specially well known, to illustrate a point.   [3] Ibid. 90.   [4] Ibid. 220.

Or take Agamemnon. In his words and actions in the assembly he is a ridiculous figure, but in the Chryseis episode more dignified and kingly. When Briseis is dragged off, Achilles

> wept and drew aside and sat apart from his comrades,[1]

but Agamemnon puts the woman on board ship himself and hands her over, though he has not long before said that he thinks more of her than of his wife. Here is nothing shameful, no yielding to love. Note also what Phoenix says, after his father has cursed him because of the concubine:

> I planned to kill him with the sharp edge of bronze;
> but some immortal stopped my wrath, and made me think
> of what the folk would say, and all the reproaches:
> I did not want to be called my father's murderer.[2]

p. 27   Aristarchus excised these lines, alarmed by them; but they are right in the situation. Phoenix is showing Achilles what anger is like and what men dare do out of anger, unless they use their reason and listen to soothing words. Phoenix also cites Meleager as having been angry with his fellow citizens, but then pacified. He rightly finds fault with the emotion, but praises, as both honourable and expedient, Meleager's resistance, opposition, control, and repentance. In this passage, the difference is obvious. Where the intention is less clear, a distinction must be made by drawing the student's attention in some such way as the following.

If Nausicaa's remark to the maids—

> I wish I had a husband like that
> living here; I wish he wanted to stay[3]—

was made frivolously because when she saw the stranger Odysseus she felt towards him like Calypso, because she was a spoilt girl and now marriageable, then her forwardness and lack of control deserve censure; but if she perceived Odysseus' character from his words and admired his sensible conversation, and so comes to pray for a husband like that rather than one of the nautical gentlemen and good dancers of her own country— then she deserves admiration.

Again, when Penelope converses amiably with the suitors, and they give her clothes and gold and other ornaments, Odysseus is pleased

> because she took their presents and charmed their hearts.[4]

---

[1] *Iliad* 1. 349.
[2] *Iliad* 9. 458. These lines are not in our texts of Homer, which thus seems to have been 'expurgated' as Plutarch reports.
[3] *Odyssey* 6. 244.
[4] Ibid. 18. 282.

If it is her acceptance of presents and her greed that pleases him, this is living off immoral earnings to a degree worse than Poliagros in the comedy:

O happy Poliagros,
with his heavenly goat that brings in the money![1]

But if Odysseus thought he would have them more under his thumb because of their expectations—they would be confident and not see what was coming—then his pleasure and confidence are justified. Similarly with his counting the treasure the Phaeacians left with him before they sailed away. If he was really afraid for the money

for fear they had gone away with something on the ship,[2]

then indeed—given his desolate situation and the total uncertainty about his own fate—his avarice deserves pity or disgust. But if, as some say, he was uncertain whether this really was Ithaca, and thought the safe transport of the treasure an indication of the Phaeacians' good faith—they would not otherwise have kept their hands off the money if they had landed him, with no profit to themselves, in a country not his own—then he uses a perfectly sound argument, and we should commend his common sense. Some actually disapprove of his being put ashore like this, if it really happened while he was asleep. They say the Etruscans preserve a tradition that Odysseus was naturally sleepy, and bad company to most people for this reason. They approve it only if the sleep was not genuine—that is to say, if he felt ashamed to send the Phaeacians away without presents and hospitality, but was unable to conceal himself from his enemies if he had them with him, and therefore covered up his difficulty by pretending to be asleep.

If we point out these things to young people, we shall stop any tendency to deterioration of character, and encourage the pursuit and choice of the better course, because we unhesitatingly accord blame to the one and praise to the other. This is especially necessary in tragedies which contain plausible and unscrupulous speeches concerned with disreputable or immoral actions. When Sophocles says,

From evil actions good words never come,[3]

it is just not true. He himself often attaches smiling words and kind explanations to bad ways and atrocious deeds. As for his colleague [Euripides], you know how *he* makes Phaedra actually reproach Theseus p. 28 as though it was because of his infidelities that she has fallen in love

---

[1] Unknown (*com. adesp.* 8 Kock).   [2] *Odyssey* 13. 216.   [3] Fr. 755.

with Hippolytus;[1] and we have another example in the language assigned to Helen about Hecuba in the *Trojan Women*, where she decides that it is Hecuba who really should be punished, because she was the adulterer's mother! The young student must beware of thinking this neat or smart. He must not smile indulgently at the ingenuity. The words of vice should be more detestable to him even than the deeds!

It is thus always useful to inquire into the reason for what is said. Cato as a child used always to do what his attendant told him—but he always asked why. There is no need to listen to poets as though they were lawgivers or tutors unless their subject stands up to examination—which it will if it is good. If it is bad, it will be seen as vain and futile. Now many people inquire acutely into the rationale and significance of lines like

> And not to put the pourer above the bowl
> while they are drinking;[2]

or

> The man who can reach another chariot from his own
> must thrust with his spear.[3]

But they accept without question dicta on graver matters:

> It enslaves a man, however bold he is,
> to know a mother's or father's evil deeds;[4]

and

> he who fares badly should have lowly thoughts.[5]

Yet these sayings touch the character and cause confusion in life, because they produce bad decisions and unworthy opinions, unless we accustom ourselves always to ask *why* the man who fares badly should have lowly thoughts, instead of resisting fortune and raising himself above humiliation. And why, if I am the son of a bad, foolish father, but myself decent and sensible, should I not be proud of my good character? Must I be humbled and cast down because of my father's stupidity? If you react and resist like this, instead of bowing to every word as to a gust of wind, and if you remember that 'it is a lazy man who takes fright at everything that is said', you will soon be free of many of these false and unhelpful statements.

So much for the ways of ensuring that reading poetry does no harm.

---

[1] Not in the extant version of *Hippolytus*: see W. S. Barrett, *Euripides: Hippolytus*, Oxford, 1964, p. 18.

[2] Hesiod, *Works and Days* 744.

[3] *Iliad* 4. 306.

[4] Euripides, *Hippolytus* 424.

[5] Euripides, fr. 957.

C. COMPARISON OF ARISTOPHANES AND MENANDER

This is an epitome: i.e. we possess only an abridgement, made up partly of Plutarch's own words and partly of connecting summaries. Plutarch's preference for the more polished writer is interesting; his appreciation of Aristophanes is less than that of the second-century archaists who followed him.—*Moralia* 853 a ff., Loeb, vol. x.

In general, Plutarch greatly prefers Menander. His detailed argument is 853 as follows.

Coarseness, vulgarity, and triviality of language are to be found in Aristophanes, but not in Menander. Aristophanes' style captivates the ordinary, uneducated reader for whom he writes, but disgusts the educated. This is due to its antitheses, rhymes, and puns. Menander thinks such tricks need careful handling, and employs them sparingly and with due thought. Aristophanes has them often, with no regard to occasion, and with a frigid effect.

[Examples of puns follow.]

Aristophanes' vocabulary, then, shows many contradictions and inequalities: a tragic element and a comic; the pretentious and the prosaic; the obscure and the commonplace; grandeur and elevation; vulgar garrulity and nauseating nonsense. Despite this, his style fails even to assign appropriate and suitable language to individual characters— grandeur to a king, cleverness to an orator, simplicity to a woman, prosaic words to an ordinary man, vulgarity to a street-lounger. Instead, it puts any words in the mouth of any character, as though out of a hat. You can't tell if it's a son talking or a father, a farmer or a god, an old woman or a hero.[1]

Menander's language, on the other hand, is so polished and its constituents so harmoniously united that, despite the varied emotions and characters involved and the fact that it has to suit all kinds of personages, it gives a single impression and maintains its uniformity by means of common, everyday words that are in normal use. Should the action however demand something fanciful or impressive, he opens all the stops of his instrument, as it were, and then quickly and convincingly closes them again and restores the tone to its usual quality. Of all the famous craftsmen there have been, no cobbler has made a shoe, no costumier

[1] Cf. Horace, *The Art of Poetry*, 114 ff. (above, p. 282).

a mask, no tailor a cloak, that would fit at the same time a man, a woman, a boy, an old man, and a household slave. Yet Menander has so contrived his language as to make it appropriate to every nature, disposition, and period of life. And he did this though he began young and died at the height of his productive career—at the age when, according to Aristotle, writers make most progress in style. A comparison between Menander's first plays and those of his middle and late period would show what fresh achievements he would have added had he lived.[1]

Some playwrights compose for the multitude and the common people, some for the few. To find one whose manner suited both factions is difficult. Aristophanes satisfies neither the many nor the intelligent. His poetry is like a retired prostitute who pretends to be a married woman. Ordinary folk find its wilfulness intolerable; those who pretend to taste are disgusted by the licence and the malice. Menander on the other hand, as well as having charm, never needs anything outside his own powers. In the theatre, the lecture-room, the dinner-party, his poetry provides reading, study, and entertainment for a wider public than that commanded by any other Greek masterpiece. He shows what mastery of language really is. He approaches every point with inescapable persuasiveness, and has under control every resource of sound and meaning that Greek affords. What good reason has an educated man for going to the theatre, except to see Menander? What else fills the theatres with learned men, when a comic character takes the stage? To whom should the dinner-table yield place and Bacchus give way more rightfully? Just as painters, when their eyes are tired, turn to the colours of grass and flowers, so Menander is a rest for philosophers and students from their unrelieved and intense pursuits; he invites the mind to a flowery and shady meadow, fanned by breezes . . .

Athens produced many good comic actors at the time . . . Menander's comedies have the salt of abundant, cheerful wit, derived, one might imagine, from the same sea whence Aphrodite sprang. Aristophanes' saltiness, on the other hand, is rough and bitter, with a sharpness to sting and inflame. Where his reputed ingenuity lies, in speeches or characters, I have no notion. Whatever he imitates he makes worse; smartness becomes malice instead of urbanity, rusticity becomes silliness instead of simplicity, humour is not amusing but absurd, love not joyous but indecent. He seems not to have written his poetry for respectable people at all; the impropriety and indecency appear to be intended for the licentious, the invective and bitterness for the spiteful and malicious.

---

[1] The idea that authors make progress between their earlier and later works is to be noted: it is unusual in ancient thinking.

D. ON READING COMEDY AT DINNER

We give a brief extract (711 f–712 d) from Plutarch's *Table Talk* (*Quaestiones Convivales* 7. 8. 4–10, Loeb *Moralia*, vol. ix).

Old Comedy is unsuitable for drinkers because of its unevenness. The seriousness and outspokenness of what are called the 'parabases'[1] are too unrelieved and intense, while the tendency to jests and buffoonery is altogether excessive and unrestrained, and improper expressions and indecent words abound. Moreover, just as at princely dinners every guest has his own wine waiter, so every reader needs his own grammarian to explain all the details . . . so that the party becomes a class-room, or else the jokes go by ineffectively and without significance.

But to New Comedy there can be no possible objection. It is so closely associated with drinking that one might as well do without the wine as without Menander in arranging the party. The plot is dressed in pleasing, pedestrian language, such that the sober will not despise it nor the drunk take annoyance; useful and simple maxims, slipping in quietly, incline even the toughest characters to better ways and soften the heart, using the wine as a melting fire. Moreover, the combination of seriousness and fun might have been invented on purpose to amuse and do good to persons who have taken drink and are relaxed. The love interest also is appropriate for men who have drunk and are shortly going to join their wives in bed.[2] In all his plays, there is no homosexual love, and the seductions of virgins end decently in marriage. As for the prostitutes, if they are bold and forward, the affair is checked by punishment or repentance in the young man; if they are good and return the hero's love, either a proper father is discovered for the girl or the affair is prolonged by a period which brings a humane relationship of respect. In ordinary life, all this is perhaps not worth attention; but in drinking the pleasure and elegance of these plays may well have an educational effect that helps to mould the character in the likeness of the kindness and humanity they represent.

[1] i.e. the addresses and songs given by the chorus, often used for discussions of politics and personalities.
[2] Cf. Xenophon, *Symposium* 9. 7.

13

TWO CRITICS OF HISTORY

Ancient historians often criticize one another; Thucydides attacks Herodotus by implication (1. 22), Polybius openly criticizes Timaeus and other predecessors (Book 12). The following extracts however are not from historians. Plutarch's *The Malice of Herodotus* (*Moralia* 854 ff., Loeb vol. xii) is an ingenious essay motivated by rather unreal indignation. Plutarch was a Boeotian, Herodotus had failed to conceal the pro-Persian sympathies of the Boeotians in the great Persian war. We give only the first few sections, which deal with more general matters and contain revealing hints on the aims and methods of historians.

Cf. also Cicero's remarks on history, above, pp. 255 ff.

A. MALICE IN HISTORY

My dear Alexander,[1]
Herodotus' simple style, the effortless and facile veneer which covers his facts, has deceived many. Even more have been taken in by his personality. Plato says that it is the utmost unrighteousness to seem righteous when you are not.[2] It is also true that it is the deepest malice to mimic good temper and simplicity in a way hard to detect.

Though Herodotus spares no one, he shows his malice most towards the Boeotians and Corinthians. So it is our natural duty to refute him in defence both of our ancestors and of the truth, in this aspect of his work. To enumerate all his lies and fictions would need a library.

Terrible is the face of Persuasion,

said Sophocles.[3] This is especially true when a style of charm and power makes it possible to conceal the writer's eccentricities and nature. Philip told the Greeks who were deserting him and going over to Flamininus that they were getting a smoother collar, but a heavier one.[4] Herodotus' malice is smoother and softer than Theopompus', but it grips and hurts more—like a wind forced through a narrow passage compared with a wind in the open.

My best plan, I think, is to make a general outline of the common footprints and recognition-tokens, as it were, of disingenuous and hostile

---

[1] The addressee is a friend, but cannot be identified for certain.
[2] *Republic* 2, 361 a.   [3] Fr. 781 Nauck.
[4] Cf. Plutarch's *Life of Flamininus* 10 for a version of this story.

narrative. I shall then classify the individual passages under these head-ings, if they fit.

(i) A writer is unkind if he uses hard words and expressions where more moderate ones are available: e.g. calling Nicias a fanatic, instead of 'too much inclined to religious observance',[1] or speaking of Cleon's 'rashness and lunacy' instead of his 'frivolity'.[2] This is to get a kick out of the facts by a lively description.

(ii) When there is some discreditable circumstance not relevant to the history, and the writer seizes on it and foists it on to a context where it is not needed, expanding and complicating the story to include someone's misfortune or eccentric or evil action, here too he is plainly taking pleasure in speaking ill. Though Cleon had abundant faults, Thucydides nowhere clearly expounds them. He only has a single word for the demagogue Hyperbolus—'a worthless character', he says,[3] and lets it go at that. Philistus in fact left out all the crimes committed by Dionysius against non-Greeks unless they were closely connected with Greek events.

Digressions and excursuses in history are usually devoted to myth and prehistory, and also to encomia; to use a digression for abuse and censure is to fall victim to the tragedian's curse,

picking out the disasters from human life.[4]

(iii) This, as is self-evident, is the opposite of the omission of the good and honourable. People think this feature unobjectionable, but it is a characteristic of malice, if the omission belongs to a topic relevant to the history. Grudging praise is no fairer than enthusiastic blame; indeed, it may be worse.

(iv) Another mark of unkindness in history is the choice of the less creditable version when there are two or more available accounts of the same event. Sophists are allowed, for professional reasons or for reputa-tion, to take the worse cause sometimes and dress it up; they are not trying to produce powerful conviction, and do not deny that they often make paradoxical statements in incredible causes. The historian does his duty if he states as true what he knows, and in cases of doubt says that the more creditable story seems to him to be true. Many omit the less creditable altogether. Ephorus, after saying that Themistocles knew of Pausanias' treason and of his negotiations with the king's generals, continues: 'He was not convinced, however, and would not join him, although Pausanias communicated the plan to him and encouraged him to share his own hopes.'[5] Thucydides simply leaves out this story, implying that he rejected it.

[1] Thuc. 7. 50.   [2] Ibid. 4. 28.   [3] Ibid. 8. 73.
[4] Unknown (*trag. adesp.* 388 Nauck).   [5] Fr. 189 Jacoby.

(v) Where the facts are established, but the motives and intentions obscure, it is unkind and malicious to make the worse conjecture—as the comic poets do when they say that Pericles fanned the war because of Aspasia or Phidias,[1] not out of an honourable ambition to put down the pride of the Peloponnesians and not yield to Sparta in anything. It is obvious that there is extreme jealousy and malice in the man who assigns bad reasons to famous deeds and laudable actions and is led on by his slanders to weird suspicions about unseen motives, because he cannot find fault with the overt act. This is exemplified by those who attribute the murder of the tyrant Alexander by Thebe to feminine jealousy and passion rather than to a noble heart and a hatred of evil; or again by those who say that Cato killed himself because he was afraid of a horrible death at the hands of Caesar.[2]

(vi) A historical narrative also admits malice in the actual manner of the deed, e.g. if it is said to have been done (*a*) for money and not for virtue's sake, as some say of Philip, (*b*) without trouble or difficulty, as some say of Alexander, (*c*) by luck not judgement, as some say of Timotheus, when they paint pictures of the cities going into the trap while he was asleep.[3] Writers who deny the moral worth, effort, excellence, and personal responsibility in actions obviously detract from their greatness and nobility.

(vii) Persons who openly abuse those they want to attack can properly be charged with bad temper, rashness, and madness if they show no restraint; those who shoot their arrows of slander from under cover, as it were, and then turn about and retreat, saying they do not believe what they very much want *us* to believe, earn the reproach of meanness as well as that of the malice they are trying to deny.

(viii) Juxtaposing praise and blame leads to the same sort of result. Aristoxenus, for instance, after saying of Socrates that he was uneducated, ignorant, and licentious, added, 'but there was no injustice in him'. Malice inserts praise in advance to lend credit to its accusations in the same way that flattery of skill and ingenuity sometimes mix some mild censure in with all their long praises, making frankness, as it were, a sauce to flattery.

B. *HOW TO WRITE HISTORY*

How to Write History, from which the following excerpts are taken is light in tone and in intention; but it is one of the more illuminating extant texts on

---

[1] For such stories cf. Aristoph. *Acharnians* 523 ff., and Plutarch, *Pericles* 24, 30–2.
[2] For Cato's heroism, see Plutarch's *Life*, esp. 72.
[3] Cf. Plutarch, *Sulla* 6.

historiography. Written about A.D. 165, it satirizes some contemporary archaists, who wrote about the Parthian wars with all the mannerisms of Herodotus and Thucydides. Lucian clearly draws on textbooks; but his debt to Thucydides Book 1 cannot be missed.—Loeb Lucian, vol. vi; Grube 336–8; text with commentary by H. Homeyer, Munich, 1965.

I. HISTORY, POETRY, AND PANEGYRIC
(§§ 6 13)

Advice has a double function: it teaches us to choose some courses and 6 to avoid others. Let us first explain what a historian must avoid, and from what faults he must be free. Then we may consider what means he should adopt to be sure of striking the right, direct path. We shall say then what kind of beginning he needs, what order he should impose on events, the limits of each subject, what is best passed in silence and what deserves to be dwelt on, what should be hurried over, and how it all ought to be put into words and the words put together. Postponing these issues for the moment, let us deal first with the vices incident to bad historians.

It would be a lengthy task, and not germane to the issue, to enumerate the general faults common to all literature—faults of language, word-order, thought, and technical inadequacy of other kinds. These are, as I 7 said, common to all literature. The faults of history you will discover to be what I have often thought them when I have myself been listening to historians—especially if you open your ears to them all. It will not be out of place to mention incidentally, *exempli gratia*, some existing works.

The first error to consider is a serious one. It is that many writers neglect research into facts and dwell instead on the praises of rulers and generals. They magnify the merits of their own men, and unduly disparage the enemy's. They do not see that the isthmus that divides history from encomium is no narrow strip. There is a great wall built between them. To use a musicians' phrase, they are two whole octaves apart. The encomiast is concerned with one thing only—to praise and gladden his subject by any and every means. If he has to lie to achieve his end, it doesn't much worry him. History, on the other hand, cannot tolerate the least fragment of untruth—any more than the windpipe, or so the doctors tell us, tolerates objects that enter it when swallowed.

Secondly: these people seem to be ignorant of the distinction between 8 the professions and rules of poetry and poems on the one hand, and of history on the other. Poetry enjoys unqualified freedom. Its sole law is the poet's will. He is possessed and inspired by the Muses. If he wants to harness a team of winged horses, or make people run on water or over the top of the corn, nobody complains. When the poets' Zeus suspends earth and sea from a single chain and swings it around, people aren't afraid of the chain breaking and the universe crashing to destruction.[1] If they want to praise Agamemnon, there is no one to prevent them saying his head and eyes are like Zeus, his chest like Zeus' brother Poseidon, his belt like Ares; the son of Atreus and Aërope, in fact, has to be a compound of all the gods, because no one of them alone, Zeus or Poseidon or Ares, suffices to fill the demands of his beauty. If history admits any flattery of this sort, it becomes a sort of prose poetry.[2] Without the grandiloquence of poetry, it presents all its monstrosities in an unmetrical form, and thus more conspicuously. It is a great, indeed an enormous mistake not to understand the distinction between poetry and history, but to try to introduce into the latter the embellishments of the former—fable, encomia, and all their exaggerations. It is as if one were to take some very tough, rugged athlete, dress him up in pink, and all the gear of a high-class prostitute, and rub red and white on his face. What a hideous and ridiculous figure he would cut in his finery!

9   I don't say one ought never to praise anyone in history. But it must be done in season, and within limits determined by the need to avoid wearying readers in the future. The future, indeed, must be the guiding consideration in these matters, as I shall demonstrate shortly.

Those who divide history into two—the element of pleasure and the element of utility—and thereby find a home for encomium as giving the reader pleasure and delight, are definitely on the wrong track. For one thing, their division is unsound. History has one function and one goal—utility; and this is achieved only by truth. It is indeed better if pleasure is added thereto—just as it is a good thing for an athlete to possess beauty, but if he doesn't—well, there will be nothing to prevent Nicostratus son of Isidotus, a grand fellow and stronger than both his adversaries, from becoming 'successor to Heracles' despite his hideous ugliness, and despite the fact that one adversary was the beautiful Alcaeus of Miletus—whom, they said, Nicostratus was himself in love with. Similarly history, if she has a side-line in pleasure, will attract many lovers; but so long as she maintains with integrity her own single special function of disclosing the truth, she will not have to bother much about good looks.

10   There is more to be said. In history, anything really fictional does not even give pleasure; while any element of encomium is obnoxious to the reader, whichever way it goes—if you are thinking, that is, not of the

[1] *Iliad* 8. 19 ff.
[2] *pezē poiētikē* (cf. Lat. *pedestris*). For another view of the relation of poetry and history see Quint. 10. 1. 31 (above, p. 385).

common mob but of those who will listen judiciously or even with malevolence. Nothing will escape these people. They see sharper than Argus, and have eyes all over. They weigh up every sentence with the precision of a money-changer, so as to reject the counterfeit and accept only the true, lawful currency, with its proper mark. This is the audience to have in your mind's eye when you write history. Never mind about the rest, even if they hurst themselves with praise. If you neglect the real critics and season your history too highly with fables and encomia and such flattering stuff, you will soon make it look like Heracles in Lydia. You must have seen pictures of Heracles as Omphale's slave, got up in a very peculiar manner. Omphale wears the lion's skin and wields the club, pretending to be Heracles. The hero himself is in saffron and purple, carding wool, and Omphale is beating him with her shoe. Worst of all, the clothes hang on him loosely, and don't fit well. In fact, that masculine deity is very thoroughly and shockingly unmanned.

Still, the majority may very well commend you for this. Only the few 11 whom you despise will have a good laugh, when they see how unorganized, unharmonious, and badly stuck together it all is. Everything has its own appropriate beauty. Change this, and the change of use destroys the beautiful effect.

I say nothing of the fact that praise pleases, at most, one person, its subject, but is disagreeable to everyone else—especially if it is violently exaggerated: and this is what usually happens, thanks to the common habit of pursuing the subject's good will and dwelling on the theme until the flattery is patent to all. They do not even know how to do it according to the rules. They make no attempt to conceal their sycophancy; they just fall to with a will, and produce a great mass of blatant implausibilities.

Consequently, they fail to achieve their main object. The subjects of 12 their praises, especially if they are men of a spirited cast of mind, come to dislike and despise them as flatterers. Aristobulus once composed an account of a duel between Alexander and Porus. He made a particular point of reading this passage aloud, because he thought he would give the king great pleasure by inventing heroic actions for him and attributing to him imaginary deeds far in excess of the truth. Alexander however seized the book—they were sailing on the Hydaspes—and threw it straight into the water. 'And that's what I ought to do to you, Aristobulus', he said, 'for the duels you fight on my behalf, and the elephants you kill with a single spear.' It was entirely natural that Alexander should be angry. He had no use either for the audacity of the architect who promised to turn Mount Athos into a statue of him, and re-shape the mountain to the likeness of the king. He recognized the man at once for the flatterer

13 he was, and stopped employing him. So where is the pleasure in all this, except for anyone foolish enough to enjoy praises which can be refuted out of hand? Ugly men—and especially women—who tell painters to paint them as pretty as possible are like this. They think they will actually look better if the painter gives them more rosy colour, and mixes plenty of white in his paints. Many historians behave like this, watching the present moment and their own interest and the profit they expect out of their history. They deserve dislike; so far as the present moment is concerned, they are blatant and unskilful flatterers, while they make their whole enterprise suspect in the eyes of posterity by their exaggerations.

And if you think pleasure an indispensable element in history—well, there are pleasures to be found in other kinds of literary refinement which are not incompatible with truth. Yet most historians neglect them in favour of quite unsuitable insertions.

2. THE IDEAL HISTORIAN AND HIS WORK
(§§ 34-64)

34 The best historian, then, must come already equipped with two vital qualifications: political understanding and power of expression. The first of these is a gift of nature that comes untaught. The second he should have acquired by long practice, continuous effort, and imitation of the ancients. These are not matters of art, and no advice is needed from me. My book does not claim to make people quick and intelligent if they are not so by nature. If it *could* bring about such a transformation, turn lead into gold, tin into silver, Conon into Titormus, or Leotrophides into Milo,[1] it would be beyond price!

35 Then what is the use of technique and advice? Not in producing qualities, but in the proper use of those there are. Iccus, Herodicus, Theon, and the other trainers would never guarantee to take Perdiccas—if indeed it was he, and not Antiochus the son of Seleucus, who fell in love with his stepmother and wasted away to a skeleton[2]—and turn him into an Olympic victor or a fit rival for Theagenes of Thasos or Polydamas of Scotussa! What they do promise is to take good material for gymnastics and make it much better by art. We do not claim to turn *anyone* into a historian. We do claim to indicate to the naturally intelligent who are well trained in literature certain correct methods—if they *are* judged correct—the use of which will give a quicker and easier road to the goal.

36 Of course, the intelligent man also needs technical instruction where he is

[1] i.e. small, weak men into strong giants.
[2] A romance of Hellenistic history: see, e.g., Plutarch, *Demetrius* 38.

ignorant. If he didn't, he would be able to play the lyre or the *aulos*,[1] or do anything else, without learning—whereas, in fact, he can't do any of these things if he hasn't learnt, though if he were only shown the way he could learn easily enough and manage quite well for himself.

What we want, then, is a pupil of good abilities in understanding and 37 expression, a sharp-eyed fellow, the sort who could manage affairs if they were put into his hands. He should have a soldier's understanding, as well as a civilian's, and experience in command. He ought to have been in an army camp at some time, and observed soldiers exercise or drill. He should be acquainted with arms and machines, and understand what is meant by 'in column' and 'in line', how companies and cavalry operate[2] . . ., what is meant by 'moving off' and 'moving round'. He mustn't be a stay-at-home or the sort of man to take what he's told on trust. Above all, he must be independent-minded, and neither fear anyone 38 nor hope for anything. If he does, he will be like a bad judge who sells decisions out of favour or malice. He must not be upset by Philip's having his eye shot out at Olynthus by the Amphipolitan archer, Aster; Philip must be shown as he is. He must not be troubled either if Alexander is bound to be angry at a straight description of his brutal murder of Clitus at dinner. Cleon's power in the assembly and domination of the rostrum must not deter him from saying that the man was a ruinous lunatic. The whole Athenian nation must not deter him, if he is relating the Sicilian disaster, the capture of Demosthenes, and the death of Nicias, with the details of how thirsty they were, what the water they drank was like, and how many of them were killed drinking.[3] He will realize, and rightly, that no rational person will blame him for relating foolish or unhappy actions as they occurred. After all, he only reports them, he doesn't cause them. If the fleet is beaten, he didn't sink the ships. If the army is routed, he's not the pursuer—unless he forgot to say his prayers as he should! If silence or contradiction could have put things right, it would have been easy for Thucydides, with a stroke of the pen, to demolish the cross-wall at Epipolae, sink Hermocrates' trireme, send a spear through the wretched Gylippus while he was still building the wall and digging ditches across the roads, and finally throw the Syracusans into the quarries, while securing all Sicily and Italy for Athens in accordance with Alcibiades' original hopes. But of course what is once done Clotho cannot unravel nor Atropos reverse.

[1] Cf. above, p. 497.
[2] Text uncertain.
[3] The last three examples come from Thucydides: 3. 36 etc. for Cleon; 7. 57 ff. for the Sicilian disaster; 7. 84, for the drinking water (cf. 'Longinus' 38. 3, above, p. 496).

39   The one function of the historian, then, is to relate things as they happened. He cannot do this if he is Artaxerxes' doctor [1] and therefore afraid of him, or if he is hoping for a red tunic, a gold necklace, and a Nisaean horse as the reward of his praises. Honest Xenophon won't do that. Nor will Thucydides; even if he dislikes people for private reasons, he will put the public interest far higher, and think truth more important than his personal feud. If he has a friend, he will nevertheless not refrain from criticism. This, as I said, is the one special feature of history. Truth is the only goddess to whom the potential historian has to sacrifice; he need not trouble with anything else. His single criterion, his one exact standard, is to bear in mind not his present hearers, but his future readers.

40   Slaves of this day and age are properly counted as flatterers, and this is something that history has rejected from the very beginning—just as athletes reject beauticians. There is a remark attributed to Alexander which is to the point: 'Onesicritus,' he said, 'I should have liked to come back to life for a bit after dying, so as to find out how people are reading this story then. Don't be surprised if they praise and welcome it now; they imagine such an attitude will be a considerable bait to attract my goodwill.'[2] Homer, of course, writes what is for the most part fable; but some people have been induced to believe what he says about Achilles, simply on the ground that he was not writing about a living person; they cannot find any reason why he should have lied.

41   This then is the historian I want—fearless, incorruptible, free, the friend of truth and plain speaking. Let him, as the comic poet says, call a fig a fig, a tub a tub. Let him give nothing to hatred or friendship; unsparing, unpitying, neither ashamed nor shy, he should be an equal judge, fair to all, but giving none more than his due. In his books, he should be a stranger and a stateless person, independent, subject to no ruler, not calculating what so-and-so will think, but reporting what was done. Thucydides laid down these rules definitively, distinguishing the

42   good from the bad in history with great wisdom. He saw that Herodotus was particularly admired—to the extent indeed that his books were called Muses. So Thucydides describes his own writing as a possession for all time, not an exhibition-piece for the moment.[3] He does not welcome fable, but bequeaths to posterity a true account of events. He introduces also an argument from utility, and defines the purpose of history in a very

---

[1] Ctesias, a Greek doctor at the court of Artaxerxes II, who saw the revolt of Cyrus from the other side. His work on Persian history is known from long extracts in Photius, and was attractive and romantic.

[2] Onesicritus of Astypalaea wrote a moralizing (Cynic) history of Alexander not long after the events.

[3] Thuc. I. 22.

sensible way: 'if the same sort of thing happens again', he says, 'people will be able to handle their problems better by referring to the record of the past.'

The style of the historian

So much for our potential historian's attitude of mind. I turn next to his 43 language and force of style.

There is no need for him to sharpen his teeth to proficiency in the vehement, cutting style of close-packed periods and intricate arguments, or indeed in rhetorical force (*deinotēs*) of any kind. He needs a more peaceful disposition. His thought should be orderly and concise, his diction clear and business-like, calculated to express the subject with the utmost clarity. As we proposed outspokenness and truth as the his- 44 torian's aims in terms of his outlook, so, as to his language, his one primary aim is the clear expression and plain description of fact, not in recondite or out-of-the-way words, nor yet in common or vulgar ones, but in such terms as the masses will comprehend and the learned approve. Ornament should be restricted to unobjectionable and unaffected figures. Other- wise, the style will be a hotch-potch.

The thought must have some community and affinity with poetry, 45 which, like history, has grandeur and elevation. This is especially so when it is involved in military confrontations, battles, and naval engage- ments. Then we need a poetical breeze to carry the boat forward and drive her high on the crest of the waves. The language however must keep its feet on the ground. It will rise in keeping with the splendour and grandeur of the story, reflecting this as closely as possible; but it will not be outlandish or extravagant, because there would then be a great risk of its being swept away into a sort of poetic frenzy. This is where the curb is needed, and where you must really be careful. Literature is subject to the staggers, like a horse, and this is a serious complaint. Better let your thoughts ride, and your style follow on foot, catching hold of the saddle- flap so as not to be left behind.

Word-arrangement [1] should be controlled and moderate: not too much 46 separation and distinctness, for that gives a rough effect, nor yet the almost completely rhythmical continuity that many writers adopt; this is as much a fault as the other is disagreeable.

A historian must not be careless about the collection of facts. He must 47 investigate the same matters over and over again, with pain and effort. If he can, he should go to the site, and see with his own eyes. If this is impossible, he must pay attention to the most impartial informants,

---

[1] *Sunthesis.* Cf. Dionysius' general account, above, pp. 321 ff.

those whom he thinks least likely to add to or subtract from the facts out of favour or prejudice. At this stage, he has to be capable of conjecturing and putting together the most plausible account.

48 Having collected all or most of his material, let him first construct an aide-mémoire (*hupomnēma*) out of it, and compose a text as yet unbeautified and unarticulated. He can then add the order and the ornament, colour it with language, give it figures and rhythm.

49 Let him make himself like Zeus in Homer, who looks one moment at the land of thė mare-milking Thracians, and the next moment at Mysia;[1] similarly, the historian should one moment look at *our* situation, and expound it to us as it seems to him from his lofty look-out, and the next moment do the same for the Persians; then, if there is a battle, he should put the two together. In the battle itself, he ought not to look exclusively at one area or one man on horse or on foot, unless there is a Brasidas leaping ashore, or a Demosthenes cutting away the landing gangway.[2] He must first keep his eye on the generals; he must have heard their exhortations and know the nature and intention of their dispositions. When the armies engage, let both be in his view; he has to weigh events 50 in the balance, and join in both pursuit and flight. All this must be subject to a limit; he mustn't go on till satiety is reached, or in a tasteless or immature fashion. Let him leave the scene without embarrassment. If need be, he can halt one set of events and pass to another, to return later when required. He should always be in a hurry, and must do his best to be in two places at once, flying from Armenia to Media, and then with a flap of his wings to Iberia and on to Italy, so as never to miss an 51 important event.[3] His mind should be like a mirror, clean, polished, accurately centred, reproducing the shapes of things exactly as it receives them, without any distortion or perversion of colour or form. Historians are not like orators. What they have to say exists, and *will* be said, because it has really happened. All that is needed is arrangement and expression. Historians therefore have to consider not what to say, but how to say it. We should conceive of them as in the same position as artists like Phidias or Praxiteles or Alcamenes. These did not make the gold, silver, ivory, and other materials; they were there already, provided by Elis or Athens or Argos. The sculptors only shaped and sawed the ivory, smoothed and glued and moulded and plated with gold. Their art consisted in managing the material for the purposes required. Well, that is also the historian's position. He has to organize his facts skilfully,

---

[1] *Iliad* 13. 4 ff.   [2] Thuc. 4. 12.
[3] Lucian envisages the situation of the Parthian wars: so Iberia is probably the Caucasian country, not Spain. Tacitus' *Annals* is a good illustration of the type of history of which Lucian is thinking.

and express them as vividly as he can. If the hearer then imagines he can see the events happen, and praises this, the work of our historical Phidias has reached its consummation and won its due meed of praise.

Prooemia

His preparations complete, the historian will begin without a formal 52 prooemium, unless the subject really demands preliminary treatment in the introduction. In effect, however, the statement of the projected subject will amount to a prooemium. When there is a formal prologue, the his- 53 torian will have two objects in mind, not three like an orator: he will omit the appeal to goodwill, while ensuring his readers' attention and ease of understanding. Attention will be secured if it is made clear that the subject is important, essential, close to home, or of practical utility. Clarity and ease of comprehension are given by explaining causes and defining the main heads of events. The best historians have always used this sort of 54 introduction. Herodotus' aim was 'that great and wonderful events be not forgotten in time, revealing as they do Greek victories and barbarian defeats'. Thucydides 'expected the war to be great and famous and more important than any that went before'—and great indeed were the events that befell in it.

Narrative

After the prooemium, long or short according to the subject, let there be a 55 smooth and easy transition to the narrative. *All* the rest of the history is a long narrative.[1] So let it have narrative excellences to adorn it, advancing smoothly and evenly, with nothing obtruding and nothing lying in the background. A studied clarity should mark both the diction, as I said above, and the connections of the facts. Everything should be finished and polished. Only when the first point has been completed should it lead on to the next, which should be, as it were, the next link of the chain. There must be no sharp break, no multiplicity of juxtaposed narratives. One thing should not only lie adjacent to the next, but be related to it and overlap it at the edges.

Rapidity is always useful, especially if there is a lot of material. It is 56 secured not so much by words and phrases as by the treatment of the subject. That is, you should pass quickly over the trivial and unnecessary, and develop the significant points at adequate length. Much should be

---

[1] In a speech, narrative occupies a place normally between prooemium and proofs and argumentation; Lucian treats history as a special kind of rhetorical composition which is only prooemium and narrative.

omitted. After all, if you are giving a dinner to your friends and every-thing is ready, you don't put salt fish and porridge on the table in the midst of the cakes, poultry, entrées, wild boar, hare, and choice cuts of fish, simply because they are ready too! You forget the cheaper articles altogether.

Descriptions

57 Moderation is especially necessary in descriptions of mountains, forts, and rivers. You mustn't give the impression of a tasteless display of virtuosity or of neglecting the history to show off your own talents. Just add a few necessary details for clarity's sake, and then pass on. Avoid the snares of the subject, keep off the dainty fare. Homer, the sublime, is a model for you: poet as he is, he passes quickly over Tantalos, Ixion, Tityos, and the rest. If Parthenius or Euphorion or Callimachus had been responsible, how many lines do you think it would have taken to get the water to Tantalus' lips or make Ixion revolve?[1] Or—better—think of the way Thucydides uses this manner for a little, and then quickly abandons it, after describing a machine or explaining the plan of a siege, if it's essential information—e.g. the plan of Epipolae or the harbour of Syracuse. His narrative of the plague[2] may seem long-winded; but con-sider the facts, and you will soon appreciate his rapidity and see how the multifarious details grip and detain him despite his haste.

Speeches, encomia, invective, myths

58 If you have to introduce a character making a speech, let the content of it be, first, suitable to the speaker and the situation, secondly (like the rest of the book) as lucid as possible—though you do indeed have licence to be rhetorical here and to demonstrate your stylistic ingenuity (deinotēs).

59   Encomia and invectives should be sparing, circumspect, honest, well-argued, rapid, and opportune. After all, your characters are not in court. You don't want to find yourself liable to the same criticism as Theo-pompus, who condemns most of his personages with real malice and makes a regular business of it, acting as prosecutor rather than historian.

60   Relevant myths should be narrated, but you should not commit your-self to the truth of them; leave that to the reader. Take no risks, come down on neither side.

---

[1] Note the disparaging reference to the great Alexandrian poets.
[2] 2. 47 ff., much imitated—cf. Procopius, Wars 2. 22 ff. on the plague of A.D. 542.

Posterity is the historian's judge

Remember, in general, my refrain: don't write with your eyes only on 61
the present, for your contemporaries to praise and honour you; make all
eternity your goal, write for posterity, ask the future to reward your
writing, so that it can be said of you, 'He was a free man, outspoken,
there was no flattery or subservience in him, he was always for the truth.'
A wise man would rate such a testimonial above all the ephemeral
ambitions of the present.[1]

Remember what the Cnidian architect did? He built the tower of Pha- 62
ros, that grandest and loveliest of buildings, to house a fire-signal for
sailors far out at sea, to save them from being wrecked on Paraetonia—a
terrible and fatal coast, they say, if you run on the reefs. And having
built it, he inscribed his own name on the stones inside, and then plastered
them over and inscribed on the outside the name of the reigning monarch.
He knew—and so it turned out—that the outside inscription would be 63
worn away with the plaster, and instead would appear the words:

> Sostratus, son of Dexiphanes, of Cnidus,
> to the preserving Gods,
> for men who sail the seas.

He did not look only to the moment and his own brief life, but to the now 64
and the always, as long as the tower stands and his skill abides. And so
must history also be written—with honesty and hope for the future,
not with flattery to gratify present recipients of praise. Here is your standard and rule for a proper history. If a few people judge by it, I shall be
content, and my purpose will be fulfilled.

If not—well, I shall have rolled my jar on the Kraneion.[2]

---

[1] Cf. 'Longinus' 14. 3 (above, p. 476).
[2] When Philip's army was approaching, the Corinthians busied themselves with
defence preparations. Nobody could find any use for Diogenes; so he rolled his jar (in
which he lived) up and down the hill, not to seem the only man idle.

14

SECOND- AND THIRD-CENTURY TEXTS

We group in this chapter a few short texts rather later in date than the preceding, and of varying significance.

A. VIRGIL, THEOCRITUS, AND HOMER
Aulus Gellius 9. 9

For Gellius see above, pp. 370–1. Discussion of Virgil's models and his debt to them doubtless began earlier; it is prominent also in the Virgil commentaries of late antiquity (Servius, Macrobius).

1 When striking thoughts in Greek poetry have to be translated and imitated, they say that one shouldn't always go out of one's way to
2 ensure literal faithfulness. Many features lose their attraction if they are
3 taken over by main force, as it were kicking and struggling. Virgil, therefore, showed skill and forethought in not translating everything when reproducing passages of Homer, Hesiod, Apollonius, Parthenius, Callimachus, Theocritus, and some others.
4 For instance, recently we had the *Bucolics* of both Theocritus and Virgil read to us at table; and we noticed that Virgil left out something that is remarkably nice in the Greek but could not and should not be
5 translated. Yet what he substituted for his omission is almost more agreeable and pretty.

> Klearista pelts the herd with apples, as he
> drives his goats by, and prettily pouts her lips.[1]

Compare

6
> Galatea aims an apple at me, naughty girl,
> and flees to the willows—and wants to be seen first.[2]

7 Here is another intentional omission that we noticed. It's very nice in the Greek:

> Tityrus, dearly beloved, feed my goats
> and drive them to the spring, Tityrus. Take care
> of the yellow he-goat: he may butt.[3]

[1] Theocr. 5. 88 f. [2] Virgil, *Ecl.* 3. 64 f. [3] Theocr. 3. 3 ff.

How could Virgil get over 'dearly-beloved'? The expression is no ordi- 8
nary one, its charm is all its own. So he left that out, and translated 9
the rest quite prettily, except that he calls *caper* what Theocritus called
a he-goat—though, according to Marcus Varro, Latin only uses *caper* of 10
a castrated goat.

> Tityrus, till I come back (I'm not going far) feed my goats, 11
> then drive them to drink, Tityrus, and as you go
> take care not to get in the way of the goat—he butts.[1]

And while I'm talking of translation, I recall that I heard from the 12
pupils of Valerius Probus (a learned man and a perceptive reader and
critic of old writings) that Probus used to say that Virgil made no more
unfortunate translation of Homer than his version of the delightful
lines about Nausicaa.

> Just as Artemis goes over the mountain, quiver full,
> over tall Taygetos or Erymanthos,
> rejoicing in the boars and the fleet deer:
> with her the nymphs, daughters of aegis-bearing Zeus,
> sport in the fields; and Leto's heart rejoices.
> She is a head taller than all of them
> and easily recognized—though all are beautiful.[2]

Compare

> Just as on the banks of Eurotas or the slopes of Cythnus 13
> Diana plies her dances: a thousand Oreads follow,
> swarming around her. On her shoulder
> she bears a quiver, and as she paces she overtops all:
> happiness touches Leto's silent heart.[3]

Probus (they said) thought first of all that in Homer the girl Nausicaa 14
playing among her friends in a solitary spot is rightly and aptly compared
with Diana hunting on the mountain ridges among the goddesses of the
countryside; but that Virgil had by no means made an appropriate simile.
Dido, walking in the middle of the city among the Tyrian elders, grave
in dress and walk, 'intent on her task' (as Virgil himself says) 'and on her
future kingdom', can have nothing that fits the games and hunting of
Diana. Again, Homer talks fairly and openly of Diana's enthusiasm and 15
pleasure in her hunt, while Virgil, after saying nothing about the goddess
hunting, merely makes her 'bear a quiver on her shoulder' as though it
were a burden. Probus was extremely surprised at one feature of the

---

[1] *Ecl.* 9. 23 ff.   [2] *Odyssey* 6. 102 ff.   [3] *Aeneid* 1. 498 ff.

Virgil: Homer's Leto feels a genuine inward delight that goes to the heart—that is the meaning of 'Leto's heart rejoices'; Virgil, wanting to imitate this, made the joy sluggish, trivial, hesitant, and (as it were)

16 superficial: for that was how Probus took 'touches'. And besides all that, Virgil had apparently left out the choicest part of the whole passage in making so little of

and easily recognized—though all are beautiful.

17 For there could be no greater or more conclusive compliment to her beauty than to say that she alone stood out among all those beautiful women, she alone was easily distinguished from all the rest.

B. VIRGIL AND PINDAR
Aulus Gellius 17. 10

1 The philosopher Favorinus,[1] as I recall, once discussed the poets Pindar and Virgil when he had gone in the hot season to a friend's villa at Anzio and I had come from Rome to see him. He said something like this:

2 'The friends and intimates of Virgil, among the impressions of his genius and character that they recorded for posterity, remark that he used

3 to say he produced verses in a bear-like manner. The bear brings forth its young unshaped and formless, but by licking them it contrives later to mould its offspring and give shape to them; similarly (Virgil said) the products of his genius, while still new, were inchoate and imperfect, but by cultivating and working over them he gave them lines and features.

4 That this most acute of men was being frank and correct here', proceeded

5 Favorinus, 'is witnessed by the facts. For what he left perfect and polished, with the last touch supplied by taste and selectivity, is aflower with every

6 excellence of poetic beauty. What he left for revision, but could not finish because his death intervened, is quite unworthy of the name of this

7 most elegant and tasteful of poets. Thus it was that, hard-pressed by illness and seeing death approach, he pressingly begged his dearest friends to burn the *Aeneid*, which he had not yet filed to perfection.

8 'Among the places that one thinks should have been revised and corrected is in particular the passage about Etna. Wanting to rival old Pindar's poem on the nature and the burning of the mountain, he amassed material and language of such a kind that, at least here, he is more unnatural and turgid even than Pindar, whose eloquence has been judged too rich and gross.

[1] See A. Barigazzi, *Favorino di Arelate*, Firenze, 1966, 122 ff.

'To show you what I mean, I will recite Pindar's poem on Mount 9
Etna, as far as I remember it:

> From its depths belches forth fire untouchable,
> in pure fountains: by day rivers roll forth a flood of smoke,
> blazing: but at night rocks are borne
> by the red rolling flame to the deep sea-plain, crashing;
> that monster sends up dreadful fountains
> of fire: a fantastic sight to see,
> a wonder for men there to hear.[1]

Listen now', Favorinus went on, 'to Virgil's lines, which I should be 10
right in saying that he started rather than completed:

> The harbour itself lies wide, untouched by the winds'
> approach: but hard by thunders Etna with dreadful crash;
> sometimes bursting a dark cloud into the sky,
> smoking with pitchy whirl, and incandescent ash.
> It raises fire-balls, licking the stars.
> Sometimes rocks, torn mountain entrails,
> it lifts, belches out: groaningly rolls into daylight
> liquefied stones: seethes up from lowest depths.[2]

First of all,' he said, 'Pindar kept to the facts, and tells us the truth about 11
what happened there, what the eye actually saw—namely that by day
Etna smoked, by night it flamed. Virgil, however, anxious to look for 12
words that resound and crash, makes no distinction, and mixes day and
night up. Again, the Greek poet brilliantly described the fountains of 13
fire belching forth from the depths, rivers of smoke aflow, dark whirl-
ing wreaths of flame carrying (as it were) fiery snakes down to the sea-
coasts. But our poet, wanting to translate 'a flood of smoke blazing', 14
grossly and tastelessly piled up 'a dark cloud smoking with pitchy whirl
and ashes'. Again 'fire-balls' for 'fountains' is a harsh and improper meta- 15
phor. 'Licking the stars' is another empty and pointless addition. Further, 16
to speak of 'a dark cloud smoking with pitchy whirl and incandescent 17
ash' is something hardly interpretable or even intelligible. Things that 18
are incandescent do not normally smoke nor are they dark. Or else he
used 'incandescent' in a vulgar and illicit way for 'hot'—not 'fiery' or
'shining'. Of course, in fact 'incandescent' (*candens*) is connected with
whiteness (*candor*), not heat (*calor*). As to causing stones and rocks to be 19
belched forth and lifted up and then immediately liquefy and groan and
roll into daylight—none of this is in Pindar. No one ever heard such a
thing; it is the most monstrous of monsters.'

---

[1] Pindar, *Pythian* 1. 21 ff.   [2] *Aeneid* 3. 570 ff.

C. IMAGINATION

This is a passage from a religious work of the early third century, Philostratus' *Life of Apollonius of Tyana* (6. 19: Loeb edn. by F. C. Conybeare). Apollonius complains of the ridiculous and peculiar representations of the gods among the Ethiopians. The sage Thespesion attempts to answer him.

'How are your statues made then?' asked Thespesion angrily.

'In the most beautiful and pious way that statues of gods can be fashioned.'

'You must be talking of the statue of Zeus at Olympia, of Athena, of Aphrodite of Cnidos, Hera of Argos, and all those other beautiful figures in the full bloom of youth?'

'Not only those. Other peoples' statuary all in all measures up to the standards of propriety, while you, it seems, ridicule the gods and don't really believe in them.'

'Did Phidias and Praxiteles and the rest go up to heaven,[1] then, and take an impression of the gods' appearances so as to reproduce it, or was there some other influence controlling their work?'

'Indeed there was—something rich in wisdom.'

'What? You can't find anything other than imitation (*mimēsis*) surely.'

'Yes; imagination (*phantasia*) did this work, a more cunning craftsman than your imitation. Imitation will fashion what she has seen, imagination also what she has not seen. She will form her conception with reference to reality. Amazement (*ekplēxis*) often baffles imitation; nothing baffles imagination. She marches undismayed to her own end . . .'

D. MALE AND FEMALE STYLES

The following extract from a treatise on music is included partly as an illustration of a kind of verbal criticism which, however unconvincing, was much practised in antiquity, and partly for its curious philosophizing account of 'male' and 'female' styles.

Aristides Quintilianus—date unknown, perhaps third or fourth century A.D.—based his work largely on Aristoxenus; he has strong Pythagorean or Neoplatonist leanings.

Text edited by R. P. Winnington-Ingram, Leipzig, 1963; no English translation. This passage (2. 7–9) = pp. 65. 10 ff. Winnington-Ingram.

2. 7   It remains to explain what kinds of tune and rhythm will control natural
(65. 10) reactions. Part of what I am going to say has been said by some older

---

[1] Cicero, *Orator* 8–9 (and cf. Sen. *Controv.* 10. 5. 8) advances the view that Phidias had a 'vision of beauty' in his mind when he made a statue of Zeus or Athena; Plotinus (5. 8. 1) expresses more clearly the concept of the artist copying from the forms. This answer to Plato's attack on art becomes evident only late in antiquity; but it may well have Hellenistic roots.

writers, but other parts are still wrapped in silence. This is not because of any ignorance or malice on the part of their authors. It would be wicked to make such a suggestion about philosophers who have had a musical initiation.[1] But the truth is that, though they set out some things in written form, the more secret doctrines were preserved orally. The explanation of this lies in the persevering enthusiasm the men of those days showed in their pursuit of the noblest studies. Nowadays however there is so much—let me be careful what I say—lack of education around, that the moderately cultivated may well be content if they can find a book which contains some sort of clear account.

The musical educator has to aim at four objects: appropriate thought, diction, harmony, and rhythm. Thought inevitably comes first. No decision to choose or avoid is made without it. Diction is a representation (*mimēsis*) of thought, and is of primary necessity in hearing and persuading our neighbour. With the addition of the qualities of acute and grave, and by means of intervals, it gives rise, in its confused state, to harmony, and when brought to order by words that accord, to rhythm.

But since music is a therapy for ills of the soul, we must first consider how and why these ills arise, since if this is not defined the next part of my argument will remain obscure.

When the soul is withdrawn from the world and conversing with 2. 8 higher things, it dwells, we believe, with reason, and is free from desire. But when it leans down to this world, and tries to learn by experience the ways of life on earth, it comes to need a body and seeks out an appropriate one. It then perceives the double nature there is in bodies, the male and the female. These of course exist not only in animate beings but in things directed by nature alone—plants, metals, perfumes. For here too a duality appears, one character or the other being displayed in the tenderness, smoothness, pleasing colour, or sweet odour of the objects, or in the opposites of these qualities. In herself, the soul is simple and uniform; but when clothed in this human shape of ours, she conceals her natural beauty, and is shaped, partly by her own will and partly under compulsion, to the location and configuration of her integument. Thus she not only desires body, but a body of a particular kind. She loves either male or female, sometimes one or the other by itself, sometimes a weird and extraordinary mixture of the two. And if souls fail to find a body such as they want naturally, they bring about changes by their own activities and assimilate the body to themselves. Then feminine looks bloom on men, so that their life is seen to be feminine too, and masculine looks are seen on women, whereby we can infer a similarity of character also. There are beardless men and bearded women, males with languishing

[1] Pythagoreans.

eyes and women with militant gaze. In each case, one can detect a character corresponding to the outward form. It is the inclination towards male or female or both that forms the soul's emotional characteristics. The feminine is too relaxed; the desires are in harmony with it. The masculine is vigorous and active; in accord with it is the spirited or angry element. Pain and pleasure abound in the feminine part of the soul and the feminine kind of human being, anger and boldness in the masculine. Again, there are combinations of these factors: pain with pleasure, anger with boldness, boldness with pleasure and pain, anger again with both, and other combinations of each with one or more of the others. Hence one could invent innumerable images of emotions seen in their complex variety.

Besides these natural differences in individuals, there are differences of thought. One man is delighted with white, one admires black, one finds pleasure in sweet things, another in bitter. The contraries exist, as I said, both in emotional reactions and in the external objects by attending to which our minds are said to acquire imaginative impressions; consequently, each of us takes pleasure in what most closely resembles our own emotional state. In the first place, we can see the contrast in visual objects. Colours and shapes which are pretty and tend to the dainty may be distinguished as feminine, the grim and anxiety-provoking as masculine. In the world of sound, we may associate the smooth and bland with the feminine, the harsh with the masculine. I need not go into more detail. We may say in general that all sensible objects which entice us to pleasure and gently relax the mind are to be reckoned as feminine, while anything that excites anxiety or activity belongs to the realm of the male. Those (68. 4) that do neither or both should be assigned to an intermediate category . . .

2. 9   Intellectual assent in ordinary life arises in the first place either from (68. 13) the felicitous understanding of the self-taught or from subsequent conviction. Repetition of an idea by many is just as efficacious in producing a quality of character as is scientific doctrine. The mind contains in itself types and images of everything, and is shaped at any given moment by the thoughts excited by words; as a result of this habituation and exercise it then imperceptibly stabilizes a happy or unhappy condition. In general terms, there are two types of moral education. One is therapeutic, whereby we correct vice. This has itself two subdivisions: the reductive (*meiotic*), by which, being unable to convince all at once, we lead the learner to emotional peace (*apatheia*) by gradual reductions; and the destructive (*anairetic*), when we bring him at one move to a complete conversion. The other main type is the beneficial; one species of this is the conservative, which stabilizes the optimum condition and maintains it as it is by education, and the other is the developing or *prosthetic*

which endeavours by fresh additions to raise moderate virtue to supreme excellence.

Education by ideas involves two techniques: if what is needed for mind-winning (*psuchagōgia*) can be found expressed in the existing material, we shall use this; if not, we shall track down what we need by special methods. The most useful of these are: epithets, metalepsis, metaphor, simile, synecdoche, periphrasis, allegory, etc.

Observe how Homer attempts to express the slow rising of the sun. He needs this for what he is about to say about the burial of the heroes in the twilight. He uses epithets which signify slowness. However, as these would not be properly used of the swiftest of the stars, he makes his main statement apply to the sun's light:

> Then was the sun newly striking the fields,

and applies the epithets to the slow-moving element of water:

> From the *soft* stream of the *deep* river Ocean
> ascending heaven.[1]

Here he gives us both the slowness of the water's movement, and the cause of the slowness, in 'the *deep* river Ocean'. For any piece of shallow water is easily moved, swirling in the hollow of the ground, but depth is something slow and steady, dissipating its impulse through many parts of the cavity beneath it. He also indicates the leisureliness of the ascent; for coming up from a depth is naturally a longer process.

On another occasion, in order to express rapidity of rising, he gives the sun an animated and impulsive movement:

> Up rose the sun, and left the lovely lake.[2]

Here he adds charm to the expression by using the feminine noun *limnē* (lake) for the ocean. Again, in giving a complete description of sunrise, he adorns his description with features agreeable in colour and smell, but he applies these not to the sun, but to Dawn, who is a female personage:

> Dawn with her saffron robe spread over the earth.[3]

And:

> When the first Dawn appeared, with rosy fingers.[4]

In another passage, on the other hand, his object is to make us tense with the description of military formations:

> Black with shields, with lances shuddering.[5]

[1] *Iliad* 7. 421–3.   [2] *Odyssey* 3. 1.   [3] *Iliad* 8. 1.
[4] e.g. *Iliad* 1. 477.   [5] *Iliad* 4. 282.

The metaphorical language here achieves an effect which the natural use of words could not. 'Black' is almost as effective on the ear as on the eye, and the notion of a shudder, because of its association with fear, expresses the anxiety of war.

To take another instance. For vividness (*enargeia*), Homer writes:

> All the feet and heads of many-fountained Ida
> were shaken.[1]

This transference from the naturally movable—the human body—to the immovable intensifies our conception of confusion. Again, take two contrasting examples of the same subject. The story of Ares and Aphrodite[2] is told in harsh terms—'they coupled', 'secretly', 'he disgraced . . .'. The first of these phrases expresses the impurity resulting from pleasure, the second the blameworthiness of the deed, the third the disgraceful wrongdoing. With Odysseus and Penelope, on the other hand, he adorns his description with dignified words, to express an act that is lawful and right:

> rejoicing they came to the right (*thesmos*) of their ancient bed.[3]

Finally, in the case of a union neither blameworthy by law nor commendable, he expresses this intermediate status by a combination of opposites in the sense:

> I never mounted the bed or slept with her, as is
> the way of men and women.[4]

When trope will not serve the turn, we can use simile. Homer makes us tense with:

> as when a goatherd from his look-out sees a storm-cloud,[5]

and relaxes us with:

> and the flower is like milk.[6]

There are many white things. He has chosen the one that also expresses sweetness.

Again, in the lament of Achilles,[7] he uses more words which obscure the mind—*black* cloud, *smoky* dust, *black* ash—and few that are brighter. The death of Euphorbus,[8] on the other hand, he wants to relate brilliantly,

---

[1] *Iliad* 20. 59.
[2] *Odyssey* 8. 266 ff.
[3] Ibid. 23. 296.
[4] *Iliad* 9. 133.
[5] Ibid. 4. 275.
[6] *Odyssey* 10. 304.
[7] *Iliad* 18. 22 ff.
[8] Ibid. 17. 51 ff.

as a relief from the emotion connected with Patroclus. The brighter words therefore predominate here: 'hair like the graces', brilliant materials like gold and silver, flourishing olives, open ground, springs of water gushing forth, pleasant breezes—the whole making a precious and brilliant piece of elegant charm (*anthos*).

Grandeur and distinction are produced by synecdoche in the passage:

Straight they advanced to the well-built wall with a great shouting, holding high their *dry oxen*.[1]

Here, elevation is given to the words by the extent of the intervals;[2] and because the word 'shield' is indecorous in a context of grandeur (*hadrotēs*) he uses the word 'ox', which stresses the size of the object; and then, because this does not fit 'holding up', he adds 'dry'. Thus, by means of the idea of lightness which goes with dryness, he both lends plausibility to the action and makes the thought a present of a vivid image that is beyond criticism.

In another passage, Homer writes:

and the great heaven trumpeted around.[3]

This expression raises the story of the battle to a more grandiose tone, but, since the word is indecorous as used of the heavens, Homer tries to recover propriety by a special procedure, magnifying the sound of the trumpet by the epithet 'great', and making the sound come from every part of the heavens by adding the preposition 'around'.

Humble words obviously produce simplicity: for example

setting a poor chair and a little table.[4]

Observe too how the variety provided by periphrases gives vividness to the style and charm to the words; for example, when Homer wants to mention the characters of young heroes with the proper excellence of each, he says 'Eteoclean might' and 'Telemachus' holy might'[5]— indicating Eteocles' superiority in strength and Telemachus' dearness to the gods because of his virtuous character.

Allegories, in which a number of words in a context are used in a transferred sense, divert the mind to a different tone. Observe how when Homer chooses to speak of those fallen in battle in such a way as to

---

[1] *Iliad* 12. 137 f.
[2] i.e. the hiatuses in the Greek: *anaschomenoi ekion megalō alalētō*.
[3] *Iliad* 21. 388 (cf. 'Longinus' 9. 6, above, p. 469).
[4] *Odyssey* 20. 259.   [5] *Iliad* 4. 386, *Odyssey* 16. 476.

rouse neither emotion nor grief, he does so by the image of the gathering of corn:

> Men soon have their fill of strife;
> the straw, that the bronze strews on the ground, is abundant,
> but the harvest is little.[1]

(73. 6)

E. POETRY AND PROSE

Aristides, the greatest of the second-century sophists, begins his 'Hymn to Sarapis' (45) with a passage on the differences between prose and poetry, in which he expands ideas he found in Isocrates (*Evagoras* 9–11). For prose hymns, cf. Menander, below, p. 579.
  Text: ed. Keil, pp. 352–6.
  A. Boulanger, *Aelius Aristide*, Paris, 1923, 303 ff.

1 Blessed is the race of poets and exempt from all troubles. Not only may they initiate subjects of whatever kind they wish, false, sometimes unconvincing, with no basis at all if we look at it properly—they also handle them as they will, with thoughts and notions some of which would be unintelligible without what goes before and after. We understand and accept them only because it is all said in one piece—and we feel very pleased at having understood. Sometimes they tell the beginning of something and leave out the rest, as though they have given it up; sometimes they rob it of the beginning, or take out the middle, and think 2 all well: they have a despotic power over their thoughts. Again, there is nothing they cannot venture or contrive. They suspend gods from the machine, embark them on ships with any fellow passengers they like, and represent them not only sitting down with human beings but drinking 3 with them and carrying lamps to give light.[2] And think of their magnificence and (this is where I started!) blessedness, and how, in Homer's words, 'in ease they live', when they are composing their hymns and paeans to the gods! In a couple of strophes or periods the whole thing is complete. First, they give us 'Delos girdled by the main', or 'Zeus who hurls the thunder' or 'deep-roaring sea', and then straight to Heracles' arrival among the Hyperboreans, or Iamos the prophet of old, or Heracles and Antaeus;[3] then, with the addition of Minos or Rhadamanthys, Phasis or Danube, or a declaration that poets are 'the Muses' flock' 4 and invincible in their skill, they think their hymn complete. Nor do laymen expect more of them. Indeed we honour them and think them so

---

[1] *Iliad* 19. 221–3.
[2] An allusion to the activities of Athena in the *Odyssey* (2. 270 ff., 3. 51 ff., 19. 34).
[3] Cf. Pindar, *Olympian* 3. 11 ff., 6. 43, 50, *Isthmian* 3. 70 ff.

very holy that we have handed over to them the composition of hymns and addresses to the gods, as though they were in truth their prophets. But the capacity to propound an appropriate subject, the well-thought-out arrangement of details, the preciseness (within human limits) of presentation—these are qualities we think unnecessary in regard to the gods. For all other occasions we use prose speech (*logos*)—encomia of festivals and heroic deeds, narratives of wars, invention of fables, contests in court. *Logos* is at hand for everything—but towards the gods who gave it us we do not think it right to use it! It is in prose that we lay down the procedures even of rituals and sacrifices, when we write laws; but hymns, no—they are not to be composed like this. Is it that the poets need the 5 gods, but we—? Let me not say it! The poets themselves confess that 'all men have need of gods'. All men should therefore honour them according to their several capacities. Are poets alone beloved of god? Is it from 6 them that the gods most like to receive gifts? Then why did we not make the poets the sole priests of the gods? 'The oracular prophets of the gods 7 give instructions in metre.' No: the priestess at Delphi, the priestesses at Dodona, Trophonios, the dreams that Asclepios and Sarapis send, speak for the most part without metre. Indeed, it is more natural for 8 man to use prose—just as it is more natural to walk than to ride. It is not true that metre was invented first, and then speech and conversation, nor did poets lay down the words to use: words and prose came first, and then, to provide a certain grace and fascination of the mind (*psuchagōgia*), came poetry, for she makes such things. So in honouring nature we should be honouring the ordinance and will of the gods; and if, as the poets themselves say, the first and oldest is also best, we should be doing it more honour by approaching the gods, who laid down all these things, with addresses in this style; after all, we are not ashamed of talking to one another unmetrically.

I say this not to dishonour the poets, nor to rob them of their rank, 9 but to show, on their own admission, that we might properly add these new sacrifices to the existing ones. And if naturalness is in everything more acceptable to the gods, we may reasonably expect to give them more pleasure by this kind of honour than by the other. The gods too would honour us the more if we assigned seniority where they do. Metre indeed gives the poets their profession's fame, but from the point of view of utility it is much more our affair. For in poetry, metre measures 10 only the hexameter or the iambic line if it fills the verse, but in prose it gives measure to the whole context and penetrates everything (starting with the author's name).[1] It allows no excess or falling short, but makes us give

---

[1] Presumably the author's name in the title.

everything its due. It forbids the insertion of unnecessary words—a ridiculous thing—for the sake of the metre; when it comes to periods, it requires self-completeness—the most difficult measure of all. Finally, as I said, it sees that everything is in proportion and has fulfilled the goal proposed . . .[1]

13 I am aware, as I said, that it is much easier to do this in song than in prose, and that such endeavours have been handed over to the poets. And reasonably so. They have many advantages, and the absolute power to do what they will. We must . . . in truth remain in measure and remember ourselves, like soldiers keeping formation.

[1] This argument—and the passage §§ 11–12, here omitted—is difficult and sophistical: *metron* means both 'metre' and 'measure'. Aristides is trying to show that the rhythmical demands of prose are just as exacting, and more beneficial.

15

LATER GREEK RHETORIC

A. HERMOGENES, *ON TYPES*

We can select only a very little from the great mass of late Greek rhetorical writing. Hermogenes of Tarsus (born *c.* A.D. 160) was a brilliant young student whom the emperor Marcus Aurelius made a detour to hear. His name is attached to a number of treatises on rhetorical subjects. *Peri ideōn*, *On Types of Style*, is authentic, and is much the most important.

The *ideai* are stylistic types or qualities found in all authors. They are something like the *aretai*, virtues, with which Theophrastus and Dionysius had operated, but Hermogenes distinguishes many more nuances even than Dionysius. It is difficult to find English equivalents for these delicate discriminations. One group of *ideai* is headed by *saphēneia* (clarity), with *katharotēs* (purity) and *eukrineia* (distinctness); a second is composed of *megethos* (grandeur) with its various specialized forms: *semnotēs*, *trachutēs*, *deinotēs*, *lamprotēs*, *akmē*, *peribolē* (solemnity, asperity, vehemence, brilliance, florescence, abundance); the third comprises the qualities roughly opposed to the 'grand' group—*ēthos* (character-fulness), and its concomitants *apheleia*, *alētheia*, *drimutēs* (simplicity, truthful-ness, sharpness) and some others. It will be seen that the first group corresponds roughly to the necessary virtues of the earlier writers, and that the other two represent the two sides of the basic antithesis between grandeur and emotion on the one hand, and simplicity and 'manners' on the other (cf. Dionysius, above, p. 331).

We excerpt passages to show Hermogenes' general principles, his attitude to Demosthenes as the exemplar of all types,[1] and these general concepts of *megethos* and *ēthos*. The final passage chosen illustrates his handling of individual authors. The translation sometimes abridges. Hermogenes is a diffuse author and repeats himself often to make his points clear to his pupils.

Text: H. Rabe, Leipzig, 1913.

Discussion: D. Hagedorn, *Zur Ideenlehre des Hermogenes*, Göttingen, 1964.

I. INTRODUCTION: GENERAL CONCEPTS

Perhaps the most necessary subject for the orator to understand is p. 213 Rabe that of the 'types' (*ideai*) of style: what are their characteristics and how are they produced? Without this knowledge, one cannot know how to judge excellence and craftsmanship, or the lack of them, in other writers, ancient or modern; and if one wishes oneself to be a craftsman in words,

---

[1] Especially the public speeches and above all *On the Crown* (*Oration* 18)—witness the concentration of the quotations from this minutely studied speech.

fine and noble words such as the ancients used, then this branch of study is indispensable—unless one is prepared to deviate widely from standards of good workmanship. Imitation (*mimēsis*) and emulation (*zēlos*) of the ancients cannot in my opinion be successful, however well-endowed the writer, if they depend simply on experience and some sort of irrational knack. Indeed, natural advantages rushing towards random objectives without science or principle may well lead to greater disasters;[1] whereas with a knowledge and understanding of this subject even a student of moderate ability will not fail. Of course it is better to have natural advantages on one's side also: the success will be the greater. But failing this, let us achieve what can be achieved by the process of learning and teaching, which depends on nothing outside our control. Indeed, the less well endowed may well overtake the more favoured, just by dint of exercise and practice on the right lines.

The study of 'types', then, is important and necessary to the future writer and the future critic, and even more so to one who would be both. No wonder therefore if we find it a difficult subject, not capable of simple treatment. Nothing good is easily obtained; and it would surprise me if there is anything better for man, who is a *logical* creature, than fine and good *logoi* and all the types of them.[2]

Before I proceed to actual instruction on the various topics involved, I must make one preliminary point. We are not here concerned with the 'type' peculiar to Plato or Demosthenes or any individual writer; that will be discussed later. For the moment, the question before us is to consider each quality in itself, and explain what sort of thing solemnity (*semnotēs*) is, and how it is produced, and similarly with asperity, simplicity, and the rest. However, the reason why we need this subject is for the study of individual famous writers. Consequently, if we put before ourselves the author whose style possesses most variety and the most striking combination of all the 'types', we shall find that in discussing him we have discussed them all. If we can explain the general and the particular features of such a writer, their origin, composition, nature and essence, we shall have given an accurate account of every type of style. We shall have explained how they may be combined, and how, as a result of combinations of the same types, the whole style (*logos*) can become poetical or unpoetical, panegyrical, deliberative, forensic, or what you will.

Now the man who, more than anyone else, handled language in this way and diversified his writing continuously is, in my opinion, Demosthenes. Thus in considering him and what may be found in his work,

[1] Cf. 'Longinus' 2. 2, above, p. 463.
[2] The point depends on the range of meaning of *logos*, which includes both 'word' and 'reason': cf. 'Longinus' 36. 3, above, p. 495.

we shall also be considering all the 'types' of style. I would beg the reader not to criticize this approach or this critical judgement until he has heard all that I am going to say. I suspect that if attention is given to what follows I shall earn admiration, especially for distinctness, rather than criticism.

The main point is this. Demosthenes' mastery of political oratory is such that, if one considers him with some sophistication, it is not very difficult to see how he is always combining styles, not separating his deliberative manner rigorously from the forensic or panegyrical, nor indeed abandoning any of these styles when concentrating on one of them. What is very difficult indeed is to discover the stylistic elements which he uses to form his own style as he does—the elements which, in combination with one another, compose all manners, including the panegyrical. Nor is it less difficult to express these plainly when one has actually uncovered them. To my knowledge, no one has yet dealt with them with exactness; those who have touched on the subject have done so in a muddled and diffident way, so that their accounts are thoroughly confused. For instance, those who have some repute as exponents of Demosthenes, because they have investigated him in detail, to the limit of their ability, without however troubling much about general principles— solemnity, simplicity, the other 'types' in themselves—may indeed prove instructive on Demosthenes or the parts of Demosthenes they claim to discuss, but do nothing to inform us about style and 'types' of writing in general, in metre, poetry or prose.

Difficult as it is to discover these things and expound them distinctly, avoiding our predecessors' failures, the attempt must nevertheless be made by the method I have proposed. If we can enumerate and describe the elements and first principles of Demosthenic style, and say how they are produced and combined, and what effect various kinds of combination have, we may find that we have given an account of style in general. To quote the great orator himself, 'this is a large undertaking, but the execution will answer for itself here and now; let whoso wishes be my judge.'[1]

The factors which make up the style of Demosthenes, considered as a unity, are the following: clarity (*saphēneia*), grandeur (*megethos*), beauty (*kallos*), rapidity (*gorgotēs*), 'character' (*ēthos*), sincerity (*alētheia*), and vehemence (*deinotēs*). By 'as a unity', I mean that all these are interwoven and interpenetrating: that is what Demosthenes' style is like. Of these 'types', some stand by themselves and exist separately, others have subordinate 'types' under them, which help to produce them; others again have one or more parts in common. In general terms, some are genera consisting

216

217

218

[1] Demosthenes 4. 15.

of species, some overlap other 'types' in respect of some specific difference, though distinct in all other ways, while others remain on their own and need no additional help. What I mean will become clearer as we proceed to discuss each 'type' separately.

We must first state the elements of which all speech is made up, and without which no kind of speech can exist. This will make it easier to follow when we have before us the subordinate qualities we have mentioned, and have to explain their genesis.

All speech has a thought or thoughts, an approach (*methodos*) corresponding to the thought, and diction appropriate to these. Diction has its own characteristics; it involves figures, cola, word-arrangement, pauses, and rhythm. Rhythm is the product of the two preceding, since to arrange the parts of speech in a particular way and to bring speech to a pause in a particular way will produce rhythm of a particular kind.

219 This may be obscure, and so I will clarify it by an example. Suppose we aim to produce sweetness. The thoughts appropriate to sweetness are those connected with myth or the like, and certain others, which we will discuss in the section on sweetness. The 'approaches' consist in handling the subject as the main theme and in narrative fashion, not allusively or in any other manner. The appropriate diction is that which makes much use of adjectives, has a sharp flavour, and is poetical without being elevated or diffuse by nature. Any diction associated with purity of style will also do. Within the sphere of diction, the figures to be recommended are generally those involving straightforward expression without interruptions. The cola should be commatic in scale or not much bigger. The arrangement of words should be relaxed because of the character of the diction, but not wholly without coherence, since sweetness must achieve some of its pleasurable effect by means of rhythm; its metrical basis should be anapaestic or dactylic. A full discussion of rhythm and word-arrangement would involve syllables and letters, since these, together with clausulae, are the elements of rhythm, as will become clear later. The clausula appropriate to sweetness, corresponding to this word-arrangement, is the firmly-based kind. Rhythm, like shape, follows arrangement and clausulae of a certain kind, although it is separate from all of them—just as when stones or timbers of a certain kind are put together to make a house or a ship in a certain way and with certain

220 limits set to the operation, the shape of the house or ship is thereby determined, though it is actually something distinct from the manner of putting together and from the limit set to the operation.

All kinds of style, then, are to be seen under the following heads, and depend on the following factors: thought, approach (*methodos*), diction, figure, colon, word-arrangement, clausula, rhythm. I am aware that these need further clarification, and I do not think, as some do, that they might be clarified by proposing examples. They do indeed need exemplification, but I do not agree that clarity would follow if we were to exemplify them now. Indeed, the discussion would be greatly prolonged by the addition here of examples of these various points, and greater confusion would probably result. It has not been my purpose here to talk about 'sweetness' —we shall discuss it in greater detail later—except so far as to show how any one type of writing may be produced in its pure state. I hope, as I said, that we may thereby be better equipped to study the rest of the subject. I return to the main point.

This being so, and every 'type' being produced in these ways, it is 221 difficult or impossible to find in any ancient writer a specimen of style belonging to one type in all respects—theme, approach, diction, and the rest. What gives every writer his particular character is the predominance in him of qualities appropriate to a given type. I exclude Demosthenes. Unlike the rest, he has not got an abnormal preponderance of any one type, though there is one part or species of one type that he does employ more than others—abundance (*peribolē*). (The discussion of grandeur and abundance which is to follow is the place to explain in detail his practice in this respect.) But the preponderance is confined to one fraction of a single type: all the others he uses in their due place, according due weight to each. Elevated and brilliant thoughts are scaled down by special approaches or figures or by some other means; the delicate or trivial is similarly roused to life and given new stature. In fact he mixes every quality on the same principles with elements not peculiar or particularly appropriate to it, and by thus diversifying his style makes everything fit together and form a unity in which all the various types interpenetrate. So all beauties merge in the one supremely beautiful style, the Demosthenic.

Strictly speaking, then, a single style cannot be found in any ancient 222 writer. No doubt it is in principle a fault to construct one's style in a single form without variety. But—to recapitulate—different authors exceed the norm in different features and this is how their styles come to be characterized in one way or another. By 'exceeding the norm' I do not mean that they use a large number of the factors that make up a type (approach, figures, word-order, pause, etc.), although this might have some significance, but rather that they make special use of the most vital factors in each type. This is what most helps to produce the type, and 'exceed the norm' means 'use the most important factors' in it. It sometimes happens that an author who employs every other means, and indeed 'exceeds the norm' in them, but falls short in these, actually fails to achieve the stylistic effort to which the means he *has* used are appropriate.

We must turn now to the effect of the factors that, as we said, contribute to types of style.

First, and always most important, is the thought. Second comes the diction, third the figure—the figure of diction I mean, because the figure of thought, in other words the approach, is my fourth factor, though this position in the list does not correspond to its value in 'vehemence'
223 (*deinotēs*), when it may be said, as will be explained, to hold the first place. Word-arrangement and clausula may be placed last, though sometimes they are not least in importance, especially in poetry. One of them without the other can indeed make little or no contribution to style, but together, and combined with rhythm, they can do much. In fact, the musicians may raise the point that they ought to be put before thought. Rhythm, they will tell us, by itself, and without articulate speech, is more effective than any type of style. Appropriate rhythms produce pleasure in the mind more than any panegyrical speech, pain more than any rhetorical appeal to pity, anger more than any violent and vehement talk, and so on. We will not quarrel with the musicians for teasing us about all these points; let rhythm come first or last or in the middle, just as anyone likes. What I hope to show is the nature of the rhythms appropriate to each quality, limiting myself to the extent to which it is possible to apply rhythm to prose without making a song out of it. If rhythm is as important in this situation as it is in music generally,
224 let it come first: if not, it shall come in its proper place. My own view is that rhythm does sometimes contribute much to the quality of style, but not as much as they say.

2. DIGNITY, GRANDEUR, SOLEMNITY

241 The discussion of grandeur (*megethos*) naturally follows that of clarity, because clarity must be accompanied by a certain grandeur, 'bulk' (*onkos*), and dignity, since the commonplace (*to euteles*) is next door to great clarity, and this is the opposite of grandeur. Demosthenes, I am convinced, recognized this. Since it is an absolute necessity for the style of the practical orator to be clear, he consistently used the elements that produce clarity, but as this involved a danger of his style declining into a rather workaday manner, he combined them with elements that produce
241. 21 grandeur, and was especially strong in the quality of 'abundance' (*peribolē*) . . .
242. 3 　　The qualities that produce grandeur, 'bulk', and dignity are therefore the following: solemnity, abundance, asperity, brilliance, florescence (*akmē*), vehemence—though this last, as will be seen when we come to discuss it,

is not very different from asperity. Of these, solemnity and abundance exist on their own, whereas all the others are combined (or not combined) with others in some respect, having some areas in common and some distinct. I shall therefore discuss solemnity now, and the rest later. Abundance does indeed, as I said before, exist on its own, but I postpone the treatment of it because Demosthenes excels in it and the reason why he employs it to achieve 'bulk' cannot be understood until we have learned about asperity, brilliance, florescence, and vehemence.

First, then, solemnity. Its opposite, I suggest, is simplicity (*apheleia*), which we shall discuss in the section on 'character' (*ēthos*).

Solemn thoughts include in the first place things said of the gods *qua* gods. Things like

The son of Kronos spoke, and clasped his wife in his arms[1]

are not spoken of gods *qua* gods: they are far removed from solemnity 243 of thought, and partake more of the nature of charm (*hēdonē*) and sweetness. They are expressions of human emotion—in general terms, they are poetical, and pleasure is the main aim of poetry. An example of something said of gods *qua* gods is: 'He was good, and no good being has any envy of anything', or: 'God wanted all things to be good and nothing bad, so far as possible', or again: 'God took all that was visible, when it was not at rest but moving in disharmony and disorder, and reduced it from disorder to order, thinking this in every way better.'[2] Many such thoughts can be found in Plato (these are from the *Timaeus*); they are not to be found in the orators, for Hyperides' *Deliacus*[3] is more poetical and mythical —I need not here explain why. There are however in Demosthenes, and here and there in the other orators, thoughts of a second or third order of solemnity. The first order, as I said, comprises thoughts about gods *qua* gods; the second are thoughts about truly divine things—e.g. an inquiry into the nature and causes of the seasons, the nature and revolution of the universe, movements of earth or sea, thunderbolts, and so 244 on. Now if these subjects are handled only with respect to causes, they have power only to make the writing *solemn*, not to give it practical value as oratory. For where is the practical oratory in the passage of Herodotus about 'the sun, driven away in the winter season',[4] or in Plato's 'The circular path of the universe, including all the kinds in its ambit, compresses them in every direction, and allows no empty space; in consequence, fire passes through everything, next comes air, the second most subtle, and so on with the others . . .'?[5] Or again, where is the relevance to practical oratory of inquiries into earthquakes, the flood and

[1] *Iliad* 14. 346. [2] Plato, *Timaeus* 29 e, 30 a.
[3] Cf. 'Longinus' 35 (above, p. 493). [4] 2. 24. [5] *Timaeus* 58 a.

ebb of water, the impact of thunderbolts, or any such matters? Considered in this way, such thoughts make the context solemn without being in a practical sense oratorical. They form therefore the *second* class of 'solemn' thoughts.

If however one handles such topics not with a view to inquiry into causes but as a description (*ekphrasis*), the result will be both solemn and practical. There is an example in Aristides' speech against Callixenus,[1] who had advised against granting burial to the ten generals, when they had been executed as a result of a single vote. Aristides on their behalf described the storm. 'It was a bolt from heaven that prevented them, 245 Callixenus, beyond description and beyond bearing. The battle had scarce begun when the sea swelled, and a brisk Hellespontine gale got up . . .'

The third group of thoughts conducive to solemnity comprises matters which are by nature divine, but are commonly seen in human affairs—e.g. the immortality of the soul, justice, temperance, or the like, or some discussion of life in general or the definition of law or nature. For instance: 'Law is an invention and gift of the gods', or 'Law is common, ordered, the same for all; nature is without order, peculiar to the individual', or 'The end of all men's life is death, even though a man should keep himself shut up at home . . .', or 'All human life is governed by nature and laws'.[2] In brief, all universal and general statements possess in some measure solemnity of thought, especially if the universality is consistently maintained. If you add a special detail, the effect is changed: 'A bad thing, men of Athens, a bad thing is an informer, a thoroughly malicious, fault-finding creature; but this little fellow was *born* a trickster.'[3] The addition of the detail has changed the effect; a combination of the universal and the particular produces the style of practical oratory and of abundance, but not necessarily that of solemnity.

246   The fourth type of solemn effect is produced by thought concerned with matters entirely human, but great and glorious: the battles of Marathon or Plataea or Salamis, Athos and the Hellespont, and so forth. The addition of a *fabulous* solemnity accompanied by charm, as in Herodotus (e.g. the Iacchus story)[4] makes a further difference.

So much for the thoughts appropriate to solemnity: the appropriate approaches (*methodoi*) are forms of exposition involving direct statement without hesitation. (i) When we aim at consistent solemnity we must speak exactly and with dignity, as though we are certain, and not with any hesitation. 'Be they gods or heroes'[5] is solemn in thought, but the

---

[1] An example from a second-century sophistic *suasoria*. This speech of Aristides is lost: see A. Boulanger, *Aelius Aristide*, Paris, 1923, 157, n. 1.

[2] [Dem.] 25. 15–16; Dem. 18. 97.

[3] Dem. 18. 242.

[4] Herod. 8. 65.

[5] Dem. 23. 70.

expression of doubt gives it more of the character of practical oratory and persuasion. (ii) The allegorical approach, if consistently maintained, also produces solemnity: 'The great leader in heaven, Zeus, rides his winged chariot . . .'[1] This happens, however, only when the writer does not choose everyday, commonplace matter for his allegory; if he does, the result is not solemnity but writing characterized by another kind of thought, the commonplace. (iii) Another feature of the solemn approach is the use of suggestive hints to indicate darkly, in the manner of the mysteries and initiations, something within the sphere of solemn thoughts. By appearing to know, but to be unable to reveal, we give an impression of grandeur and solemnity: e.g. 'verily being' or 'he was good . . .' in Plato.[2] Plato in fact in one passage expands this approach: 'To discover this is difficult, to reveal it to all on discovery, impossible.' Such approaches are valuable in amplifying solemnity when the thoughts concerned are by nature solemn; hints like this however do not produce solemnity in subjects of practical concern—they have a different effect.

From the thoughts and approaches of solemnity we pass to the diction. This includes, first, all broad sounds which make us open our mouths wide, so as to give a pompous impression, and, as it were, force us into a manner which some speakers deliberately cultivate. This applies especially to words containing many long 'a's or 'o's. Thus Plato tells us how some people call *oiōnistikē* (augury) *ōōnistikē* 'to make it more solemn'.[3] Similarly with 'a'. Theocritus represents a man as angry with women who speak Doric and use the a continually in their broad accent.[4] Long 'o' and 'a' particularly elevate and enlarge words if they occur in the closing syllables: . . . *hēgemōn en ouranō Zeus* ('. . . leader in heaven, Zeus').

A second class of solemn words is made up of those containing a short 'o' by itself, ending in a long syllable, as in *Orontēs*. We must add also words which contain a number of long syllables or diphthongs, and those which end in such sounds, except the diphthong 'ei'. Recurrent 'i', however, does not make for solemnity, since it contracts the mouth instead of opening it, and produces a rictus.

Thirdly: tropical expressions are solemn and grand, but their use involves considerable risks. Moderate tropes do indeed give the desired effect: 'putting forward good hopes'[5] instead of 'hoping for good' is an example, because—you see this?—the expression is so moderate that the trope is not even noticed. Any excess, however, produces asperity: for

[1] Plato, *Phaedrus* 246 e.
[2] *Timaeus* 28 c, 29 e, for these passages.
[3] *Phaedrus* 244 d.
[4] Theocritus 15. 87 ff.: the two women are talking in a crowd in a street in Alexandria.
[5] Dem. 18. 97.

example 'the cities were sick'.[1] This expression needed explanation—
'the politicians accepted bribes . . .' is simply explanation of 'sick'.

Further excess makes for even greater harshness: 'hamstrung', 'sold
himself', 'robbery with violence to Greece'.[2] To go further still in the
same direction produces coarseness and indeed vulgarity. One could not
find an example of this, indeed, in Demosthenes—there aren't any—but
249 our friends the bogus sophists would yield many. They call vultures
(whose attentions they deserve themselves) 'living tombs',[3] and use many
other such frigid expressions. Tragedy, which contains many instances
of such things, and poets like Pindar who have a tragic style, are their
downfall. There may well be things to say in defence of the use of language
in this way by these writers—Pindar and the tragedians, I mean—but
it does not belong to the present occasion, and must be postponed. For
writers who use crassitudes like this in oratory, I find no excuse.

Fourthly: nouns and nominal diction also produce solemnity. By
'nominal diction', I mean diction involving a conversion from verb to
noun, and the use of participles, pronouns, etc. In the solemn manner
one should use as few verbs as possible. Thucydides always aims at this;
he has done it most noticeably in the description of the revolution at
Corcyra.[4] Apart from the verb 'was considered', everything is nouns or in
nominal form: 'irrational daring was considered loyal courage, cautious
delay specious cowardice, discretion a cloak for unmanliness', etc. (I
am not here concerned with the element of harshness or asperity in the
250 passage.) Similar is a passage of Demosthenes,[5] on the effect of which he
comments himself: 'words, he said, do not strengthen associations': then
comes the comment—'a very solemn way of putting the point'.

So much for diction: the figures appropriate to solemnity are those
which also give purity: i.e. directness and the like. 'Confirmations'
(*epikriseis*), whether to be regarded as thoughts or figures, are solemn:
'But to pay them in speech what honour remains is enjoined by the law,
and is our duty';[6] 'They were willing to give themselves up to danger for
the sake of honour and glory, and their decision was honourable and right.'[7]
All this sort of thing is solemn and dignified. 'Confirmations' combined
with expressions of doubt, on the other hand, are characterful (*ēthikai*)
but not solemn: 'I am no lover of invective, but I am bound to say . . .'
Any touch of doubt or hesitation lends an individual character to a
passage. A speaker who wishes to give his words dignity and solemnity
needs to be dogmatic: 'Philip had no way of putting an end to, or getting

---

[1] Dem. 18. 45.   [2] Dem. 3. 31, 19. 6, 9. 22.
[3] Gorgias: cf. 'Longinus' 3. 2, above, p. 464.
[4] Thuc. 3. 82.   [5] Dem. 18. 35.
[6] Plato, *Menexenus* 236 d.   [7] Dem. 18. 97.

out of, his war with us.' If you say 'I imagine Philip had . . .' you produce an effect of 'character' (*ēthos*). On the other hand, to attribute something of what you are going to say to your own opinion *is* dignified and solemn: 'What I want to say is this . . .';[1] 'Agamemnon seems to me to have been the most powerful ruler of the time . . .'[2]

'Apostrophe' and 'hypostrophe' are not appropriate to the solemn manner or to the pure: indeed, they undermine and destroy them, because they break the piece up by interruptions and upset the free run, making it 251 more ordinary and oratorical. Compare the effect of the phrase 'whether they dwell in a great city or a small' placed in the middle of the sentence 'the whole life of men is governed by nature and by laws'.[3] To arrange the clauses in the order I have just given them would produce a different effect from that given by dividing the sentence by hypostrophe and writing 'the whole life of men, whether they dwell in a great city or a small, is governed by nature and laws'. This last is rapid, as well as being oratorical, and solemn; the other would be solemn and homogeneous in a pure manner. This therefore is the treatment to be adopted if the speech is to remain solemn throughout; otherwise, we should prefer the other.

As to cola: 'solemn' cola are the 'pure' cola—i.e. the shorter ones. They should be as it were aphorisms. 'Every soul is undying, for the ever-moving is undying'.[4] 'Law is the invention and gift of the gods, and the decision of intelligent men'.[5] There may however be longer cola for some necessary reason in a context of solemnity.

As to word-arrangement: the 'solemn' types are those which are not fussy about vowel-clashes, but are broadly speaking dactylic, anapaestic, or paeonic, sometimes iambic, and especially spondaic. Forms based on the epitrite thus suit the solemn manner, while trochaic and ionic rhythms 252 do not . . .

[We omit some examples.]

Clausulae in the 'solemn' manner again follow the same principles as 253. 11 those in the 'pure'. The sentence must rest on one of the feet appropriate to solemnity, and with no catalexis, so that the 'basis' does not become trochaic, or the rhythm turn hurried instead of steady. It will be steady if it ends in a noun or nominal expression at least three syllables long:

eis toutonī ton agōna.[6]

Alternatively, there may be a majority of long syllables at the clausula, 254

---

[1] Dem. 9. 20.   [2] Thuc. 1. 9.   [3] [Dem.] 25. 15.
[4] Plato, *Phaedrus* 245 c.
[5] [Dem.] 25. 16.   [6] Dem. 18. 1 ('to this contest').

so that a double spondee or any epitrite other than the fourth forms the 'basis':

hapās ho tōn anthrōpōn bios phusei kai nomois dioikeitai.[1]

The rhythm has a particularly solemn base if the clausula has last, or next to last, a broad sound which forces the mouth open—a point I made above in connection with solemn *diction*.

The nature of the rhythm should be clear from the above. Note however that if the general rhythmical character is epitritic or dactylic or the like, but the clausula fails to terminate in such a way that what follows (?) has the kind of feet appropriate to solemnity, the rhythm is not solemn. This principle is true of all 'types'. If a composition is formed of feet of a certain nature, which are supposed to produce a certain type, but the clausulae are not formed of complete feet of the same kind, but the feet are broken up, the rhythm is changed and becomes appropriate to a different manner from that associated with the feet of which the whole **254. 21** context was composed.

3. 'CHARACTER', SIMPLICITY

321. 19 'Character' (*ēthos*) in speech is produced by moderation (*epieikeia*) and simplicity, and also by the genuineness and sincerity apparent in it. Weightiness also is involved in writing in character, though it is not an essential part of it, as simplicity, moderation, genuineness, and sincerity all are. Nor indeed can it be seen on its own—it needs with it simpli-**322** city or moderation or some other characterful quality. This will be clearer after a discussion of the several qualities.

Simplicity

The thoughts of simplicity are in general those of purity. Thoughts common to mankind, reaching, or believed to reach, everyman, with nothing deep or sophisticated about them, are obviously simple and pure. 'Think me a villain, but let him go'[2] is an example. It is generally agreed, too, that pure thoughts will necessarily be simple, and vice versa. Simple in a more special sense are the characters who are unaffected and childish—not to say silly—to some degree.

For example, it gives this effect to go over events or tell a story that is unnecessary and that no one has asked for. There is much in Anacreon

---

[1] [Dem.] 25. 15, quoted more than once already: 'the whole life of man is governed by nature and by laws.'

[2] Dem. 19. 8.

of this kind, and in Theocritus' pastorals, and in many other writers: for example,

I'm serenading Amaryllis, while my goats graze on the mountain,[1]

and the context. Now as the examples we gave under 'purity' were of a more oratorical and contentious kind ('think me a villain, but let him go' 323 is perhaps of this sort also), and as we gave no instances of pure and simple thoughts in other kinds of prose writing, something more must be said now. I make no separation of 'pure' thoughts as a category distinct from 'simple', nor of 'simple' as distinct from 'pure'. What I mean is that of these 'pure and simple' thoughts, some suit oratory better than others, and some do not suit it at all. These last are the thoughts that are strictly peculiar to simplicity, as I said, though at the same time perfectly 'pure'. They are, for example, the thoughts of infants, men of infantile mind, women, countrymen, and generally speaking simple, guileless folk of any kind. 'How lovely grandpa is, mother!' 'They are bad men', said Cyrus of the Assyrians, 'and they ride bad horses.'[2] See how simple the thought is! Or again:

Sweet is the murmuring, goatherd, and yonder pine . . .[3]

—and indeed most, if not all, bucolic poetry. There are similar passages in Anacreon, while in Menander one could find innumerable such things, spoken by women or young men in love or cooks or similar characters. And in general, because the characters of all such personages (gluttons, 324 countrymen, etc.) fall under the head of 'character', all or most of them must come under simplicity: they are what are strictly called 'character' elements. It should be noted also that 'pure' thoughts in this sense, which are also simple, are essential and useful if one is reporting what in the narrow sense is called a 'character' personage; otherwise they have no relevance to oratorical writing.

'Simple' also are thoughts that appear to border on the vulgar. These are found when one speaks about vulgar or ordinary matters. For example, in the speech against Stephanus for false witness, we have the phrase 'showered the nuts over him', and again 'strip the rose-garden'. In the Appeal against Eubulides, we find the speaker saying that his mother used to sell ribbons in the market.[4] This sort of thing is common in private speeches, even commoner in Lysias. In public speeches it is rare, and is introduced with some degree of apology: for example the phrase 'riots without his mask'[5] is raised above the level of utter vulgarity by the addition

---

[1] Theocr. 3. 1. [2] Xenophon, *Cyropaedia* 1. 3. 2, 1. 4. 19.
[3] Theocr. 1. 1.
[4] Dem. 45. 74; 57. 31, 35. [5] Dem. 19. 287.

of the spontaneous 'the appalling Kyrebion' and 'in the processions'.
325 Again: '. . . how your mother made use of the daily weddings in the hut
by the Hero of the Splints, and brought you up as a lovely statue or a
supreme third-part actor'.¹ This is of the same general type, even if it is
introduced with vehemence, for the subject is vulgar; but it earns its
defence with the phrase 'daily weddings', the vehemence, the irony, and so
on. Again: the phrase 'squashing the brown snakes' and the whole passage
down to 'and all the other names the old women called you' is of this kind,
but it is justified by the fact that Demosthenes deprecates what is said
himself, because these were words used by old women.² There is another
passage which some people have—perhaps rightly—obelized and deleted
because of its extreme vulgarity. It is the one that begins: 'She wandered
around all the summer, crying baked beans . . .' This might be suitable
in a private speech, but could not possibly do in a public speech, or one
with that level of dignity, or in regard to a person or event of that kind.
Similar is the passage, obelized by some, in the speech against Neaera:
'ply her profession through three openings'. This is very vulgar, even if
it is vigorous.³

'Simple' also are thoughts occurring in arguments drawn from irrational animals. 'The ox strikes with his horn, the horse with his hoof,
326 the dog with his mouth, the boar with his tusk'.⁴ A very similar effect is
given by arguments from plants, though these have even more simplicity
of sentiment in them, being close to 'sweetness' and thus common in the
poets. In the poets indeed these features may possess grandeur, and this
is not surprising: for one thing, they do not use examples of this kind in
quantity, as we do in prose, but take just one, and this does not make the
whole context simple; and secondly, poets are naturally concerned with
the grand as well as the pleasant, and therefore elevate their subject by
diction or figures even if in its own nature it is simple and pleasant.

More about 'sweetness' anon. The foregoing example gains in simplicity by having a number of distinct parts. Now this multiplication of
parts is a matter not of the thought appropriate to simplicity but of the
method or approach. In the expression 'Except for harvesters and others
working for hire',⁵ if one were to remove the indefiniteness and dwell on
the details, one would make the passage 'simple': for example 'except
for harvesters and diggers and binders and shepherds and herdsmen'.
This dwelling on details would produce great simplicity.

Simple and character-revealing in thought is also the appeal to an
oath rather than to facts. 'I call on all the gods and goddesses of the land

---

¹ Dem. 18. 129.   ² Ibid. 260.
³ These passages are not in our Demosthenes MSS.: the obelizers have prevailed.
⁴ Xen. *Cyropaedia* 2. 3. 9.   ⁵ Dem. 18. 51.

of Attica, and on Apollo of Delphi.' 'First, men of Athens, I pray to all 327 gods and goddesses.'[1] There are countless such examples in Demosthenes and all these oaths are 'in character' (*ēthika*) and simple. So also if one binds the audience or one's opponent by an oath; this is not a debating move, like 'For the sake of Zeus and the gods, do not accept . . .'[2] and the like, but a matter of convincing character and persuasiveness. On the other hand, if one were to process (*methodeuein*) a debating proof or something else in such a way that it falls into the figure of an oath, this is something different, and not simple or 'in character'. For it is then no longer an oath, but a processed form of something else. Retaining its original force, it acquires additional qualities through the process adopted. 'No, by those of our ancestors who risked their lives at Marathon . . .'[3] This is a notable example and proof of the fact that it was the city's habit to fight and take risks for the liberty of Greece, so 'processed' as to fall into an oath; the result is thus splendour and grandeur, not simplicity and 327. 21 character.

4. THE PURELY 'PANEGYRIC' MODE AND ITS EXPONENTS

It is not very easy to say anything about the purely 'panegyric',[4] except 403. 21 that all the elements which produce the finest, Platonic panegyric can, by their isolated predominance, produce a kind of panegyric mode: viz. solemnity by itself, simplicity, sweetness, purity, care, all the qualities 404 mentioned above. Those ancient writers who have the highest reputation for panegyric evidently wrote in this manner. They form my present subject.

But first, some remarks by way of necessary preface. The best panegyric must possess grandeur with charm, ornament, and clarity, as well as realistic representation of character and all the other things discussed in our section on the panegyrical style. Not only poetry and prose in general (*logographia*) possess these qualities. History has them in abundance. Historians must therefore definitely be placed among the panegyrists. They do indeed belong here, for their aims are grandeur and pleasure and all the other usual objects, even if they do not attain them in the same way as Plato. They must therefore be discussed here. First,

---

[1] Dem. 18. 141, 1.   [2] Ibid. 19. 78.
[3] Ibid. 18. 208; cf. 'Longinus' 16 (above, p. 480).
[4] An extended sense of this term. Of the three branches of oratory—forensic, deliberative, epideictic or panegyric—the last can be regarded as in a sense covering also all non-oratorical prose; thus Hermogenes is able to regard Plato as the great 'panegyrist', and history also as a species of 'panegyric'. The term here does not mean only 'encomiastic'.

however, we must proceed to writers distinguished in panegyric in the school of Plato, especially as some practised history as well as other sorts of prose-writing—for example, Xenophon, with whom I begin.

Xenophon is a particularly simple writer. He is stronger on this side than in the other aspects of the panegyric manner. He makes ample use of the pleasures of simplicity, rather more sparing use of the sweetness resulting, for example, from myths and the like. For example, in his pleasant account of dogs, he produces his effect by intensification of simplicity, not by anything naturally peculiar to sweetness.[1] On the other hand, the character and emotion in the story of Abradates and Panthea[2] acquire their great pleasurableness from the mythical fiction: similarly with Tigranes and his wife Armenia.[3] Such sweetnesses, as I said, he uses sparingly; but he does use them. He often touches grandeur in thought, but brings it down to earth and forces it into a simple mould by his methods, diction, and everything related to diction, Xenophon is as pure and distinct as any writer there is; he likes tartness and sharpness— qualities we discussed in connection with sweetness and simplicity. He shows great care and study, within the limits of a simple, unaffected style. Indeed, his simplicity is much simpler than Plato's, because it arises in the subject-matter, not only in the diction and accompanying qualities. Each wrote a *Symposium*: Xenophon does not refuse to describe —and with charm—entrances of dancing-girls, dance-figures, kisses, and so on. Plato 'leaves all that to the women',[4] to use his own phrase, and guides the simplicity of the subject in a more solemn direction. Xenophon maintains similar characteristics in his historical works. 'They wore garlands of straw'; 'they talked to the slaves as though they were deaf and dumb'; 'they had to bend over the bowl and drink like cattle'.[5] The charm of such passages is due to their surpassing simplicity, which Plato does not match. Xenophon also excels in the representation of persons, when he is concerned with simple, unaffected, tender, and pleasing characters, for instance the boy Cyrus. There is nothing like this in Plato, except what is to do with young boys—Theaetetus or some similar character— but this is not to be compared with the boy Cyrus, the lady Armenia, or the like. It is also a peculiarity of Xenophon to use at intervals poetical expressions which are by nature sharply distinguished from the rest of his diction—for example *porsunein* for 'to provide'.

Aeschines (the Socratic) may well come next after Xenophon. He too is an outstanding example of the simple writer, but he uses the pure and distinct manner even more than the simple. He is thus more delicate in diction than Xenophon, with (once again) a fair number of more solemn

---

[1] *Cynegeticus.* [2] *Cyropaedia* 5.1, 6.1, 6.4, 7.3. [3] Ibid. 3. 1. 36.
[4] Plato, *Symp.* 176 e. [5] Xenophon, *Anabasis* 4. 5. 32.

thoughts and a moderate use of the charms of fable and the fabulous. You might say he excels Xenophon in delicacy as much as Xenophon's 407 simplicity excels that of Plato. He is much purer, and more careful than Xenophon, yet still within the limits of the simple manner.

Nicostratus,[1] who deserves or demands mention next, is as simple as any of these, but more delicate and pure. His style is exceptionally slight (*huperischnon*), with no grandeur except in the thought. He likes fables and their charms—indeed, he has invented many fables himself, and not only Aesopic ones but such as could be the subject of plays. He is extremely careful in arrangement, but without violating his simplicity . . .   407. 18

I come next to the distinguished historians. The Olympic, Panathenaic, 407. 21 and indeed Panegyric speeches of Isocrates and Lysias—despite their title!—are clearly something different. They possess a certain panegyric element, such as a deliberative or forensic speech might admit, but even 408 if they did belong to this category because (in particular) of Isocrates' artistry in word-order, what has been said of them in the discussion of deliberative and forensic orators still suffices. We must now discuss the historians other than Xenophon, whose style we have already considered.

The most panegyrical of the historical panegyrists, then, is Herodotus. This is because he abounds in charm as well as purity and distinctness. His thoughts are almost all mythical, his language is throughout poetical. He often displays grandeur of thought, but it is his care and the richness of his artistry that ensures the double achievement of grandeur and charm. Most of his rhythms in word-arrangements and clausulae are dactylic, anapaestic, spondaic, and in general solemn. His representations of character and emotion are among the finest and most poetical there are; this indeed is how he achieves so much grandeur, notably in Book 7 in the conversation of Xerxes with Artabanus and the latter's reply on human destiny.[2]

In approaching Thucydides, I have one preliminary point to make clear. 409 That I mention him after Herodotus and the others carries no implication that I regard him as their inferior in literary skill and capacity. I should certainly not put Herodotus after Nicostratus or Aeschines, nor indeed after Xenophon, in terms of power and skill—especially as we are discussing the panegyric mode. I have simply followed the order dictated by the sequence of the discussion of this style, placing the historians in a separate category from the other panegyrists. I then placed Herodotus

---

[1] A sophist and philosopher of the second century A.D. None of his works survive. The novel *Lucius or the Ass* has been attributed to him without solid reason (C. A. Behr, *Aelius Aristides*, Amsterdam, 1968, 13, n. 34).

[2] 7. 46 ff.

first among the historians, because he is more panegyrical and more charming not only than Thucydides but than any other practitioner in this manner. Of Thucydides indeed, it might be doubted into which category he falls; he is as much forensic and deliberative as panegyrical, in his thought and the elaboration with which he introduces every point. Let him however occupy his proper place, by genre and by his superiority to some and (it may be) inferiority to others in literary capacity. I shall merely describe him as he is.

Thucydides aims at grandeur, and he does in a sense achieve it—but not the grandeur that I think he wanted. He aims, I fancy, at solemnity, 410 the proper quality of panegyrical grandeur, but he obviously goes too far in the direction of roughness, harshness, and hence obscurity. This is true especially of his diction, but also of his word-arrangement. He takes great trouble over artistic adornment, but here too aims at sublimity and great grandeur, with the result that he overshoots the mark in hyperbole and novel word-order—whence comes harshness, and then obscurity. He is extremely dignified, and his thought possesses a remarkable combination of the oratorical and the solemn. Nothing even in his historical narrative goes unelaborated.

In his 'methods' or approaches, he is quite different. He introduces even his elaborations with some notable piece of grandeur or the like, and thus is almost wholly without sweetness. Where this does occur, it is conspicuously alien to the style: for instance 'Tereus who took Procne the daughter of Pandion from Athens as his wife' etc.[1] Were there no such instances, one would have cause for surprise that his writing does sometimes achieve charm; virtually no other individual style, that chooses 411 and perfects some particular manner, can appear pure without making at any rate some contact with all the other possible manners. As a historian, Thucydides employs representation (*mimēsis*) in his speeches and in some dialogues,[2] but he has the same characteristics here—indeed, they are even more marked. In his actual narrative he is less harsh and rough with many pure and distinct passages, far surpassing (in this and in much else) his teacher Antiphon.

Hecataeus of Miletus, from whom Herodotus learned much, is pure and lucid, and sometimes shows considerable charm. His pure, unmixed Ionic, without the variety of that of Herodotus, makes him less poetical in diction. Nor is he as studied or as ornamental in diction; his charms thus are far inferior to Herodotus', despite the fact that almost his whole subject is myth and narrative of that character. On the other hand, not only is his subject capable of giving rise to any kind of style, but his

---

[1] Thuc. 2. 29.
[2] Notably the Melian Dialogue in Book 5.

diction, and the features associated with diction—figures, cola, word-order, rhythm, clausulae—are well adapted to produce charm and sweet-ness like that of Herodotus, and indeed any other of the various kinds of writing. Hecataeus' inferiority, it seems, is thus due to his failure to take sufficient care about accuracy and ornament of diction.

It seemed unnecessary here to discuss Theopompus, Ephorus, Hellani- 412 cus, Philistus, and their like. For one thing, it is easy to characterize them on the basis of the theory of types, and of our discussions of individual authors. Secondly, their styles have, to the best of my knowledge, never been thought worthy of imitation or rivalry by Greeks, as have those of Thucydides, Herodotus, Hecataeus, Xenophon, and some others.

B. ON INVENTED HYMNS

This piece and the next come from treatises on 'epideictic' ('display') oratory attributed to a rhetor called Menander, and probably dating from the third century A.D. They illustrate the concern of the later rhetoric for unreal themes. Many of the prescriptions these handbooks offer are clearly much older than the books themselves, and afford useful parallels for the interpretation of the Greek and Latin poetry of the Empire.

Text: L. Spengel, *Rhetores Graeci*, iii. The first piece deals with hymns to the gods involving myths made up for the occasion. Spengel 340 ff.

The first point to note about 'invented' hymns is that they cannot easily be written for the famous gods, whose origins and powers are well known, but usually relate to minor gods or demigods; for example Eros in Plato is at one time said to have existed before the earth, at another to be the child of Aphrodite; later on again he is represented as born of Poverty and Plenty, as controlling the art of medicine, and as bringing together the halves of the original human body.[1] Plato invents these hymns, which relate to the nature, power, and birth of the divinity, with great ingenuity. This licence comes to prose-writers from the poets. Poets invent Deimos (Terror) and Phobos (Fear) as companions of Ares, Phugē (Flight) as a friend of Phobos, and Sleep as the brother of Death. I myself made Logos (Reason) the brother of Zeus (? to make a sort of summary of moral philosophy). The next thing is to explain what rules must be observed in invented hymns. First, they should not be separate from the whole but continuous with it and this condition will be ful-filled if the invention is taken from the main subject (?) and is not remote from it. Secondly, the fiction must be constructed in a facile, elegant, and by no means disagreeable manner: for example the Muses as the daughters

[1] *Symposium* 178 d, 180 d, 186 b, 191 c, 203 b.

of Memory, or the like. For some inventions are disagreeable even to hear, for instance that Athena sprang from the head of Zeus. This may indeed do very well in some other circumstances, if it is meant allegorically, but the invention is plainly disagreeable. Thirdly, in all our fiction we should take proofs from reality, as I have done, and as Homer often does. Fourthly: invented hymns should be consistent with themselves and not involve contradictory or conflicting elements, as in the story that Zeus came before all things and is the father of all gods, and yet married Themis, Cronos' former wife. For if he was before all things, he was before Themis; but if Themis was before Zeus, Zeus was not before all things. Fifthly: excessive length and elaboration are to be avoided. Some recent writers, having invented the new demigod Jealousy, make Envy her head-dress, and Strife her girdle. Pausanias[1] has a particular inclination to this sort of elaboration. Old and new can be made one both in poetry and more particularly in prose.

The style for such hymns should be chosen with an eye to the subject. If you invent a human story, it should be simple and neat—by 'human story', I mean something not terrifying or supernatural: Poverty or Insomnia or the like. If it *is* something supernatural, adopt a more solemn style. This kind of hymn, it should be noted, shows great talent and is a sign of inventiveness.

C. PROPEMPTICA (VALEDICTIONS)

Spengel 395 ff. See, in general, *Oxford Classical Dictionary*, s.v. Propempticon.

A valedictory speech is one which speeds its subject on his journey with good wishes. It likes delicacy and the charm of old-world stories. There are many varieties of valediction. The first admits advice in some part, while other parts of the speech give opportunities for encomiastic and amatory passages, if the speaker so wishes. Advice is in place when a superior is sending off an inferior (e.g. a teacher his pupil), because his own position gives him a character which makes advice appropriate. A second type allows the expression of a loving and passionate attitude to the departing person without the addition of advice; this is when the reputation and position of the two parties are equal, e.g. when a friend sends off a friend. Even if the speaker in these circumstances is superior to his departing companion, the common title of friend and their mutual affection deprive him of his advisory position. A third type gives greater scope for encomium—indeed it consists almost entirely of this: this is when one wants to present as a valediction what is really an encomium.

---

[1] A second-century sophist. See Philostratus, *Lives of the Sophists* 2. 13.

For example, we may be saying good-bye to a governor at the end of his term of office or because he is moving to another city. In saying this, I do not mean to deprive any of the varieties I have mentioned of the emotions of love. The valedictory speech always rejoices in these. What I am trying to show is that there are times for making greater use of it, and times for making less. In the case of the governor, one can include the desire and love of entire cities for him.

SUGGESTED DIVISION OF A VALEDICTORY SPEECH

Let us suppose a young man sending off a friend. He will complain to Fortune or to the Loves, as though he had suffered some extraordinary and unexpected blow, because they do not allow the bond of friendship to hold firm, but keep injecting new desires to make the man who agreed and consented to maintain indissoluble friendship again feel love for his country and want to see his parents, forgetting as it were the treaty of friendship he made with his friend. Alternatively, the speaker can approach the audience as though they were a jury, with a charge against his friend, pretending he is making a claim in accordance with his agreement with him; then you can proceed by urging your hearers not to allow him to transgress, and you can support your argument by historical instances or by parallels: as historical instances you have the inseparable friendships between Theseus and Heracles, Diomedes and Sthenelus, Euryalus ⟨and Nisus⟩.[1]

Parallels may be drawn from animals: one can point out that horses and cattle associating together in herds, and birds also, find separation painful. At a later point in the speech, you will perhaps recall the exercises, the wrestling, the gymnastics you have shared with him.

After this address to the audience as jury, you may introduce, as a third point, an encomium of the city—a plea, as it were, to stay at home. 'Love of Athens, her mysteries and ceremonies, does not even so grip you so fast—no, nor her libraries and lecture-halls, the literary enthusiasm of her teachers—the Areopagus, the Lyceum, the Academy, the beauties of the acropolis, so laboriously and yet so delightfully wrought! I fear you had no love:

> What shall become of our treaties and oaths?[2]

How proud I was of my friends! How I thought I had fortified myself with my friend! And now I am left as naked as Ajax without his shield;

---

[1] Text uncertain. If 'Nisus' is rightly supplied, the allusion is to the story in *Aeneid* 9. It is unusual to find a Greek author referring to a Latin classic.
[2] *Iliad* 2. 339.

I shall dwell in desert places and solitudes, I shall be called a misanthrope, like Timon. Why form a friendship, only to be hurt when my friend breaks the bond? Happy the wild beasts that are content with a solitary life!'[1]

This kind of material will occupy the first part of the valedictory speech . . . When you come to the rest, you should again complain of having failed to persuade him as you wished, and you can then conclude: 'Since the decision has been taken, and I have lost, let us run with his wishes.' Thus you will come to the regular topics of encomia. 'Happy parents of such offspring! Happy city for your sake! You will gladden your parents by your success, you will be your city's champion in courts of law, in rhetorical competitions, on embassies, in literary rivalries.' To give support to this, you can say you have personal experience of his uprightness and self-control, his wisdom and courage, his excellence as a speaker, and so have his teachers and all his friends. If possible, you should relate episodes here to demonstrate his excellence. You can say he will be useful to emperors when they recognize him for his outstanding qualities, and may one day be head of a school—though not as Isocrates, Isaeus, Lysias, and the like were.[2] This is appropriate if the subject of the valedictory address is a highly educated person; it will fit him if you praise him by saying that he may perhaps be head of a school and educate the young. If you say anything about him which is not true, everybody will know it, and you will lose credit, make yourself suspect for other occasions, and thereafter have an uphill job with your audience. One must always fall in with what is commonly agreed. In the case of such a man, you can say also that when there were literary competitions at the festival of the Muses, he was praised by the teachers above all his contemporaries. As Ephorus and Theopompus, Isocrates' pupils, won garlands for being better than the others—Isocrates used to offer a garland every month as a prize for the best of his pupils—so your friend was seen to be the best and was thought worthy of praises no less valuable than any garland.

Since physical beauty contributes to happiness, write also of what he was like to look at. Describe his beard, eyes, hair, and so on. To elevate your description and avoid the scandal which might come from admiring his beauty, make his appearance dignified and serious, saying that he adds to his beauty by the purity of his manners and by the fact that he does not give himself easily to many, but lives only with the best men, the best speeches, and the best books.

After that, you will have an opportunity of praising his native city:

---

[1] Cf. *Aeneid* 4. 551.

[2] Presumably because these all wrote speeches for others, and did not act in public life themselves, while the young man here praised has the highest political ambitions.

it is splendid and glorious, no less than the most famous cities, and he will be seen there in his splendour in a splendid and prosperous setting.

Finally, ask him to remember old acquaintance, kindness, and friendship. You should bid him ease the pain of separation by talk and memory. If he is going by land, describe the journey and the country through which he travels—how he will pass, maybe, through Thrace, praised and honoured for his oratory, how he will be admired in Lydia and Phrygia. If he is going by sea, you should call to mind the deities of the sea, Egyptian Proteus, Glaucus of Anthedon, Nereus, who will escort him and race beside the ship; the dolphins and whales shall rejoice, fawning or fleeing as Poseidon escorts the ship. Let the ship go on her way 'bearing the god-like hero', until in your speech you bring her into port; then conclude with a prayer, asking the gods for every blessing on him.

INDEXES

I. INDEX OF GREEK AND LATIN TERMS

Only words used technically in Literary Criticism are included; cross-references are to the General Index.

II. INDEX OF PROPER NAMES

Figures in bold type denote references of major importance.

253, 307 f., 309 ff., 314 f., 341, 361, 392, 397, 408, 452, 475 f., 562, 567 f., 575 f.; faults of, 465 f., 489, 491 f., 494 f.; cited for stylistic comment, 142, 146, 174, 177 f., 183 f., 205, 210, 213 f., 330, 488 f., 491 f.; cited for content, 6, 161, 168, 245, 509, 534, 579; and Demosthenes, 230, 408, 452, 475; and Xenophon, 576; and Cicero, 399

Pliny the younger (c. A.D. 61–112, consul 100, orator and letter writer), 423 ff.

Plotinus (A.D. 205–70, the Neoplatonist philosopher), 552 n.

Plutarch (see 507 n.), 5 f., 507 ff.

Polemo (4th–3rd cent. B.C., Academic philosopher), 236

Pollio, Asinius (76 B.C.–A.D. 4, politician, writer, and friend of Horace and Virgil), 271 f., 357, 369, 383 f., 397, 402 f., 406, 424, 439, 441 f., 445, 448 f., 454, 457. See also Asinii

Polus (5th cent. B.C., early teacher of rhetoric), 76

Polybius (c. 200–after 118 B.C., the historian), 304, 326, 534

Polyclitus (of Argos, 5th cent. B.C.: the sculptor of the Doryphorus), 225, 227, 405, 424, 495

Polycrates (4th cent. B.C., rhetorician, famous for his 'Accusation of Socrates'), 195, 311

Polyeuctus (Attic orator contemporary with Demosthenes), 151

Polygnotus (5th cent. B.C., painter), 42, 92, 99, 225, 405 f.

Polyidus (otherwise unknown sophist), 112, 114

Pompeius, Sextus (uncle of the great Pompey, philosopher), 232

Pompeius, Sextus (son of the great Pompey, defeated by Octavian's fleet and killed 36 B.C.), 353 f.

Pompeius Silo (rhetor), 351, 356

Pompey (108–48 B.C., Roman general and politician), 245, 350 ff., 354, 456 f.

Pomponius Secundus (1st cent. A.D., poet and consular), 395, 439

Ponticus (epic poet), 293

Pope, Alexander, 463 n.

Pratys (a rhapsode), 154

Praxiphanes (3rd cent. B.C., Peripatetic philosopher), 172, 185

Praxiteles (4th cent. B.C., the sculptor), 406, 544, 552

Probus, Valerius (of Berytus, 1st cent. A.D., scholar), 549 f.

Prodicus (of Ceos, 5th cent. B.C., sophist much interested in the meanings of words), 68, 76, 160, 220, 226

Propertius (Sextus, c. 50–before 2 B.C., the elegiac poet), 293, 295, 394

Protagoras (of Abdera, 5th cent. B.C., sophist), 68, 76, 117, 143, 220, 223, 226

Proteus (versatile minor sea-god), 311

Protogenes (of Caunus, 4th cent. B.C., painter and sculptor), 225, 405

Proust, 137 n.

Psaon (of Plataea, 3rd cent. B.C., Hellenistic historian), 326

Publicola, Pedius (perhaps the quaestor of 41 B.C.), 270

Pyrrhonians (followers of Pyrrhon of Elis, i.e. sceptical philosophers), 235

Pythagoras (of Samos and Croton, 6th cent. B.C., thinker), 234, 419

Pythagoreans, 273, 300, 553 n.

Pythia (i.e. the prophetess at the Delphic oracle), 476

Quintilian (see 372 n.), 344, 372 ff.

Quintilius (Augustan poet, d. 23 B.C., friend of Horace and Virgil), 291

Quirinus (i.e. Romulus), 270

Rabirius (Gaius, defended by Cicero for treason in 63 B.C.), 246

Rabirius (Gaius, Augustan epic poet), 393

Regulus, Marcus Aquillius (orator and informer of Neronian and Flavian times), 425, 441 n.

Rhodian oratory, 407, 458

Roscius (the most famous Roman actor, 1st cent. B.C.), 274, 444

Ruskin, John, 153 n.

Sacerdos, Nicetes (see n. in text), 441

Salii, 274 n.

Sallust (distinguished Roman historian, writing after 44 B.C., terse and archaistic in style), 356, 366, 379, 385, 395 f., 402

Santra (Roman grammarian of Ciceronian period), 407

III. GENERAL INDEX

Greek and Latin equivalents are normally added only where they have been mentioned in the body of the text; it is *not* to be supposed that they have been consistently translated throughout.

niques of producing, 151–2, 208–10, 258, 483, 486–7, 490, 556–7. *See also* Visualization

Vocabulary, acquisition of, 381–2. *See also* Words

Wit (*asteiotēs, urbanitas*), 150–5, 396–8. *See also* Laughter

Words, all appropriate somewhere, 334, 381; choice of, 323–5, 335; arrangement of (*sunthesis, compositio*), 205, 262, 280–1, 321–43 *passim* (types of arrangement [*charaktēres*], viz. austere, smooth, mixed, 313, 331, 338–41), 369, 496–9, 543, 571. *See also* Archaic, Dialect, Euphonious, Low, Rare, Sublime words, Neologisms, Usage, Vocabulary

Written and spoken speeches, 155–7, 412–13, 424–5